A CRITICAL AND EXEGETICAL COMMENTARY

ON

THE EPISTLE TO THE GALATIANS

BY

ERNEST DE WITT BURTON

The International Critical Commentary

A CRITICAL AND EXEGETICAL COMMENTARY

ON

THE EPISTLE TO THE GALATIANS

BY

ERNEST DE WITT BURTON

PROFESSOR OF NEW TESTAMENT INTERPRETATION IN THE
UNIVERSITY OF CHICAGO

EDINBURGH
T. & T. CLARK LTD, 36 GEORGE STREET

PRINTED IN SCOTLAND BY
MORRISON AND GIBB LIMITED
EDINBURGH AND LONDON
FOR

T. & T. CLARK LTD., EDINBURGH

0 567 05029 7

LATEST IMPRESSION . . 1980

PREFACE

WHEN in 1896 I began work upon the Epistle to the Galatians with definite reference to the preparation of this Commentary, it was with a clear conviction that if I was to make any appreciable contribution to the understanding of the epistle, it would be by confining myself to a few of the several lines of study which an interpreter might properly and profitably undertake. I decided not to attempt an exhaustive study of the history of the interpretation of the epistle, or of the rabbinic writings and method of exegesis. Convinced that, despite all that had been done in the study of the vocabulary of the New Testament, much remained still to be done, and strongly inclined to expect that such study would aid materially in the recovery of the primary elements of the thought of the apostle Paul, persuaded also that such lexicographical work would prepare the way for a clearer perception of the course of thought of the epistle, I determined, while not wholly neglecting other lines of study, to give my chief attention, first, to a fresh historical study of the vocabulary of the letter, and then to an endeavour to trace its course of thought with exactness and to state it with clearness.

When the study of the religions of the Roman empire, commonly known as the mystery religions, came into prominence, I gave some study to them, with the result that I became convinced that the contribution which a thorough investigation of them would make to the interpretation of this epistle, would not justify the postponement of the publication of this work for the period of years which such investigation would require.

Meantime, a growing sense of the close relationship between the experiences of the early Christian church, as these are disclosed in the letter, and those through which Christianity of our own day is passing, had greatly increased my sense of the practical value of the letter to the church of to-day, and begotten a strong desire to make this clear to my readers.

Whether I have been justified in thus emphasising these three things, meanings of words, course of thought, relation of the problems discussed by the apostle to those of our own day, others must judge. The choice at any rate was deliberately made and has been persistently followed.

Of the lexicographical studies which were made in pursuance of this plan, one, which consumed many months and was extended over years, proved in character and bulk unsuited to be included in this volume, and was published separately under the title, *Spirit, Soul and Flesh: The Usage of* Πνεῦμα, Ψυχή *and* Σάρξ *in Greek Writings and Translated Works from the Earliest Period to* 180 *A. D.; and of their Equivalents . . . in the Hebrew Old Testament.* Chicago, 1918. The other studies of this character the publishers have graciously consented to include in this volume, the longer ones in an appendix at the end of the volume, the shorter ones scattered through it.

In the quarter of a century in which I have made this Commentary the chief centre of my work as a student of the New Testament, I have called to my assistance in the collection of material and to a certain extent in the study of it, a goodly number of those who have been studying in my classes, chiefly Fellows of the University of Chicago. To all such I wish to express my appreciation of their services. But I desire especially to mention Professor Arthur Wakefield Slaten, Ph.D., of the Young Men's Christian Association College in Chicago, who for a period of nearly five years worked with me in almost daily fellowship, and to whom I am deeply indebted for his patient and skilful assistance, and Professor Benjamin Willard Robinson, Ph.D., of the Chicago Theological Seminary, who has generously read the proofs of the book, and made me many valuable suggestions. The list of others, authors whose books I have used, and colleagues whom I have consulted, is far too long to be printed here.   ERNEST D. BURTON.

July 1, 1920.

CONTENTS

ABBREVIATIONS.

It is assumed that references to the books of the Bible and the O. T. Apocrypha, and to the classical and Jewish-Greek authors will be self-explanatory. The notation is that of the standard editions. In the references to Aristotle the figures first following the author's name refer to the Paris edition of his works, those in parenthesis to page, column, and line of the Editio Borussica (Berlin). In the case of Josephus the figures preceding the parenthesis refer to the books and sections of the edition of B. Niese, 7 vols., Berlin, 1887–95, those in parenthesis to the chapter and sections indicated in Whiston's English translation. In the case of Philo the figures before the parenthesis denote the sections of the edition of Cohn and Wendland, 6 vols., Berlin, 1896–1915, those in parenthesis the sections of the edition of Richter, to which also the notation of Yonge's English translation correspond. For explanation of the abbreviations employed in the text critical notes and not found in this list the reader is referred to the section on the Text, pp. lxxiv ff., and to the works on Textual Criticism there listed. References to authors, both ancient and modern, supposed to be easily interpreted by reference to the Bibliography are not included in this list. The titles of works infrequently referred to are in general not included in the following list but are printed fully enough for identification when the works are mentioned.

AJT. = *The American Journal of Theology.*

Ambrst. = Ambrosiaster. *Ca.* 305 A. D. See Ltft., p. 232; *DCB.*

ARV. = *The Holy Bible*, Revised, American Standard Edition. New York, 1901.

Aug. = Aurelius Augustinus. *Ca.* 394. See Ltft., p. 232; *DCB.*

AV. = *The Holy Bible.* Authorised Version of 1611.

BDB. = Brown, Driver, and Briggs, *Hebrew and English Lexicon.* Boston, 1906.

Beng. = Bengel. See Bibliography, p. lxxxiii.

BGU. = *Ägyptische Urkunden aus den königlichen Museen zu Berlin : Griechische Urkunden I–IV.* Berlin, 1895.

Boeckh, *C. I. G.* = *Corpus Inscriptionum Græcarum* edidit Augustus Boeckius, Berlin, 1828–77.

Bl.–D. = Blass, F., *Grammatik des neutestamentlichen Griechisch.* Göttingen, 1896. Vierte völlig neugearbeitete Auflage, besorgt von Albert De Brunner, 1913.

B*MT* = Burton, Ernest De Witt, *Syntax of the Moods and Tenses in New Testament Greek.* Third edition. Chicago, 1898.

B*SSF.* = Burton, Ernest De Witt, *Spirit, Soul, and Flesh.* Chicago, 1918.

Butt. = Buttmann, A., *A Grammar of the New Testament Greek.* E. T. by J. H. Thayer. Andover, 1873.

Bous. = Bousset, Wilhelm. See Bibliography, p. lxxxvi.

Bous. *Rel. d. Jud.* = Bousset, W., *Religion des Judentums im neutestamentlichen Zeitalter.* Zweite Aufl. Berlin, 1906.

BW. = *The Biblical World.*

BZ. = *Biblische Zeitschrift.*

Cal. = Calov. See Bibliography, p. lxxxiii.

Calv. = Calvin. See Bibliography, p. lxxxiii, and S. and H., p. ciii.

Cf. = *Confer*, compare.

Ch.*AP.* = Charles, R. H., *Apocrypha and Pseudepigrapha of the Old Testament.* 2 vols. Oxford, 1913.

Chrys. = Joannes Chrysostomus. † 407. See Ltft., p. 228.

Cremer = Cremer, H., *Biblisch-theologisches Wörterbuch der neutestamentlichen Gräcität.* Zehnte völlig durchgearbeitete Auflage herausgegeben von Julius Kögel. Gotha, 1911–15.

Cyr. = Cyril of Alexandria. † 444. See *DCB*.

Cyr^hr = Cyril of Jerusalem. † 386. See *DCB*.

Dal.*WJ.* = Dalman, *The Words of Jesus.* Edinburgh, 1902.

Dam. = Joannes Damascenus. † *ca.* 756. See S. and H., p. c.; *DCB*.

DCB. = *Dictionary of Christian Biography, Literature, Sects, and Doctrines.* Edited by Wm. Smith and Henry Wace. 4 vols. London 1877–87.

De.*BS.* = Deissmann, *Bible Studies.* Edinburgh, 1901.

de W. = de Wette, M. L. See Bibliography, p. lxxxiv.

Dib.*Gwt.* = Dibelius, *Die Geisterwelt im Glauben des Paulus.* Göttingen, 1909.

Did. = Διδαχὴ τῶν δώδεκα Ἀποστόλων. Various editions.

Ell. = Ellicott, C. J. See Bibliography, p. lxxxiv.

Encyc. Bib. = *Encyclopedia Biblica.* Edited by T. K. Cheyne and J. S. Black. 4 vols. London, 1899–1903.

Epiph. = Epiphanius. † 404. See *DCB*.

Erasm. = Erasmus. See Bibliography, p. lxxxiii

Est. = Estius. See Bibliography, p. lxxxiii.

E. T. = English translation.

Euthal. = Euthalius. 459. See Ltft., p. 230, and *DCB*.

Frit. = Fritzsche, K. F. A. See Bibliography, p. lxxxiv.

Gild. *Syn.* = Gildersleeve, Basil L., *Syntax of Classical Greek from Homer to Demosthenes.* 2 vols. New York, 1900, 1911.

GMT = Gildersleeve, Basil L., *Syntax of the Moods and Tenses of the Greek Verb*. Revised and enlarged. Boston, 1889.

Grimm = Grimm, C. L. W., *Lexicon Græco-Latinum in Libros Novi Testamenti*. (Based on the *Clavis Novi Testamenti Philologica* of C. G. Wilke.) Editio secunda, emendata et aucta. Leipzig, 1879.

Grot. = Grotius, Hugo. See Bibliography, p. lxxxiii.

HDB = *Dictionary of the Bible*. Edited by James Hastings. 5 vols Edinburgh and New York, 1898–1905.

Hier. = Eusebius Hieronymus (Jerome). † 420. See Ltft., p. 232, and *DCB*.

Hilg. = Hilgenfeld, Adolf. See Bibliography, p. lxxxiv.

Introd. = Introduction.

Iren. = Irenæus. † 190. See *DCB*.

JBL = *The Journal of Biblical Literature*.

Jelf = Jelf, W. E., *A Grammar of the Greek Language*. Fifth edition. Oxford, 1881.

JfpT. = *Jahrbuch für protestantische Theologie*.

Just. Mart. = Justin Martyr. *Ca.* 150.

Ka.*AP.* = Kautzsch, Emil, *Apocryphen und Pseudepigraphen des Alten Testaments*. 2 vols. Tübingen, 1900.

Kühner-Gerth = Kühner, Raphael, *Ausführliche Grammatik der griechischen Sprache*. Dritte Auflage in neuer Bearbeitung, besorgt von Bernhard Gerth. 2 vols. Leipzig, 1898, 1904.

L. & S. = Liddell, H. G., and Scott, R., *Greek English Lexicon*. Seventh edition revised. New York, 1882.

Ln. = Lachmann, C., *Novum Testamentum Græce et Latine*. (Ed. major) 2 vols. Berlin, 1842, 1850.

Ltft. = Lightfoot, J. B. See Bibliography, p. lxxxv.

Luth. = Luther, M. See Bibliography, p. lxxxiii, and S. and H., p. ciii.

Lxx = *The Old Testament in Greek according to the Septuagint*. Quotations are from the edition of H. B. Swete. 3 vols. Cambridge, 1887–94.

M. and M. *Voc.* = Moulton, J. H., and Milligan, G., *Vocabulary of the Greek New Testament*. 1914–.

Mcion. = Marcion. See *DCB*.

MGNTG. = Moulton, J. H., *A Grammar of New Testament Greek*. Vol. I. Prolegomena. Edinburgh, 1906.

Mey. = Meyer, H. A. W. See Bibliography, p. lxxxiv.

Moff. = Moffatt, Jas., *Introduction to the Literature of the New Testament*. Edinburgh and New York, 1911.

ms., mss. = manuscript, manuscripts.

Oecum. = Oecumenius. Tenth century. See Ltft., p. 234; S. and H., p. c.

Ols. = Olshausen, H. See Bibliography, p. lxxxiv.

Or. = Origenes. †253. See Ltft., p. 227, and *DCB*.

Pap. Amh. = *The Amherst Papyri.* 2 vols. Edited by B. P. Grenfell and A. S. Hunt. London 1900–1.

Pap. Gd. *Cairo* = *Greek Papyri from the Cairo Museum.* Edited by E. J. Goodspeed. Chicago, 1902.

Pap. Kar. = *Papyri from Karanis.* Edited by E. J. Goodspeed, in *University of Chicago Studies in Classical Philology.* Chicago, 1900.

Pap. Lond. = *Greek Papyri in the British Museum.* Vols. I, II, edited by F. G. Kenyon; vol. III, by F. G. Kenyon and H. I. Bell; vol. IV, by H. I. Bell. London, 1893–1910.

Pap. Oxyr. = *The Oxyrhynchus Papyri.* Vols. I–VI, X–XIII, edited by B. P. Grenfell and A. S. Hunt; vols. VII–IX by A. S. Hunt. London 1898–1919.

Pap. Tebt. = *The Tebtunis Papyri.* Vol. I edited by B. P. Grenfell, A. S. Hunt, and J. G. Smyly; vol. II by B. P. Grenfell, A. S. Hunt, and E. J. Goodspeed. London, 1902–7.

Patr. Ap. = Apostolic Fathers.

Pelag. = Pelagius. *Ca.* 410. See Ltft., p. 233; S. and H., p. ci; *DCB*.

Pollux, *Onom.* = Pollux, Julius, *Onomasticon,* various editions.

PRE. = *Real-Encyclopädie für protestantische Theologie und Kirche.* Dritte Auflage, herausgegeben von A. Hauck, 1896–1913.

Preusch. = Preuschen, Erwin, *Vollständiges - Griechisch - Deutsches Handwörterbuch zu den Schriften des Neuen Testaments und der übrigen urchristlichen Literatur.* Giessen, 1910.

PThR. = *Princeton Theological Review.*

q. v. = *quod vide,* which see.

Rad. = Radermacher, L., *Neutestamentliche Grammatik.* Tübingen, 1911.

Ram. = Ramsay, W. M. See Bibliography, p. lxxxvi. Also Introd., p. xxiv.

Rob. = Robertson, Archibald T., *Grammar of the Greek New Testament.* New York, 1914.

Rück. = Rückert, Leopold Immanuel. See Bibliography, p. lxxxiv.

RV. = *The Holy Bible, Revised.* Oxford, N. T., 1881, O. T. 1884.

S. and H. = Sanday, Wm., and Headlam, A. C., *A Critical and Exegetical Commentary on the Epistle to the Romans.* Edinburgh and New York, 1895.

Schm. = Schmiedel, P. W.

Schr. = Schürer, *Geschichte des Jüdischen Volkes im Zeitalter Jesu Christi.* Vierte Auflage, 1901–9.

Sd. = Soden, Hermann Freiherr von, *Die Schriften des Neuen Testaments.* Göttingen, 1902–13. Handausgabe (*Griechisches Neues Testament*), 1913.

Seml. = Semler. See Bibliography, p. lxxxiii.

Sief. = Sieffert, F. See Bibliography, p. lxxxv.

Sl.*QN.* = Siaten, Arthur Wakefield, *Qualitative Nouns in the Pauline Epistles.* Chicago, 1918.

Smith, *DB = William Smith's Dictionary of the Bible.* Revised and edited by H. B. Hackett and Ezra Abbot. Boston, 1867.

SNT. = *Die Schriften des Neuen Testaments,* herausgegeben von J. Weiss. Zweite Auflage. Göttingen, 1907–8.

Th.St.u.Krit. = *Theologische Studien und Kritiken.*

Tdf. = Tischendorf, Constantin, *Novum Testamentum Græce.* Editio octava crit. maj. Leipzig, 1869–72.

Tert. = Tertullian. † *ca. 223.* See *DCB.*

Th. = Thayer, Joseph Henry, *A Greek English Lexicon of the New Testament.* New York, 1886. Rev. edition, 1889.

Thdrt. = Theodoretus. † *ca.* 458. See Ltft., p. 230; *DCB.*

Thphyl. = Theophylactus. *Ca.* 1077.

TR. = Textus Receptus, the Greek text of the New Testament as commonly accepted from 1516 till the modern critical period.

Tr. = Tregelles, *Greek New Testament.* London, 1857–79.

u. s. = *ut supra,* as above.

Vg. = Vulgate, text of the Latin Bible.

Victorin. = C. Marius Victorinus. *Ca.* 360 A. D. See Ltft., p. 231; *DCB.*

W. = Winer, G. B., *Grammatik des neutestamentlichen Sprachidioms.* Various editions and translations.

WM. = Eng. translation of the sixth edition of the preceding (1867) by W. F. Moulton. Third edition revised. Edinburgh, 1882.

WSchm. = Winer, G. B., *Grammatik,* etc., *u. s.* Achte Auflage neu bearbeitet von P. Schmiedel. Theil I. Göttingen, 1894.

Weizs. = Weizsäcker, C., *Das apostolische Zeitalter.* Zweite Aufl. Freiburg, i. B. 1892. *Das Neue Testament,* übersetzt von C. Weizsäcker.

Wetst. = Wetstein. See Bibliography, p. lxxxiii.

WH. = Westcott, B. F., and Hort, F. J. A., *The New Testament in the original Greek.* London, 1881. Vol. I, Text; vol. II, Introduction and Appendix.

b

Wies. = Wieseler, Karl.   See Bibli-
     ography, p. lxxxv.

Ws. = Weiss, Bernhard.   See Bib-
     liography, p. lxxxviii.

ZhTh. = *Zeitschrift für nistorische
     Theologie.*

ZntW. = *Zeitschrift für die neutesta-
     mentliche Wissenschaft.*

ZwTh. = *Zeitschrift für wissenschaft-
     liche Theologie.*

ZkWkL. = *Zeitschrift für kirchliche
     Wissenschaft und kirchliches
     Leben.*

INTRODUCTION

I. GALATIA AND THE GALATIANS

Gιeek authors use the terms Κελτοί, Κέλται, and Γαλάται, Latin authors the similar terms Celtæ, Galatæ, and Galli, without clear discrimination.* In Polybius and Pausanias Κελτοί and Γαλάται are used synonymously, as in Greek writers generally Κέλται and Γαλάται are.† Thus Polybius though commonly using the name Κελτοί (see 3. 40, 41, 60, 67–74; cf. 3. 59) of the people whom he describes in 3. 37 as occupying the country from Narbo to the Pyrenees, yet occasionally calls them Γαλάται (3. 40; cf. 3. 3), and their country Γαλατία (3. 59). In 3. 62, 65, he uses the adjective Γαλατικός. Similarly Pausanias 10¹⁹ᶠᶠ· uses Κελτοί and Γαλάται interchangeably of the Gauls who invaded Greece. Diodorus Siculus, 5. 32¹, however, distinguishes between the Γαλάται of the north and the Κέλται of the south.‡

On the question whether the names Κελτοί, Κέλται and Γαλάται were etymologically variant forms of the same name or of diverse origin, scholars have been divided, Niese, for example, identifying them,§ Contzen,‖ Tarn,¶ and apparently most other modern philologists regarding them as of diverse origin. D'Arbois de Jubainville** apparently regards the words

---

* Κελτοί: Hdt. 2³³; Xen. *Hell.* 7. 1²⁰; Pausan. 1⁴; Polyb. 3. 60, etc. Κέλται: Strabo, 4. 1¹.
Γαλάται: Pausan. 1³·⁴; Polyb. 2. 15. Celtæ: Cæsar *B. G.* 1¹. Galatæ: Cic. *ad Att.*, VI 5²; Tacit. *Ann.* 15⁶. Galli: Cæsar *B. G.* 1¹. Various compounds occur both in Greek and Latin. Thus Κελτολίγυες: Strabo, 4. 6³. Κελτοσκύθαι: Strabo, 1. 2²⁷; Ἑλληνογαλάται: Diod. Sic. 5. 32⁵. Γαλλογραικοί, Γαλλογραικία: Strabo, 2. 5³¹; 12. 5¹ (cited by Woodhouse, *Encyc. Bib.*). Gallogræcia: Livy 38¹²; Gallogræci: Livy 38¹⁷.

† Tarn, *Antigonos Gonatas*, p. 141, f. n. 11.

‡ Niese, art. "Galli" in *Pauly-Wissowa*, discounts this passage in Diodorus as late evidence. Tarn, *op. cit. ibid.*, takes issue with Niese on this point, holding that Diodorus is here quoting Posidonius. Even so, however, the evidence would be later than Polybius.

§ Art. "Galli" in *Pauly-Wissowa, init.*

‖ *Die Wanderung der Kelten*, Leipzig, 1861, p. 3.   ¶ *Op. cit.*, p. 141.

** "Les Celtes, les Galates, les Gaulois," in *Revue Archéologique*, xxx 2 (1875), p. 4 *ff.*

xvii

as etymologically distinct, but the people as ethnographically identical.

Related to this linguistic question, but not identical with it, is that of the nature of the tie uniting the various tribes which were grouped together under the terms Κέλται or Γαλάται, or both. Was the basis of this grouping racial, the tribes being of ultimately common origin; or linguistic, tribes of perhaps different origin having come to speak related languages; or cultural, different races sharing in a common civilisation; or economic and military, the several tribes participating in a common migratory movement?* Related to this in turn is the question, whence and when these Celtic or Gallic peoples came into western Europe. All these questions pertain to a period long previous to that with which we are concerned, and lie outside the scope of an introduction to Paul's Epistle to the Galatians.

Of more immediate interest, however, are the eastward movements of the Gauls, which led to the ultimate settlement of a portion of the race in Asia Minor and the establishment of an eastern Gaul in which, or in an extension of which bearing its name, Paul was in process of time to preach the gospel and found churches. The stages of the process seem to have been as follows:

1. Under a chieftain whose name or title was Brennus the Gauls invaded Italy in B. C. 390 and captured Rome, although the capitol itself resisted the siege successfully (Polyb. 2. 18). The attack upon Rome seems to have been a punitive expedition, and when it was completed and indemnity extorted from the Romans the invaders retired (Livy 5³⁴ᶠᶠ·; Polyb. 2. 19–21). Polybius calls these Gauls Γαλάται and Κελτοί (cf. 2. 22 f.), their country Γαλατία.

2. A second Brennus, about 281 B. C., led another eastward movement which had as its object the finding of a new home for the overcrowded Gauls. Routed by the Ætolians at Delphi, the Gauls withdrew from Greece and, joining an-

---

* Ripley, *Races of Europe*, pp. 124–128; 470–475; 490–492; McCulloch, art. "Celts" in Hastings, *Dict. Rel. and Eth.*

other detachment of the same general stream of eastward moving Celts, invaded Asia Minor (Livy 38[16]).

> Tarn, *op. cit.* pp. 439 *ff.* holds that the common treatment of the Gallic attack upon Delphi as constituting the invasion of Greece is incorrect. He regards the latter as part of a general home-seeking movement of the Gauls, of which the former was an incident. He bases his opinion upon the Koan decree of B. C. 278, which distinguishes between two divisions of the Gauls who invaded Greece, one of which attacked Delphi. Tarn admits, however, that the events were very early confused. The source for our knowledge of the details of these events is Pausanias, Bk. 10 *passim,* esp. 10[23ff].

3. At first overrunning the whole peninsula, they were later, about 239 B. C., defeated by Attalus I, king of Pergamum. As a result of this defeat they were confined to a territory somewhat north and east of the centre, bounded on the north by Bithynia and Paphlagonia, on the east by Pontus, on the south by Cappadocia and Lycaonia, and on the west by Phrygia, and traversed by the rivers Halys and Sangarius. In 189 B. C. this eastern Gaul, called by the Greeks Galatia, or Gallogræcia, shared the fate of the rest of Asia Minor and came under the power of the Romans, its status being that of a dependent kingdom (Strabo, 12.5[1]).

4. In the latter half of the first century B. C. Galatia was materially increased in extent. On the death of Deiotarus, king of Galatia, about B. C. 40, Antony conferred the kingdom of Galatia with the eastern part of Paphlagonia, on Kastor, son-in-law of Deiotarus, and to Amyntas, secretary of the late Deiotarus, gave a new kingdom, comprising portions of Pisidia and Phrygia. A few years later, B. C. 36, Kastor died, and his Paphlagonian dominion was given to his brother, but his Galatian realm to Amyntas, who also retained his Phrygio-Pisidian dominion. In the same year he also received a part of Pamphylia. To unite these two separated territories, Galatia and Phrygio-Pisidia, Amyntas was given, also, Lycaonia, or a considerable portion of it. After the battle of Actium Augustus gave to Amyntas the country of Cilicia Tracheia.*

* Ramsay, *Com. on Galatians,* pp. 101, 109 *ff.*; Perrot, *De Galatia Provincia Romana,* cap. II, esp. pp. 42 *f.*

5. When in B. C. 25 Amyntas was killed in the war with the Homonades, his kingdom was converted into a Roman province, but the part of Pamphylia which had belonged to him was restored to that province, and Cilicia Tracheia was given to Archelaus. In B. C. 5 a large part of Paphlagonia was added to Galatia, and at some time before, or in, the reign of Claudius (41–54 A. D.), the territory of the Homonades.*

This situation gave rise to a double use of the term Γαλατία as applied to a territory in Asia Minor, the newer, official sense, not at once or wholly displacing the older, ethnographic sense. The former is found in the following passages from Pliny, Tacitus, and Ptolemy:

Pliny, *Hist. Nat.* 5. 146, 147 (42): Simul dicendum videtur et de Galatia, quæ superposita agros maiori ex parte Phrygiæ tenet caputque quondam eius Gordium. Qui partem eam insidere Gallorum Tolistobogi et Voturi et Ambitouti vocantur, qui Mæoniæ et Paphlagoniæ regionem Trogmi. Prætenditur Cappadocia a septentrione et solis ortu, cujus uberrimam partem occupavere Tectosages ac Toutobodiaci. Et gentes quidem hæ. Populi vero ac tetrarchiæ omnes numero CXCV. Oppida Tectosagum Ancyra, Trogmorum Tavium, Tolistobogiorum Pisinuus. Præter hos celebres Actalenses, Alassenses, Comenses, Didienses, Hierorenses, Lystreni, Neapolitani, Œandenses, Seleucenses, Sebasteni, Timoniacenses, Thebaseni. Attingit Galatia et Pamphyliæ Cabaliam et Milyas qui circa Barim sunt et Cyllanicum et Oroandicum Pisidiæ tractum, item Lycaoniæ partem Obizenen.

Tacitus, *Hist.* 2⁹: Galatiam ac Pamphyliam provincias Calpurnio Asprenati regendas Galba permiserat.

Tacitus, *Ann.* 13³⁵: Igitur dimissis quibus senectus aut valetudo adversa erat, supplementum petivit. Et habiti per Galatiam Cappadociamque dilectus.

Ptolemy 5⁴: Ἡ Γαλατία περιορίζεται ἀπὸ μὲν δύσεως Βιθυνίᾳ καὶ μέρει τῆς Ἀσίας κατὰ τὴν ἐκτεθειμμένην γραμμὴν ἀπὸ τῆς μεσημβρίας Παμφυλίᾳ ἀπὸ τοῦ εἰρημένου πρὸς τῇ Ἀσίᾳ πέρατος ἕως τοῦ κατὰ παράλληλον ἔχοντος ζᾶ δ᾽ λβ᾽γίβ ἀπὸ δὲ ἀναταλῶν Καππαδοκίας μέρει τῷ ἀπὸ τοῦ εἰρημένου πέρατος μέχρι τοῦ Πόντου.

It appears also in Boeckh, *C. I. G.* 3991:

Ἐπίτροπον Τιβερίου Κλαυδίου Καίσαρος Σεβαστοῦ Γερμανικοῦ καὶ Νέρωνος Κλαυδίου Καίσαρος Σεβαστοῦ Γερμανικοῦ Γαλατικῆς ἐπαρχείας τὸν ἑαυτοῦ εὐεργέτην καὶ κτίστην.

* *Encyc. Bib.* vol. II, col. 1591.

On the other hand, Memnon, a resident of Asia Minor, writing in the second century, refers to the land inhabited by the Celtic tribes as "the now so-called Galatia."

οὗτοι δὲ πολλὴν ἐπελθόντες χώραν αὖθις ἀνεχώρησαν, καὶ τῆς αἱρεθείσης αὐτοῖς ἀπετέμνοντο τὴν νῦν Γαλατίαν καλουμένην, εἰς τρεῖς μοίρας ταύτην διανείμαντες. *Fragg. Hist. Græc.* Ed. Didot. III 536.

Other inscriptions (*C. I. G.* 4016, 4017, 4031, 4039, p. 102), bear no decisive testimony, being capable of interpretation in either sense. See Perrot, *op. cit.*, p. 102. *Cf.* Sief. *Kom.* p. 11; *contra* Zahn, *Introd.* pp. 184 *ff.*, and Ram. in *Stud. Bib. et Eccl.* IV 26–38.

II. WHERE WERE THE GALATIAN CHURCHES?

A. The Alternative Opinions.

The facts narrated in the preceding paragraphs respecting the gradual extension of the term Γαλατία over larger areas, show that in the period when Paul was writing his letters the term was used in more than one sense of an eastern territory, denoting, on the one hand, the district of which the people of Gallic blood who came from the West had gained control before the incoming of the Roman power, and, on the other hand, the whole of the territory which constituted the Roman province of Galatia, including both the district just named and the adjacent portions of Lycaonia, Pisidia, and Phrygia. These two usages being both in existence in Paul's day, he may have used it in either sense. In itself the answer to the question in which sense he employed the word would not of necessity determine the location of the churches of Galatia to which our epistle was addressed, since churches in either part of Galatia, or a group partly in one and partly in the other, would be in the province. But it happens that the statements of the Book of Acts concerning the apostle's missionary journeys in Asia Minor and the relation of these statements to the evidence of the epistle are such that, if we assume the historicity of the former, the determination of Paul's use of the word Galatia will determine also the location of the churches.

In Acts, chaps. 13, 14, it is related that Paul visited Pamphylia, Pisidia, and Lycaonia, and founded churches in Derbe, Lystra, Iconium, and Antioch ($13^{13, 14}$ $14^{1, 6, 21-24}$). This journey and these churches were evidently in the province of Galatia, but in its southern portion, not in the part of the province which was known as Galatia before the days of Amyntas. There is no intimation that at this time Paul entered the northern portion of the province, and such an extension of his journey northward is practically excluded by Acts 14^{23-26}. If at any time he founded churches in this latter region, it was doubtless neither at this time, nor on what is commonly called his third missionary journey (Acts 18^{23}), but on the second, in the period referred to in Acts 16^6. Whether it is probable that churches were founded at this time will be considered later. What is important to point out here is that if there were Christian churches founded by Paul in the northern, more strictly Gallic portion of the province of Galatia, the letter to the Galatians can not have been addressed both to this group and to the churches of the southern, non-Gallic part of the province. For the letter itself, especially 3^{1-3} $4^{13\,\mathrm{ff}}$, clearly implies that the churches addressed were all founded in the same period, on one general occasion; whereas the two groups of churches, if such there were, were founded one group on one journey, and the other on another, some years later. This being the case, if when Paul wrote his epistle there were churches in northern Galatia founded by him, these churches, being in Galatia in whatever sense the term was used, must have been included in the term "the churches of Galatia," and the churches of southern Galatia excluded. But in that event, since these southern churches were located in Galatia in the larger, Roman, sense, Paul could not have been using the term in that sense, but in its older, narrower, ethnographic sense. In short, if there were any churches in northern Galatia when the letter was written, Paul's letter was addressed to them only, and he used the term in the ethnographic sense.

On the other hand, if Paul used the term Galatia in the Roman sense as designating the province, then since it is certain that there were churches in the southern, non-Gallic portion of the province, these must have been included in the apostle's phrase, "the churches of Galatia," and, for the same reason that excluded these churches on the former hypothesis, the northern churches are now themselves excluded. Indeed, the latter could not on this hypothesis have existed when the letter was written; for, had they been in existence, they must have been included in the phrase, "the churches of Galatia," but, on the other hand, could not have been included along with the churches of southern Galatia, because they were not founded on the same journey as the latter.

On the basis, therefore, of the Acts narrative, and the evidence of the letter that "the churches of Galatia" to which it was addressed constituted one group founded on the same general occasion, we must exclude any hypothesis that the letter was addressed to churches in both parts of the province, and make our choice between the two hypotheses: (a) that Paul founded churches in northern Galatia on his second missionary journey, and addressed the letter to them and them only, using the term Galatia in its older, ethnographic sense; and (b) that he founded no churches in northern Galatia, and that he addressed his letter to the churches of Derbe, Lystra, Iconium, and (Pisidian) Antioch, using the term Galatia in the political sense.

> There is indeed a third possibility, viz., that he founded churches in northern Galatia on his second missionary journey, but that he wrote his letter before founding these churches, and addressed it to the only churches then existing in Galatia, those of the southern part of the province. But this hypothesis will not, in fact, require separate consideration, for the examination of the evidence for the other two will incidentally suffice to show its improbability.

It is incumbent upon us, therefore, to consider these two crucial questions, viz., what was Paul's use of the term Galatia, and whether he founded churches in northern Galatia.

B. The History of Opinion.

Before considering these questions, however, it will be well to sketch briefly the history of opinion on the matter of the location of the churches.

Ancient interpreters took it for granted without discussion that the churches were in the northern, Gallic, part of the province (*cf.* Zahn, *Kom.* p. 12), and this view has been adopted in modern times by Neander, *Pflanzung u. Leitung*, 1838; Conybeare and Howson, *St. Paul*, 1851, and various later editions; Hilgenfeld, *Einleitung*, 1875; Farrar, *St. Paul*, 1880; Holsten, *Evangelium des Paulus*, 1880; H. J. Holtzmann, *Einleitung*, 1886; Schürer, *Jahrb. für prot. Theol.* vol. XVIII, 1892; Godet, *Introduction*, 1894; Jülicher, *Einleitung*, 1894[1], 1906[6]; Chase in *Expositor*, Ser. IV, vols. VIII, IX; Mommsen, "Die Rechtsverhältnisse des Apostels Paulus," in *ZntW*. 1901, p. 86; Schmiedel in *Encyc. Bib.* vol. II, cols. 1596–1616; Steinmann, *Die Abfassungszeit des Galaterbriefs*, 1906; *Der Leserkreis des Galaterbriefs*, 1908; Moffatt, *Introduction*, 1911; and by the following commentators on the epistle: Hilgenfeld, 1852; Wieseler, 1859; Meyer, 1841 and various later editions; Lightfoot, 1865 and various later editions; Ellicott, 1865; Alford, 1849[1], 1871[5]; Sieffert, 1899[6]; Findlay, in *Exp. Grk. Test.* 1910

The South-Galatian view was first proposed by J. J. Schmidt, rector of Ilfeld, whom J. D. Michaelis combated in his *Einleitung*[4], 1788. (See Zahn, *Einleit.*[2] I 130, E. T. p. 183, but for 1199 read 1788); then advocated more at length by Mynster in *Einleitung in den Brief an die Galatèr* in his *Kleinere Schriften*, 1825; by Böttger, *Beiträge*, 1837; and Thiersch, *Die Kirche im apostolischen Zeitalter*, 1852[1], 1879[3]. It received fresh attention when Perrot advocated it in his *De Galatia Provincia Romana*, 1867, and since his day has been defended by Renan, *St. Paul*, 1869, and various later editions; Hausrath, *Neutestamentliche Zeitgeschichte;* by Ramsay, who has written voluminously in its defence (*Church in the Roman Empire*, 1893[1], 1895[4]; *Studia Biblia et Ecclesiastica*, vol. IV, 1896; *Historical Commentary on Galatians*, 1900, and various essays, especially in *The Expositor*); Rendall, in *The Expositor*, Ser. IV, vol. IX; Gifford, in *The Expositor*, Ser. IV, vol. X; Clemen, "Die Adressaten des Galaterbriefs," in *ZwTh.* XXXVII 396–423; also *Paulus*, vol. I, 1904; McGiffert, *Apostolic Age*, 1897; Askwith, *The Epistle to the Galatians: Its Destination and Date*, 1899; Bartlet, *Apostolic Age*, 1899; J. Weiss, art. "Kleinasien," in PRE. vol. X; Bacon, *Introd. to N. T.* 1900; Woodhouse in *Encyc. Bib.* vol. II, col. 1592 *ff.*; Zahn, *Einleitung*[2], 1900, E. T., 1909[1], 1917[2]; *Kommentar*, 1905; Lake, *The Earlier Epistles of St. Paul*, 1911; Emmet, in *The Readers' Commentary*, 1912.

Of the above discussions those of Lightfoot, Chase, Schmiedel, and Moffatt on the North-Galatian side, and those of Ramsay, Woodhouse, Zahn, Clemen, and Lake on the South-Galatian side, are most worthy of consultation.

From this sketch of the history of opinion, we return to consider the evidence on which a decision of the question must be based, and under the two heads named above.

C. Paul's Use of the Term Γαλατία

1. The letter is addressed ταῖς ἐκκλησίαις τῆς Γαλατίας. It is apparently the habit of the apostle, in speaking of churches, either to name the individual church by the city in which it was located or by the person in whose house it met, or grouping them together, to follow the Roman political divisions, and to designate each group by the name of the Roman province in which it belonged.   See, on the one hand, 1 Thes. 1[1] 2 Thes. 1[1] 1 Cor. 1[2] 2 Cor. 1[1a] Rom. 16[1, 5] 1 Cor. 16[19b] Col. 4[15] Phm. [2], the four latter being cases of a church in a house, the rest churches in a city; and, on the other hand, 2 Cor. 8[1] (ἐν ταῖς ἐκκλησίαις τῆς Μακεδονίας) 1 Cor. 16[19a] 2 Cor. 1[1b].

Indeed, it seems to be Paul's habit not simply in the designation of churches, but in general, to use the geographical terms that were officially recognised by the Roman Government. Thus he uses names of cities, Antioch, Ephesus, Troas, Thessalonica, Philippi, Athens, Corinth, Jerusalem, Rome, and of Roman provinces, Judæa, Syria, Cilicia, Asia, Macedonia, Achaia, but never Lycaonia, Pisidia, Mysia or Lydia.

It is indeed contended by Schm. (*Encyc. Bib.* vol. II, col. 1604), and by Sief. that some of these terms may be used by Paul in their popular ethnographic sense rather than in their strictly political sense.   This is doubtless to be admitted, but the absence of any terms that are unambiguously ethnographic and non-political, and of any clear case of the employment of a term of double meaning in the non-political sense leaves little ground for this hypothesis.

To this uniform employment of Roman terms Judæa can not be cited as an exception.   For throughout the period in which those letters of Paul were written in which he mentions Judæa (see 1 Thes. 2[14] Gal. 1[22]

2 Cor. 1[16] Rom. 15[31]), Judæa was a Roman province under procurators, and though it sustained in this period as in the years 6–41 A. D. a kind of dependence on the province of Syria (Schürer, *Gesch. d. Jüd. V.*[3], vol. I, p. 564, E. T. I ii 165) it was clearly recognised as a province under its own governor. See more fully in detached note on Judæa, pp. 435 *f.* Nor is it probable that Illyricum in Rom. 15[19] is an exception. For in Paul's day this term was the name of a Roman province, extending northwest along the Adriatic from the river Drilon to the Arsia (Mommsen, *Provinces of the Roman Empire*, I 24 *f.*; art. "Illyricum," in *Encyc. Bib.* and *HDB* i vol. ed.) and to its border Paul may quite possibly have penetrated. The argument of Woodhouse in *Encyc. Bib.* vol. II, col. 2161, that μέχρι in Rom. 15[19] must mean "into," and that because we have no other evidence that Paul ever went into the province of Illyricum, we must assume that by Illyricum he meant Illyris Græca, that portion of Macedonia which adjoins Illyricum on the southeast, is, to say the least, inconclusive. For neither does μέχρι naturally mean "into," nor is it explained why, if Paul meant Illyris, he should have written Ἰλλυρικόν; nor have we any more evidence that Paul went into or to Illyris Græca, than we have respecting Illyricum, this passage furnishing all that we possess in either case.

In 1 Cor. 16[1], which is of peculiar interest because of its use of the very name with whose usage we are concerned, there is a reference to the collection of money for the Christians of Jerusalem, which is also spoken of in 2 Cor., chaps. 8, 9, and in Rom. 15[26]. From these passages it is clear that during the two years or so next preceding the writing of the Epistle to the Romans and Paul's last visit to Jerusalem, he gave much attention to the gathering of gifts for the poor Christians of Jerusalem from among his Gentile churches. The Corinthian passages show that in the gathering of the funds he engaged the services of his fellow-missionaries, and Acts 20[4] suggests that in the transmission of the gifts to Jerusalem he associated with himself representatives of the churches from which the gifts came. Now it is significant that whenever in his epistles he speaks of this enterprise he uses the names of the provinces (see 2 Cor. 8[1] 9[2, 4] Rom. 15[26]) and in such way as to imply that he made the province the unit and pitted the churches of one province against those of another in friendly rivalry. This suggests that Galatia in 1 Cor. 16[1] is itself a province-name. It does not, indeed, exclude the possibility that in Galatia there were two groups of churches, those of southern Galatia and those of northern Galatia. But independently of that question, it has a bearing on the apostle's usage of geographical terms, and in connection with 2 Cor. 8[18-24], esp. [20], and Acts 20[4] it also favours the opinion that there was but one group of Galatian churches, viz., those of southern Galatia. And this in turn confirms the view that Paul's use of terms is exclusively Roman. For the names mentioned in Acts 20⁴, compared with 1 Cor. 16³, suggest that as he had gathered the money by provinces, so he selected the representatives of the churches who were to accompany him to Jerusalem on the same basis. In that case Sopater, Aristarchus, Secundus, and probably Luke himself, represented Macedonia. The absence of representatives from Achaia is strange, especially in view of 16³; it has been suggested and is not improbable that the Corinthians, modifying the suggestion of Paul in 1 Cor. 16³, ⁴, or possibly taking it in the sense which they had the discernment to recognise to be his real thought, designated Paul as their representative. Tychicus and Trophimus are the delegates from Asia, and Gaius and Timothy from Galatia. But as both these latter are from southern Galatia, northern Galatia is unrepresented, a situation not, indeed, impossible if the churches of Galatia in 1 Cor. 16¹ means those of northern Galatia, or those of both northern and southern Galatia, but in either case improbable. Of the three hypotheses, then, (a) that "the churches of Galatia," in 1 Cor. 16¹ are the churches of northern Galatia, the name being used ethnographically; (b) that the term is used provincially, but the churches were of two groups, those of northern Galatia and those of southern Galatia, and (c) that the term is used provincially and the churches are those of southern Galatia, there being none in northern Galatia, the third is most consistent with the evidence. The first not only makes the use of the term different from that which is usual with Paul, but is at variance with the natural implication of Acts 20⁴ by putting the churches in one region and the delegates in another. The second is open to the second of these objections and also finds in Corinthians a different use of the phrase and term from that which occurs in Galatians. The third is consistent with all the evidence.

The evidence of the Pauline epistles is, therefore, decidedly more favourable to a uniformly Roman use of geographical terms by the apostle and the view that by Galatia he means both in 1 Cor. 16¹ and Gal. 1², the Roman province, than to a mixed usage such as is found, for example, in Acts.

This judgment is somewhat confirmed by 1 Pet. 1¹. Galatia being there grouped along with Pontus, Cappadocia, Asia, and Bithynia, all of which are provinces, is itself presumably the name of a province, and there is a certain measure of probability that the author of this letter, who gives evidence of acquaintance with the ideas of the apostle Paul and probably knew of his letters, knew also what he meant by Galatia. But this argument is not very weighty.

It is still further somewhat confirmed by the facts respecting the usage of geographical terms in general. The extension of a name to cover a larger territory and to include territories formerly bearing other names is a common historical phenomenon. It occurs as the result of conquest, bestowal of territory by a superior power, or in the case of cities by growth and incorporation. Now the general proceeding in such cases is that it is precisely the name that is spread over a larger territory that loses its original narrower significance. The names of the absorbed territories remain as official or unofficial designations of subdivisions of the larger territory because they have received no new significance, while the territory whose name has been extended over the larger area either retains no distinctive name or acquires a new one. Thus, when the name France, which formerly designated a comparatively small area around Paris, was gradually extended over the whole kingdom of the Capetian kings, the original France came to be known as Île de France. When Brandenburg and Prussia (Borussia) came under the rule of a single king, and, the intervening territory being added, the name Prussia was extended to cover the whole kingdom, the original Prussia came to be known as East Prussia, and the intervening territory as West Prussia. As the names of cities, London, New York, Boston, Chicago, have been extended to include the suburbs, the latter have retained their names as official or unofficial designations, but the original territory has either had no distinctive name, or has acquired some new name. It can not, indeed, be affirmed that this is the invariable practice. Where changes in the extent of territory designated by a certain name are frequent and in both directions, involving now increase and now decrease, there is a natural tendency on the part of a later writer to continue to use the term in its original sense or to waver between the different senses without always conforming his usage exactly to that of the time of which he is at the moment speaking. See detached note on ’Ιουδαία with its discussion of the usage of Josephus, pp. 435 *f.*

In respect to Galatia there was, from 189 B. C. to the time of Paul, for the most part, only extension of the term. For fuller details see pp. xix *ff.*, and literature there referred to. From the year 25 B. C. to the time when Paul wrote, that is to say, for seventy-five years covering the whole period of his life, Γαλατία had been the official designation of a Roman province; that province had been in large part of unchanged extent, including both the territory within which the Gauls had been confined by Attalus, king of Pergamum, about 240 B. C. and the territory south of this, viz., Lycaonia, Pisidia, and part of Phrygia. During practically his whole lifetime, viz., from 5 B. C., it had included a part of Paphlagonia, also.

Yet these general considerations are obviously not decisive, and, in view of the evidence cited above on pages xx ff., showing that in the case of the term Γαλατία the more extended, political usage did not wholly supersede the older, narrower, ethnographic usage, they are of value only as somewhat confirming the probability that the wider and later usage was the common one.

It has been urged, indeed, and the contention has been supported by the weighty authority of Mommsen (*op. cit.* p. xxiv), that Paul could not have addressed the inhabitants of the cities of southern Galatia as Galatians, as he does the recipients of the letter in 3[1], but that the term necessarily designates inhabitants of Gallic Galatia. The argument perhaps assumes a greater difference between the populations of northern and southern Galatia respectively than actually existed. Both were doubtless of very much mixed blood, with Gallic elements in both regions. (See Rendall, "The Galatians of St. Paul," in *Expositor*, Ser. IV, vol. IX, pp. 254 ff., esp. 256 f.) Nor does it seem possible to name any other term which would be inclusive enough for his purpose. If the churches addressed were those of Derbe, Lystra, Iconium, and Antioch, which he founded on his first missionary journey, he could not well address their members by any single term except Galatians.

D. Did Paul Found Churches in Northern Galatia?

For the discussion of this question there is, unfortunately, but little evidence in the epistles of Paul independent of his use of the term Galatia, and even such as there is, is of significance only in connection with the evidence of the Book of Acts.

1. Paul's illness in Galatia.

In Gal. 4[13] Paul says that he preached the gospel to the Galatians on the first occasion (τὸ πρότερον) because of a weakness of the flesh. Whatever the meaning of τὸ πρότερον (see more fully on 4[13]), it is clear that the passage refers to the original evangelisation of the Galatians. That this occurred δι' ἀσθένειαν signifies either that Paul was detained by illness in a country which he had intended merely to pass through, or that he was obliged for his health's sake to visit a country which otherwise he would not have visited at that time, and that in either case he availed himself of the opportunity to deliver his Christian message to the inhabitants of the region. The latter part of the same verse with its reference to that in his flesh which was a trial to them implies that the illness was of a more or less repellent nature, and that, even if it occurred before he entered Galatia and was the occasion of his going there, it continued while he was there. If the churches to which he was writing were those of southern Galatia, the illness here referred to must have occurred in Pamphylia or at Pisidian Antioch on his first missionary journey (Acts 13[13, 14]). Ram. has made the suggestion that Paul contracted malarial fever in the coast lands of Pamphylia, and for this reason sought the highlands of southern Galatia instead of either continuing his work in Pamphylia or pushing on into Asia, as he had intended to do. It is perhaps equally possible that having gone to Pisidian Antioch with the intention of going to Asia and being detained there by illness, he abandoned for the time his plan of entering Asia, and turned eastward into the cities of Lycaonia.

If the churches were in northern Galatia he must have fallen ill at Pisidian Antioch on his second missionary journey or at some place in that vicinity, and been led to betake himself to northern Galatia; or having already, for some other reason, gone into northern Galatia from Antioch or Iconium, with the intention of passing through, he must have become ill there, and in either case must have used the period of his detention in preaching to the Galatians. The relation of his illness to the evidence of Acts will be discussed more fully below. Taken by itself it furnishes no ground of decision for either North-Galatian or South-Galatian view.

2. The evidence of Acts 16[6] and Acts 18[23].

Incidental use has been made of Acts above to show that the churches addressed by Paul were either in southern Galatia or northern Galatia, not both. The Acts evidence must now be examined more fully.

In Acts 16⁶ we read: διῆλθον δὲ τὴν Φρυγίαν καὶ Γαλατικὴν χώραν, κωλυθέντες ὑπὸ τοῦ ἁγίου πνεύματος λαλῆσαι τόν λόγον ἐν τῇ Ἀσίᾳ, ἐλθόντες δὲ κατὰ τὴν Μυσίαν ἐπείραζον εἰς τὴν Βιθυνίαν πορευθῆναι καὶ οὐκ εἴασεν αὐτοὺς τὸ πνεῦμα Ἰησοῦ.*

In v.¹ᵃ it is related that the travellers had visited Derbe and Lystra; vv.¹ᵇ⁻³ having related the story of the circumcision of Timothy, v.⁴ states that they went on their way through the cities, v.⁵ adding that the churches were strengthened in their faith and increased in number. Inasmuch as Paul's plan, as set forth in 15³⁶, was to visit the brethren in the cities wherein he and Barnabas had previously preached, and as in 16¹ they were moving westward through the southern part of the province of Galatia, it is natural to suppose that "the cities" of v.⁴ are Iconium and Antioch, and that "the churches" of v.⁵ are the churches of those cities. A visit to Iconium is, indeed, almost implied in v.².†

The most obvious and, indeed, only natural explanation of the phrase τὴν Φρυγίαν καὶ Γαλατικὴν χώραν in v.⁶ is that Φρυγίαν and Γαλατικήν are both adjectives and both limit χώραν. Geographical names ending in -ια were originally employed as adjectives, and their customary use as nouns with an article preceding is a reminiscence of their use as adjectives with χώρα. The presence of such an adjective with an article

* The above is the text adopted by Tdf. WH. al. διῆλθον is the reading of ℵABCD 81, 440, 614, al.²⁰ Syr. (psh. harcl.) Sah. Boh. Aeth. Epiph. al. διελθόντες is the reading of HLP al. longe plu. Chr. Thdrt. Ltft. adopts the latter reading on the ground that the indicative is open to suspicion as an attempt to simplify the grammar of a sentence which is rendered awkward by the accumulation of participles. But it is not certain that the scribal mind did not work in the reverse way, and against this doubtful probability the strong preponderance of external evidence leaves no room for reasonable doubt. Ramsay's adoption of διελθόντες in St. Paul, p. 195, after rejecting it in Church in the Rom. Emp.⁴ p. 484, looks suspiciously like controlling evidence by theory.

† Professor Chase, in Expositor, Ser. IV, vol. VIII, p. 408, contends that μὲν οὖν of v.₅ is correlative with δέ of v.⁶, and that the paragraph properly begins with v.⁵, or at least that there is a close connection between these two verses. But this contention can not be maintained. μὲν οὖν may introduce the concluding clause of a paragraph without reference to any δέ in the following sentence. See Th. under μέν, II 4. The instances which Chase himself cites, taken together, make against his view. Nothing, therefore, can be deduced from this either way. V.⁶ may begin a new paragraph, as in RV., indeed, probably does so, and this v. may, so far as μὲν οὖν is concerned, be a repetition of preceding verses. But that the paragraph begins here does not prove that it is a repetition.

ι

before it and the word χώρα after it almost of necessity marks
the intervening word ending in -ια as an adjective and the
joining of the words Φρυγίαν and Γαλατικήν by καί, with the
article before the first one only, implies that the region designated by χώρα is one, Phrygian and Galatian. In what sense
it is one, whether in that it was inhabited throughout by a
mixed Phrygian-Galatian population, or that it was in one
sense (e. g. ethnographically) Phrygian, and in another (e. g.
politically) Galatian, or that it constituted one physiographic
region, composed of two parts politically or ethnographically,
Phrygian and Galatian respectively, is not decisively indicated.
The unity which is implied may even be only that of the journey referred to, the two districts constituting one in the mind
of the writer because they were traversed in a single journey.

The contention of Moff. *Introd.* p. 93, following Chase, *op. cit.*
pp. 404 *ff.*, that Φρυγίαν is a noun and χώραν is limited by Γαλατικήν
only, can not be supported by Acts 2¹⁰, where Φρυγία is indeed substantively used, but is shown to be so used by the absence of χώρα;
nor by Acts 18²³; for, though the words are the same as in 16⁶, it is
not certain that Φρυγίαν is a noun, nor if it is, can it be inferred that
it is so also in 16⁶, since it is the order of words alone that in 18²³ tends
to establish the substantive character of Φρυγίαν, and that order is
not found in 16⁶; nor by Acts 19²¹, διελθὼν τὴν Μακεδονίαν καὶ 'Αχαίαν,
nor by 27⁵, τὴν Κιλικίαν καὶ Παμφυλίαν; for, though these passages
both illustrate the familiar fact that words in -ια may be used substantively, and show that, when two geographical terms are joined
by καί and the article precedes the first only, the unity thus implied
is not necessarily political or geographical, but may be only that of
the itinerary, they carry no implication respecting the grammatical
construction of such a phrase as that of 16⁶. On the other hand, while
Ltft. and Ram. are right in claiming a presumption in favour of the
view that the country referred to is in some sense one, it is not of
necessity the case that this one country is in one sense Phrygian and
in another Galatian. See, *e. g.*, Acts 17¹⁸, τῶν 'Επικουρίων καὶ Στοϊκῶν
φιλοσοφῶν.* Such a meaning is indeed possible, but neither Ltft.

* Ram.'s contention that the fact that these words are in the plural makes the example
irrelevant and his demand for an instance with Φιλόσοφος in the singular are not convincing.
A philosopher can not, indeed, be one half Epicurean and one half Stoic, but a group of
philosophers may be so, and so, also, may a country be one half Phrygian and one half Galatian.
An example of a collective singular noun with two adjectives would, indeed, be more pertinent, but a plural of persons is more like a singular geographical term than the singular of
a personal name, which Ram. demands.

nor Ram. have cited any examples of such a use of words. Chase, *op. cit.*, states the grammatical principle quite correctly: "From the point of view of the writer they are invested with a kind of unity sufficiently defined by the context." It is, indeed, surprisingly difficult to cite examples of phrases similar in structure to the phrases which Acts employs here and in 18²³. An examination of all the passages in which Josephus uses the words Ἰουδαία, Ἰδουμαία, Σαμαρία, Σαμαρίτις, Γαλιλαία, or Περαία, fails to discover a single example. The expression τῆς Ἰτουραίας καὶ Τραχωνίτιδος χώρας in Lk. 3¹ [has been appealed to on both sides, but apparently can not, for lack of exact knowledge of the political status of the region in Luke's day, be counted as furnishing decisive evidence on either side. See Geo. Adam Smith in *Expositor*, Ser. IV, vol. IX, p. 231.

It remains then to ask what region in the vicinity of Antioch or Iconium capable of being described as in any sense Phrygian and Galatian also meets the further requirements of the context. The possible hypotheses may be conveniently presented by considering the various views of modern scholars.

The following writers suppose that the phrase refers to, or includes, northern Galatia, and that on the journey churches were founded in northern Galatia.

Ltft. takes Φρυγίαν and Γαλατικήν as adjectives both limiting χώραν and both used ethnographically. First translating the phrase, "the Phrygian and Galatian country" and interpreting it as designating "some region which might be said to belong either to Phrygia or Galatia, or the parts of each continuous to the other" (*Com.* p. 20), he presently translates it "the region of Phrygia and Galatia," adding: "The country which was now evangelised might be called indifferently Phrygia or Galatia. It was, in fact, the land originally inhabited by Phrygians but subsequently occupied by Gauls" (*Com.* p. 22). The actual journey Ltft. supposes to have extended to Pessinus, Ancyra, and Tavium. The grammatical exegesis is sound, but neither the inference that the country referred to is in one sense Phrygian and in another sense Galatian, nor the specific contention that it was Phrygian in its original population and Galatian in its later, follows from the grammatical premise or from any other evidence. To establish Ltft.'s opinion it would be necessary to show from the context that the only Phrygian and Galatian country that meets the conditions of Acts 16⁶ ᶠᶠ· is that to which he refers the phrase; or at least that no other so well meets the conditions. This is not the case, but on the contrary, his interpretation encounters a serious difficulty in v.⁷,

ἐλθόντες δὲ κατὰ τὴν Μυσίαν ἐπείραζον εἰς τὴν Βιθυνίαν πορευθῆναι.
Taken together, the two verses represent the missionaries as turning
back from Asia to pass through the Phrygian and Galatian country,
and in the course of that journey reaching a point at which they were
over against Mysia with Bithynia as an alternative destination. But
a journey from Pisidian Antioch to Pessinus, Ancyra, and Tavium
would at no point have brought the travellers "over against Mysia,"
in the most probable sense of that phrase, viz., at a point where Mysia
lay on a line at right angles with the direction in which they were travelling, nor in the possible sense of "opposite," i. e., facing it. Even if
"passed through the Phrygian and Galatian country" be supposed,
as is very improbable, to refer to a journey into the Phrygian and
Galatian country and out again in approximately the reverse direction, say from Antioch northeast to Tavium or Ancyra, and westward
to Dorylaion or Nakoleia, they could not be said at any time to have
come κατὰ Μυσίαν, since in the whole of the return journey they
would have been facing Mysia, and at no point over against it. At
Nakoleia, Dorylaion, or Kotiaion, e. g., they would have been κατὰ
Βιθυνίαν, not κατὰ Μυσίαν. Nor can κατά* be taken in its occasional
sense of "near," since they would have been near Mysia only when
they had practically passed Bithynia. Nor is it easy to adjust this
interpretation to the statement of Gal. 4¹³ considered above. Was
northern Galatia a place to which a sick man would go from Pisidian
Antioch for his health? Or if Paul is supposed to have been passing
through northern Galatia and to have been detained there by illness,
what was his destination? Is it likely that with Paul's predilection
for work in the centres of population he would have planned to pass
through northern Galatia without preaching for the sake of reaching
Paphlagonia or Pontus?

Chase ("The Galatia of the Acts" in *Expositor*, Ser. IV, vol. VIII,
pp. 401–419), with whom, also, Wendt substantially agrees in the
later editions of his *Apostelgeschichte*, interprets τὴν Φρυγίαν καὶ
Γαλατικὴν χώραν as meaning "Phrygia and the Galatian region,"
and finds the two districts thus referred to in the country between
the cities of Lycaonia and Pisidia, which Paul was leaving behind,
and Bithynia on the north. Between these cities of the south
and Bithynia, Chase says "districts known as Phrygia and Galatia
lie." "Forbidden to turn westward, the travellers . . . bent their
steps northward, passing along the road, it seems likely, which led
through Phrygia to Nakoleia. At this point they turned aside and

* On the use of κατά see L. & S. κατά B. I 3, and *cf.* Hdt. 1⁷⁶; Thuc. 6⁶⁵, ¹⁰⁴; Acts 27⁷, but
also Blass on Acts 16⁷ (cited by Ram., art. "Mysia" in *HDB*). On κατά, meaning "opposite," "facing," see Æsch. *Theb.* 505; Xen. *Hell.* 4². For the meaning "at" or "near" see
Hdt. 3⁶⁴; Æsch. *Theb.* 528.

ıntered the Galatian district on the east. We may conjecture that they halted at Pessinus." This interpretation again fails to do justice to κατὰ Μυσίαν. By shortening the journey eastward as compared with that proposed by Ltft., the difficulty is made somewhat less glaring, but not removed. To express the idea of Chase the author should have omitted the reference to the Galatian region in v.⁶ and after v.⁷ have inserted a statement to the effect that they entered Galatia and again returning passed by Mysia, etc. The view also encounters the difficulty that it finds no probable place for the illness which became the occasion of the preaching in Pessinus.

Sief. (Kom.⁶, pp. 9–17, esp. 15) interprets τὴν Φρυγίαν καὶ Γαλα-τικὴν χώραν of Acts 16⁶ as designating the country northeast of Pisidian Antioch and supposes that the journey here spoken of probably passed to the west of the Sultan Dagh and brought the apostle to Pessinus via Kinnaborion and Ammorion. The churches of Galatia he would locate in Pessinus, Germa, and neighbouring places. Schm. (Encyc. Bib. vol. II, col. 1600, 1606 f.) and Moff. (Introd. pp. 92–95) adopt substantially the same view though with less specific definition of the route and location of the churches.

The following writers, differing in their interpretation of the geographical phrase, are agreed in the opinion that the passage does not refer to the founding of churches:

Ram. holds that the reference is to the western half of the southern portion of the province of Galatia, the region of Iconium and Antioch, being called Phrygian because ethnographically so, and Galatian because politically so. Church in the Roman Empire⁴, p. 77; St. Paul, pp. 180 f.; Stud. Bib. et Eccl. IV 56; on the diversity of interpretations advocated by Ram., see Schm. in Encyc. Bib. vol. II, col. 1598, 1601 f.

Apparently, indeed, the author of Acts has already narrated the passage through this country in v.⁴. But Ram. explains vv.⁴, ⁵ not as a continuation of the narrative, but as a (parenthetical) description of Paul's procedure in the churches, the narrative being continued in v.⁶, vv.¹⁻³ covering Derbe and Lystra, v.⁶ Iconium and Antioch. The further objection to his view that the remainder of v.⁶, "having been forbidden by the Holy Spirit to speak the word in Asia," naturally implies that at the beginning of their journey the travellers were already on the borders of Asia, Ram. seeks to obviate by supposing κωλυθέντες to be a participle of subsequent action, referring to an event which took place after the journey through the Phrygian and Galatian country. Later Greek, in particular the second half of Acts, seems to furnish examples of an aorist participle standing after the principal

verb and denoting an action subsequent to that of the verb.* But
κωλυθέντες does not seem to be an example of this rather rare usage.
The most probable occurrences of it, in Acts at least, are of two classes:
(a) Instances in which the participle follows closely upon the verb
and expresses an action in close relation to the verb, approximating
in force a participle of identical action. So, e. g., Acts 25¹³, where
ἀσπασάμενοι, while not denoting an action identical with that of
κατήντησαν, is intimately associated with it as its purpose. Similarly, in *Test. XII Patr.* Reub. 3, μὴ ἁψάμενος is not identical with
ἐπένθει, but is its immediate consequence. A probable, though
perhaps not certain, case of similar character is found in Jos. *Contra
Ap.* 1³³ (7), συγγράψαντες. (b) Instances in which the participle is
far removed from the verb, and, the complications of the sentence
obscuring the relation of the different parts of the sentence to one
another, an additional fact is loosely added at the end by an aorist
participle. Examples of this form are found in Acts 23³⁵ 24²³. In
Acts 16⁶, on the other hand, we have neither form. The sentence is
short and uninvolved, but the action denoted by the participle, if subsequent to that of the verb, is not involved in it as purpose or result,
but marks a distinctly new and important stage of the narrative.

When to these considerations it is added that the interpretation of
κωλυθέντες as a participle of subsequent action involves taking
vv.⁴,⁵ as parenthetical, and the first part of v.⁶ as in effect a repetition
of these vv., the weight of objection to the view as a whole compels
its rejection. Taking vv.⁴,⁵ in their obvious sense as referring to a
journey beyond Lystra, v.⁶ as an addition to what has already been
said, and the participle in what is in this connection its equally obvious
force, viz., as expressing the cause of the action denoted by the verb,
the whole passage is self-consistent and simple. Ram.'s view breaks
down under an accumulation of improbabilities. The opinion expressed by Gifford (*op. cit.* p. 18) is that previously reached by the
present writer, viz., that while the supposed grammatical usage is
itself possible, and Ram.'s view can not be said to have "shipwrecked
on the rock of Greek grammar" (as Chase affirms), the present passage
can not be regarded as an example of that usage.

Gifford interpreting κατὰ τὴν Μυσίαν in v.⁷ as meaning "over against
Mysia," *i. e.*, at a point where the road to Mysia lay at right angles to

* BMT 145; cf. Gifford in *Expositor*, Ser. IV, vol. X (1894), pp. 17 ff.; and *contra* Rob.
p. 861. For exx. of this usage additional to those cited in B*MT*, see Pind. *Pyth. IV* 189,
ἐπαινήσας; *Test. XII Patr.* Reub. 3, 15, ἁψάμενος (cited by Gifford from Sanday); Clem.
Alex. *Protrept.* (*Cohortatio ad gentes*), chap. 2: μίγνυται δράκων γενόμενος, ὃς ἦν ἐλεγχθείς
(Migne. col. 76): "He makes his approach as a dragon, his identity being afterwards discovered"; *Chronicon Paschale*, pref. quoted by Routh, *Reliquiæ Sacræ*, I 161, ἐπιτεθέντος.
That the exx. of this usage are scattered over several centuries of time, some being earlier,
some later than N. T., does not, perhaps, diminish their value.

the course which the travellers were up to that point pursuing, supposes the phrase τὴν Φρυγίαν καὶ Γαλατικὴν χώραν to designate the
frontier of Phrygia and Galatia (apparently taking the latter term as
the name of the province), and to refer to the country between Pisidian
Antioch and the point at which the road to Troas branches from the
road to Bithynia, probably Nakoleia. This view is similar to that of
Chase as respects the route followed, differing, however, in that it
does not assume a journey eastward to Pessinus and the founding of
churches. The principal difficulty with Gifford's suggestion is that
a line drawn from Antioch to Nakoleia apparently lies so far from the
Galatian border that the country through which one would pass would
be much more naturally called simply Φρυγίαν. Yet it is, perhaps,
possible that the road actually taken, for reasons unknown to us,
passed so far to the east as to make this expression wholly natural.

Zahn prefers to take the article with Φρυγίαν only and to interpret
the lack of the article with Γαλατικὴν χώραν as indicating that Paul
and his companions only touched upon a part of the region so designated. This interpretation is manifestly untenable on grammatical
grounds. The suggestion supposed to be conveyed could not be indicated by the omission of the article. As his second choice Zahn proposes the view that the article belongs to both nouns, and the whole
phrase refers to territory which was partly in Phrygia and partly in
Galatia, both terms being ethnographically understood. Such a journey starting from Antioch would, perhaps, include Amorion, Pessinus,
Germa, and Nakoleia or Dorylaion. *Einleitung*, I 136; E. T. I 187 *ff.*,
esp. 189 *fin.*; *Com.*, p. 16. See also Moff. *Introd.* pp. 92 *f.* Such an
interpretation is grammatically sound and otherwise entirely unobjectionable. Rather better than Gifford's, it accounts for the use of
Γαλατικὴν χώραν in preference to Γαλατίαν, or Γαλατικὴν ἐπαρχείαν,
which would naturally have been chosen if, as Gifford apparently supposes, the Acts writer was speaking of the province of Galatia.

As concerns the purpose and result of the journey, the evidence of Acts at least seems clearly on the side of the writers of
this second group. The Acts narrative says nothing about
founding churches in the region named in 16⁶. Indeed the
impression which the whole passage makes is that the writer
knew of no evangelising, or at least of no prolonged or successful work, from the time when the missionaries left "the cities"
(v.⁴) till they arrived at Philippi in obedience to the vision received at Troas (v.⁹). Forbidden to speak the word in Asia,
turned back from Bithynia, passing by Mysia, only when they

reach Troas do they find a way open to them. Certainly the author would scarcely have described the journey through the Phrygian and Galatian country in the brief language of vv.[6, 7a] if he had known that at this time Paul founded a group of churches. This does not prove that no churches were founded, but it raises the question whether Zahn is not right in locating the journey much as Moff. Sief. and Schm. do, but in holding that no churches were founded. Before deciding this question, however, the evidence of Acts 18[23] must be considered.

This sentence reads: διερχόμενος καθεξῆς τὴν Γαλατικὴν χώραν καὶ Φρυγίαν, στηρίζων πάντας τοὺς μαθητάς.

Advocates of the North-Galatian theory generally interpret the phrase τὴν Γαλατικὴν χώραν καὶ Φρυγίαν as referring to the same territory called in 16[6] τὴν Φρυγίαν καὶ Γαλατικὴν χώραν, ascribing the difference in order to the different direction of approach, and looking upon the confirmation of the disciples as evidence that on the journey mentioned in 16[6] the apostle founded churches. It must be questioned whether either of these assumptions is sound. There is, indeed, a presumption in favour of the view that two phrases employing exactly the same terms (though in different order) and standing in the same author, use the individual terms in the same sense. But there is distinctly less probability that the two phrases as a whole mean the same thing, for the change of order may itself be significant. Nor is it probable that the difference in order is due simply to the difference in the direction of journey. For if, as we have maintained above, both Φρυγίαν and Γαλατικήν are adjectives limiting χώραν in 16[6], we should expect here τὴν Γαλατικὴν καὶ Φρυγίαν χώραν if the two expressions were intended to denote the same territory traversed in opposite directions.* The probability is therefore

---

* Mt. 24[45] shows, indeed, that Φρυγίαν may be an adjective limiting χώραν, despite its position. But such an order is apparently poetic or rhetorical and not likely to be found in a plain geographical statement. The examples cited by Ram. *St. Paul*, p. 211, are not really parallel cases. The first one is a case of distributive apposition, the general term preceding the noun and specific terms following it. The other passages are not examples of two adjectives limiting the same noun, one preceding the noun with the article, the other following it without the article, but of a series of proper adjectives, each preceded by an article and each denoting a different object, the noun being expressed with the first and supplied with the others.

that Φρυγίαν is a noun. Γαλατικήν is, of course, clearly here, as in 16⁶, an adjective. The unity indicated by the single article is presumably that of the journey only.

Where, then, are these two regions which were traversed in this one journey? V.²² names Antioch of Syria as the point of departure. Chap. 19¹ names Ephesus as the point of arrival. Between these two extremes, Paul has passed through the Galatian country and Phrygia. Whether "the upper country" (ἀνωτερικὰ μέρη) referred to in 19¹ is the same as the Galatian region and Phrygia, being referred to here resumptively, or the territory between Phrygia and Ephesus, is not wholly certain, nor particularly important for our present purpose. It is generally and probably rightly understood of the highlands of Asia in contrast with the coast plain. It is evident that the writer has not given a complete itinerary, but has only mentioned some points in which he was specially interested. If, as on his previous journey, Paul went entirely by land, he must have passed through the Syrian Gates and northern Syria. Thence he might, indeed, as Schm. suggests, have gone north through Cappadocia. But Schm.'s reason for this route, that if he had gone through Cilicia the narrative would have spoken of confirming the churches in that region, is not convincing. It is certainly as probable, if not more so, that his route lay through Cilicia as far as Tarsus, thence through the Cilician Gates to the point at which the roads branch, one arm going westward to Lycaonia, and the other northward through Cappadocia.

From this point three routes are possible. He may have taken the northern road to Tavium, and thence westward through Ancyra. This is the route for which Ltft.'s theory that he had on the previous journey founded churches in these cities would naturally call. Emerging from the Galatian country he would come into Phrygia and so through the mountains of the eastern part of the province of Asia to Ephesus.

On the other hand, he might have left the great western road soon after passing through the Cilician Gates and travelling *via* Tyana and the road south of Lake Tatta (or possibly *via* Iconium) have come to Pessinus in the western part of old Galatia and so on through Phrygia to Ephesus. Such a route could hardly have been dictated solely by a desire to reach Ephesus, since it was far from being the shortest or easiest. In this case we may with Moff. suppose that "the disciples" are those in the churches founded on the previous journey, or with Zahn that he had founded no church and "all the disciples" are the scattered Christians in these regions. In either case τὴν Γαλατικὴν χώραν is old Galatia, but the part passed through is the extreme western part only. Φρυγία is the eastern part of Asia.

But still again, he may have taken the route westward through

Derbe, Lystra, Iconium, and Pisidian Antioch, and thence on directly westward to Ephesus. The last explanation makes the language cover a larger part of the country actually passed through than either of the others. It is, however, an objection to it that it supposes Γαλατικήν to be used in a different sense from any that can reasonably be attached to it in 16⁶, taking Γαλατικὴν χώραν in a political sense, which is contrary to the usual practice of the Acts author and to the use of Φρυγίαν which he immediately joined with it.

It is against any view that finds in Acts 18²³ a second visit to the Galatian churches supposed to have been founded on the second journey (Acts 16⁶) that while the Acts author definitely speaks of the *churches* founded in southern Galatia and elsewhere (14²³ 15⁴¹ 16⁵) here he speaks only of disciples (but *cf.* also 14²²). This, together with the absence of any mention of the founding of churches in 16⁶ᶠ·, favours the view of Zahn that while there were scattered disciples in this region (found or made on his previous journey) there were no churches. This evidence could, indeed, be set aside if there were strong opposing reasons. But the contrary is the case. All forms of the North-Galatian view with its hypothesis of churches in old Galatia labour under the disadvantage that its sole evidence for the existence of any churches in northern Galatia is found in two passages, both somewhat obscure, in a writer who, though doubtless in general trustworthy, is not always accurate. To create on the basis of such evidence a group of churches of Galatia, when we already have perfectly clear evidence of another group of churches which could be properly so called, and which fulfil all the conditions necessary to be met by the term as used by Paul, is of more than doubtful legitimacy.

It may be objected to Zahn's view that it is strange that the term Γαλατικήν in Acts should refer to an entirely different region from that to which Paul refers in his term Γαλατία. But it is to be answered that Luke has apparently taken no pains to conform his use of geographical terms to that of Paul, and that in particular he gives no evidence of intending to furnish the background of the Epistle to the Galatians, never using the word "church" in connection with Γαλατική. On the other hand, the analogy of similar cases suggests the possibility if not the probability that when the name Γαλατία was extended to cover the Lycaonian, Pisidian, and Phrygian territory a. new name, Γαλατικὴ χώρα should have been coined to describe old Galatia. See above, p. xxviii.

It may also be said against Zahn's view that it is incredible that Paul on his way to visit scattered disciples in western ethnographic Galatia should pass by southern Galatia without visiting the churches of that region; to which it may be answered that a motive similar to that ascribed to Paul in Acts 20¹⁶, together with a desire to foster the Christian movement represented by scattered disciples in the Galatian country, may have led him to avoid the cities of southern Galatia. Of course it is also possible that the cities of southern Galatia were visited at this time, but that, as the Acts writer says nothing about the churches of Syria and Cilicia, though Paul must have passed through these regions, he for some unknown reason ignores the cities of southern Galatia though this journey included them. The omission of the second group is no more strange than that of the first.

We conclude, therefore, that so far as concerns Acts 16⁶ᶠᶠ· and 18²³ the interpretation which best satisfies all the evidence is that which supposes that the journey of Acts 16⁶ ran a little east of north from Antioch, possibly passing around the Sultan Dagh and through Amorion and Pessinus, and that it was undertaken not for evangelisation but as a means of reaching some other territory in which the apostle expected to work, perhaps Bithynia. The point at which they were κατὰ τὴν Μυσίαν would be not Nakoleia or Kotiaion, but some point further east, perhaps Pessinus itself. Why this route was chosen rather than the apparently more direct route through Nakoleia and Dorylaion must be a matter wholly of conjecture. At Pessinus, of course, might have occurred the preaching because of sickness (Gal. 4¹³), and the consequent founding of the Galatian churches. But there is no suggestion of this in the Acts narrative, and no presumption in favour of it. For the journey of Acts 18²³ there is no more probable route than that through the Cicilian Gates and *via* Tyana and Lake Tatta.

3. Some minor considerations derived from Paul's Epistles.

It remains to consider certain items of evidence that have in themselves little weight, but which have filled a more or less prominent place in previous discussions of the problem.

a. The epistle represents the people addressed as warmhearted, impulsive, and fickle. These characteristics have been pointed to as indicating their Gallic blood, and hence as tending to show that the churches were in northern Galatia. But warmheartedness and fickleness seem to have been equally characteristic of the Lycaonian people (with Acts 14$^{8-18}$ *cf.* Acts 14$^{19, 20}$), and the evidence of the letter is too general in character to enable us to draw any conclusion whatever from this evidence.

b. It has been said to be improbable that the scene between Peter and Paul depicted in Gal. 2$^{11-21}$ occurred before the second missionary journey, since in that case Paul must have proposed to Barnabas to accompany him on another journey after he had found him unstable on an important point. But if this incident of Gal. 2$^{11-21}$ is put after the second missionary journey, then Galatians, since it narrates the incident, must also itself be later than the second missionary journey. But if it was written on the third journey, since Gal. 4^{13} implies that Paul had visited the Galatians but twice, these Galatians can not be those of southern Galatia, because on his third missionary journey he visited them for the third time. Hence, it is inferred, we must place this incident after the second journey, the letter on the third journey, and the churches in northern Galatia. In reply it is to be said that, aside from the indecisive character of the evidence of τὸ πρότερον (see on 4^{13}), this argument overlooks three possibilities that can not be ignored: (a) that the incident of Gal. 2$^{11-21}$ may have deterred Barnabas from accepting Paul's proposal rather than Paul from making it; (b) that even if the incident occurred after the second journey, the letter may still have been written before the third journey, viz., at Antioch between the second and third journeys, and just after the Antioch incident; (c) that the third journey may not have included a visit to the churches of southern Galatia, and hence the letter, even if written on the latter part of that journey, may have been preceded by only two visits to the churches of southern Galatia.

c. Inasmuch as Barnabas was with Paul on his first missionary journey when the churches of southern Galatia were founded, but did not accompany him on his second journey, and, hence, would not be known personally to the North-Galatian churches, if there were such, the fact that the letter mentions him without explanation or identification is somewhat in favour of the South-Galatian theory. But the fact can not be regarded as strong evidence. The letter does not imply that the readers knew him in person, and they might know him by name if he had never been among them.

d. The statement of Gal. 2^5 that Paul refused to yield to the pressure brought upon him in Jerusalem "that the truth of the gospel might continue with you" is understood by some to imply that at the time of the conference in Jerusalem he had already preached the gospel to the Galatians, hence that they were South-Galatians. But the "you" of this passage may mean the Gentiles in general, not the Galatians in particular.

e. The people of Lystra took Paul and Barnabas for gods (Acts 14[11]). Paul says the Galatians received him as an angel of God (Gal. 4[14]). But the parallel is not close enough to prove anything more than that the Galatians and Lycaonians were both warmhearted, impulsive people.

f. The allusion in Gal. 5[11] to the charge that Paul still preached circumcision seems an echo of the use made among the Galatians of his circumcision of Timothy. Now, as Timothy was a South-Galatian, it is particularly probable that the judaisers would use this fact against him in southern Galatia. True, but the story might easily be told in northern Galatia, though the event occurred in southern Galatia.

g. The "marks of the Lord Jesus," Gal. 6[17], have been interpreted to refer to the scourging at Philippi, and the inference has been drawn that the letter was written on the second missionary journey, and that accordingly the churches were in southern Galatia, since at this time he had not yet been twice (4[13]) in northern Galatia. But it is equally plausible (and equally inconclusive; cf. b above) to refer these marks to the experience referred to in 1 Cor. 15[32] or 2 Cor. 1[8], and to argue that the letter must belong to the third missionary journey and that the churches could not be in southern Galatia, since when Paul was at Ephesus he had on the South-Galatian theory been in southern Galatia three times.

h. It is said that Paul would not have gone into northern Galatia, where Greek was comparatively unknown. Jerome does, indeed, testify that the Gallic language was still spoken in this region three hundred years after Paul wrote. But the same passage characterises Greek as the common language of the Orient, and the use of Greek in inscriptions of Ancyra belonging to the time of Tiberius (Boeckh, C. I. G. 4011, 4039, cited by Mommsen, Provinces of the Roman Empire, I 369) indicates that the country was bilingual in Paul's day also.

i. It is said that Paul would certainly have kept to the main highways, hence would not have passed through northern Galatia. This argument can apply only to the second missionary journey; for if on that journey he had founded churches in Pessinus, Ancyra, and Tavium these churches would themselves have furnished a sufficient reason for a subsequent journey into that region. The question, therefore, reduces itself to the inquiry whether under the circumstances indicated in Acts 16[6] and Gal. 4[13] Paul would have gone northeast into northern Galatia. This question has already been discussed at length.

In view of all the extant evidence we conclude that the balance of probability is in favour of the South-Galatian view. The North-Galatian theory in the form advocated by Sief. Schm. and Moff. is not impossible. If in place of the incomplete and obscure, possibly inaccurate, language of Acts 16[6] and 18[23] we had clear and definite evidence, this evidence might prove the existence of North-Galatian churches founded by Paul before the writing of this letter. If so, this would, as indicated above, in turn prove that Paul's letter was written to them. But the evidence as it stands is not sufficient to bear the weight of theory which this hypothesis involves, including, as it does, the very existence of churches of whose existence we have no direct or definite evidence. On the basis of the existing evidence the most probable view is that of Zahn, viz., that on his second missionary journey Paul passed through the western edge of old Galatia, there finding or making a few disciples, but founding no churches; and that his letter to the churches of Galatia was written not to the Galatians of this region, but to the churches of Derbe, Lystra, Iconium, and Pisidian Antioch.

III. THE TIME AND PLACE OF WRITING.

There is no evidence by which to determine with accuracy the time in Paul's life at which he wrote his letter to the Galatians. All that can be done is to fix certain limits of time within which it was written.

1. It must obviously have been written after the events narrated in chaps. 1 and 2. Of these the conference at Jerusalem (2^{1-10}) is expressly said to have taken place fourteen years after the conversion of Paul, or more probably fourteen years after his previous visit to Jerusalem, which itself took place three years after his conversion.

2. The points of coincidence between this narrative and that of Acts, chap. 15, are so many and of such character as practically to establish the identity of the two events.* The Acts

* See detached note, p. 117; Weizs. *Apost. Zeit.*[3], p. 168; E. T. I 199 *ff.*; McGiffert, *Apostolic Age.* p. 208; Ltft. *Com. on Gal.* pp. 123 *ff.*, and other commentaries on Gal.; Wendt, *Apostelgeschichte*, cap. 15, in Meyer's *Kommentar*, and other commentaries on Acts.

narrative places the conference "no little time" after the return of Paul and Barnabas to Antioch from their first missionary journey. We thus have a double dating of the event, that of Gal. 2¹, which locates it from fourteen to seventeen years after the conversion of Paul and that of the Acts narrative, which places it between the apostle's first and second missionary journeys.

3. The visit of Peter to Antioch narrated in 2¹¹⁻¹⁴ presumably followed the conference in Jerusalem, and is naturally assigned to the period of Paul's stay in Antioch referred to in Acts 15³⁵. Thus the earliest possible date for the writing of the letter is the latter portion of that period.

4. The phrase τὸ πρότερον in Gal. 4¹³ has often been appealed to as decisive evidence that before writing this letter Paul had made two evangelistic journeys into Galatia. Taken alone the words do not seem with certainty to prove this (see note on τὸ πρότερον, pp. 239 ff.). But when the evidence of 4¹⁶, ²⁰ (q. v.; cf. 1⁹, also) that Paul had communicated with the Galatians between the original preaching of the gospel to them (4¹⁴) and the writing of the letter is taken into account, the simplest explanation of all the data is that Paul had made two visits to Galatia before writing the letter. On this supposition the letter must have been written not only after the visit of Peter to Antioch (Acts 15³⁵) but after the journey of Acts 16¹⁻⁵. Time must also be allowed for the apostle to have gone some distance from Galatia, for the visit of the judaising missionaries, for such success as they had achieved in their effort to win the Galatians to their conception of the way of salvation, and for the carrying of the news to Paul. See Gal.1⁶, ⁷ 5⁷⁻¹², and discussion under "Occasion and Purpose" below. As these conditions could scarcely have been fulfilled before the arrival of the apostle in Corinth as narrated in Acts 18¹, we may regard it as improbable that the letter was written before that event. On the North-Galatian view and the supposition that Paul had visited the churches twice before writing the letter, it must have been written after Acts 18²³.

5. The phrase οὕτως ταχέως in 1⁶ shows that the letter was

written at no long time after the conversion of the Galatians, but furnishes no ground of choice among dates which are on other grounds possible. See on 1^6.

6. If within the period of the apostle's life after Acts 18^1 we seek to determine a more definite date, some weight must be given to such evidence as the relation between Galatians and Romans. The latter, presenting calmly and deliberately views similar in substance to those which the former expresses with the heat of controversy, was probably written after Galatians. Of somewhat similar character is the relation between Galatians and 1 and 2 Corinthians. The situation reflected in the latter, showing the representatives of the judaistic tendency opposing Paul's work in Achaia, probably arose after the situation described in Galatians was created in Galatia, the judaisers presumably moving westward in their attack upon Paul's work. But inasmuch as the letter was manifestly written while the situation that arose in Galatia was still acute, and not long after the visit of the judaisers, it is most probably to be assigned to a period before the coming of the judaisers to Corinth; in other words, not later than the early part of the apostle's two years and three months in Ephesus (Acts $19^{1\text{-}22}$). Yet this argument can not be strongly pressed. The missionaries to Galatia and Achaia were not at all certainly the same persons, and the delegation to Corinth may have gone there before the other group arrived in Galatia.

7. Some consideration is also due to the fact that the letters of the apostle taken together show that his controversy with his legalistic opponents made a deep impression on his thinking and, for some years at least, filled a large place in his thoughts. From 1 Corinthians to Colossians every letter shows at least some marks of this controversy, while of several of them it is the central theme. But in 1 and 2 Thessalonians we find no reference whatever to this matter. This fact creates a certain probability that Galatians was not written till after 1 and 2 Thessalonians. But the force of this argument is largely destroyed by the fact that the letters to the Thessalonians must have been written in any case after the conference

at Jerusalem, and, therefore, after the judaistic controversy had come to fill a large place in the apostle's thought.

But if, as is on the whole probable, Galatians was written after the arrival at Corinth on his second missionary journey, and before Romans on his third missionary journey, there are several places and times at which it may have been written, of which four are perhaps most worthy of consideration. If it was written to the churches of southern Galatia it may date from (1) Corinth in the period of Acts 18[1-17], and either before or after the writing of 1 Thessalonians, (2) Antioch in the period of Acts 18[22, 23a], (3) Ephesus in the period covered by Acts, chap. 19, or (4) Macedonia or Achaia in the period covered by Acts 20[1-3].

> Mynster (*Einleitung in den Brief an die Galater*, in *Kleinere Schriften*, 1825), Zahn (*Einleitung in d. N. T.*[3], pp. 139–142, E. T. pp. 193 *ff.*, esp. 196–199), Bacon (*Introduction to the N. T.*, p. 58), and Rendall (*Expositor*, Ser. IV, vol. IX; *Exp. Grk. Test.*, vol. III, p. 146) assign it to Corinth before the writing of 1 Thessalonians, thus making it the first of all the apostle's letters. Renan (*St. Paul*, p. 313) and Ramsay (*St. Paul the Traveller*, pp. 189 *ff.*; *Commentary*, pp. 242 *ff.*) date it from Antioch in the period of Acts 18[23a], while Askwith (*Epistle to the Galatians*, chaps. VII, VIII) dates it from Macedonia after 2 Corinthians.

In favour of Antioch in the period of Acts 18[23] as against Corinth on the second missionary journey, it is to be said that information concerning affairs in Galatia (the efforts of the judaisers and their success with the Galatians) would more easily reach the apostle in Antioch of Syria than in Macedonia or Achaia. It has also been suggested by Ram. (*Traveller*, pp. 189 *ff.*) that the letter gives evidence that the apostle had full information of the state of affairs such as would not easily have been obtained by a letter, and implies, therefore, that he had received knowledge by a personal messenger. As such messenger no one would be more probable than Timothy, himself a Galatian. But Timothy was with Paul at Corinth for some time, as 1 and 2 Thessalonians show. Only then, towards the latter part of the Corinthian residence, could he have left

d

Paul for Galatia, and in that case could have joined Paul at no more probable place than Antioch. Indeed, it is a very natural hypothesis that at or about the time when Paul left Corinth to go to Syria by water, he sent Timothy to go as far as Ephesus by water and thence through Asia Minor overland for the double purpose of visiting his home once more and of gathering information concerning the churches. In that case, whether originally expecting to go through to Antioch or to await Paul in Galatia, it would be natural for Timothy, when he learned the state of affairs in Galatia, to hasten forward to Antioch to inform Paul. The prominence of the incident at Antioch (2^{11-21}) would also be easily explained if the apostle wrote from Antioch, as also the fact that though writing to several churches, one of which was at Pisidian Antioch, he nevertheless speaks of Antioch in Syria simply as Antioch. To the possible objection that Paul would hardly have written to the Galatians from Syrian Antioch between his second and third missionary journeys, since he must have been on the point of going to Galatia himself, it is sufficient to answer that we have no means of knowing how long he was still to tarry at Antioch when he wrote, and that his conduct in relation to the church at Corinth (see esp. 2 Cor. 1^{23} 2^1) shows that he had a preference for dealing with such troubles as that which existed in Galatia by correspondence and messenger rather than by a personal visit.

But none of these reasons is very weighty. It must be confessed, moreover, that the supposition that the letter was written at Antioch to the churches of southern Galatia between the second and third missionary journeys does not comport well with what seems to be the most probable interpretation of Acts 18^{23}, viz., that the apostle passed by these churches on the third journey; cf. p. xl. If his effort to retain the loyalty of the churches to his gospel was successful he would certainly wish to confirm this result by a visit; if it was unsuccessful (unless, indeed, utterly and hopelessly so, in which case the letter would probably not have been preserved), he would certainly wish to attempt to accomplish by a visit what he had

failed to achieve by his letter. If, indeed, Acts 18[23] can be so
interpreted as to imply a journey through southern Galatia, then
the expression "confirming all the disciples" would appropriately describe the purpose and effect of a visit following the
letter, assumed to be successful, but in itself furnishes no strong
evidence that the letter had been written.

The case for Antioch is, therefore, not very strong, and as
against Ephesus on the third missionary journey, it is even
less so than against Corinth on the second. Nor can
τὸ πρότερον (4[13]) be urged against Ephesus on the ground
that at that time Paul would have been in Galatia three times,
for, as shown above, it is not certain or even probable that the
journey of Acts 18[23] included the churches of Galatia. If there
is any weight in Ram.'s argument respecting the probability of
Timothy bringing the apostle personal information, this applies
almost equally well to Ephesus as the place of writing. For if
Paul did not visit the churches of southern Galatia in the journey of Acts 18[23] he may very well have sent Timothy by that
route, and have received Timothy's report at Ephesus.

The arguments by which Askwith supports his contention
in favour of Macedonia on the third missionary journey are
not all equally forcible, but there is no strong counter argument, and this location of the letter very interestingly accounts
for the language of Gal. 6[7, 8] and its parallelism with 2 Cor. 9[6].
Yet neither is this a decisive or strong argument for his view.

Apparently, therefore, we must remain contented without
any strong reason for deciding whether the letter, if destined
for the churches of southern Galatia, was written in the latter
part of the apostle's stay at Corinth on his second missionary
journey, or at Antioch between the second and third journeys,
or at Ephesus on the third journey, or still later on this journey, in Macedonia or Achaia. If there is any balance of probability it seems to be in favour of Ephesus.

On the supposition that the letter was written to churches in northern
Galatia founded on the second missionary journey (Acts 16[6]), and
that the evidence of the epistle indicates that he had visited them a
second time, the letter, as already pointed out, must have been writ-

ten after Acts 18²³. On the other hand, his journeys after leaving Corinth at the end of his third missionary journey (Acts 20³) are such as to make the writing of the letter after this latter time improbable, as is also the relation of Galatians to Romans. As between Ephesus and Macedonia, or between either of these and Achaia, there is little ground for choice. The argument of Ltft. that it must be placed after the Corinthian letters because of its close affinity to Romans is of little weight, especially in view of the fact that Romans was probably a circular letter and may have been composed some months before the Roman copy was sent from Corinth.

Continental scholars who hold the North-Galatian view generally place the letter at Ephesus. So Mey. Ws. Sief. Godet, Stein. Similarly Holtzmann places it on the journey to Ephesus, or soon after the arrival there, and Jülicher during the Ephesus ministry, but while on a missionary journey out from that city. Conybeare and Howson, and after them Ltft., argue for Corinth on the same journey; so also Salmon. On the whole, there is no more probable date for the letter than Ephesus on the third missionary journey, whether it was written to northern or southern Galatia.

Lake, *Earlier Epistles of St. Paul*, pp. 279 *ff.*, identifying the visit to Jerusalem of Gal. 2¹⁻¹⁰ with that of Acts, chaps. 11 and 12, and denying that the τὸ πρότερον of 4¹³ implies two visits to Galatia, places the writing of the letter before the Council at Jerusalem recorded in Acts, chap. 15. In this he agrees substantially with Emmet (*Galatians*, pp. XIV *ff.*), and Round (*The Date of . . . Galatians*), and, as concerns the identification of the visit of Gal. 2¹⁻¹⁰ with that of Acts 11³⁰, with Ram. and Weber. But against this identification the meaning and tense of ἐσπούδασα in 2¹⁰ are strong if not decisive evidence (see *ad loc.*), while the many points of agreement between Gal. 2¹⁻¹⁰ and Acts, chap. 15, constitute on the whole decisive evidence for the reference of these two passages to the same event. See detached note, p. 117. It is indeed true that it is impossible to suppose that the account in Acts, chap. 15, is in all respects accurate if it refers to the incident of Gal. 2¹⁻¹⁰; but it is more probable that this narrative is inaccurate in its statement of the terms of the agreement, or in assigning them to this occasion, than that, if the incident of Acts 2¹⁻¹⁰ occurred on the occasion of the visit of Acts 11³⁰, and the agreement stated in Gal. 2⁹, ¹⁰ was reached at that time, the whole question was reopened, and an event so like the former one occurred some two years later.

Turner, art. "Chronology" in H*DB*, vol. I, p. 424, col. a (*cf.* also Zahn, *Kom.* pp. 110 *ff.*), holds that the visit of Peter to Antioch (Gal. 2¹¹⁻¹⁴) preceded the events of Gal. 2¹⁻¹⁰. Identifying the conference of 2¹⁻¹⁰ with that of Acts, chap. 15, Turner also identifies the τινὲς ἀπὸ Ἰακώβου of Gal. 2¹² with the τινὲς κατελθόντες ἀπὸ τῆς Ἰουδαίας

INTRODUCTION

of Acts 15[1]. Ram. *Traveller*, pp. 158 *ff.*; *Com.* pp. 304 *ff.*, making
Gal. 2[1-10] refer to the visit narrated in Acts 11[30], leaves Gal. 2[11-14] in
the position in relation to 2[1-10] in which it stands in Galatians. As indicated above he dates the letter in the period of Acts 18[23]. The result in
both cases is, without affecting the date of the letter, to place the Antioch incident at a longer interval before the writing of it than the more
common view, which identifies Gal. 2[1] with Acts 15[2] and leaves the
order of Gal. chap. 2 undisturbed. Zahn, agreeing with Ram. in
identifying Gal. 2[1] with Acts 11[30] and with Turner in placing Gal. 2[11-14]
before 2[1-10], puts the Antioch incident still further back, even before
Paul's first missionary journey, but still puts the writing of the letter
as Ram. does, after Acts, chap. 15, viz., at Corinth, in the period of
Acts 18[11]. There is little or nothing to be said against the date to
which these writers assign the letter, but quite as little to be said in
favour of the position to which they assign the Antioch incident.
The transposition of the parts of Gal. chap. 2, to which Turner and
Zahn resort, is indeed not explicitly excluded by an ἔπειτα at the
beginning of 2[11], but neither is there anything to support it in the
language of the passage, while it does distinct violence to the psycho-
logical probabilities of the situation. As is pointed out in detail in
the exegesis of the passage, the question which arose at Antioch is
distinctly different from that which was discussed at Jerusalem, but
one to which the ignoring of ultimate issues which characterised the
Jerusalem conference, and the compromise in which it issued, was
almost certain to give rise. The position, moreover, which Paul was
driven to take at Antioch was definitely in advance of that which
he took at Jerusalem, involving a virtual repudiation not of one statute
of the law, but of all, and this not only for the Gentiles, but in principle
for the Jews. The reversal of the order in which he has narrated the
events is, therefore, an unwarranted violence to the record. It may,
indeed, not unreasonably be said that the Antioch incident could
scarcely have happened after the events of Acts, chap. 15, as narrated
in that passage; for the question that apparently arose as a new issue
at Antioch is already settled in decisions recorded in Acts, chap. 15.
But in view of all the evidence, the solution of this difficulty lies neither
in denying the general identity of the event of Gal. 2[1-10] with that of
Acts, chap. 15, nor in putting Acts, chap. 15 after Gal. 2[1-11], but in
recognising that the Acts narrative is inaccurate in its statement of the
outcome of the conference, either colouring the decision actually
reached, or ascribing to this time a decision reached on some other and,
presumably, later occasion.

The view of McGiffert and Bartlet, adopted also by Emmet, that
the two visits to Galatia implied in τὸ πρότερον of Gal. 4[13] are the outward and return parts of the journey through southern Galatia on the

lii INTRODUCTION

first missionary journey, on which is based the conclusion that the letter was written before the second missionary journey, is discussed on p. 241. McGiffert's argument that if Paul had visited the Galatian churches since the conference of Acts, chap. 15, he would have had no occasion to give them the full account of it in Gal. 2^{1-10}, as of something of which they had not heard before, ignores the hint of the letter (1^9 4^{18}) that he had already discussed the matter with them, and the possibility, not to say probability, that the acute situation which existed when he wrote the letter called for a fresh statement of the matter, and probably a fuller one than he had previously felt to be necessary.

The reduction of the above statements, which are expressed in terms of periods of the apostle's life, to calendar dates involves the whole problem of the chronology of the apostle's life. Without entering at length into this question, which lies outside the scope of this Introduction, it may suffice to point out that if, as seems to be proved by an inscription found at Delphi (see *Report of the Palestine Exploration Fund*, April, 1908; Deissmann, *St. Paul*, Appendix II; *American Journal of Theology*, XXI 299), Gallio became proconsul of Achaia in the summer of 51 A. D., we arrive at 50 or 51 as the date for the writing of Galatians in case it was written at Corinth on the second missionary journey. If it was written at Antioch between his first and second journeys, it falls into 51 or 52; if at Ephesus, on the third journey, in all probability into 52; if in Macedonia or at Corinth, on the third missionary journey, at some time in 54 or 55. If we identify the conference of Gal. 2^{1-10} with that of Acts, chap. 15, assume, as is generally held, that Herod Agrippa I died in 44 A. D., and, on the ground of the position of the narrative of this event in Acts, assign the visit of Acts 11^{30} 12^{25} to a date not later than about 46 A. D., it will follow that the first visit to Galatia (Acts, chaps. 13, 14) occurred not far from 46, and the second visit of Paul to Jerusalem (Gal. 2^{1-10}) not far from 48. This date is consistent with the apostle's location of the event as occurring seventeen years after his conversion (see on 2^1), the resultant date of his conversion being about 31 A. D.

The argument for the later date (34 or 35) based on 1 Cor. 11^{32*} falls to the ground with the recognition of the fact that the presence of the ethnarch of Aretas in Damascus does not imply that Damascus was in the dominion of Aretas. See on 1^{17}.

IV. OCCASION AND PURPOSE OF THE LETTER.

It is fortunate for the interpreter of the letter to the Galatians that while the location of the churches is in dispute and the time and place of writing can be determined, if at all, only by a balance of probabilities resting on indirect evidence, the question for whose answer these matters are of chief importance, can be decided with a good degree of certainty and on independent grounds. The previous relations of the writer and his readers, the circumstances that led to the writing of the letter, the purpose for which it was written, these appear with great clearness in the letter itself.

The Galatians to whom the letter was written were Gentile Christians, converted from heathenism (4^8), evidently under the preaching of Paul (1$^{8, 9}$ 4^{13}; cf. 3$^{1ff.}$). Paul's first preaching to them was occasioned by illness on his part (4^{13}); intending to go in some other direction, he was led by illness to go to Galatia, or being on his way through Galatia and not intending to tarry there, he was led to do so by illness. He proclaimed to them Jesus Christ and him crucified, preaching that men could through faith in Jesus the Christ escape from the present evil age and attain the approval of God apart from works of law (3$^{1, 2}$). He imposed on his converts no Jewish ordinances, but taught a purely spiritual Christianity (3$^{2, 3}$ 4$^{8-11}$ 5$^{3, 4}$). The Galatians received him and his gospel with enthusiasm (4$^{12-15}$). They were baptised (3^{27}) and received the gift of the Holy Spirit, miracles wrought among them giving evidence of his presence (3$^{2-5}$). That Paul visited them a second time is made practically certain by the evidence of 1^9 4$^{13, 20}$ (q. v.). Possibly before the second visit there had been false teachers among them (1^9), but if so the defection had not been serious (1^6 5^7). More recently, however, a serious attempt had

---

* See Burton, *Records and Letters of the Apostolic Age*, pp. 204 f.

been made to draw them away from the gospel as Paul had preached it to them (1^7 5^{12}). This new doctrine opposed to Paul's was of a judaistic and legalistic type. Its advocates evidently endeavoured to win the Galatians to it by appealing to the promises to Abraham and his seed recorded in the Old Testament. Though the letter makes no definite quotation from the language of these teachers it is easily evident from the counter argument of the apostle in chapters 3 and 4 that they had taught the Galatians either that salvation was possible only to those who were, by blood or adoption, children of Abraham, or that the highest privileges belonged only to these. See especially $3^{7,\ 9,\ 14}$ $4^{21\text{-}31}$. They had laid chief stress upon circumcision, this being the initiatory rite by which a Gentile was adopted into the family of Abraham. Though they had cautiously abstained from endeavouring to impose upon the Galatians the whole Jewish law, or from pointing out that this was logically involved in what they demanded (5^3), they had induced them to adopt the Jewish feasts and fasts (4^{10}).

To these doctrinal elements of the controversy, themselves sufficient to arouse deep feeling and sharp antagonisms, there was added a personal element still more conducive to embitterment. The letter itself furnishes evidence, which is confirmed by 1 and 2 Corinthians, that the apostolic office or function was clearly recognised as one of great importance in the Christian community, and that the question who could legitimately claim it was one on which there was sharp difference of opinion. An apostle was much more than a local elder or itinerant missionary. He was a divinely commissioned founder of Christian churches, indeed, more, of the Christian church œcumenical. With their effort to keep the Christian movement within the Jewish church, including proselytes from other religions, the judaisers naturally associated the contention that the apostolate was limited to those who were appointed by Jesus or by those whom he appointed. With their denial of the distinctive doctrines of Paul they associated a denial of his right to teach them as an apostle. This denial seems to have taken the form of representing Paul as a renegade follower of the

Twelve, a man who knew nothing of Christianity except what he had learned from the Twelve, and preached this in a perverted form. This appears from the nature of Paul's defence of his independent authority as an apostle in the first two chapters of the letter, and indicates that with their theory of a limited apostolate the judaisers had associated the claim that the apostolic commission must proceed from the circle of the original Twelve. See detached note on Ἀπόστολος, pp. 363 ff.

This double attack of the judaisers upon the apostle and his doctrine and the attempt to convert the Galatians to their view was upon the point of succeeding when Paul learned of the state of affairs. The Galatians were already giving up the gospel which Paul had taught them (1^6); he feared that his labour on them was wasted (4^{11}); yet in a hopeful moment he was confident in the Lord that they would not be carried away (5^{10}).

Such is the situation that gave rise to the letter. In a sense Paul had a double purpose, partly to defend himself, partly to defend his gospel, but only in a sense. The defence of himself was forced on the apostle by the relation in which the question of his apostleship stood to the truth of his gospel. Considerable space is necessarily devoted in the first third of the letter to the personal matter, since it was of little use for the apostle to argue, and of no use to affirm, what constituted the true gospel, while his readers doubted his claim to be an authorised expounder of the gospel. Towards the end he carefully guards his doctrine from certain specious but false and mischievous inferences from it ($5^{13ff.}$), and touches upon a few other minor matters. But the central purpose of the letter is to arrest the progress of the judaising propaganda with its perverted gospel of salvation through works of law, which the Galatians were on the very point of accepting, and to win them back to faith in Jesus Christ apart from works of law, the gospel which Paul himself had taught them.

Incidentally the letter affords us most important information which we can not suppose to have been any part of the apostle's plan to transmit to us, but which is not on that account the less valuable. No other letter contains so full and objective a piece of autobiography as that which he has given us in the first two chapters of this letter. Informing as are 1 and 2 Corinthians, 1 Thessalonians and Philippians, these chapters are even more so.

Not less valuable is the contribution of the letter to the history of the apostolic age. It carries us into the very heart of the controversy between the narrow, judaistic conception of the gospel, and that more enlightened, broader view of which Paul was the chief champion in the first age of the church. The story is told, indeed, in part in Acts, but as it was conceived years after the event; in the letter we have not so much an account of the controversy as a voice out of the conflict itself. The information is first-hand; the colours have the freshness and vividness of nature. Not least important for us to-day is the testimony which the letter bears to the limits of that controversy. A just interpretation of the second chapter shows most clearly not that Peter and Paul were in sharp antagonism to one another, representatives of opposing factions, but that, while they did not altogether agree in their conceptions of religious truth, and while Peter lacked the steadiness of vision necessary to make him stand firmly for the more liberal view, yet neither he nor even James directly opposed Paul's view, or his claim to be an apostle of Christ. The opponents of Paul were certain "false brethren . . . who came in privily to spy out our liberty." They had, indeed, influence enough with the Jerusalem apostles to lead the latter to urge Paul to pursue a compromising course; but when Paul refused, the pillar-apostles virtually took his side and gave to him hands of fellowship, recognising the legitimacy of his mission to the Gentiles.

Yet the recognition of the fact that there were really three parties to the controversy rather than two leaves its significance but little diminished and its bitterness unchanged. The sharpness of the apostle's language both in Galatians and 2 Corinthians was doubtless called forth by at least an equal bitterness on the side of his opponents. The questions at issue

were fundamental (see below, § V) and the discussion of them
was no calm academic debate, but a veritable contest for large
stakes between men of intense conviction and deep feeling.
Nor was it significant for Galatia and Corinth and Jerusalem
only, nor for that age alone. Had no one arisen in that age
to espouse the view for which Paul contended, or had the controversy issued in a victory for the judaistic party, the whole
history of Christianity must have been different from what it
has been. Christianity would have been only a sect of Judaism, and as such would probably have been of relatively little
force in the history of the world, or would even have been lost
altogether, becoming reabsorbed into the community from
which it came. The letter to the Galatians is a first-hand
document from the heart of one of the most significant controversies in the history of religion.

V. THE QUESTIONS AT ISSUE.

The above statement of the occasion of the letter is sufficient
to show that the controversy in which it played a part had to
do with certain questions which were of fundamental importance for early Christianity. These questions did not first
come to the surface in Galatia, but neither did they become
prominent at the beginning of Paul's career, nor were they all
stated and discussed with equal explicitness. The one which
came most clearly into the foreground and was probably also
the first to be debated was whether Gentiles who, attracted by
the message of the gospel, were disposed to accept it must be
circumcised in order to be recognised as members of the Christian community and to participate in the salvation which the
gospel brought to those who received it. To this question
Gal. 3[1-3] shows clearly that Paul had, before beginning his
evangelistic work in Galatia, returned a definitely negative
answer. This epistle furnishes evidence which, though not
explicit in its individual items, is on the whole sufficient to
show that this position of the apostle was not at first strongly
opposed by the Jerusalem church (see 1[24] and notes thereon).
The statement of Gal. 1[23, 24] that when the churches of Judæa

heard of Paul's work in Syria and Cilicia they glorified God in him, taken with the evidence that Paul's convictions about the relation of his gospel to the Gentiles were formed very early in his career as a Christian, makes it probable that there was at first no strong sentiment in the Jerusalem church against recognising Gentiles who accepted the gospel message as members of the new fellowship and community. That presently, however, there arose a conflict of opinion on the subject was apparently due to two causes. On the one hand, there were added to the Christian community in Judæa certain men of strongly conservative tendencies who were convinced that Christianity ought to be built strictly on the basis of the Abrahamic covenant, and that the Christian sect ought to differ from other Jewish sects, in particular from the Pharisaic sect, only by the addition of the doctrine of the Messiahship of Jesus, and in no case by any subtraction from the doctrines or requirements of the Old Testament religion as currently interpreted. On the other hand, as the effects of the evangelistic activity of Paul became more manifest and better known to the church at Jerusalem, the real extent and serious nature of his departure from the views and practices now becoming current in the mother church doubtless became more evident. As a result of these two influences the question of the obligation of the Gentile Christians to be circumcised came to an issue in the incident narrated by Paul in Gal. $2^{1\text{-}10}$. The debate which took place on that occasion was apparently limited to this one question of the circumcision of Gentile Christians. The Jerusalem apostles at first urging Paul to conform, at least in the case of Titus, to the views of the ultraconservative element, were at length persuaded to throw their influence on the side of Paul's view, to give their approval to his way of winning the Gentiles to faith in Christ, and not to insist upon circumcision. See the commentary on this passage.

But the decision of this question speedily opened another one. In the Antioch church, in which there were both Jews and Gentiles, it became customary not only not to circumcise the Gentile members, but for Jews to eat with the Gentiles, doubtless also for Gentiles to eat with the Jews. It is true that our only explicit record is an account of what took place after Peter came to Antioch. Yet that he was responsible for the custom in which he at first participated is contrary to all probability. The table-fellowship at Antioch was clearly the product of Pauline liberalism, not of Petrine caution or compromise. On the relation of the narrative of Acts, chap. 10, to the matter, see pp. 116 *f.*

That the Gentiles with whom Jewish Christians were eating were not conforming to the laws of the Old Testament concerning food, and that the table-fellowship of the Jews with Gentiles involved violation of the Old Testament law by the Jews, also, is the clear implication of the whole narrative. It is not, indeed, impossible that the Jewish legalists in their zeal to "build a hedge about the law" had laid down a rule against association of Jews and Gentiles in general (*cf.* Acts 10²⁸). But that in the present case the requirement of the law, of which the more strenuous rule, in so far as it was observed or enforced, was an expansion by tradition, was distinctly in mind as the crux of the controversy is shown by several considerations. In the first place Paul speaks in Gal. 2¹² of Peter's *eating* with the Gentiles, implying that the question at issue was one not only of association but of food. In the second place, Paul's interpretation of Peter's withdrawal from fellowship with the Gentiles as an attempt to compel the Gentiles to conform to Jewish custom (Gal. 2¹⁴) implies that the fellowship could be resumed on condition that the Gentiles observed the Jewish law; which obviously would not be the case if those who came from James protested against fellowship between Jews and Gentiles in general, or even against table-fellowship in particular, without reference to whether it involved a disregard of the law of foods. In the third place, the apostle's quick transition from the discussion of the matter of Jews and Gentiles eating together, in vv.¹²⁻¹⁴, to that of the observance of *law* in vv.¹⁵ᶠᶠ·, makes it evident that it was a statute of the law, not a tradition, the observance of which was at issue. Even the narrative in Acts, chap. 15, though manifestly not a wholly correct report of what took place in Jerusalem and having no direct reference to the Antioch incident, nevertheless shows how early the food law played a part in the question of the freedom of the Gentiles.

But if the food on the tables of the Gentiles was not restricted to that which the Levitical law permitted, then it is evident, first, that the Gentiles had generalised the decision respecting circumcision and concluded that no Jewish statutes were binding upon them, or at least had extended the principle to another group of statutes; and, second, what is even more significant, that the Jews had acted on the principle that the law which was not binding on the Gentiles was not binding on them.

These two new questions came to issue in the discussion between Peter and Paul at Antioch as narrated in $2^{11ff.}$. And on this occasion Paul squarely took the position that the law of foods was not only not binding on Jewish Christians, but that they must not obey it under circumstances like those at Antioch, which made their observance of it a compulsion of the Gentiles to do the same.

By this contention Paul in effect denied the authority of the Old Testament statutes over either Jews or Gentiles, at least over those who accepted Jesus as the Son of God. That he did this not only in effect, but with recognition of the fact that this position on circumcision and foods carried with it the general principle, is indicated by his employment, both in his narrative of what he said to Peter and in his discussion of the question later in the epistle, of the general term "law." This is also confirmed by the fact that in writing to the Corinthians (1 Cor. 6^{12}; cf. 10^{23}) he refused to make the authority of the law the basis of his stern reproof of sexual immorality. Though his principle, "All things are lawful," was quoted in justification of gross immorality, he would not withdraw it, but reaffirmed it and rested his case against sexual crime solely on the Christian ground that all things are not expedient, and that by fornication the members of Christ become members of a harlot, i. e., enter into a relationship which destroys the Christian's vital fellowship with Christ. To Paul it was not circumcision and foods, and festival days only that could not be enforced by law; nor ceremonies only; nothing could be insisted upon in the name of law.

Yet in rejecting the authority of the Old Testament statutes, Paul did not reject the teachings of the Old Testament *in toto*. While quoting from the Old Testament the dicta of that legalism which he emphatically rejects (3^{10}), he more frequently quotes from it sentiments which he heartily approves. But, more important, he affirms that the whole law is fulfilled in one word to which he gives his unqualified assent (5^{14}), a sentence which in view of his clear rejection of certain clear requirements of the law can only mean that he saw in the law, along with many statutes that were for him of no value, certain fundamental principles which he had come to regard as constituting the real essence and substance of the law. Thus Paul neither approves nor disapproves all that the Jewish church had canonised, but assumes towards it a discriminative attitude, finding much in it that is true and most valuable, but denying that being in the Old Testament of itself makes a teaching or command authoritative. This discriminative attitude towards the Old Testament, coupled with the apostle's clear recognition of its value as a whole and his insistence, despite his dissent from many of its precepts, upon connecting the Christian religion historically with that of the Old Testament, is most significant. Though he has left us no definite statement to this effect, possibly never formulated the matter in this way in his own mind, he in effect accepted the principle that while each generation is the heir of all the ages, it is also the critic of all, and the arbiter of its own religion. His conduct implied that not what was held in the past, though it stood in sacred scriptures with an affirmation of its perpetual authority, was determinative for the conviction and conduct of living men, but that the criterion for belief and action was to be found in their own interpretation of human experience, their own experience and that of past generations as far as known to them. Religion is not then, for him, static, but fluid, in constant evolution under the influence of men's understanding of the experience of the race.

This rejection of the authority of the Old Testament as such, coupled with the apostle's kindred contention that the gospel was for all nations as they were, *i. e.*, without entrance into the Jewish community or subjection to Jewish law, raised squarely the issue whether Christianity was to be a potentially universal religion or was to continue, as it was at first, a sect of Judaism, differing mainly by one doctrine from current Pharisaism.   On this question Paul took clear issue with the conservative party among the believers in the Messiahship of Jesus.   The inspiration of his mission was a vision of a church universal worshipping the one God and Father, and accepting Jesus as Lord and Saviour—a church into which men should come from every nation and religion, not through the vestibule of Judaism and the acceptance of the law of Moses and the rites of the Old Testament, but straight from where they were and through the single and open door of faith in Jesus Christ.   His opponents also believed in one God and in Jesus as his Messiah, but they could not consent or conceive that men should enter the Christian community except through an acceptance of Judaism, or that the Christian church should be anything else than a specific expression of the Jewish religious community.

But Paul brought the question of authority in religion to the front in another way also.   When the conservative brethren at Jerusalem, whom Paul in his intensity of feeling denounces as false brethren, took up arms against his doctrine of the freedom of the Gentiles and his practical application of it to circumcision and foods, they found it necessary to deny his right to assume to be an expositor of Christianity, and to claim substantially that such authority was vested in those who had received it from Jesus while he was alive on earth.   This affirmation Paul denied, claiming that he had an independent right to preach the gospel by virtue of the revelation of Jesus to him as the Son of God ($1^{1ff.\ 11f.}$).   Yet in claiming for himself this right to preach the gospel without hindrance or permission from the Twelve he conceded to them equally with himself the title of apostle (1^{17}), and the same right to preach within their sphere of action the convictions which they held (2^9).   It is true, indeed, that he was severe in his denunciation of those who endeavoured to undo his own work (1⁸), and was outspoken in his condemnation of those whom he regarded as false apostles (2 Cor. 11¹³). But this is but the extreme affirmation of his own divinely conferred commission, and an evidence that zeal to make converts was not for him a necessary proof of a divine commission or a right spirit. It in no way contravenes what we are now affirming that what he claimed for himself, viz., a divine commission and a corresponding responsibility, he freely admitted might be possessed by other men who did not wholly agree with him. Sitting in council with them he neither consented to conform his own course of action or message to their practice nor demanded that they should conform theirs to his. The gospel of the circumcision and the gospel of the uncircumcision had certain elements in common, but they were by no means identical. Yet he claimed for himself the right and duty to preach his gospel, and admitted the right and duty of the other apostles to preach theirs.

Thus to his rejection of the authority of Old Testament statutes over the conduct of the men of his time, he added in effect the denial that there was any central doctrinal authority for the Christian community as a whole. Claiming the right to teach to the Gentiles a religion stripped of all legalism and reduced to a few religious and ethical principles, he conceded to his fellow-apostles the right to attempt to win the Jews to faith in Jesus while leaving them still in the practice of a strict legalism. That both parties alike had this right to preach according to their conviction, demanded that each should recognise the other's right. Such recognition Paul freely granted to his fellow-apostles and claimed for himself. Thus without expounding in detail a doctrine of the seat of authority in religion, he in reality raised the whole question, and by implication took a very positive position, not against conference and consultation or consideration for the rights of others—these he insisted on—but against the authority of community or council, and in favour of the right of the individual to deliver the message he believes God has given him, and if he gives credible evidence of a real divine commission, to go forward with his work without interference.

But in connection with this principle of liberty in religion there arose in the mind of the apostle, as doubtless also in the minds both of his converts and his critics, further questions. What is the essence of true religion? How is moral character achieved? To men who had been wont to think of religion as authoritatively defined for them in certain sacred books, of morality as consisting in obedience to the statutes contained in these books, and of acceptance with God as conditioned upon such obedience and membership in the community whose uniting tie and basis of unity was a relation to the covenant recorded in the books, it was a serious question what became of religion and morality if there was no longer any authoritative book or any centralised ecclesiastical authority. Precisely this question Paul never states in these words, but with the question itself he deals explicitly and directly. Religion, he says in effect, is not conformity to statutes, or non-conformity, but a spiritual relation to God expressed in the word "faith," and an ethical attitude towards man, summed up in the word "love" (Gal. 5^6). Morality, he affirms, is not achieved by keeping rules, but by living in fellowship with the Spirit of God and in consequent love towards men, issuing in conduct that makes for their welfare (5^{16-23}). Thus he makes religion personal rather than ecclesiastical, and morality a social relation grounded in religion. This is not a new doctrine. It had been announced by the prophets of Israel long before. It is the doctrine which the synoptic gospels tell us Jesus taught. But not even the teaching of Jesus had sufficed to make it the dominant thought of those who early joined the company of his followers, and it was a novelty, indeed, in the Graeco-Roman world. It has never been accepted wholeheartedly by any considerable portion of the Christian church. It is not to-day the real creed of any great part of Christendom.

In this short epistle, written doubtless in haste and some heat, Paul has raised some of the most fundamental and far-reaching questions that can be raised in the field of religion.

The positions which he took were in the main not those that were generally accepted in his day or have been accepted since. He was not the first to announce them, but as held by him they were mainly the product of his own experience and thinking. The writing of the Epistle to the Galatians was an epochal event in the history of religious thought. It is matter for profound regret that its vital contentions were so soon lost out of the consciousness of the Christian church.

VI. GENUINENESS AND INTEGRITY.

The question of the genuineness of Galatians is not easily detached from the larger questions, how Christianity arose, whether there was an apostle Paul who was a factor in its origin, and if so whether he wrote any letters at all. It can not be settled by the comparison of this letter with some other letter which is accepted as certainly written by Paul. For there is no other letter which has any better claim to be regarded as his work than Galatians itself. But neither can it be best discussed without reference to the other letters. As has been shown in considering its occasion, the letter itself discloses, largely incidentally and without apparent effort or intention, a situation so complex, so vital, so self-consistent, so psychologically credible as to make it very improbable that it is a work of art cunningly framed to create the impression that a situation which existed only in the writer's mind was an actual one. This fact is itself a strong reason for believing that the letter is a natural product of the situation which it reflects. Yet the question whether the letter was really written, as it professes to have been, by Paul, an early preacher of the Christian gospel and a founder of churches among the Gentiles, can best be dealt with in connection with the same question respecting some, at least, of the other letters which bear his name. For the real question is what hypothesis best accounts for all the data; more specifically whether the total evidence of the letters considered in relation to all other pertinent evidence renders it most probable that they are all genuine products of real situations,

which they severally disclose, or that the whole group is manu-
factured, a work of art and literary device, or that while some
are of the former kind, there are others whose qualities bring
them under suspicion. Thus, in the same process, we select
the genuine, if any such there are, and fix the standard by
which to test the doubtful. In the attempt to select the documents of early Christianity which, furnishing first-hand and
basic testimony respecting that period, should constitute the
standard by which to assign the other books to their proper
place, Galatians has always been included in the normative
group by those who have found in the New Testament collection any books that were what they professed to be. On the
other hand, its own claims to be from Paul and the claim of
the church that it belonged to the first century have been
denied only in connection with a general denial that we have
any first-century Christian literature, or that there was any
first-century apostle Paul. The reason for this is not far to
seek. The situation out of which Galatians purports to spring
and which it professes to reflect is a very definite and concrete
one with strongly marked features. These features are largely
repeated in certain other letters that also purport to come from
Paul, with somewhat less close resemblance in still other letters bearing Paul's name, and in the Book of Acts. No one
book can without arbitrariness be assumed to be the standard
by which to test all the rest. No single book can arbitrarily
be excluded from consideration or postponed for secondary consideration. But if in the examination of all the books purport-
ing to come from the first age of the church, it proves to be a
difficult task to restore from them all a self-consistent account
of the whole situation, then it is not an irrational but a reasonable course to inquire whether there is any group which unitedly
reflects a situation which is self-consistent, psychologically possible, and in general not lacking in verisimilitude; and then in
turn to make this group and the situation it discloses the point
of departure for determining the relation of the rest to this
situation. F. C. Baur and the Tübingen School may have
been, probably were, somewhat arbitrary in limiting their

normative group to Galatians, 1 and 2 Corinthians, and Romans. But their error was not in including these four in this group, nor chiefly in beginning with these, but in that having begun with these, they excluded such other letters as 1 Thessalonians, Philippians, and Philemon on insufficient grounds. For our present purpose we shall not go far wrong if with Baur we begin with the four letters that he accepted.

Beginning thus, we find that these four letters all claim to have been written by a Paul who describes himself as an apostle of Jesus Christ, and that they all present a clearly defined picture of him, which, however they differ among themselves in important features, is yet consistent in the total result, and singularly life-like. In respect to the region of his work, his relation to the other apostles and to parties in the church, his conception of Jesus and his attitude towards him, the outstanding elements of his religion, the characteristics of his mind and temper, they in part agree, in part supplement one another. Their differences are never greater than would be probable in the case of letters written by the same man in the same general period of his life but in different places and under different circumstances.

> It is not necessary for the purpose of this argument to inquire whether every part of the Epistle to the Romans, as we possess it, was written by Paul, or how many epistles have been combined in our so-called 2 Corinthians, or whether the editor has added some lines of his own. The possibility of editorship including both arrangement and some additions does not materially affect the significance of the substantial and striking consistency and complementariness of the testimony of the several letters to the character and career of their author. Nor, as indicated above, is it necessary at this point to discuss the question whether 1 and 2 Thessalonians, Philippians, Philemon, Colossians, and Ephesians have equal claim to genuineness with the four which Baur and his school accepted. The course of action which the internal evidence of the letters and the history of criticism combine to make most practicable is that which is indicated above.

It is not strange, therefore, that from the second century to the present Galatians has been generally accepted as written by Paul and as constituting, therefore, a first-hand source of knowledge concerning his life, his controversies, and his convictions.

Consistently with the general practice of the time, and what we find to be the case in respect to other New Testament books, there is a considerable period after the writing of the letter in which we find traces, indeed, of its influence on other Christian writers but no explicit mention of it by the name either of the author or of the persons addressed.

There are certain coincidences of language between Galatians and 1 Peter, which some writers take to be evidence of a use of Galatians by the author of the Petrine epistle. Von Soden (cited by Bigg, *St. Peter and St. Jude*, in *Int. Crit. Com.* p. 20) finds such relationship between 1 Pet. 1[4ff.] and Gal. 3[23] 4[7]; between 1 Pet. 2[16] and Gal. 5[13]; and between 1 Pet. 3[6] and Gal. 4[24]. O. D. Foster, *The Literary Relations of the First Epistle of Peter*, New Haven, 1913, finds a still longer list of coincidences, which he ascribes to dependence of 1 Peter on Galatians. If, as is probable, we should recognise a dependence of 1 Peter upon Romans (Sanday and Headlam, *Com. on Romans*, pp. LXXIV *ff.*) it is not improbable that the writer knew Galatians also. But the passages cited are not in themselves altogether conclusive evidence of such knowledge.

Probable reminiscences of the language of Galatians are found in Barn. 19[8]: κοινωνήσεις ἐν πᾶσιν τῷ πλησίον σου (Gal. 6[6]); Clem. Rom. 49[6]: διὰ τὴν ἀγάπην, ἣν ἔσχεν πρὸς ἡμᾶς, τὸ αἷμα αὐτοῦ ἔδωκεν ὑπὲρ ἡμῶν Ἰησοῦς Χριστὸς ὁ κύριος ἡμῶν, ἐν θελήματι θεοῦ, καὶ τὴν σάρκα ὑπὲρ τῆς σαρκὸς ἡμῶν καὶ τὴν ψυχὴν ὑπὲρ τῶν ψυχῶν ἡμῶν (Gal. 1[4]). Clearer parallels appear in Polyc. *Phil.* 3[2, 3]: Παύλου . . . ὃς καὶ αὐτὸς ὑμῖν ἔγραψεν ἐπιστολάς, εἰς ἃς ἐὰν ἐγκύπτητε, δυνήσεσθε οἰκοδομεῖσθαι εἰς τὴν δοθεῖσαν ὑμῖν πίστιν, ἥτις ἐστὶ μήτηρ πάντων ὑμῶν (Gal. 4[26]); *Phil.* 5[1], εἰδότες οὖν ὅτι θεὸς οὐ μυκτηρίζεται (Gal. 6[7]; note the coincidence of the anarthrous θεός in both cases, and *cf.* com. *l. c.*); Phil. 12[2]: *qui credituri sunt in Dominum nostrum et Deum Jesum Christum et in ipsius patrem qui resuscitavit eum a mortuis* (Gal. 1[1]); Just. Mart. *Dial.* 95[1]: ἐπικατάρατος γὰρ εἴρηται (sc. Μωυσῆς) πᾶς ὃς οὐκ ἐμμένει ἐν τοῖς γεγραμμένοις ἐν τῷ βιβλίῳ τοῦ νόμου τοῦ ποιῆσαι αὐτά (Gal. 3[10]; Lxx read: ἐν πᾶσιν τοῖς λόγοις τοῦ νόμου τούτου ποιῆσαι αὐτούς). For other possible influences of the letters on early Christian literature, *cf.* Charteris, *Canonicity*, pp. 233 *f.*; Gregory, *Canon and Text*, pp. 201 *f.*; Moff. *Introd.* p. 107.

As early as about the middle of the second century there existed lists of the letters of Paul, in which Galatians is included.

From Tertullian, *Adv. Marc.* V, and from Epiph. *Haer.* XLII, we learn that Marcion accepted ten epistles of Paul, though somewhat modifying their text. These ten were Galatians, 1 and 2 Corinthians, Romans, 1 and 2 Thessalonians, Laodiceans (Ephesians?), Colossians, Philippians, and Philemon. Both writers name them in the same order except that Epiphanius puts Philemon before Philippians. The agreement of a free-lance such as Marcion with the orthodox party is more significant of the state of early Christian opinion than would be its acceptance by either alone. Marcion's reference to the Epistle to the Galatians is apparently the first extant mention of it by name.

The Muratorian Canon, which Gregory (*op. cit.*, p. 129) dates about 170 A. D. and most others before 200 A. D. at latest (for different opinions see Jülicher, *Einl.*², p. 146) includes Galatians among the epistles of Paul.

From about 175 A. D. quotations from the epistle with citation of it by name, or express quotation of its language are found.

Irenæus quotes Gal. 4⁸, ⁹ expressly ascribing it to Paul (*Haer.* 3. 6⁵), and 3¹⁹ 4⁴, ⁵, speaking of these passages as in the Epistle to the Galatians. (*Haer.* 3. 7², 16³; 5. 21¹). See Charteris, *op. cit.*, p. 235.

Clement of Alexandria, *Strom.* 3¹⁶, says that "Paul writing to the Galatians says, τεκνία μου οὓς πάλιν ὠδίνω, ἄχρις οὗ μορφωθῇ Χριστὸς ἐν ὑμῖν" (Gal. 4¹⁹).

Origen, *Con. Celsum*, v.⁶⁴, quotes Celsus as saying that men who differ widely among themselves, and in their quarrels inveigh most shamefully against one another, may all be heard saying, "The world is crucified to me and I to the world": ἐμοὶ κόσμος ἐσταύρωται, κἀγὼ τῷ κόσμῳ (Gal. 6¹⁴).

From the end of the second century quotations from our epistle are frequent, and no question of its Pauline authorship was raised until the nineteenth century. Even since that time few scholars have doubted it.

To Bruno Bauer apparently belongs the distinction of being the first person to question the genuineness of Galatians.* In opposition

---

* Edward Evanson, an English deist previously a clergyman of the Church of England, in his work on the *Dissonance of our Four Generally Received Evangelists*, 1792, directing his criticism especially against the fourth gospel, denied also the genuineness of Romans, Ephesians, and Colossians, and expressed doubts about Philippians, Titus, and Philemon, but raised no question about Galatians. *Cf.* Sief. *Kom.* p. 26; Knowling, *Testimony of St. Paul to Christ*, p. 38. Steck, *Galaterbrief*, p. 4, seems to be in error in saying that Evanson embraced in his denial all the books of the New Testament with the possible exception of Luke. I have not myself seen Evanson.

to the well-known view of F. C. Baur and the Tübingen school that the chief factor in the production of the genuine literary remains of the apostolic age was the controversy between the judaistic party in the church and the opposing liberal tendency represented by Paul, and that Galatians, 1 and 2 Corinthians, and Romans were the products on the Pauline side of this conflict, B. Bauer in his *Kritik der paulinischen Briefe*, Berlin, 1850–52, assigned practically all the books of the New Testament, including all the so-called letters of Paul, to the second century. But, like Evanson before him, Bauer found no followers.

In 1882 Professor A. D. Loman of Amsterdam began the publication of a series of Essays in *Theologisch Tijdschrift* under the title "Quæstiones Paulinæ," in which, though recognising the existence of Paul, of whom we gain our most trustworthy knowledge in the "we-sections" of Acts, he maintained that we have no letters from Paul, and that all the letters accepted by Baur are in reality attempts to present an idealised Paul.

A. Pierson, who in 1878 had incidentally expressed doubts of the genuineness of the Epistle to the Galatians, in 1886 joined with S. A. Naber in a volume entitled, *Verisimilia: Laceram conditionem Novi Testamenti exemplis illustrarunt et ab origine repetierunt.* They explained all the New Testament books as the result of a Christian working-over of books produced originally by a liberal school of Jewish thought. The Pauline epistles in particular are the product of the editorial work of a certain Paulus Episcopus of the second century.

Rudolf Steck, in *Der Galaterbrief nach seiner Echtheit untersucht*, Berlin, 1888, maintains the historicity of the apostle Paul, but holds that like Jesus he wrote nothing. The four principal letters ascribed to Paul he maintains to have been written in the order: Romans, 1 Corinthians, 2 Corinthians, Galatians, by the Pauline School, the last being based upon the earlier ones.

Van Manen at first vigorously opposed the views of Loman, but later himself advocated similar opinions. In his article "Paul," in *Encyc. Bib.* vol. III, col. 3603 *ff.*, he contends that "we possess no epistles of Paul" (col. 3631), "and various reasons lead us so far as the canonical text [of Galatians] is concerned to think of a Catholic adaptation of a letter previously read in the circle of the Marcionites, although we are no longer in a position to restore the older form" (col. 3627).

It is no longer necessary to discuss these views at length. They belong already to the history of opinion rather than to living issues. Outside the limited circle of the writers named above and a very few others* they have won no adherents either in England or America or on the Continent. The verdict of Germany as expressed by H. J. Holtzmann is accepted by scholars generally. "For ten years a determined effort was made by Holland and Switzerland to ascribe all of the epistles of Paul as not genuine to the second century. This attempt has found no support from German theology" (*New World*, June, 1894, p. 215).

The student who is interested may consult the works above referred to for the views of the writers themselves, and for criticism of their views: Zahn, *ZkWkL*, 1889, pp. 451–466; Gloel, *Die jüngste Kritik des Galaterbriefes*, Erlangen, 1890; Schmidt, *Der Galaterbrief im Feuer der neuesten Kritik*, Leipzig, 1892; Godet, *Introduction to the Epistles of St. Paul*, 1894, pp. 230 ff.; Knowling, *Witness of the Epistles*, London, 1892, chap. III; and *Testimony of St. Paul to Christ*, New York, 1905, Preface and Lectures I and III; Schmiedel, article, "Galatians," in *Encyc. Bib.* vol. II, cols. 1617–1623; Clemen, *Paulus*, Giessen, 1904, vol. I, pp. 6–42; Lake, *Earlier Epistles of St. Paul*, London, 1911, chap. VII; cf. also literature referred to by Moff. *Introd.*, p. 107, Knowling, and Schmiedel, *op. cit.*

Modern criticism as represented by scholars of all schools of thought, with the few exceptions noted, ratifies the tradition of centuries that the letter to the Galatians was written, as it claims to have been, by Paul, the Christian apostle of the first century. The internal evidence of the letter, with the vivid disclosure of a commanding personality and a tense and intensely interesting situation, and the correspondence of that situation with that which is reflected in the other literature professing to come from the same author and period, supplemented by the external evidence, rather meagre though it is, furnish no ground or occasion, indeed, for any other opinion.

* J. Friedrich, *Die Unechtheit des Galaterbriefs*, 1891; Kalthoff, *Die Entstehung des Christenthums*, 1904; Johnson, *Antiqua Mater*, 1887; Robertson, *Pagan Christs*. *Cf.* Knowling and Clemen, *op. cit.*

VII. ANALYSIS OF THE LETTER.

I. INTRODUCTION. 1^{1-10}.

    1. Salutation, including assertion of the writer's apos-
tolic authority 1^{1-5}.

    2. Expression of indignant surprise at the threatened
abandonment of his teaching by the Galatians, in
which is disclosed the occasion of the letter 1^{6-10}.

II. PERSONAL PORTION OF THE LETTER.

    The general theme established by proving the apostle's
independence of all human authority and direct
relation to Christ: 1^{11}–2^{21}.

    1. Proposition: Paul received his gospel not from men,
but immediately from God $1^{11\ 12}$.

    2. Evidence substantiating the preceding assertion of
his independence of human authority drawn from
various periods of his life 1^{13}–2^{21}.

        a. Evidence drawn from his life before his conver
sion $1^{13,\ 14}$.

        b. Evidence drawn from the circumstances of his
conversion and his conduct immediately thereafter 1^{15-17}.

        c. Evidence drawn from a visit to Jerusalem three
years after his conversion 1^{18-20}.

        d. Evidence drawn from the period of his stay in
Syria and Cilicia 1^{21-24}.

        e. Evidence drawn from his conduct on a visit to
Jerusalem fourteen years after the preceding
one 2^{1-10}.

        f. Evidence drawn from his conduct in resisting
Peter at Antioch 2^{11-14}.

        g. Continuation and expansion of his address at
Antioch so stated as to be for the Galatians,
also an exposition of the gospel which he
preached 2^{15-21}.

III. Refutatory Portion of the Letter.

The doctrine that men, both Jews and Gentiles, become acceptable to God through faith rather than by works of law, defended by refutation of the arguments of the judaisers, and chiefly by showing that the "heirs of Abraham" are such by faith, not by works of law. Chaps. 3, 4.

1. Appeal to the early Christian experience of the Galatians 3^{1-5}.

2. Argument from the faith of Abraham, refuting the contention of his opponents that only through conformity to law could men become "sons of Abraham" 3^{6-9}.

3. Counter argument, showing that those whose standing is fixed by law are by the logic of the legalists under the curse of the law 3^{10-14}.

4. Argument from the irrevocableness of a covenant and the priority of the covenant made with Abraham to the law, to the effect that the covenant is still in force 3^{15-18}.

5. Answer to the objection that the preceding argument leaves the law without a reason for being 3^{19-22}.

6. Characterisation of the condition under law and, in contrast with it, the condition since faith came: then we were held in custody under law; now we are all sons of God, heirs of the promise 3^{23-29}.

7. Continuation of the argument for the inferiority of the condition under law, with the use of the illustration of guardianship 4^{1-7}.

8. Description of the former condition of the Galatians as one of bondage to gods not really such, and exhortation to them not to return to that state 4^{8-11}.

9. Affectionate appeal to the Galatians to enter fully into their freedom from law, referring to their

former enthusiastic reception of the apostle and affection for him 4[12-20].

10. A supplementary argument, based on an allegorical use of the story of the two sons of Abraham, and intended to convince the Galatians that they are joining the wrong branch of the family 4[21-31].

IV. HORTATORY PORTION OF THE LETTER. 5[1]-6[10]

1. Exhortations directly connected with the doctrine of the letter 5[1]-6[5].

    a. Appeal to the Galatians to stand fast in their freedom in Christ 5[1-12].

    b. Exhortation not to convert their liberty in Christ into an occasion for yielding to the impulse of the flesh 5[13-26].

    c. Exhortation to restore those who fall, and to bear one another's burdens 6[1-5].

2. Exhortations having a less direct relation to the principal subject of the epistle 6[6-10].

V. CONCLUSION OF THE LETTER. 6[11-18]

1. Final warning against the judaisers 6[11-16].

2. Appeal enforced by reference to his own sufferings 6[17].

3. Final benediction 6[18].

VIII. THE TEXT.

Accepting in general the principles of Westcott and Hort, the author of this commentary has diligently examined the available evidence for the text of Galatians in the light of those principles. The result has naturally been the acceptance for the most part of the Westcott and Hort text; yet in a few cases the evidence has seemed to require the adoption of a different reading from that preferred by those eminent scholars.

The evidence has been gained almost wholly from Tischendorf, *Novum Testamentum Græce*, ed. oct. crit. maj. Leipzig, 1872. Use has also been made of Souter, *Novum Testamentum Græce*, Oxford, 1910, and, for the ms. H., of the reproductions of it by Omont, Robinson, and Lake. See below, p. lxxvi. The notation is that of Gregory as found in *Die griechischen Handschriften des Neuen Testaments*, Leipzig, 1908.

The epistle is found in whole or in part in twenty-one uncial manuscripts, being complete in sixteen of them. The five instances in which it is incomplete are noted in the following list:

ℵ. *Codex Sinaiticus.* Fourth century. In Imperial Library, Petrograd. Edited by Tischendorf, 1862; photographic reproduction by H. and K. Lake, Oxford, 1911.

A. *Codex Alexandrinus.* Fifth century. In British Museum, London. Edited by Woide, 1786; N. T. portion by Cowper, 1860; Hansell, 1864; in photographic facsimile, by E. Maunde Thompson, 1879; and again in photographic simile by F. G. Kenyon in 1909.

B. *Codex Vaticanus.* Fourth century. In Vatican Library, Rome. Photographic facsimile by Cozza-Luzi, 1889; and a second issued by the Hoepli publishing house, 1904.

C. *Codex Ephræmi Rescriptus.* Fifth century. In National Library, Paris. As its name implies, it is a palimpsest, the text of the Syrian Father Ephrem being written over the original biblical text. New Testament portion edited by Tischendorf, 1843. Contains Gal. 1^{21}, ἔπειτα to the end, except that certain leaves are damaged on the edge, causing the loss of a few words. So *e. g.* ξῆλος or ξῆλοι, Gal. 5^{20}.

Dᴾ. *Codex Claromontanus.* Sixth century. In National Library, Paris. Greek-Latin. Edited by Tischendorf, 1852.

Eᴾ. *Codex Sangermanensis.* Ninth century. In Petrograd. Greek-Latin. A copy, not very good, of

Codex Claromontanus. Hence not cited in the evidence.

F. *Codex Augiensis.* Ninth century. In Trinity College, Cambridge. Greek-Latin. Edited by Scrivener, 1859. Closely related to *Codex Bœrnerianus.* See Gregory, *Textkritik*, pp. 113 *f.*

Fᵃ. *Codex Parisiensis Coislinianus I.* Seventh century. In National Library, Paris. Edited by Tischendorf in *Mon. Sac. Ined.* 1846. Contains Gal. $4^{21, 22}$.

Gᴾ. *Codex Bœrnerianus.* Ninth century. In Royal Library, Dresden. Greek-Latin. Edited by Matthæi, 1791; photographic reproduction issued by the Hiersemann publishing house, Leipzig, 1909.

H. Sixth century. The fragments of this ms. are scattered in six European libraries. The portion at Athos contains Gal. 1^{1-4} 2^{14-17}; that in the Imperial Library at Petrograd Gal. 1^{4-10} 2^{9-14}; that in the National Library in Paris Gal. $4^{30}-5^{5}$. The portions known at that time were published by Tischendorf in *Mon. Sac. Ined.* Bd. VIII; Duchesne published the Athos and Paris fragments in *Archives des Missons sc. et lit.* Ser. III, vol. 3, pp. 420–429, Paris, 1876; and H. Omont published the entire ms. as then known (forty-one leaves) in *Notice sur un très ancien manuscrit grec en onciales des épîtres de Saint Paul, conservé à la Bibliothèque Nationale*, Paris, 1889; which is republished in *Notices et Extraits des manuscrits de la Bibliothèque Nationale*, vol. 33, pp. 145–192, Paris, 1890. From the offset on opposite leaves J. A. Robinson published sixteen pages of the ms., including Gal. 4^{27-30} 5^{6-10}, in *Texts and Studies*, vol. III, No. 3, Cambridge, 1895. Kirsopp Lake reproduced the Athos fragments in facsimile and a transcribed text in *Facsimiles of the Athos Fragment of Codex H of the Pauline Epistles*, Oxford, 1905. The citations of the text in this commentary are made from the publications of Omont, Robinson, and Lake.

K. *Codex Mosquensis.* Ninth century. In Moscow.

L. *Codex Angelicus.* Ninth century. In Angelica Library in Rome.

N[p]. *Codex Petropolitanus.* Ninth century. In Imperial Library, Petrograd. Contains Gal. 5^{12}–6^4.

P. *Codex Porphyrianus.* Ninth century. In Imperial Library, Petrograd. Published by Tischendorf in *Mon. Sac. Ined.* Bd. V, 1865.

Ψ. Eighth or ninth century. At the monastery of the Laura on Mt. Athos; unpublished. See Gregory, *Textkritik*, p. 94; Kenyon, *Textual Criticism of N. T.* p. 120.

056. Tenth century. In National Library, Paris. See Gregory, *Textkritik*, p. 296, No. 19, p. 1047.

062. Fourth or fifth century. In Damascus. Contains only Gal. 4^{15}–5^{14}. See Gregory, *Textkritik*, p. 1047.

075. Tenth century. In National Library, Athens. See Gregory, *Textkritik*, p. 309, No. 382, p. 1061.

0142. Tenth century. In Royal Library, Munich. See Gregory, *Textkritik*, p. 267, No. 46, p. 1081.

0150. Tenth century. In Patmos. See Gregory, *Textkritik*, p. 311, No. 413, p. 1081.

0151. Twelfth century. In Patmos. See Gregory, *Textkritik*, p. 311, Nos. 1 and 14, p. 1081.

The text of the last seven mss. was not available for use in the text-critical notes of this commentary.

Of the approximately six hundred cursive manuscripts which contain the epistle in whole or in part, almost all of them in whole, Tischendorf cites the evidence of sixty-six, manifestly, however, for the most part only when they sustain the readings of the more ancient authorities, and some of them only once or twice. These sixty-six are 1, 2, 3, 4, 5*, 6, 10, 31, 32, 33, 39, 42, 88, 93, 101, 102, 103, 104, 122, 181, 205, 206, 209, 216, 218, 234, 242, 263, 309, 314, 319, 322, 323, 326, 327, 328, 330, 336, 356, 424², 429, 431, 436, 440, 442, 450, 460, 462, 463, 464, 479, 489, 605, 618, 642, 1905, 1906, 1908, 1911, 1912, 1913, 1924, 1927, 1944, 1955, 2125.

The readings for which Tischendorf cites these mss. are almost exclusively such as would be classed as pre-Syrian by Westcott and Hort. The attestation of the rival reading is in most cases either exclusively Syrian, or Western and Syrian. The pre-Syrian element is most clearly marked in the following six mss.:

31 (Tdf. 37) the so-called Leicester Codex. Fifteenth century. At Leicester, England. Described by J. Rendel Harris in *The Origin of the Leicester Codex of the New Testament*, London, 1887.

33 (Tdf. 17). Ninth or tenth century. In National Library, Paris. Called by Eichhorn "the queen of the cursives." Cited by Tischendorf in Galatians more frequently than any other cursive. Contains the Prophets as well as Gospels, Acts, Cath. Epp. and Paul.

424 (Tdf. Paul 67). Eleventh century. In Vienna. It is in the corrections of the second hand (424²) that the pre-Syrian element especially appears. See Westcott and Hort, *Introd.* § 212, p. 155.

436 (Tdf. 80). Eleventh century. In the Vatican Library, Rome.

442 (Tdf. 73). Thirteenth century. In Upsala.

1908 (Tdf. 47). Eleventh century. In Bodleian Library, Oxford.

The estimate of the testimony of certain groups of manuscripts which one gains from a study of the text of Galatians is in general quite in accordance with the value which Westcott

---

* But according to Gregory, *Textkritik*, p. 295, this ms. does not contain any part of Galatians.

and Hort ascribe to these groups in the Pauline epistles in general.

In the following one hundred and two instances (which include, it is believed, all except those in which either the variation or its attestation is unimportant) ℵ and B agree and are supported by various groups of other uncials: $1^{4, 10, 16, 18, 24}$ $2^{4, 5 (2)*, 6, 8, 9 (2), 10, 11, 12, 13, 14 (3), 16 (4), 18}$ $3^{1, 2, 6, 8, 10, 12, 13, 16, 17 (2), 19, 22, 23 (2), 24, 29 (2)}$ $4^{2, 4, 6 (2), 7 (2), 8 (2), 14, 15 (3), 17 (2), 18, 19, 21, 25, 26, 30 (2), 31}$ $5^{1 (5), 4, 7 (2), 10 (2), 12, 13, 14 (2), 15, 17, 19, 20 (2), 21, 23 (2), 24, 25}$ $6^{1 (2), 3, 8 (2), 9, 10, 12 (2), 13, 14 (2), 15, 16, 17}$. In 2^{12} ἦλθεν, which is the reading of ℵBDFG 39, 442, is undoubtedly an error, though manifestly very ancient. In 6^{12} transcriptional probability is against διώκωνται, the reading of ℵBD, but intrinsic probability is strongly in its favour. In nearly half the remaining instances internal evidence, chiefly transcriptional probability, is clearly on the side of the reading of ℵB; in a considerable number of cases the external attestation of the rival reading is so weak as to leave no room for doubt that the reading of ℵB is the original; in no case other than the two named is there any strong evidence for the reading opposed to that of ℵB.

ℵ and B agree in supporting a reading unsupported by other uncials whose text is available in eight passages, viz., $3^{7, 10, 14}$ $4^{9, 18, 19}$ 5^{21} 6^{10}. In 4^{9} ℵ and B stand quite alone. In 3^{7} their reading is found also in early fathers, in 3^{14} in two ancient versions, Syr. (psh.) and Aeth., but in no other Greek manuscript so far as noted. In the other passages their reading is supported by good cursives. Of the eight passages the ℵB reading is unquestionably correct in 6^{10}; almost unquestionably wrong in 4^{18}; in all the other instances it is accepted or given the preference by Westcott and Hort, and doubtless rightly, except in 4^{9}, where δουλεῦσαι seems clearly to be a corruption of the original text.

ℵ and B are opposed to one another in forty-four instances. In sixteen of these ℵ is accompanied by A and by either C or P or both, and B is accompanied by FG (once G only) or D,

---

* Figures in parentheses indicate the number of instances within the verse.

sometimes by both. The sixteen passages are $1^{3, 11, 15, 17, 18}$; $2^{6, 14, 20}$ $4^{14, 23, 25, 28}$ 5^{26} $6^{2, 7, 13}$. Tried by internal evidence neither group can be said to be uniformly superior to the other. The reading of אA (C) (P) is preferred by Westcott and Hort in twelve of the sixteen instances; viz. in $1^{3, 15, 17, 18}$ $2^{6, 20}$ $4^{23, 28}$ 5^{26} $6^{2, 7, 13}$. Their judgment seems open to question in reference to 1^{15} 2^6 4^{28}, but in the other nine cases there seems no reason for doubt.

In seven instances אACP, and in two instances אAP (C being lacking), are accompanied also by DFG, and B stands opposed to them supported by good cursives (33, 424^2), versions or fathers, but by no weighty uncial authority. These nine passages are $1^{4, 12}$ $2^{13, 16}$ $3^{19, 21}$ 5^6 $6^{11, 15}$. In five of these passages the B reading is probably the original. In 6^{15} Westcott and Hort are clearly right in accepting the reading of B without alternative. In all the rest they give both readings, one in the text, the other in the margin, preferring the אAC reading in four of the passages.

In the remaining nineteen cases in which א and B are opposed to one another the division of evidence varies greatly. The B reading seems clearly preferable in 1^9 $3^{13, 28}$ ($\epsilon\hat{\iota}s$ $\dot{\epsilon}\sigma\tau\dot{\epsilon}$ $\dot{\epsilon}\nu$ $X\rho\iota\sigma\tau\hat{\omega}$ $I\eta\sigma o\hat{v}$) $6^{9, 17}$; the א reading in 4^3 4^{23} ($\dot{a}\lambda\lambda'$) 4^{23} ($\mu\dot{\epsilon}\nu$). In the other cases neither is clearly the original, but the B reading is probably so in 1^8 ($\epsilon\dot{v}a\gamma\gamma\epsilon\lambda\dot{\iota}\zeta\eta\tau a\iota$) 2^{16} 3^{28} ($\pi\dot{a}\nu\tau\epsilon s$) 4^{25} $5^{1, 20}$ ($\zeta\hat{\eta}\lambda os$) 6^{18}; the א reading in 5^{17}. In 1^8 ($\dot{v}\mu\hat{\iota}\nu$) 3^{21} 5^{20} ($\dot{\epsilon}\rho\iota\theta\dot{\iota}a\iota$), perhaps neither is original.

On the whole it appears that when א and B support different readings ACP are much more likely to be associated with א, and DFG somewhat more likely to be with B. Thus A agrees with א thirty times, with B seven times; C agrees with א twenty-one times, with B nine times; P agrees with א twenty-eight times, with B five times. D agrees with א nineteen times, with B twenty times. FG agree with א sixteen times, with B twenty-two times. There is a slight preponderance of probability in favour of a reading of א supported by A and either C or P as against the rival reading of B with its various support; but a reading of א without at least two of the group

ACP is very rarely original. The אACP group is stronger without the support of DFG than with it. In the instances in which the cursive 33 is quoted it agrees with א eight times, with B ten times. It is almost invariably on the side of the more probable reading, but it is possible that the record would be somewhat different if it had been cited in all the forty-four cases in which א and B are on opposite sides.

It is not within the scope of this commentary to discuss the textual theory of Von Soden, nor has it been judged practicable to cite the evidence which he has assembled in addition to that of Tischendorf. His text of Galatians differs all told in forty-six readings from that of Westcott and Hort. But this number gives an exaggerated impression of the real difference between the two texts. Of the forty-six instances of disagreement one (ὁ σάρξ, 5¹⁷) is the result of a palpable misprint in Von Soden. Nine are differences in the spelling of a word as, e. g., by the addition or omission of ν movable. Three pertain to order of words, not affecting the sense. In eleven Westcott and Hort and Von Soden adopt the same reading, but Westcott and Hort admit an alternative reading which Von Soden ignores (1⁸, ¹⁵, ²¹ 2⁶, ¹³, ²¹ 4²³ 5⁶ 6¹, ⁴, ¹⁸). In eleven Von Soden adopts (in ten cases without alternative, in one with alternative) the reading to which Westcott and Hort give their second preference: viz., in 1⁴ περί for ὑπέρ; in 3¹⁹ οὗ for ἄν; in 3²¹ ἐκ νόμου ἦν ἄν for ἐν νόμῳ ἄν ἦν; in 4⁹ δουλεύειν for δουλεῦσαι; in 4²³ διὰ τῆς for δι'; in 4²⁸ ὑμεῖς . . . ἐστέ for ἡμεῖς . . . ἐσμέν; in 5²⁰ ἔρεις, ξῆλοι for ἔρις, ξῆλος; in 6¹² τοῦ χριστοῦ for τοῦ χριστοῦ ['Ιησοῦ]; in 5²¹ καί in brackets for καί in the margin. In eleven cases Von Soden adopts a reading which is not recognised by Westcott and Hort and involves more than spelling or order of words, viz., in 1⁸ εὐαγγελίζηται for εὐαγγελίσηται; in 3²³ συγκεκλεισμένοι for συνκλειόμενοι; in 4²⁵ γάρ for δέ; in 4³⁰ κληρονομήσῃ for κληρονομήσει; in 6⁹ ἐκκακῶμεν for ἐνκακῶμεν; in 5¹⁷ δέ for γάρ; in 6¹⁰ ἔχομεν for ἔχωμεν; in 3¹ adds [ἐν ὑμῖν] after ἐσταυρωμένος; in 4²⁷ [πάντων] after μήτηρ; in 5²¹ [φόνοι] after φθόνοι; and in 6¹⁷ κυρίου before 'Ιησοῦ. With the exception of 5²¹ none of these differences affects the meaning of the passage further than in the shade of the thought or explicitness of expression.

In a number of instances the reading adopted by Von Soden had before the publication of his text already been adopted for the present work in preference to that of Westcott and Hort. So, e. g., in 1^8 εὐαγγελίζηται, 2^{14} οὐχί, 3^{21} ἐκ νόμου, 4^9 δουλεύειν, 4^{28} ὑμεῖς . . . ἐστέ.

An examination of the whole series fails to disclose any clear and constant principle underlying the text of Von Soden. But it is evident that he gives to B much less weight than do Westcott and Hort, rates אAC higher than they do, yet puts DFG still higher, and even at times prefers a reading supported by KLP to its rival supported by all the other uncials.

For a discussion of the evidence of the ancient versions and the fathers the reader is referred to the standard treatises on Textual Criticism, such as Gregory, *Textkritik des Neuen Testaments*, vol. II, Leipzig, 1902; *Canon and Text of the New Testament*, New York, 1907; Kenyon, *Textual Criticism of the New Testament*[2], London, 1912.

IX. BIBLIOGRAPHY.*

This list does not include general works on Introduction to the New Testament or to the Pauline Epistles, or general treatises on the Life of Paul or the Apostolic Age, or New Testament Theology. Many treatises on special topics not included in this list are referred to in the body of the commentary.

I. COMMENTARIES.

For a list of Patristic Commentaries on the Epistle to the Galatians with characterisation of them, see Lightfoot, J. B., *St. Paul's Epistle to the Galatians*, pp. 227–236; and Turner, C. H., "Greek Patristic Commentaries on the Pauline Epistles" in *HDB*, vol. V, pp. 484 *ff.*   See also Sanday and Headlam, *Commentary on the Epistle to the Romans*, pp. xcviii *ff.*

---

* The intention has been in general to give the date of the first edition of each work listed and to indicate the existence of later editions when such were published. But as not all the works cited were at hand and as first editions were often inaccessible exactness of statement can not be guaranteed in every case. The Commentaries marked with a * are of exceptional interest or value.

Faber, J., *Epistolæ divi Pauli Apostoli: cum Commentariis.* Paris, 1517.

*Luther, Martin, *In Epistolam Pauli ad Galatas Commentarius.* Leipzig, 1519. German edition, 1525.

*——, *In Epistolam S. Pauli ad Galatas Commentarius ex Prælectione D. M. Lutheri collectus.* Wittenberg, 1535. (Not a revised edition of the preceding, but a distinct and larger work. See preface to the edition of J. C. Irmischer, Erlangen, 1843, 1844.) Many other editions and translations. For characterisation, see S. and H., p. ciii.

Erasmus, Desiderius (Roterodamus), *In Epistolam Pauli ad Galatas Paraphrasis,* Leipzig, 1519.

Bugenhagen, J., *Adnotationes in Epistolas ad Galatas,* etc. Basle, 1527.

Bullinger, Heinrich, *Commentarii in omnes Epistolas Apostolorum.* 1537.

Cajetan, Thomas de Vio, *In omnes D. Pauli et aliorum Epistolas Commentarii.* Lyons, 1539.

*Calvin, J., *Commentarii in quatuor Pauli Epistolas* (Gal. Eph. Phil. Col.). Geneva, 1548.

*——, *In omnes Pauli Apostoli Epistolas Commentarii.* Geneva, 1565. Various later editions and translations.

Béze, Theodore de, *Novum Testamentum . . . ejusdem Th. Bezæ Annotationes.* Geneva, 1565.

Prime, John, *Exposition and Observations upon St. Paul to the Galatians.* Oxford, 1587.

Piscator, Johannes, *Commentarii in omnes Libros Novi Testamenti.* Herborn, 1613.

Estius, Guilelmus, *In omnes Pauli Epistolas Commentarii.* Douay, 1614.

Lapide, Cornelius a (C. Van den Steen), *Commentarius in omnes D. Pauli Epistolas.* Antwerp, 1614. Numerous later editions.

Orellius, Johann, *Commentarius in Epistolam Pauli ad Galatas.* Racov, 1628.

Grotius, Hugo (Huig van Groot), *Annotationes in Novum Testamentum.* Paris, 1644. See S. and H., p. civ.

Cocceius, Johannes (Johann Koch), *Commentarius in Epistolam ad Galatas.* Leyden, 1665.

Calov, Abraham, in *Biblia Novi Testamenti illustrata.* Frankfort, 1676.

Locke, John, *A Paraphrase and Notes on St. Paul to the Galatians, Corinthians,* etc. London, 1705.

*Bengel, Johann Albrecht, in *Gnomon Novi Testamenti.* Tübingen, 1742. See S. and H., p. ciii.

Michaelis, Johann David, *Paraphrasis und Anmerkungen über die Briefe Pauli an die Galater, Epheser,* etc. Bremen, 1750. Ed. altera, 1769.

Wetstein (or Wettstein), J. J., *Novum Testamentum Græcum.* Amsterdam, 1751, 1752.

Semler, Johann Salomo, *Paraphrasis Epistolæ ad Galatas, cum Prolegomenis, Notis,* etc. Magdeburg, 1779.

Matthaei, P. F., *Pauli Epistolæ ad Galatas, Ephesios, et Philippenses.* Ed. altera, Rigæ, 1784.

Mayer, F. G., *Der Brief Pauli an die Galater*, etc.   Vienna, 1788.

Borger, E. A., *Interpretatio Epistolæ Pauli ad Galatas*.   Leyden, 1807.

Rosenmüller, Ernst Friedrich Karl, in *Scholia in Novum Testamentum*. Leipzig, 1815.

*Winer, Georg Benedict, *Pauli ad Galatas Epistola*. *Latine vertit et perpetua Annotatione illustravit.* Leipzig, 1821. Ed. quarta, 1859.

Flatt, Karl Christian, *Vorlesungen über die Briefe Pauli an die Galater und Epheser.* Tübingen, 1828.

Paulus, Heinrich Eberhard Gottlob, *Des Apostels Paulus Lehrbriefe an die Galater- und Römerchristen.* Heidelberg, 1831.

Rückert, Leopold Immanuel, *Commentar über den Brief Pauli an die Galater.* Leipzig, 1833.

Matthies, Konrad Stephan, *Erklärung des Briefes an die Galater.* Greifswald, 1833.

Usteri, L., *Kommentar über den Galaterbrief.* Zürich, 1833.

Fritzsche, Karl Friedrich August, *Commentarius de nonnullis Epistolæ ad Galatas Locis.* Rostock, 1833–4.

Schott, H. A., *Epistolæ Pauli ad Thessalonicenses et Galatas.* Leipzig, 1834.

Olshausen, Hermann, in *Biblischer Kommentar über sämmtliche Schriften des Neuen Testaments.* Fortgesetzt von Ebrard und Wiesinger. Königsberg, 1830–62 (Gal. 1840). E. T. by A. C. Kendrick, New York, 1858.

*Meyer, Heinrich August Wilhelm, *Kritisch-exegetisches Handbuch über den Brief an die Galater.* Göttingen, 1841, in *Kritisch-exegetischer Kommentar über das Neue Testament*, 1832–59. E. T., with bibliography, by Venables and Dickson. Edinburgh, 1873–85. Various later editions. See also under Sieffert.

*Wette, Martin Leberecht de, *Kurze Erklärung des Briefes an die Galater,* etc. Leipzig, 1841, in *Kurzgefasstes exegetisches Handbuch zum Neuen Testament*, 1836–48. Various later editions.

Baumgarten-Crusius, Ludwig Friedrich Otto, *Kommentar über den Brief Pauli an die Galater,* herausgegeben von E. J. Kimmel. Jena, 1845.

Haldane, James Alexander, *An Exposition of the Epistle to the Galatians.* London, 1848.

Alford, Henry, in *The Greek Testament . . . a Critical Exegetical Commentary.* London, 1849–61. Various subsequent editions.

*Hilgenfeld, Adolph, *Der Galaterbrief übersetzt, in seinen geschichtlichen Beziehungen untersucht und erklärt.* Leipzig, 1852.

Brown, John, *An Exposition of the Epistle of Paul to the Galatians.* Edinburgh, 1853.

*Ellicott, Charles John, *A Critical and Grammatical Commentary on St. Paul's Epistle to the Galatians.* London, 1854. Various subsequent editions.

*Jowett, Benjamin, *The Epistles of St. Paul to the Thessalonians, Galatians, and Romans.* London, 1855. Edited by L. Campbell, London, 1894.

Webster, W., and Wilkinson, W. F., *The Greek Testament with Notes Grammatical and Exegetical.* London, 1855–61.

Wordsworth, Christopher, in *The New Testament in the Original Greek.* London, 1856–60. 5th ed., 1867, 1868.

Bagge, H. J. T., *St. Paul's Epistle to the Galatians.* London, 1857.

Ewald, Heinrich, in *Sendschreiben des Apostels Paulus.* Göttingen, 1857.

Bisping, August, in *Exegetisches Handbuch zu den Briefen des Apostels Pauli.* Münster, 1857.

*Wieseler, Karl, *Commentar über den Brief Pauli an die Galater.* Göttingen, 1859.

Holsten, Carl, *Inhalt und Gedankengang des Pauli Briefes an die Galater.* Rostock, 1859.

Schmoller, Otto, *Der Brief Pauli an die Galater.* Bielefeld, 1862, in *Theologisch-homiletisches Bibelwerk,* herausgegeben von J. P. Lange. Various later editions. E. T. by C. C. Starbuck.

Gwynne, G. J., *Commentary on St. Paul's Epistle to the Galatians.* Dubli 1863.

Kamphausen, Adolph Herman Heinrich, in *Bunsen's Bibelwerk.* Leipzi 1864.

*Lightfoot, Joseph Barber, *Saint Paul's Epistle to the Galatians.* London, 1865. 2d ed., revised, 1866. Various later editions.

Reithmayr, F. X., *Commentar zum Briefe an die Galater.* München, 1865.

Carey, Sir Stafford, *The Epistle of the Apostle Paul to the Galatians.* London, 1867.

Eadie, John, *Commentary on the Greek Text of the Epistle of Paul to the Galatians.* Edinburgh, 1869.

Brandes, Friedrich, *Des Apostels Paulus Sendschreiben an die Galater.* Wiesbaden, 1869.

Holsten, Carl, *Das Evangelium des Paulus.* Th. I. Abth. 1. Berlin, 1880.

Sieffert, Friedrich, *Der Brief an die Galater,* in *Kritisch-exegetischer Kommentar über das Neue Testament,* begründet von H. A. W. Meyer. Göttingen, 1880. Sieffert's first edition is counted as the sixth in the Meyer series. The edition cited in this work is the ninth, 1899.

Howson, J. S., in *The Bible Commentary,* edited by F. C. Cook. New York, 1881.

Schaff, Philip, in *A Popular Commentary on the New Testament.* New York, 1882.

Schroeder, Friedrich, *Der Brief Pauli an die Galater.* Heidelberg, 1882.

Philippi, Friedrich Adolph, *Erklärung des Briefes Pauli an die Galater.* Gütersloh, 1884.

Boise, James Robinson, *Notes, Critical and Explanatory on Paul's Epistle to the Galatians.* Chicago, 1885.

Beet, Joseph Agar, *A Commentary on St. Paul's Epistle to the Galatians.* London, 1885. Later editions.

Zöckler, Otto, in *Kurzgefasster Kommentar zu den heiligen Schriften Alten und Neuen Testamentes*, herausgegeben von Strack und Zöckler. Nordlingen, 1887. Later editions.

Wood, William Spicer, *Studies in Saint Paul's Epistle to the Galatians*. London, 1887.

Findlay, G. G., in *The Expositor's Bible*. New York, 1888.

Baljon, J. M. S., *Exegetisch-kritische verhandeling over den brief van Paulus aan de Galatiërs*. Leyden, 1889.

Hovey, Alvah, in *An American Commentary on the New Testament*. Philadelphia, 1890.

Perowne, E. B., in *Cambridge Bible for Schools and Colleges*. Cambridge, 1890.

Schlatter, A., *Der Galaterbrief ausgelegt für Bibelleser*. Stuttgart, 1890.

Lipsius, R. A., in *Hand-Commentar zum Neuen Testament*, bearbeitet von H. J. Holtzmann *et al.* Freiburg, 1891.

*Ramsay, W. M., *A Historical Commentary on St. Paul's Epistle to the Galatians*. London and New York, 1900.

Rendall, Frederick, in *The Expositor's Greek Testament*, vol. III. London and New York, 1903.

Bousset, Wilhelm, in *Die Schriften des Neuen Testaments*. Göttingen, 1907. 2te Aufl., 1908.

Williams, A. L., in *Cambridge Greek Testament*. Cambridge, 1910.

Adeney, W. F., in *The New Century Bible*. Edinburgh, 1911.

*Emmet, Cyril, in *Reader's Commentary*, edited by Dawson Walker. London, 1912.

MacKenzie, W. D., in *Westminster New Testament*. London, 1912.

Girdlestone, R. B., *St. Paul's Epistle to the Galatians*. London, 1913.

II. TREATISES.

1. THE DESTINATION OF THE EPISTLE.

Perrot, Georges, *De Galatia Provincia Romana*. Paris, 1867.

Sieffert, *Galatien und seine ersten Christengemeinden*, in *ZhTh.*, vol. XLI, 1871.

Grimm, Willibald, *Über die Nationalität der kleinasiatischen Galatern*, in *Th.St.u.Kr.*, 1876.

Schürer, Emil, *Was ist unter Γαλατία in der Überschrift des Galaterbriefes zu verstehen?* in *JfpT.*, vol. XVIII, 1892.

Gifford, E. H., *The Churches of Galatia*, in *Expositor*, Ser. IV, vol. X, 1894.

Clemen, Carl, *Die Adressaten des Galaterbriefes*, in *ZwTh.*, 1894.

Votaw, Clyde W., *Location of the Galatian Churches*, in *BW.*, vol. III, 1894.

Zöckler, Otto, *Wo lag das biblische Galatien?* in *Th.St.u.Kr.*, 1895.

Ramsay, W. M., *The "Galatia" of St. Paul and the Galatic Territory of Acts*, in *Studia Biblica et Ecclesiastica*, vol. IV, 1896.

Askwith, E. H., *The Epistle to the Galatians. An Essay on its Destination and Date.* London, 1899.

Weber, Valentin, *Die Adressaten des Galaterbriefes. Beweis der rein-südlichen Theorie.* Ravensburg, 1900.

Steinmann, Alphons, *Der Leserkreis des Galaterbriefes.* Münster i. W., 1908.

Moffatt, J., *Destination of Galatians* (Review of Steinmann, *Leserkreis des Galaterbriefes*), in *AJT.*, vol. XIII, 1909.

2. THE DATE OF THE EPISTLE.

Meister, *Kritische Ermittelung der Abfassungszeit der Briefe des heiligen Paulus.* Regensburg, 1874.

Clemen, Carl, *Die Chronologie der paulinischen Briefe aufs Neue untersucht.* Halle, 1893.

Rendall, Frederick, *The Galatians of St. Paul and the Date of the Epistle,* in *Expositor,* Ser. IV, vol. IX, pp. 254–264, 1894.

Askwith, E. H., *The Epistle to the Galatians. An Essay on its Destination and Date.* London, 1899.

Weber, Valentin, *Die Abfassung des Galaterbriefes vor dem Apostelkonzil.* Ravensburg, 1900.

Briggs, Emily, *The Date of the Epistle of St. Paul to the Galatians,* in *New World,* vol. IX, 1900.

Aberle, *Chronologie des Apostels Paulus von seiner Bekehrung bis zur Abfassung des Galaterbriefes,* in *BZ.*, vol. I, 1903.

——, *Chronologie des Apostels Paulus vom Apostelkonzil bis zum Märtyrertode des Paulus in Rom,* in *BZ.*, vol. III, 1905.

Round, Douglass, *The Date of St. Paul's Epistle to the Galatians.* Cambridge, 1906.

Steinmann, Alphons, *Die Abfassungszeit des Galaterbriefes.* Münster i. W., 1906. With extensive bibliography.

3. GENUINENESS AND INTEGRITY.

Steck, Rudolf, *Der Galaterbrief nach seiner Echtheit untersucht, nebst kritischen Bemerkungen zu den paulinischen Hauptbriefen.* Berlin, 1888.

Lindemann, Rudolf, *Die Echtheit der paulinischen Hauptbriefe gegen Stecks Umsturzversuch vertheidigt.* Zürich, 1889.

Völter, D., *Die Composition der paulinischen Hauptbriefe.* Vol. I. Tübingen, 1890.

Weiss, Bernhard, *The Present Status of the Inquiry concerning the Genuineness of the Pauline Epistles.* Chicago, 1897; also in *AJT.*, vol. I, 1897.

For further references, see pp. lxxi *f.*

4. THE TEXT OF THE EPISTLE.

Zimmer, Friedrich, *Zur Textkritik des Galaterbriefes,* in *ZwTh.*, 1881, 1882.

Baljon, J. M. S., *De tekst der brieven van Paulus,* etc. Utrecht, 1884.

Corssen, Peter, *Epistola ad Galatas ad Fidem optimorum Codicum Vulgatæ recognovit Prolegomenis instruxit Vulgatam cum antiquioribus Versionibus comparavit*. Berlin, 1885.

Zimmer, Friedrich, *Der Galaterbrief im altlateinischen Text als Grundlage für einen textkritischen Apparatus der vetus Latina*. Königsberg, 1887.

Weiss, Bernhard, *Die paulinischen Briefe und der Hebräerbrief im berichtigten Text*. Leipzig, 1896.

——, *Textkritik der paulinischen Briefe*, in *Texte u. Untersuchungen z. Geschichte d. altchristlichen Literatur*, vol. XIV, 3. Leipzig, 1896.

Hemphill, W. L., *Codex Coxianus of the Homilies of Chrysostom on Ephesians and his Commentary on Galatians*. Norwood, 1916.

See further references in *Encyc. Bib.*, vol. II, col. 1626.

5. THE APOSTOLIC CONFERENCE AND DECREE.

Bertheau, Carl, *Einige Bemerkungen über die Stelle Gal. 2 und ihr Verhältniss zur Apostelgeschichte*. Hamburg, 1854.

Holtzmann, H. J., *Der Apostelconvent*, in *ZwTh.*, 1882, 1883.

Zimmer, Friedrich, *Galaterbrief und Apostelgeschichte*, 1887.

Hilgenfeld, A., *Die neuesten Vertheidiger des Aposteldecrets*, in *ZwTh.*, 1891.

Dobschütz, Ernst von, *Probleme des apostolischen Zeitalters*. Leipzig, 1904.

Völter, D., *Paulus und seine Briefe*. Strassburg, 1905.

Kreyenbühl, J., *Der Apostel Paulus und die Urgemeinde*, in *ZntW.*, 1907.

Bacon, B. W., *Acts versus Galatians: The Crux of Apostolic History*, in *AJT.*, vol. XI, 1907.

For further references see p. xliv, and Lipsius, *op. cit. sup.*

III. THE TEACHING OF THE EPISTLE.

Holsten, Carl, *Zum Evangelium des Paulus u. Petrus*. Rostock, 1848.

——, *Das Evangelium des Paulus*. Th. II. Berlin, 1898.

Sabatier, A., *L'Apôtre Paul. Esquisse d'une Histoire de sa Pensée*. Paris, 3d ed., 1870. E. T. by A. M. Hellier, London, 1891.

Pfleiderer, Otto, *Der Paulinismus*. Leipzig, 1873. E. T. by Edward Peters, London, 1877.

Cler, Samuel, *La Notion de La Foi dans Saint Paul. Étude de Théologie Biblique*. Alençon, 1886.

Gloel, Johannes, *Der heilige Geist in der Heilsverkündigung des Paulus*. Halle, 1888.

Everling, Otto, *Die paulinische Angelologie und Dämonologie*. Göttingen, 1888.

Stevens, George Barker, *The Pauline Theology*. New York, 1892.

Grafe, Eduard, *Die paulinische Lehre vom Gesetz nach den vier Hauptbriefen*. Freiburg, 2te Aufl., 1893.

Kabisch, Richard, *Die Eschatologie des Paulus*. Göttingen, 1893.

Bruce, Alexander Balmain, *St. Paul's Conception of Christianity*. Edinburgh and New York, 1894.

Teichmann, Ernst, *Die paulinischen Vorstellungen von Auferstehung und Gericht und ihre Beziehung zur jüdischen Apokalyptik*. Freiburg, 1896.

Somerville, David, *St. Paul's Conception of Christ*. Edinburgh, 1897.

Simon, Theodore, *Die Psychologie des Apostels Paulus*. Göttingen, 1897.

Wernle, Paul, *Der Christ und die Sünde bei Paulus*. Freiburg, 1897.

Feine, Paul, *Das gesetzesfreie Evangelium des Paulus*. Leipzig, 1899.

Thackeray, Henry St. John, *The Relation of St. Paul to Contemporary Jewish Thought*. London, 1900.

Mommsen, Theodor, *Die Rechtsverhälinisse des Apostels Paulus*, in *ZntW.*, 1901.

Wernle, Paul, *Die Anfänge unserer Religion*. Tübingen, 1901.

Feine, Paul, *Jesus Christus und Paulus*. Leipzig, 1902.

Brückner, Martin, *Die Entstehung der paulinischen Christologie*. Strassburg, 1903.

Vos, Gerhardus, *The Alleged Legalism in Paul's Doctrine of Justification*, in *PThR.*, 1903.

Sokolowski, Emil, *Die Begriffe Geist und Leben bei Paulus*. Göttingen, 1903.

Kennedy, H. A. A., *St. Paul's Conception of the Last Things*. New York, 1904.

Monteil, S. *Essai sur la Christologie de Saint Paul*. Paris, 1906.

Arnal, Jean, *La Notion de l'Esprit, sa Genèse et son Évolution dans la Théologie Chrétienne*. Paris, 1907.

DuBose, William Parcher, *The Gospel according to St. Paul*. New York, 1907.

Olschewski, Wilhelm, *Die Wurzeln der paulinischen Christologie*. Königsberg, 1909.

Macintosh, Douglas C., *The Pragmatic Element in the Teaching of Paul*, in *AJT.*, vol. XIV, 1910.

Gardner, Percy, *The Religious Experience of St. Paul*. New York, 1911.

Dewick, E. C., *Primitive Christian Eschatology*. Cambridge, 1912.

Boysson, A. de, *La Loi et la Foi*. Paris, 1912.

Williams, E. J. Watson, *A Plea for a Reconsideration of St. Paul's Doctrine of Justification*. London, 1912.

Wetter, Gillis Piton, *Der Vergeltungsgedanke bei Paulus*. Göttingen, 1912.

Rostron, S. Nowell, *The Christology of St. Paul*. London, 1912.

Westcott, F. B., *St. Paul and Justification*. London and New York, 1913.

Prat, F. *La Théologie de Saint Paul*. Paris, 1913. Contains bibliography.

Ramsay, W. M., *The Teaching of Paul in Terms of the Present Day*. London, 1913.

Hatch, William Henry Paine, *The Pauline Idea of Faith in Its Relation to Jewish-Hellenistic Religion*. Cambridge, 1917.

Morgan, W. *The Religion and Theology of Paul*. Edinburgh, 1917.

THE EPISTLE TO THE GALATIANS.

I. INTRODUCTION (1^{1-10}).

1. *Salutation, including the assertion of the writer's apostolic commission* (1^{1-5}).

The apostle Paul, writing to the churches of Galatia (who had received the gospel from him, but were already, under the influence of preachers who held a different type of Christian thought, on the point of abandoning the gospel as Paul had taught it to them to accept the teachings of these other preachers), affirms in the very salutation of the letter his *direct* commission as an apostle from Jesus Christ and God the Father, making mention also in this connection, doubtless as against the declaration or insinuation of his opponents that only a personal follower of Jesus could be an apostle, of the fact that the Christ still lives, having been raised from the dead by the Father. Invoking upon them grace and peace from God the Father and the Lord Jesus Christ, he adds to this usual element of his epistolary salutation a characterisation of Jesus Christ, emphasising his mission of Saviour of men from their sins, as against the conception of law as the means of salvation, which the preachers who had succeeded him in Galatia held.

Paul, an apostle, not from men nor through man, but through Jesus Christ and God the Father who raised him from the dead, ²and all the brethren that are with me, to the churches of Galatia: ³grace to you and peace from God our Father and the Lord Jesus Christ, ⁴who gave himself for our sins, that he might deliver us out of the present evil age, according to the will of our God and Father, ⁵to whom be the glory for ever. Amen.

I   I

1. Παῦλος ἀπόστολος, "Paul an apostle." By the addition
of the word ἀπόστολος to his name, at the very opening of the
epistle Paul claims to be one who is divinely commissioned to
preach the gospel of Christ and authorised to plant Christianity.
The apostleship as conceived by him involved the idea of the
church œcumenical, Christianity as an organic whole, not simply isolated centres of effort, and of divine appointment in relation to it. To the apostles was committed the task of laying
the foundations of the church (1 Cor. 3[6, 10] Eph. 3[20]) and among
those who were endowed with the gifts of the Spirit for the
building up of the church they constituted the highest rank
(1 Cor., chap. 12, esp. v. [28]; cf. Eph. 4[11, 12]). These facts gave
to them a responsibility and right above that of any other class
in the church. While this was apparently generally recognised
there was much controversy over the question to whom this
responsibility and right belonged. In Paul's view they belonged
neither exclusively to any individual nor to a college of apostles
as such. The function of the apostle, neither limited on the
one side to a local church, nor extended on the other to the
whole world, was defined as respects each apostle or group of
apostles by the divine commission which made them apostles. See Rom. 1[1, 5], in which S. and H. rightly translate
ἐν πᾶσιν τοῖς ἔθνεσιν "among all the Gentiles"; 1 Cor. 9[2];
but esp. Gal. 2[8]. Respecting the origin of the apostolic
order or class, the qualifications, rights, and responsibilities of
an apostle, and the limitations of his authority, see detached
note on Ἀπόστολος, p. 363. It is evident from what follows
in the epistle both that Paul's representation of the content of the gospel had been declared to be incorrect by those
who had visited Galatia since Paul was there, and that they
had denied his right to assume the function or claim the rights
of an apostle. This denial Paul meets, in the very salutation
with which the letter opens, by the affirmation of his apostleship, which he claims to possess not to the exclusion of others,
but along with others; note the absence of the article before
ἀπόστολος and cf. 1[17] 2[8]. The title is certainly not here, and
probably not in the salutation of any of his letters, a mere title

of dignity, but involves an assertion, the maintenance of which is essential to the purpose of the letter. *Cf.* 1 Cor. 1¹ 2 Cor. 1¹ Rom. 1¹ 1 Thes. 2⁶, etc.

οὐκ ἀπ᾽ ἀνθρώπων οὐδὲ δι᾽ ἀνθρώπου "not from men nor through man." The first phrase denies that Paul's apostleship had a human source, the second that it had come to him through a human channel, by human agency. Paul claims not only to be an apostle, but to have an apostleship which is in no sense indirect, dependent, or secondary. This fact is important for the understanding of the whole personal portion of the letter. It is evident that his opponents were substantially in agreement with Paul himself in holding that the right of self-directed presentation of the gospel, and the laying of foundations, belonged to the apostles as a definite class in the church. Apparently, also, they held respecting apostles much the same view which Acts 1²¹, ²² represents Peter as holding respecting the Eleven, viz.: that authority to add to the number lay with the Jerusalem church. With this idea of the basis on which additions to the Eleven were to be made they apparently associated the view that any one whose teaching differed from that of the Jerusalem church, in which the influence of James and the Twelve was dominant, was either an altogether unauthorised and false teacher, or a renegade associate or representative of the Twelve and a perverter of the true teaching; in either case no true apostle. It is not wholly clear in which class Paul's critics had placed him. But the nature of his reply, in which he denies with emphasis any kind of dependence on men in general (1¹, ¹¹), or the apostles in particular (1¹⁶, ¹⁷), combined with the facts mentioned in 1¹⁸⁻²⁴ in themselves considered, makes it probable that his opponents looked upon him, not indeed as having been commissioned as an *apostle* by the Twelve, but as one who having received instruction from them had perverted their teaching, and thereby deprived himself of all right as a Christian teacher. His claim to be an *apostle* they would doubtless have treated as wholly groundless. This denial of authority he answers, not as Barnabas or Mark might have done, with the assertion that he was true to the teaching of the Twelve, but

by affirming that he possessed an independent apostleship, neither
derived from a human source nor through a human channel.

The preposition ἀπό expresses source in its simplest and most general
form; hence it is the most natural preposition to use to express clearly
the idea of source as distinguished from that of agency expressed by διά.
By οὐκ ἀπ' . . . ἀνθρώπου the apostle denies definitely and specifically
that either the source or the agency of his apostleship was human.

The phrase οὐκ ἀπ' ἀνθρώπων is evidently qualitative, denying human
origin in the broadest possible way without of itself directing the mind
to any particular persons. Even the generic plural with the article,
οἱ ἄνθρωποι, is used very freely in N. T., not to denote the totality
of the race, but in reference to any group of men thought of as actually
existing, though unnamed and unidentified. See Mt. 5[13, 16, 19] 6[1, 15]
Rom. 14[18] 1 Cor. 1[25] Col. 2[8, 22]. But the noun without the article is more
clearly and emphatically qualitative, being nearly equivalent in the
genitive to the adjective "human," or with ἐξ or ἀπό to the phrase
"of human origin." See Rom. 1[18], πᾶσαν . . . ἀδικίαν ἀνθρώπων,
"every form of human iniquity"; 1 Cor. 2[5], μὴ . . . ἐν σοφίᾳ ἀνθρώπων
ἀλλ' ἐν δυνάμει θεοῦ, "not in human wisdom but in divine power"; also
Phil. 2[7] Mt. 15[9] 21[25, 26]. It is in this broad sense that Paul uses the
phrase here. Yet vv. [16, 17] leave no doubt that in using it he has
especially in mind the primitive apostles, or the Christian church in
Jerusalem, in which they were the dominant influence, it being from
this source that his opponents would hold that he ought to have derived
his apostleship in order to make it valid. In like manner, although
the singular is much less commonly used with qualitative force than
the plural, οὐδὲ δι' ἀνθρώπου is probably to be taken simply as denying
human agency, and is better translated "through man" than "through
a man." Cf. Acts 17[29] Rom. 1[23] 3[5] Gal. 1[11, 12] 2[6].

Though it is evidently no part of the apostle's purpose in this verse
to set forth his conception of the nature or mission of Christ, yet his
language indirectly and partially reflects his thought on that subject.
The antithesis between οὐδὲ δι' ἀνθρώπου and διὰ Ἰησοῦ Χριστοῦ, even
though to the latter is joined καὶ θεοῦ πατρός, and the very fact of the
close association of Ἰησοῦ Χριστοῦ with θεοῦ πατρός after the one
preposition διά, combine to indicate that Paul distinguished Jesus
Christ from men; not indeed in the sense that he denied that he was
man (cf. 1 Cor. 15[21]), but that this term did not state the whole, or
even the most important truth about him. Even had Paul believed
that his apostleship came from God through his fellow apostles, he
could never have written οὐδὲ δι' ἀνθρώπου, ἀλλὰ διὰ τῶν ἀποστόλων
καὶ θεοῦ πατρός, or even ἀλλὰ διὰ τῶν ἀποστόλων καὶ ἀπὸ θεοῦ πατρός.
See detached note on Πατήρ as applied to God, p. 384, and on The
Titles and Predicates of Jesus, p. 392.

The change from the plural, ἀνθρώπων, to the singular, ἀνθρώπου, is probably purely stylistic, it being natural to think of a possible human 'source of authority as composed of a group of men, and of the agent of its transmission as a single person. The plural may, indeed, be in some measure due to the fact that the source of authority which he had particularly in mind to deny was a group, the apostles. But there is no corresponding explanation of the singular. Zahn interprets οὐδὲ δι' ἀνθρώπου as a denial of a charge that he had received his apostleship through a certain unnamed person, most probably Barnabas. But this view overlooks the fact that Paul is here denying, not that he received his apostleship in the way in which they alleged he had, but that he had obtained it as they alleged he (not having been one of the original group) must have received it if it were genuine. They did not say, "You received your apostleship from men, and through a man, therefore it is not genuine," but "You *should* thus have received it," and Paul's answer is that he received it in a way far above this, which made human source and human agency wholly superfluous.

ἀλλὰ διὰ Ἰησοῦ Χριστοῦ καὶ θεοῦ πατρός "but through Jesus Christ and God the Father." Three facts are specially noticeable in reference to this expression: (1) the use of διά rather than ἀπό, indicating that the apostle is speaking not simply of a source of his apostleship between which and himself there intervenes an agent, but of the channel through which it came to him, or of the immediate source of it (see on meanings of διά below); (2) the addition of καὶ θεοῦ πατρός to Ἰησοῦ Χριστοῦ, showing that he is not thinking simply of the agency through which his apostleship came to him, but also of the source, than which, being ultimate, there can be no higher; (3) the governing of both substantives by the one preposition but once expressed, showing that Jesus Christ and God the Father are not separated in his mind as sustaining different relations to his apostleship, but are conceived of jointly and as sustaining one relation. Taken together, therefore, the whole expression bears the meaning "directly from Jesus Christ and God the Father." Had he thought of Christ as the agent and God as the source he must have written διὰ Ἰησοῦ Χριστοῦ καὶ ἀπὸ θεοῦ πατρός; if of God and Christ, as jointly source only, ἀπὸ Ἰησοῦ Χριστοῦ καὶ θεοῦ πατρός, which, however, would not have furnished a proper antithesis to δι' ἀνθρώπου, since it would have left open the possibility of a human channel.

Διά with the genitive, in addition to its use with reference to spatial and temporal relations, expresses means or instrument, which with a personal object merges into the idea of agency; but in three ways: (a) Expressing mediate agency. This use of the preposition grows naturally and most directly out of the spatial sense of the preposition "through," the governed substantive being thought of as standing between the source of power and the person or thing affected, and as transmitting the power. See, *e. g.*, Rom. 1² 5¹ 1 Cor. 2¹⁰ *et freq.* (b) The idea of mediateness falling into the background or disappearing, διά is used with a word denoting that which is at the same time source and agent; in such cases, while the preposition itself perhaps expresses only agency, the conception of mediateness implying something behind the agent is lost, and the fact that the agent is also source is separately expressed or implied in the nature of the case. See Th. *s. v.* A. III 1 and such passages as Rom. 11³⁶ 1 Cor. 1⁹. (c) The idea of agency merging into that of conditioning cause (viz. that which, though not the instrument of the action, or its ultimate source, is necessary to its accomplishment), διά is used with reference to that which, so to speak, stands behind the action and renders it possible. So, *e. g.*, Acts 1² Rom. 1⁸ 15³⁰ 1 Thes. 4².

In the phrase δι' ἀνθρώπου, διά evidently expresses mediate agency, since source is separately expressed by ἀπ' ἀνθρώπων, and the thought of man as a conditioning cause standing behind and rendering possible the action by which Paul became an apostle is excluded by the obvious nature of the facts. But the διά with 'Ιησοῦ Χριστοῦ, though evidently suggested by the use of διά with ἀνθρώπου, is used rather with the second meaning (b). The idea of mediateness is not required by any antithetical ἀπό, and in respect to θεοῦ πατρός, which is also governed by this same διά, the idea of mediateness is excluded, since it can not be supposed that the apostle thinks of a more ultimate source than God of which God is the agent.* Nor is it probable that the idea of mediateness is present even in respect to 'Ιησοῦ Χριστοῦ, since neither is ἀπό used with θεοῦ πατρός nor is διά even repeated before it; instead the two substantives are closely bound together under the government of one preposition, which probably therefore has the same force with both of them. The whole phrase διά 'Ιησοῦ . . . πατρός is accordingly antithetical not to δι' ἀνθρώπου only, but to ἀπ' ἀνθρώπων and δι' ἀνθρώπου, being the positive correlative of the negative οὐκ . . . ἀνθρώπου.

τοῦ ἐγείραντος αὐτὸν ἐκ νεκρῶν, " who raised him from the dead." By this characterisation of God Paul reminds his

* *Cf.* Philo, *Leg. Alleg.* I 41 (13): τὰ μὲν καὶ ὑπὸ θεοῦ γίνεται καὶ δι' αὐτοῦ, τὰ δὲ ὑπὸ θεοῦ μέν, οὐ δι' αὐτοῦ δέ. He illustrates this general statement by the assertion that the mind of man is created both by and through God, the irrational parts of the soul by God but not through God, being produced through the reasoning power that rules in the soul.

readers, who may have been told that Paul could not be an apostle because he was not a follower of Jesus in the flesh, that Jesus rose from the dead, and that it was the risen Christ who had given him his commission.

Of the apostle's motive for adding this expression there have been many theories. See a considerable number of them in Sief. That of Wies., who regards the reference to the resurrection as intended to substantiate on the one hand the superhuman nature and divine sonship of Jesus, which is implied in οὐδὲ δι' ἀνθρώπου and in the association of Jesus with the Father, and on the other hand the fatherhood of God, intrudes into the sentence a Christological and theological interest which is quite foreign to its purpose. The words οὐδὲ . . . πατρός undoubtedly reflect incidentally the apostle's conception of God and Christ, but they are themselves introduced for the purpose of establishing the main point, Paul's independent apostleship, and it is wholly improbable that the added words, τοῦ ἐγείραντος, etc., were injected to confirm the incidentally reflected thought. Sief. himself, taking in general the same view, goes beyond probability in supposing that the phrase conveys a reference to the resurrection of Christ as that through which God manifested his paternal love to the Son in the highest degree and established him in the full status of Son, this fact being in turn the basis on which Paul's call into the apostleship is made possible. The evident emphasis of the sentence upon Paul's apostleship, its independence and its validity, makes it improbable that there underlay it, unexpressed, any such elaborate and indirect reasoning. Nor is the fact that τοῦ ἐγείραντος limits θεοῦ πατρός sufficient to set this objection aside. Having, according to his usual custom (enforced in this case by special reasons) joined the names of Christ and God closely together, the only way in which he could then make reference to the fact of the resurrection without inconvenient circumlocution was by a phrase limiting θεοῦ πατρός. A similar objection holds against most of the interpretations enumerated by Sief., and against that of Beet, who introduces the thought that the Father, when raising Jesus from the dead, with a view to the proclamation of the gospel throughout the world, was himself taking part personally in the mission of the apostles.

The word ἐγείρω is Paul's regular term for the raising from the dead. He uses it in this sense 35 times, in 10 instances in the active, in 25 in the passive (exclusive of Eph. and the pastorals), only twice in any other sense (Rom. 13[11] Phil. 1[17]). He employs ἀνίστημι of rising from the dead in 1 Thes. 4[14, 16] only. In the gospels and Acts both terms are used with approximately equal frequency, except that Mt. has a decided preference for ἐγείρω (pass.), using ἀνίστημι but once,

though it appears as a variant in three other passages also. There is
apparently little or no distinction in thought between the two terms.
The general usage of ἐγείρω suggests a waking out of sleep, that of
ἀνίστημι a rising up from a recumbent position, but this distinction
affects the terms as used of the resurrection from the dead at most
merely in the outward form of the thought. Both verbs are frequently
followed by ἐκ νεκρῶν. For ἐγείρω (act.), see Rom. 4²⁴ 8¹¹ 10⁹; (pass.),
Rom. 6⁴, ⁹ 1 Cor. 15¹², ²⁰. Only rarely do ἐκ τῶν νεκρῶν (see 1 Thes.
1¹⁰, where, however, AC omit τῶν and WH. bracket it, and Eph. 5¹⁴, a
quotation from some unidentified source) and ἀπὸ τῶν νεκρῶν (Mt. 14²)
occur. The omission of the article is probably due to the expression
being a fixed prepositional phrase. See Slaten, *Qualitative Nouns in
the Pauline Epistles*, p. 25, Chicago, 1918.

2. καὶ οἱ σὺν ἐμοὶ πάντες ἀδελφοί, "and all the brethren
that are with me." The term "brethren" is one which according to Paul's usage and that of the early Christians generally
(1 Thes. 1⁴ 2¹ 1 Cor. 5¹¹ 6⁵⁻⁸ 8¹², *et freq.* in Paul; Jas. 1² 1 Pet. 5¹²
1 Jn. 3¹³ Rev. 12¹⁰; Clem. Rom. 1¹; Ign. *Philad.* 5¹—much less
frequent in the early fathers than in N. T.) usually meant "fellow-Christians." See below on v. ¹¹. The fact that it is Paul's
usual habit to join with himself in the address of a letter one or
two of his closest companions and fellow-labourers (see esp. 1
Cor. 1¹ and *cf.* 16²⁰; 2 Cor. 1¹ and *cf.* 13¹¹, ¹²; Phil. 1¹, and *cf.* 4²¹, ²²;
Col. 1¹ and *cf.* 4¹⁰, ¹², ¹⁴), the distinction which he apparently
makes in Phil. 4²¹, ²² between "the brethren with him" and the
resident Christians, and the fact that a temporary sojourner in
a place would more naturally refer to the residents of the place
as "those with whom I am staying" or more generally as "the
brethren of such a place," than "the brethren that are with
me," makes it probable that the phrase here designates not the
Christians of the place in general (as Wies., Zahn, and Bous.
maintain), but his fellow-missionaries (so Hilg., Ltft., Ell.,
Sief., Beet).

The purpose of this association of his companions with himself in
the writing of the letter does not clearly appear. If the persons thus
named took any part in the composition of the letter, we are unable
now to detect their part, or even that they had any such. Even in
1 Thes. where Paul uses the first person plural in the first two chapters
and part of the third (*cf.* Frame on 1. 1) it is probable that while the

pronoun at first includes the companions named at the beginning, they took no actual part in the composition of the letter, being only in the background of his thought, as 2^{18} itself shows. But in Gal. the almost uniform use of the first person singular for the author, not only in narrative passages (such as $1^{12-19, 21, 22}$ 2^{1-14} 4^{13-15}) and in those in which the pronoun might be supposed to be rhetorically used for the Christian believer as such (2^{18-21}), but in those in which the writer speaks of himself as such, referring to what he is at the moment saying (1^6, $^{10, 11, 20}$ 3^2, $^{15, 17}$ 4^1, $^{12, 16-21}$ 5^2, ^{3}, $^{10-12, 16}$ 6^{17}), practically excludes the possibility of any partnership in the writing of the letter. The first person plural is usually "we Jews," or "we Christians." Only in $1^{8, 9}$ can it be taken as an epistolary plural referring to Paul himself (see Dick, *Der schriftstellerische Plural bei Paulus*, 1900), and even here more probably (see on those vv.) as a designation of the apostle and his companions. But in 1^9, at least, these are apparently referred to, not as with him at the moment of writing, but when he was preaching in Galatia; and that "the brethren with me" here referred to were his companions in Galatia is rather improbable, since had those who shared with him in the preaching of the gospel in Galatia been with the apostle at the moment of writing it is likely that, instead of there being no other reference to them in the letter than this obscure one, they would have received at least as much recognition as in 1 Thes. Paul gives to Timothy and Silas. Nor does it seem likely that the brethren here referred to are intended to be understood as indorsing the apostle's statements. The mention of them seems rather, as in Paul's salutations generally, mainly at least, an act of courtesy, though doubtless carrying with it the implication that the brethren were aware of his writing the letter, and were not averse to being mentioned in it.

The question who these brethren were is, of course, inseparably connected with the question where and when the letter was written. If it was written to the churches of southern Galatia from Corinth on the second missionary journey (see *Introd.*, pp. xlvii *ff.*) we can name none who were more probably included than Silas and Timothy, who were with Paul in Macedonia and Achaia on this journey, his first into that region (1 Thes. 1^1 3^1, ^{2}, ^{6} 2 Thes. 1^1 2 Cor. 1^{19} Acts 17^{10}, ^{14} 18^5). If it was written from Antioch between the second and third journeys, Timothy or Titus was very likely among those referred to. Both were with Paul on the latter journey (2 Cor. 1^1 2^{18}). Titus had been with Paul in Antioch before the writing of this letter (Gal. 2^1), perhaps about three years before, and was sent by him to Corinth in connection with the trouble in the Corinthian church (2 Cor. $2^{12, 13}$ 7^6 12^{18}), probably about three years after the writing of the letter to the Galatians, if it was written at Antioch; but his movements in the interval we can not trace. If it was sent from Ephesus or Macedonia, there is a still wider range of possibilities (1 Cor. 1[1, 11] 16[10-12, 17] 2 Cor. 1[1] 2[13] 8[16-24]. That the Galatians knew who were referred to, or would be informed by those who bore the letter, is rendered probable by the very omission of the names. On the use of the term ἀδελφός, see on 1[11].

ταῖς ἐκκλησίαις τῆς Γαλατίας· "to the churches of Galatia." On the location of these churches see *Introd.*, p. xxi. On the use of the word ἐκκλησία in N. T. see detached note, p. 417. The most notable characteristic of this salutation is the total lack of such commendatory words as are found in the address of all other Pauline letters (see below). This is commonly and doubtless rightly explained as reflecting the apostle's perturbation of mind mingled with indignation against the fickle Galatians. *Cf.* on θαυμάζω, v. [6].

1 and 2 Thes. are addressed τῇ ἐκκλησίᾳ Θεσσαλονικέων ἐν θεῷ πατρὶ καὶ κυρίῳ Ἰησοῦ Χριστῷ, with ἡμῶν after πατρί in 2 Thes. In 1 and 2 Cor. the address is τῇ ἐκκλησίᾳ τοῦ θεοῦ τῇ οὔσῃ ἐν Κορίνθῳ, the first letter adding ἡγιασμένοις ἐν Χριστῷ Ἰησοῦ, κλητοῖς ἁγίοις etc., the second adding σὺν τοῖς ἁγίοις πᾶσιν, etc. None of the later Pauline letters, from Rom. on, have the term ἐκκλησία in the address, but all those addressed to communities have a phrase designating the members of the community and always including the word ἅγιος.

3. χάρις ὑμῖν καὶ εἰρήνη "grace to you and peace." These words form a part of the benediction which in every Pauline letter is included in the opening salutation, usually forming the last words of it. The first word is perhaps connected with the common Greek salutation χαίρειν, with which also the Ep. of Jas. begins (Jas. 1[1], *cf.* Mayor, *The Epistle of St. James*, pp. 30, 31; Acts 15[23] 23[26]), but, if so, is a decidedly Christian version of it. εἰρήνη is the Greek word which represents the Semitic salutation, Hebrew, שָׁלוֹם, Aramaic, שְׁלָם, used both in personal greeting (Lk. 10[6] 24[36]) and at the beginning of a letter (Ezr. 4[17] 5[7]). Yet this term also takes on a deeper religious significance than it commonly bore as a salutation among the Hebrews. χάρις is a comprehensive term for that favour of God towards men which is the basis of their salvation. It includes the ideas of love, forbearance, desire to save. εἰρήνη denotes the blessed state of well-being into which men are brought and in which

they are kept by the divine χάρις. For a fuller discussion, see detached notes, pp. 423 and 424. The words stand without the article because the thought of the sentence calls for a qualitative not an individualising representation of grace and peace. Cf., on the other hand, Gal. 6¹⁸.

ἀπὸ θεοῦ πατρὸς ἡμῶν καὶ κυρίου Ἰησοῦ Χριστοῦ, "from God our Father and the Lord Jesus Christ." These words also, or a phrase but slightly different from them, are found in the salutation of every Pauline letter except 1 Thes. and Col. They are undoubtedly to be taken as limiting both χάρις and εἰρήνη. It is characteristic of the apostle's method of thought that he joins together God the Father and Christ the Lord as jointly source of grace and peace. Any attempt to discriminate sharply their respective shares in the bestowment of these blessings would lead us away from the apostle's thought. The entire sentence constitutes in effect a prayer for the Galatians that God the Father and the Lord Jesus Christ may be gracious to them, may look upon them not in wrath, but in favour that brings salvation, and that (as a consequence) they may be in a state of spiritual well-being.

Concerning θεοῦ πατρός, see detached note, on Πατήρ as applied to God pp. 384 ff., and on κυρίου as applied to Christ, see detached note on the *Titles and Predicates of Jesus*, pp. 399 ff.

Ἡμῶν stands after πατρός in אAP 33 al plu. 20 fu. demid. Chr. Ambrst.; after κυρίου in BDFGHKL, 31, 1908, al 20 fere d e f g Vg. Syr. (psh. harcl. pal.) Arm. Goth. Victorin. Hier.; in Boh. Aeth. in both places. The external evidence is indecisive; the reading of אAP, etc., may be regarded as non-Western and its rival as Western, or it may be Alexandrian and its rival non-Alexandrian. Intrinsic probability favours the reading of אAP (after πατρός); see Rom. 1⁷ 1 Cor. 1² 2 Cor. 1² Eph. 1² Phil. 1² Col. 1² Phm. 3 (*contra* Eph. 6²³ 2 Thes. 1² 1 Tim. 1² 2 Tim. 1² Tit. 1⁴), and transcriptional probability is certainly not against it. On the whole the preponderance of probability is slightly on the side of πατρὸς ἡμῶν.

4. τοῦ δόντος ἑαυτὸν ὑπὲρ τῶν ἁμαρτιῶν ἡμῶν "who gave himself for our sins." In itself the expression τὸ δοῦναι ἑαυτόν may perfectly well refer to a devotion of one's self in service,

but the general usage of Paul so associates the death of Christ
with deliverance from sin as to leave no reasonable doubt that
he here refers especially if not exclusively to Jesus' voluntary
surrender of himself in his death.   See Rom. 5⁶˒ ⁸ 1 Cor. 15³ Gal.
2²⁰.   Similarly ὑπὲρ τ. ἀμ. ἡμ. in itself means (to achieve something) "in relation to our sins."   But Paul's conception of sin
and its effects on men and the relation of Jesus' death to it, as
elsewhere expressed, and the following expression, ὅπως . . .
πονηροῦ, leave no doubt that in his thought deliverance from
sins is that which is to be achieved in respect to them.   Since
the apostle elsewhere associates the death of Jesus with deliverance both from the power of sin over one's life (Rom. 6¹⁻¹¹)
and from the condemnation under which it brings men (chap.
3¹³˒ ¹⁴ Rom. 3²³⁻²⁶ 5⁹˒ ¹⁰), either of these aspects of salvation may
be in mind here.   But as the association of the death with the
forensic aspect is somewhat more frequent in Paul, and as it is
this phase which is prominent in this epistle, it is probably this
that the apostle has chiefly in mind here.   On the meaning of
ἁμαρτία, see detached note, pp. 436 ff.

On the usage of δοῦναι ἑαυτόν, see Polyb. 8.18¹¹: οὕτως ἔφη δώσειν ὁ
Βῶλις ἑαυτὸν εἰς τὴν χρείαν: "So Bolis said he would give himself
to the matter"; 10. 6¹⁰: ἐπὶ πράξεις αὐτὸν ἔδωκε τελέως παρὰ τοῖς
πολλοῖς ἀπηλπισμένας: "He undertook affairs regarded by most as perfectly hopeless"; 1 Mac. 2⁵⁰ᶠ˙ and exx. from papyri and inscriptions
referred to by Nägeli, Wortschatz, p. 50, in none of which does it seem
to mean to lay down one's life.   On the other hand, see Jos. Ant. 2. 144
(6⁸).   For a discussion of δοῦναι τὴν ψυχὴν αὐτοῦ in Mk. 10⁴⁵ Mt.
20²⁸, and of τὴν ψυχὴν θεῖναι in Jn. 10¹⁵, see Burton, Smith, and Smith,
Biblical Ideas of Atonement, pp. 114 ff.

The preposition ὑπέρ primarily signifies "over" in a local sense, but
it is not so used in N. T.   Its common use there is in the sense "on
behalf of," "for the benefit of," followed by a personal term.   See,
e. g., chap. 2²⁰ 1 Cor. 1¹³ Rom. 5⁶ᶠ˙.   The modification of this meaning
which the preposition necessarily undergoes when used with an abstract
noun gives it a telic force, "to accomplish something for, or in respect
to," the thing to be accomplished being in each case implied in the
nature of the thing which stands as the object of the preposition.   With
most abstract nouns the meaning is approximately "for the promotion
of": thus in Jn. 11⁴, ὑπὲρ τῆς δόξης τοῦ θεοῦ, "for the promotion or
manifestation of the glory of God"; 2 Cor. 1⁶, ὑπὲρ τῆς ἡμῶν παρα-

κλήσεως, "for your comfort, that you may be comforted"; and Phil.
2¹³, καὶ τὸ θέλειν καὶ τὸ ἐνεργεῖν ὑπὲρ τῆς εὐδοκίας. "both the willing and
the working for the accomplishment of that which is well pleasing (to
God)." Cf. also Jn. 6⁵¹ Rom. 15⁸ 16⁴ 2 Cor. 13⁸ Eph. 6²⁰ 2 Thes. 1⁵
Heb. 13¹⁷. With ἁμαρτιῶν and words of similar import, the meaning
"on behalf of" naturally becomes not "for the promotion of," but "for
the deliverance from," or with the genitive ἡμῶν following, "to deliver
us from our sins." The possibility that the apostle had in mind a still
more definite meaning can for reasons given above neither be excluded
nor established.

ℵᶜBH33,424² al. read ὑπέρ. ℵ*ADFGKLP al. 50 fere read περί.
The latter testimony is apparently Western and Syrian. Cf. Introd.
p. lxxx. Intrinsic probability is in favour of ὑπέρ; for though Paul
uses both prepositions with both meanings, "concerning" and "on
behalf of," he employs περί much more commonly in the former sense
and ὑπέρ in the latter.

ὅπως ἐξέληται ἡμᾶς ἐκ τοῦ αἰῶνος τοῦ ἐνεστῶτος πονηροῦ
"that he might deliver us out of the present evil age." On
αἰών and ἐνεστώς see detached notes pp. 426, 432. The phrase
ὁ αἰὼν ὁ ἐνεστώς, here only in N. T., but manifestly the
equivalent of the more usual ὁ αἰὼν οὗτος, is primarily a phrase
of time denoting the (then) present period of the world's history
as distinguished from the coming age, ὁ αἰὼν ὁ μέλλων. Its
evil character is implied in 1 Cor. 1²⁰ and Rom. 12², and apparently always assumed, but here only is the adjective πονηρός
directly attached to αἰών. Its position here gives it special
emphasis.* ἐξέληται denotes not a removal from, but a rescue from the power of. Cf. Acts 7¹⁰, ³⁴ 12¹¹ 23²⁷ 26¹⁷, in all which
cases the emphasis of the word is upon the idea of rescue. It
occurs in Paul's epistles here only. Cf. Jn. 17¹⁵. The whole
clause expresses the purpose for which the Lord Jesus Christ
gave himself for our sins, and thus presents from a different
point of view the thought of ὑπὲρ τῶν ἁμαρτιῶν ἡμῶν.

The very presence of these words (v. 4) at this point is itself
a significant fact. In all the other Pauline letters the salutation closes with the benediction, though not always in exactly
the same form, and the next paragraph is introduced by an

---

* An interesting parallel, the only other observed instance of αἰὼν ἐνεστώς, is found in an
inscription of 37 A. D., ὡς ἂν τοῦ ἡδίστου ἀνθρώποις αἰῶνο(ς) νῦν ἐνεστῶτος (Dittenberger,
Sylloge, 364. 9); quoted by M. and M Voc. s. v., who suggest that αἰών means "period of life,"
but without obvious ground; it seems clearly to mean "age" (of human history).

expression of thanksgiving or an ascription of praise to God. The addition of this verse with its reference to the death of Christ for the salvation of men is undoubtedly occasioned by the nature of the erroneous teaching which was propagated among the Galatians by the judaising opponents of Paul, and which this letter was written to combat. As in opposition to their personal attack on him he affirmed his independent apostleship (v.[1]), so here against their legalistic conception of the value of works of law, he sets forth even in the salutation the divine way of deliverance provided in Christ's gift of himself for us according to the will of God.

It remains to be considered whether the deliverance here referred to is (a) ethical, having reference to emancipation from the moral influence of this present evil age (cf. Rom. 8[2]), or (b) present judicial, consisting essentially in justification, through the death of Christ (cf. Rom. 5[9a, 10]), or (c) eschatological, being deliverance from the wrath of God which will fall upon the wicked at the coming of the Lord (cf. 1 Thes. 5[2, 3, 9, 23] Rom. 5[9b]). There is no doubt that Paul held the current Jewish doctrine of the two ages (see detached note on Αἰών, p. 426), and though he never definitely places the coming of the Lord in judgment on the wicked and salvation for believers at the boundary-line between the two ages, his language is most naturally understood as implying this, and there is in any case no doubt that in his thought salvation was achieved in the full sense not before but at the coming of the Lord (cf. Rom. 5[9] 13[11] 1 Thes. loc. cit.). The associations of the phrase are therefore eschatological. Nor can it be urged against the interpretation of the whole expression as eschatological that the thought of the future salvation distinctly as such is usually associated by Paul not with the death of Jesus but with his resurrection (so Zahn; cf. Rom. 5[10] 6[5] 1 Cor. 15[12ff.] Phil. 3[10]). For though this is true, it is also true that in several of the passages the death is closely associated with the resurrection, and in 1 Thes. 5[9, 10], the deliverance from wrath at the coming of the Lord (cf. v.[23]) is definitely made to result from the death of Christ. There are, however, two valid objections to the supposition that the reference of the phrase is chiefly eschatological. The first is the use of the word ἐξέληται. The present age is to end at the coming of the Lord. Salvation at that time consists not in deliverance from this age, but from the wrath of God. Had the apostle's thought at this point been, as it is in Rom. 5[10, 11], definitely eschatological, he would naturally have written ὅπως ἐξέληται ἡμᾶς ἀπὸ τῆς ὀργῆς τοῦ θεοῦ ἐν τῇ παρουσίᾳ τοῦ κυρίου. The second reason is found in the general atmosphere and purpose of the epistle. Its thought is concentrated on the way of acceptance with God in the present life; eschatological references are few and indirect; it is improbable, therefore, that in the salutation, which bears clear marks of being written under the influence of the controversial situation with which the epistle deals, the idea of the salvation achieved at the coming of the Lord should fill a prominent place. As between the judicial and the ethical conceptions, it is doubtful whether we should exclude either (*cf.* on ὑπὲρ τ. ἁμ. ἡμ. above).* To limit the reference to the ethical phase would be to exclude that aspect of the significance of Christ's death which the apostle usually emphasises (see Rom. 3[24, 25] 5[6-10] Gal. 3[13]), and which precisely in this epistle, which deals so largely with justification, we should least expect to be forgotten. But, on the other hand, the appropriateness of the words to describe the ethical aspect, and the absence of any phraseology expressly limiting the thought to the judicial aspect (as, *e. g.*, in Rom. 8[1] and Gal. 3[13]), seem to forbid the exclusion of the former. That Paul sometimes associated the morally transforming power of Christ with his death clearly appears from Gal. 2[20, 21] and Rom. 6[10, 11] (*cf.* also a clear expression of this idea in 1 Pet. 1[18, 19]). Probably, therefore, we must include the judicial aspect, and not exclude the ethical. That the apostle has the law chiefly in mind as an element of the present evil age from which the Christ by his death is to deliver men (see Bous. *ad loc.*) is improbable, not indeed because the thought itself is un-Pauline (see Rom. 10[4]), but because the phrase "present evil age" is too general and inclusive to suggest a single element of that age so little characteristic of it as a whole as was the law.

κατὰ τὸ θέλημα τοῦ θεοῦ καὶ πατρὸς ἡμῶν, "according to the will of our God and Father." Whether these words are to be taken as limiting (a) δόντος or (b) ἐξέληται, or (c), the whole complex idea expressed by τοῦ δόντος . . . πονηροῦ (πονηροῦ alone is manifestly out of the question), can not be decisively determined. Most probably, however, the third construction is the true one. Twice before in this paragraph the apostle has closely associated together Jesus Christ and God the Father, first as the source of his own apostleship (v.[1]) and then as the source of grace and peace to those to whom he is writing. The present phrase emphasises once more essentially the same

* The idea of removal from the present life by death or translation is itself naturally suggested by the words ἐκ τ. αἰ. τ. ἐνεστ. πον., but is rendered improbable by the usage of the word ἐξέληται (see above) and decisively excluded by the wholly un-Pauline character of the thought that the salvation through Christ shortens the earthly life of the saved.

thought, affirming that in the salvation provided for us (the pronouns ἡμῶν and ἡμᾶς in v.⁴ include both the apostle and his readers) through Christ's gift of himself for us, God our Father also participates, the gift and its purpose being according to his will. Concerning the construction of ἡμῶν and the translation of τοῦ θεοῦ καὶ πατρὸς ἡμῶν, see detached note on Πατήρ *as applied to God*, pp. 388 *f.*

5. ᾧ ἡ δόξα εἰς τοὺς αἰῶνας τῶν αἰώνων· ἀμήν. "to whom be the glory for ever and ever. Amen." An ascription of praise to God for the gift of Christ and the deliverance accomplished through it. δόξα (here only in Gal.) is frequent in Paul, with considerable variation of meaning. See Th. *s. v.* and Kennedy, *St. Paul's Conception of the Last Things*, pp. 229 *ff.* Its sense here, "praise," comes down from the classic times, and is frequent in N. T. The article, when occurring, seems almost invariably to convey a reference to something which has just been mentioned; in this case, no doubt, the redeeming work of Christ. *Cf.* Rom. 11³⁶ 16²⁷ Eph. 3²¹ Phil. 4²⁰ 2 Tim. 4¹⁸ Heb. 13²¹ 1 Pet. 4¹¹. Contrast Lk. 2¹⁴ (where, however, the poetic form may rather be the cause of the omission of the article); Rom. 15⁷ Phil. 2¹¹. The generic (or intensive) force of the article, such as apparently occurs in Rev. 7¹² and perhaps in 2 Pet. 3¹⁸, is possible but less probable than the demonstrative force suggested above. On εἰς τ. αἰ. τ. αἰώνων, see detached note on Αἰών, p. 426.

Ἀμήν (Heb. אָמֵן, an adverb derived from אָמַן "to be firm," Hiphil, "to believe," "to trust") is carried over into the N. T. vocabulary from the Hebrew. It is used in O. T. as confirming an oath (Num. 5²² *et al.*), as the solemn conclusion and confirmation of a doxology (Neh. 8⁶ Ps. 41¹⁴, etc.), and otherwise. The Lxx usually translate it by γένοιτο, but occasionally transliterate (1 Chron. 16³⁶ Neh. 5¹³ 8⁶ 1 Esd. 9⁴⁷ Tob. 8⁸ 14¹⁵), but none of these instances are at the end of a doxology or benediction. This usage, of which 3 Mac. 7²³ (see also 4 Mac. 18²⁴) apparently furnishes the earliest example, may have arisen from the custom of the congregation responding "Amen" to the prayer offered by the leader. *Cf.* Neh. 8⁶ 1 Cor. 14¹⁶, and Frame on 1 Thes. 3¹³, also M. and M. *Voc. s. v.*

On the relation between the salutations of the Pauline and other

N. T. letters, and the methods of beginning letters current among Greek, Roman, Jewish, and early Christian writers, see extended and instructive note in Hilgenfeld, *Der Galaterbrief*, 1852, pp. 99 *ff.*; also respecting the classical Greek and Latin forms, Fritzsche on Rom. 1¹; Wendland, *Handbuch zum Neuen Testament*, III 3, Beilage 15, pp. 411 *ff.*; Ziemann, *De Epistularum graecarum formulis*, in *Diss. phil. Hal.* XVIII 4, 1910. Respecting the evidence of the papyri, see Lietzmann, *Griechische Papyri*, 1905; Witkowski, *Epistulae graecae privatae*, 1906, and Milligan, *Selections from the Greek Papyri*, 1910. *Cf.* Frame on 1 Thes. 1¹. See also Mayor, *The Epistle of St. James*, pp. 30, 31. The following are typical examples: Πλάτων 'Αρχύτᾳ Ταραντίνῳ εὖ πράττειν (Epistle IX, Ed. Hermann, p. 58). M. Cicero salutem dicit P. Lentulo Procos. (Ed. Mueller, IV 1, pp. 1 *ff.*); לְדָרְיָוֶשׁ מַלְכָּא שְׁלָמָא כֹלָּא (Ezr. 5⁷); τοῖς ἀδελφοῖς τοῖς κατ' Αἴγυπτον 'Ιουδαίοις χαίρειν οἱ ἀδελφοὶ οἱ ἐν 'Ιεροσολύμοις 'Ιουδαῖοι καὶ οἱ ἐν τῇ χώρᾳ τῆς 'Ιουδαίας, εἰρήνην ἀγαθήν (2 Mac. 1¹). καὶ οἱ ἐν τῇ 'Ιουδαίᾳ καὶ ἡ γερουσία καὶ 'Ιούδας 'Αριστοβούλῳ · · · χαίρειν καὶ ὑγιαίνειν (2 Mac. 1¹⁰). Κλαύδιος Λυσίας τῷ κρατίστῳ ἡγεμόνι Φιλίκι χαίρειν (Acts 23²⁶; *cf.* Acts 15²³). 'Ιωάνης ταῖς ἑπτὰ ἐκκλησίαις ταῖς ἐν τῇ 'Ασίᾳ· χάρις ὑμῖν καὶ εἰρήνη (Rev. 1⁴). Πολύκαρπος · · · τῇ ἐκκλησίᾳ τοῦ θεοῦ τῇ παροικούσῃ Φιλίπποις· ἔλεος ὑμῖν καὶ εἰρήνη παρὰ θεοῦ (Polyc. *Phil.*). The following, from Milligan's *Selections*, show the usage of the papyri: Πολυκράτης τῶι πατρὶ χαίρειν. 'Απολλώνιος Πτολεμαίωι τῶ πατρὶ χαίρειν. 'Ιλαρίων [α] "Αλιτι τῆι ἀδελφῆι πλεῖστα χαίρειν. Θέων Τυράννωι τῶι τιμιωτάτωι πλεῖστα χαίρειν.

These and other examples cited by the writers above referred to show (1) that both Greeks and Romans, if not also the Hebrews, frequently began a letter with the writer's name; (2) that the naming of the person or persons addressed, usually in the dative, but sometimes in the vocative, was the general custom among Greeks, Romans, and Hebrews; (3) that to these two it was customary among the Hebrews to add the word שָׁלוֹם, or if writing in Greek, εἰρήνη, among the Greeks χαίρειν, with or without the addition of λέγει, and among the Romans *salutem* with or without *dicit;* (4) that the early Christian writers followed in general the usages then current in the Roman world, but in the exercise of that liberty which these usages themselves sanctioned, combined elements derived on the one side from the Greek custom and on the other from the Hebrew, and introduced also distinctly Christian elements. As a result there seems to have been created almost a standard Christian form (note the resemblance between the salutation of the Pauline letters, those ascribed to Peter, 2 and 3 Jn., the salutation of Rev. 1⁴, and those used by Clem. Rom. and Polycarp), yet one which was freely modified by each writer in adaptation to the particular occasion and persons addressed. Note the variations from the usual form in Jas. and the Ignatian letters, and the lack of salutation in 1 Jn.

2

and Heb., though these latter are perhaps rather literary epistles than letters in the stricter sense. See Deissmann, *Bible Studies*, chap. I. In the creation of this general Christian form for beginning letters, the dates of the literature would suggest that Paul exerted a special influence, though there can hardly have been any slavish, perhaps not even a conscious, copying of his form by others.

2. *Expression of indignant surprise at the threatened abandonment of his teaching by the Galatians, in which is disclosed the occasion of the letter* (1[6-10]).

In place of the expression of thanksgiving or of praise to God with which in all the letters that bear Paul's name, except 1 Tim. and Titus, the paragraph immediately following the address and salutation opens, there stands in this letter an expression of surprise and indignation; surprise that the Galatians are so quickly abandoning the gospel as they had received it from the apostle, and are on the point of accepting from others a perversion of it; indignation at those who are troubling them and seeking to pervert the gospel of the Christ. In this expression there is disclosed, as usually in the second paragraph of the apostle's letters, the occasion of the epistle.

[6]*I marvel that ye are so quickly turning away from him who called you in the grace of Christ unto a different gospel, [7]which is not another except in the sense that there are some who are troubling you and desire to pervert the gospel of the Christ. [8]But even if we or an angel from heaven shall preach unto you a gospel not in accordance with that which we preached to you, let him be accursed. [9]As we said before, so now I say again, if any one is preaching to you a gospel not in accordance with that which ye received, let him be accursed. [10]For am I now seeking the favour of men, or of God? Or am I now seeking to please men? If I were still pleasing men I should not be a servant of Christ.*

6. Θαυμάζω ὅτι οὕτως ταχέως μεϊατίθεσθε ἀπὸ τοῦ καλέσαντος ὑμᾶς ἐν χάριτι Χριστοῦ "I marvel that ye are so quickly turning away from him who called you in the grace of Christ." The present tense of the verb μετατίθεσθε indicates clearly that when the apostle wrote the apostasy of the Galatians was as yet only in process. They were, so to speak, on the point, or more exactly in the very act, of turning. The mind of the apostle wavers while he writes between hope and fear as to the outcome ($4^{20,}$ 5^{10}). The word ταχέως might conceivably refer to the rapid development of the apostatising movement after it was once begun. But it is equally suitable to the usage of the word to take it in the sense of "soon" (*cf.* 1 Cor. 4^{19} Phil. $2^{19,\ 24}$ Mt. 5^{25} Mk. 9^{39}), and it is certainly far more probable that the apostle is here speaking of the brevity of the interval than of the rapidity of the process. The point from which this interval, which seems to the apostle so brief, is reckoned is left unstated, but that of which one most naturally thinks in speaking of an apostasy is the time of the original acceptance of that which is now abandoned—in this case the gospel—and this is also suggested by ἀπὸ τοῦ καλέσαντος and εἰς ἕτερον εὐαγγέλιον.

Little help is afforded by this expression towards the determination of the date of the letter, since such a change as is here spoken of would doubtless seem to the apostle to have been quickly made if it took place at any time within a few years after the conversion of the Galatians.

It is grammatically possible to take τοῦ καλέσαντος as limiting Χριστοῦ and so to render "from the Christ who called you in grace." On this order of words see *BMT* 427; Gild. *Synt.* 622, and *cf.* Gal. 3^{17}. The thought thus yielded would moreover be wholly appropriate to this situation, since the apostasy of the Galatians was from Christ and his grace. But Paul's general use of the verb καλέω (see below) must be regarded as a decisive objection to referring the phrase to Christ (as is done by Hier. Luth. Calv. Beng. *et al.*; *cf.* Wies. and Sief. *ad loc.*) or to Paul (as by Paulus, cited by Wies.), and as a convincing reason for here referring it to God (so Chrys. Wies. Mey. Sief. Ell. Ltft.).

> The verb μετατίθημι, meaning in the active, "to transfer," "to remove" (see, *e. g.*, Heb. 11^5) or "to alter," "to pervert" (Jude 4), is used in the middle or pass. with various constructions in the sense "to change [one's opinion]". Hdt. 7^{18}: ἐγὼ μὲν καὶ αὐτὸς τράπομαι καὶ τὴν γνώμην μετατίθεμαι: "I myself am changing and altering my opinion;"

Plato, *Rep.* 345 B: φανερῶς μετατίθεσο καὶ ἡμᾶς μὴ ἐξαπάτα: "Change your mind openly, and do not [attempt to] deceive us." Followed by ἀπό, as here, in 2 Mac. 7²⁴, it means "to turn from," "to apostatise from," μεταθέμενον ἀπὸ τῶν πατρίων, "on condition of having apostatised from the ancestral [laws]." With πρός, instead of εἰς as here, "to turn to" in Polyb. 26. 2⁶.

For various interpretations of οὕτως ταχέως, see Sief. who himself takes it to mean "rapidly," "swiftly since it began."

In fifteen passages in the letters ascribed to Paul the writer attributes "calling" to God (Rom. 4¹⁷ 8³⁰ 9¹¹, ²⁴ 1 Cor. 1⁹ 7¹⁵, ¹⁷ Gal. 1¹⁵ 1 Thes. 2¹² 4⁷ 5²⁴ 2 Tim. 1⁹, using the verb καλέω; Rom. 11²⁹ 1 Cor. 1²⁶ Eph. 1¹⁸ Phil. 3¹⁴ 2 Tim. 1⁹, using κλῆσις), and never, except in the sense of "naming" or "inviting to a feast," to any one else. The main features of the apostle's conception of this divine act appear clearly in the passages cited. It is in execution of his predetermined purpose (Rom. 8²⁸⁻³⁰ 2 Thes. 2¹³, ¹⁴; *cf.* 2 Tim. 1⁹); an act of grace, not in accordance with men's deserts (Gal. 1¹⁵; *cf.* 2 Tim. 1⁹); it is the divine initiative of the Christian life (1 Cor. 7¹⁷⁻²²), by which God summons men into the fellowship of his Son Jesus Christ (1 Cor. 1⁹; *cf.* Rom. 8²⁹, ³⁰), to live in sanctification (1 Thes. 4⁷), and peace (1 Cor. 7¹⁵ Col. 3¹⁵), and to attain unto salvation (2 Thes. 2¹⁴), God's kingdom and glory (1 Thes. 2¹²; *cf.* also 1 Tim. 6¹²). Though always spoken of as God's act, it may take place through the preaching of the gospel by men (2 Thes. 2¹⁴), and it is doubtless to the divine call, brought to the Galatians through his own preaching, that the apostle here refers.

Paul's use of the terms "call" and "calling" is in general such as to suggest that he thought of those only as called who obeyed the divine summons (see esp. Rom. 8²⁸⁻³⁰); of a rejected call at least he never speaks. Yet the present passage evidently speaks of the Galatians as on the point or in the act of turning from him who had called them. This apostasy, moreover, the apostle evidently regarded as a most serious matter, vitally affecting their relation to Christ (see esp. 5²⁻⁴). It can not therefore be unqualifiedly affirmed that Paul always conceived of "calling" as effectual in the sense that all who were called were surely destined unto eternal life.

On the meaning of χάρις. see on v.³. Modern commentators have generally given to the preposition ἐν either its instrumental force (see Th. ἐν, I 5 d), or its causal and basal sense (see Th. I 6 c). In either case the grace of Christ is that which is manifested in his gift of himself for men, and is conceived of specially in its relation to their entrance into the kingdom of God; in the latter case, it is that on the ground of which, by virtue of which, men are called; in the former case, it is that by which the calling takes place. To these views there is no decisive objection either in the usage of the phrase "grace of

Christ" (see 2 Cor. 8⁹ Rom. 5¹⁵) or in the use of the preposition ἐν
(see Th. *u. s.*).   But (a) the grace of Christ is more commonly spoken
of by Paul in its relation to the Christian in his Christian life (see
Rom. 16²⁰ 2 Cor. 12⁹ 13¹⁴ Gal. 6¹⁸ Phil. 4²³ 1 Thes. 5²⁸ 2 Thes. 3¹⁸; *cf.*
also Rom. 5², and the benedictions in connection with the salutation
of all the letters).   (b) In the expression καλέω ἐν as used elsewhere
by Paul (Rom. 9⁷ does not properly come into account, being from
the Lxx, and καλέω not being used in its special Pauline sense of the
divine call into the kingdom), ἐν is never either instrumental or causal,
except possibly in 1 Cor. 7²², but almost uniformly marks its object as
the state or sphere in which the one called is, either (1) when he is
called (1 Cor. 7¹⁸,²⁰,²⁴), or (2) as the result of his call.   In this latter
case the phrase is pregnant and bears the meaning "call to be in"
(1 Thes. 4⁷ 1 Cor. 7¹⁵ Col. 3¹⁵ (ἐν ἑνὶ σώματι) Eph. 4⁴; *cf.* Th. ἐν I 7, and
εἰς in 1 Cor. 1⁹ Col. 3¹⁵ 2 Thes. 2¹⁴).   Usage evidently favours the metaphorical local sense of the preposition, and, since χάριτι is evidently
not the sphere in which the Galatians were when they were called, the
pregnant use of the phrase is the more probable.   (c) The sense yielded
for this passage by taking χάριτι as referring to the state in which the
Galatians were called to be is much more suitable to the connection
than that given by either of the other constructions.   In speaking of a
change of position on their part, it is more natural to refer to the state
in which by God's call they are or should be than to emphasise the
basis or instrument of God's call.   The remarkable and surprising fact
about their apostasy was that they were abandoning the position of
grace, *i. e.*, the relation towards God which made them the objects of
the grace of Christ and participators in its benefits, to put themselves
under law, which could only award them their sad deserts.   On Paul's
view of the nature of the change *cf.* 5⁴ 3¹⁰⁻¹⁴.   It is a further objection
to the view that ἐν is basal that while redemption is conceived of by
Paul as based on the work of Christ (Rom. 3²⁴), it is difficult to suppose
that he would speak of God's call as being on the ground of the grace
of Christ.   It is rather his thought that the work of Christ has its basis
in the love of God.   See Rom. 5⁸ ᶠᶠ..   Nor is the thought that the call
of God is by means of Christ's grace materially easier, for the expansion
of this into "the announcement of the grace of Christ" is unwarranted
by the language.

The absence of the article before χάριτι has the effect, and is doubtless due to the intention, of giving the word qualitative rather than
individualising force.   This in turn emphasises the folly of the conduct of the Galatians.   This shade of meaning can not well be expressed
in English (which requires a definite article before "grace" because of
the phrase that follows it) except by some such periphrasis as, "I marvel that ye are so quickly turning away from grace, that of Christ."

εἰς ἕτερον εὐαγγέλιον, "unto a different gospel." On the meaning of the word ἕτερον, see detached note, p. 420. On εὐαγγέλιον, see detached note, p. 422. It is evident that in the present passage, as indeed generally in this epistle, it is the doctrinal aspect of the gospel that the apostle has specially in mind. The questions at issue between Paul and his judaistic opponents did not at all concern the historical facts of the life of Jesus, nor did they so far as known have to do with the methods of carrying on the gospel work. They pertained rather to the way of acceptance with God and the significance of the Christ in relation to such acceptance. They were thus distinctly doctrinal questions.

The preposition εἰς denotes mental direction (cf. Acts. 26[18] Rom. 2[4] 1 Tim. 1[6]) and in view of the meaning and tense of μετατίθεσθε signifies "towards, with inclination to accept." That Paul calls the teaching of his opponents in Galatia a different "gospel" doubtless reflects the fact that they claimed for it the name "gospel," "good tidings"; they may even have described it in contrast with Paul's preaching, as a different gospel, ἕτερον εὐαγγέλιον. In what sense Paul was willing to apply to it the term "gospel" appears in what follows.

7. ὃ οὐκ ἔστιν ἄλλο, εἰ μή "which is not another except in the sense that." The relative ὅ should undoubtedly be taken as referring neither to εὐαγγέλιον alone, nor to the whole statement μετατίθεσθε . . . εὐαγγέλιον (reasons given below), but, as the manifest emphasis upon ἕτερον in the preceding clause and the use of the partly antithetical ἄλλο in this clause suggests, to ἕτερον εὐαγγέλιον taken as a single term and designating the erroneous teaching of the judaisers. The clause is thus a qualification of the preceding statement, intended to exclude the possible implication that that which the Galatians were urged to accept was really a gospel which might legitimately be substituted for that which Paul preached. On εἰ μή meaning "except" and introducing not a protasis but an exception, see Th. εἰ, III 8 c; BMT 274, 471. On εἰ μή meaning "except that," see Mk. 6[5] Rom. 14[14], and cf. Th. εἰ, III 8 b.

Οὐκ ἄλλο εἰ μή is taken in the sense "nothing else than" by Winer (Com. ad loc.), Grot., Rück.. as also hv Grimm (Th. εἰ III 8 c ε), ARV.

marg., and Ram. (first choice; see also below), ὅ being in this case referred not to ἕτερον εὐαγγέλιον, but to the fact related in μετατίθεσθε . . . εὐαγγέλιον. To this construction there are several objections: (1) It makes the antithesis between ἕτερον and ἄλλο only seeming and accidental, which is in view of Paul's usage rather improbable. See below on N. T. usage of these words. (2) It necessitates the supposition that Paul left the application of the term εὐαγγέλιον to the teaching of the judaisers unretracted. (3) The reference of ὅ to the whole preceding sentence is awkward and improbable. Following immediately upon ἕτερον εὐαγγέλιον, and agreeing with it in gender and number, ὅ could scarcely be taken by the reader otherwise than as referring to this expression. If Paul had intended ὅ to refer to the entire preceding clause he would naturally have written ἅ (cf. 4²⁴) or τοῦτο γάρ ἐστιν or τοῦτο δέ ἐστιν.* (4) It gives to οὐκ ἄλλο εἰ μή the sense "not other than" (denying qualitative distinction), which is unsustained by usage. See for classical writers Jelf, 773. 5 860. 7; Kühner-Gerth, 597 m. For this idea the Lxx use οὐκ ἀλλ' ἤ (Gen. 28¹⁷), τί (= οὐκ) ἄλλο ἤ (Mal. 2¹⁶), οὐκ εἰ μή (Neh. 2²); N. T. writers use οὐκ ἄλλος ἀλλ' ἤ (2 Cor. 1¹³), οὐκ εἰ μή (1 Cor. 10¹³), τίς (= οὐκ) εἰ μή (Rom. 11¹⁵ Eph. 4⁹), but neither Lxx nor N. T. use οὐκ ἄλλος εἰ μή.†

By a still older view (Chrys., Thdrt., Luth., Beza, Beng., Koppe, de W., and Hilg., cited by Sief. ad loc.) ὅ is referred to εὐαγγέλιον in the sense of the true gospel, the relative clause is taken as equivalent to οὐ γάρ ἐστιν ἄλλο, and the εἰ μή clause is taken as adversative. This view is now generally recognised to be erroneous, and requires no

---

* The relative ὅ might indeed be taken to refer to ἕτερον εὐαγγέλιον, the expression οὐκ ἄλλο εἰ μή being still interpreted as meaning "not other than" or "nothing else than," and against this the objection of Sief. (cf. also Wies.) that in that case ὅτι must have been inserted, as in 2 Cor. 12¹³, or εἰσίν omitted, is hardly valid in view of Mk. 6⁵ Rom. 14¹⁴. But there would still remain the first and fourth objections, and these, taken together, are decisive against this interpretation.

† The idea of qualitative non-distinction ("not other than," "the same as") is, of course, not the same as (numerical) exception to a negative statement ("no other except," "none beside," or "not except"). For this latter the Lxx use οὐκ ἄλλος πλήν (Exod. 8¹⁰ Isa. 45¹¹ᵃ Bel. 41); οὐκ ἔτι πλήν (Deut. 4³⁵), ἐκτὸς ἄλλος οὐκ (Isa. 26¹³). οὐκ παρέξ (Isa. 45²¹ᵇ), οὐκ εἰ μή (Neh. 2¹²). N. T. writers use most commonly οὐκ (or οὐδείς, μηδείς) εἰ μή (Mt. 11¹⁷ 17⁸ 21¹⁹ Rom. 7⁷ 13¹· ⁸ 1 Cor. 1¹⁴, etc.), once οὐκ ἄλλος πλήν (Mk. 12³²; quotation from Lxx), once ἕτερος οὐκ εἰ μή (Gal. 1¹⁹), and once ἄλλος οὐκ εἰ μή (Jn. 6²²). These last two expressions most closely resemble the one before us in v.⁷, Jn. 6²¹. being the only exact verbal parallel (and not even this in order of words) found in either Lxx or N. T. But in both these passages what is expressed is not qualitative non-distinction, but exception (rather loosely attached) to a preceding negative statement. They furnish no argument, therefore, for taking the present passage in the sense "not other than," but in so far as they weigh at all favour taking εἰ μή as introducing an exceptive clause, qualifying the preceding relatively complete statement, rather than as coalescing with the preceding ἄλλο to express a single idea, "not other than," "equivalent to saying." The use of οὐδεὶς ἄλλος in Jn. 15¹⁴ Acts 4¹². meaning "no one else," and of οὐδὲν ἄλλο in Gal. 5¹⁰ in the sense "nothing else" creates some probability that if Paul had meant here "nothing else than" he would have written οὐδὲν ἄλλο instead of οὐκ ἄλλο. But the fact that nowhere in Lxx or N. T. is οὐδὲν ἄλλο used in a phrase meaning "nothing else than" forbids laying stress on this argument.

extended discussion. Each element of it is in itself impossible: ὅ can not refer to εὐαγγέλιον alone in the sense of the (true) gospel, since this would involve an abrupt dropping from the mind of the emphatic element in the antecedent clause, and the mental substitution of a word (τό) having practically the opposite force; ὅ οὐκ ἔστιν might possibly mean "for it is not," but can not mean, as this interpretation requires, "there is not," since the substantive element of ὅ in this case altogether disappears; nor can εἰ μή be merely adversative in force (see on 1¹⁹).

Ram., as stated above, prefers the first of these views, but as his second choice translates "another gospel, which is not different (from mine), except in so far as certain persons pervert the gospel of Christ." ἕτερον εὐαγγέλιον he refers to the teaching of the Twelve, which Paul affirms to be not really different from his own; the perverters of this gospel, which is common to Paul and the Twelve, he supposes to be the judaisers. Aside from the question whether Paul could by this language convey so complex an idea, and whether Paul really regarded his gospel as quite so closely identical with that of the Twelve as this interpretation supposes, the crucial question is whether it does justice to the relative meanings of ἕτερος and ἄλλος, and to this question it seems necessary to return a negative answer, and consequently to reject Ram.'s interpretation of the passage. See detached note on Ἕτερος and Ἄλλος, p. 420.

The balance of evidence therefore seems to require taking ἕτερον as meaning "different," ἄλλο in the sense "another" (additional) and translating ὅ οὐκ ἔστιν ἄλλο εἰ μή as above, "which is not another except in the sense that." The only alternative is not, with Ram., to reverse this distinction between ἕτερος and ἄλλος, but to suppose that the two terms are entirely synonymous, the change being simply for variety of expression. In the latter case both words might consistently with Greek usage in general mean either "another" (second) numerically distinct, or "different." But the interpretation advocated above is more probable than either of these latter. In any case εἰ μή retains its exceptive force, meaning here "except (in the sense that)."

τινές εἰσιν οἱ ταράσσοντες ὑμᾶς καὶ θέλοντες μεταστρέψαι τὸ εὐαγγέλιον τοῦ χριστοῦ. "there are some who are troubling you and desire to pervert the gospel of the Christ." This is the first mention of those who were preaching the other gospel among the Galatians. The present tense of the verb indicates that they are still in Galatia, and that this letter is intended to combat them while they are in the very midst of their work. The verb ταράσσω, prop. "to agitate physically" (Jn. 5⁷), much more frequently in N. T. means "to disturb mentally," with excitement, perplexity, or fear (Mt. 2³ Jn. 14¹ Acts 15²⁴). Concerning the participle, or other attributive, with the article after an indefinite word like τινές or a noun without the article, see W. XVIII 3; XX 4 (WM. pp. 136, 174), B*MT* 424, Bl. § 412 (73²), Rad. p. 93, Gild. *Syn.* p. 283, Rob. p. 277. W. implies that τινές is here subject and οἱ ταρ. pred.; but the attributive construction is more probable; *cf.* chaps. 2²⁰ 3²¹. Observe in the use of θέλοντες another indication that the Galatians have not yet succumbed to the influence of the judaising missionaries. The troubling is a present fact. The perversion is as yet only a wish of the disturbers.

Μεταστρέφω (in N. T. Acts 2²⁰, here, and Jas. 4⁹ only) means (1) "to turn," "to transfer," (2) "to change from one thing into another or from one state to another"; whether for better or for worse is not involved in the meaning of the word (Deut. 23⁵ Sir. 11³¹[³³]); yet when the thing changed is right and good, to change it is naturally thought of as being to pervert it.

On the meaning of χριστός, see detached note on *The Titles and Predicates of Jesus*, III, pp. 395 *ff.* Note that we should here translate "the gospel of the Christ," χριστός with the article being here, as usually, and always after τὸ εὐαγγέλιον, not a proper name but a descriptive title, with tacit identification of the person referred to; as one would say "the Governor" or "the President," leaving the hearer to supply the personal identification.

8. ἀλλὰ καὶ ἐὰν ἡμεῖς ἢ ἄγγελος ἐξ οὐρανοῦ εὐαγγελίζηται ὑμῖν παρ' ὃ εὐηγγελισάμεθα ὑμῖν, ἀνάθεμα ἔστω. "But even if we or an angel from heaven shall preach unto you a gospel not in accordance with that which we preached to you, let him be accursed." This strong language shows how serious Paul considered the differences between his gospel and that which the Jewish Christian preachers were promulgating in Galatia. Contrast the language of Phil. 1¹⁵⁻¹⁸. The antithesis expressed by ἀλλά is probably between the disposition, which he suspects some of his readers may feel, to regard the gospel of Paul and that of the judaisers as, after all, not so very different, and his own strong sense of the serious difference between them. The clause, so far as ἡμεῖς ἢ ἄγγελος ἐξ οὐρανοῦ is concerned, is concessive, being unfavourable to the fulfilment of the apodosis, ἀνάθεμα ἔστω, and the καὶ is intensive, marking the extreme nature of the supposition. It is, of course, only rhetorically a possibility. In respect to the following words, παρ' ὅ, etc., the clause is causally conditional. See BMT 278, 281, 285 b. On the meaning of ἄγγελος, see on 4[14].

ℵA Dial[108] Ath. Cy[hr] Euthal. al. read εὐαγγελίσηται; BDFGHL al. pler. Bas. read εὐαγγελίζηται; Eus. Chr. Thdrt. Dam. have both -σηται and -ζηται; KP 442, 460, 1908 al. read -ζεται. External evidence is indecisive as between -σηται and -ζηται. Intrinsically it is a little more probable that Paul would write -ζηται, implying a continuous propagand-ism, rather than -σηται, which might suggest a single occasion of preach-ing, contrary to the apostle's doctrine. Transcriptional probability also favours -ζηται as more easily than either of the other forms, accounting for all the readings, each of the others arising from -ζηται by the change of a single letter. It is also more probable that scribes would give to the apostle's anathema a harsher form by changing -ζηται to -σηται than that they would soften it by the reverse change. Ln. (mg.) Tdf. WH. read -σηται. Ln. (txt.) Tr. Alf. Ell. Ltft. Weiss, Sief. Sd. read -ζηται.

ℵ°AD°KLP al. pler. d f Vg. Syr. (psh. harcl. pal.) Boh. read ὑμῖν after εὐαγγελ.; BH have it before the verb; ℵ*F[gr.] G g omit it; D* Ath. Cy[hr] read ὑμᾶς after εὐαγγελ. The reading ὑμᾶς may be set aside as weakly attested and probably due to the influence of ὑμᾶς in v.[9], yet it bears a certain testimony to the presence of a pronoun at this point. The witnesses to ὑμῖν before the verb and those to ὑμῖν after it furnish strong testimony to its presence in one place or the other, with a prob-ability in favour of the latter position.

Εὐαγγελίζομαι occurs first so far as observed in Aristoph. Eq. 643, λόγους ἀγαθοὺς εὐαγγελίσασθαι τινι (see Dalman, Words of Jesus, pp. 102 ff.). The active occurs first apparently in the Lxx, but is found also in secular writers after N. T. In the Lxx it is a translation of בִּשֵּׂר, "to bring tidings," "to bring good news." In N. T. it is found in the active (Rev. 10[7] 14[6] only), in the middle frequently, and in the passive. The middle is accompanied by an accusative of content, with or without a dative of indirect object (Lk. 4[43] 8[1]), or by a dative (Rom. 1[15]) or accusative (Acts 8[40]) of the person to whom the message is delivered without an accusative of content, or is used absolutely (1 Cor. 1[17]). Except in Lk. 1[19] and 1 Thes. 3[6] the accusative of content refers to the "gospel" message of salvation or to some phase of it. When used absolutely or in the passive the reference is to the proclamation of the gospel in the N. T. sense of the word. See note on εὐαγγέλιον, p. 422. Paul uses the word in the middle only, both with and without accusative of content (see Rom. 1[15] 15[20] 1 Cor. 1[17] 9 [16, 18] 15[1, 2] 2 Cor. 10[16] 11[7] Gal. 1[8, 9, 11, 16, 23] 4[13]), and always, except in 1 Thes. 3[6] Rom. 10[15] and this verse and the next, with reference to the preaching of his gospel. By the addition of παρ' ὅ, etc., here and in v. [8], the word is given a more general reference than to Paul's gospel in particular, yet doubtless still refers to the preaching of the Christian gospel, not to the announcement of good tidings in general. It is equivalent to εὐαγγέλιον κηρύσσειν, with εὐαγγέλιον in the same breadth of meaning which is implied in ἕτερον εὐαγγέλιον of v. [6]. On other ways of expressing substantially the same idea as that of this v., see 1 Cor. 3[11] 2 Cor. 11[4].

It has been much disputed whether παρά in παρ' ὅ signifies "contrary to," or "besides." But the room for dispute which usage permits is very narrow. The metaphorical uses of παρά in the New Testament are as follows:

1. Beyond, passing a certain limit. (a) Beyond the measure or limit of: (i) in excess of (Rom. 12[3] 2 Cor. 8[3] Heb. 11[11] also Heb. 2[7, 9]); (ii) in greater degree than (Luke 13[2, 4] Rom. 1[25] 14[5] Heb. 1[9]); (iii) in transgression of, contrary to (Acts 18[13] Rom. 1[26] 4[18] 11[24] 16[17]); (b) after comparatives, than (Luke 3[13] Heb. 1[4] 3[3] 9[23] 11[4] 12[24]); (c) after ἄλλος, than, except (1 Cor. 3[11] and freq. in Greek writers).

2. Aside from, except, lacking, used with a numeral, 2 Cor. 11[24], and in Greek writers with other expressions suggesting number or quantity.

3. Because of (1 Cor. 12[15, 16]).

The use in the present passage evidently falls neither under 2 nor 3; nor under 1 (a) (i) or (ii); nor, because of the absence of a comparative or ἄλλος, under (b) or (c). The meaning "beside, in addition to," does not exist in N. T., nor have instances of it been pointed out in the Lxx or Greek writers. The nearest approach to it is that which is illustrated in 1 Cor. 3[11]; but this sense apparently occurs only after ἄλλος, which is not found in the present passage. It remains therefore to take παρά in this verse, and the following, in the sense common in classical writers and in N. T., "contrary to," 1, (a) (iii) above. It should be observed, however, that the fundamental meaning of παρά is "by the side of," then "beyond," and that it acquires the meaning "contrary to" from the conception of that which goes beyond (and so transgresses) the limits of the object. This fundamental idea seems usually at least to linger in the word, suggesting not so much direct contradiction or denial, or on the other side merely addition, as exceeding the limits of a thing, e. g., a law or teaching—and so non-accordance with it. Cf. Rob., p. 616. This meaning suggested by the original sense of the preposition and by its usage is entirely appropriate to the present passage. The evidence of the letter as a whole indicates that the teachings of the judaisers, which Paul evidently has in mind here, were neither, on the one side, additions to his own teaching in the same spirit as his, nor, on the other side, direct contradictions and denials of his, but additions which were actually subversive in effect. The translation "other than" (RV., *cf*. Weizsäcker) is not quite accurate, because it suggests any variation whatever from Paul's message. "Contrary to" (RV. mg.) slightly exaggerates this idea of contrariety, suggesting direct contradiction. "Not in accordance with" or "at variance with" seems to come nearest to expressing the idea of the Greek.

The words ἀνάθεμα and ἀνάθημα were originally simply variant spellings of the same word. The latter word meant in Homer "an ornament," in Herodotus, *et al.*, "votive offering" set up in a temple. "Votive offering" is perhaps in fact the older sense. In this sense ἀνάθεμα appears in Greek writers from Theocritus down. In the Lxx, however, it is used to translate חֵרֶם, a thing devoted to God for destruction, a thing accursed. In the mss. of the Lxx and Apocr. ἀνάθημα and ἀνάθεμα are for the most part consistently distinguished, the former signifying "a votive offering," the latter "a thing accursed, devoted to destruction" (Lev. 27²⁸ Deut. 13¹⁷ ⁽¹⁸⁾), etc., or "a curse" (Deut. 13¹⁵⁽¹⁶⁾ 20¹⁷). But variant readings appear in Deut. 7²⁶ *bis* Jud. 16¹⁹ ⁽²³⁾ 3 Mac. 3¹⁷. In N. T. ἀνάθημα, found only in Lk. 21⁵ (even here אADX read ἀνάθεμα), means "a votive offering"; ἀνάθεμα in Rom. 9³ 1 Cor. 12³ 16²² means "a thing (or rather a person) accursed"; in Acts 23¹⁴ "a curse," a vow taken with an oath, a meaning found also in an Attic inscription of the first or second century A. D. (see Deissmann in *ZntW*. II 342), and hence doubtless a current use of the term in Common Greek, as it is also in modern Grk. *Cf.* M. and M. *Voc. s. v.* The former of these two meanings differs from the common Lxx sense of ἀνάθεμα in that it denotes not so much a thing devoted to God to be destroyed (see, *e. g.*, Josh. 6¹⁷⁻²¹) as one under the curse of God. See esp. Rom. 9³. In this sense the word must be taken in the present passage. How this condemnation of God would express itself is not conveyed in this word. Taken in their literal sense the words ἀνάθεμα ἔστω (on the use of the imper. see Rob. p. 939) are the opposite of the benediction in v. ³; they are a petition that the person referred to may be deprived of God's grace, and instead be the object of his disapproval. Precisely what thought the expression represented in Paul's mind is difficult to determine, because it is impossible to know precisely how largely the hyperbole of impassioned feeling entered into the words. For the evidence that ἀνάθεμα does not here or in N. T. generally refer to excommunication, as some older interpreters maintained, see Wieseler's extended note on this passage.

9. ὡς προειρήκαμεν, καὶ ἄρτι πάλιν λέγω, "As we said before so now I say again." The προ- in προειρήκαμεν may mean "before" either in the sense "on a former occasion," as, *e. g.*, in

2 Cor. 7³ Heb. 4⁷, or in a predictive sense "before the event spoken of," as in Mk. 13²³ Rom. 9²⁹ 2 Cor. 13². The two ideas are indeed not mutually exclusive. But the fact that v.⁹ᵇ, which is distinctly said to be a repetition of the utterance referred to in προειρήκαμεν, is not a prediction shows that προ- refers to a previous utterance of these words. This previous utterance, however, is not that of v.⁸, but something said on a previous occasion, as e. g., on a visit to Galatia, or in a previous letter. Paul does, indeed, not infrequently use a plural in speaking of himself alone, and even change abruptly from plural to singular (see 1 Thes. 2¹⁸ 3¹, ⁶ 2 Cor. 1¹³ f., ²³ 10² 11²¹, and Dick, *Der schriftstellerische Plural bei Paulus*, pp. 143 *ff*.), and προειρήκαμεν could in itself refer to something just said in the letter (see 2 Cor. 7³). But the use of ἄρτι here implying difference of time between the two utterances excludes the supposition that he is here referring to words just written down. Since we know of no previous letter to the Galatians, the previous utterance was probably made by Paul (or by Paul and his companions—on this point the plural can not in view of 2 Cor. 1¹³ f. and other passages cited above be said to be decisive) when he was in Galatia. On which of the two occasions on which he had probably already visited the Galatians (4¹³) this warning was given, depends somewhat on the question of the chronology of these visits, itself turning in large part on the location of the churches. See *Introd.*, p. xxi. The very fact that he felt it necessary to utter such a warning as this suggests an already existing danger. If the churches, being in northern Galatia, were founded on his second missionary journey, there might easily have been occasion for such a warning on his first visit to them. If, on the other hand, the churches were in southern Galatia, and hence founded on the first missionary journey, it is less probable that he had occasion at that time to utter so pointed a warning, and more likely that he refers to something said on the occasion of his second visit.

The perfect tense of προειρήκαμεν marks this saying as not simply a past fact, but as one of which the result remains, doubtless in that they remember (or may be assumed to remember) the utterance of the saying. B*MT* 74, 85. The tense therefore conveys an appeal to their memory of the utterance. This reference to the existing result of the saying can not be expressed in English except by an interjected clause, "as we told you and you remember," and inasmuch as the use of the English perfect in such a connection suggests a recent action— in this case most naturally an utterance just made in the preceding sentence—the best translation is the simple past, which though it leaves unexpressed a part of the meaning of the Greek, has at least the advantage of not expressing anything not conveyed by the Greek. B*MT* 82.

The strict force of καί before ἄρτι is doubtless adverbial, "also," but English idiom in such a case prefers the simple "so." *Cf.* Jn. 6⁵⁷ 13³² 1 Cor. 15⁴⁹. The fuller and more definitely comparative expression οὕτως καί occurs 1 Cor. 15²² Gal. 4²⁹, etc. ἄρτι, frequent in papyri, of strictly present time (M. and M. *Voc. s. v.*), is cited by Nägeli; *Wortschatz*, p. 78, as a word of the unliterary Κοινή; yet see numerous classical exx. in L. & S.

εἴ τις ὑμᾶς εὐαγγελίζεται παρ' ὃ παρελάβετε, ἀνάθεμα ἔστω. "If any one is preaching to you a gospel not in accordance with that which ye received, let him be accursed." This sentence differs from that of v. ⁸ in two respects which affect the thought: (1) the element of concession and improbability disappears in the omission of ἡμεῖς ἢ ἄγγελος ἐξ οὐρανοῦ; (2) the form of the condition that suggests future possibility is displaced by that which expresses simple present supposition, and which is often used when the condition is known to be actually fulfilled. The result is to bring the supposition closer home to the actual case, and since it was known both to Paul and his readers that the condition εἴ τις . . . παρελάβετε was at that very time in process of fulfilment, to apply the ἀνάθεμα ἔστω directly to those who were then preaching in Galatia.

10. ἄρτι γὰρ ἀνθρώπους πείθω ἢ τὸν θεόν; "For am I now seeking the favour of men, or of God?" ἄρτι, now, *i. e.*, in these utterances. The apostle evidently refers to a charge that on previous occasions or in other utterances he had shaped his words so as to win the favour of men. A similar charge was made by his opponents at Corinth, 2 Cor. 10¹. πείθω means "to win the favour of," "to conciliate," as in 2 Mac. 4⁴⁵ Mt. 28¹⁴ Acts 12²⁰. The present tense, by reason simply of the meaning of the word and the idea of action in progress suggested by the tense, has the meaning, " to seek the favour of." B*MT* 11; G*MT* 25.

The force of γάρ is difficult to determine. If, indeed, as Win. Th. Preusch. *et al.* affirm, γάρ has a conclusive or illative force (derived, as some maintain, from its etymological sense as compounded of γέ and ἄρα), this meaning would be most suitable. The apostle would in that case draw from his preceding sentence the inference, expressed in a rhetorical question, that he is not pleasing men (as has been charged against him), but God. Or if it had the asseverative force attributed to it by Hoogeveen *et al.* (see Misener, *The Meaning of Γάρ*, Baltimore, 1904), this would also yield a suitable meaning: "Surely I am not now pleasing men, am I?" But most of the N. T. passages cited by Th. *et al.* as examples of the illative sense are as well or better explained as in some sense causal, and though there remain a very few which it is difficult to account for except on the assumption of an asseverative or illative force, whether primitive or derived (see Acts 16[17] Phil. 1[8]), yet in view of the preponderance of evidence and judgment that all the uses of γάρ are to be explained from its causal force (see Misener, *op. cit.*), and the fact that the only two N. T. cases that obstinately refuse to be reduced to this category are in condensed exclamatory phrases, we do not seem to be justified in assuming any other than a causal force here. In that case it must be either confirmatory—"and I mean what I say, for am I now?" etc.—or, explanatory and defensive, justifying the use of the strong and harsh language of vv.[8, 9]— "and this I am justified in saying, for am I now?" etc. Of these two explanations the second is the more probable, since the preceding expression is already sufficiently strong and would naturally call for justification rather than confirmation. To this as to any form of the view that makes γάρ causal, it is indeed an objection that the clause introduced by γάρ ought naturally to be either a positive assertion, or a question the answer to which is to the opponent in argument so evident and unquestionable that it has the value of a proved assertion. See, *e. g.*, Jn. 7[41] Acts 8[31] 19[35] 1 Cor. 11[22]. But this latter is precisely what this question does not furnish. To those to whom Paul is addressing himself it is by no means self-evident and unquestionable that he is concerned to win the favour of God and not of men. But ἄρτι with its backward reference to the strong language of the preceding sentences suggests that this language itself is appealed to as evidence that the apostle is not now seeking to please men but God, which fact, as γάρ shows, he in turn employs to justify the language. It is as if one reproved for undue severity should reply, "My language at least proves that I am no flatterer," the answer tacitly implying that this fact justified the severity. Such a mode of expression is not impossible to one writing under strong emotion, and this interpretation furnishes the most probable explanation of both ἄρτι and γάρ.

ἢ ζητῶ ἀνθρώποις ἀρέσκειν; "Or am I seeking to please men?" These words only repeat a little more distinctly the thought of the preceding clause, ζητῶ ἀρέσκειν taking the place of πείθω and expressing the idea of attempt more definitely.

εἰ ἔτι ἀνθρώποις ἤρεσκον, Χριστοῦ δοῦλος οὐκ ἂν ἤμην. "If I were still pleasing men, I should not be a servant of Christ." A supposition contrary to fact (BMT 248), implying that he is no longer pleasing men, and that he is a servant of Christ. The imperfect ἤρεσκον is doubtless like the πείθω above, conative, not resultative. This is the usual force of the progressive tenses in verbs of pleasing, persuading, and the like, which by their meaning suggest effort, and there is no occasion to regard the present instance as exceptional. That which the apostle says would prove him not to be a servant of Christ is, not a being pleasing to men, but an endeavour to please men. The expression is moreover comparative rather than absolute, signifying not the intention under any circumstances or in any degree to please men, but to please men in preference to God, as is implied in the preceding ἀνθρώπους . . . ἢ τὸν θεόν, and for his own advantage and convenience as the whole context suggests. There is no contradiction, therefore, between this assertion and that of 1 Cor. 10³³: πάντα πᾶσιν ἀρέσκω, μὴ ζητῶν τὸ ἐμαυτοῦ σύμφορον ἀλλὰ τὸ τῶν πολλῶν, ἵνα σωθῶσιν. The meaning ascribed to the sentence by some of the Greek expositors and by a few moderns, according to which it expresses the course which the apostle would voluntarily have pursued if he had been seeking to win the approval of men, "I would not have entered the service of Christ but would have remained a Pharisee," would almost of necessity have been expressed by οὐκ ἂν ἐγενόμην "I should not have become." On Χριστοῦ without the article, as a proper name, cf. on τοῦ χριστοῦ in v.⁷, and detached note on The Titles and Predicates of Jesus, III, p. 396. The whole sentence εἰ ἔτι . . . ἤμην is doubtless, though its relation to the preceding is not marked by any conjunction (the

γάρ of TR. having no sufficient authority), a confirmation of
the implied answer to the questions of the first part of the verse.
The appeal, however, is not to the *fact* that he was a servant of
Christ—this his opponents to whose criticisms he is at this
moment addressing himself, would not have conceded—but to
his own consciousness of the incongruity of men-pleasing and
the service of Christ. It is as if he should say: "Surely I am
not now a men-pleaser, for I myself recognise that that would
make me no longer a servant of Christ."

The connection of this verse with v.⁹ is so obviously close,
and vv. ¹¹,¹² so clearly enter upon a new phase of the letter,
that it is difficult to see how WH. could have made the
paragraph begin at v.¹⁰. RV. is obviously right in beginning
it at v. ¹¹.

It has been urged against taking ἤρεσκον as conative that the closely
preceding ἀρέσκειν is evidently not conative, since the idea of attempt
is separately expressed in ζητῶ. The objection, however, is of little
force. The Greek verb ἀρέσκω in the present system means either "to
be pleasing to" or (as nearly as it can be expressed in English) "to
seek to please." With a verb which by its tense suggests the idea of
attempt, but only suggests it, the conative idea may be separately
expressed, as in ζητῶ ἀρέσκειν, or may be left to be conveyed by the
tense only, as in ἤρεσκον.

Ἔτι "still" (1) primarily a temporal particle marking action as
continuing, "then as before," or "now as heretofore," is also used (2)
to denote quantitative or numerical addition (ἔτι ἕνα ἢ δύο, "one or two
more," Mt. 18¹⁶), and (3) logical opposition (τί ἔτι κἀγὼ ὡς ἁμαρτωλὸς
κρίνομαι: "why am I nevertheless judged as a sinner?" Rom. 3⁷). The
second and third uses, of course, spring from the first, and occasional
instances occur in which one or the other of these derived ideas is associated with the temporal idea and modifies it. See, *e. g.*, Heb. 11⁴. In
the present passage ἔτι might be (a) purely temporal, the comparison
being with his pre-Christian life when he was not a servant of Christ;
(b) purely temporal, the comparison being with a previous period of
his Christian life when he was seeking to please men and, consequently,
was not a servant of Christ; (c) purely temporal, the comparison being
with a previous period of his Christian life, when, *as alleged by his opponents*, he was seeking to please men; or (d) temporal and adversative,
ἔτι, meaning "still, despite all that I have passed through." The
interpretation (b) is excluded by the practical impossibility that Paul
could characterise any part of his Christian life as one in which he

was not a servant of Christ. The adversative rendering (d) is rendered improbable by the fact that his recent experiences were not such as to be specially calculated to eradicate the tendency to men-pleasing; rather, if anything, there was in them a temptation to seek to please men, a temptation to which his opponents alleged he had yielded. The interpretation (c) probably is correct to this extent, that the apostle has in mind the charges that have been made against him respecting his recent conduct as a Christian apostle, and means to say that whatever may have been alleged respecting that past conduct, now at least it cannot be charged that he is still seeking to please men. Yet it is doubtful whether the reference is solely to an alleged pleasing of men, and in so far as ἔτι implies a comparison with anything actual in the past, it must be with the days of his Phariseeism. For though Paul was perhaps less affected by the desire for the praise of men (Mt. 6². ⁵. ¹⁶ 23⁵ ff.), having more desire for righteousness and divine approval, than most of his fellow Pharisees (Gal. 1¹⁴ Phil. 3⁵), yet he would doubtless not hesitate to characterise that period of his life as one of men-pleasing as compared with his Christian life. The thought is therefore probably: "If I were still pleasing men, as was the case in the days of my Phariseeism, and as my opponents allege has been recently the case, I should not be a servant of Christ."

Δοῦλος, properly "a slave, a bondservant," is frequently used by N. T. writers to express their relation and that of believers in general to Christ and to God. The fundamental idea of the word is subjection, subservience, with which are associated more or less constantly the ideas of proprietorship by a master and service to him. The δοῦλος is subject to his master (κύριος, δεσπότης), belongs to him as his property, and renders him service. As applied to the Christian and describing his relation to Christ or God the word carries with it all three of these ideas, with varying degrees of emphasis in different cases, the fundamental idea of subjection, obedience, on the whole predominating. At the same time the conception of the slave as one who serves unintelligently and obeys from fear, is definitely excluded from the idea of the δοῦλος Χριστοῦ as held by Paul and other N. T. writers; δουλεία in this sense is denied, and υἱοθεσία affirmed in its place (Gal. 4¹⁻⁷ Rom. 8¹⁵. ¹⁶; cf. also Jn. 15¹⁵ Eph. 6⁵⁻⁸). The statement of Cremer correctly represents the thought of N. T. in general: "The normal moral relation of man to God is that of a δοῦλος τοῦ θεοῦ, whose own will though perfectly free is bound to God." It is evidently such a full but free service of Christ that Paul has in mind here in the use of the term δοῦλος Χριστοῦ. The effort to please men conflicts with and excludes unreserved obedience to Christ. Cf. Deissmann, New Light from the Ancient East, p. 381.

II. PERSONAL PORTION OF THE LETTER.

1. *Proposition: Paul received the gospel not from men, but immediately from God ($1^{11, 12}$).*

Beginning with these verses, the apostle addresses him-self to the refutation of the charges and criticisms of the judaising teachers, and to the re-establishment of himself and his gospel in the confidence of the Galatians; and first of all, doubtless as against an assertion of his opponents that he had never received (from Jerusalem) a commission authorising him to set himself up as a teacher of the religion of Jesus, he affirms his entire independence of all human authority or commission, and his possession of his gospel by virtue of a divine revelation of Jesus Christ.

^{11}For I declare to you, brethren, that the gospel that was preached by me is not according to man; ^{12}for neither did I receive it from man, nor was I taught it, but it came to me through revelation of Jesus Christ.

11. Γνωρίζω γὰρ ὑμῖν, ἀδελφοί, "For I declare to you, breth-ren." The verb γνωρίζω suggests a somewhat formal or solemn assertion. *Cf.* 1 Cor. 12^3 15^1 2 Cor. 8^1 Eph. 1^9, the similar ex-pression οὐ θέλω ἀγνοεῖν in Rom. 1^{13} 11^{25} 1 Cor. 10^1 12^1 2 Cor. 1^8 1 Thes. 4^{13}, and M. and M. *Voc.* on γνωρίζω and γινώσκω. The assertion that follows is in effect the proposition to the prov-ing of which the whole argument of 1^{13}–2^{21} is directed. This relation of vv. $^{11, 12}$ to what follows remains the same whether we read δέ or γάρ. Only in the latter case the apostle (as in Rom. 1^{16}) has attached his leading proposition to a preceding statement as a justification of it, not, however, of v. ^{10}, which is itself a mere appendix to vv. $^{6-9}$ and almost parenthetical, but of the whole passage, vv. $^{6-9}$, as an expression of his surprise at their apostasy and his stern denunciation of those who are

leading them astray. See a somewhat similar use of γάρ at
the beginning of a new division of the argument in Rom. 1¹⁸; cf.
also Rom. 1¹⁶, ¹⁷. The word "brethren," ἀδελφοί, doubtless
here, as almost invariably in Paul's epistles, signifies fellow-
Christians. See more fully in fine print below, and on v. ².

Γάρ after γνωρίζω is the reading of ℵ*BD*FG 33 d f g Vg. Dam.
Victorin. Hier. Aug.; δέ: ℵ*AD^b et o KLP, the major portion of the
cursives. Syr. (psh. harcl. pal.) Boh. Or^int. Chr. Euthal. Cyr. Thdrt.
al. The preponderance of evidence for γάρ is very slight. Both readings
must be very ancient. γάρ is the reading of the distinctively Western
authorities, and δέ apparently of the Alexandrian text. But which in
this case diverged from the original can not be decided by genealogical
evidence. The group BDFG supporting γάρ, and that supporting
δέ, viz., ℵAP al., each support readings well attested by internal
evidence. See *Introd.*, p. lxxx. The addition of 33 to the former group
in this case somewhat strengthens it, and throws the balance of evidence
slightly in favour of γάρ. Internal evidence gives no decided ground of
preference for either against the other, and the question must apparently be left about as it is by WH., γάρ in the text as a little more probably right, δέ on the margin as almost equally well attested. If δέ
is the true reading, it is probably resumptive in force (Th. *s. v.* 7;
W. LIII. 7 b; Rob. p. 1185 *init.*), marking a return to the main thought
of the superhuman authority of the gospel after the partial digression
of v. ¹⁰.

Among the Jews it was customary to recognise as brethren all the
members of a given family or tribe (Lev. 25²⁵ Num. 16¹⁰), and indeed
all members of the nation (Lev. 19¹⁷ Deut. 1¹⁶ 2 Mac. 1¹ Acts 7²
Rom. 9³). Papyri of the second century B. C. show that members of
the same religious community were called ἀδελφοί. See M. and M.
Voc. s. v. The habit of the Christians to call one another brethren
may have been the product in part of both these older usages. In the
Christian usage the basis of the relation is purely religious, family and
national lines, as well as lines of merely personal friendship, being dis-
regarded. Thus while the brethren mentioned in v.² were presumably
Jews, those who are here addressed as brethren were Gentiles. *Cf.*
also Acts 15²³. According to the gospels Jesus had taught that they are
his brethren who do God's will, and they brethren to one another
who unite in recognising Jesus himself as Master. Mk. 3³¹⁻³⁴ Mt. 23⁸.
In Paul the emphasis of the term is upon the fraternal, affectionate,
mutually regardful attitude of Christians to one another (1 Cor. 5¹¹ 6⁵⁻⁸
8¹¹⁻¹³ 15⁵⁸ 2 Cor. 1¹ 2¹³ Rom. 14¹⁰, ¹³, ¹⁵), though the suggestion of a common relationship to Christ and God is not wholly lacking (see Rom.

8¹⁶, ¹⁷, ²⁹), and the use of it constitutes an appeal to all those relations of affection and fellowship which Christians sustain to one another by virtue of their common faith, and membership in one body (1 Cor. 12¹ᶠᶠ·).   On later Christian usage, see Harnack, *Mission and Expansion of Christianity*,² I 405 *f.*

τὸ εὐαγγέλιον τὸ εὐαγγελισθὲν ὑπ' ἐμοῦ ὅτι οὐκ ἔστιν κατὰ ἄνθρωπον· "that the gospel that was preached by me is not according to man." τὸ εὐαγγέλιον, logically the subject of ἔστιν, is, by a species of attraction common both in classical writers and N. T. (Jelf 898. 2; W. LXVI 5 a) introduced as the object of γνωρίζω. On the meaning of εὐαγγέλιον, see detached note, p. 422, and on εὐαγγελισθέν see on v.⁸. On the use of the verb with an accusative of content, or in the passive with a subject denoting the gospel or its content, see vv. ¹⁶,²³ Lk. 8¹ 16¹⁶ 1 Cor. 15¹ 2 Cor. 11⁷. The aorist tense, εὐαγγελισθέν, is probably used in preference to the present because Paul has in mind at this moment the gospel not as that which he is wont to preach, or is now preaching, but as that which was preached by him to the Galatians. That the gospel preached by him is always the same is at once suggested, however, by the use of the present tense, ἔστιν. A converse use of aorist and present occurs with similar effect in 2², ἀνεθέμην αὐτοῖς τὸ εὐαγγέλιον ὃ κηρύσσω.

Κατὰ ἄνθρωπον, a phrase used by Greek writers from Aeschyl. down (see Wetst. on Rom. 3⁵), but in N. T. by Paul only, is of very general significance, the noun being neither on the one hand generic (which would require τὸν ἄνθρωπον) nor individually indefinite, "a man," but merely qualitative. The preposition signifies "according to," "agreeably to," "according to the will or thought of," or "after the manner of" (see it used similarly in the phrases κατὰ θεόν, Rom. 8²⁷ 2 Cor. 7⁹, ¹¹, κατὰ κύριον, 2 Cor. 11⁷, and κατὰ Χριστὸν Ἰησοῦν, Rom. 15⁵), and the whole phrase means "human" or "humanly," "from a human point of view," "according to human will or thought": Rom. 3⁵ 1 Cor. 3¹ 9⁸ 15²² Gal. 3¹⁵. Respecting its precise force here there are three possibilities: (a) As in 1 Cor. 9⁸ it may signify "according to the thought of man," *i. e.*, of human authority; (b) under the influence of the idea of a message in εὐαγγέλιον it may mean "of human origin"; (c) it may convey simply the general idea "human" without more exact discrimination. There is no decisive ground of choice among these, but the last seems more consistent both with the usage of the phrase and with the context; notice that v. [12] covers both source and method of origin, and does not specifically mention authority. The suggestion of Bous. (*SNT.*) that it means "self-originated," "eigene Phantasie," is not sustained by usage, and is excluded by the next two clauses, οὐδέ . . . ἐδιδάχθην, in which it is in effect defined.

12. οὐδὲ γὰρ ἐγὼ παρὰ ἀνθρώπου παρέλαβον αὐτό, "for neither did I receive it from man." This is the first step of the proof of the preceding general statement that his gospel is not a human message. Like the proposition itself it is negative, denying human source. οὐδέ coupled with γάρ may (1) serve to introduce a statement of what is at the same time a fact additional to the one already stated and an evidence for it, as is the case especially in arguments from analogy (see Lk. 20[36] Jn. 5[22] Acts 4[12] Rom. 8[7]), or (2) οὐδέ may throw its force upon a single term of the sentence, suggesting a comparison of the case mentioned with some other case previously mentioned or in mind. On this latter view the comparison would doubtless be with the Twelve, who, it is taken for granted, received the gospel otherwise than from man. This comparison itself, however, may be of either one of two kinds: (a) It may be comparison simply and, so to speak, on equal terms, "For neither did I any more than they receive it, etc." (*Cf.* Jn. 7[5], as interpreted in AV., "for neither did his brethren believe on him." See also a similar use of οὐδέ without γάρ in Mk. 11[26]; or (b) it may be ascensive comparison: "For not even I, of whom, not being of the Twelve, it might have been supposed that I must have received the gospel from men, received it thus" (*cf.* Gal. 6[13]). Of these three views the first (maintained by Sief.) is most in accord with N. T. usage of οὐδὲ γάρ (see exx. above), but is objectionable because the statement here made can not easily be thought of as a co-ordinate addition to the preceding, and because the presence of ἐγώ, emphatic by the mere fact of its insertion, almost requires that οὐδέ shall be interpreted as throwing its force upon it. The second view, 2(a), is more probable than the third, 2(b); the implication of the latter that his receiving his gospel otherwise than from man is in a

sense an extreme case seems foreign to the state of mind of the
apostle as it appears in this chapter. The objection that there
is no ground for assuming a comparison with the Twelve is
without force; the whole tenor of this chapter and the following goes to show that Paul's commission had been declared to
be inferior to that of the Twelve, and that he has this in mind
throughout his defence; when, therefore, by the use of ἐγώ he
indicates that he is comparing himself with some one else as
respects the source of his gospel, we scarcely need to be informed
that the unexpressed term of the comparison is the Twelve.

The verb παραλαμβάνω bears in N. T. two meanings: (1) "To take to
or along with one's self," "to accept." (2) "To receive something
transmitted to one." The latter is the uniform or all but uniform use
in Paul. 1 Cor. 11²³ 15¹,³ Gal. 1⁹ Phil. 4⁹ Col. 2⁶ (?) 4¹⁷ (?) 1 Thes. 2¹³
4¹ 2 Thes. 3⁶, and is the undoubted meaning here.

παρὰ ἀνθρώπου. The original force of παρά with the genitive is "from
beside," denoting procession from a position beside or with some one.
In N. T. precisely this sense is rare (Jn. 15²⁶ 16²⁷), but in the majority
of instances the meaning is one which is derived from this. Thus both
in Greek writers and in N. T. it is used after verbs of learning, hearing,
inquiring, issuing, receiving, yet often in a sense scarcely distinguishable from that of ἀπό. With Mk. 5³⁵ cf. Lk. 8⁴⁹, and with Mt. 12²⁸ cf.
Lk. 11¹⁶. When used after a verb which implies transmission, especially a compound of παρά, παρά before the noun apparently acquires
by association the sense "along from," marking its object as source,
but at the same time as transmitter from a more ultimate source.
Such seems to be the force of the preposition in 1 Thes. 2¹³ 4¹ 2 Thes. 3⁶;
it is also entirely appropriate to the first instance of its occurrence in
Phil. 4¹⁸; its use the second time may be due either to the fact that
Paul avoided the suggestion of a different relation in the two cases
which a change to ἀπό would have conveyed, or even to a desire deli-
cately to hint a divine source back of the Philippians themselves, making them also transmitters. This latter instance seems in any case
to be strongly against the view of Winer (WM. p. 463ƒ. n.) and Mey.
on 1 Cor. 11²³ that παρά means "directly from." On the other hand,
Ltft.'s view that "where the idea of transmission is prominent παρά
will be used in preference to ἀπό," whether the object be the immediate
or the remote source, is not sustained by the evidence as a whole.
Not only is παρά often used of ultimate source, with no suggestion of
transmission, but ἀπό is used, in 1 Cor. 11²³ at least, when the idea of
transmission is suggested by the verb, and in every instance where

παρά is used before a transmitting source, the idea of transmission is suggested by the verb or context, and the object is the mediate source. To this rule Phil. 4¹⁸ is, as remarked above, probably no exception. The force of παρά accordingly in the present phrase παρὰ ἀνθρώπου, joined with παρέλαβον, which distinctly suggests receiving by transmission, is probably "along from," and taken with οὐδέ the phrase denies that the gospel which Paul preached was received by him from men as the intermediate source. This, of course, carries with it, also, the denial of man as the ultimate source, since the supposition of an ultimate human source with a divine mediate source is excluded by its own absurdity. In effect, therefore, παρά in the present phrase covers the ground more specifically covered in v.¹ by ἀπό and διά.

Ἀνθρώπου is probably to be taken as in δι' ἀνθρώπου in v.¹ in the most general qualitative sense, not as having reference to any individual; it is hence to be translated "from man," rather than "from a man." Cf. on v.¹, and see Jn. 5³⁴.

οὔτε ἐδιδάχθην, "nor was I taught it." To the denial of man as the source from which he received his gospel the apostle adds as a correlative statement a denial of *instruction* as the *method* by which he obtained it. This was, of course, precisely the method by which the great majority of the Christians and even of the Christian teachers of that day had received the gospel. It had been communicated to them by other men. Cf. the case of Apollos, Acts 18²⁵, ²⁶, of Timothy, 2 Tim. 3¹⁴, and the frequent use of the word "teach" in reference to the work of apostles and preachers in general: Acts 4¹⁸ 5²⁸ 20²⁰ 1 Cor. 4¹⁷ Col. 1²⁸, etc. The apostle characterises his as an exceptional case. As a pupil of the Pharisees he had been taught something very different from the gospel, but he had had no connection with those who at the beginning were the teachers of the gospel. See the reference to these facts in vv.¹³⁻¹⁷.

Οὐδέ before ἐδιδ. is read by ℵAD*FGP 31, 104, 326, 436, 442 Boh. Eus. Chr. Euthal. Cyr. Thdrt. Dam.; οὔτε by BD°KL Oec. al. Since the latter evidence proves that οὔτε is not simply an idiosyncrasy of B., and the Western authorities are almost unanimously on the side of οὐδέ, the probability is that οὐδέ is a Western digression from the original reading οὔτε, produced either by accidental assimilation to the preceding οὐδέ or by correction of the unusual combination οὐδέ . . . οὔτε. Cf. WM. pp. 617 f.

The οὔτε before ἐδιδ. can not be regarded as strictly correlative to οὐδέ at the beginning of the verse, since οὐδέ and οὔτε are not correlative conjunctions (WM. p. 617), the "neither . . . nor" of the English translation by its suggestion of this relation to that extent misrepresenting the Greek. Nor would the clauses be correlative if οὐδέ be read instead of οὔτε here (see below), since οὐδέ . . . οὐδέ express not correlation—the first looking forward to the second and the second back to the first—but successive negation, each οὐδέ looking backward and adding a negation to one already in mind. With the reading οὔτε, however, the second clause is introduced as correlative to the first, though the first had been expressed with a backward look to the preceding sentence, not with a forward look to the present clause.

ἀλλὰ δι' ἀποκαλύψεως Ἰησοῦ Χριστοῦ. "but it came to me through revelation of Jesus Christ." A verb such as is suggested by παρέλαβον and ἐδιδάχθην is of necessity to be supplied in thought with δι' ἀποκαλύψεως, yet not ἐδιδάχθην itself, since there is a manifest contrast between instruction and revelation, the first being denied and the latter affirmed, as the method by which the apostle obtained his gospel. On the meaning of ἀποκάλυψις, see detached note on Ἀποκαλύπτω and Ἀποκάλυψις, p. 433. It is evident that the apostle is here using the term in its third sense, viz., a divine disclosure of a person or truth, involving also perception of that which is revealed by the person to whom the disclosure is made. He is speaking neither of an epiphany of Jesus as a world event, nor of a disclosure of him which, being made to men at large, as, e. g., through his life and death, might be perceived by some and fall ineffectual upon others, but of a personal experience, divine in its origin (cf. οὐδὲ . . . παρὰ ἀνθρώπου), personal to himself and effectual.

It has been much disputed whether Ἰησοῦ Χριστοῦ is an objective or subjective genitive, whether Christ is the revealed or the revealer. According to the former interpretation, Paul in effect affirms that Jesus Christ had been revealed to him, and in such way that that revelation carried with it the substance of the gospel. If Christ is the revealer, it is doubtless the gospel that is revealed. It is in favour of the former view (1) that Paul is wont to speak of God as the author of revelations; and of Christ as the one revealed, not as the revealer: see for

the former usage 1 Cor. 2¹⁰ 2 Cor. 12¹, and for the latter 1 **Cor.**
1⁷ 2 Thes. 1⁷ Gal 1¹⁶; (2) that this latter usage occurs in this
very context (v.¹⁶) where Paul, apparently speaking of the
same fact to which he here refers, uses the phrase ἀποκαλύψαι
τὸν υἱὸν αὐτοῦ ἐν ἐμοί, in which Jesus is unambiguously represented as the one revealed. It may be urged in favour of the
second interpretation (1) that the phrase thus understood furnishes the proper antithesis to παρὰ ἀνθρώπου and ἐδιδάχθην,
affirming Christ as the source and revelation as the method
over against man as the source and instruction as the method;
(2) that the gospel, especially the gospel of Paul as distinguished
from the Jewish-Christian conception of the gospel, requires as
its source a revelation of larger and more definite content than
is implied when the genitive is taken as objective. But these
arguments are by no means decisive. Paul is not wont to pre-
serve his antitheses perfect in form, and the first view as truly
as the second preserves it substantially, since it is self-evident
that if Christ was revealed to him (or in him) God was the
revealer. As to whether a revelation of which Christ was the
content was adequate to be the source of his gospel, there is
much reason to believe that in his conception of Jesus obtained
by the revelation of him there were virtually involved for Paul
all the essential and distinctive features of his gospel. Thus it
certainly included the resurrection of Jesus, and as an inference
from it his divine sonship (Rom. 1⁴); these in view of Paul's
previous attitude towards the law might, probably did, lead him
to recognise the futility of righteousness by law, this in turn
preparing the way at least for the recognition of faith as the
true principle of the religious life; this accepted may have led
to the conviction that the Gentile could be justified without
circumcision. While it can not perhaps be proved that precisely this was the order of Paul's thought, his various references to his experience find their most natural explanation in
this view, that the new conception of Jesus which Paul gained
by the revelation of Christ in him furnished the premise from
which the essential elements of his gospel were derived. See
Phil. 3⁴⁻⁹ Gal. 2¹⁹ Rom. 7²⁵ 3²⁹, ³⁰, and v.¹⁶ of this chap., where

he closely connects the two extremes of the experience attributed to him, viz., the revelation of Christ and the mission to
the Gentiles. See also Acts 26$^{16, 17}$, where a similar connection
occurs. It seems, therefore, more probable that the genitive
'Ιησοῦ Χριστοῦ is objective, and that the apostle refers to a
divinely given revelation of Jesus Christ which carried with it
the conviction that he was the Son of God. See further on v.^{16}.

Ἀποκαλύψεως, being without the article, may be either indefinite, "a
revelation" or qualitative, "revelation." In the former case the reference is to a single specific though unidentified experience. In the
latter case the phrase simply describes the method by which the gospel
was received without reference to singleness or multiplicity of experience. The reference in the apostle's mind may be to the Damascus experience only (cf. vv. $^{16, 17}$) or may include any revelations
by which Christ was made known to him. In the absence of evidence
of specific reference "by revelation" is preferable to "by a revelation"
as a translation of the phrase.

2. *Evidence substantiating the preceding assertion of his
independence of human authority* (vv.$^{11, 12}$) *drawn
from various periods of his life* (1^{13}–2^{21}).

(a) Evidence drawn from his life before his conversion
($1^{13, 14}$).

To substantiate the statement of vv.$^{11, 12}$ the apostle appeals to the facts of his life, some of them at least already
known to his readers; he begins with his life before his conversion to faith in Jesus. The evidence in the nature of the
case is directed towards the negative part of the proposition.
That which sustained the positive assertion he could affirm,
but could not appeal to as known to others.

^{13}*For ye have heard of my manner of life formerly in the religion
of the Jews, that beyond measure I persecuted the church of God
and ravaged it.* ^{14}*And I was advancing in the religion of the
Jews beyond many who were of equal age with me in my nation,
being more exceedingly zealous than they of the traditions of my
fathers.*

13. Ἠκούσατε γὰρ τὴν ἐμὴν ἀναστροφήν ποτε ἐν τῷ Ἰουδαϊσμῷ, "For ye have heard of my manner of life formerly in

the religion of the Jews." With this sentence Paul introduces
the evidence which his own career furnished that he had not
received the gospel from man or by instruction. The force of
γάρ in the present sentence extends in effect into, if not through,
the second chapter. The argument is cumulative in character.
Its first step is to the effect that he was not, previous to his
conversion, under Christian influence at all, but was, on the
contrary, a violent opposer of the Christian church. From
whom the Galatians had heard (ἠκούσατε) the story of his pre-
Christian life Paul does not say; most probably it was from
himself. If so, this reflects in an interesting way his probable
habit of making use of his own experience in presenting the
gospel. *Cf.* Acts, chap. 22, and esp. chap. 26. On the tense
of ἠκούσατε, see BMT 46, 52.

'Αναστροφή, meaning in classical writers "return," etc., first appears in the second century B. C. in the sense "manner of life,"
"conduct" (Polyb. 4. 82¹), which sense it also has in the very few
instances in which it is found in the Apocr.: Tob. 4¹⁴ 2 Mac. 3²¹ (it is
not found in the Lxx, canonical books, and though it stands in the
Roman edition at 2 Mac. 5⁸ it is without the support of either of the
uncials which contain the passage, viz. AV.); this is also its regular
meaning in N. T. (Eph. 4²² 1 Tim. 4¹² Heb. 13⁷ Jas. 3¹³ 1 Pet. 1¹⁵, ¹⁸ 2¹²
3¹, ², ¹⁶ 2 Pet. 2⁷ 3¹¹).

On the position of ποτέ see Butt. p. 91, and *cf.* Phil. 4¹⁰ 1 Cor. 9⁷; also
(cited by Sief. *ad loc.*), Plato, *Legg.* III 685 D, ἡ τῆς Τροίας ἅλωσις
τὸ δεύτερον, "the capture of Troy the second time"; Soph. *O. T.* 1043,
τοῦ τυράννου τῆςδε γῆς πάλαι ποτέ, "the long-ago ruler of this land."

'Ιουδαϊσμός, "the Jews' religion," occurs in N. T. only in this and
the following verse; for exx. outside N. T. see 2 Mac. 2²¹ 8¹ 14³⁸ *bis*
4 Mac. 4²⁶. In the passages in Mac. it denotes the Jewish religion in
contrast with the Hellenism which the Syrian kings were endeavouring
to force upon the Jews; here, of course, the prevalent Judaism with its
rejection of Jesus in contrast with the faith of the followers of Jesus as
the Messiah. The very use of the term in this way is significant of
the apostle's conception of the relation between his former and his
present faith, indicating that he held the latter, and had presented it
to the Galatians, not as a type of Judaism, but as an independent
religion distinct from that of the Jews. Though the word Christianity
was probably not yet in use, the fact was in existence.

ὅτι καθ' ὑπερβολὴν ἐδίωκον τὴν ἐκκλησίαν τοῦ θεοῦ καὶ ἐπόρθουν αὐτήν, "that beyond measure I persecuted the church of

God and ravaged it." This whole clause and the following one
are epexegetic of τὴν ἐμὴν ἀναστροφήν, not, however, defining
in full the content of that phrase, but setting forth that element
of it which the apostle has in mind as bearing on his argument.
That he stood thus in intense hostility to the church is evidence
that he was not of those who through the influence of association with Christians, and as a result of instruction (cf. οὔτε
ἐδιδάχθην, v. 12) were led to receive the gospel.

The word ὑπερβολή and the specific phrase καθ' ὑπερβολήν are classical,
but are used in N. T. only by Paul. The phrase occurs in Rom. 7¹³
1 Cor. 12³¹ 2 Cor. 1⁸ 4¹⁷, always in the sense "exceeding (ly)," "superior."

The imperfects, ἐδίωκον and ἐπόρθουν, representing the actions
denoted by them as in progress, bring out clearly the continuance of
the persecuting activity. The latter verb, meaning in itself not simply
"to injure," but "to destroy," "to ruin," has here, as commonly in
the progressive tenses, a conative force. See L. & S. s. v. and BMT 23,
and compare on πείθω and ἤρεσκον in v. ¹⁰. διώκω, used from Homer
down, meaning "to pursue," frequently carries the associated idea of
hostile purpose, and so comes in classical writers to mean "to prose-
cute" (ὁ διώκων is "the prosecutor," ὁ φεύγων, "the defendant"), and in
the Lxx (Jer. 17¹⁸) and N. T. "to persecute" (Rom. 12¹⁴ 1 Cor. 4¹²
et freq.). πορθέω, used from Homer down as a military term, meaning
"to destroy," "to ravage" (cities), and from Æschylus, of violence to
persons, is not found in the Lxx (canonical books) or Apocr., but
occurs in 4 Mac. 4²³ 11⁴ of persons. In N. T. it is found in this epistle
here and v. ²³ and in Acts 9²¹, always of Paul.

On ἐκκλησία in N. T. see detached note, p. 417. Two facts are
notable about the expression employed here, ἡ ἐκκλησία τοῦ θεοῦ:
(1) the use of the singular to denote not a local body but the Christian
community at large. Cf. the different use of the word in vv. ², ²² 1 Cor.
1² 2 Cor. 1¹; and for the evidence that the phrase has this œcumenical
meaning here, see the detached note referred to above. (2) the characterisation of this community as the church of God. The first of
these facts shows that Paul had not only formed the conception of
churches as local assemblies and communities of Christians (vv. ², ²²),
but had already united these local communities in his thought into
one entity—the church. The second fact shows that this body already
stood in his mind as the chosen people of God, and indicates how
fully, in his thought, the Christian church had succeeded to the position once occupied by Israel. Paul's employment of this phrase in
this particular place was probably due to his sense of the wrongful-
ness of his persecution as directed against the church of God. Cf. 1
Cor. 15⁹. Incidentally it may be noticed that inasmuch as the church

which Paul persecuted was a Jewish church, not only in that it was composed of Jews, but probably mainly of those who still observed the Jewish law, his characterisation of it as the church of God shows how far he was from denying the legitimacy of Jewish Christianity in itself. *Cf.* also 1 Thes. 2¹⁴, and see *Introd.*, pp. lxii *f.*

14. καὶ προέκοπτον ἐν τῷ Ἰουδαϊσμῷ ὑπὲρ πολλοὺς συνηλικιώτας ἐν τῷ γένει μου, "and I was advancing in the religion of the Jews beyond many who were of equal age with me in my nation." As in the preceding part of the sentence, so here the action is presented not as a mere fact but as continuing. *Cf.* Lk. 2⁵². The nature of this advance in Judaism is not defined. *Cf.* below on ὑπάρχων. Increasing knowledge of those things which constituted the learning of the Jewish schools, a more perfect realisation of the Jewish (in his case specifically the Pharisaic) ideal of conduct, higher standing and official position in the Pharisaic order, may all have been included in the experience, and in his thought as here expressed; but, as Phil. 3⁵, ⁶ would suggest, especially the achievement of righteousness according to the standards and ideals of Pharisaism. His progress, he adds, not only carried him beyond his own former attainments, but by it he outstripped many of his contemporaries, making more rapid progress than they.

On ἐν τῷ γένει μου, *cf.* 2 Cor. 11²⁶ Phil. 3⁵. Though γένος varies in inclusiveness from family to race in the largest sense, yet the etymological sense (*cf.* γίνομαι, γεννάω, etc.) is so far retained that the word almost invariably refers to what is determined by origin, not by choice. In Jos. *Ant.* 13. 297 (10⁶) we find indeed the phrase τὸ Σαδδουκαίων γένος. Yet this is not N. T. usage, and in view of the use of the term Ἰουδαϊσμός, indicating that to his Gentile readers Paul is describing his life from the general national point of view, without reference to distinction of sects, and in the absence of any qualifying phrase giving to it a narrower sense than usual, it can not be understood to have specific reference to the sect of the Pharisees.

περισσοτέρως ζηλωτὴς ὑπάρχων τῶν πατρικῶν μου παραδόσεων. "being more exceedingly zealous than they of the traditions of my fathers." περισσοτέρως is in form and force a comparative; the unexpressed member of the comparison is doubtless to be supplied from the πολλοὺς συνηλικιώτας. The

participle ὑπάρχων is probably causal, though not emphatically
so, "because I was more exceedingly zealous than they." See a
similar use of ὑπάρχων in similar position in Acts 19⁴⁰ 1 Cor. 11⁷
2 Cor. 8¹⁷. Ell. and Sief. take it as a participle of closer definition, defining that in which the action of προέκοπτον takes
place. But this interpretation mistakes either the meaning or
the tense-force of προέκοπτον, taking it in a sense impossible
to it, "I was in advance of." The whole phrase accounts for
his extraordinary advancement as compared with his fellows.
Though ὑπάρχων is grammatically subordinate to προέκοπτον
the fact expressed by it is, even more emphatically than that
conveyed by the verb, an evidence of that which the apostle is
here endeavouring to establish, viz., that he was not at the
time referred to under such influences or in such frame of mind
as to make reception of the gospel by him from human hands
or by instruction possible. The limitation of ζηλωτής by τῶν
πατρικῶν παραδόσεων makes it probable that it is not to be
taken as a class name meaning a Zealot, a member of the
Zealot party (see Th. s. v. and Dict. Bib.), but rather as an
adjective meaning "zealous for," "zealously devoted to."
Aside from the question whether the Zealots and Pharisees
were so related to one another that one could be a member of
both parties (Phil. 3⁵ shows that Paul was a Pharisee), there
is no clear or even probable N. T. instance of ζηλωτής used as a
class name, and at the same time limited by an objective genitive, and the passages cited by Ltft. do not at all prove that
Paul belonged to this party. As an adjective the word does
not define the exact relation to that which is expressed by the
genitive, but is general enough to refer to zeal to acquire, to
observe, to defend, according to the nature of the case. In the
present instance it evidently includes the two latter ideas.
Cf. Acts 21²⁰ 22³; the sense is slightly different in Tit. 2¹⁴
1 Pet. 3¹³.

πapáδoσις itself signifies an act of transmission or that which is transmitted (in N. T. always in the latter sense and with reference to instruction or information), without indicating the method of transmission, or implying any lapse of time such as is usually associated with

the English word tradition. Thus Paul uses it of his own instructions, both oral and written, 1 Cor. 11² 2 Thes. 2¹⁵ (though possibly referring to elements of his teaching received from others), and Josephus of his own written narrative, *Con. Ap.* 1. 50 (9), 53 (10). Here, however, the addition of πατρικῶν μου distinctly describes the παράδοσις as transmitted from previous generations, and the similarity of the phrase to παράδοσις τῶν πρεσβυτέρων (Mt. 15² Mk. 7³, ⁵, where it is contrasted with the laws of Moses), and to τὰ ἐκ παραδόσεως τῶν πατέρων, Jos. *Ant.* 13. 297 (10⁶),* where the things derived by tradition from the fathers and not written in the laws of Moses are contrasted with those which are thus written, makes it clear that Paul refers to the well-known orally transmitted traditions which were observed by the Pharisees. There is no reason, however, especially in view of the fact that Paul is writing to Gentiles, to take πατρικῶν μου otherwise than simply in the national sense (*cf.* ἐν τῷ γένει μου above), describing the traditions as derived from his national ancestors, not from his (Pharisaic) fathers in contrast with those of other Jews, or of the Sadducees. *Cf.* the passage cited above from Josephus, in which the traditions observed by the Pharisees are described not as coming from the Pharisees, but from the fathers, and criticised not on the ground of their Pharisaic origin, but as being observed by the Pharisees as authoritative. *Cf.* also Mk. 7³, ⁵.

(b) Evidence of his independent apostleship drawn from the circumstances of his conversion and his conduct immediately thereafter (1¹⁵⁻¹⁷).

Passing from the evidence of his pre-Christian life, the apostle now draws evidence from the conversion-experience and his conduct immediately thereafter.

¹⁵*And when it pleased him who from my mother's womb had set me apart, and who called me through his grace, ¹⁶to reveal his Son in me, that I might preach him among the Gentiles, immediately I communicated not with flesh and blood, ¹⁷nor did I go up to Jerusalem to those that were apostles before me, but I went away into Arabia and again I returned to Damascus.*

---

* νῦν δὲ δηλῶσαι βούλομαι, ὅτι νόμιμά τινα παρέδοσαν τῷ δήμῳ οἱ Φαρισαῖοι ἐκ πατέρων διαδοχῆς, ἅπερ οὐκ ἀναγέγραπται ἐν τοῖς Μωυσέως νόμοις, καὶ διὰ τοῦτο ταῦτα τὸ Σαδδουκαίων γένος ἐκβάλλει, λέγον ἐκεῖνα δεῖν ἡγεῖσθαι νόμιμα·τὰ γεγραμμένα, τὰ δ᾽ ἐκ παραδόσεως τῶν πατέρων μὴ τηρεῖν: "And now I wish to show that the Pharisees transmitted to the people certain usages received from the fathers which are not recorded in the laws of Moses, and on this account the sect of the Sadducees rejects them, saying that it is necessary to regard as obligatory those things that are written, but not to observe the things handed down by tradition from the fathers."

15. Ὅτε δὲ εὐδόκησεν ὁ ἀφορίσας με ἐκ κοιλίας μητρός μου καὶ καλέσας διὰ τῆς χάριτος αὐτοῦ **(16)** ἀποκαλύψαι τὸν υἱὸν αὐτοῦ ἐν ἐμοί "And when it pleased him who from my mother's womb had set me apart, and who called me through his grace, to reveal his Son in me." The affirmation of this sentence that after his conversion, as before, the apostle kept himself apart from the Twelve is not antithetical to that of the preceding, but continues his argument; δέ should, therefore, be translated "and," rather than "but" (RV.). For the purposes of his argument the central element of the statement of vv. ¹⁵⁻¹⁷ is in v. ¹⁶ᵇ: "immediately I communicated not with flesh and blood." For this statement, however, pertaining to his conduct immediately after his conversion to faith in Jesus, he prepares the way in vv. ¹⁵, ¹⁶ᵃ by referring to certain antecedents of his conversion. All these he ascribes to God; for that ὁ ἀφορίσας . . . καὶ καλέσας refers to God, and ἀποκαλύψαι to a divine act, is evident from the nature of the acts referred to. See esp. on the Pauline usage of καλέω, v. ⁶, and detached note on Ἀποκαλύπτω and Ἀποκάλυψις, p. 433. Of the three antecedents here named the first and second, expressed by ἀφορίσας and καλέσας are associated together grammatically, the participles being under one article and joined by καί. But it is the second and third that are most closely associated in time, ἀφορίσας being dated from his birth, while the events denoted by καλέσας and ἀποκαλύψαι, as the usage of the word καλέω shows, are elements or immediate antecedents of the conversion-experience.

By the emphasis which in his references to these antecedents of his conversion he throws upon the divine activity and grace (note ἐν χάριτι) and by dating the first of these back to the very beginning of his life he incidentally strengthens his argument for his own independent divine commission. He whom God himself from his birth set apart to be a preacher of the gospel to the Gentiles and whom by his grace he called into that service can not be dependent on men for his commission or subject to their control.

The question whether the phrase ἀποκαλύψαι . . . ἐν ἐμοί

refers to a subjective revelation in and for the apostle or to an objective manifestation of Christ in and through him to others (on which Ell., *e. g.*, holds the former, and Ltft. the latter view) can not be answered simply by an appeal to the meaning or usage of the preposition ἐν. ἐν ἐμοί can of itself mean nothing else than "in me." But it may equally well represent in the mind of the writer the thought "within me," with no reference to any effect upon any one else (*cf.* Rom. 1¹⁹ Gal. 2²⁰), or "in my case" and thus (impliedly) "by means of me to others" (*cf.* v.²⁴ 1 Cor. 4⁶ 1 Tim. 1¹⁶). Which of these two represents the apostle's thought must be decided by other evidence than the mere force of the preposition. (a) The meaning of the verb ἀποκαλύπτω. As pointed out in the detached note on this word, p. 433, with rare exceptions, if any, ἀποκαλύπτω denotes a disclosure of something by the removal of that which hitherto concealed it, and, especially, a subjective revelation to an individual mind. Now it is evident that only the revelation of Christ to Paul, not the public manifestation or presentation of him to the world in and through Paul, could be thought of either in general as a disclosure of what was previously hidden (since Christ had already been preached in the world but had been hidden in his true character from Paul), or specifically as a subjective revelation. The choice of the word ἀποκαλύπτω, therefore, is favourable to the former of the two views named above. (b) Such being the case as respects the meaning of ἀποκαλύπτω, it is evident that the idea of a manifestation of Christ in and through Paul to others could hardly have been expressed simply by ἐν ἐμοί, but would require διὰ ἐμοῦ or some such addition as τῷ κόσμῳ. (c) The connection with ἵνα εὐαγγελίζωμαι also favours the reference to an experience in itself affecting Paul only. This revelation is defined by the passage as the third stage of the apostle's preparation for his public proclamation of Christ (not, as Ltft. makes it, an integral part of his entrance on that ministry; εὐαγγελίζωμαι. αὐτόν defines his ministry, to which the divine ἀποκαλύψαι, equally with the ἀφορίσαι and the καλέσαι, were preparatory). For this preaching an inward revelation to Paul of the Son of

God, whom he was to preach, was a natural and necessary preparation; a manifestation of Christ in and through him to others is too nearly identical with the preaching itself to be spoken of as having that preaching for its purpose. (d) V.[12] clearly speaks of a revelation of Christ to Paul by which he received his gospel. The similarity of the terms used here and the close connection of the thought—Paul is here proving what he there affirmed—make it probable that the terms mean the same and the fact referred to is the same here as there. (e) Even aside from any similarity of terminology it is evident that the whole subject of discourse in this paragraph is not how Paul made known his gospel, but how he received it; the reference of the central term of this sentence to the presentation of Christ to others involves an impossible digression from the theme of the whole passage.

The apostle's use of the phrase "Son of God" and v.[12] are either alone sufficient to make it clear that by τὸν υἱὸν αὐτοῦ he means Jesus, while the time of the event of which he speaks and the phrase ἐν ἐμοί make it certain that it is the risen Jesus of whom he speaks. Though grammatically the direct object of ἀποκαλύψαι, τὸν υἱὸν αὐτοῦ is undoubtedly to be taken as expressing the conception of Jesus which he obtained in the revelation; it is thus in effect equivalent to Ἰησοῦν ὡς (or εἶναι) τὸν υἱὸν αὐτοῦ. On the question, which is very important for the understanding of the genesis of Paul's gospel, especially his Christology, what aspect of the divine sonship of Jesus he has chiefly in mind as having been revealed to him in the Damascus experience, and for the evidence that he refers especially to sonship as involving moral likeness to God and hence revelation of God, see detached note on *The Titles and Predicates of Jesus*, V, p. 408, and *cf.* esp. 2 Cor. 4[6].

TR. with אADKLP al. pler. d Boh. Arm. Eth. Or. Dial. Eus. Epiph. ps-Ath. Chr. Cyr. Euthal. Severian Thdrt. Dam. Ir[int.] Aug. al. insert ὁ θεός after εὐδόκησεν. The text as above, without ὁ θεός, is attested by BFG 1905 f g Vg. Syr. (psh. harcl.) Eus. Epiph. Chr. Thdrt. Ir[int.] Victorin. Ambrst. Hier. al. Transcriptional probability strongly favours the text without ὁ θεός as the original, since there is an obvious motive for the (correct) interpretative gloss, but none for its omission. In view of the indecisive character of the external evidence the internal evidence must be regarded as decisive for the omission.

The verb εὐδοκέω (the earliest extant instances of which are found in the Lxx, where it stands most often as the translation of the Hebrew verb רָצָה, "to accept," "approve," "delight in," "be pleased," and which is found in secular writers from Polybius down) has two general uses: (1) "to accept," "to be pleased with," "to take delight in," followed by an acc., dat., or εἰς with the acc., or ἐν with the dat.: Gen. 33¹⁰ Ps. 51¹⁶ 1 Chron. 29³ Ps. 77⁷ Sir. 9¹² 1 Mac. 8¹ Mt. 3¹⁷ 12¹⁸ 2 Thes. 2¹²; (2) "to see fit," "to consent," "to choose," followed by an infinitive, or with an infinitive understood. Ps. 40¹³ (only Lxx instance); 1 Mac. 6²² 14⁴¹, ⁴⁶, ⁴⁷ Lk. 12³² Rom. 15²⁶ 1 Cor. 1²¹ 2 Cor. 5⁸ Col. 1¹⁹ 1 Thes. 2⁸ 3¹. In this latter sense and construction the verb seems often to convey the subsidiary implication that the purpose referred to is kindly or gracious towards those affected by the action expressed by the infinitive; especially is this true when the verb is used of God. See Ps. 40¹³ 2 Mac. 14³⁵ Lk. 12³² Col. 1¹⁹; cf. the use of εὐδοκία (which had clearly acquired as one of its senses "good-will," "favour") in Ps. 51¹⁸ Sir. 32 (35)¹⁴ Ps. Sol. 8³⁹ Lk. 2¹⁴ Phil. 2¹⁵, and see S. and H. on Rom. 10¹: "In this sense it came to be used almost technically of the good-will of God to man." It is doubtless with such an implication of the gracious character of the divine act that Paul uses the verb in this place. The clause emphasises at the same time the tact that he owed his "call" to God and that the call itself was an act of divine grace.

'Αφορίζειν signifies not "to remove from a place," but "to mark off from something else," "to separate or set apart from others" (Mt. 13⁴⁹ 25³² Lk. 6²² Acts 19⁹ 2 Cor. 6¹⁷ Gal. 2¹² Lev. 13⁴, ⁵, ⁵⁴ et freq. in Lxx and in classical writers); esp. to set apart for a particular service, this latter occurring in Aristot., Pol. 6. 8¹¹ (1322 b²⁶); Lxx (Ex. 13¹² Deut. 4⁴¹, etc.); and N. T. (Acts 13² Rom. 1¹). In view of this meaning of ἀφορίζειν, ἐκ κοιλίας μητρός μου must be taken, according to what is in any case its usual sense, as a phrase of time meaning "from birth." See Judg. 16¹⁷ Ps. 22¹⁰ 71⁶ Isa. 49¹ (Job 1²¹ 38⁸ only otherwise); Lk. 1¹⁵ Jn. 9¹ Acts 3² 14⁸ (Mt. 19¹² only otherwise). Cf. also Jer. 1⁵.

On the Pauline usage of the word καλέω, see on v.⁶ and on the meaning of χάρις, see detached note, p. 423. διά is manifestly instrumental, but not in the stricter and more usual sense of the term. It marks its object not as that which, standing, so to speak, between the doer of the action and its effect, is the instrument through which the action is accomplished (as, e. g., Rom. 15¹⁸ Gal. 3¹⁹ 5¹³ et freq.), but rather as that which standing behind the action renders it possible; so, e. g., Acts 1² Rom. 1⁸ 1 Thes. 4². Cf. note on διά instrumental under v.¹. The phrase διὰ χάριτος αὐτοῦ may be rendered, "by virtue of his grace," "in the exercise of his grace."

ἵνα εὐαγγελίζωμαι αὐτὸν ἐν τοῖς ἔθνεσιν, "that I might preach him among the Gentiles." The verb εὐαγγ. itself characterises the message as glad tidings, or perhaps rather as the glad message, the gospel (cf. on v.[8]), while αὐτόν (acc. of content; cf. for this construction v.[23] 1 Cor. 15[1] 2 Cor. 11[7] Eph. 2[17] and Delbrück, *Vergleichende Syntax*, § 179), referring to τὸν υἱὸν αὐτοῦ defines its substance. A similar thought of the content of the gospel as summed up in Christ himself is expressed in Rom. 15[19, 20] 1 Cor. 1[23] 2 Cor. 1[19] Phil. 1[15]. The use of the present tense εὐαγγελίζωμαι, following the aorists ἀφορίσας, καλέσας, and ἀποκαλύψαι indicates that the apostle has distinctly in mind that these definite events had for their purpose a continued preaching of the gospel. Cf. 1 Thes. 4[12] Phil. 2[19] Eph. 4[28]. Accurately but somewhat awkwardly rendered into English the clause would read, "that I might continue to preach him, as glad tidings (or as the good news) among the Gentiles."

In a few instances, chiefly in the phrases πολλὰ ἔθνη and πάντα τὰ ἔθνη as they occur in O. T. quotations, the word ἔθνη is used by Paul in the general sense meaning "nations." But otherwise and almost uniformly it means "Gentiles" as distinguished from Jews. This is most clearly the sense in this letter, except perhaps in 3[8b]; see 2[2, 8, 9, 12, 14, 15] 3[8a, 14]. Undoubtedly then Paul means here to define the divinely intended sphere of his preaching as among the Gentiles. Whether he recognised this fact at the time of the revelation which had this preaching as its purpose, or whether the perception of this definition of his work came later, this passage does not decide. According to Acts 26[17] it came in connection with his conversion. The preposition ἐν is important, indicating that the scope of his mission as conceived by him was not simply the Gentiles (for this he must have written εὐαγγελίζωμαι αὐτὸν τοῖς ἔθνεσιν) but *among* the Gentiles, and by implication included all who were in Gentile lands. Cf. on 2[2, 8].

εὐθέως οὐ προσανεθέμην σαρκὶ καὶ αἵματι, "immediately I conferred not with flesh and blood." The negative οὐ limits προσανεθέμην, not εὐθέως, which in that case it must have preceded, as in Lk. 21[9]; and this being so, εὐθέως must be taken with the whole sentence as far as Ἀραβίαν, not simply οὐ προσανεθέμην, since by its meaning εὐθέως calls for

an affirmation, not simply a statement of non-action. Zahn's
contention that the time of the departure to Arabia is not
fixed except as within the three years of v.[18] is therefore without ground. Place for the events of Acts 9[19b-22] must be found
not at this point but after v.[17]. Ltft. gives the sense correctly:
"Forthwith instead of conferring with flesh and blood. . . I
departed," etc.

Σαρκί καὶ αἵματι, primarily denoting the parts of a living physical
body (Heb. 2[14]) is here used by metonymy, as σάρξ alone more frequently is, for a being having such a body, *i. e.*, for a corporeally conditioned living being, in contrast with beings of a higher order, especially
with God. *Cf.* Sir. 14[18] 17[31] Eph. 6[12] and esp. Mt. 16[17]. See detached
note on Πνεῦμα and Σάρξ, p. 492. προσανεθέμην (here and 2[6] only in
N. T.) signifies "to betake one's self to," "to hold conference with," "to
communicate" whether for receiving or imparting. (See Chrysipp. ap.
Suid. *s. v.* νεόττος [Bernhardy, 959]: ὄναρ γὰρ τινά φησι θεασάμενον . . .
προσαναθέσθαι ὀνειροκρίτῃ: "For he says that a certain man having had
a dream conferred with the interpreter of dreams"; Luc. *Jup. Trag.* 1;
Diod. Sic. 17. 116[4], τοῖς μάντεσι προσαναθέμενος περὶ τοῦ σημείου, "conferring with the soothsayer concerning the sign." See extended note in
Zahn *ad loc.* pp. 64*f.* In 2[6], where the verb is limited by an acc. and
dat., impartation is apparently what is in mind; here, primarily at least,
receiving, as is indicated by the general subject of discourse, viz., the
source of his gospel; yet note the double aspect of the act referred to
in the passages quoted above, involving narrating the dream or the
sign and receiving advice concerning it.

17. οὐδὲ ἀνῆλθον εἰς Ἱεροσόλυμα πρὸς τοὺς πρὸ ἐμοῦ
ἀποστόλους, "nor did I go up to Jerusalem to those that
were apostles before me." The reference is, of course, particularly to the Twelve, yet would include any, such as James,
who had been recognised as apostles before Paul himself received the apostolic office. The preposition πρό is evidently
used in its temporal sense. The reference to Jerusalem indicates that at this time Jerusalem was the headquarters of the
Christian movement as conducted by the Twelve, and that
they or the leaders among them still resided there. The use
of the phrase τοὺς πρὸ ἐμοῦ ἀποστόλους involves the recognition of the apostleship of the Twelve, and implies that Paul
regarded his apostleship and that of the Twelve as of essen-

tially the same character.   *Cf*. detached note on Ἀπόστολος,
p. 363.   It possibly suggests that he regarded himself as already
at the time referred to, an apostle, but does not necessarily
involve this.

οὐδὲ ἀνῆλθον: אAKLP al. pler. It. Vg. Syr. (harcl-txt.) Arm. Aeth. Boh.
Chr. Euthal. Cyr. Thrdt. Dam. Victorin. Ambrst. Aug. Hier.; οὐδὲ
ἀπῆλθον: BDFG 103, 181, 429, 462, Syr. (psh. harcl-mg.) Bas. Thphl.
The attestation of ἀπ- seems to be Western, that of ἀν- Alexandrian and
Syrian.   Either reading might arise by assimilation, ἀνῆλθον under the
influence of v. ¹⁸, ἀπῆλθον under that of ¹⁷ᵇ, but the former more easily
because of the εἰς Ἱεροσόλυμα.   Because it was common usage to speak
of going up to Jerusalem (as in v. ¹⁸; *cf*. M. and M. *Voc. s. v.*) ἀπῆλθον
would be more likely to be changed to ἀνῆλθον than the reverse, but
for the same reason intrinsic probability is on the side of ἀνῆλθον, and
the latter is in this case perhaps of greater weight.   The preponderance of evidence is but slightly in favour of ἀνῆλθον.   So Tdf. WH.
Ltft. Sief. Sd. *et al. Contra* Zahn.

ἀλλὰ ἀπῆλθον εἰς Ἀραβίαν, "but I went away into Arabia."
The purpose of this visit to Arabia, though not specifically
stated, is clearly implied in οὐ προσανεθέμην σαρκὶ καὶ αἵματι
above.   By that phrase the apostle denies not only that he
sought instruction from the Twelve in particular, but that he
put himself in communication with men at all, excluding not
only the receiving of instruction, but the imparting of it.   The
only natural, almost the only possible, implication is that he
sought communion with God, a thought sufficiently indicated
on the one side by the antithesis of "flesh and blood" and on
the other by the mention of the relatively desert land to which
he went.   The view of some of the early fathers (adopted
substantially by Bous.) that he sought no instruction from
men, but having received his message hastened to Arabia to
preach the gospel to the "barbarous and savage people" of this
foreign land (for fuller statement of the early views see Ltft.,
p. 90) is not sustained by the language.   He must in that case
have written not προσανεθέμην, but some such expression as
οὐκ ἐζήτησε διδασκαλίαν.   Nor is it in accordance with psy-
chological probability.   The revelation of Jesus as the Son of
God must at once have undermined that structure of Pharisaic

thought which he had hitherto accepted, and, no doubt, furnished also the premises of an entirely new system of thought.
But the replacement of the ruined structure with a new one
built on the new premises and as complete as the materials
and his power of thought enabled him to make it, however
urgent the necessity for it, could not have been the work of
an hour or a day. The process would have been simpler had
the acceptance of Jesus as the Christ been, as it was to some
of his fellow Jews, the mere addition to Judaism of the belief
that Jesus was the long-expected Messiah; it would have been
simpler if the acceptance of Jesus had been to him what it
doubtless was to many of his Gentile converts, the acceptance
of a new religion with an almost total displacement of former
religious views and practices. To Paul the revelation of Jesus
as the Son of God meant neither of these, but a revolutionary
revision of his former beliefs, which issued in a conception of religion which differed from the primitive Christian faith as commonly held by Jewish Christians perhaps even more than the
latter differed from current Judaism. Only prolonged thought
could enable him to see just how much of the old was to be
abandoned, how much revised, how much retained unchanged.
Many days would be needed to construct out of the material
new and old even so much of a new system as would enable
him to begin his work as a preacher of the new faith. A period
of retirement in which he should in some measure accomplish
this necessary task is both more consistent with his language
and in itself more probable than an impetuous plunging into
evangelism. Particularly improbable is the selection of Arabia
(see below on the meaning of the word) as a place of preaching.
Aside from the question whether there were Jews in Arabia,
and whether Paul at this early period recognised with sufficient
clearness his mission to the Gentiles to lead him to seek at once
a Gentile field of effort, it is clear alike from his letters and
from the narrative of Acts that Paul had a strong preference
for work in the centres of population and of civilised life. A
withdrawal to a region like that of Arabia, sparsely inhabited
and comparatively untouched by either Jewish or Roman civ-

ilisation is almost certainly, unless Paul's disposition in this respect underwent a radical change, not a missionary enterprise but a withdrawal from contact with men.

The term Ἀραβία (Heb. ערב, originally simply "desert") is applied by Greek writers from Herodotus down to the whole or various portions of that vast peninsula that lies between the Red Sea on the southwest and the Persian Gulf and the Euphrates River on the northeast, and extends to the ocean on the southeast. See Hdt. 2¹¹ 3¹⁰⁷⁻¹¹³ 4³⁹ (*Encyc. Bib.*). Its northwestern boundary was somewhat vague, but the term generally included the Sinaitic peninsula, and excluded Palestine and Phœnicia. Within this great territory, inhabited doubtless by many nomad tribes, the kingdom of the Nabateans established itself some time previous to 312 B. C. (see *Encyc. Bib.* art. "Nabateans"). In Jos. *Ant.* 14. 15 ff. (1⁴), which refers to the time of Hyrcanus II and Antipater, father of Herod, Aretas, known from other sources to be king of the Nabateans, is spoken of as king of the Arabians (*cf.* also 2 Mac. 5⁸); his country is said to border upon Judea and its capital to be Petra. 2 Cor. 11³² has been interpreted as showing that at the time to which our present passage refers the Nabatean dominion included Damascus. See Schürer, *Gesch. des jüd. Volkes*,² vol. I, pp. 726 ff. In that case Paul would seem to say that he went from a city of Arabia into Arabia, which would be like saying that one went from London into England. But it is known that Pompey gave Damascus to Syria, and the coins of Damascus show that down to 34 A. D. (between 34 and 62 A. D. evidence is lacking) it was under Rome; while a passage which Josephus (*Ant.* 14. 117 [7²]) quotes from Strabo refers to an ethnarch of the Jews in Alexandria, and thus indicates that the title ethnarch might be applied to one who acted as governor of the people of a given nationality residing in a foreign city. It is probable, therefore, that at the time of which Paul is speaking, though there was an ethnarch of the Nabateans in the city, Damascus was not under Nabatean rule, hence not in Arabia. This both removes all difficulty from this sentence, and makes it practically certain that by Ἀραβία Paul means the Nabatean kingdom. See Clemen, *Paulus*, I 83; Lake, *Earlier Epistles of St. Paul*, pp. 321 ff.*

Into what portion of the kingdom Paul went the sentence does not, of course, indicate. That the Sinaitic peninsula was sometimes included in Arabia is shown in 4²⁵, which, if the clause is a genuine part of the epistle, shows also that Paul so included it. But this does not

---

* Zahn, *Neue kirchl. Zeitschr.*, 1904, pp. 34–41, and following him, Bachmann, *Der zweite Brief d. Paulus an die Korinther*, p. 383, think that the ethnarch had jurisdiction over (nomad?) Nabateans in the vicinity of Damascus. But while this supposition comports well with ἐφρούρει τὴν πόλιν, it is less accordant with ἐν Δαμασκῷ.

prove that it was to this peninsula that Paul went. If it is necessary to suppose that he went to a city, Petra in the south and Bostra in the north are among the possibilities. There is nothing to necessitate the supposition that he went far from Damascus, nor anything to exclude a far-distant journey except that if he had gone far to the south a return to Damascus would perhaps have been improbable.

καὶ πάλιν ὑπέστρεψα εἰς Δαμασκόν. "and again I returned to Damascus." An indirect assertion that the experience described above (ἀποκαλύψαι τὸν υἱὸν αὐτοῦ ἐν ἐμοί) occurred at Damascus (cf. Acts 9¹⁻²² and parallels); from which, however, it neither follows that the ἀποκάλυψις here spoken of must because of Acts 9³, ⁴ be interpreted as an external appearance of Jesus, nor that the narrative in Acts is to be interpreted as referring to an experience wholly subjective. The identity of place, Damascus, and the evident fact that both passages refer to the experience by which Paul was led to abandon his opposition to Jesus and accept him as the Christ, require us to refer both statements to the same general occasion; but not (nor are we permitted), to govern the interpretation of one expression by the other. As shown above our present passage deals only with the subjective element of the experience. For the apostle's own interpretation of the character of the event viewed objectively, cf. 1 Cor. 9¹ 15¹⁻⁸.

(c) Evidence of his independent apostleship drawn from a visit to Jerusalem three years after his conversion (1¹⁸⁻²⁰).

The apostle now takes up the circumstances of his first visit to Jerusalem after his Damascus experience, finding in it evidence that he was conscious of a source of truth independent of men.

¹⁸*Then after three years I went up to Jerusalem to visit Cephas, and I remained with him fifteen days,* ¹⁹*and no other of the apostles did I see except James the brother of the Lord.* ²⁰*Now as respects the things which I write to you, behold, before God, I am not lying.*

18. Ἔπειτα μετὰ τρία ἔτη ἀνῆλθον εἰς Ἱεροσόλυμα ἱστορῆσαι Κηφᾶν, "Then after three years I went up to Jerusalem to visit Cephas." The phrase "after three years" is argumentative in purpose, not merely chronological. The mention of the period subsequent to his conversion during which he voluntarily abstained from contact with the apostles at Jerusalem tends to show his entire independence of them. The three years are therefore doubtless to be reckoned not from his return to Damascus, but from the crisis of his life which preceded his departure from Damascus. The exact length of the interval can not be determined from this phrase, which is probably a round number (cf. Acts 20³¹, and with it Acts 19⁸, ¹⁰, ²²). In reckoning the years of their kings the later Jews apparently counted the years from one New Year's Day, the 1st of Abib (or Nisan) to another, and the fraction of a year on either side as a year. See Wieseler, *Chronological Synopsis of the Four Gospels*, pp. 53 ff. But we do not know that Paul would have followed the same method in a statement such as this. It is not possible in any case to determine how large a part of the three years was spent in Arabia.

Κηφᾶν is the reading of ℵ*AB 33, 424², 1912, Syr. (psh. hcl-mg. pal.) Boh. Aeth. The Western and Syrian authorities generally read Πέτρον, which is evidently the substitution of the more familiar for the less familiar name of the apostle.

The verb ἱστορέω (cognate with ἵστωρ, ἵδρις, οἶδα) is found in Greek writers from Herodotus down, meaning "to inquire"; in Aristotle and later writers in the sense "to narrate," "to report"; it has this sense also in 1 Esdr. 1³¹ ⁽³³⁾, ⁴⁰ ⁽⁴²⁾, the only passages in biblical Greek beside the present one in which the word occurs at all; it occurs in Plut. *Thes.* 30⁴; *Pomp.* 40¹; Polyb. 3. 48¹², with the meaning "to visit" (places), and in Jos. (*Ant.* 8. 46 [2⁵] *Bell.* 6. 81 [1⁸]); Clem. Rom. (8²⁴) meaning "to visit" (persons). See Hilg. and Ell. *ad loc.* The sense in the present passage is evidently that which is found also in Josephus. By the use of this word Paul characterises his journey as having had for its purpose personal acquaintance with Peter, rather than the receiving of instruction. *Cf.* v. ¹², and see below on πρὸς αὐτόν.

καὶ ἐπέμεινα πρὸς αὐτὸν ἡμέρας δεκαπέντε· "And I remained with him fifteen days." The use of the phrase πρὸς αὐτόν, with its personal pronoun in the singular, referring definitely to Peter, rather than πρός with a plural pronoun or an adverb of place, emphasises the purely personal character of the visit.

On the preposition πρός with the accusative after a verb not expressing motion, cf. Th. s. v. I 2 b, and for exx. in Paul see I Thes. 3⁴ Gal. 2⁵ 4¹⁸, ²⁰, etc. The mention of the brief duration of the stay is intended, especially in contrast with the three years of absence from Jerusalem, to show how impossible it was to regard him as a disciple of the Twelve, learning all that he knew of the gospel from them. Cf. οὔτε ἐδιδάχθην, v. ¹².

19. ἕτερον δὲ τῶν ἀποστόλων οὐκ εἶδον, εἰ μὴ Ἰάκωβον τὸν ἀδελφὸν τοῦ κυρίου. "and no other of the apostles did I see except James the brother of the Lord." On the use of ἕτερον, see detached note, p. 420. It is evidently used here in its closest approximation to ἄλλος, denoting merely numerical non-identity, not qualitative distinction. εἰ μή means here, as always before a noun, "except." The only question is whether εἰ μὴ Ἰάκωβον, etc., is an exception to the whole of the preceding statement ἕτερον . . . οὐκ εἶδον, or only a part of it, οὐκ εἶδον. Either is in accordance with usage (see Th. εἰ, III 8 c β, and such cases as Lk. 4²⁶, ²⁷ Rom. 11¹⁵, etc.). In this passage, however, the view which would make the exception apply to a part only of the preceding assertion is excluded, since Paul certainly can not mean to say that he saw no one in Jerusalem except Peter and James, or even, according at least to Acts 9²⁷, no person of importance. The phrase must probably be taken as stating an exception to the whole of the preceding assertion, and as implying that James was an apostle. The assumption that the term ἀπόστολος is applied to James in a broad and loose sense only (so Sief., e. g.) is without good ground in usage and is especially unjustified in view of the fact that the term ἀποστόλων under which James is by the exceptive phrase included, refers primarily to the Twelve. Cf. detached note on Ἀπόστολος, p. 363.

James, here designated the brother of the Lord, is doubtless the same who is similarly spoken of in Mk. 6³, and simply as James in Gal. 2⁹, ¹² I Cor. 15⁷ Acts 15¹³ 21¹⁸; cf. also Jn. 7⁵ I Cor. 9⁵. He is never mentioned as one of the Twelve; it is rather to be supposed that he was brought to believe in Jesus by the vision recorded in I Cor. 15⁷. He early took a prominent place in the church at Jerusalem (Gal 2⁹, ¹² Acts 15¹³ff.), and was known in later tradition as the first bishop of

that church (Eus. *Hist. Eccl.* II 1). The view of Jerome which identifies James the brother of the Lord with James the son of Alphæus
(see defence of it by Meyrick in Smith, *DB* art. "James," and criticism by Mayor in H*DB* art. "Brethren of the Lord") rests on no
good evidence. Nor is there any positive evidence for the theory
that he was older than Jesus, being the son of Joseph and a wife previous to Mary. See Ltft.'s defence of this (Epiphanian) view in Dissertation II, appended to his *Galatians*, and reprinted as Dissertation I,
in his *Dissertations on the Apostolic Age;* and Farrar's argument for the
(Helvidian) view that the brothers of the Lord were sons of Joseph
and Mary, in *Early Days of Christianity*, chap. XIX, and in Smith, *DB*
art. "Brothers of the Lord"; also Mayor, *op. cit.*, and Cone, art.
"James" in *Encyc. Bib.* Mt. 1²⁵ and Lk. 1⁷ naturally imply that the
early church knew of children of Mary younger than Jesus. It does
not indeed follow that all the six children named in Mk. 6³ were borne
by her. But neither is there any direct evidence that there were children of Joseph by a former marriage. Jn. 19²⁶, ²⁷ might suggest it (*cf.*
Ltft. *u. s.*) but its late date and the uncertainty whether the statement
is in intent historical or symbolic diminish its value for historical purposes. On the other hand the implication of the infancy narrative of
Mt. and Lk. that Joseph was not the father of Jesus and hence that
his sons by a former marriage were not brothers of Jesus, can not be
cited against the Epiphanian view; for not only does this presuppose a
strictness in the use of the term brother which is unsustained by usage,
but the evidence of this passage as to the time at which the title "brother
of the Lord" was given to James, and the evidence of the Pauline letters in general (*cf.* on 4⁴) as to the time when the theory of the virgin
birth of Jesus became current, make it nearly certain that the former
much preceded the latter.

20. ἃ δὲ γράφω ὑμῖν, ἰδοὺ ἐνώπιον τοῦ θεοῦ ὅτι οὐ ψεύδομαι.
"Now as respects the things which I write to you, behold, before God, I am not lying." For similar affirmations of Paul
that in the presence of God he is speaking truly, see 1 Thes. 2⁵
2 Cor. 1²³ 11³¹. Its use here shows clearly that the facts just
stated are given not simply for their historical value, but as
evidence of what he has before asserted, his independence of
the Twelve. ἃ γράφω doubtless refers to all that precedes, from
v.¹³ (or ¹⁵) on. Even so one can not but wonder why Paul
should use such very strong language unless he had been
charged with misstating the facts about his visits to the other
apostles.

(d) Evidence of his independent apostleship drawn from the period of his stay in Syria and Cilicia (1^{21-24}).

The apostle now turns to a period, which 2^1 compared with 1^{18} shows to have been eleven or even fourteen years, during which he was out of Judea and not in touch with the other apostles, yet was carrying on his work as a preacher of the gospel.

[21]Then I went into the regions of Syria and Cilicia, [22]and I was unknown by face to the churches of Judea that are in Christ; [23]only they heard (kept hearing), Our former persecutor is now preaching the faith which formerly he ravaged; and they glorified God in me.

21. Ἔπειτα ἦλθον εἰς τὰ κλίματα τῆς Συρίας καὶ τῆς Κιλικίας. "Then I went into the regions of Syria and Cilicia." That this was a period of preaching, not, like that in Arabia, of retirement, is implied in v.[23], εὐαγγελίζεται. On the question whether he had yet begun to work distinctively for the Gentiles in these regions, see below on v.[24].

> The repetition of the article before Κιλικίας is very unusual. The two regions being adjacent and both nouns limiting κλίματα, one would expect a single article, standing before the first one. See, e. g., Acts 1^8 8^1 9^{16} $15^{23, 41}$ 27^5; Jos. *Ant.* 8. 36 (2^2) 12. 154 (4^1); *Bell.* 2. 95 (6^2) 2. 247 (12^2), which reflect the all but uniform usage of N. T. and Josephus, to which *Ant.* 13. 175 (4^4) and 12. 233 (4^{11}) are not really exceptions. Note especially Acts 15^{23}, κατὰ τὴν Ἀντιόχειαν καὶ Συρίαν καὶ Κιλικίαν. In Acts 15^{41}, where Συρίαν and Κιλικίαν occur in the same order, the article is inserted before Κιλικίαν by BD cat²⁶⁰ Thphyl^b only. This strong preponderance of usage makes the second article in the present passage a very difficult reading, but even more strongly points to the secondary character of the reading without it, sustained by ℵ*33, 241, 1908. That some mss. should have omitted it in conformity with common usage is not strange; that all the rest should have inserted it, departing thereby both from usage and the original text, is almost impossible.

22. ἤμην δὲ ἀγνοούμενος τῷ προσώπῳ ταῖς ἐκκλησίαις τῆς Ἰουδαίας ταῖς ἐν Χριστῷ, "and I was unknown by face to the churches of Judea that are in Christ." The periphrastic form of the imperfect tends to emphasise the continuance of

the state, "I remained unknown." The motive of these statements of the apostle respecting his departure into Syria and Cilicia and the non-acquaintance of the Judean churches with him is doubtless to show that his work during this period was not in that region in which it would have been if he had placed himself under the direction of the Twelve, but that, on the contrary, he began at once an independent mission. This, rather than, *e. g.*, the intention to show that he was not under the influence or instruction of these churches, is what is required by the nature of the argument, which has to do not with his contact with Christians in general, but with his subjection to the influence of the leaders of primitive Christianity. On the expression ταῖς ἐκκλησίαις . . . ἐν Χριστῷ, *cf.* 1 Thes. 1¹ 2¹⁴ 2 Thes. 1¹ Phil 1¹. On the force of the preposition as meaning "in fellowship with," see Th. *s. v.* I 6 b, and *cf.* 5⁶. The expression characterises the churches referred to as Christian as distinguished from Jewish, but reflects also the apostle's conception of the intimacy of the fellowship between these communities and the risen Jesus.

In itself the phrase "churches of Judea" of course includes that of Jerusalem. Nor is that church excluded by the fact of Paul's persecution of it, since this would not necessarily involve his meeting face to face those whom he persecuted, and, moreover, some years elapsed between the events referred to in v.¹³ and those here recorded; nor by the visit of Paul to Jerusalem, as recorded in vv.¹⁸, ¹⁹, since the statement that he was unknown can hardly be taken so literally as to mean that no member of the church had ever seen him. In favour of the more inclusive use of the term is also 1 Thes. 2¹⁴, where a similar phrase is employed without the exclusion of Jerusalem. Nor can Acts 9²⁶⁻²⁹ be regarded as a serious argument against the more inclusive sense of the term. For, though v.²⁹ manifestly implies such an acquaintance of Paul with the Christians of Jerusalem as to contradict his statement here if it includes Jerusalem, and though v.²⁹ itself might be accepted as not directly contradicted by vv.¹⁸, ¹⁹ of the present passage, yet the conflict between the first-hand testimony of the latter and vv.²⁷, ²⁸ of the Acts passage is such as to call in question the accuracy in details of the whole section in Acts. Acts 26²⁰ is even more at variance with Paul's statement here, unless it refers to a period subsequent to the period covered by Gal. 1¹⁸⁻²⁴. Nor can Jn. 3²² be cited as evidence that 'Ιουδαία can mean Judea exclusive of Jerusalem, the language there being ἡ Ἰουδαία γῆ, not ἡ Ἰουδαία alone; nor Mt. 3⁵, Ἱεροσόλυμα καὶ πᾶσα ἡ Ἰουδαία (cf. Paris and all France); nor Jos. Ant. 10. 184 (9⁷): ἔρημος πᾶσα ἡ Ἰουδαία καὶ Ἱεροσόλυμα καὶ ὁ ναός διέμεινεν, since as the temple is in Jerusalem, so may Jerusalem be in Judea. On the other hand it can not justly be urged, as is done by Bous., that a statement pertaining to the churches of Judea exclusive of Jerusalem would be without force, since, as pointed out above, the reference is in any case probably not to these churches as a source of instruction, but as those among whom he would probably have been working if he had put himself under the guidance of the Twelve. While, therefore, in speaking of "the churches of Judea" Paul may have had chiefly in mind those outside of Jerusalem, the word Judea can not apparently designate the territory outside Jerusalem as distinguished from the city. Of the location of the churches of Judea outside of Jerusalem we have no exact knowledge. On the extent of the territory covered by the term, see detached note on Ἰουδαία, pp. 435 f.

23. μόνον δὲ ἀκούοντες ἦσαν ὅτι Ὁ διώκων ἡμᾶς ποτὲ νῦν εὐαγγελίζεται τὴν πίστιν ἥν ποτε ἐπόρθει, "only they heard (kept hearing), Our former persecutor is now preaching the faith which formerly he ravaged." μόνον doubtless limits the whole statement, indicating that it constitutes the only exception to the ignorance of him referred to in the preceding clause. The logical subject of the sentence is the members of the churches mentioned in v. ²²; note the gender of the participle ἀκούοντες. ὅτι is recitative, the following words being shown by the pronoun ἡμᾶς to be a direct quotation. The present participle διώκων describes the persecution as a thing in progress, assigning it to the past, in contrast with the present νῦν. The aorist would have presented it simply as a (past) fact. Cf. GMT 140, BMT 127. ἡμᾶς refers, of course, not directly to those to whom he was unknown by face, but to Christians in general. On εὐαγγελίζεται see v. ⁸. πίστιν is not the body of Christian doctrine, in which sense the word is never used by Paul, but the faith in Christ which the preachers of the gospel bade men exercise. Concerning its nature see more fully under 2²⁰. On ἥν ποτε ἐπόρθει cf. v. ¹³. What is there described as a ravaging of the church is here called a ravaging of the faith, which is the principle of the church's life; the aim of Paul's persecution was the extermination of the church and its faith in Jesus as the Christ. The tense is here, as there, conative.

24. καὶ ἐδόξαζον ἐν ἐμοὶ τὸν θεόν. "and they glorified God
in me," *i. e.*, found in me occasion and reason for praising God.
On this use of ἐν of that which constitutes the ground or basis
of an action (derived from the use of the preposition to denote
the sphere within which the action takes place) see Th. I 6 c,
though the classification at this point is far from satisfactory;
W. XLVIII a (3) c; Ell. *ad loc.*, though here also the matter is
stated with unnecessary obscurity; and such passages as Mt. 6⁷
Acts 7²⁹ Rom. 2¹⁷, ²³ 5⁹ Gal. 3¹¹, ¹⁴. The satisfaction which the
churches of Judea found in Paul's missionary activity in this
period is in sharp contrast with the opposition to him which
later developed in Jerusalem. See 2¹⁻¹⁰. Of the several explanations that might be given of the more friendly attitude of
the early period, (a) that Paul had not yet begun to preach
the gospel of freedom from the law, or (b) that though he
was doing so the Christians of Judea were not aware of this
aspect of his work, or (c) that the strenuous opposition to the
offering of the gospel to the Gentiles apart from the law had
not yet developed in the churches of Judea, the first is probably true in the sense and to the extent that Paul had not yet
had occasion to assume a polemic attitude in the matter; but
in any other sense seems excluded by his repeated implication
that the gospel which he now preached he had preached from
the beginning (see 1¹¹ 2² and comment). But in that case there
is little room for the second. The third is, moreover, the one
most consistent with the testimony of this letter; see especially
2⁴, with its distinct implication that the opponents of Paul's
liberalism were a recent and pernicious addition to the Jerusalem church. And this in turn suggests that the apostle's reason
for adding the statement καὶ ἐδόξαζον . . . ἐμοί was incidentally to give strength to his contention for the legitimacy of
his mission by intimating, what 2⁴ says more clearly, that the
opposition to him was a recent matter, and did not represent the
original attitude of the Judean Christians. On the other hand,
it must not be forgotten that his main contention throughout
this chapter and the next is not that he had been approved by
the Judean Christians, but that he had from the first acted

independently. The whole sentence μόνον . . . ἐν ἐμοί is a momentary digression from that point of view.

(e) Evidence of his independent apostleship drawn from his conduct on a visit to Jerusalem fourteen years after the preceding one (2¹⁻¹⁰).

Following, as before, a chronological order, the apostle now narrates the circumstances of a very important occasion on which he came in contact with those who were apostles before him. At the outset he calls attention to the length of his absence from Jerusalem, fourteen years, during which, so it is implied, he had had no contact with the Jerusalem apostles; then to the fact that when he went up it was not at their command, but in obedience to divine revelation; then, indicating that the question at issue was then, as now in Galatia, the circumcision of the Gentiles who had accepted his gospel, he tells how he laid his gospel before the Jerusalem Christians, and in a private session before the pillars of the church, James and Cephas and John, since he recognised that their disapproval of his preaching might render of no avail his future work and undo what he had already done. Though, out of consideration for the opponents of his gospel of freedom from law, who had crept into the Jerusalem church for the purpose of robbing the Christians of their freedom and bringing them into bondage to the law, the apostles urged him to circumcise Titus, a Greek Christian who was with him, he refused to do so; and so far from his yielding to the authority or persuasion of these eminent men, whose eminent past did not weigh with him, as it did not with God, they imparted nothing new to him, but when they perceived that God, who had commissioned Peter to present the gospel to the Jews, had given to Paul also a commission to the Gentiles, these leaders of the church cordially agreed to a division of the territory and of responsibility. Paul and Barnabas were to preach among the Gentiles, Peter among the Jews, and the only additional stipulation was that Paul and Barnabas should remember the poor among the Jewish Christians, which thing, Paul affirms, he gladly did.

Then after fourteen years I again went up to Jerusalem, with Barnabas, taking Titus also along. ²And I went up in accordance with [a] revelation. And I laid before them the gospel which I preach among the Gentiles,—but privately before the men of eminence—lest perchance I should run or had run in vain. ³But not even Titus, who was with me and was a Greek, was compelled to be circumcised (⁴now it was because of the false brethren surreptitiously brought in, who sneaked in to spy out our freedom which we have in Christ Jesus, that they might bring us into bondage [that his circumcision was urged], ⁵to whom not for an hour did we yield by way of the subjection [demanded]), that the truth of the gospel might continue with you. ⁶And from those who were accounted to be something—what they once were matters not to me—God accepts not the person of man—for to me the men of eminence taught nothing new—⁷but on the contrary when they saw that I had been entrusted with the gospel to the uncircumcised as Peter with the gospel to the circumcised—⁸for he who wrought for Peter unto an apostleship to the circumcised wrought also for me unto an apostleship to the Gentiles—⁹and when, I say, they perceived the grace that had been given to me, James and Cephas and John, who were accounted pillars, gave to me and to Barnabas right hands of fellowship, that we should go among the Gentiles and they among the circumcised, ¹⁰provided only that we should remember the poor, which very thing I have also taken pains to do.

1. Ἔπειτα διὰ δεκατεσσάρων ἐτῶν πάλιν ἀνέβην εἰς Ἱεροσό-λυμα "Then after fourteen years I again went up to Jerusalem." Since for the purposes of his argument that he had not been dependent on the other apostles (*cf.* 1¹², ¹⁷) it is his contacts with them that it is pertinent to mention, the fact that he speaks of these as visits to Jerusalem (*cf.* 1¹⁸) indicates that throughout the period of which he is speaking Jerusalem was the headquarters of the apostles. And this being the case the denial, by implication, that he had been in Jerusalem is the strongest possible way of denying communication with the Twelve. It follows also that, had there been other visits to Jerusalem in this period, he must have mentioned them, unless indeed they had been made under conditions which excluded communication with the Twelve, and this fact had been well known to his readers. Even in that case he would naturally have spoken of them and appealed to the well-known absence of the apostles or have spoken, not of going to Jerusalem, but of seeing those who were apostles before him.

Ἔπειτα, primarily a particle of chronological succession, clearly has this force here, as is suggested by διά . . . ἐτῶν. The ἔπειτα . . . ἔπειτα . . . ἔπειτα of 1[18, 21] and the present v. mark the successive steps of a chronological series, and at the same time of the apostle's argument, because he is arranging it on a chronological framework; they thus acquire as in some other cases (see 1 Thes. 4[17] 1 Cor. 15[46]) a secondary logical force. That διά may mean "after the lapse of" is clearly shown by Hdt. 3[27]; Soph. Ph. 758; Xen. Cyr. 1. 4[28], and other passages cited by L. & S. s. v. A. II 2, and by W. XLVII i. (b) (WM. p. 475), and that this use was current in Jewish Greek appears from Deut. 9[11] Mk. 2[1] Acts 24[17]. That this rather than "throughout," the only alternative meaning in chronological expressions, is the meaning here is evident from the unsuitableness of "throughout" to the verb ἀνέβην. On the question whether the period is to be reckoned from the same starting point as the three years previously named (1[18]) or from the end of that period, there is room for difference of opinion. Wies. Ell. Alf. hold the former view; Ltft. Mey. Beet, Sief. Lip. Zahn, Bous. the latter. For the exposition of the apostle's thought at this point the question is of little consequence. His purpose is evidently to emphasise the limited amount of his communication with the Twelve as tending to show that he did not receive his gospel from them, and for this purpose it matters little whether the period during which he had no communication with the Twelve was fourteen years or eleven. For the chronology of the life of Paul, however, the question is of more significance. While it is impossible to determine with certainty which view is correct, the balance of probability seems to favour reckoning the fourteen years as subsequent to the three years. The nature of his argument requires him to mention not how long after his conversion he made this visit, but during how long a period he remained without personal communication with the other apostles, which period would be reckoned, of course, from his latest preceding visit. This argument is somewhat strengthened by the use of the preposition διά, which, meaning properly "through," and coming to signify "after" only through the thought of a period passed through, also suggests that the period of fourteen years constitutes a unit in the apostle's mind—an unbroken period of non-communication with the apostles.

The substitution of τεσσάρων for δεκατεσσάρων (advocated by Grot.
Seml. *et al*., named by Sief. and Zahn *ad loc*.), resting as it does on no
external evidence, calls for no refutation. The supposed difficulties
of the chronology of the apostle's life based on δεκατεσσάρων are insufficient to justify this purely conjectural emendation of the text.

For the doubt whether πάλιν belonged to the original text expressed
by Zahn and Bous. there seems slight justification. It is lacking in
no ancient ms., though standing in DFG d g Goth. Aeth. after ἀνέβην,
and in but one ancient version, the Boh. The quotation of the sentence without it by Mcion. Iren. Ambrst. Chrys. seems insufficient
evidence that the original text lacked it.

μετὰ Βαρνάβα, "with Barnabas," *i. e*., accompanied by him,
as in Mt. 16²⁷ 1 Thes. 3¹³ 2 Thes. 1⁷, rather than accompanying
him, as in Mt. 25¹⁰ 26⁴⁷ Acts 7⁴⁵; for the remainder of the narrative, especially the constant use of the first person singular,
implies that Paul and not Barnabas was the chief speaker and
leader of the party.

συνπαραλαβὼν καὶ Τίτον· "taking Titus also along." Titus
is thus assigned to a distinctly subordinate position as one
"taken along," and the members of the party evidently ranked
in the order, Paul, Barnabas, Titus. The apostle says nothing
at this point concerning the reason for taking Titus with him.
But the specific mention of the fact and the part that Titus
played in the subsequent events (vv. ³⁻⁵) suggest that Paul
intended to make his a test-case for the whole question of the
circumcision of the Gentile Christians.

Concerning the tense of the participle συνπαραλαβών, see B*MT* 149,
and *cf*. Acts 12²⁵. The act denoted by the participle, though coinciding
in time with the action of the principal verb, is expressed by an aorist
rather than a present participle, because it is conceived of as a simple
fact, not as an action in progress, least of all as one within the time of
which the action of the principal verb falls.

2. ἀνέβην δὲ κατὰ ἀποκάλυψιν· "and I went up in accordance with [a] revelation," *i. e*., in obedience to such [a]
revelation. The word ἀποκάλυψις evidently has the same
meaning here as in 1¹² (see the discussion there and detached
note on Ἀποκαλύπτω and Ἀποκάλυψις, p. 433), but refers in

this case to a disclosure of the divine will respecting a specific
matter, not, as there, to a revelation of the person Jesus in his
true character. Concerning the specific method in which the
divine will that he should go to Jerusalem was disclosed to
him, and whether directly to him or through some other person, the apostle says nothing. Nor can it be determined
whether the word is here used indefinitely, referring to a
(specific) revelation, or with merely qualitative force, describing revelation as the method by which he obtained his conviction that he ought to go to Jerusalem. On the former point,
however, *cf.* 2 Cor. 12¹ᶠᶠ· Acts 13¹ 16⁷, ⁹ 21¹¹ 27²³ᶠᶠ·.

For a similar use of the preposition κατά *cf.* Acts 23³¹ Rom. 16²⁶ 2 Thes.
3⁶. "In accordance with," being the more usual and exact meaning of
κατά, is to be preferred to the nearly equivalent sense, "because of."
In Rom. 16²⁵ and Eph. 3³, though the phrase is the same, the sense is
different.

καὶ ἀνεθέμην αὐτοῖς τὸ εὐαγγέλιον ὃ κηρύσσω ἐν τοῖς
ἔθνεσιν, "And I laid before them the gospel which I preach
among the Gentiles." The pronoun αὐτοῖς, having no definitely expressed antecedent, is to be taken as referring in
general to those whom he visited in Jerusalem, *i. e.*, the Christian community. Concerning the word εὐαγγέλιον, see detached note, p. 422; the use of the term here is doubtless the
same as in 1⁶. The questions at issue between Paul and those
of a different opinion in Jerusalem were not historical, nor practical in the sense that they pertained to the methods of gospel
work, but doctrinal, having to do with the significance of the
work of Christ, the conditions of salvation, the obligations of
believers. The use of the present tense, κηρύσσω, reflects the
apostle's thought that he is still at the time of writing preaching the same gospel which he had been preaching before he
made this visit to Jerusalem. *Cf.* the similar implication,
though with a reverse use of tenses, in 1¹¹. The use of a past
tense, ἐκήρυξεν, would almost have suggested that what he
then preached he was now no longer preaching. "Among the
Gentiles," the apostle says, suggesting that he not only preached

to the Gentiles but to the Jews also, so far as they were in
Gentile lands. Note the same phrase in 1^{16} and εἰς τὰ ἔθνη
in 2^8, all of which indicate that Paul conceived his apostleship
to be not simply to the Gentile people but to the people of Gentile lands.

> Ἀνατίθημι, found from Homer down, is apparently used only in later
> writers in the sense " to present " (matter for consideration). See 2
> Mac. 3^9; Acts 25^{14}, only N. T. instance, and cf. M. & M. Voc. s. v.

κατ' ἰδίαν δὲ τοῖς δοκοῦσιν, "but privately before the men of
eminence." Those who are here designated as οἱ δοκοῦντες
are evidently the same who in v. ^{6} are called οἱ δοκοῦντες and
οἱ δοκοῦντες εἶναί τι, and in v. ^{9} οἱ δοκοῦντες στύλοι εἶναι,
and in v. ^{9} are also identified as James and Cephas and John.
See note in fine print below. By these phrases the three men
named are described as the influential men, the leaders, of the
Christian community in Jerusalem. There is nothing in the
present passage or in the usage of the words to indicate that
they are used with irony.

On the question whether this phrase refers to the same interview spoken of in ἀνεθέμην . . . ἔθνεσιν, so that τοῖς δοκοῦσιν
is merely a more definite designation of αὐτοῖς, or to a different
one, so that there was both a public and a private meeting at
which Paul set forth his gospel, probability is in favour of the
latter; for although an epexegetic limitation may certainly be
conjoined to what precedes by δέ, yet it is Paul's usual habit
in such cases to repeat the word which the added phrase is to
limit (cf. ἀνέβην in this v.; Rom. 3^{22} 9^{30} 1 Cor. 1^{16} 2^6 Phil. 2^8—
in 1 Cor. 3^{15} it is otherwise). In this case, moreover, it is difficult to suppose that Paul should have used the very general
αὐτοῖς if, indeed, he meant only three men, or to see why if he
referred to but one interview he should not have written simply
καὶ ἀνεθέμην τοῖς δοκοῦσιν τὸ εὐαγγέλιον, etc. Among modern interpreters Wies. Ell. Ltft. Mey. Weizs. Holst. Sief.
Lip. Zahn, Bous. et al., understand the language to imply two
interviews; Zeller, Neander, Alf. Beet. Vernon Bartlet (in
Expositor, Oct., 1899), Emmet, et al., but one.

On the use of κατ' ἰδίαν, which can not mean "especially" (as Bous. *et al.*) but only "privately," *cf.* Mt. 17¹⁹ Mk. 4³⁴ 9²⁸ etc.; Ign. *Smyrn.* 7²: πρέπον οὖν ἐστίν . . . μήτε κατ' ἰδίαν περὶ αὐτῶν λαλεῖν μήτε κοινῇ.

The phrase οἱ δοκοῦντες, vv.², ⁶ᵇ is an example of a usage rare in ancient Greek literature. The participle alone, as here, is found in Eur. *Hec.* 295 and *Troiad.* 613, both times in the sense "men of standing and consequence, men of esteem." There is no hint of any derogatory flavour in the phrase. In Herodian 6. 1³, sometimes cited under this head, τοὺς δοκοῦντας has a predicate in καὶ σεμνοτάτους καὶ . . . σωφρονεστάτους following. The meaning is "those esteemed both most dignified and most sober." With this *cf.* οἱ δοκοῦντες στύλοι, v. ⁹. The expression οἱ δοκοῦντες εἶναί τι which Paul uses in v. ⁶ᵃ (and from which, as Zahn holds, the shorter form is derived by ellipsis) is found in the same form and meaning in Plato, *Gorg.* 472 A, where it is synonymous with εὐδοκίμους a few lines above; *cf.* also *Euthyd.* 303 C, where the phrase is the same, except that the εἶναί τι is inverted. The same phrase, however, is used also in the sense "those who think themselves something"; so Plut. *Apophth. lacon.* 49, and probably Plato, *Apol.* 35 A. The meanings of the word δοκεῖν itself as used in these or similar phrases are as follows: 1. "To be accounted, esteemed" (a) in the indifferent sense of the word. See vv.⁶ᵃ, ⁹; *cf.* Plato, *Apol.* 35 A; Plut. *Aristid.* 1⁷; Epictet. *Enchir.* 13: κἂν δόξῃς τισιν εἶναί τις, ἀπίστει σεαυτῷ. 2 Mac. 9¹⁰ (?) Mk. 10⁴² 1 Cor. 12²² (?) (b) in the definitely honourable sense, "to be highly esteemed," as in vv.², ⁶ᵇ. 2. "To account one's self," as in Gal. 6³ 1 Cor. 3¹⁸ 8² 10¹² Jas. 1²⁶ Prov. 26¹². For an especially close parallel to Gal. 6³ see Plato, *Apol.* 41 E. Thus in all of the four instances in the present passage the word has substantially the same meaning, differing only in that in vv.⁶ᵃ, ⁹ the word is colourless, the standing of those referred to being expressed in the predicate, while in vv. ², ⁶ᵇ, the predicate is omitted and the verb itself carries the idea of high standing.

μή πως εἰς κενὸν τρέχω ἢ ἔδραμον. "lest perchance I should run or had run in vain." μή πως expresses apprehension (see more fully below). The whole phrase implies that the apostle saw in the existing situation a danger that his work on behalf of the Gentiles, both past and future, might be rendered ineffectual by the opposition of the Jerusalem church, or of certain men in it, and the disapproval of the apostles, and that fearing this, he sought to avert it. The ground of his apprehension is, of course, not a doubt concerning the truth of the gospel which he preached—it would be an impossible incon-

gruity on his part to attribute to himself such a doubt in the
very midst of his strenuous insistence upon the truth and divine
source of that gospel—but rather, no doubt, the conviction
that the disapproval of his work by the leading apostles in
Jerusalem would seriously interfere with that work and to a
serious degree render it ineffectual. The apostle's conduct
throughout his career, notably in the matter of the collection
for the poor of Jerusalem, and his own last visit to Jerusalem
(see 1 Cor. 16$^{1-3}$ 2 Cor. chs. 8, 9, esp. 9$^{12-15}$ Rom. 15$^{25-32}$, esp. v. ^{31}),
show clearly that it was to him a matter of the utmost impor-
tance, not only to prevent the forcing of the Jewish law upon
the Gentiles, but at the same time to maintain the unity of the
Christian movement, avoiding any division into a Jewish and
a Gentile branch. To this end he was willing to divert energy
and time from his work of preaching to the Gentiles in order to
raise money for the Jewish Christians, and to delay his journey
to the west in order personally to carry this money to Jerusalem. His unshaken confidence in the divine origin and the
truth of his own gospel did not prevent his seeing that the
rupture which would result from a refusal of the pillar apostles,
the leaders of the Jewish part of the church, to recognise the
legitimacy of his mission and gospel and so of Gentile Christianity on a non-legal basis, would be disastrous alike to the Jewish and the Gentile parties which would thus be created.

Εἰς κενόν found also in Lxx (Lev. 26^{20} Job 39^{16} Mic. 1^{14} Isa. 29^8, etc.);
Jos. *Ant.* 19. 27 (1^4), 96 (1^{13}); *Bell.* 1. 275 (14^1); in late Greek writers
(Diod. Sic. 19. 9^5) and in the N. T. by Paul (1 Thes. 3^5 2 Cor. 6^1 Phil.
2^{16}) is with him always, as usually in the Lxx, a phrase of result meaning
"uselessly," "without effect." Running, as a figure of speech for effort directed to an end, is not uncommon with Paul (1 Cor. 9$^{24, 26}$
Gal. 5^7 Phil. 2^{16}; see also Phil. 3^{14} 2 Tim. 4^7).

The clause μή . . . ἔδραμον has been explained: (1) As an indirect
question, "whether perhaps I was running or had run in vain." τρέχω
is in this case a present indicative, retained from the direct form. So
Usteri, assuming an ellipsis of "in order that I might learn from them,"
Wies., who assumes an ellipsis of "in order that they might perceive,"
and Sief., who supplies "to put to test the question," and emphasises
the fact that since μή expects a negative answer the apostle implies
no doubt respecting the result of his work, but only the abstract

possibility of its fruitlessness. (2) As a final clause, "that I might not
run or have run in vain" (so Frit. Beet). (3) As an object clause
after a verb a verb implied, "fearing lest I should run or had run
in vain." τρέχω is in that case most probably a pres. subj., referring
to a continued (fruitless) effort in the future. A pres. ind. would be
possible (GMT 369.1) referring to a then existing situation, but is a
much less probable complement and antithesis to ἔδραμον than a pres.
subj. referring to the future. Cf. 1 Thes. 3⁵. So Ltft. Ell. (?), Lip.
(though apparently confusing it with the preceding interpretation). To
the first of these it is to be objected that it involves a doubtful use of
μή πως. Goodwin (GMT 369 fn. 1) distinguishing clearly, as Sief. following Kühner (II 1037, 1042, but cf. Kühner-Gerth, II 391 fn., which
corrects Kühner's error) fails to do, between the indirect question and
the clause of fear, maintains (L. & S. sub. μή πως, however, contra) that
μή is never used in classical writers in an indirect question. Sief., indeed, alleges that this indirect interrogative use is common in later
Greek, but cites no evidence. μή πως is certainly not so used in Paul,
with whom it is always a final particle, occurring in a pure final clause,
or in a clause of fear, or in an object clause after verbs of precaution
(1 Cor. 8⁹ 9²⁷ 2 Cor. 2⁷ 9⁴ 11³ 12²⁰ Gal. 4¹¹ 1 Thes. 3⁵; it is not used by
other N. T. writers) and there is no certain instance of μή so used
in N. T.; Lk. 11³⁵, which is generally so taken, is at best a doubtful
case. To the second interpretation it is a decisive objection that a
past tense of the indicative is used in final clauses only after a hypothetical statement contrary to fact and to express an unattained purpose. Neither of these conditions is fulfilled here. The verb ἀνεθέμην
expresses a fact, not what would have been under certain circumstances, and the apostle certainly does not mean to characterise the
purpose that he might not run in vain as unattained. The attempt
of Frit., approved by W. LVI 2 (b) β (WM. p. 633), to give the
sentence a hypothetical character by explaining it, "that I might
not, as might easily have happened if I had not communicated my
teaching in Jerusalem, have run in vain," is not only artificial, but
after all fails to make the principal clause ἀνεθέμην, etc., an unreal hypothesis. See GMT 333, 336. The third interpretation is consistent
both with general Greek usage and with Paul's use of μή πως, and is
the only probable one. It involves, of course, the implication of a
purpose of the apostle's action, viz., to avert what he feared, that his
future work should be fruitless, or his past work be undone. But such
implication is common in clauses of fear. When the verb of fear is expressed, the μή clause expresses by implication the purpose of an action previously mentioned or about to be mentioned (Acts 23¹⁰ 2 Cor.
12²⁰); when the fear is only implied the μή clause, denoting the object
of apprehension, conveys by implication the purpose of the immediately
preceding verb (2 Cor. 9⁴ 1 Thes. 3⁵). The use of the aorist indicative

following a statement of fact suffices, however, to show that in this case the clause expresses primarily an object of apprehension. The objection of Sief. to this interpretation, that Paul certainly could not have implied that his fear of his past work being rendered fruitless was actually realised, rests upon a misunderstanding of the force of a past tense in such cases. This implies not that the fear has been realised —in this case one would not express fear at all, but regret—but that the event is past, and the outcome, which is the real object of fear, as yet unknown or undetermined. *Cf. GMT* 369; B*MT* 227, and see chap. 4[11], where the object clause refers to a past fact, the outcome of which is, however, not only as yet unknown to him, but quite possibly yet to be determined by the course which the Galatians should pursue in response to the letter he was then writing.

3. ἀλλ' οὐδὲ Τίτος ὁ σὺν ἐμοί, Ἕλλην ὤν, ἠναγκάσθη περι-τμηθῆναι· "But not even Titus, who was with me, and was a Greek, was compelled to be circumcised." In antithesis to the possibility of his work proving fruitless (by reason of the opposition of the Jerusalem church and apostles) Paul here sets forth the fact that on this very occasion and in a test-case his view prevailed. For ἀλλά introducing the evidence disproving a previously suggested hypothesis, see Rom. 4[2] 1 Cor. 2[9]. The fact of the presence of Titus with the apostle had already been mentioned in the preceding sentence. Its repetition here in ὁ σὺν ἐμοί is evidently, therefore, for an argumentative purpose, and doubtless as emphasising the significance of the fact that he was not circumcised. It is upon this element of the sentence especially that οὐδέ "not even" throws its emphasis. The opponents of Paul, the "false brethren" desired, of course, the circumcision of all Gentile Christians. But so far were they from carrying through their demand that not even Titus, who was there on the ground at the time, and to whom the demand would first of all apply, was circumcised. The non-circumcision of Titus, therefore, was in reality a decision of the principle. The phrase ὁ σὺν ἐμοί is thus concessive in effect. See B*MT* 428. The participial phrase, Ἕλλην ὤν, adds a fact, probably like ὁ σὺν ἐμοί, known to the readers, but necessary to be borne in mind in order to appreciate the significance of the fact about to be stated. Like the preceding phrase it also is concessive

(B*MT* 437), "though he was a Greek" (and hence uncircumcised; not of course, "although a Greek and hence under pre-
eminent obligation to be circumcised," which neither Paul nor
his opponents would have claimed). Though the Greek construction is different in the two phrases, the thought is best
expressed in English by joining them as in the translation given
above. Segond also renders "qui était avec moi et qui était
Grec." The term Ἕλλην is doubtless to be taken in its broad
sense of "Gentile," as in Rom. 1¹⁶ 2⁹, ¹⁰ *et freq.*, a usage which
occurs also in Jos. *Ant.* 20. 262 (11²), and in the Christian
Fathers (Th.). This is the first mention of circumcision in the
epistle. The fact so well known to Paul and his readers as to
require no explicit mention, but clearly brought out later in
the letter, that the legalistic party insisted most strenuously
upon circumcision, is here incidentally implied. ἠναγκάσθη is
undoubtedly to be taken as a resultative aorist (B*MT* 42), and
οὐδὲ ἠναγκάσθη denies not the attempt to compel but the success of the attempt. That the attempt was (unsuccessfully)
made is clearly implied in the context.

> The argument of Sief. for his interpretation, making οὐδὲ ἠναγκάσθη
> a denial that pressure was brought to bear on Paul, *i. e.*, by the
> apostles, confuses the distinction between the meaning of the word
> and the force of its tense. ἀναγκάζω is used consistently throughout
> N. T. in the present and imperfect with conative force (Acts 26¹¹
> Gal. 2¹⁴ 6¹²), signifying "to apply pressure," "to (seek to) compel"; in
> the aorist, on the other hand, consistently with a resultative sense, in
> the active "to compel," in the passive, "to be forced" (Mt. 14²² Mk.
> 6⁴⁵ Lk. 14²³ Acts 28¹⁹ 2 Cor. 12¹¹). What, therefore, the aorist with
> οὐκ denies is simply the result. Whether that result did not ensue be-
> cause no pressure was applied, or because the pressure was successfully
> resisted, can be determined only by the connection. The fact, how-
> ever, that the imperfect with οὐκ would have clearly expressed the
> thought that no effort was made, and the clear implication in the con-
> text that effort was made are practically decisive for the present case.
> Sief.'s contention that the context excludes effort on the part of the
> apostles to have Titus circumcised is unsupported by the context, and
> involves a misapprehension of Paul's contention throughout the pas-
> sage; this is not that the apostles did not disagree with him, and always
> approved his position, but that he was independent of them; in this
> particular matter, that they yielded to him. See esp. v. ⁷ with its clear

implication of a change of front on the part of the apostles. For other
interpretations of οὐκ . . . περιτμηθῆναι, see below on the various constructions ascribed to διὰ . . . ψευδαδέλφους.

4. διὰ δὲ τοὺς παρεισάκτους ψευδαδέλφους, "now it was
because of the false brethren surreptitiously brought in."
The question what this phrase limits, *i. e.*, what it was that
was done because of the false brethren, is one of the most
difficult of all those raised by the passage. The most probable
view is that it is to be associated with the idea of pressure, ur-
gency, implied in οὐδὲ ἠναγκάσθη. The meaning may then be
expressed thus: "And not even Titus . . . was compelled to be
circumcised, and (what shows more fully the significance of the
fact) it was urged because of the false brethren." If this is
correct it follows that there were three parties to the situation
under discussion in Jerusalem. There were, first, Paul and
Barnabas, who stood for the policy of receiving Gentiles as
Christians without circumcision; on the other hand, there were
those whom Paul characterises as false brethren, and who
contended that the Gentile Christians must be circumcised; and
finally there were those who for the sake of the second party
urged that Paul should waive his scruples and consent to the
circumcision of Titus. This third party evidently consisted of
the pillar apostles, with whom Paul held private conference (v.[3])
and who because of Paul's representations finally themselves
yielded and gave assent to Paul's view (vv.[7-9]). With the
second party it does not appear that Paul came into direct
contact; they are at least mentioned only as persons for whose
sake, not by whom, certain things were done. It is thus clearly
implied that they who in person urged the circumcision of
Titus (οἱ δοκοῦντες) did not themselves regard it as necessary
except as a matter of expediency, as a concession to the feelings
or convictions of those whom Paul designates as false brethren,
but who were evidently regarded by the other apostles rather
as persons whose prejudices or convictions, however mis-
taken, it was desirable to consider. On the question whether
the apostles carried their conciliatory policy to the extent of
urging the circumcision of all Gentile converts, see fn. p. 91.

Παρείσαχτος, a word not found in extant classical writings, is nevertheless given by the ancient lexicographers, Hesych. Phot. and Suid.
Cf. Frit. Opuscula, pp. 181 ff. (Th.); Sief. ad loc., p. 101, fn. In view
of the frequent use of the passive of verbs in later Greek in a middle
sense, and of the definition of this word by Hesych. Phot. and Suid.
by the neutral term ἀλλότριος, it is doubtful whether the passive sense
can be insisted upon, as if these false brethren had been brought in by
others.   The relative clause, οἵτινες etc., distinctly makes the men
themselves active in their entrance into the church, which though by
no means excluding the thought that some within were interested in
bringing them in, throws the emphasis upon their own activity in the
matter.   Nor is the idea of surreptitiousness, secrecy, at all clearly
emphasised.   That they are alien to the body into which they have
come is what the term both etymologically and by usage suggests.
ψευδάδελφος, used elsewhere in N. T. only 2 Cor. 11²⁶, evidently means
those who profess to be brethren, i. e., to be true members of the
Christian body, but are not so in fact.   Cf. Paul's use of the term
ψευδαπόστολος, 2 Cor. 11¹³.   These words παρεισάκτους ψευδαδέλφους
express, of course, Paul's judgment concerning these men when he
wrote.   That they were so looked upon by the other apostles at the
time of the events here referred to does not necessarily follow.

The community into which "the false brethren" had made
their way is unnamed.   That they had made their influence
felt in Antioch, if not also generally among the churches having Gentile members, and that they came from Jerusalem and
were in some sense representatives of that church, is implied in
the very fact that Paul and Barnabas came up to Jerusalem
about the matter.   If, therefore, παρεισάκτους and παρεισῆλθον
refer to a visit to a church, we should mentally supply with
them "into the church at Antioch," or "into the churches
among the Gentiles."   But if, as is more probable, these words
refer to incorporation into the membership of the body, then
the reference is either to the church at Jerusalem, which is
favoured by the facts above cited as indicating that they were
actually from Jerusalem, or the Christian community in general, which is favoured by the indefiniteness of the language
here employed and the fact that the apostle's indignation is
most naturally explained if he is thinking of these men not as
additions to the Jerusalem church in particular, with which he
was not directly concerned, but as an element of discord in the

Christian community. In either case it is clear that they emanated from Jerusalem and were exerting their influence as a foreign element at Antioch or in general in the churches having Gentile members. See further, par. 12, p. 117.

Of the numerous constructions which have been adopted for the phrase διὰ . . . ψευδαδέλφους the following may be named:

1. Those which make it limit some following word. (a) εἴξαμεν. So, omitting οἷς οὐδέ (in v. ⁵; cf. textual note below), Tert. et al., and in modern times Zahn. This yields the sense, "but because of the false brethren . . . I yielded for a brief space." This may be dismissed because based on a text insufficiently supported by textual evidence, and giving the impossible sense that Paul yielded by way of the subjection demanded by the false brethren that the truth of the gospel might continue with the Gentiles.* (b) So, retaining οἷς οὐδέ, but assuming that the insertion of οἷς involves an anacoluthon, Wies. p. 110; Philippi; and substantially so Weizs. Ap. Zeit. p. 155. Cf. Butt. p. 385. Paul, it is supposed, having intended at first to make διὰ . . . ψευδαδ. limit οὐκ εἴξαμεν directly, was led by the length of the sentence to insert οἷς, thus changing the thought from an assertion that on their account he did not yield into a denial that he yielded to them, and leaving διὰ . . . ψευδαδ. without a regimen. The objection of Sief. (ad loc., p. 98) to this interpretation that these two conceptions "yielded on account of" and "yielded to" are so different that the one could not be merged in the other is of little force; for certainly Paul might naturally think of a yielding to a demand made for the sake of the false brethren as in effect a yielding to them. Nor can the fact of the anacoluthon itself be urged against this view, since anacolutha are common in Paul, and especially so in this very paragraph. The real objection to this interpretation lies in the difficulty of supposing that Paul could say that he refused to circumcise Titus because it was requested for the sake of the false brethren, or as Wies. in effect makes it, by them. Is it to be supposed that, when the very question at issue was the legitimacy of the gospel which offered itself to the Gentiles without legal requirement, he would have consented to circumcise Titus, if only the request had not been made for the sake of the false brethren? Weizs., indeed, interprets διὰ . . . ψευδαδ. as giving not the decisive reason, but for the urging of which Titus would have been circumcised, but a contributory reason, which made his course all

---

* Zahn, like Tert. before him, finds the yielding and the subjection to have been to the pillar apostles and in the fact of coming to Jerusalem to submit this question to the apostles there (not in the circumcision of Titus, which he maintains Paul denies to have taken place) yet supposes that it was not demanded by the apostles, but more probably by the Antioch church. See Com. pp. 93 f. A stranger distortion of the record it would be hard to imagine.

the more necessary—a meaning which has much to commend it, but, which it seems would have necessitated the insertion of some such word as μάλιστα (*cf.* chap. 6¹⁰).

2. Those which make διά . . . ψευδαδ. limit what precedes, introducing an epexegetic addition to the preceding statement. So Sief., who, joining this verse closely to the words ἠναγκάσθη περιτμηθῆναι and making οὐκ limit the whole phrase, finds in the sentence the meaning that no attempt was made for the sake of the false brethren to compel Titus to be circumcised. In other words, though the leading men might not unnaturally have urged the circumcision of Titus for the sake of the false brethren, no such compulsion was in fact applied. Aside from the improbable sense given to οὐδὲ . . . ἠναγκάσθη (see on v. ⁴), this involves an extremely difficult if not impossible sense of δέ, concerning which see on v. ². To have yielded this meaning διά . . . ψευδαδ. must have stood in the least prominent position in the midst of the sentence, not subjoined and emphasised by δέ, or if for the sake of making the denial of Titus's circumcision—the fact itself—unequivocal, it was necessary that the words διά . . . ψευδαδ. should stand apart, then they must have become a phrase of concession or opposition, expressing the thought, "though urged by," or "in spite of the false brethren," or have been introduced by οὐδέ, "and not even for the sake of the false brethren." *Cf.* on οὐδέ under 1¹². Mey. also joins this phrase closely to what precedes, but to the whole expression οὐδὲ . . . περιτμηθῆναι, and finds in it the reason why Titus was not circumcised, *i. e.*, because the false brethren urged it. If this relates to Paul, constituting his reason for refusing to consent to the circumcision of Titus, it is open to the same objection as 1 (b) above, viz., it implies that but for the advocacy of it by the false brethren Paul would have had no objection to the circumcision of Titus. If, on the other hand, the phrase is understood to refer to the motives of the eminent Jerusalem brethren, giving their reason for not asking for or consenting to the circumcision, then we have the representation that the false brethren urged the circumcision of Titus, and that the Jerusalem apostles opposed it not on principle, but because it was being urged by the false brethren; a view which attributes to them a degree of opposition to the legalistic party in the Jewish portion of the church, and of championship of the freedom of the Gentiles, which does not comport with the otherwise known history of the apostolic age, and which would, it would seem, have made this council itself unnecessary. Had the facts, moreover, been what this interpretation makes them, Paul could hardly have failed to bring out with greater distinctness what would have been so much to the advantage of his case, as he has done, *e. g.*, in vv. ⁷⁻⁹.

The joining of the phrase with ἀνεθέμην, or ἀνέβην, advocated by some of the older modern expositors (see in Sief.), scarcely calls for discussion. These interpretations yield a not unreasonable sense, and avoid many of the difficulties encountered by the other constructions, but it is hardly conceivable that the reader would be expected to supply mentally a word left so far behind.

3. Those which make διά . . . ψευδαδ. limit something supplied from the preceding. (a) οὐκ ἠναγκάσθη περιτμηθῆναι (Ell.) or οὐκ περιετμήθη (Frit. cited by Ltft.). This is not materially different from making it limit οὐδέ . . . περιτμηθῆναι already expressed, as is done by Mey., and is open to the same objections. (b) περιετμήθη, Rück. et al.; advocated by Hort. (WH. II app. p. 121). According to this interpretation οὐ throws its whole force on ἠναγκάσθη, only the compulsion, not the circumcision, being denied; δέ is adversative, and introduces the statement of the reason why Titus, though not compelled, was nevertheless circumcised, viz., because of the false brethren. This is perhaps the most improbable of all the proposed interpretations. If the circumcision of Titus was carried through without Paul's consent, then how could he have said that it was not compelled? If with his consent and, as he says, because of the false brethren, how could he say that he had not yielded to them for so much as an hour? What was such consent but precisely ἡ ὑποταγή, the surrender which they demanded (cf. on τῇ ὑποταγῇ, v. 5) ? And with what honesty could he have maintained that he had pursued this course at Jerusalem, "that the truth of the gospel might continue with you," when in fact he had on that occasion surrendered the very thing which was to him the key to the whole situation so far as concerned the relation of the Gentile to the law and to Christ? Cf. 5^{1-4}. In fact, any view which assumes that Titus was circumcised involves the conclusion that Paul surrendered his case under compulsion or through wavering, and that in his present argument he made a disingenuous and unsuccessful attempt to prove that he did not surrender it. (c) The thought of (unsuccessful) pressure implied in οὐδέ . . . ἠναγκάσθη. This view (set forth in the larger print above), and well advocated by Ltft. pp. 105, 106, yields a clear and consistent account of what took place, showing the Jerusalem apostles standing between the extremists on both sides, advising Paul to consent to the circumcision of Titus for the sake of peace, while Paul, seeing in such a yielding a surrender of vital principle to the false representatives of Christianity, persistently refused; it accounts at the same time for the insertion of the phrase, and for the characterisation of the men referred to as false brethren, etc., showing at the same time the extent to which the Jerusalem apostles could, from Paul's point of view, be led astray, so as even to advocate a course dictated by regard for those who were in reality only false brethren, and suggesting a contributory reason for his resistance, that the demand for the circumcision of Titus originated with spies from without, men who had no proper place in the church at all. This view alone brings this portion

of the paragraph into line with the apostle's general argument by which
he aims to show his entire independence, even of the other apostles.

If it be judged too harsh and difficult to supply from the preceding
language the thought, "this was urged," the most reasonable alternative
view is that of Wies. *et al.* (1[(b)] above). From a purely linguistic point
of view this interpretation is perhaps the easiest of all that have been
proposed, and if it could be supposed, with Weizs., that Paul would refer in this unqualified way to a reason which was, after all, only contributory, it would be the most probable interpretation of the passage.

οἵτινες παρεισῆλθον κατασκοπῆσαι τὴν ἐλευθερίαν ἡμῶν
"who sneaked in to spy out our freedom." The liberty of which
the apostle here speaks is, of course, the freedom of the Christian from bondage to the law, which would have been surrendered in principle if the Gentile Christians had been compelled to be circumcised. *Cf.* 4[8, 9, 11-31], and esp. 5[1-3, 13]. That
he calls it "our freedom" (*cf.* ὑμᾶς at the end of v. [5]) shows that
although the obligation of the Gentile to be circumcised was
the particular question at issue, this was in the apostle's mind
only a part of a larger question, which concerned both Jewish
and Gentile Christians, or else that Paul is for the moment
associating himself with the Gentile Christians as those whose
case he represents. The Antioch incident (vv. [11-21]) shows how
closely the question of the freedom of the Jews was connected
with that of the liberty of the Gentile Christians, both in fact
and in the apostle's mind. Yet there is nothing in his narrative to indicate that in the discussion at Jerusalem the freedom of the Gentile was explicitly considered in relation to anything except circumcision. Still less is it to be assumed that
the question of the obligation of the Jewish Christians in respect to foods or defilement by association with Gentile Christians was at this time brought up. Rather does the expression
"that the truth of the gospel might continue with you" suggest that at this time the only question raised pertained to the
Gentiles, and this is further confirmed by the situation which
afterwards arose at Antioch, in which the question of foods and
particularly the obligation of the Jews in respect to them appears as one on which an agreement had not been previously
reached.

Παρεισέρχομαι is a verb not uncommon in later Greek, meaning literally
"to come in alongside," but usually (not, however, in Rom. 5²⁰) implying stealth.   See exx., cited by Th.; and esp. Luc. *Asin.* 15, εἰ λύκος
παρεισέλθοι (Sief.).   κατασκοπέω, "to spy out," with the associated idea
of hostile intent, purpose to destroy (Grk. writers from Xenophon
down, Lxx, here only in N. T.) is here nearly equivalent to "stealthily
to destroy."

ἣν ἔχομεν ἐν Χριστῷ Ἰησοῦ, "which we have in Christ Jesus."
The preposition ἐν is probably used here to mark its object as
the causal ground or basis of the freedom which we possess,
the person by reason of whom and on the basis of whose work
we have this freedom.   See Th. ἐν, I 6c, and Acts 13³⁹ Rom.
3²⁴ 5⁹ and note on v. ¹⁷ below.   Others (see Ell., *e. g., h. l.* and
v. ¹⁷) take ἐν in the sense "in mystical union with," a meaning
which the word sometimes has in Paul.   But in view of the
clear instances of the causal sense both before names of Christ
and other words, it is certainly to be preferred here where the
so-called mystical sense itself becomes intelligible only by adding to it a causal sense, making it mean "by virtue of our
union with."

ἵνα ἡμᾶς καταδουλώσουσιν, "that they might bring us
into bondage," *i. e.*, to the law, implying an already possessed freedom.   Observe the active voice of the verb, excluding the sense to bring into bondage to themselves, and *cf.*
4⁹⁽ ¹⁰ 4²¹–5¹.   Undue stress must not be laid on ἡμᾶς as meaning
or including Jewish Christians (*cf.* on ἐλευθερίαν ἡμῶν above),
yet its obvious reference is to Christians in general, not to Gentile Christians exclusively.   The whole phraseology descriptive
of these "false brethren" implies, as Weizs. has well pointed
out (*Ap. Zeit.* pp. 216–222, E. T., I 257–263) that they were
distinct and different from the original constituents of the
church, a foreign element, introduced at a relatively late date,
distinguished not only from the apostles but from the primitive church in general, and this not only personally but in their
spirit and aims.   By κατασκοπῆσαι and ἵνα καταδουλώσουσιν
Paul definitely charges that these men entered the church for
a propagandist purpose, that they joined the Christian com-

munity in order to make it legalistic, and implies that previous to their coming non-legalistic views were, if not generally
held, at least tolerated. *Cf.* also on 1²⁴. As concerns the apostle's reflection upon the character of these men and the un-
worthiness of their motive, some allowance must necessarily
be made for the heat of controversy; but that fact does not
seem to affect the legitimacy of the inferences from his statement as to the state of opinion in the Jewish church and of
practice among Gentile Christians. These facts have an important bearing on the question of the relation of Paul's narrative in this chapter to that of Acts, chaps. 6, 7, 10, 11. The
recent entrance of these men into the church and the implication as to the condition of things before they came suggest that
the representation of Acts that the Jerusalem church was in
the early days of its history tolerant of non-legalistic views,
and not unwilling to look with favour on the acceptance of
Gentiles as Christians, is not in itself improbable. It is at
least not in conflict with the testimony of this letter.

On the use of a future in a pure final clause, see B*MT* 198 and *cf.*
Lk. 14¹⁰ 20¹⁰ Acts 21²⁴, 28²⁷ Rom. 3⁴.

5. οἷς οὐδὲ πρὸς ὥραν εἴξαμεν τῇ ὑποταγῇ, "to whom not for
an hour did we yield by way of the subjection (demanded)."
Though the request that Paul and those with him should yield
was made not by, but because of, the false brethren, he clearly
saw that to grant the request would be in effect to surrender
to the latter. Hence the dative here instead of διὰ οὕς, corresponding to διὰ τοὺς ψευδαδέλφους. The article before
ὑποταγῇ is restrictive, showing that the word is used not simply with qualitative force, but refers to the particular obedience which was demanded. The phrase is therefore epexegetic of εἴξαμεν, indicating wherein the yielding would have
consisted if it had taken place, and the negative denies the
yielding, not simply a certain kind of yielding. This fact excludes any interpretation which supposes that Paul meant
simply to deny that he yielded obediently, *i. e.*, to a recognised
authority, while tacitly admitting a conciliatory yielding (as is

maintained by those who hold that he really circumcised Titus).
For this thought he must have used the dative without the
article. *Cf.* Phil. 1[15-18] 1 Thes. 4[4, 5].

On πρὸς ὥραν, meaning "for a short time," see 2 Cor. 7[8] 1 Thes. 2[17]
Phm.[15], where, as in the present passage, ὥρα is not a definite measure of time, a twelfth of a day, but merely a (relatively) short time;
in the cases cited, some days or weeks; in the present passage
rather, as we should say in English, "a moment," "an instant." *Cf.*,
not as exactly similar instances, but as illustrating the flexibility of the
word, Mt. 10[19] 26[40, 45, 55].

Οἷς οὐδὲ πρὸς ὥραν. The reading at this point has been the subject of
extended discussion, especially by Klostermann, *Probleme im Apos-
teltexte*, pp. 36 *ff.*, Sief. *Com. ad loc.*, and Zahn *Com. ad loc.* and Ex-
curs. I. The principal evidence may be summarised as follows:

πρὸς ὥραν (without οἷς οὐδέ): D* d e plur. codd. lat. et gr. ap. Victorin.
codd. lat. ap. Hier. al. Iren[int.] Tert. Victorin. Ambrst. Pelag.

οὐδὲ πρὸς ὥραν: codd. gr. et lat. ap. Ambrst., quidam (codd.?) ap.
Victorin. Mcion, Syr. (psh.), and (accg. to Sief.) one ms. of Vg.

οἷς πρὸς ὥραν: Jerome quotes certain persons as asserting: *et hoc esse
quod in codicibus legatur Latinis*, "*quibus ad horam cessimus.*" Prima-
sius (XI 209, quoted by Klostermann, p. 83; *cf.* Plummer, *Com. on 2
Corinthians*, p. lv) says: *Latinus habet: "quibus ad horam cessimus."*
Sedulius: *Male in Latinis codicibus legitur: "quibus ad horam cessimus."*

οἷς οὐδὲ πρὸς ὥραν: ℵABCD[corr] FGKLP, 33, and Grk. mss. generally, f g Vg. Syr. (psh. harcl.) Boh. Arm. Aeth. codd. gr. ap. Hieron.;
also Bas. Epiph. Euthal. Thdrt. Damas. Aug. Ambr. Hier.

Klostermann and Zahn adopt the first reading. Tdf. Treg. WH. Ws.
RV. and modern interpreters generally, the fourth. The evidence
shows clearly that the difficulty of the latter reading was early felt,
and that, for whatever reason, a syntactically easier text was current
among the Latins. The evidence against οἷς οὐδέ, however, is not
sufficient to overcome the strong preponderance in its favour, or the
improbability that any one would have introduced the anacoluthic οἷς.
But since the reading οἷς without οὐδέ is very weakly attested it remains to accept the reading which has both οἷς and οὐδέ.

ἵνα ἡ ἀλήθεια τοῦ εὐαγγελίου διαμείνῃ πρὸς ὑμᾶς. "that
the truth of the gospel might continue with you." The clause
states the purpose of his refusing to yield. To make it a statement of the purpose of the yielding as Zahn does, omitting *οἷς
οὐδέ* is, especially in view of the *τῇ* before *ὑποταγῇ*, to represent
Paul as making the absurd statement that, in order that the

truth of the gospel that men are free from law might abide
with the Gentiles, he yielded to the demand of the legalists and
did as they required. It is also to convert a paragraph which
is put forth as an evidence that he had always maintained his
independence of men into a weak apology for having conceded
the authority of the Twelve. The term εὐαγγέλιον evidently
has here the same sense as in v.² and in 1⁷ (cf. the notes on
those vv., and note word ἀλήθεια here). The genitive is a
possessive genitive, the truth is the truth contained in, and so
belonging to, the gospel. Cf. ἡ τῶν νόμων ἀλήθει[α], Papyri in
Brit. Mus. II p. 280, cited by M. and M. Voc. The effect of
the triumph of the view of Paul's opponents would have been
to rob the Gentiles of the truth of the gospel, leaving them a
perverted, false gospel. See 1⁷. The verb διαμείνῃ implies
that at the time referred to the truth of the gospel, i. e., the
gospel in its true form as he preached it, not in the perverted
form preached by the judaisers, had already been given to
those to whom he refers under ὑμᾶς.

Πρός meaning properly "towards" and then "with," usually of persons in company and communication with others (1 Thes. 3⁴ 2 Thes. 2⁵
3¹⁰ Gal. 1¹⁸ 4¹⁸, ²⁰) is here used like μετά in Phil. 4⁹, of the presence of an
impersonal thing with men. The idea of possession is not in the preposition, but is suggested by the context and the nature of the thing
spoken of. ὑμᾶς may refer specifically to the Galatians, to whom he
is writing, in which case it is implied that they had already received
the gospel at the time of this Jerusalem conference. But the more
general interpretation of ὑμᾶς as meaning simply "you Gentiles" is
so easy, and the inclusion of the Galatians with the Gentiles in the
class on behalf of whom Paul then took his stand is so natural, even
though historically the Galatians only later participated in the benefit
of his action, that it would be hazardous to lay any great weight on this
word in the determination of chronological questions. The most that
can safely be said is that διαμείνῃ πρὸς ὑμᾶς receives its most obvious interpretation if the Galatians are supposed to have been already in possession of the gospel at the time here referred to. See Introduction, p. xlii.

6. ἀπὸ δὲ τῶν δοκούντων εἶναί τι "And from those who were
accounted to be something." On τῶν δοκούντων, etc., cf. v.².
The verb which this phrase was to have limited is left unexpressed, the construction being changed when the thought is

resumed after the parenthesis ὁποῖοι, etc. The apostle doubtless had in mind when he began the sentence παρέλαβον οὐδέν
(cf. 1¹²) or some equivalent expression. The sentence seems
not adversative, but continuative; to the statement that when
the pillar apostles took up, in a sense, the cause of the false
brethren, he did not for a moment yield to the latter, he adds
as further evidence of his entire independence of the apostles
that (in this discussion) they taught him nothing new.

—ὁποῖοί ποτε ἦσαν οὐδέν μοι διαφέρει— "what they once were
matters not to me." ὁποῖοι, a qualitative word, meaning "of
what kind" (cf. 1 Thes. 1⁹ 1 Cor. 3¹³ Jas. 1²⁴), here evidently
refers not to personal character but to rank or standing, and
doubtless specifically to that standing which the three here
referred to had by reason of their personal relation to Jesus
while he was in the flesh, in the case of James as his brother, in
the case of Peter and John as his personal followers. This fact
of their past history was undoubtedly appealed to by the opponents of Paul as giving them standing and authority wholly
superior to any that he could claim. Cf. 2 Cor. 5¹⁶ 10⁷. Paul
answers here substantially as afterwards to the Corinthians in
reply to much the same argument, that facts of this sort do
not concern him, have no significance. Apostleship rests on a
present relation to the heavenly Christ, a spiritual experience,
open to him equally with them. The whole parenthetical sentence, though introduced without a conjunction, serves as a
justification of the depreciation of the apostles which he had
begun to express in the preceding clause—or perhaps more
exactly as an answer in advance to the thought which the apostle foresaw would be raised by that statement when completed,
viz.: But if you received nothing from them, that is certainly
to your disadvantage; were they not personal companions of
Jesus, the original and authoritative bearers of the gospel?
What valid commission or message can you have except as you
derived it from them?

With a verb of past time ποτέ (enclitic) may mean (a) "ever," "at
any time"; (b) "at some time," "once," "formerly"; (c) "ever," with
intensive force, like the Latin cunque, and the English "ever" in "who-

ever," "whatever." The last meaning is that which is preferred in RV.—"whatsoever they were." But this use is unusual in classical Greek, and has no example in N. T. The second meaning, on the other hand, is frequent in N. T., especially in Paul (chap. 1¹³, ²³ Rom. 7⁹, etc.), and is appropriate in this connection, directing the thought to a particular (undefined but easily understood) period of past time referred to by ἦσαν. There can therefore be no doubt that it is the meaning here intended. The first meaning is not impossible, but less appropriate because suggesting various possible past periods or points of time, instead of the one, Jesus' lifetime, which gives point to the sentence.

The above interpretation of ποτε and substantially of the sentence is adopted by Wies. Hilg. Ltft. and many others from the Latin Vg. down. Win. and Lip., though taking ποτε in the sense of *cunque*, by referring ἦσαν to the time of Jesus' life on earth reach substantially the same interpretation of the clause. Ell. Sief., *et al.*, take ποτε in the sense of *cunque*, and understand the clause to refer to the esteem in which these men were held at the time of the events spoken of; whatsoever they were, *i. e.*, whatever prestige, standing, they had in Jerusalem at this time. Sief. supplies as subject for διαφέρει the thought "to obtain authorisation from them"; making the sentence mean: "whatever their standing in Jerusalem, it is of no consequence to me to secure their authorisation or commission." But the clause ὁποῖοί ποτε ἦσαν (*cf.* 1 Cor. 3¹³) itself is a suitable subject, and the supplying of a subject unnecessary.

—πρόσωπον θεὸς ἀνθρώπου οὐ λαμβάνει—"God accepts not the person of man." To accept the person—literally face—of one is to base one's judgment and action on external and irrelevant considerations. *Cf.* Mt. 22¹⁶ Mk. 12¹⁴ Lk. 20²¹. Such, in the judgment of Paul, were mere natural kinship with Jesus, such as James had, or personal companionship with him during his earthly life, such as the Twelve had. *Cf.* 2 Cor. 5¹², where Paul uses ἐν προσώπῳ with reference to the realm of external things. This second parenthesis in its turn gives a reason justifying the statement of the first. The former advantages of these men signify nothing to me, for God takes no account of such external considerations. Concerning the emphasis on θεός see the textual note.

As between θεός and ὁ θεός external evidence alone is indecisive. ℵAP 33, 88, 103, 122,* 442, 463, 1912, Chrys. al. insert the article.

BCDFGKL al. plcr. Eus. Thdrt. Dam. omit it. Sheer accident would be as likely to operate on one side as on the other. At first sight intrinsic probability seems to make for the genuineness of the article, since the N. T. writers, and Paul in particular, rarely use θεός as subject without the article. Yet the use of θεός without the article, because employed with qualitative force with emphasis upon the divine attributes, especially in contrast with man, is an established usage of which there are numerous examples in Paul (see 1 Thes. 1⁹ 2⁴ 1 Cor. 2⁵ 3⁹⋅¹⁶) and a few in the nominative (1 Thes. 2⁵ Gal. 6⁷ 2 Cor. 5¹⁹). Inasmuch, therefore, as there is in this passage just such a contrast, it would be in accordance with Pauline usage to omit the article, and the balance of intrinsic probability is apparently on this side. Transcriptional probability is also in its favour, since the scribe would be more likely to convert the unusual θεός into ὁ θεός than the reverse.

ἐμοὶ γὰρ οἱ δοκοῦντες οὐδὲν προσανέθεντο, "for to me the men of eminence taught nothing new." In these words the apostle evidently says what he began to say in ἀπὸ δὲ τῶν δοκούντων, giving it now the specific form that the Jerusalem apostles imposed on him no burden (of doctrine or practice), or imparted nothing to him in addition to what he already knew. See discussion of προσανέθεντο below. γάρ may be justificatory, introducing a statement which justifies the seemingly harsh language of the two preceding statements, or explicative, the thought overleaping the parenthetical statements just preceding, and the new clause introduced by γάρ putting in a different form the thought already partly expressed in ἀπὸ δὲ τῶν δοκούντων. The latter is simpler and for that reason more probable.

The uses of the verb προσανατίθεμαι (Mid.) clearly attested outside of the present passage are three: (1) "To offer or dedicate beside": Boeckh. C. I. G. 2782. (2) "To confer with": Gal. 1¹⁶ (q. v.); Diod. Sic. 17. 116⁴; Luc. Jup. Trag. 1. (3) "To lay upon one's self in addition, to undertake besides": Xen. Mem. 2.1⁸. Beside these there have been proposed for the present passage: (4) "To lay upon in addition." i. e. (3) taken actively instead of with a middle sense. Cf. Pollux, I 9⁹⁹. (5) (equiv. to προστίθημι) "To add," "to bestow something not possessed before": Chrys., et al.; (6) (adding to the sense of ἀνατίθεμαι in 2² and Acts 25¹⁴, that of πρός in composition, "besides," "in addition"), "To set forth in addition," i. e., in this connection, "to teach in addition to what I had already learned." The word "impart" in RV. might per-

haps represent either (4), (5), (6), possibly even (2). The first meaning is evidently impossible here. The second can be applied only by
taking οὐδέν as an accusative of respect, "in respect to nothing did
they confer with me," and then there still remains the fact that in the
other instances of the verb used in this sense the conference is chiefly
for the sake of learning, but here the reference must be to conferring
for the purpose of teaching. This renders it very difficult, taking the
word in the sense illustrated in 1¹⁶, to find in οὐδὲν προσανατίθεσθαι,
as Ltft. does, the sense "to impart no fresh knowledge," or as Ell.
does, taking πρός as directive only, the meaning "to communicate
nothing," "to address no communications." Zahn, indeed, takes the
verb as in 1¹⁶, and interprets the sentence as meaning, "for they laid
nothing before me for decision, they did not make me their judge."
This Zahn interprets as an explanation and justification of οὐδέν μοι
διαφέρει, in that it gives a reason why he did not regard their high
standing as he might have been tempted to do if he had been acting
as judge of their affairs. Vv.⁷ᶠᶠ· then state that, on the contrary, they
acted as his judges and pronounced favourable judgment on him. The
interpretation is lexicographically possible, but logically difficult to the
point of impossibility. It compels the supposition either that in ἐμοὶ
γὰρ οἱ, etc. Paul said the opposite of what he set out to say in ἀπὸ δὲ
τῶν δοκούντων, or else that, having begun in the latter phrase to say
that from the men of esteem he received a favourable judgment, he
interrupted himself to belittle the value of their judgment. It makes
the apostle, moreover, admit a dependence upon the pillar apostles
which it is the whole purpose of 1¹¹⁻2²¹ to disprove. The third sense is
rendered impossible for the present passage by the presence of ἐμοί.
"To lay no additional burden on themselves for me" is without meaning in this connection. The fourth meaning does not occur elsewhere,
the voucher being only for the reflexive sense (3), "to lay a burden upon
one's self." Sief. infers from the fact that ἀνατίθεμαι is found in the
active sense (Xen. Cyr. 8.5⁴), as well as in the reflexive that the compound προσανατίθεμαι may also occur in the active sense. The fifth
sense, though adopted by many interpreters, ancient and modern,
seems least defensible, being neither attested by any clear instance
(unless Chrysostom's adoption of it constitutes such an instance) nor
based on attested use of ἀνατίθημι. The sixth meaning is easily derived from ἀνατίθημι; the absence of any actual occurrence of it elsewhere renders it, like the fourth, conjectural, but not impossible, in
view of the difficulty of all the well-attested senses. Our choice of
interpretations must lie between the fourth, advocated by Sief. (who
also cites for it Bretschn. Rück. Lechl. Pfleid. Zeller, Lip.), and the
sixth. Both satisfy the requirements of the context—for the apostle
is evidently here, as throughout the paragraph, presenting the evidence
of his independence of the Jerusalem apostles. But the sixth is, on

the whole, slightly to be preferred: it is more consonant with the thought of ἀπὸ δὲ τῶν δοκούντων, in which the apostle apparently began to say what he here expresses in a different syntactical form, and with the words πρόσωπον . . . λαμβάνει, which seem to have been written, as pointed out above, in anticipation of these words.

7. ἀλλὰ τοὐναντίον ἰδόντες ὅτι πεπίστευμαι τὸ εὐαγγέλιον τῆς ἀκροβυστίας καθὼς Πέτρος τῆς περιτομῆς, "but on the contrary when they saw that I had been entrusted with the gospel to the uncircumcised as Peter with the gospel to the circumcised." ἀλλὰ (Germ. "sondern") introduces the positive side of the fact which is negatively stated in ἐμοὶ γάρ, etc. The participle ἰδόντες, giving the reason for the fact about to be stated, δεξιὰς ἔδωκαν, v.⁹, implies that what they had learned led them to take this step, and so that they had in some sense changed their minds. There is an obvious relation between the words of this v. and v.². But whether the decision of the Jerusalem apostles to recognise Paul's right of leadership in the Gentile field was based on his statement of the content of his gospel (v.²), or on his story of how he received it (1¹⁵), or on the recital of its results, or in part on the spirit which he himself manifested, or on all these combined, is not here stated. The last supposition is perhaps the most probable.*

That Paul regarded the distinction between the gospel of the uncircumcision entrusted to him and that of the circumcision entrusted to Peter as fundamentally not one of content but of the persons to whom it was addressed is plain from that which this verse implies and the next verse distinctly affirms, that the same God commissioned both Paul and Peter each for his own work. It is implied, moreover, that this essential identity of

* Nor is it wholly clear precisely to what extent they had changed their minds. If the interpretation of v. ⁴ advocated at that point is correct, they had urged the circumcision of Titus on grounds of expediency rather than of principle. They can not therefore have stood for the circumcision of Gentile Christians in general as a matter of intrinsic necessity. But whether in asking for the circumcision of Titus for the sake of the legalists, they had also asked that for like reasons Paul should circumcise all his Gentile converts, does not clearly appear. Consistency would have required that they should do so, since the circumcision of Titus could have had little significance if it were not to be regarded as a precedent. But it is not certain that they were as intent upon logical consistency as upon securing a peaceful settlement of the matter.

both messages was recognised by the Jerusalem apostles as well
as by Paul; for it was their recognition of the divine source of
Paul's apostleship, which of course they claimed for their own,
that, Paul says, led them to give to him and to Barnabas hands
of fellowship. At the same time it is evident that Paul, contending for the right to preach this one gospel to the Gentiles
without demanding that they should accept circumcision, and
so to make it in content also a gospel of uncircumcision, expected that Peter also would preach it to the circumcised Jews
without demanding that they should abandon circumcision.
Thus even in content there was an important and far-reaching
difference between the gospel that Paul preached and that
which Peter preached, the difference, in fact, between a legalistic
and a non-legalistic gospel. But even this difference, it is important to note, sprang from a fundamental identity of principle, viz., that the one message of salvation is to be offered
to men, as they are, whether circumcised or uncircumcised.
Whether this principle was clearly recognised by the Jerusalem
apostles is not certain, but that it was for Paul not only im-
plicit but explicit seems clear from chap. 5^6 1 Cor. $7^{17\text{-}24}$. Thus
for him at least the one gospel itself involved the principle of
adaptation to men's opinions and convictions, and consequent
mutual tolerance. And for such tolerance he contended as
essential. For differences of opinion and practice in the Christian community there must be room, but not for intolerance of
such differences. That in other things as well as in circumcision
there might be a difference of practice on the part of those who
received the one gospel in accordance with the circumstances
of those addressed and the convictions of those who preached,
is logically involved in the decision respecting circumcision, and
is clearly implied in the terms of v. ^{9} (*q. v.*). But there is nothing in the present passage ($2^{1\text{-}10}$) to indicate that other matters
were explicitly discussed at this time or that the applicability
of the principle to other questions, such, *e. g.*, as clean and unclean foods, the Sabbath, and fasting, was explicitly recognised.

The genitives τῆς ἀκροβυστίας and τῆς περιτομῆς can not be more
accurately described than as genitives of connection, being practically

equivalent to τοῖς ἐν ἀκροβυστίᾳ (in uncircumcision) and τοῖς περιτε-
τμημένοις. *Cf.* vv. ⁸, ⁹ and 1 Cor. 7¹⁸ Rom. 4⁹. Both nouns are used by
metonymy, ἀκροβυστία by double metonymy, the word signifying, first,
"*membrum virile*," then "uncircumcision," then "uncircumcised person";
on the form of the word, see Th. and M. and M. *Voc. s. v.* The word
εὐαγγέλιον, referring primarily, no doubt, to the content of the message
(*cf.* on 1⁷, ¹¹ 2² and detached note on εὐαγγέλιον, p. 422), by the addition
of the genitives denoting to whom the message is to be presented
acquires a secondary reference to the work of presenting it.

For the construction of εὐαγγέλιον with πεπίστευμαι, see W. XXXII 5
(WM. p. 287), Butt., p. 190, and Rom. 3² 1 Cor. 9¹⁷ 1 Tim. 1¹¹. The
perfect tense has here—and appropriately—its regular force, denoting
a past fact and its existing result. B*MT* 74. Its translation by the
pluperfect is necessitated by the fact that it stands in indirect discourse
after a past tense. B*MT* 353.

That in this verse and the following Paul speaks only of himself (as
also in vv.⁵, ⁶) and Peter, omitting mention of Barnabas on the one
side and of James and John on the other, doubtless reflects the fact
that Paul was recognised as the leader of the work among the Gentiles,
and Peter as the leader, not indeed of the Jewish Christian church, but
of the missionary work of the Jerusalem party. When in v.⁹ the reference is again to the conference, Barnabas is again named, though after
Paul, and James is named first among the three Jerusalem apostles.

8. ὁ γὰρ ἐνεργήσας Πέτρῳ εἰς ἀποστολὴν τῆς περιτομῆς ἐνήργησεν καὶ ἐμοὶ εἰς τὰ ἔθνη, "for he who wrought for
Peter unto an apostleship to the circumcised wrought also
for me unto an apostleship to the Gentiles." This parenthetical v. is confirmatory of the implied assertion of v. ⁷, being
intended either as a statement of the reasoning by which the
pillar apostles reached their conviction there stated, or more
probably of Paul's own thought by which he supports and confirms their conclusion. Conceding without reserve Peter's
apostleship and its divine source, Paul justifies their recognition
of his own claim to apostleship by appeal to his own equal and
like experience of God.

Whether the appeal is to the inner experience of each by which they
were endowed for their work, or to the known results, in the way of
converts, etc., of his work and Peter's, depends upon the precise
sense in which Paul used the words ἐνεργήσας and ἐνήργησεν. The usage
of ἐνεργέω in 1 Cor. 12⁶, ¹¹, where it refers to the work of the Spirit of

God in men, fitting and endowing each for his own work, suggests the first view. But Phil. 2¹³, where in the second instance ἐνεργεῖν means specifically " to effect, to produce results,",shows that Paul might easily use the word here with reference to the divine activity in accomplishing results through himself and Peter, perhaps preferring it to κατεργάζομαι (see Rom. 15¹⁸) because it is intransitive and because it more distinctly suggests the divine energy by which the results were accomplished. The argument on this view would be similar to that of 1 Cor. 9¹, but also wholly appropriate to the present connection, and more forcible than a reference to the inner experience of Peter and himself, which would be known only to each of them respectively.

In ὁ γὰρ ἐνεργήσας, as in some other passages, Paul refers to God by a descriptive epithet without the insertion of the word θεός. See 1⁶, ¹⁵ and notes; Col. 3¹⁰. To understand ὁ ἐνεργήσας of Christ rather than God, would not be consistent with Paul's usual method of expression concerning the apostleship. Save where as in Gal. 1¹ the two ideas coalesce in the representation of God and Christ as immediate source, it is his habit to speak of God as its source and Christ as the agent or mediator of it (Rom. 1⁵ 15¹⁵ 1 Cor. 15¹⁰ Eph. 3², ⁷ Gal. 1¹⁵; cf. also on his use of the verb ἐνεργέω 1 Cor. 12⁶ Phil. 2¹³).

The dative Πέτρῳ is a dative of advantage, not governed by ἐν in composition, ἐνεργήσας not being a verb compounded with ἐν, but derived from ἐνεργής or ἐνεργός = ἐν ἔργῳ, "effective," and meaning "to be operative, to work."

'Αποστολή, here as always in N. T. (see Acts 1²⁵ Rom. 1⁵ 1 Cor. 9²; it is otherwise in classical Greek and the Lxx) refers specifically to the office and work of an apostle of Christ; see on 1¹. The omission of the article gives the word qualitative force. The preposition εἰς expresses not mere reference but purpose or result, "for or unto the creation of," i. e., "so as to make him an apostle."

Τῆς περιτομῆς is here, as in v. ⁷, by metonymy for "the circumcised." εἰς τὰ ἔθνη is manifestly a condensed expression equivalent to εἰς ἀποστολὴν τῶν εθνῶν, or the like, used for brevity's sake or through negligence. That ἀποστολήν is omitted because of an unwillingness on Paul's part to claim apostleship for himself is excluded alike by the whole thought of the sentence and by 1¹.

9. καὶ γνόντες τὴν χάριν τὴν δοθεῖσάν μοι, 'Ιάκωβος καὶ Κηφᾶς καὶ 'Ιωάνης, οἱ δοκοῦντες στύλοι εἶναι, δεξιὰς ἔδωκαν ἐμοὶ καὶ Βαρνάβᾳ κοινωνίας, "and when, I say, they perceived the grace that had been given to me, James and Cephas and John, who were accounted to be pillars, gave to me and to Barnabas right hands of fellowship." These words resume the thought of v. [7], virtually repeating ἰδόντες ὅτι πεπίστευμαι, etc., and completing what was there begun. It is an overrefinement to attempt to discover a marked difference between ἰδόντες and γνόντες. The "grace that was given to me" is manifestly the grace of God or Christ (on the word χάρις, see 1[3] and detached note p. 423), including especially the entrusting to him of the gospel to the uncircumcised (v.[7]), but not necessarily excluding that manifested in the results which he had been able to accomplish. Cf. Rom. 1[5], δι᾿ οὗ [sc. Ἰησοῦ Χριστοῦ] ἐλάβομεν χάριν καὶ ἀποστολὴν εἰς ὑπακοὴν πίστεως ἐν πᾶσιν τοῖς ἔθνεσιν. See also 1 Cor. 3[10] 15[10] Eph. 3[2, 7, 8] 4[7]. On the question how the other apostles came to recognise that God had given him this grace, cf. on v.[7]. The giving of right hands is in token of a mutual compact, while κοινωνίας defines that compact as one of partnership. See more fully below in fine print.

The placing of the name of James first is probably the reflection of a certain prominence of James in the action here spoken of and of his influence in the decision, even above that of Peter. Thus while Peter is mentioned in vv. [7, 8], as in some sense the apostle of the circumcision, i. e., as the leader in missionary work among the Jews, James was apparently the man of greatest influence in the settlement of a question of policy, involving one of doctrine in the more practical sense. Cf. on vv. [7, 8].

The substitution of Πέτρος for Κηφᾶς, and the placing of it before Ἰάκωβος (DFG d f g Vg. Syr. [psh. harcl.] Tert. Hier. al.) like the reading Πέτρον for Κηφᾶν in 1[18] (q. v.), and Πέτρος for Κηφᾶς in v.[11] and Πέτρῳ for Κηφᾷ in v.[14], is a Western corruption. In vv.[7, 8], on the other hand, Πέτρος and Πέτρῳ are undoubtedly the correct readings.

The custom of giving the hand as a pledge of friendship or agreement existed both among the Hebrews and the Greeks, though probably derived by the Hebrews from some outside source. Cf. the passages cited by Ltft., indicating its existence among the Persians (Corn. Nep. Dat. c. 10; Diod. Sic. 16. 43[3]; Justinus XI 15[13]); and showing its prevalence among the Parthians and other adjacent peoples (Jos. Ant. 18.328 (9[3])); and notice in Gen. 24[2, 9] 25[33] 31[45-49] 33[10, 11] other methods of confirming an agreement or expressing friendship. The Hebrew expression is "to give the hand," יָד נָתַן: 2 Ki. 10[15] Ezr. 10[19] Ezek. 17[18] 1 Chr. 29[24] 2 Chr. 30[8] Lam. 5[6], in the last three instances implying submission. In Greek writers χείρ, χεὶρ δεξιτερή, or χεὶρ δεξιά, or δεξιά alone, are

used with various verbs, such as λαμβάνω, ἐμβάλλω, δίδωμι, in speaking of
pledges received or given: Hom. *Il.* VI 233: χεῖράς τ' ἀλλήλων λαβέτην.
Od. I 121: χεῖρ' ἕλε δεξιτερήν. Soph. *Ph.* 813: ἔμβαλλε χειρὸς πίστιν.
Tr. 1181: ἔμβαλλε χεῖρα δεξιάν. Xen. *An.* I. 6⁶: δεξιὰν ἔλαβον καὶ ἔδωκα.
2. 5⁹, δεξιὰς δεδομένας. In a papyrus of the second century A. D. the
expression μὴ φυλάσσ[ι]ν σου τὴν δεξιάν, "not to keep your pledge"
(Grenfell, Hunt, and Hogarth, *Fayum Towns and their Papyri*, 124¹³),
indicates that δεξιά had acquired the meaning "pledge." In the Jewish
Greek writings διδόναι δεξιάν (or δεξιάς) is a token of a friendly compact. See 1 Mac. 6⁵⁸ 11⁵⁰, ⁶², ⁶⁶ 13⁵⁰ 2 Mac. 11²⁶ 12¹¹ 13²²; Jos. *Ant.*
18. 328 (9³), 20. 62 (3²). In none of these cases does the giving of the hand
indicate submission, but a pledge of friendship, in most cases from the
superior power to the inferior. Notice esp. the use of δοῦναι and λαβεῖν
in 1 Mac. 11⁶⁶ 13⁵⁰ 2 Mac. 12¹¹, ¹², but also in 2 Mac. 13²², where in the
case of a mutual compact the same person both gives and receives δεξιάν.
κοινωνίας, "fellowship, partnership," implying a friendly participation in
the same work (*cf.* Phil. 1⁵) defines that which the giving of the right
hands expressed, and to which the givers pledged themselves. It thus
excludes the idea of surrender or submission which the phrase "to give
the hand" without qualification (1 Chr. 29²⁴) might suggest, or that of
superiority which usually accompanies its use in 1 and 2 Mac. The
genitive can hardly be defined grammatically more exactly than as a
genitive of inner connection. WM. pp. 235 *ff.*

On δοκοῦντες στύλοι εἶναι, see note on οἱ δοκοῦντες, v. ². The term
"pillars" as a designation of those upon whom responsibility rests, is
found in classical, Jewish, and Christian writers. Thus in Eur. *Iph. T.*
57: στύλοι γὰρ οἴκων παῖδές εἰσιν ἄρσενες. Æsch. *Ag.* 898: στῦλον
ποδήρη, μονογενὲς τέκνον πατρί. *Cf.* exx. from Rabbinic writings in
Schöttgen, *Horae Hebraicae, ad loc.*, and for early Christian writers, see
Clem. Rom. 5², οἱ μέγιστοι καὶ δικαιότατοι στύλοι, referring to the apostles,
of whom Peter and Paul are especially named.

ἵνα ἡμεῖς εἰς τὰ ἔθνη, αὐτοὶ δὲ εἰς τὴν περιτομήν· "that
we should go (or preach the gospel) among the Gentiles, and
they among the circumcised." A verb such as ἔλθωμεν or
εὐαγγελισώμεθα is to be supplied in the first part, and a corresponding predicate for αὐτοί in the second part. On the
omission of the verb after ἵνα, see Th. ἵνα II 4 c, and *cf.* Rom.
4¹⁶ 1 Cor. 1³¹ 2 Cor. 8¹³. The clause defines the content of the
agreement implied in δεξιὰς ἔδωκαν . . . κοινωνίας. See
BMT 217 (b) and *cf.* John 9²². αὐτοί stands in antithesis to
ἡμεῖς, and is thus slightly emphatic, but not properly intensive.

See Butt. p. 107. The whole sentence of v. [9] marks the complete victory of the apostle on this memorable occasion, the
significance of which lies not in that the apostles approved him,
which of itself might signify dependence on them instead of
the independence on which he has been insisting ever since his
strong affirmation of it in $1^{11, 12}$, but in that his view prevailed
as against the opposition of the legalists and the timid compromise which the apostles themselves at first wished to follow.

Was the division of the field here described territorial or
racial? Was it understood that Paul and Barnabas were to
go to Gentile lands, and, though having it as their distinctive
aim to reach the Gentiles, preach to all whom they found, while
the other apostles took as their territory the Jewish home
lands? Or were the Gentiles in any and every land or city
assigned to Paul and Barnabas and the Jews in the same land
and city to Peter, James, and John? The use of the terms
ἔθνη and περιτομή, which designate the people rather than the
territory, seems at first sight to indicate a personal, or rather
racial, division. And no doubt it was this in a sense. The
basis on which it rested was a difference between Jews and
Gentiles as peoples, not between the lands in which they lived.
Unquestionably, too, the mission of Paul and Barnabas was
chiefly a mission to and for the Gentiles, and that of the others
to and for the Jews. Yet on the other hand it must be observed
that Paul has used not a simple dative or πρός with the accusative, but εἰς, and that, despite some apparent or even a few
real exceptions to the general rule, the distinction between these
constructions severally, whether we assume here an omitted
ἔλθωμεν, εὐαγγελισώμεθα, or κηρύσσωμεν, is with a good
degree of consistency maintained throughout N. T. The dative
after verbs such as εὐαγγ. and κηρύσ. (the rare cases after verbs
of motion need not come into account here) is a dative of indirect object denoting the persons addressed. πρός with words
denoting persons individually or collectively denotes personal
approach or address; εἰς with names of places means "into"
or "to"; with personal designations "among" (i. e., to and
among), never being used with singular personal nouns (save

in such special idioms as εἰς ἑαυτὸν ἐλθεῖν), but only with plurals or collectives. The use of the phrase εἰς τὰ ἔθνη rather than τοῖς ἔθνεσιν, therefore favours the conclusion that the division, though on a basis of preponderant nationality, was nevertheless territorial rather than racial. This conclusion is, moreover, confirmed by the fact that twice in this epistle (1¹⁶ 2²) Paul has spoken unambiguously of the Gentiles as those among (ἐν) whom he preached the gospel, and that he has nowhere in this epistle or elsewhere used the preposition εἰς after εὐαγγε-λίζομαι or κηρύσσω to express the thought "to preach to" (on 1 Thes. 2⁹, the only possible exception, see below). The whole evidence, therefore, clearly indicates that the meaning of the agreement was that Paul and Barnabas were to preach the gos-pel in Gentile lands, the other apostles in Jewish lands. On the question whether the division of territory involved a differ-ence in the content of the message, see on v. ⁷.

For instances of the dative after verbs of speaking, see 4¹³ 1 Cor. 3¹ 15¹, ² 2 Cor. 11⁷ Rom. 1¹⁵ 3¹⁹ 7¹ Acts 8⁵ 10⁴². The dative is the most frequent construction with εὐαγγελίζομαι. For πρός with the accusa-tive (occurring only Rev. 10⁷ after εὐαγγελίζομαι, never after κηρύσσω, frequently after πορεύομαι and esp. ἔρχομαι), see 1¹⁷ᶠᶠ· 1 Thes. 2¹⁸ 2 Cor. 1¹⁶, ¹⁶ Rom. 1¹⁰, ¹³ 15²², ²³, ²⁹, ³² Mt. 10⁶ Lk. 16³⁰ 18¹⁶ Jn. 14¹², ²⁸. For εἰς with personal nouns, see 1 Pet. 1²⁵ (only instance after εὐαγγ· when the noun is personal, but cf. 2 Cor. 10¹⁶) Mk. 1³⁹ 13¹⁰ Lk. 24⁴⁷ 1 Thes. 2⁹ (after κηρύσσω) Mt. 15²⁴ Lk. 11⁴⁹ Acts 22²¹ 26¹⁷ (after ἀποστέλλω and ἐξαπος-τέλλω) Jn. 9³⁹ 21²³ Acts 20²⁹ (after ἔρχομαι, ἐξέρχ· and εἰσέρχ·) Jn. 7³⁵ Acts 18⁶ (after πορεύομαι). The usage of ἐν after κηρύσσω (chap. 2² Acts 9²⁰ 2 Cor. 1¹⁹ Col. 1²³ 1 Tim. 3¹⁶), together with the use of distinctly local terms after εἰς (Mk. 1³⁹ Lk. 4⁴⁴), leaves no room for doubt that εἰς after κηρύσσω means "among" rather than "unto." On 1 Thes. 2⁹, see Bornemann ad loc. and on Mk. 13¹⁰ Lk. 24⁴⁷, see WM. p. 267. Similar reasoning based on the use of the dative after εὐαγγελίζομαι (chap. 4¹³ 1 Cor. 15¹, ² 2 Cor. 11⁷ Rom. 1¹⁵) and the employment of the phrase εὐαγγελίζομαι ἐν in this epistle (1¹⁶) and of εὐαγγ· εἰς (2 Cor. 10¹⁶; on 1 Pet. 1²⁵, see WM. p. 267) leads to a similar conclusion respecting εἰς after this verb. Concerning εἰς after verbs like πορεύομαι, etc., Jn. 7³⁵, μὴ εἰς τὴν διασπορὰν τῶν Ἑλλήνων μέλλει πορεύεσθαι καὶ διδάσκειν τοὺς Ἕλληνας, is particularly instructive since the persons to be addressed are expressly distinguished from those among (εἰς) whom Jesus is sup-posed to be going. If in Acts 18⁶ εἰς certainly verges towards the mean-

ing "unto" (denoting address rather than location), yet the total evidence leaves no room for doubt that εἰς uniformly, or all but uniformly,
retains its local sense after all the verbs here under consideration.

10. μόνον τῶν πτωχῶν ἵνα μνημονεύωμεν, "provided only
that we should remember the poor." ἐθέλησαν or some similar
verb might be supplied before this clause. See G*MT* 332,
Butt. p. 241. But it is better in the absence of a verb to make
the clause co-ordinate in construction with the preceding ἵνα
clause, ἵνα . . . περιτομήν, and dependent on the idea of
agreement implied in δεξιὰς ἔδωκαν. On this understanding
the clause is not a request added to the agreement, but a part
of the agreement itself. μόνον limits the whole clause and indicates that it contains the only qualification of the agreement
already stated in general terms. On the use of μόνον, introducing a qualification of a preceding statement or of its apparent implications, see 1²³ 5¹³, and esp. 1 Cor. 7³⁹. To the general
agreement that the field be divided between them, each group
maintaining entire independence in its own territory, there is
added as the only qualification of this independence and sep-
arateness the specification that the apostles to the Gentiles
shall continue to remember the poor, *i. e.*, manifestly the poor
among the Christians on the other side of the dividing line (*cf.*
Sief. *ad loc.*). The tense of μνημονεύωμεν, denoting continued
action (B*MT* 96), indicates either that the course of action
referred to is one which having already been begun is to be
continued, or that there is distinctly in mind a practice (not
a single instance) of it in the future. The former as the more
common implication of a present tense in the dependent moods
is somewhat more probable.

ὃ καὶ ἐσπούδασα αὐτὸ τοῦτο ποιῆσαι. "which very thing I
have also taken pains to do." On the strengthening of ὃ by
αὐτό, see Butt. p. 109. The verb σπουδάζω in N. T. signifies not simply "to be willing," nor, on the other hand, "to do
with eagerness," but "to make diligent effort" to do a thing
(1 Thes. 2¹⁷ of unsuccessful effort; everywhere else in exhortations); *cf.* Jth. 13¹⋅ ¹², "to make haste" to do a thing. Apparently, therefore, it can not refer simply to the apostle's state of

mind, but either to a previous or subsequent activity on his part. Against the supposition that the reference is to an effort in which Paul and Barnabas had jointly taken part (*cf.* Acts 11³⁰) is the singular number of ἐσπούδασα. A reference to an effort on behalf of the poor at that very time in progress is impossible in view of the meaning and tense of ἐσπούδασα, to which also its singular number adds further force. This would have required an imperfect tense, and in all probability, since Barnabas was with Paul at the time, the plural number (notice the number of μνημονεύωμεν)—ἐσπουδάζομεν ποιεῖν or ἐποιοῦμεν. There is apparently a slight hint in the present tense of μνημονεύωμεν of a previous remembrance of the poor on the part of one or both of them (it would be overpressing the plural to say both of them), in ἐσπούδασα a reference to Paul's subsequent diligence in fulfilling the stipulation then made.

Respecting the argument of the whole paragraph, it should be noticed that while the apostle's objective point is precisely not to prove that he was in agreement with the Twelve, but independent of them, yet by the facts which he advances to prove his independence he at the same time excludes the interpretation which his judaistic opponents would have been glad to put upon his conduct, viz., that he was in disagreement with the Twelve, they right and he wrong, and shows that, though they at first disagreed with him as to what was expedient to do, in the end they cordially admitted that he was right.

f. Evidence of his independence of all human authority drawn from his conduct in resisting Peter at Antioch (2¹¹⁻¹⁴).

In this passage the apostle relates one of the most significant incidents of the whole series from the point of view of his independence of the apostles. Peter, coming down to Antioch evidently with no hostile intent or critical spirit, and probably arriving in Paul's absence, is attracted by the spectacle of Jewish and Gentile Christians living together in harmony in one community, joins himself for the time to this community and, following the practice of the Jews of the church, eats with the Gentile members. Presently, however, there appeared at An-

tioch certain men who came from Jerusalem as the representatives of James. These men, doubtless contending that
Peter's conduct in eating with the Gentiles was not only not
required by the Jerusalem agreement, but was in fact contrary
to it, since it involved disregard of the law by Jewish Christians,
brought such pressure to bear upon Peter that he gradually dis-
continued his social fellowship with the Gentile Christians.
So influential was this change in Peter's practice that all the
Jewish members of the church ceased to eat with their Gentile
fellow-Christians, and as a result of this even Barnabas, who
at Jerusalem had with Paul championed the freedom of the
Gentiles, also followed Peter's example. Thus the church was
divided, socially at least, into two, and by this fact pressure
was brought upon the Gentiles to take up the observance of
the Jewish law of foods, since so only could the unity of the
church be restored. At this point Paul, perhaps returning
from an absence from Antioch, for it is difficult to suppose that
matters would have reached this pass while he was present, or
possibly delaying action so long as the question pertained to
the conduct of the Jews only, and interfering only when it
became also a question of the subjection of the Gentiles to the
Jewish law—at this point, at any rate, Paul boldly rebuked
Peter, claiming that Peter's own previous conduct showed that
he recognised that the law was not binding even upon Jewish
Christians, and that it was therefore unjustifiable and hypo-
critical for him, by refusing to eat with the Gentiles, in effect
to endeavour to bring them under the law. By this incident
a new phase of the question discussed at Jerusalem was brought
to the front, viz.: whether the Jewish Christian was also released from the obligation to keep the law, as well as the Gentile; and, by the inclusion of foods as well as circumcision
among the matters brought into controversy, the question of
the obligation of statutes in general was raised. The essentially
contradictory character of the compromise reached at Jerusalem having also in this way been brought to light, Paul, so
far from recognising the authority of Peter as the representative of the Jerusalem apostles to dictate his course of action,

resisted him openly, and following out the logic not of that to
which he had consented at Jerusalem, viz., the continuance of
legal practices by the Jewish Christians, but of that for which
he had contended, viz., the freedom of the Gentiles from obligation to conform to the statutes of the law, boldly claimed
that even Jewish Christians were not under law, and must not
obey its statutes when such obedience involved compulsion of
the Gentiles to do the same.   In no way could he more effectively have affirmed his independence as a Christian apostle
of all human authority.

[11]*And when Cephas came to Antioch I resisted him to the face,
because he stood condemned.   [12]For before certain came from
James he was eating with the Gentiles.   But when they came
he gradually drew back and separated himself, fearing the
circumcised.   [13]And there joined him in the hypocrisy the rest
of the Jews also, so that even Barnabas was carried along with
their hypocrisy.   [14]But when I saw that they were not pursuing a
straightforward course in relation to the truth of the gospel, I said
to Cephas in the presence of everybody, If thou, though a Jew,
livest after the manner of the Gentiles and not after that of the
Jews, how is it that thou dost constrain the Gentiles to live after the
Jewish manner?*

11. Ὅτε δὲ ἦλθεν Κηφᾶς εἰς Ἀντιόχειαν, κατὰ πρόσωπον
αὐτῷ ἀντέστην, ὅτι κατεγνωσμένος ἦν· "And when Cephas came
to Antioch, I resisted him to the face, because he stood condemned."   The antithesis between the right hands of fellowship (v. [9]) and Paul's resistance of Peter at Antioch suggests
the translation of δέ by "but."   But the paragraph is simply
continuative of the argument begun in [11], and extending to
and through this paragraph.   By one more event in which he
came into contact with the Jerusalem leaders he enforces his
argument that he had never admitted their authority over him,
but had acted with the consciousness of having independent
guidance for his conduct.

The Antioch here referred to is unquestionably not the Pisidian
Antioch, but the more famous Syrian city, which is regularly spoken
of simply as Antioch, without further title to designate it.   See Acts

11¹⁹ *et freq.* *Cf.* Acts. 13¹⁴. This temporal clause evidently denotes the time of the fact about to be stated, only in a general way, not as if it occurred immediately upon Peter's arrival; for the following verses show that in fact a considerable series of events must have elapsed before Paul took his stand against Peter. Concerning the time of the whole incident, see *Introd.* pp. 1 f.

The phrase κατὰ πρόσωπον conveys in itself no implication of hostility, but only of "face to face" encounter (Acts 25¹⁶ 2 Cor. 10¹). ἀντέστην reflects the fact that to Paul Peter seemed to have made the initiative aggression. For while the verb is used both of passive resistance (lit. "to stand against") and active counter opposition (*cf.* Acts 13⁸ 2 Tim. 3⁸), yet it usually or invariably implies an initiative attack in some sense from the other side. This was furnished in the present instance by the conduct of Peter, which though not necessarily so in intention was in effect an attack on the position which Paul was maintaining at Antioch.

Of the various senses in which the verb καταγινώσκω is used by classical writers, two only can be considered here: (a) "to accuse," (b) "to condemn." Of these the latter is evidently much more appropriate in a clause in which Paul gives the reason for resisting Peter. The participle is predicative, and best taken as forming with ἦν a pluperfect of existing state (B*MT* 90, 91, 430; Gal. 4³ Mt. 9³⁶ 26⁴³ Mk. 1⁶ Lk. 1⁷). It comes to practically the same thing to take κατεγνωσμένος as having the force of an adjective meaning "guilty" (Sief. cites Herodian, 5, 15¹, ἐλέγχειν ἐπειρᾶτο εἰκότως κατεγνωσμένην, Luc. *De salt.* 952; Clem. Hom. 17¹³; with which compare also, as illustrating the adjectival use of participles in N. T., Acts 8⁷ Gal. 1²² Eph. 2¹² 4⁸ Col. 1²¹; B*MT* 429). A phrase of agency denoting by whom he had been condemned is not in any case necessary, nor is it necessary definitely to supply it in thought. Probably Paul's thought is that Peter's own action condemned him. Notice the following clause introduced by γάρ. The perfect is used with similar implication in Rom. 14²³ Jn. 3¹⁸; Jos. *Bell.* 2.135 (8⁶), cited by Ltft. To supply "by the Gentile Christians in Antioch" is to add to the text what is neither suggested by the context nor appropriate to it. For since the purpose of the apostle in narrating this event is still to show his own independence of the other apostles, a condemnation of Peter's action by the Gentile Christians in Antioch is an irrelevant detail, and especially so as the reason for Paul's action in rebuking Peter.

12. πρὸ τοῦ γὰρ ἐλθεῖν τινὰς ἀπὸ Ἰακώβου μετὰ τῶν ἐθνῶν συνήσθιεν. "For before certain came from James he was eating with the Gentiles." Not this clause alone but the whole sentence (v.¹²) gives the reason why Peter stood condemned,

and so the proof (γάρ) of κατεγνωσμένος. ἐθνῶν refers, of
course, chiefly or exclusively to the Gentile Christians, as in
Rom. 15[16] 16[4], and in v.[14] below, and συνήσθιεν, without doubt,
to sharing with them in their ordinary meals, as in Lk. 15[2] Acts
11[3]. The imperfect tense implies that he did this, not on a single
occasion, but repeatedly or habitually. The significance of the
act lay in the fact that he thereby exposed himself to the lia-
bility of eating food forbidden by the O. T. law of clean and
unclean foods (Lev. chap. 11), and thus in effect declared it not
binding upon him.* The question thus brought to the front
was, it should be clearly observed, quite distinct from that one
which was the centre of discussion at Jerusalem. There it was
the obligation of the Gentile Christian to observe the law, and
particularly in the matter of circumcision; here it involves the
obligation of the Jewish Christian to keep the law, and particularly in the matter of food. By his action in eating with
Gentile Christians, whose freedom from the law had been expressly granted at Jerusalem so far as concerned circumcision,
and who had doubtless exercised a like freedom in respect to
foods, Peter went beyond anything which the action at Jerusalem directly called for, and in effect declared the Jew also,
as well as the Gentile, to be free from the law. It does not
indeed follow that he would have been prepared to apply the
principle consistently to other prescriptions of the law, and to
affirm, e. g., that the Jewish Christian need not circumcise his
children. Nevertheless, the broad question whether any statute
of the law was binding upon Gentile or Jew was now brought
out into clear light, and on this question Peter by his conduct
took a position which was of great significance.

Yet it can scarcely have been Peter's conduct that first raised
the question. The custom of Jewish Christians eating with
Gentiles he no doubt found in existence when he came to
Antioch and fell in with it because it appealed to him as right,
although contrary to his previous practice. It is wholly im-

---

*On the Jewish feeling respecting Jews eating with Gentiles, see Jubil. 22[16] Tob. 1[10, 11]
Dan. 1[8] Esth. Lxx chap. 28 Jth. 12[1ff.] 3 Mac. 3[4, 7]; Jos. Ant. 4.137 (6[8]); cited by Bous. Rel.
d. Jud.[3], p. 192; Acts 10[28] 11[3].

probable that not finding it in existence he himself suggested it, or that if he had already been in the habit of eating with Gentiles in Judea, he would have been deterred from continuing to do so in Antioch by the arrival of the messengers from James.   The Antioch practice was clearly an expression of the "freedom in Christ Jesus" which Paul advocated, but in all probability a new expression, developed since the conference at Jerusalem (vv.[1-10]).   It was probably only after that event, in which the full Christianity of the Gentile Christians was recognised even at Jerusalem, that the Jewish Christians at Antioch gained courage to break over their scruples as Jews, and eat with their Gentile brothers in the church.   Nor is there any special reason to think that Paul would have pressed the matter at the beginning.   Concerning, as it did, not the freedom of the Gentiles, but the adherence of the Jews to their own ancestral custom enforced by O. T. statute, in consistency with his principles (1 Cor. $7^{14ff.}$) and the course he pursued at Jerusalem, where he stood for the freedom of the Gentiles but assumed apparently without demurrer that the Jews would continue to observe the law, it would probably seem to him not a matter to be pressed, but left to the gradual enlightenment of the Jewish Christians themselves.   It is difficult to see, moreover, how, if the Jewish Christians in Antioch had before the conference at Jerusalem already begun to disregard the Jewish law of foods, this should not have been even more a burning question at Jerusalem than the circumcision of the Gentiles.   Certainly it would have been more difficult for the legalistic party to yield in the former than in the latter matter.   Probability, therefore, points to the time between Paul's return to Antioch and Peter's arrival there as that in which the Jewish Christians at Antioch began to eat with their Gentile brethren.

If this is correct it furnishes, moreover, a natural explanation of the visit to Antioch both of Peter and of the representatives of James.   If news of this new departure at Antioch had come to Jerusalem it might easily seem to Peter that inasmuch as it affected not simply the Gentiles, but also the Jewish Christians, it concerned him as the apostle of the latter to know what was going on. Especially would this be the case if there was any uncertainty in his mind as to whether the division of the field agreed to at Jerusalem assigned to him the Jews, or Jewish lands. See on 2⁹. Even if he had come expecting to disapprove what he found, it would be by no means uncharacteristic of him that, captivated with the picture of Christian unity which he saw, he should, instead of reproving, have himself adopted the new custom. And if in turn news of this state of affairs, including Peter's unexpected conduct, reached Jerusalem, this would furnish natural occasion for the visit of the representatives of James; for to James as well as to the more extreme legalists such conduct might seem not only to violate the Jerusalem agreement, but to create a most serious obstacle to the development of the Christian faith among the Jews.

And this in turn makes clear the important fact that the situation at Antioch was not the result of repudiation of the Jerusalem agreement by any of the parties to it, but was simply the coming to the surface of the contradictory convictions which were only imperfectly harmonised in the compromise in which the Jerusalem conference issued. A new aspect of the question which underlay the discussion at Jerusalem had now come to the front and raised a question concerning which precisely opposite decisions might easily seem to different persons to be involved in the Jerusalem decision. The brethren at Antioch might naturally seem to themselves to be only following out what was logically involved in the Jerusalem decision, when they found in the recognition of uncircumcised Gentile believers as brethren the warrant for full fellowship with them on equal terms, and, in the virtual declaration of the non-essentiality of circumcision, ground for the inference that the O. T. statutes were no longer binding, and ought not to be observed to the detriment of the unity of the Christian community. The Jerusalem brethren, on the other hand, might with equal sincerity maintain that they had never expressed or intimated the belief that the Jews could disregard the statutes of the law, and that the tacit understanding of the Jerusalem decision was that these statutes should be regarded as still in force for the Jews, whatever concessions were made in respect to the Gentiles. It was this derivation of contrary conclusions from the Jerusalem compromise and Peter's wavering between the two interpretations that created the Antioch situation.

Whether ἀπὸ Ἰακώβου limits τινάς or ἐλθεῖν it is impossible to determine with certainty. The fact that the subject of an infinitive somewhat more frequently precedes it than follows it (see Votaw, *Inf. in Bib. Gr.* p. 58; *cf.* Mt. 6⁸ Lk. 22¹⁵; *contra* Lk. 2²¹ Gal. 3²³) slightly favours explaining the position of τινάς as due to the desire to bring it into connection with ἀπὸ Ἰακώβου. Yet the rarity of any limitation of an indefinite pronoun by any phrase except a partitive one is against this construction. In either case the mention of the personal name, James, the same, of course, who is named in v.¹² and in 1¹⁹, implies that the persons spoken of were sent by him or in some sense represented him. That they did not belong to those whom in v.⁴ Paul calls "false brethren" is probable not only from the fact that Paul does not so describe them, but designates them as representing James, who was of the mediating party, but also from the fact, brought out above, that these messengers of James to Antioch probably contended not for obedience to the Jewish law by Gentile Christians, but for the keeping of the Jerusalem compact as they not unnaturally interpreted it.

ὅτε δὲ ἦλθον, ὑπέστελλεν καὶ ἀφώριζεν ἑαυτόν, φοβούμενος τοὺς ἐκ περιτομῆς. "But when they came, he gradually drew back and separated himself, fearing the circumcised." The verb ὑποστέλλω, used, especially by Polybius, of the drawing back of troops in order to place them under shelter, itself suggests a retreat from motives of caution; ἑαυτόν is the object of both verbs. The imperfect tense is very expressive, indicating that Peter took this step not at once, immediately on the arrival of the men from James, but gradually, under the pressure, as the next phrase implies, of their criticism. The force of the tense can hardly be otherwise expressed than by the word "gradually." For a possible parallel instance of the use of the tense, see Acts 18⁵. The circumcised from fear of whom Peter reversed his course of action are manifestly those Jewish Christians who came from James. That Peter should have been to such an extent under their domination illustrates both his own instability and the extent to which the legalistic party had developed and acquired influence in the Jerusalem church and Jewish Christianity generally. In view of this statement it is by no means incredible that at that later time referred to in Acts 21²⁰ such a situation as is there described should have developed. *Cf.* on 1²⁴.

Ἦλθεν (understood by Origen (1³⁸⁶) to refer to James, ἐλθόντος Ἰακώβου) though supported by אBD*FG 39, 442, and the old Latin must be either a primitive error or a Western corruption. See WH. *Introd.* p. 224, and *App.* p. 121. The reading ἦλθον is supported by ACDᵇ ᵉᵗ ᶜEHKLP, the great body of later manuscripts and the ancient versions with the exception of the old Latin.

Περιτομή is probably not used here as above, by metonymy for "the circumcised"—observe the presence of the article there and its omission here—but in its proper sense. The preposition expresses source, *i. e.*, not of existence but of standing and character (*cf.* Th. ἐκ, II 7, though the characterisation of the use is not quite broad enough), and the phrase means simply "the circumcised," "the Jews." This rather than "converts from Judaism" (Ltft.) seems to be the regular sense of this phrase, found also in Rom. 4¹² Col. 4¹¹ Acts 10⁴⁵ 11². *Cf.* the expression ὁ ἐκ πίστεως, chap. 3⁷⁺ ⁹ Rom. 3²⁶ 4¹⁶; ὁ ἐκ νόμου, Rom. 4¹⁴; see also Gal. 3¹⁰.

13. καὶ συνυπεκρίθησαν αὐτῷ καὶ οἱ λοιποὶ Ἰουδαῖοι, ὥστε καὶ Βαρνάβας συναπήχθη αὐτῶν τῇ ὑποκρίσει· "And there joined him in the hypocrisy the rest of the Jews also, so that even Barnabas was carried along with their hypocrisy." Hypocrisy, consisting essentially in the concealment of one's real character, feelings, etc., under the guise of conduct implying something different (ὑποκρίνεσθαι* is "to answer from under," *i. e.*, from under a mask as the actor did, playing a part; *cf.* Lk. 20²⁰), usually takes the form of concealing wrong feelings, character, etc., under the pretence of better ones. In the present case, however, the knowledge, judgment, and feelings which were concealed were worse only from the point of view of the Jews of whom Peter and those who joined with him were afraid. From Paul's point of view it was their better

---

* On the compound συνυποκρίνομαι, see Polyb. 3. 92⁵, 5. 49⁷; Plut. *Marius*, 14¹⁷; here only in N. T.

knowledge which they cloaked under a mask of worse, the usual type of hypocrisy which proceeds from fear. By the characterisation of this conduct as hypocrisy Paul implies that there had been no real change of conviction on the part of Peter and the rest, but only conduct which belied their real convictions. "The rest of the Jews" are manifestly the other Jewish Christians in Antioch, from which it is evident that it was not Peter only who had eaten with the Gentile Christians but the Jewish Christians generally. That even Barnabas, who shared with Paul the apostleship to the Gentiles, yielded to the pressure exerted by the brethren from Jerusalem shows again how strong was the influence exerted by the latter.

Καί (after αὐτῷ) is the reading of ℵACDFGHKLP al. pler. d g Syr. (psh. harcl.) Arm. Aeth. Victorin. Ambrst. Hier. Or. It is omitted by B f Vg. Boh. Goth. Or. (Sout.). Neither external nor internal evidence is decisive; but its omission from the small number of authorities which do not contain it, either from pure inadvertence or from a feeling that it was superfluous, seems somewhat more probable than its addition to the great body of authorities.

Τῇ ὑποκρίσει may be either a dative of accompaniment—"swept along with their hypocrisy"—dependent on the σύν in composition (cf. Eph. 5¹¹ Phil. 4¹⁴ Rom. 12¹⁶ et freq.) or perhaps, a little more probably, a dative of agent, "by their hypocrisy," "with them" being implied in σύν. On the use of the verb συναπάγω, found also in Xen. and Lxx, cf. esp. 2 Pet. 3¹⁷.

14. ἀλλ᾿ ὅτε εἶδον ὅτι οὐκ ὀρθοποδοῦσιν πρὸς τὴν ἀλήθειαν τοῦ εὐαγγελίου, "But when I saw that they were not pursuing a straightforward course in relation to the truth of the gospel." The natural implication of this sentence and indeed of the preceding narrative is that all the events thus far related, the coming of the emissaries of James, the retreat of Peter from his first position, the like action of the rest of the Jewish Christians and even of Barnabas, took place before Paul himself took a position of open opposition to Peter. Had Paul, then, been in Antioch all this time, either holding his peace while the whole Jewish element in the church took a position which he judged to be wrong, or unable, without open opposition to

Peter, to stem the tide, and reluctant to resort to this? The latter alternative is the more probable, if he was actually present. But the most probable explanation of the facts, neither directly supported nor opposed by anything in the passage itself, is that Paul was absent during the early part of Peter's stay in Antioch.

It is indeed possible to suppose that Paul's activity in the matter was due not to his arrival in Antioch but to a new perception (note the word εἶδον) of the significance of the question at issue. Possibly he himself had not, till this controversy cleared the air, seen how far the principles of the gospel that he preached must carry him in his anti-legalism, had offered no active opposition to Peter's attempt to bring the Jewish Christians under the law, and only when the movement began to spread to the Gentile Christians (see v. 14 *fin.*) saw clearly that the only position consistent with the gospel was that if the law was not binding upon the Gentile, neither could it be really so upon the Jew, and that when obedience to it by Gentile or Jew became an obstacle in the way of the gospel, then both Jew and Gentile must cease to obey its statutes. But on this hypothesis Paul himself was involved only less deeply than Peter in the latter's confusion of thought and it is therefore hardly likely that he would have spoken in the words of sharp condemnation of Peter which he employs in v. 11 and in this verse.

The verb ὀρθοποδέω, used only here (and in later eccl. writers where its use may be traced to this passage, Ltft.), means "to make a straight path" rather than "to walk erect." *Cf.* ὀρθόποδες βαίνοντες, Nicander, *Al.* 419; and Sophocles, *Greek Lexicon of Rom. and Byz. Period. Cf.* Paul's frequent use of περιπατέω, "to walk," as a figure for moral conduct, chap. 5¹⁶ Rom. 6⁴ 8⁴, etc. The present word is apparently not simply a general ethical term for doing right, but, as the context implies, denotes straightforward, unwavering, and sincere conduct in contrast with the pursuing of a‾crooked, wavering, and more or less insincere course, such as Paul has just attributed to Peter and those who followed him. The present tense describes the fact from the point of view of Paul's original perception of it—"they are not acting straightforwardly." It is not, however, a historical present (Sief.) but the present of the direct form retained in indirect discourse even after a past tense (*BMT* 341 [b]). The preposition πρός probably means "towards," "in relation to" (chap. 6¹⁰ 2 Cor. 1¹² Col. 4⁵), and the phrase πρός . . . εὐαγγ· constitutes a definitive limitation of ὀρθοποδοῦσιν, yielding the sense "pursue a straight course in relation to the truth of the gospel," "to deal honestly and consistently with it,

not juggling, or warping, or misrepresenting it." πρός may indeed
mean "in conformity with" (Lk. 12⁴⁷ 2 Cor. 5¹⁰ Eph. 3⁴; so Th. Ltft.
Ell. Sief.), and the phrase constitute an epexegesis of ὀρθοποδοῦσιν,
yielding the sense "pursuing a straightforward (righteous) course, viz.,
one in accordance with the truth of the gospel." But the fact that
Paul regularly employs κατά with περιπατέω in the sense "in conformity to" (2 Cor. 10². ³ Rom. 14¹⁵ etc.) is against this latter view,
while the former is more in accordance with the context, which refers
not so much to conformity to the truth of the gospel as to an attitude
(of straightforwardness or crookedness) towards it. The interpretation
of πρός in the sense of (motion) towards, making the truth of the gospel
the goal of their action, involves a sense possible to πρός, but out of
harmony with the context. The phrase, "the truth of the gospel," is
doubtless used here in the same sense as in v. ⁵, q. v.

εἶπον τῷ Κηφᾷ ἔμπροσθεν πάντων "I said to Cephas in
the presence of everybody." The omission of the article before
πάντων makes the statement very general, not simply before
those who have just been mentioned (τῶν πάντων) but when all
the members of the church were present. Cf. 1 Cor. 11¹⁸ 14²³,
and esp. 1 Tim. 5²⁰.

How much of what follows was actually uttered on this occasion it is impossible to say with certainty. Only the first sentence (v. ¹⁴ᵇ) contains unmistakable evidence of having been
addressed to Peter, and the absence of any direct address in the
remainder of the chapter makes it unlikely that through the
whole of it Paul is still quoting what he said to Peter. Yet on
the other hand it is improbable that he intends to limit his
report of his words on that occasion to a single sentence. He
passes imperceptibly from the report of his former words into
argument on the theme itself, and the line between the two
can not be detected.

Εἰ σὺ Ἰουδαῖος ὑπάρχων ἐθνικῶς καὶ οὐχὶ Ἰουδαϊκῶς ζῇς,
πῶς τὰ ἔθνη ἀναγκάζεις Ἰουδαΐζειν; "If thou, though a Jew,
livest after the manner of the Gentiles, and not after that of
the Jews, how is it that thou dost constrain the Gentiles to live
after the Jewish manner?" The terms ἐθνικῶς and Ἰουδαϊκῶς
manifestly refer to the living according to Gentile and Jewish
customs respectively, especially in the matter of foods. The

conditional clause evidently refers, as is often the case with a
simple present supposition, to an admitted fact. (B*MT* 244.)
It is an overpressing of the present tense to maintain that it
must refer to an act at that very time in progress, which is
plainly excluded by the preceding narrative. Grammatically
it is doubtless to be taken not as a present for an imperfect, but
as a general present, describing a habit or mental attitude which,
being illustrated by a recent act, may itself be assumed to be
still in force (*cf*. Mk. 2[7] Mt. 12[26 ff.] Acts 22[7, 8] 23[3, 4] Ps. 89[42, 43]).
The use of it implies that Peter had not really in principle abandoned the Gentile way of life, though temporarily from fear
returning to the Jewish way of living. In English we should
probably say in such a case, "If you can live," or "If your
convictions permit you to live."   Over against this recent practice Paul forcibly sets forth Peter's inconsistency in compelling
the Gentiles to follow the Jewish mode of life.   The words
ἀναγκάζεις 'Ιουδαΐζειν are of crucial importance for the understanding of Paul's position. They show what he regarded as
the significance if not the deliberate intent of Peter's conduct
in refusing longer to eat with the Gentile Christians.   Under
the circumstances this amounted not simply to maintaining the
validity of the Jewish law for Jewish Christians, but involved
the forcing of Jewish practices upon the Gentile Christians.
By his refusal any longer to eat with them and by the adoption
under his influence of the same course on the part of the Jewish members of the Antioch church, he left to the Gentiles no
choice but either to conform to the Jewish law of foods, or suffer
a line of division to be drawn through the church.   It was this
element of coercion brought to bear on the Gentile Christians
that made the matter one of direct concern to Paul.   Against
efforts to maintain the observance of the Jewish law on the part
of Jewish Christians, he would doubtless have had nothing to
say so long as they were confined to Jewish communities, concerned the Jews only, and did not affect the Gentiles.   Had
Peter, when he came to Antioch, chosen from the first to abstain
from eating with the Gentiles on the ground that his relation
to the Jewish Christians made it inexpedient, Paul would prob-

ably have made no objection. But when Peter, having first associated freely with the Gentiles, afterwards under pressure from the men that came from James, drew back, carrying all the other Jewish Christians with him, and forcing the Gentile Christians to choose between subjection to the Jewish law and the disruption of their church, this conduct involved an interference with the freedom of the Gentiles which was of most vital concern to Paul as the apostle of the Gentiles and defender of their freedom. That he interpreted the creation of such a situation as a forcing of the Gentile Christians to judaise, ignoring the possibility of escape from this by creating a division of the church, is itself of significance as showing how important to him was the maintenance of the unity of the church as against any division into Jewish and Gentile wings, and confirms the interpretation given above to μή πως . . . ἔδραμον (v.²), and of εἰς τὰ ἔθνη (v.⁹).

> To the men who came from James it might have seemed an entirely feasible course that the Gentiles should constitute a separate—from their point of view a second-rank—Christian body. Has not a similar thing sometimes happened for other reasons on a modern mission field? They might have justified their course in the matter on the ground that they were not dictating to the Gentile Christians what course they should pursue; it did not concern them which horn of the dilemma the Gentiles chose, whether they elected to observe the Jewish law, or to constitute a separate body from the Jewish believers; they were concerning themselves only with the conduct of Jewish Christians. Even Peter might have assumed somewhat the same position, maintaining that he was dealing only with the question of the obligation of the Jews in the matter of foods; for the action of the Gentiles the latter were themselves responsible. To Paul the matter did not appear thus. To a territorial division of the field he had indeed consented at Jerusalem; but the creation of a division between the Jewish and Gentile Christians in the Gentile territory was evidently to him intolerable and out of the question.

Thus in the maintenance of the freedom of the Gentiles Paul was forced to take a position respecting the validity of the law for the Jews and concerning the unity of the Christian community in Gentile cities. The former at least was decidedly in

advance of the position taken at Jerusalem, though logically
involved in it. The Jerusalem decision was essentially a compromise between contradictories, the validity of the law, and
its non-validity. The practical decision that the Jewish Christians should continue to observe the law and the Gentiles be
free from it left it undecided which of these principles should
take precedence over the other when they should come into
that conflict which was sooner or later inevitable. The visit of
Peter to Antioch and the subsequent arrival of the men from
James precipitated the conflict. The Jerusalem brethren practically took the position that the first half of the Jerusalem
agreement must be kept at any cost—the Jewish Christian
must keep the law whatever the effect in respect to the Gentile
Christians. Paul, carrying to its logical issue the principle
which underlay the position which he had taken at Jerusalem,
maintained that the Gentile Christians must not be forced to
keep the law, even if to avoid such forcing the Jews themselves
had to abandon the law. In Antioch much more clearly than
at Jerusalem the issue was made between legalism and anti-
legalism. It was incidental to the event at Antioch, but from
the point of view from which Paul introduced the matter here,
a matter of primary importance that on this occasion more
decisively than ever before he declared his independence of
Jerusalem and her apostles.

The oldest and most trustworthy mss. are divided between οὐχ
and οὐχί before Ἰουδαϊκῶς, the former being the reading of ℵ*ACP
31, 33, the latter that of ℵᶜBD* and a few cursives. Dᵇ ᵉᵗ ᶜFGK ˢⁱˡ L
and most of the cursives read οὐκ. WH., adopting οὐκ with the margin:
"οὐχ MSS." apparently judge that οὐχ is a primitive error and οὐχί
a derivative from it. But the grounds of this decision are not easy to
discover. In view of Acts 2⁷ Rom. 3²⁷, οὐχί can not be judged to be
impossible, and in view of its strong attestation is probably to be
accepted as the original reading, of which οὐχ is a corruption arising
from the accidental omission of one ι, or from the substitution of the
more familiar for the less familiar form.

Πῶς used as here in the sense of "how is it that," nearly equivalent
to "why," expressing surprise or displeasure, is of not uncommon
occurrence both in classical and biblical writers. See Hom. *Il.* IV 26;
Aesch. *Pers.* 798; Soph. *El.* 407; Mt. 22¹² Jn. 4⁹ Acts 2⁸, etc.

'Ἀναγκάζεις is undoubtedly conative, referring not to an accomplished result, but to the intention or tendency of Peter's action. BMT 11.

'Ιουδαΐζειν, "to follow the Jewish way of life"; i. e., to observe the Jewish law, occurs in the same sense in the Lxx of Esth. 8¹⁷: καὶ πολλοὶ τῶν ἐθνῶν περιετέμνοντο καὶ ἰουδάϊζον διὰ τὸν φόβον τῶν 'Ιουδαίων, in Ignat. Mag. 10³: ἄτοπόν ἐστιν 'Ιησοῦν Χριστὸν λαλεῖν καὶ ἰουδαΐζειν, and in Ev. Nic. 2; Plut. Cic. 7³. In the sense "to favour the Jews," it is found in Jos. Bell. 2. 463 (18²).

'Ιουδαῖος ὑπάρχων, standing in opposition to ἐθνικῶς ζῇς, is concessive. The view of Ltft. that ὑπάρχων has reference to the original, natural state, being nearly equivalent to φύσει ὤν, is but slenderly supported by evidence. Certainly this is not the invariable force of ὑπάρχω in N. T. Cf. chap. 1¹⁴ Acts 2³⁰ 4³⁴, etc.

The term ἐθνικῶς occurs here only in Bib. Gr.; elsewhere only in later writers; cf. ἐθνικός, Mt. 5⁴⁷ 6⁷ 18¹⁷ 3 Jn. ⁷. 'Ιουδαϊκῶς occurs here only in Bib. Gr.; elsewhere in Jos. Bell. 6. 17 (1³); cf.'Ιουδαϊκός, Tit. 1¹⁴ 2 Mac. 13²¹; Jos. Ant. 20. 258 (11¹). On the meaning of ζῇς, see note on ζάω, p. 134.

GAL. 2¹⁻¹⁴ AND ACTS, CHAPS. 10, 11, 15.

The discussion of the bearing of the historical data furnished by this chapter on the interpretation and criticism of the narrative of Acts belongs rather to the interpretation of the latter book than to the present task. It may not be amiss, however, to point out certain results of the interpretation of Galatians which are of concern to the student of the life of Paul.

1. A visit to Jerusalem between that of Gal. 1¹⁸ and that of 2¹ is rendered improbable by the constant implication of the apostle that Jerusalem was the headquarters of the Jewish church and its leaders, combined with his implied assertion that he is enumerating in succession the occasions of his contact with these leaders. See more fully on 2¹, and contra, Steinmann, Abfassungszeit des Galaterbriefes, pp. 127 ff.

2. That the visit to Jerusalem recorded in 2¹⁻¹⁰ was for the purpose of relieving the poor of Jerusalem is excluded by the aorist tense of ἐσπούδασα in 2¹⁰. Cf. on v. ³.

3. The subject for the discussion of which Paul went to Jerusalem on the occasion recorded in 2¹ was specifically the necessity of circumcising Gentiles who believed in Christ and wished to join the Christian community. Cf. on vv.²,³, pp. 69, 75

4. The defenders of the freedom of the Gentiles were Paul and Barnabas, Titus being present also as a representative of the Gentile element in the church from which Paul and Barnabas came, presumably Antioch.

5. Paul presented the matter in Jerusalem both publicly, and privately before the eminent men of the church, James and Peter and John. *Cf.* on v. ².

6. These latter at first, for the sake of certain extreme legalists who had recently come into the church, desired that Titus should be circumcised, but finally, convinced by Paul's presentation of his gospel, yielded and gave their cordial assent to the prosecution of the Gentile mission according to the convictions of Paul, reserving to themselves the work among the Jews. *Cf.* on vv. ⁴, ⁷, ⁹.

7. Of any discussion at Jerusalem of the question of the obligation of the Gentile Christians in respect to foods there is no intimation in Paul's narrative; and any decision restricting their liberty in this matter is decisively excluded by the statement that the only qualification of the entire and strict division of the field between himself and Peter, with implication that each was to follow his own conviction in his own field (since without this implied provision the question that was raised was still as much unsettled as ever), was that he and Barnabas should remember the poor of the Jewish Christian community. *Cf.* p. 99.

8. Paul's account of the subsequent incident at Antioch also excludes the possibility of fellowship between Jews and Gentiles in the church having been agreed to at Jerusalem either on the basis of the Gentiles conforming to the Jewish law of foods or of the Jews disregarding their law. It is practically certain, therefore, that the practice of Jewish and Gentile Christians eating together in disregard of the Jewish law arose at Antioch, independent of any decision at Jerusalem, and probably subsequent to the Jerusalem conference. *Cf.* on v.¹², p. 105.

9. What the previous practice of the Gentile Christians at Antioch was is nowhere explicitly stated. It is highly improbable, however, that the silence of the Jerusalem conference with reference to food was due to the Gentiles having already adopted the Jewish law of food. Having refused to be circumcised, as the case of Titus shows they had, it is not likely that they conformed to the law in respect to food. But if not, the Jerusalem legalists, since they did not press the question of food in the Jerusalem conference, were less insistent on conformity to the law in respect to this matter than in reference to circumcision, or in respect to the former matter were unable to gain from the pillar apostles the measure of support that they obtained in respect to the latter. In either case it is evident that the Jerusalem church did not in the early days insist upon the Gentile Christians practising a thoroughgoing and consistent legalism.

10. The reference of Paul to the recent incoming of the extreme legalistic element into the Jerusalem church, and the evidence of 1²⁴ (*q. v.*) also indicate that the Jerusalem church was at first disposed to be hospitable towards the acceptance of Gentiles as Christians, and that the question was not an acute one until it became so through the in-

coming of the legalistic element. When this occurred the Jerusalem apostles endeavoured to conciliate the legalists, but by conviction at first, and at length on the practical question also, sided with Paul so far as concerned the freedom of the Gentiles. *Cf.* pp. 77, 97.

11. This being the case, though Paul does not specifically mention the coming of the legalists to Antioch, such a visit is the most probable explanation of his coming to Jerusalem.

12. The presence of these men in the private conference at Jerusalem is excluded by the very assertion that it was private, but there is nothing in it either to prove or disprove their presence in the public conference.

13. The impossibility of identifying the event which Paul narrates in 2^{1-10} with the visit of Acts 11^{27-30} (*cf.* 2 above), and the many similarities between Paul's narrative in 2^{1-10} and that of Acts 15 make it necessary to suppose that these latter both refer to the same event; while the differences between the two accounts (*cf.* 7 and 8, above) compel the conclusion that the Acts narrative is inaccurate as to the result of the conference; it has perhaps introduced here an event that belongs somewhere else. From the argument of Gal. $1^{11}-2^{21}$ (*cf.* 1 above) it also follows that Acts 11^{27-30} is inaccurate.

14. From 8 and 10 it follows that before the events of Gal. 2^{1-10} the apostles at Jerusalem might have looked with favour upon the conversion of Gentiles to Christianity without the full acceptance of the Jewish statutes, and might have interpreted such an experience as that narrated of Peter in Acts, chap. 10, symbolically, as indicating that Gentiles to whom God gave his Spirit could not be rejected by them; yet that it is wholly improbable, not to say impossible, that they should also have interpreted it as indicating the abolition of the Jewish law of foods for themselves. *Cf.* Acts 11^3, and p. 105 above.

g. Continuation and expansion of Paul's address at Antioch, so stated as to be for the Galatians also an exposition of the gospel which he preached (2^{15-21}).

Having in the preceding verses, $^{11-14}$, narrated the incident of his controversy with Peter in Antioch, he passes in these to discuss the question on its merits, yet at first having still in mind the Antioch situation and mentally addressing Peter, if not quoting from what he said to him. When he leaves the Antioch situation behind, or whether he really does so at all, it is impossible to say. The argument is at first an appeal to the course which both he and Peter had followed in seeking justification in Christ, whereby they confessed the worthlessness of works of law. He then raises and answers the objection to his position that since his premises had led him and Peter to abandon and disregard the statutes of the law, they had made Christ a minister of sin, denying the premise of this objection that violation of law is sin, and affirming, on the contrary, that one becomes a transgressor by insisting upon obedience to the statutes of the law. This paradoxical statement he in turn sustains by the affirmation that he—speaking now emphatically of his own experience—through law died to law, *i. e.*, by his experience under law was forced to abandon it, in order to live to God. The legitimacy of his anti-legalistic course he still further defends by maintaining that in his death to law he became a sharer in the death of Christ, and that in his new life Christ lives in him, his own impulses and will being displaced by those of the Christ, and his life being sustained by faith upon the Son of God who loved him and gave himself for him. Finally he denies that in so doing he is making of no account the grace of God manifest in giving the law, pointing out that the premise of this objection that God intended law as the means of justification makes the death of Christ needless, a thing which no believer in Christ would affirm or admit.

15We though Jews by nature and not sinners of Gentile origin, 16yet knowing that a man is not justified by works of law, but only through faith in Christ Jesus, even we believed in Christ Jesus, that we might be justified by faith in Christ and not by works of law, because by works of law " shall no flesh be justified." 17But if through seeking to be justified in Christ, we ourselves also were found to be sinners, is Christ therefore a minister of sin? By no means. 18For if the things that I broke down, these I build up again, I show myself a transgressor. 19For I through law died to law that I might live to God. 20I have been crucified with Christ, and it is no longer I that live, but Christ that liveth in me, and the life that I now live in the flesh, I live in faith, faith which is in the Son of God, who loved me and gave himself for me. 21I do not make of no effect the grace of God; for if righteousness is through law, Christ died needlessly.

15. Ἡμεῖς φύσει Ἰουδαῖοι καὶ οὐκ ἐξ ἐθνῶν ἁμαρτωλοί, "We though Jews by nature and not sinners of Gentile origin." The clause is concessive in relation to καὶ ἡμεῖς . . . ἐπιστεύσαμεν, etc., below: though possessing by virtue of birth all the advantages of knowledge of law (cf. Rom. 3¹, ²), and hence of opportunity of obeying it and achieving righteousness through it (cf. Phil. 3⁵, ⁶), and not men born outside the law, and hence in the natural course of events possessing none of the advantages of it.

On the use of φύσει, cf. Rom. 2²⁷ 11²¹⁻²⁴. ἐξ ἐθνῶν (note the omission of the article) is qualitative in force. The phrase is one of origin, exactly antithetical in thought, though not perfectly so in form to φύσει Ἰουδαῖοι. ἁμαρτωλοί is evidently used not in its strict sense denoting persons guilty of sin, not perfectly righteous (see detached note on Ἁμαρτία p. 436), but, as often in N. T., "persons (from the point of view of the speaker or from that which he for the moment adopts) pre-eminently sinful," "sinners above others," "habitual transgressors of law." So of the publicans and other Jews, who at least from the Pharisaic point of view were guilty of specific violation of the law, Lk. 7³⁴, ³⁷ 15¹, ², etc., and of the Gentiles, like our word "heathen," Mk. 14⁴¹ Lk. 24⁷; cf. 1 Mac. 1³⁴: καὶ ἔθηκαν ἐκεῖ ἔθνος ἁμαρτωλόν, ἄνδρας παρανόμους. Tob. 13⁶: δεικνύω τὴν ἰσχὺν καὶ τὴν μεγαλωσύνην αὐτοῦ ἔθνει ἁμαρτωλῶν.

16. εἰδότες δὲ ὅτι οὐ δικαιοῦται ἄνθρωπος ἐξ ἔργων νόμου "yet knowing that a man is not justified by works of law." In antithesis to the preceding concessive phrase this is causal, giving the reason for the ἐπιστεύσαμεν of the principal clause. To be justified, δικαιοῦσθαι, is to be accounted by God acceptable to him, to be approved of God, accepted as being such as God desires man to be. In the word δικαιόω we have one of those great words of the Pauline vocabulary, a right understanding of which is of the highest importance for the interpretation of this letter and of the Pauline theology. But an adequate conception of its meaning can hardly be conveyed in a phrase; still less can the definition of it be justified in a sentence. For a fuller discussion intended to set the word in its true historic light and to present the evidence which sustains the definition thus reached, see the detached note on Δίκαιος, Δικαιοσύνη, and Δικαιόω, p. 460, in particular under VI, N. T. usage,

C. 2 (b), p. 473. ἄνθρωπος is used in its wholly indefinite
sense, as equivalent to τὶς. *Cf.* Rom. 3²⁸ 1 Cor. 4¹ 11²⁸.

We meet here for the first time in this letter the phrase ἐξ
ἔργων νόμου, which in this letter and in the epistle to the Romans
plays so important a part in the apostle's discussion of the
basis of acceptance with God.   Like δικαιόω, the phrase calls
for an extended historical investigation, for which see detached
note on Νόμος, p. 443.   νόμου is here evidently used qualitatively, and in its legalistic sense, denoting divine law viewed as
a purely legalistic system made up of statutes, on the basis of
obedience or disobedience to which men are approved or condemned as a matter of debt without grace.   This is divine law
as the legalist defined it.   In the apostle's thought it stands
for a reality only in that it constitutes a single element of the
divine law detached from all other elements and aspects of
divine revelation; by such detachment it misrepresents the will
of God and his real attitude towards men.   By ἔργα νόμου Paul
means deeds of obedience to formal statutes done in the legalistic spirit, with the expectation of thereby meriting and securing divine approval and award, such obedience, in other words,
as the legalists rendered to the law of the O. T. as expanded
and interpreted by them.   Though νόμος in this sense had no
existence as representing the basis of justification in the divine
government, yet ἔργα νόμου had a very real existence in the
thought and practice of men who conceived of the divine law
after this fashion.   The preposition ἐξ properly denotes source,
in this case the source of justification.   Since, however, justification is an act of God, while ἔργα νόμου are deeds of men, the
preposition in effect marks its object as a conditioning cause,
whose inadequacy for the justification of men the apostle says
he and Peter already knew.   The translation of this phrase
here and constantly in RV. by "the works of the law," retained
also in ARV., and in general the ignoring of the qualitative
use of νόμος and other like terms, is a serious defect of these
translations.   *Cf.* Slaten, *Qualitative Nouns in the Pauline
Epistles*, pp. 39 *f.*

ἐὰν μὴ διὰ πίστεως Χριστοῦ Ἰησοῦ, "but only through faith

in Christ Jesus." ἐὰν μή is properly exceptive, not adversative (*cf.* on 1¹⁹), but it may introduce an exception to the preceding statement taken as a whole or to the principal part of it—in this case to οὐ δικαιοῦται ἄνθρωπος ἐξ ἔργων νόμου or to οὐ δικαιοῦται ἄνθρωπος alone. The latter alternative is clearly to be chosen here, since the former would yield the thought that a man can be justified by works of law if this be accompanied by faith, a thought never expressed by the apostle and wholly at variance with his doctrine as unambiguously expressed in several passages. See, *e. g.*, the latter part of this verse and 3¹⁰⁻¹⁴, where faith and works of law are set in sharp antithesis with one another. But since the word "except" in English is always understood to introduce an exception to the whole of what precedes, it is necessary to resort to the paraphrastic translation "but only."

In πίστις, as in δικαιόω and νόμος, we have a word of central importance in the vocabulary of Paul. It signifies an acceptance of that which accredits itself as true, and a corresponding trust in a person which dominates the life and conduct. Its personal object is God, or especially Christ as the revelation of God. For fuller discussion, see detached note on Πίστις and Πιστεύω, p. 475, esp. V B. II 2 (e), p. 482. The following clause by its relation to the present clause evidently defines both the specific nature of the faith here referred to and the relation of Christ Jesus to it. Χριστοῦ Ἰησοῦ is therefore to be taken as an objective genitive, expressing substantially the same relation to πίστις which is expressed after the verb by εἰς Χριστὸν Ἰησοῦν.

On the view of Haussleiter, *Der Glaube Jesu Christi u. der christliche Glaube*, Leipzig, 1891, that the genitive in such cases is subjective, the phrase denoting the faith which Christ exercised, see the brief note in S. and H. on Rom. 3²². The evidence that πίστις like ἐλπίς and ἀγάπη may take an objective genitive is too clear to be questioned (*cf.* Mk. 11²² Acts 3¹⁶ Col. 2¹² 2 Thes. 2¹³). This once established, the context in the present case (see esp. the phrase εἰς Χριστὸν Ἰησοῦν ἐπιστεύσαμεν) is decisive for its acceptance here; and the meaning here in turn practically decides the meaning of the phrase throughout this epistle. See 2²⁰ 3²².

The preposition διά, properly denoting channel and then means, here marks its object as the means through which one secures justification, and so, in effect, the conditioning cause, that in man by virtue of which he is justified by God. To draw any sharp distinction between διά as here used and ἐκ in ἐξ ἔργων νόμου above or in ἐκ πίστεως below is unjustifiable refinement, not legitimate exegesis.

After διὰ πίστεως ℵCDFGKLP al. pler. It. Vg. al. read Ἰησοῦ Χριστοῦ. Χριστοῦ Ἰησοῦ, on the other hand, is the reading of AB 33, some mss. of Vg. Victorin. Aug. An examination of all the occurrences of the title Χριστός, Ἰησοῦς Χριστός, or Χριστὸς Ἰησοῦς in this epistle indicates a preference of the scribes for the form Χρ. or Χρ. Ἰησ. after ἐν, but elsewhere for Ἰησ. Χρ. rather than Χρ. Ἰησ.; thus in $1^{1, 12}$ $3^{1, 22}$ $6^{14, 18}$ Ἰησ. Χρ. occurs (not after ἐν) without variant or with unimportant variation. In 1^{22} $2^{4, 17}$ $3^{26, 28}$ 5^{6} ἐν Χριστῷ or ἐν Χριστῷ Ἰησοῦ occurs without important variation. Cf. also 6^{15}, where ἐν Χριστῷ Ἰησοῦ is doubtless an addition to the original text, but attested by a large number of authorities without variation in the form of the name. In 3^{22}, where the correct text is undoubtedly Ἰησοῦ Χριστοῦ, L reads ἐν Χριστῷ Ἰησοῦ. On the other hand, there are exceptions: in the present passage, 2^{16a}, after διὰ πίστεως there is, as shown above, good authority for both Χριστοῦ Ἰησοῦ and Ἰησοῦ Χριστοῦ; in 2^{16b}, after εἰς most authorities read Ἰησοῦν Χριστόν, but B 322, 429, Syr. (psh. harcl.) Boh. Aeth., etc., read Χριστὸν Ἰησοῦν, which Tdf. adopts and WH. prefer; in 5^{24} τοῦ χριστοῦ Ἰησοῦ is doubtless the original reading, but many authorities omit Ἰησοῦ; in 3^{14} authorities are divided between ἐν Χριστῷ Ἰησοῦ and ἐν Ἰησοῦ Χριστῷ. Only in 4^{14} has Χρ. Ιη. not after ἐν been allowed to stand without variation; in 6^{12} only B 31 are cited for Χριστοῦ Ἰησοῦ, all others reading τοῦ Χριστοῦ. The evidence of the other Pauline epistles points in the same direction. ἐν Χριστῷ and ἐν Χριστῷ Ἰησοῦ occur often, with frequent variations in the mss. between the two forms, but in no Greek ms. of these epistles has the form ἐν Ἰησοῦ Χριστῷ been noted. In 2 Thes. 1^{1} occurs the form ἐν . . . κυρίῳ Ἰησοῦ Χριστῷ. Some authorities omit κυρίῳ and transpose to Χριστῷ Ἰησοῦ. In Phil. 3^{14} to ἐν Χριστῷ Ἰησοῦ some Western authorities add κυρίῳ after ἐν and then transpose to Ἰησοῦ Χριστῷ. See also Rom. 14^{14} Phil. 2^{19} where numerous authorities convert ἐν κυρίῳ Ἰησοῦ, into ἐν Χριστῷ Ἰησοῦ. In other words, while this evidence shows that it was the apostle's usual habit to write Χριστῷ or Χριστῷ Ἰησοῦ after ἐν and to prefer the form Ἰησ. Χρ. rather than Χρ. Ἰησ. in other positions, yet it also shows (a) that he allowed himself a certain liberty in the matter, and (b) that the tendency of the scribes was (as was natural) to conform his text to his usual habit. The evidence therefore tends to confirm the general estimate of the testimony of AB and points to the conclusion that in such cases as the present passage ($2^{16a\, and\, b}$) 3^{14} (q. v.) 5^{24}, it is the apostle

who has departed from his usual habit; most of the scribes have conformed the text to it.

καὶ ἡμεῖς εἰς Χριστὸν Ἰησοῦν ἐπιστεύσαμεν, ἵνα δικαιωθῶμεν
ἐκ πίστεως Χριστοῦ καὶ οὐκ ἐξ ἔργων νόμου, "even we believed in Christ Jesus, that we might be justified by faith in
Christ and not by works of law." On the significance of the
individual words, the qualitative force of the anarthrous nouns
and the force of the genitive after πίστεως, see comment on
the former part of the verse. καί, throwing its emphasis on
ἡμεῖς, itself emphatic by the very fact of being expressed, especially after having already been expressed at the beginning
of the sentence, serves to recall ἡμεῖς φύσει Ἰουδαῖοι of v.[15].
ἐπιστεύσαμεν εἰς expresses in its fullest and most definite form
the act of Christian faith, the committal of one's self to Christ
on the basis of the acceptance of the message concerning him.
See the detached note on Πίστις and Πιστεύω, pp. 475–485,
esp. V A. 2, p. 480.

The emphasis of ἵνα . . . νόμου, which expresses the purpose of
ἐπιστεύσαμεν, is evidently upon the verb, not upon its limitations; the
latter ἐκ πίστεως, etc., are in effect a re-assertion of the condition on
which alone justification is possible. For a somewhat similar instance
of emphasis upon one element of a clause, see Rom. 6[17]. ἐκ πίστεως
differs from διὰ πίστεως in the former clause rather in the form than
in the substance of the thought expressed, διά denoting the means by
which, ἐκ that in consequence of which, one is justified. Cf. Th. ἐκ
II 6, and for examples indicating the practical equivalence of the two
expressions, see (for διά) chap. 3[26] Rom. 3[22, 25] Eph. 2[8] 3[12, 17]; (for ἐκ)
chap. 3[7, 8, 9] Rom. 1[17] 3[26] 4[16] 5[1] 9[30, 32]; and especially Rom. 3[30], where,
as here, the two prepositions occur in adjacent clauses.

On the reasons for preferring the reading, εἰς Χριστὸν Ἰησοῦν, see
on Χριστοῦ Ἰησοῦ above.

ὅτι ἐξ ἔργων νόμου " οὐ δικαιωθήσεται πᾶσα σάρξ." "because
by works of law shall no flesh be justified." This clause, added
at the end of a verse which has already twice expressed in effect
the same thought, is evidently intended to confirm what has
been said by the authority of scripture. The words οὐ δικαιωθήσεται πᾶσα σάρξ are from Ps. 143[2], following substantially

the Lxx (which itself renders the Hebrew exactly) except that
ἐνώπιόν σου, "before thee," is omitted and πᾶσα σάρξ substituted for πᾶς ζῶν of the Lxx. The word σάρξ, here used by
metonymy for a materially conditioned being, is practically
equivalent to ἄνθρωπος. See detached note on Πνεῦμα and
Σάρξ, p. 486, esp. p. 492. The words ἐξ ἔργων νόμου, which
are essential to the apostle's purpose, are not in the psalm.
There is, however, a basis for them in the preceding line, "Enter
not into judgment with thy servant," which gives to the words
that Paul has quoted the sense, "no man can be justified if
judged on a basis of merit, all grace and mercy on God's part
being excluded." The words added are therefore a correct
interpretative gloss. Indeed, the teaching of the apostle on
this point is a re-exposition in clearer form of a doctrine already
taught by the Hebrew prophets.

17. εἰ δὲ ζητοῦντες δικαιωθῆναι ἐν Χριστῷ "But if through
seeking to be justified in Christ." The most frequent use
of this oft-recurring Pauline phrase ἐν Χριστῷ is that by
which, representing Christ as the sphere within which the
Christian lives, it expresses the intimate fellowship of the believer with Christ. See Th. ἐν, I 6 b. Cf. Frame on 1 Thes. 1¹
and literature there referred to, esp. Deissmann, *Die neutestamentliche Formel " In Christo Jesu."* But this can be adopted
here only by assuming that by an ellipsis of some such words as
διὰ τὸ εἶναι the phrase ἐν Χριστῷ really stands for "by virtue of
being in Christ." For this reason and because ἐν with δικαιόω
usually has its causal and basal sense (see Th. ἐν I 6 c) it is
best to give it the latter force here. Cf. for this use of ἐν
3¹¹: ἐν νόμῳ οὐδεὶς δικαιοῦται. Rom. 3²⁴, διὰ τῆς ἀπολυτρώ-
σεως τῆς ἐν Χριστῷ Ἰησοῦ. Rom. 5⁹, δικαιωθέντες νῦν ἐν τῷ
αἵματι αὐτοῦ. Acts 13³⁹: ἀπὸ πάντων ὧν οὐκ ἠδυνήθητε ἐν
νόμῳ Μωυσέως δικαιωθῆναι ἐν τούτῳ πᾶς ὁ πιστεύων δικαιοῦται. Thus interpreted the expression ἐν Χριστῷ is in a sense
the complement of διὰ πίστεως or ἐκ πίστεως of the preceding
v., the former expressing that on which justification rests, that
which renders it possible, the latter the subjective conditioning
cause.

εὑρέθημεν καὶ αὐτοὶ ἁμαρτωλοί, "we ourselves also were found to be sinners." The emphatic pronoun αὐτοί, indicating that the apostle has definite persons or a definite class in mind, is most naturally understood to refer to Paul and Peter, and indicates that Paul is still maintaining the point of view of his address to Peter. The addition of καί in connection with αὐτοί and ἁμαρτωλοί carries the thought back to the expression οὐκ ἐξ ἐθνῶν ἁμαρτωλοί in v.[15] and indicates that ἁμαρτωλοί is to be taken here in the sense suggested by that verse, "men outside of the law," "violators of the law," having reference to the disregard of the statutes of the law, especially those concerning clean and unclean meats, which statutes Paul, and for a time Peter also, had violated, and which Paul maintained ought not under the circumstances existing at Antioch to be kept. That they had become sinners by seeking to be justified in Christ, Paul would admit in the sense that they had become violators of law, but deny what the judaisers would affirm, that this was equivalent to saying that they had become actual sinners, wrongdoers, violators of God's will. The supposed case, ζητοῦντες . . . ἁμαρτωλοί, Paul probably takes from the mouth of an actual or supposed objector, and accepts it as a correct statement of the situation in a sense of the words which he recognises as current. For confirmation of this interpretation, see on μὴ γένοιτο below.

> The passive force of εὑρέθημεν "were discovered" [by some one] can not be pressed. Not only is it true in general that many passives have in later Greek a middle or intransitive force (Butt. p. 52), so that εὑρέθημεν might easily mean, "we found ourselves," but it is clear from N. T. examples that εὑρέθην in particular had the sense "prove to be," "turn out to be," almost "to become," without special thought of the discovery of the fact. See 1 Cor. 4[2] 2 Cor. 5[3] Acts 5[39], etc. Yet it is also possible that the apostle has in mind, and is in a measure quoting here the language of his opponents, who, referring to his violation of the statutes of the law, would put their charge in the form: "You who profess to be seeking to be justified in Christ are found sinners." Cf. Rom. 7[10] 1 Cor. 15[15] 2 Cor. 11[12] 1 Pet. 1[7].

ἄρα Χριστὸς ἁμαρτίας διάκονος; "is Christ therefore a minister of sin?" The sentence is to be taken as a question rather

than an assertion because of the following μὴ γένοιτο, which in
Paul regularly follows a rhetorical question.* ἁμαρτίας διάκονος
is not ἁμαρτίας δοῦλος, "one who is in bondage to sin" (cf.
Jn. 8³⁴), but "one who ministers to sin," one who furthers the
interests of sin, promotes, encourages it. Cf. Rom. 15⁸ 2 Cor.
3⁶ 11¹⁵. Whatever the meaning of ἁμαρτωλοί above (on this,
as will appear below, interpreters disagree), the noun ἁμαρτία
is doubtless to be taken here in its proper sense, "conduct
which is not in accordance with true righteousness." The
noun ἁμαρτία is apparently never used in the formal sense,
violation of law, in N. T., and though in view of the use of
ἁμαρτωλός the possibility of it could not be denied, yet the
absence of any example of it is against it and the nature of the
argument here even more decisively so. The conclusion which
Paul by μὴ γένοιτο emphatically rejects manifestly pertains
not to sin in any formal or Pharisaic sense, but to veritable
guilty wrong-doing. The whole speciousness of the objection
which Paul is answering turns on the seeming identity, the real
diversity, of the conceptions of sin implied in ἁματωλοί and
ἁμαρτίας respectively. See detached note on Ἁμαρτία, p. 436.

μὴ γένοιτο· "by no means," lit. "let it not be." This phrase
used in N. T. almost exclusively by Paul (elsewhere in Lk.
20¹⁶ only) is uniformly employed by him to repel as abhorrent
to him a suggested thought. When standing alone (it is otherwise only in 6¹⁴) it invariably follows a rhetorical question and
rejects the suggested thought as one which the previous premises, themselves accepted as true, do not justify; and usually
(1 Cor. 6¹⁵ and possibly Rom. 11¹ are the only exceptions),
a conclusion which may be speciously but falsely deduced
from his own previous statements. See chap. 3²¹ Rom. 3⁴, ⁶ 6², ¹⁵
7⁷, ¹³ 9¹⁴ 11¹¹. These facts concerning Paul's usage of this phrase

* Whether we are to read ἆρα or ἄρα there seems to be no decisive reason to determine;
the sentence being a question and that question being whether a certain inference follows
from a supposed situation. ἆρα, which is an interrogative particle, leaves the illative element
unexpressed, while ἄρα, an illative particle, leaves the interrogation unexpressed. But ἄρα
being frequent in Paul, whereas there is no clear instance of ἆρα in his writings, the presumption is perhaps slightly in favour of the former. The difference of meaning is not great.
Of the hesitation or bewilderment which lexicographers say is suggested by ἆρα, there is no
trace here.

are important. They not only show that the preceding words
must, as stated above, be taken as a question, but make it
practically certain that what μὴ γένοιτο denies is not the supposition εἰ . . . ἁμαρτωλοί and with it the conclusion based
upon it, but the validity of the deduction of the conclusion
from the premises. The apostle accepts the premises; denies
that the conclusion follows. In other words, he admits that they
became sinners, violators of law, by seeking to be justified in
Christ, but denies that from this fact one can legitimately draw
the conclusion which his opponents allege to follow and by
which they seek to discredit his position, viz., that Christ is
therefore a minister of sin.

Of this sentence as a whole there have been very many interpretations. It will be sufficient here to direct attention to a few. The differences between them may be most easily made clear by setting down
the three propositions which are involved in the verse: (1) We are seeking to be justified in Christ. (2) We were found sinners. (3) Christ
is a minister of sin. Proposition (1) Paul undoubtedly accepts; proposition (3) he undoubtedly denies. All interpretations agree that "sin"
is used in proposition (3) in its strict and proper Pauline sense, veritable wrong-doing. The differences of interpretation turn mainly upon
two questions: What is the sense of the word " sinners," ἁμαρτωλοί, in
prop. (2)? Is (2) admitted or denied?

According to the view of many commentators, both ancient and
modern,* ἁμαρτωλοί is used in a sense corresponding to that of ἁμαρτίας
in the next clause, " sinners " in the proper sense of the word, and μὴ
γένοιτο denies both (2) and (3); it is tacitly assumed that they stand or
fall together, as must indeed be the case if ἁμαρτωλοί and ἁμαρτίας correspond in meaning. This interpretation takes on two slightly different
forms, according as εἰ . . . διάκονος is supposed to be an affirmation
of an objector quoted by Paul, or a question put by Paul himself. In
the former case the objector, a legalist Jewish Christian, tacitly assuming that violation of law is sin, reasons that by their abandonment of
law in their effort to obtain justification in Christ the Jewish Christians
have themselves become sinners and thus have made Christ a minister of sin, from the objector's point of view a *reductio ad absurdum*
which discredits the whole Pauline position. To this Paul replies deny-

* Sief. cites as holding substantially this view, but with various modifications: Chrys.
Thdrt. Oecum. Thphyl. Erasm. Luth. Cast. Calv. Cal. Est. Wolf. Wetst. Seml. Koppe, Borg.
Fl. Win. Ust. Matth. Schott. B–Cr. de W. Hilg. Ew. Mey. Pfleid. Wetzel, Ws. This
is also the view of Ell.

ing that (by violating law) they have been found sinners, and denying therefore that there is any ground for affirming that they have made Christ a minister of sin. If on the other hand the sentence is a question, Paul himself asks whether in seeking to be justified in Christ (without law) they have become veritable sinners, and thus made Christ a minister of sin, and as before by μὴ γένοιτο denies that they have (by abandoning law) become sinners, and hence that there is any ground for saying that they have made Christ a minister of sin. In either case Paul uses ἁμαρτωλοί in the sense of real sinners, admits that premise and conclusion go together, and denying (on the unstated ground that abandonment of law is not sin) that they are found sinners, with it denies the conclusion. It is an objection to this interpretation in all of its forms that it disregards both the obvious force of μὴ γένοιτο in relation to the preceding sentence and the apostle's regular usage of it. As Zahn well points out, the question which μὴ γένοιτο answers (that it is a question, see above on μὴ γένοιτο) is by its very terms not an inquiry whether the premises are true, but whether the alleged conclusion follows from the premise. The placing of εὑρέθημεν in the conditional clause along with the unquestionably admitted ζητοῦντες, etc., implies that it is only Χριστὸς ἁμαρτίας διάκονος that is called in question. If εὑρέθημεν . . . ἁμαρτωλοί were also disputed the sentence ought to have been as follows: "Seeking to be justified in Christ, were we ourselves also found to be sinners, and is Christ accordingly a minister of sin?" This conclusion as to the meaning of the sentence is still further confirmed by the fact that by μὴ γένοιτο, as stated above, Paul regularly negatives a false conclusion from premises which he accepts.

Of the interpretations which, giving the necessary weight to the usage of μὴ γένοιτο, find in it a denial not of prop. (2) and a consequent denial of (3), but of the legitimacy of the deduction of the conclusion (prop. 3) from the premise (2) the correctness of which is thereby implied, the following types may be mentioned:

Wies., et al., understand ἁμαρτωλοί as meaning sinners in the strict sense, and make εὑρέθημεν . . . ἁμαρτωλοί refer to the sins which even the justified is found to commit. This view manifestly involves an idea remote from the context, and is generally regarded as incorrect by modern interpreters.

Several modern interpreters take ἁμαρτωλοί in the sense suggested by ἁμαρτωλοί in v. [15], sinners in that like the Gentiles they are outside of law, find in εὑρέθημεν . . . ἁμαρτωλοί, a consequence which Paul admits follows *logically* from the attempt to be justified in Christ, and in Χριστὸς ἁμαρτίας διάκονος an inference, the legitimacy of which Paul denies in μὴ γένοιτο. Thus it may be supposed that Paul has in mind an objector who alleges that, inasmuch as the apostle's own reasoning is to the effect that to make faith in Christ the basis of justification involves for the Jew putting himself on the plane of the Gentile, therefore he makes Christ the minister of sin; to which Paul, in reply, admits that this is his reasoning so far as the relation of the believer to law is concerned, but denies that the conclusion that Christ is the minister of sin legitimately follows. So clearly Ltft., who states his view thus: "Seeing that in order to be justified in Christ it was necessary to abandon our old ground of legal righteousness and to become sinners (*i. e.*, to put ourselves in the position of heathen), may it not be argued that Christ is thus made a minister of sin?" So also substantially Zahn, who definitely maintains that the being found sinners took place in the very fact of conversion, and that ζητοῦντες . . . Χριστῷ is practically equivalent to πιστεύοντες; and Sief., who paraphrases thus: "In that we Christians, however, on our part sought to be justified not by works of the law but in Christ only, it is proved that we, just like the heathen, are sinners; this, in fact, follows from what was just said (v. ¹⁶). This being the case is not Christ, then, with whom confessed sinners can, repudiating the righteousness based on works of law, seek justification, a promoter of sin?" In favour of this general interpretation it is to be said that it recognises the significance of μὴ γένοιτο and of the structure of the sentence, takes ἁμαρτωλοί in a sense suggested by καὶ αὐτοί, explains the introduction of παραβάτης below, which is brought in when Paul leaves behind the ambiguity of ἁμαρτωλοί, and does not make the argument turn on remote and unsuggested premises. It may be doubted, however, whether it does not err in that it goes too far afield for its explanation of the word ἁμαρτωλοί, detaches the argument too much from the situation at Antioch as depicted in vv. ¹¹⁻¹⁴, and finds the occasion for the apostle's question in a supposed logical inference from the doctrine of justification in itself rather than in the actual and recent conduct of Peter and Paul. Whether these words were actually uttered in substance at Antioch or not, the Antioch incident furnishes their background. It is probable, therefore, that the question there at issue is still in mind, and that in εὑρέθημεν καὶ αὐτοὶ ἁμαρτωλοί he refers to himself and Peter, or possibly to the Jewish Christians who had associated themselves with his movement, and describes them as becoming, or as being discovered to be, violators of the Jewish law. The sentence thus takes on a definite and concrete meaning appropriate to the context.

But this interpretation again assumes two forms, according as one supposes Paul to be replying to an objection, or himself presenting to Peter's mind an inference from his recent conduct in ceasing to eat with the Gentile Christians. In the former case the sentence means: "If, then, our seeking to be justified in Christ issued in our becoming like the Gentiles, violators of law as was the case at Antioch, and in that sense sinners, does it follow, as my critics allege, that

Christ becomes a minister of sin?" In the latter case it means: "You will admit, Peter, that it was while seeking to be justified in Christ that we were led to become violators of law at Antioch; are you willing, then, to admit that Christ is a minister of sin, as would follow from what was implied in your conduct in refusing to eat with the Gentiles, viz.: that not to obey the statutes of the law is sin?" Either of these interpretations is possible. They are alike in that they connect the thought with the Antioch event and that, recognising the usage of μὴ γένοιτο, they make the sentence a question and μὴ γένοιτο a denial of the conclusion, not of the expressed premise, and base the denial on the rejection of the suppressed premise that violation of the statutes of law is (real) sin. But it is in favour of the form which finds in them an answer to an objection that εὑρέθημεν is more suggestive of the attitude of a critic than of an original statement of Paul (see above on εὑρεθ·), and especially that μὴ γένοιτο is more naturally understood as repudiating the conclusion and false reasoning of an objector, than as a comment of the apostle on his own argument addressed to Peter. To combine the two interpretations, as Bous. apparently attempts to do, is impossible, because in the one case it is the critic of Paul's position who is supposed to allege that Paul's view makes Christ a minister of sin, and in the other case it is Paul who points out to Peter that his recent conduct issues in this impossible conclusion.

18. εἰ γὰρ ἃ κατέλυσα ταῦτα πάλιν οἰκοδομῶ, παραβάτην ἐμαυτὸν συνιστάνω, "for if the things that I broke down, these I build up again, I show myself a transgressor." By this statement the apostle sustains his μὴ γένοιτο, in which he denied the validity of the argument that by becoming a violator of law he had made Christ a minister of sin, the suppressed premise of which was that violation of law was sin. By ἃ κατέλυσα is obviously meant the statutes of the law which Paul had by his conduct declared to be invalid. The reasoning of this sentence is of the type *e contrario*. So far from its being the case that I commit sin by violating statutes of the law, it is, on the contrary, the fact that if I build up again those commands of the law which I broke down, I show myself therein a transgressor. This was precisely what Peter had done by his vacillating conduct; but Paul instead of saying either "thou" or "we," tactfully applies the statement to himself. That he uses the form of conditional sentence expressive of simple supposition, not that of condition contrary to fact, is probably due to his really having in mind Peter's conduct in building up the wall he had before broken down. The statement that not by disobeying but by obeying the statutes of the law he becomes a transgressor is, of course, obviously paradoxical and itself requires proof; this is furnished in v. ¹⁹.

On καταλύω and οἰκοδομῶ in their literal sense, cf. Mk. 15²⁹, ὁ καταλύων τὸν ναὸν καὶ οἰκοδομῶν. But as applied to a law or the like, καταλύω means "to deprive of force," "to abrogate" (cf. Mt. 5¹⁷: μὴ νομίσητε ὅτι ἦλθον καταλῦσαι τὸν νόμον ἢ τοὺς προφήτας), and οἰκοδομῶ as the antithesis of καταλύω in this sense means to "give force to," "to render or declare valid."

The word παραβάτης is doubtless chosen instead of ἁμαρτωλός in order to get rid of the ambiguity of this latter term, which lay at the basis of the opponent's fallacious reasoning. The παραβάτης is a violator of the law, not of the statutes, but of its real intent. To have added τοῦ νόμου would have been correct, but confusing as introducing a sense of νόμος quite contrary to that in which it occurs throughout the context. The apostle might naturally have precisely reversed this usage, employing παραβάτης for the technical violator of the statute, and ἁμαρτωλός for the real sinner, the man who was not acting according to God's will, and had he been quite free in the matter it is not improbable that he would have done so. But the usage of his opponents, who employed ἁμαρτωλός rather than παραβάτης for the Gentiles and those who like them did not observe the requirements of the law, compelled him to use this as the ambiguous term, and to resort to παραβάτης when he wished a strictly moral and unambiguous term. It is noticeable, however, that in the only other passage in which he uses the latter word (Rom. 2²⁵, ²⁷), it has substantially the same sense as here, designating not one who disregards the letter of the law, but one who is disobedient to its essential ethical spirit, and the passage gains in point and force by applying this forceful term to one who, obedient to the statutes, misses the real meaning of the law.

The verb συνιστάνω, late form of συνίστημι, lit. "to set together," is in N. T. employed in its active tenses with the meanings "to prove," and "to commend," in the former case usually to prove by one's action, to exhibit in one's conduct. Thus in Rom. 5⁸: συνίστησιν δὲ τὴν ἑαυτοῦ ἀγάπην εἰς ἡμᾶς ὁ θεὸς ὅτι ἔτι ἁμαρτωλῶν ὄντων ἡμῶν Χριστὸς ὑπὲρ ἡμῶν ἀπέθανεν. See also 2 Cor. 6⁴, ¹¹. There is therefore nothing in the force of the verb that requires the interpretation, "I prove that I was (in that former breaking down) a transgressor," or that opposes the interpretation, "I show myself therein (i. e., in the

present building up) a transgressor." There are indications that the
verb sometimes meant "to establish" (see Num. 27²³ 2 Mac. 14¹⁵ 3 Mac.
1¹⁹ 2²⁶, though in no case with two accusatives); but this usage does
not occur in N. T., and though appropriate to the present passage is
not demanded by it.

On the paradox involved in the statement of this verse, see Rom. 3³¹,
where the apostle maintains, and in chap. 4 endeavours to prove, that
the principle of faith, rejecting law, is not hostile to law but consonant with it; Rom. 8¹⁻⁴, where he declares in effect that the law is done
away that the requirements of the law may be fulfilled; and Gal.
chap. 5, where having in v.¹ insisted upon freedom from the law, he
nevertheless in v.¹⁴ distinctly implies the necessity of fulfilling the
law.

19. ἐγὼ γὰρ διὰ νόμου νόμῳ ἀπέθανον, "for I through law
died to law." The use of the first person, which in the preceding verse was unemphatic because Paul was speaking of what
would be equally true of any Christian, e. g., of Peter, and
applied to himself only hypothetically, becomes now emphatic.
Note the expressed ἐγώ, which together with the use of direct
assertion indicates that the apostle is now speaking of his own
personal experience. In the usage of Paul, "to die to" a thing
is to cease to have any relation to it, so that it has no further
claim upon or control over one. See Rom. 6². ¹⁰. ¹¹ 7⁶. That
to which Paul here refers in νόμου and νόμῳ is evidently law in
some sense in which it has played a part in the preceding discussion, and most obviously divine law as a legalistic system,
a body of statutes legalistically interpreted (see detached note
on Νόμος, pp. 443-460, esp. V 2 (c), p. 457). Paul would certainly not say that he had died to law conceived of as consisting in the ethical principle of love (V 2 (d)), nor to law conceived
of in the broad inclusive sense of the word (V 2 (b)). Law as a
concrete historic fact without reference to the distinction between the legalistic and ethical interpretation would be a suitable meaning of διὰ νόμου, but could apply to νόμῳ only if we
suppose that Paul thinks of dying to it not in every respect,
but as respects subjection to its statutes. On the other hand,
the legalistic meaning meets all the conditions of this verse
and the context. It was on the basis of law in this sense that

it was demanded that the Gentiles should be circumcised, and the Jewish Christians continue to obey the law of foods. It was this to which Paul refers in v. [16] in the phrase ἐξ ἔργων νόμου. It was under this that he had lived in his Pharisaic days, and under which he had ceased to live (died to it), and to this he may well have referred as that through which he had been led to take this step.

How the necessity of abandoning law was made evident to him by law, Paul does not here state. But there is no more probable explanation of his language here than that he has in mind the experience under the law to the result of which he refers in v. [16] and which he describes at length in Rom., chap. 7. There he tells how the law—by ὁ νόμος he doubtless means the Mosaic law in its legalistic interpretation—had by his experience under it taught him his own inability to meet its spiritual requirements and its own inability to make him righteous, and thus led him finally to abandon it and to seek salvation in Christ. *Cf.* also Phil. 3[5-9].

The sentence does indeed become somewhat more forcible, especially as more directly suggesting that he has divine authority for his repudiation of law, if νόμος be supposed to refer to divine law in a general sense (qualitatively considered, as is shown by the omission of the article), but with a constant shifting of emphasis from one phase to another. We may then mentally supply νόμου in this general sense after παραβάτην and read: "But if I build up again the authority of those statutes of the law which I broke down, *i. e.*, insist again upon the obligation to obey them, I become a transgressor of divine law (in its deepest meaning), for through my experience in seeking justification under it interpreted as a legalistic system, divine law itself taught me to abandon it, as a body of statutes to be obeyed." But the very complexity of the thought thus yielded is an objection to this interpretation, and the simpler, more direct and self-consistent one is probably, therefore, to be preferred.

The interpretation of διὰ νόμου according to which it refers to the fact expressed by the words διὰ τοῦ σώματος τοῦ χριστοῦ in Rom. 7[4]: ἐθανατώθητε τῷ νόμῳ διὰ τοῦ σώματος τοῦ χριστοῦ, and which assumes a reference to the curse of the law which falling upon Christ is thereby exhausted, leaving the believer in Christ free, is far less probably correct than the one proposed above. διὰ νόμου is by no means obviously equivalent to διὰ τοῦ σώματος τοῦ χριστοῦ in Rom. 7[4].

The words are different and the connection is different. There Paul is stating the objective grounds for freedom from the law; here, as the emphatic ἐγώ implies, he is appealing to personal experience. Had his thought been what this interpretation supposes, it would certainly have been more natural that he should write, ἡμεῖς διὰ (τοῦ) νόμου (τῷ) νόμῳ ἐθανατώθημεν. Moreover, it is by no means clear that Paul conceived of the law as demanding and causing the death of Christ. In chap. 3¹³ he expresses the thought that the law pronounces a curse on the sinner, from which Christ by his death frees us. But it is essential to the interpretation now under consideration that he should have thought of the law as bringing Christ to his death, and thereby ending its own dominion over men who are joined with Christ by faith—a thought which Paul has nowhere expressed. That the work of Christ should avail to avert the curse of the law from man, and to end the dominion of law, affords a basis for the statement that through Christ I died to law (cf. Rom. 8²) but not for "through law I died to law." See Sief. for defence of this general view and criticism of other interpretations, and Zahn for a criticism of it.

ἵνα θεῷ ζήσω· "that I might live to God." Cf. Rom. 6¹⁰, ¹¹ 14⁷, ⁸ 2 Cor. 5¹⁵. This clause expressing the purpose of the apostle's death to law is in effect also an argument in defence of it. It is implied that subjection to law in reality prevented the unreserved devotion of the life to God—this is one vice of legalism, that it comes between the soul and God, interposing law in place of God—and that it had to be abandoned if the life was really to be given to God. This is a most important element of Paul's anti-legalism, showing the basis of his opposition to legalism in its failure religiously, as in Rom. 7⁷⁻²⁵ he sets forth its ethical failure.

The dative θεῷ is, as in Rom. 6¹⁰, ¹¹, primarily a dative of relation in antithesis to the dative νόμῳ in the preceding clause—but while it results from the nature of the verb ἀποθνήσκω that a dative of relation after it implies separation, it results equally from the nature of the verb ζάω that the dative of relation with it involves, or at least suggests, the force of a dative of advantage, as is clearly the case also in 2 Cor. 5¹⁵. On the force of θεός without the article see p. 89.

The verb ζάω is used by the apostle Paul in four senses, which are, however, not always sharply distinguished: 1. "To be alive, to be a living being": (a) of men in contrast with dying or with the dead: 1 Thes. 4¹⁶, ¹⁷ 1 Cor. 7³⁹ 15⁴⁵ 2 Cor. 1⁸ 4¹¹ 5¹⁵* 6⁹ Rom. 6¹¹(?) 7¹, ², ³ 12¹ 14⁷, ⁸*

* Shading in these cases into meaning 2.

Phil. 1²¹, ²²; *cf.* 1 Tim. 5⁶ 2 Tim. 4¹; (b) of God, in contrast with lifeless idols: 1 Thes. 1⁹ 2 Cor. 3³ 6¹⁶ Rom. 9²⁶ 10⁵ 14¹¹; *cf.* 1 Tim. 3¹⁵ 4¹⁰; (c) metaphorically, "to enjoy life," "to live happily": 1 Thes. 3⁸ Rom. 7⁹ (?); "to have one's living": 1 Cor. 9¹⁴.

2. In an ethical or qualitative sense: "to live in a certain way" (usually ethically defined) with reference either to the source of vital power or to the direction of energy: chap. 2¹⁴, ¹⁹, ²⁰ 5²⁵ Rom. 6² 8¹², ¹³ Col. 2²⁰ 3⁷; *cf.* 2 Tim. 3¹² Tit. 2¹².

3. In quotations from O. T. in a soteriological sense: "to escape death," the penalty of sin, "to attain the divine approval," "to be justified": chap. 3¹¹ Rom. 1¹⁷ (in quotation from Hab. 2⁴); chap. 3¹² Rom. 10⁵ (quotation from Lev. 18⁵).

4. "To live after death," "to possess eternal life": 1 Thes. 5¹⁰ 2 Cor. 13⁴ Rom. 6¹⁰ 14⁹.

All the instances in this chap. fall under 2 above; those in chap. 3 under 3.

20. Χριστῷ συνεσταύρωμαι· "I have been crucified with Christ." The thought of participation with Christ in the experiences of his redemptive work is a favourite one with Paul, and the metaphors by which he expresses it are sometimes quite complicated. *Cf.* Rom. 6⁴⁻⁸ 8¹⁷ Phil. 3¹⁰ Col. 2¹²⁻¹⁴, ²⁰ 3¹⁻⁴. A literal interpretation of these expressions, as if the believer were in literal fact crucified with Christ, buried with him, raised with him, etc., is, of course, impossible. The thought which the apostle's type of mind and enthusiastic joy in the thought of fellowship with Christ led him to express in this form involves in itself three elements, which with varying degrees of emphasis are present in his several expressions of it, viz.: the participation of the believer in the benefits of Christ's experience, a spiritual fellowship with him in respect to these experiences, and the passing of the believer through a similar or analogous experience. The first element is distinctly expressed in 2 Cor. 5¹⁵ and Rom. 4²⁴, ²⁵, and is probably in mind along with the third in Col. 2²⁰ 3¹; *cf.* 2¹⁴. The second is the predominant element in Phil. 3¹⁰, and the third in Rom. 8¹⁷, while in Rom. 6⁵ both the second and the third are probably in mind. In the present instance the verb συνεσταύρωμαι indicates that the experience of Christ referred to is his death upon the cross, and the context implies that the experience of Paul here spoken of is his death to law. Whether this death to law is related to the death of Christ objectively by virtue of a participation of the believer in the effects of Christ's death (*cf.* Rom. 3[24, 25]) or subjectively by a spiritual fellowship of the believer with Christ in respect to his death (*cf.* Rom. 6[10, 11]) is not decisively indicated. On the one side, Paul has elsewhere expressed the idea that the believer is free from law by virtue of the work, specifically the death, of Christ (chap. 3[13] Col. 2[14] Eph. 3[15, 16]; *cf.* Gal. 2[4] 5[1] Rom. 10[4]), and in Col. 2[20] expressed this participation as a dying with Christ. On the other hand, while he has several times spoken of dying with Christ in the sense of entering into a spiritual fellowship with him in his death, he has nowhere clearly connected the freedom from the law with such fellowship.* Probably therefore he has here in mind rather the objective fact that the death of Christ brings to an end the reign of law (as in Rom. 10[4], and esp. Col. 2[14]) than that the individual believer is freed from law by his spiritual fellowship with Christ in death. Yet such is the many-sidedness of the apostle's thought that neither element can be decisively excluded. In either case the expression still further enforces the argument in defence of his death to law. It was brought about through law; it was necessary in order that I might live to God; it is demanded by the death of Christ on the cross, wherein he made us free from law, bringing it to an end, or by my fellowship with him in that death.

> Ltft., interpreting συνεσταύρωμαι by the use of the same word in Rom. 6[6] and by the use of the simple verb in Gal. 5[24] 6[14] refers it to a death to sin, the annihilation of old sins. Such a change in the application of a figure is by no means impossible in Paul (see the varied use of ἡμέρα in 1 Thes. 5[2-8]). But a sudden veering off from the central subject of his thought—the point which it was essential that he should carry—to an irrelevant matter is not characteristic of the apostle, and is certainly not demanded here by the mere fact that he has in another context used similar phraseology in a sense required by that context, but not harmonious with this.

ζῶ δὲ οὐκέτι ἐγώ, ζῇ δὲ ἐν ἐμοὶ Χριστός· "and it is no longer I that live, but Christ that liveth in me." The order of

* Gal. 2[4] would be an example of this manner of speaking if ἐν Χριστῷ were taken as meaning "in fellowship with Christ" rather than "on the basis of [the work of] Christ."

the Greek is very expressive even when reproduced in English: "and live no longer I, but liveth in me Christ." The first δέ is not adversative but continuative, the sentence expressing another aspect of the same fact set forth in the preceding sentence. The translation of AV. and RV., "Yet I live, yet no longer I," is wholly unwarranted; this meaning would have required ἀλλά before οὐκέτι. *Cf.* RV. mg. The second δέ is sub-adversative (Ell.), equivalent to the German "sondern," introducing the positive correlative to a preceding negative, statement. In this sentence Paul is clearly speaking of spiritual fellowship with Christ (*cf.* on v.[19]). Yet this is not a departure from the central thought of the whole passage. He has already said in v.[19] that the purpose of the dying to law was that he might devote himself directly to the service of God instead of to the keeping of commandments. He now adds that in so doing he gains a new power for the achievement of that purpose, thus further justifying his course. Saying that it is no longer "I" that live, he implies that under law it was the "I" that lived, and the emphatic ἐγώ is the same as in Rom. 7[15-20]. There, indeed, it stands in vv.[17, 20] in direct antithesis to the ἁμαρτία which is inherited from the past (*cf.* Rom. 5[12]), here over against the Christ who is the power for good in the life of one who, leaving law, turns to him in faith. But the ἐγώ is the same, the natural man having good impulses and willing the good which the law commands, but opposed by the inherited evil impulse and under law unable to do the good. On the significance of the expression ἐν ἐμοί, see Rom. 8[9, 11] 1 Cor. 2[16] Col. 1[27-29] Eph. 3[16-19]. It is, of course, the heavenly Christ of whom he speaks, who in religious experience is not distinguishable from the Spirit of God (*cf.* chap. 5[16, 18, 25]). With this spiritual being Paul feels himself to be living in such intimate fellowship, by him his whole life is so controlled, that he conceives him to be resident in him, imparting to him impulse and power, transforming him morally and working through him for and upon other men. *Cf.* 4[19]. Substantially the same fact of fellowship with Christ by which he becomes the controlling factor of the life is expressed, with a difference of form of thought rather than of essential conception of the nature of the relation, by the phrase ἐν Χριστῷ, which is more frequent in Paul than ἐν ἐμοί. Cf. 1²² 3²⁶, ²⁸ 5⁴, and Frame on 1 Thes. 1¹, and references there given to modern literature.

ὃ δὲ νῦν ζῶ ἐν σαρκί, ἐν πίστει ζῶ "and the life that I now live in the flesh, I live in faith." The sentence is continuative and epexegetic of the preceding, explaining the life which, despite his preceding affirmation that he is no longer living, he obviously still lives, by declaring that it is not an independent life of his own, but a life of faith, of dependence on the Son of God. See below.

The relative ὅ is an accusative of content, which simply puts into substantive form the content of the verb ζῶ (Delbrück, *Vergleichende Syntax*, III 1, § 179; Rob. p. 478). νῦν manifestly refers to the time subsequent to the change expressed in νόμῳ ἀπέθανον and the corresponding later phrases. ἐν σαρκί is therefore not an ethical characterisation of the life (as in Rom. 8⁷, ⁸) but refers to the body as the outward sphere in which the life is lived, in contrast with the life itself and the spiritual force by which it was lived. By this contrast and the fact that σάρξ often has an ethical sense, the phrase takes on perhaps a slightly concessive force: "the life that I now live though in the flesh is in reality a life of faith." On the use of σάρξ in general, see detached note on Πνεῦμα and Σάρξ, p. 492.

> The words ἐν πίστει stand in emphatic contrast with those which they immediately follow, a contrast heightened by the use of the same preposition ἐν in a different sense, or rather with different implication. For, while in both cases ἐν denotes the sphere in which the life is lived, in ἐν σαρκί the sphere is physical and not determinative of the nature of the life, in ἐν πίστει it is moral and is determinative of the character of the life. πίστει without the article is, like σαρκί, qualitative in force, and though properly a noun of personal action, is here conceived of rather as an atmosphere in which one lives and by which one's life is characterised. For other instances of this use of the preposition with nouns properly denoting activity or condition, see 1 Cor. 4²¹ 2 Cor. 3⁷ff. Eph. 4¹⁶ 5².

τῇ τοῦ υἱοῦ τοῦ θεοῦ "(faith) which is in the Son of God." Having in the expression ἐν πίστει described faith qualitatively as the sphere of his new life, the apostle now hastens to identify that faith by the addition of the article τῇ and a genitive expressing the object of the faith. For other instances of a qualitative noun made definite by a subjoined article and limiting phrase, see W. XX 4 (WM. p. 174); Rad. p. 93; Gild. *Syn.* p. 283; Rob. p. 777; B*MT* 424; and *cf.* chap. 1⁷ 3²¹. On the objective genitive after πίστις, see on διὰ πίστεως Χριστοῦ Ἰησοῦ, v.¹⁶. On the meaning of τοῦ υἱοῦ τοῦ θεοῦ, see detached note on *The Titles and Predicates of Jesus*, V, p. 404. What particular phase of the meaning of this title as applied to Jesus is here in mind, or why it is chosen instead of Χριστός or Χριστός Ἰησοῦς, which have been used in this passage thus far, there is nothing in the context clearly to indicate. No theory is more probable than that here, as in 1¹⁶, it is the Son of God as the revelation of God that he has in mind, and that this expression comes naturally to his lips in thinking of the love of Christ. See Rom. 8³, ³²; but notice also Rom. 5⁸ 8³⁵, ³⁹, and observe in the context of these passages the alternation of titles of Jesus while speaking of his love or the love of God, without apparent reason for the change.

<blockquote>
τοῦ υἱοῦ τοῦ θεοῦ: so אACDᵇ ᵉᵗ ᶜKLP, all the cursives, f Vg. Syr. (psh. harcl.), Boh. Sah. Arm. Eth. Goth. Clem., and other fathers. Ln. adopted the reading τοῦ θεοῦ καὶ Χριστοῦ attested by BD* FG d g. Despite its attestation by B, this is probably a Western corruption. The apostle never speaks of God expressly as the object of a Christian's faith.
</blockquote>

τοῦ ἀγαπήσαντός με καὶ παραδόντος ἑαυτὸν ὑπὲρ ἐμοῦ· "who loved me and gave himself up for me." *Cf.* the note on τοῦ δόντος ἑαυτὸν ὑπὲρ τῶν ἁμαρτιῶν ἡμῶν, chap. 1⁴. Here as there, and even more clearly because of the use of the verb παραδίδωμι (*cf.* Rom. 4²⁵ 8³² 1 Cor. 11²³ Eph. 5², ²⁵, esp. Eph. 5²) in place of the simple δίδωμι, the reference is to Christ's voluntary surrender of himself to death. The use of μέ and ἐμοῦ rather than ἡμᾶς and ἡμῶν indicates the deep personal feeling with which the apostle writes. The whole expression, while suggesting the ground of faith and the aspect of Christ's work with which faith has specially to do, is rather a spontaneous and grateful utterance of the apostle's feeling called forth by the mention of the Son of God as the object of his faith than a phrase introduced with argumentative intent. On the meaning of ἀγαπάω, see on 5¹⁴.

21. Οὐκ ἀθετῶ τὴν χάριν τοῦ θεοῦ· "I do not make of no effect the grace of God." This sentence, abruptly introduced without connective, is doubtless an answer to an objection which the apostle knows to have been urged or which he foresees may easily be urged against his doctrine. This objection, as is shown by the χάριν of this sentence and the reference to law in the next, is to the effect that he is making of no account the special grace of God to Israel in giving them the law (cf. Rom. 3³¹). Since χάρις is a favourite term of the apostle in reference to the gospel, it is not impossible that it was taken up by his critics and turned against him in some such statement as that by his doctrine of grace as against law he was really making of no account the grace of God to Israel. This criticism he answers by direct denial, which he sustains in the next sentence. It would be natural to expect him to turn the criticism upon his critics by intimating that it was they who rejected the grace of the gospel. But to have suggested this thought he must, it would seem, have used the emphatic ἐγώ.

On ἀθετῶ, "to set aside," "to reject," cf. Mk. 7⁹ 1 Thes. 4⁸ Gal. 3¹⁵; M. and M. *Voc. s. v.* On the meaning of χάρις, see on 1⁶.

εἰ γὰρ διὰ νόμου δικαιοσύνη, ἄρα Χριστὸς δωρεὰν ἀπέθανεν. "for if righteousness is through law, then Christ died needlessly." On the use of the word δικαιοσύνη, see detached note, p. 460. It is doubtless to be taken here, chiefly at least, in its forensic sense (VI B. 2, p. 469), this rather than the ethical sense having been the subject of discussion from v. ¹⁵ on, and it being this also which the apostle a little more frequently associates with the death of Christ (chap. 3¹³, ¹⁴ Rom. 3²⁴⁻²⁶ 5⁹, ¹⁰; cf. note on chap. 1⁴). διὰ νόμου is doubtless also to be taken, as throughout the passage, in its legalistic sense (see detached note on Νόμος V 2 (c), p. 457, and cf. on v. ¹⁹ above). δωρεάν means not "without result," a meaning which it apparently never has, certainly not in N. T., nor "freely," in the sense "gratuitously," "without (giving or receiving) pay," which, though a well-established meaning of the word (see Rom. 3²⁴, and *cf.* also M. and M. *Voc. s. v.*), would be wholly inappropriate here, but "without cause," "needlessly," as in Jn. 15²⁵. The protasis εἰ . . . δικαιοσύνη is in form a simple supposition, which is often used, as in chap. 1⁹ Rom. 5¹⁰, when the context makes it clear that the condition is fulfilled, but also not infrequently, as here and in 3¹⁸, where it is equally clear that in the opinion of the writer it is contrary to fact. See B*MT* 248, 249. The argument of the sentence is from a Christian point of view a *reductio ad absurdum*, and is adduced as proof of the preceding statement. If, as you affirm but I deny, men must obey the statutes of the law in order to achieve righteousness, then there was no need that Christ should die. Law in the legalistic sense, and the conception of righteousness as obtainable through it, was well established in the world. If this conception was correct, if righteousness could really be attained in this way, there was no need of a new revelation of God's way of righteousness (see Rom. 1¹⁷ 3²¹); and the death of Christ, with its demonstration of divine righteousness (Rom. 3²⁵ ᶠ·) and God's love (Rom. 5⁷⁻¹⁰) and its redemption of men from the curse of the law (see chap. 3¹³ and notes on it), was needless. That in the plan of God it came to pass (chap. 1⁴ 4⁴ Rom. 8³²) is evidence that it was not needless, and this in turn proves that righteousness through law was not God's plan for the world, and refutes the charge that denial of the validity of law to secure righteousness involves a setting aside of the grace of God.

Mey. and others understand χάριν to refer exclusively and directly to the grace of God manifest in the gospel and take οὐκ ἀθετῶ, etc., not as an answer to an objection but as an indirect condemnation of the course of Peter, the meaning being, I do not set aside the grace of God manifest in the death of Christ, as is virtually done by those who insist that righteousness is through law. The clause εἰ . . . δικαιοσύνη is then designed to prove, not, as above, that the rejection of righteousness by law does not involve a setting aside of the grace of God, but that insistence on righteousness by law does involve it. For to affirm

that righteousness is through law is to say that God's grace manifest
in his death was useless. Such an interpretation of the argument,
though not perhaps impossible, is open to two objections: first, that
the form of expression, "I do not set aside," etc., suggests a denial of
something that is said or might be speciously said against Paul's view,
rather than a claim made by himself for his view or an objection to
his opponent's view; and, secondly, that it makes the εἰ γάρ sentence
a proof of something only remotely implied in the preceding statement
instead of taking it as directly related to what is expressed in the preceding sentence, viz., that Paul's view does not involve a setting at
nought of God's grace.

III.   REFUTATORY PORTION OF THE LETTER.

THE DOCTRINE THAT MEN, BOTH JEWS AND GENTILES,
BECOME ACCEPTABLE TO GOD THROUGH FAITH
RATHER THAN BY WORKS OF LAW, DEFENDED BY
THE REFUTATION OF THE ARGUMENTS OF THE
JUDAISERS, AND CHIEFLY BY SHOWING THAT THE
"HEIRS OF ABRAHAM" ARE SUCH BY FAITH, NOT
BY WORKS OF LAW (CHAPS. 3, 4).

1. *Appeal to the early Christian experience of the Galatians* (3^{1-5}).

Leaving the defence of his doctrine through the assertion of
his own direct divine commission, the apostle now takes up
that defence by refuting the objections to it brought by his opponents, the judaisers.   Vv.$^{1-5}$ begin that refutation by appealing to the early Christian experience of the Galatians, which,
as both they and he well knew, was not in the sphere of law,
but of faith.

*Oh foolish Galatians, who bewitched you, before whose eyes Jesus
Christ was placarded crucified ?   ²This only would I learn from
you, Received ye the Spirit on ground of works of law or of a
hearing of faith ?   ³Are ye so foolish ?   Having begun with Spirit
are ye now finishing with flesh ?   ⁴Did ye suffer so many things
in vain ?   If it really is to be in vain.   ⁵He therefore that supplied*

*the Spirit richly to you and wrought miracles among you, did he
do these things on ground of works of law or of a hearing of faith?*

1. Ὦ ἀνόητοι Γαλάται, τίς ὑμᾶς ἐβάσκανεν, οἷς κατ᾽ ὀφθαλμοὺς Ἰησοῦς Χριστὸς προεγράφη ἐσταυρωμένος; "Oh foolish
Galatians, who bewitched you, before whose eyes Jesus Christ
was placarded crucified?" Returning to the situation in
Galatia itself, which he had left behind in 1⁹, but still having
in mind what he had just said in 2²¹ to the effect that the legalistic teaching of the judaisers makes the death of Christ a fact
without significance, a useless tragedy, the apostle breaks forth,
somewhat as in 1⁶, in an expression of surprise touched with
indignation that the Galatians were turning away from his
gospel of Christ crucified (*cf.* 1 Cor. 1¹⁷, ²³ 2²). To this great
fact, which Paul had set forth before the Galatians with the
clearness of a public proclamation on a bulletin-board, and
which it should, therefore, have been impossible for them ever
to forget, the preaching of the judaisers tends to blind them as
by malicious magic. The verb βασκαίνω (see below) is doubtless
used tropically with the meaning "lead astray," and the question, which is, of course, rhetorical, refers to the same persons
who in 1⁷ are spoken of as troubling them and seeking to pervert the gospel of the Christ. On the people here designated
Galatians, see Introd. pp. xxi–xliv.

The addition of τῇ ἀληθείᾳ μὴ πείθεσθαι after ἐβάσκανεν by CDᶜKLP
al. pler., is a manifest corruption under the influence of 5⁷.

Ἀνόητος, a classical word from Sophocles and Herodotus down, is
found in N. T., besides here and v. ³, in Lk. 24²⁵ Rom. 1¹⁴ 1 Tim. 6⁹
Tit. 3³. Properly a passive, "unthinkable," it has in N. T., as also
ordinarily in classical writers and regularly in the Lxx, the active sense,
"foolish," "lacking in the power of perception." 1 Tim. 6⁹ is not a real
exception, the word properly describing a person being applied by
easy metonymy to his desires. The usage of the word, both classical
and biblical, suggests failure to use one's powers of perception rather
than natural stupidity, and the context, especially v. ³, clearly points
to the former sense for the present passage. See Hdt. 1⁸⁷ 8²⁴; Xen. *An.*
2. 1¹³; *Mem.* 1. 3⁹; Plat. *Protag.* 323D; *Phil.* 12D; *Legg.* III 687D;
Prov. 15²¹ 17²⁸ Sir. 42⁸ 4 Mac. 5⁹ 8¹⁷ Lk. 24²⁵ Rom. 1¹⁴ 1 Tim. 6⁹ Tit. 3³.

The verb βασκαίνω, signifying in classical authors, to slander (Dem.

94¹⁹ 291²²), "to envy" (Dem. 464²⁴), "to bewitch" (Theocr. 5¹³ 6⁸⁹; Arist. *Probl.* 20. 34 [926 b²¹]; Herodian 2. 4¹¹) is used in the Lxx and Apocr. (Deut. 28⁵⁴, ⁵⁶ Sir. 14⁶, ⁸) with the meaning, "to envy," but very clearly has here, as in Aristot. and Theocr. *loc. cit.*, the meaning "to bewitch." For the evidence that the possibility of one person bewitching, exercising a spell upon another was matter of current belief both among Gentiles and Jews, see *HDB*, arts. "Magic," esp. vol. III, p. 208a, and "Sorcery," vol. IV, p. 605b; M. and M. *Voc. s. v.* See also Ltft. *ad loc.*; Jastrow, *The Religion of Babylonia and Assyria*, pp. 253–293; Blau, *Das altjüdische Zauberwesen*, pp. 23 *ff.* Concerning the practice of magic arts in general, *cf.* φαρμακία, chap. 5²⁰ Acts 19¹⁹, and Deissmann, *Bible Studies*, pp. 273 *ff.*, 323 *f.*, 352 *ff.* It would be overpressing the facts to infer from Paul's use of this word that he necessarily believed in the reality of magical powers, and still more so to assume that he supposed the state of mind of the Galatians to be the result of such arts. It is more probable that the word, while carrying a reference to magical arts, was used by him tropically, as we ourselves use the word "bewitch," meaning "to pervert," "to confuse the mind."

On οἷς κατ᾿ ὀφθαλμούς *cf.* Aristoph. *Ran.* 625, ἵνα σοι κατ᾿ ὀφθαλμοὺς λέγῃ, and chap. 2¹¹: κατὰ πρόσωπον αὐτῷ ἀντέστην.

Προγράφω occurs in Greek writers in three senses: (1) "to write beforehand," the προ- being temporal (Rom. 15⁴ Eph. 3³); (2) "to write publicly," "to register" (Jude 4, but by some assigned to the previous sense); (3) "to write at the head of the list." The third meaning does not occur in biblical writers and may be dismissed as wholly inappropriate to the context. To take it in the first sense as referring to O. T. prophecy, though consistent with current usage, is excluded by κατ᾿ ὀφθαλμούς; to take it in this sense and refer it to Paul's own presentation of Christ to the Galatians is forbidden by the inappropriateness of γράφω to describe the apostle's *viva voce* preaching; for if προ- be taken temporally, ἐγράφη alone remains to describe the act itself. Many commentators on this passage give to the word the sense "to paint publicly," "to depict before, or openly." So Th. Jowett, and Sief., the last-named citing, also, Calv. deW. Holst. Phil. Lips. Zöckl. *et al.* The argument for this meaning rests not upon extant instances of προγράφω in this sense, but upon the usage of the simple γράφω in the sense "to paint" and the appropriateness of the meaning "to depict publicly" to this context. But in view of the absence of vouchers for this meaning—even the instances of γράφω in the sense "to paint" are, so far at least as cited by lexicographers or commentators on this passage, much earlier than the N. T. period—and of the fact that taking προεγρ- in the meaning "to write publicly," "to placard," yields a meaning more suitable to ἐσταυρωμένος (see below), it is best to accept this latter meaning for this passage, and to understand the apostle as describing his preaching to the Galatians under the figure of public announcement or placarding of Jesus before them.

Ἐσταυρωμένος means "having been crucified," and doubtless in the sense of "having been put to death on the cross"; the perfect participle expresses an existing (in this case permanent) result of the past fact of crucifixion. To express the idea "in the act of being crucified" would require a present participle, if the thought were "in the act of being affixed to the cross," and probably if it were "hanging on the cross." For while the verb σταυρόω may be used of the affixing to the cross (Mt. 27²⁵), yet it seems usually to refer to the putting to death on the cross as a whole (Acts 2³⁶ 4¹⁰, etc.) and the participle ἐσταυρωμένος is used in N. T. of Jesus, not as having been affixed to the cross and hanging there, but invariably of him as one who was put to death on the cross, and thenceforth, though risen from the dead, the crucified one. See Mt. 28⁵ Mk. 16⁶ 1 Cor. 1¹² 2². The tense of the participle, therefore, constitutes a strong objection to taking προγράφω in the sense of "paint before," and in favour of the meaning "to placard, to post publicly"; a picture would doubtless present Jesus on the cross; the crucifixion as an accomplished fact would be matter for public writing, announcement, as it were, on a public bulletin.

Σταυρός (root: sta) occurs from Homer down, meaning a stake, used for fencing (Od. 14¹¹) or driven into the ground for a foundation (Hdt. 5¹⁶). σταυρόω used in Thuc. 7. 25⁷, meaning "to fence with stakes," first appears in Polybius with reference to a means of inflicting death (1. 86⁴), where it probably means "to crucify." Polybius also uses ἀνασταυρόω apparently in the same sense (1. 11⁵; 1. 24⁶; 1. 79⁴), but also with the meaning "to impale" (a dead body, 5. 54⁶; 8. 23²), which is its meaning in Hdt. 3¹²⁵; 6³⁰; 9⁷⁸, etc.; Thuc. 1. 110³; Plato Gorg. 473C; Xen. An. 3. 1¹⁷. In Esth. 7⁹ 8¹³ line 34 (Swete 16¹⁸) it is used of the hanging of Haman upon a gallows (עֵץ, ξύλον), said in 5¹⁴ to be fifty cubits high. In 7⁹ σταυρόω translates הָלָה, "to hang," elsewhere in this book translated with reference to the same event by κρεμάννυμι. Impalement or hanging as a method of inflicting death, or as applied to the dead body of a criminal, was practised by various ancient nations, e. g., the Assyrians (cf the Lexicons of Delitzsch and Muss-Arnolt under Zagapu and Zagipu; Schrader, Keilinschriften des A. T.³, pp. 387 f.; Code of Hammurabi, Statute 153, in Winckler, Die Gesetze Hammurabis in Umschrift u. Uebersetzung, p. 45, or R. F. Harper, The Code of Hammurabi, p. 55); the Egyptians (cf. Gen. 40²² Jos. Ant. 2. 73 [5³]); the Persians (cf. Ezra 6¹¹); but it is not always possible to determine precisely what method is referred to. Among the Jews the bodies of certain criminals were after death hanged upon a tree or impaled (Josh. 8²⁹ 10²⁶ 2 Sam. 4¹²), but there is no sufficient evidence that these methods were used for inflicting death, 2 Sam. 21⁶⁻⁹ being too obscure to sustain this conclusion. Hanging in the modern sense, of suspension causing immediate death by strangulation, is referred to as a means of committing suicide, Hdt. 2¹³¹; Thuc. 3⁸¹; 2 Sam. 17²³ Tob. 3¹⁰ Mt. 27⁵, but was probably unknown in ancient times as a means of inflicting the death penalty. Crucifixion, *i. e.*, the affixing of the body of the criminal, while still living, to an upright post (with or without a crosspiece) to which the body was nailed or otherwise fastened, death resulting from pain and hunger after hours of suffering, was not a Jewish method of punishment; though employed by Alexander Jannæus, Jos. *Bell.* 1. 17 (4⁶), it was inflicted upon Jews, as a rule, only by the Romans. With what nation or in what region this peculiarly cruel form of death penalty originated is not wholly certain. Diod. Sic. 17. 46⁴, speaking of Alexander the Great before Tyre, says: ὁ δὲ βασιλεὺς . . . τοὺς . . . νέους πάντας, ὄντας οὐκ ἐλάττους τῶν δισχιλίων, ἐκρέμασε. Romans of the later days of the republic and early days of the empire ascribed its origin to Punic Carthage, but perhaps without good evidence. Among the Romans crucifixion was for a time (but perhaps not originally) practised only in the case of slaves and the worst of criminals. When the use of it was gradually extended, especially in the provinces (Jos. *Ant.* 17. 295 [10¹⁰]; *Bell.* 5. 449–51 [11¹]) to others than these, it retained the idea of special disgrace.

The word σταυρός, properly referring to the upright stake, came through its use with reference to the implement of crucifixion to designate what we now know as a cross (in N. T. the word ξύλον is still used, Acts 5³⁰ 10³⁹ 1 Pet. 2²⁴; *cf.* Gal. 3¹³), and through the fact that it was on the cross that Jesus suffered death, came to be employed by metonymy for the death of Jesus, carrying with it by association the thought of the suffering and the disgrace in the eyes of men which that death involved and of the salvation which through it is achieved for men. See chap. 5¹¹ 6¹⁴ 1 Cor. 1¹⁸ Phil. 3¹⁸ Col. 1²⁰.

On the cross and crucifixion in general, and the crucifixion of Jesus in particular, see Cremer, *Bibl.-Theol. Wörterb. s. v.*; Zöckler, *Das Kreuz Christi;* Fulda, *Das Kreuz und die Kreuzigung;* W. W. Seymour, *The Cross in Tradition, History, and Art*, esp. the bibliography, pp. XXI–XXX; the articles "Cross" and "Hanging" in *Encyc. Bibl.* and *HDB*, and those on "Kreuz" and "Kreuzigung" in *PRE.*, and in Wetzer and Welte, *Kirchenlexikon;* Mommsen, *Römisches Strafrecht*, pp. 918 *ff*; Hitzig, art. "Crux" in Pauly-Wissowa, *Realencyclopädie d. klassischen Altertumswissenschaft* (with references to literature). On the archæology of the cross Zöckler refers especially to Lipsius, *De Cruce*, Antwerp, 1595; Zestermann, *Die bildliche Darstellung des Kreuzes u. der Kreuzigung Jesu Christi historisch entwickelt*, Leipzig, 1867; Degen, *Das Kreuz als Strafwerkzeug u. Strafe der Alten*, Aachen, 1873; the Code of Hammurabi, Statute 153 (in Winckler or Harper); Birch and Pinches,

The Bronze Ornaments of the Palace Gates of Balawat, London, 1902, Plates B2. D4 and J3.

2. τοῦτο μόνον θέλω μαθεῖν ἀφ᾽ ὑμῶν, ἐξ ἔργων νόμου τὸ πνεῦμα ἐλάβετε ἢ ἐξ ἀκοῆς πίστεως; "This only would I learn from you, Received ye the Spirit on ground of works of law or of a hearing of faith?" A forcible appeal to the experience of the Galatians. The implication of μόνον is that an answer to the question about to be asked would itself be a decisive argument. For μανθάνω in the general sense here illustrated, "to ascertain," "to find out," see Acts 23²⁷ Col. 1⁷. On ἐξ ἔργων νόμου, see detached note on Νόμος and note on 2¹⁶. ἀκοὴ πίστεως is a hearing (of the gospel) accompanied by faith (see detached note on Πίστις), in other words, a believing-hearing, acceptance, of the gospel. τὸ πνεῦμα undoubtedly refers to the Spirit of God (see detached note on Πνεῦμα and Σάρξ, and especially III B. 1 (a) in the analysis of meanings on p. 490). The receiving of the Spirit here referred to is evidently that which marked the beginning of their Christian lives; cf. ἐναρξάμενοι v.³ and see Rom. 8²³ 2 Cor. 1²² 5⁵. That the apostle has especially, though not necessarily exclusively, in mind the charismatic manifestations of the Spirit evidenced by some outward sign, such as speaking with tongues or prophesying, is indicated by the reference to δυνάμεις in v. ⁵. See also Acts 8¹⁴⁻¹⁷ 10⁴⁴⁻⁴⁷ 11¹⁶, ¹⁷ 19¹⁻⁶ 1 Cor. 12⁴⁻¹¹. The two contrasted phrases ἐξ ἔργων νόμου and ἐξ ἀκοῆς πίστεως express the leading antithesis of the whole epistle, and by this question Paul brings the issue between the two contrasted principles of religious life to the test of experience. The answer which the experience of the Galatians would supply, and which therefore did not require to be expressed, was of course ἐξ ἀκοῆς πίστεως. The testimony of these vv. that Paul in his preaching in Galatia and doubtless elsewhere, since he more than once in this epistle implicitly claims always to have preached the same gospel (see on 1¹¹ and 2²), presented his message to the Gentiles wholly divorced from any insistence upon the acceptance of O. T. teachings as such, is of capital importance, both in defining for us the content of his gospel (cf. also 1 Thes. 1¹⁰) and

as showing how completely he had early in his career as an apostle, and not simply when forced to it by controversy, repudiated the principle of scripture authority.

3. οὕτως ἀνόητοί ἐστε; ἐναρξάμενοι πνεύματι νῦν σαρκὶ ἐπιτελεῖσθε; "Are ye so foolish? having begun with Spirit, are ye now finishing with flesh?" The antithesis is twofold: beginning . . . completing; spirit . . . flesh. ἐναρξάμενοι πν. recalls ἐλαβ. πν., but instead of following up their assumed mental answer to his question, viz.: "we received the Spirit by a hearing of faith," in which faith would have been the emphatic term, the apostle transfers the emphasis to πνεῦμα, which his previous question took for granted, as an element in their early Christian experience. Apparently it seems to him that the antithesis "spirit" and "flesh" is at this point a more effective one for his purpose than "faith" and "works of law." On the meaning of the words πνεῦμα and σάρξ, see detached note, pp. 486 ff., especially the discussion of the use of these terms in antithesis, p. 494. πνεύματι doubtless refers, as does τὸ πνεῦμα above, to the Spirit of God, and σαρκί is used in a purely material sense, meaning "flesh" or "body," as that which is circumcised. That the antithesis between πνεῦμα and σάρξ is quite different in chap. 5 is no objection to this interpretation here; for in view of the fact that the precise aim of the judaisers was to induce the Galatians to be circumcised, a reference to the flesh would be naturally taken by them as referring to this, and no other meaning would be likely to occur to them. That σαρκί has a relation to ἔργα νόμου in that circumcision falls in the category of "works of law" is, of course, obvious, but σαρκί is not, therefore, to be taken as equivalent to that phrase or as denoting the natural powers of men apart from the divine Spirit, (1) because ἔργα νόμου does not in the preceding sentence stand in antithesis with πνεῦμα, and (2) because there is nothing in the context to suggest the introduction of this meaning of σάρξ. The absence of the article with both πν. and σαρ. gives them a qualitative force, and heightens the contrast between the two possible agencies of salvation: (divine) Spirit, and (material) flesh. That πνεῦμα is to be taken in a wider sense, as including both the divine Spirit which operates and the human spirit as the sphere of operation, is possible, but improbable in view of the nearness of τὸ πνεῦμα with its express reference to the divine Spirit. πνεύματι and σαρκί are doubtless instrumental datives, which is, however, no objection to taking the latter as referring to the flesh, in the material sense, for though the flesh is, strictly speaking, passive in circumcision, that aspect of the fact is a matter of indifference for the purpose of the argument.

On ἐναρξ. and ἐπιτελ. cf. Phil. 1⁶. ἐπιτελ. occurs elsewhere in N. T. in the active (Rom. 15²⁸ 2 Cor. 7¹ 8⁶, ¹¹ Phil. 1⁶ Heb. 8⁵ 9⁶) in the sense "to accomplish," "to complete," and in 1 Pet. 5⁹ in the form ἐπιτελεῖσθαι, which is probably to be taken as a middle (see Bigg ad loc.). The Lxx use the word in active and passive, not in middle. But the existence of a middle usage in Greek writers (Plat. Phil. 27C; Xen. Mem. 4. 8⁸; Polyb. 1. 40¹⁶; 2. 58¹⁰; 5. 108⁹ cited by Sief.) and the antithesis of ἐναρξ. a word of active force, favours taking ἐπιτελ. also as a middle form with active sense, "to finish, to complete."

4. τοσαῦτα ἐπάθετε εἰκῇ; εἴ γε καὶ εἰκῇ. "Did ye suffer so great things in vain? If it really is to be in vain." A reference to the great experiences through which the Galatians had already passed in their life as Christians, and in effect an appeal to them not to let these experiences be of no avail. The word ἐπάθετε is, so far as our evidence enables us to decide, a neutral term, not defining whether the experiences referred to were painful or otherwise. εἴ γε καὶ εἰκῇ shows that the question whether these experiences are to be in vain is still in doubt, depending on whether the Galatians actually yield to the persuasion of the judaisers or not. Cf., as illustrating the alternation of hope and fear in the apostle's mind, 4¹¹, ²⁰ 5¹⁰. γέ emphasises the contingency and suggests that the condition need not be fulfilled.

The verb πάσχω is in itself of neutral significance, "to experience," εὖ πάσχειν meaning "to be well off," "to receive benefits," and κακῶς or κακὰ πάσχειν, "to suffer ills"; yet πάσχω has in usage so far a predilection for use in reference to ills that πάσχειν alone signifies "to suffer" (ills), and to express the idea "to experience" (good) requires as a rule the addition of εὖ or an equivalent indication in the context.

There is indeed nothing in the immediate limitations of the word in
Jos. *Ant.* 3. 312 (15¹): τὸν θεὸν ὑπομνῆσαι μέν, ὅσα παθόντες ἐξ αὐτοῦ
(*i. e.*, θεοῦ) καὶ πηλίκων εὐεργεσιῶν μεταλαβόντες ἀχάριστοι πρὸς αὐτὸν
γένοιντο, to indicate that it is employed in a good sense, but it is
relieved of its ambiguity by the closely following πηλίκων εὐεργεσιῶν, if not, indeed, in part by ἐξ αὐτοῦ. Since there is nothing
in the context of the Galatian passage distinctly to suggest a beneficial meaning, the presumption is in favour of the more usual adverse
meaning; and this would undoubtedly be the meaning conveyed to the
Galatians if they had in fact been exposed to severe sufferings in connection with their acceptance of the gospel. On the other hand, if
they had suffered no such things this meaning would evidently be
excluded, and the word would refer to the benefits spoken of in vv. ¹, ².
If we adopt the opinion that the letter was addressed to people of
southern Galatia, we may find in Acts 14²² an intimation of persecutions
or other like sufferings to which the present passage might refer; but
no evidence that they were of sufficient severity to merit the term
τοσαῦτα. If the churches were in northern Galatia we are unable to say
whether they had suffered or not. For lack of knowledge of the circumstances, therefore, we must probably forego a decision of the
question whether the experiences were pleasant or painful, and for
this very reason understand the term πάθετε in a neutral sense, or,
more exactly, recognise that the term is for us ambiguous, though it
could hardly have been so to Paul and the Galatians. This leaves the
meaning of εἰκῇ also somewhat in doubt. If the τοσαῦτα are the
preaching of the gospel and the gift of the Spirit, then εἰκῇ means
"without effect" (as in 4¹¹); if the reference is to persecutions it probably means "needlessly," "without good cause" (Col. 2¹⁸), the implication being that if they give up the gospel which Paul preached they
will have abandoned Christ (5²⁻⁴) and might just as well have remained
as they were (note the implication of 4¹¹); or if the persecutions were
instigated by the Jews, that they might have escaped them by accepting Judaism, with its legalism, which they are now on the point of
taking on.

Τοσαῦτα in a large preponderance of cases means in the plural "so
many" (see L. & S., Th.) and, with the possible exception of Jn. 12³⁷,
always has that meaning elsewhere in N. T. The meaning "so great"
is, however, possible (see Preusch.· *s. v.*), and in view of the fact that
it is manifestly more natural for Paul to appeal to the greatness than
simply to the number of the experiences of the Galatians is perhaps
to be adopted here. So Wies. and Preusch.

Sief. finds in εἰ . . . εἰκῇ a reason for taking τοσαῦτα . . . εἰκῇ
not as a question but an exclamation, which is, of course, possible, but
not necessary because of the conditional clause; for this is, in any

case, not a true protasis of a preceding apodosis, but is to be mentally attached to some such supplied clause as, "which I am justified in saying." The dictum that εἴ γε introduces an assumption that the writer believes to be true (Vigerus, ed. Hermann, p. 831, cited by Th.), is not regarded by recent authorities as true for classical Greek (see L. & S. *sub.* γέ I 3, Kühner-Gerth, II 1, pp. 177 *f.*), and certainly does not correspond to the usage of N. T. writers. Where the assumption is one that is regarded as fulfilled (Rom. 5⁶ 2 Cor. 5³ Eph. 4²¹), it is the context that conveys the implication. In Col. 1²³ there is no such implication, and perhaps not in Eph. 3². See WM. p. 561, fn. 6, and Ell. Ltft. Sief. In the present passage the conditional clause must be understood without implication as to its fulfilment, since the context, indeed the whole letter, shows that while the apostle fears that the Galatians are about to turn back and so prove themselves τοσαῦτα παθεῖν εἰκῇ, yet he *hoped*, and was in this very appeal seek-ing, to avert this disaster. See esp. 4¹¹ 5⁷⁻¹⁰.

5. ὁ οὖν ἐπιχορηγῶν ὑμῖν τὸ πνεῦμα καὶ ἐνεργῶν δυνάμεις ἐν ὑμῖν ἐξ ἔργων νόμου ἢ ἐξ ἀκοῆς πίστεως; "He therefore that supplied the Spirit richly to you, and wrought miracles among you, did he do these things on ground of works of law or of a hearing of faith?" This sentence in effect repeats the question of v. ², and, like that, is doubtless to be understood as referring to the experiences of the Galatians in connection with and shortly after their conversion. The two participles, ἐπιχορηγῶν and ἐνεργῶν, limited by one article evidently refer to the same person, and describe related activities affecting the same persons (ὑμῖν . . . ἐν ὑμῖν). It is obvious, there-fore, that the two parts of the phrase are to be regarded as mutually interpretative. This, in turn, implies that the apostle has in mind chiefly the charismatic manifestation of the Spirit (see detached note on Πνεῦμα and Σάρξ, I D III B. 1 (a), p. 490), which attests itself in δυνάμεις and other kindred manifesta-tions (see 1 Cor. 12¹⁰ 2 Cor. 12¹², and for the use of the word δύναμις Mk. 6² Lk. 10¹³ Acts 2²², etc.). Yet it must also be borne in mind that in the view of the apostle it was one Spirit that produced alike the outward χαρίσματα and the inward moral fruit of the Spirit (chap. 5²², ²³), and hence that the latter though not included in δυνάμεις is not necessarily excluded from the thought expressed by ἐπιχορηγῶν ὑμῖν τὸ πνεῦμα;

the words ἐνεργῶν . . . ὑμῖν may be narrower in scope than
the preceding phrase.   The whole phrase ὁ οὖν . . . ἐν ὑμῖν is
a designation of God (cf. chap. 4⁶ 1 Thes. 4⁸ 2 Cor. 1²², and especially Rom. 5⁵, where the idea of abundant supply, here expressed by ἐπιχορηγῶν, is conveyed by ἐκκέχυται).   θεός is
omitted and left to be supplied in thought as in 2⁸ and probably
in 1¹⁵ also.   δυνάμεις referring to outward deeds, ἐν ὑμῖν naturally takes the meaning "among you" (cf. on ἐν τοῖς ἔθνεσιν,
1¹⁶ 2²); yet in view of the dative ὑμῖν after ἐπιχορηγῶν the
δυνάμεις must be supposed to have been wrought not prin-
cipally by Paul but by the Galatians themselves, as 1 Cor.
12¹⁰, ²⁸, ²⁹ imply was the case among the Corinthians.   2 Cor.
12¹² indeed suggests that such things were signs of the apostle,
yet probably not in the sense that he only wrought them, but
that the δυνάμεις of the apostle were in some way more notable,
or that they constituted a part of the evidence of his apostleship.   The phrases ἐξ ἔργων νόμου and ἐξ ἀκοῆς πίστεως are,
of course, to be taken as in the similar question in v. ².

'Επιχορ·, comp. of ἐπί and χορηγέω, expresses strongly the idea "to
supply abundantly."   The simple verb means to defray the expense
of providing a "chorus" at the public feast.   In view of 2 Pet. 1⁵,
ἐπιχορηγήσατε ἐν τῇ πίστει ὑμῶν τὴν ἀρετήν, and Phil. 1¹⁹ ἐπιχορηγίας
τοῦ πνεύματος, the preposition ἐπί is to be interpreted not as directive
(so Ell. Beet, Sief.), but, with Ltft., as additive and hence in effect
intensive, and, therefore, as still further emphasising the idea of abun-
dance.   Cf. 2 Cor. 9¹⁰ Col. 2¹⁹ 2 Pet. 1⁵, ¹¹.   From these participles,
ἐπιχορ· and ἐνεργ·, the unexpressed verbs of the sentence are to be
supplied, but they afford no clue to the tense of such verbs.   To this
the only guide is the fact that the apostle is still apparently speaking
of the initial Christian experience of the Galatians and, in effect, repeating here the question of v. ².   This would suggest aorists here also,
ἐπεχορήγησε and ἐνήργησε.   The participles may be either general
presents (BMT 123), in effect equivalent to nouns, "the supplier,"
"the worker," or progressive presents, and in that case participles of
identical action, since they refer to the same action as the unexpressed
principal verbs (BMT 120).   The choice of the present tense rather
than the aorist shows that the apostle has in mind an experience extended enough to be thought of as in progress, but not that it is in
progress at the time of writing (Beet), or that the participle is an
imperfect participle (Sief.; cf. BMT 127).

2. *Argument from the faith of Abraham, refuting the*
contention of his opponents that only through con-
formity to law could men become sons of Abraham
(3⁶⁻⁹).

Passing abruptly, in a subordinate clause, from the early
experience of the Galatians to the case of Abraham, the argument of the apostle revolves, from this point to the end of
chap. 4, mainly around the subject of the blessing to Abraham
and the conditions on which men may participate in it. In
these verses he affirms at the outset his fundamental contention that Abraham was justified by faith, and that so also must
all they be justified who would inherit the blessing promised to
his seed.

⁶*As "Abraham believed God and it was reckoned to him for right-*
eousness." ⁷Know, therefore, that the men of faith, these are sons
of Abraham. ⁸And the scripture, foreseeing that God would
justify the Gentiles on ground of faith, announced the gospel to
Abraham beforehand, saying, "In thee shall all the nations be
blessed." ⁹So that the men of faith are blessed with the faithful
(believing) Abraham.

6. καθὼς "'Αβραὰμ ἐπίστευσεν τῷ θεῷ, καὶ ἐλογίσθη αὐτῷ
εἰς δικαιοσύνην." "as Abraham believed God, and it was
reckoned to him for righteousness." The apostle assumes that
to his question of v.⁵ his readers will, in accordance with the
historic facts, answer: ἐξ ἀκοῆς πίστεως. To this answer he
attaches a comparison between the faith of the Galatians and
that of Abraham. The next two chapters, in which the argument revolves largely around Abraham and Abraham's sons (see
3⁷, ⁸, ¹⁴, ¹⁶, ¹⁸, ²⁹ 4²²⁻³¹), show that this is no mere incidental illustration, but fills a vital place in his argument. The fact itself
suggests, what an examination of the argument confirms, that
Paul is here replying to an argument of his opponents. This
argument, we may safely conjecture, was based on Gen. chaps.
12 and 17, especially 17¹⁰⁻¹⁴, and most especially v.¹⁴, and was
to the effect that according to O. T. no one could participate in
the blessings of God's covenant with Abraham, and so in the

messianic salvation that is inseparably associated with it, who
was not circumcised. Neither the usage of δικαιοσύνη (see detached note on Δίκαιος, Δικαιοσύνη and Δικαιόω, pp. 469 ff.),
nor that of λογίζεται εἰς (see below), is decisive as between the
two meanings: (1) "it was attributed to him as right conduct,"
i. e., "he was accounted to have acted righteously," and (2) "it
was reckoned to him as ground of acceptance." The general
context, however, dealing predominantly with righteousness in
the forensic aspect, acceptance with God, decides for the latter
meaning. Against the argument probably advanced by his
opponents in Galatia to the effect that under the covenant with
Abraham no one is acceptable to God who is not circumcised
(Gen. 17¹⁴; cf. Jub. chap. 15, esp. v.²⁶·), Paul points out that,
according to the scripture, to Abraham himself it was his faith
that was accounted as ground of acceptance.

Λογίζομαι is used in Greek writers frequently and in a variety of
applications of the general meaning "to reckon, to calculate, to deem,
to consider." To express the idea "to credit or charge something to
one's account, to put it to his account," the Greeks used λογ· τινι·
(Dem. 264¹⁶; Lev. 7⁸[¹⁸]. According to Cremer, "to account a thing
as being this or that, or having a certain value," was expressed by
λογ· with two accusatives (Xen. Cyr. 1. 2¹¹, μίαν ἄμφω τούτω τὼ ἡμέρα
λογίζονται). In the Lxx λογίζομαι is the translation of חָשַׁב, "to
reckon," "to account." In N. T. it is used with much the same variation of meanings as in cl. Gr., and the idea "to credit or charge to
one" is expressed in the same way. (Rom. 4⁴· ⁶ 2 Cor. 5¹⁹; cf. Prov.
17²⁸). "To reckon a thing or person to be this or that," or "to account
a thing as having a certain value," is expressed as it is in the Lxx,
who translate the Heb. לְ חָשַׁב by λογ· εἰς. The examples show that
this form of expression may have either of the above-named meanings; "to think (one) to be this or that," or "to count as having the
value of this or that." Thus in 1 Sam. 1¹³: ἐλογίσατο αὐτὴν Ἡλὶ εἰς
μεθύουσαν, it clearly bears the former meaning; so also Rom. 9⁸, τὰ
τέκνα τῆς ἐπαγγελίας λογίζεται εἰς σπέρμα. But in Acts 19²⁷:
κινδυνεύει . . . ἱερὸν εἰς οὐθὲν λογισθῆναι, and in Rom. 2²⁶: οὐχ ἡ
ἀκροβυστία αὐτοῦ εἰς περιτομὴν λογισθήσεται, the latter is apparently the meaning. See also Gen. 15⁶ Ps. 105 (106)³¹ Isa. 29¹⁷ 32¹⁵
40¹⁷ Lam. 4² Hos. 8¹² Wisd. 2¹⁶ 3¹⁷ 9⁶ Jas. 2²³. Even in this second class
of cases, however, the word itself conveys no implication of a reckoning above or contrary to real value, as Cremer maintains. If this

thought is conveyed it must be by the limitations of the word, not by
the word itself. There being in the present passage no such limitations, the idea of estimation contrary to fact can not legitimately be
discovered in the passage. Nor can it be imported into this passage
from Rom. 4¹⁻⁶, concerning which see in detached note on Δικαιοσύνη,
p. 470.

7. Γινώσκετε ἄρα ὅτι οἱ ἐκ πίστεως, οὗτοι υἱοί εἰσιν Ἀβραάμ. "Know therefore that the men of faith, these are
sons of Abraham." πίστις is here not specifically faith in
Jesus Christ, but, as the absence of the article suggests, and the
context with its reference on the one hand to Abraham's faith
in God and on the other to the faith of believers in Jesus clearly
indicates, faith qualitatively thought of and in a sense broad
enough to include both these forms of it. Here, as in Rom. 3³¹ff.,
Paul distinctly implies the essential oneness of faith, towards
whatever expression or revelation of God it is directed. The
preposition ἐκ describes source, yet not source of being—they
do not owe their existence to faith—but source of character and
standing, existence after a certain manner. The expression
οἱ ἐκ πίστεως, therefore, means "those who believe and whose
standing and character are determined by that faith"; men of
faith in the sense of those of whose life faith is the determinative
factor. Here appears for the first time the expression "sons of
Abraham," which with its synonyme, "seed of Abraham," is, as
pointed out above, the centre of the argument in chaps. 3 and 4.
ἄρα marks this statement as a logical consequence of the preceding. Abraham believed God, and was on that ground
accepted by God; therefore, the sons of Abraham are men of
faith. The sentence itself shows that "sons of Abraham" is
not to be taken in a genealogical, but, in the broad use of the
term, an ethical sense. The context indicates clearly that by it
Paul means those who are heirs of the promise made to Abraham, and to be fulfilled to his seed (vv. ¹⁶, ²⁹).

　　The unexpressed premise of this argument is that men become
acceptable to God and heirs of the promise on the same basis on which
Abraham himself was accepted. The ground of this premise in Paul's
mind was doubtless his conviction that God deals with all men on

the same moral basis; in other words, that there is no respect of persons with God (chap. 2⁶; cf. Rom. 2¹¹ 3²⁹, ³⁰ Sir. 35¹²). The expressed premise, derived from scripture, is that this basis was faith. Those who put forth the argument to which this was an answer would have accepted the apostle's definition of sons (or seed) of Abraham, and would probably not have directly contradicted either the expressed or the unexpressed premise of his argument, but would practically have denied the expressed premise. They had probably reached their conclusion, that to be sons of Abraham men must be circumcised, by ignoring faith as the basis of Abraham's justification, and appealing to the express assertion of scripture that the seed of Abraham must be circumcised, and that he who will not be circumcised shall be cut off from God's people, having broken his covenant (Gen. 17⁹⁻¹⁴). The apostle in turn ignores their evidence, and appeals to Gen. 15⁶. In fact the whole passage, Gen. chaps. 12–17, furnishes a basis for both lines of argument. The difference between Paul and his opponent is not in that one appealed to scripture and the other rejected it, but that each selected his scripture according to the bent of his own prejudice or experience, and ignored that which was contrary to it.

Ramsay's explanation of v.⁷ as grounded in Greek customs and usages respecting adoption, and as meaning that because among the Gentiles is found the property of Abraham, viz., his faith, therefore they must be his sons, since only a son can inherit property, ignores all the evidence that Paul is here answering judaistic arguments, and is, therefore, moving in the atmosphere not of Greek but of Old Testament thought, and goes far afield to import into the passage the far-fetched notion of faith as an inheritable property of Abraham. See his *Com. on Gal.* pp. 338 *ff.*

SONS OF ABRAHAM.

It has been suggested above that in the employment of this phrase Paul is turning against his judaising opponents a weapon which they have first endeavoured to use against him, rather than himself introducing the term to the Galatians and founding on it an argument intended to appeal to their unprejudiced minds. It is in favour of this view that the evidence that has been left us does not indicate that it was Paul's habit to commend Christ to the Gentiles either on O. T. grounds in general or in particular on the ground that through the acceptance of Jesus they would become members of the Jewish nation. See, *e. g.*, the reports of his speeches in Acts, 1 Thes., esp. 1²⁻¹⁰ 1 Cor. 2² Phil. 3²⁻⁹. There is, indeed, an approximation to this form of argument in Rom. chaps. 4 and 11. But in both these chapters the apostle is rebutting an argument put forth (or anticipated as likely to be put forth) from the side of the judaisers; chap. 4 contending that in the

case of Abraham there is nothing to disprove, but on the contrary
much to establish, the principle of the justification of uncircumcised
Gentiles through faith, and chap. 11 maintaining that the purpose of
God does not come to nought because of the rejection of Israel from
its place of peculiar privilege, but finds fulfilment in the elect people,
whether Jews or Gentiles. Moreover, precisely in respect to the
Galatians do the testimonies of vv. 1-5 and 27, 28 of this chapter, and
5²⁻⁴, indicate with special clearness that Paul's preaching to them and
their acceptance of Christ had been on an independently Christian
basis—Christ crucified, faith in him, Christian baptism, the gift of
the Spirit manifested in charismatic powers.

An examination of chaps. 3 and 4, moreover, reveals that Paul's
argument here is mainly of the nature of rebuttal. Thus the recurrent
expressions, "sons of Abraham" (3⁷), "blessed with faithful Abraham" (3⁹), "blessing of Abraham" (3¹⁴), "the covenant" and "the
seed" (3¹⁵⁻¹⁷), "Abraham's seed" (3²⁹), all of which have their basis
in Gen. 12 and 17 (cf. Gen. 12³ 17²⁻¹⁰), and the express quotation in 3⁸
of the words of Gen. 12³, all combine to indicate that the O. T. background of the discussion is largely that furnished by Gen. chaps. 12, 17.
But if we turn to these chapters it is at once clear not only that they
furnish no natural basis for a direct argument to the effect that the
Gentiles may participate in the blessing of the Abrahamic salvation
without first becoming attached to the race of his lineal descendants,
but that they furnish the premises for a strong argument for the
position which Paul is here combating. Thus in Gen. 17²⁻⁹ there is
repeated mention of a covenant between God and Abraham, an everlasting covenant with Abraham and his seed throughout their generations, a covenant of blessing on God's part and obligation on their
part, which he and his seed after him are to keep throughout their
generation, and it is said: "This is my covenant which ye shall keep
between me and you and thy seed after thee; every male among you
shall be circumcised" (v.¹⁰) . . . "and it shall be a token of a covenant
betwixt you and me" (v.¹¹). V.¹², moreover, states that this shall
apply both to him that is born in the house and to him that is bought
with money of any foreigner, and v.¹⁴ declares that "the uncircumcised
male who is not circumcised in the flesh of his foreskin, that soul shall
be cut off from his people—he hath broken my covenant." In 12³,
indeed, it is stated that in Abraham all the nations of the earth shall
be blessed (so Paul interprets the sentence), yet there is nothing in
this to intimate that they are to receive this blessing apart from a
racial relation to Abraham, and chap. 17 seems to exclude such a
thought. Indeed, it requires neither perversity nor rabbinic exegesis,
but only a reasonable adherence to the obvious meaning of the passage,
to find in these chapters the doctrine that God's covenant of blessing

was with Abraham and his seed, that none could be included in that covenant save those who being of the blood of Abraham were sealed as his seed by circumcision, or who being adopted into the nation from without also received the seal of circumcision, and that any who refused thus to receive circumcision could have no part in the people of God or the blessing to Abraham's seed, since they had "broken God's covenant." "The covenant with Abraham," "the seed of Abraham," "blessed with faithful Abraham" (*cf.* Jub. 17¹⁸ 19⁸˒⁹), "in Abraham (with an emphasis on 'in') shall all the nations of the world be blessed"—these are apparently the premises and stock phrases of the judaiser's argument—to which was doubtless added, as we can see from Gal. 5¹ᶠᶠ˙, the obvious inference that to enjoy these blessings one must be circumcised, as Gen. 17¹ᶠᶠ˙ says. To the judaiser, whose arguments Paul is answering, "seed of Abraham" meant, as to the Pharisaic author of the book of Jubilees (see chap. 15, esp. v.²⁶), the circumcised descendant of Abraham, with whom might also be included the circumcised proselyte; and to these he limited the blessing of the covenant with Abraham, and so in effect the blessing of God.

That all this would be directly contrary to Paul's position is also evident (*cf.* 5¹⁻⁴). It is scarcely less evident that in this third chapter, confronted by substantially such an argument as this, he was aiming to refute it from the same source from which it was drawn. This he does by appeal to Gen. 15⁶, "Abraham believed God, and it was reckoned to him for righteousness," which though it lay between the two passages which they had used, we may be sure the judaisers had not quoted. On the basis of this passage he puts into their favourite phrases, "seed of Abraham," "blessed with Abraham," a different content from that which they had given to them, and finds for the blessing with which all the nations were to be blessed a different ground and condition. The substitution of "sons of Abraham" for "seed of Abraham" contributes somewhat to that end, even if the former phrase, which is not in Genesis, is not original with Paul (*cf.* Jub. 15³⁰). Affirming on the basis of Gen. 15⁶ that the characteristic thing about Abraham is his faith, and taking the expression "sons of Abraham" in a sense by no means foreign to Semitic use of the term "son" as meaning those who walk in his footsteps (Rom. 4¹²), those who are like him (*cf.* sons of God in Mt. 5⁴⁵ Rom. 8¹⁴), he maintains that the men of faith are sons of Abraham. The various arguments by which the apostle endeavours to substantiate this ethical definition of sons of Abraham as against the physical definition of the judaiser, and in general to show that men obtain God's blessing not by works of law, but by faith, are to be found in this and the following chapter.

As concerns the apostle's method of refuting the argument of his opponents, it is clear that he does not resort to a grammatico-historical exegesis of Genesis, chap. 17. Aside from the fact that on such a basis his opponents must have won, such an argument would scarcely have appealed to his Galatian readers. Instead, while retaining the terminology of the Abrahamic narrative of Genesis, as the exigencies of the situation and the necessity of answering the arguments of his opponents compelled him to do, he makes his appeal to the assertions of Gen. 15⁶ that it was faith that was accounted by God as righteousness, and to the teaching of O. T. as a whole concerning the basis of acceptance with God. Circumcision, which was the chief point of contention, he does not mention, perhaps because the argument of his opponents on this point could not be directly answered. Instead he discusses the larger and underlying question, what is the real nature of God's demands on men and the basis of acceptance with him, contending that not by the fulfilment of legal statutes but by faith does a man become acceptable to God. How he would have dealt with one who admitting this central position should still have asked, "But is not circumcision nevertheless required by God?" these chapters do not show. That despite the explicit teaching of Gen. 17, he nevertheless did maintain not only that it is faith that justifies, but that circumcision was no longer required or, indeed, permissible among Gentiles, and even went further than this and denied the authority of the O. T. statutes as such, shows that he had found some means of discovering on the basis of experience what portions of O. T. were still of value for the religious life. But what kind of experience he conceived to be necessary for this purpose, and whether that kind of experience specifically called by him revelation was requisite, is not by this passage indicated.

8. προϊδοῦσα δὲ ἡ γραφὴ ὅτι ἐκ πίστεως δικαιοῖ τὰ ἔθνη ὁ θεὸς προευηγγελίσατο τῷ Ἀβραὰμ ὅτι "Ἐνευλογηθήσονται ἐν σοὶ πάντα τὰ ἔθνη." "And the scripture foreseeing that God would justify the Gentiles on ground of faith, announced the gospel to Abraham beforehand, saying, In thee shall all the nations be blessed." This is doubtless Paul's answer to an argument put forth by the judaisers to the effect that inasmuch as it is in Abraham that all the nations are to be blessed, the Gentiles to be blessed must be in Abraham, i. e., incorporated in his descendants by circumcision. Appealing to the fact that Abraham was justified by faith (the particle δέ connects this v. with v.⁷, itself deduced from v.⁶), he finds the ground and explanation of the promise that the Gentiles would be blessed in Abraham in the foreseen fact of their justification by faith after the pattern of his justification. He thus converts the very oracle which his opponents have cited (Gen. 12³) into an announcement, in advance, of his own doctrine that God will justify the Gentiles by faith. This is obviously an interpretation after the fact. For the nature of the reasoning, see fine print below.

'Η γραφή (sing.), usually at least, denotes a particular passage of scripture (see Lk. 4²¹ 2 Tim. 3¹⁶ and cf. note on 3²²), and there is no reason to depart from this usage here. The passage referred to is Gen. 12³ (cf. 18¹⁸). The participle is causal, "because the scripture foresaw." Attributing foresight to the scripture is, of course, a figure of speech for the thought that the divine foresight is expressed in the scripture in question. Cf. Philo. Leg. alleg. III 118 (40), εἰδὼς γοῦν ὁ ἱερὸς λόγος. On ἐκ πίστεως δικαιοῖ, see detached notes on Πίστις and Δικαιόω and notes on 2¹⁶ff.. δικαιοῖ is a present for a future (as is demanded by προϊδοῦσα) in indirect discourse. The choice of the present may be due in a measure to the feeling that what is here stated as then future is, in fact, a general principle, God's rule of action in all time. τὰ ἔθνη is clearly "the Gentiles," not "the nations" inclusively, since it is the former whose justification is under discussion. Had he meant to employ an inclusive phrase covering the Gentiles, he must have taken over the full phrase πάντα τὰ ἔθνη from the quotation, where it has the more inclusive sense, ἔθνη meaning "nations." προευηγγελίσατο, found neither elsewhere in N. T. nor in the Lxx or Apocr., but in Philo, Opif. mund. 34 (9); Mutat. nom. 158 (29); Schol. Soph. Trach. 335 (cf. Th. s. v., and Sief. ad loc.), is probably to be taken here specifically in the sense "announced the gospel"; this meaning accords with the usual N. T. usage of εὐαγγέλιον and its cognates, and with the fact that what Paul here represents as fore-announced, ὅτι, etc., is that which was to him the distinctive and central message of the εὐαγγέλιον.

The quotation follows the Lxx of Gen. 12³, but for πᾶσαι αἱ φυλαί substitutes πάντα τὰ ἔθνη of Gen. 18¹⁸, doubtless for the purpose of bringing in the word ἔθνη, which Paul desires because of its current use in the sense of Gentiles. For a similar reason τῆς γῆς found in both passages is omitted. No violence is, however, thereby done to the meaning of the passage, since what is true of all the families (or nations) of the earth is, of course, true of the Gentiles. But in following the Lxx with the passive ἐνευλογηθήσονται the apostle has probably missed the meaning of the Hebrew, which is, "In thee shall all the families of the earth bless themselves," i. e., shall make thee the standard of blessing, saying, "May God bless us as he blessed Abra-

ham." He doubtless takes ἐν in its causal, basal sense, meaning "on
the basis of what he is or has done," and interprets it as having reference to his faith. By virtue of his faith and the establishment in
connection with it of the principle of justification by faith a blessing is
conferred on all the Gentiles, since to them also faith is possible. Whether
the apostle has specifically in mind here the fact that Abraham, when
he believed and had his faith accounted as righteousness, was himself
uncircumcised and, therefore, himself a "Gentile" (as in Rom. 4[10, 11])
is doubtful. There is no reference to that aspect of the matter.

Paul's discovery in the language of Gen. 12[3] of the fact that God will
justify the Gentiles on ground of faith, and that, therefore, this statement is a pre-evangelic announcement of the gospel (of justification
by faith) is not, of course, based on a verbal exegesis of the sentence
as it stands either in Heb. or Lxx. The language itself and alone
will sustain neither his view nor that which we have above supposed
the judaisers to have found in it. But the effort to discover a more
definite meaning than the words themselves conveyed was on both
sides legitimate. The passage meant to the original author more
than its words simply as words expressed. The phrase ἐν σοί, in particular, is a condensed and ambiguous expression which calls for closer
definition. The judaiser doubtless found the basis of his view in a
genealogical sense of ἐν, reinforced by Gen. 17[9-14]. Paul may have
based his interpretation in part on the context of Gen. 12[3]. In its reference to Abraham's response to the divine command to leave his
father's house and go out into another land (see Heb. 11[8] for evidence
that this act of Abraham was in Paul's day accounted one of faith and
cf. v.[9] for evidence that Paul had that phase of it in mind here) he may
have found ground for interpreting ἐν σοί as meaning, "in thee, because by this exercise of faith in God thou hast given occasion to the
establishment and announcement of the principle that God's approval
and blessing are upon those that believe." If this principle is established in Abraham's case it follows not only that the blessing that the
Gentiles are to receive is divine acceptance, but that such acceptance
is on ground of faith. Secondly, he may have found in the fact that
the blessing was extended to all the nations evidence of the fact that
it was not to be bestowed on the basis of the law, since the Gentiles
were not under the law. Yet this reasoning would be precarious, since
it was easy to reply that Gen. 17 made it clear that the nations could
partake in the Abrahamic blessing only in case they joined the seed
of Abraham by circumcision. Thirdly, he may have reasoned that
the oracle ought to be interpreted in view of the fact, to him well
established by his own observation, that God was accepting Gentiles
on the basis of faith without works of law in general or circumcision in
particular. This consideration doubtless had great weight with him,

and was probably the decisive one. It must be remembered, of course, that he is not so much proving by original argument that his doctrine is sustained by scripture as refuting the argument of his opponents that the scripture sustains their view.

9. ὥστε οἱ ἐκ πίστεως εὐλογοῦνται σὺν τῷ πιστῷ Ἀβραάμ. "So that the men of faith are blessed with the faithful (believing) Abraham." A definite statement of what Paul wishes to prove by his previous argument. The emphasis is on οἱ ἐκ πίστεως as against οἱ περιτετμημένοι, or οἱ ἐξ ἔργων νόμου, of whom the judaisers affirmed that they only could inherit the blessings of the promise made to Abraham. That he here says "blessed with . . . Abraham" instead of "justified" is doubtless due to the fact that he is still using the language of his opponents. Note the similarity of this verse to v.[7] and compare notes on that v. "Blessed with Abraham" is clearly equivalent to "sons of Abraham." By the addition of the word πιστῷ (cf. Jub. 17[18] 19[8,9]) the apostle reminds his readers that the important thing about Abraham is the fact of his faith. No undue stress must be laid on the use of σύν instead of the ἐν of the quotation. It may have been his opponents' form of expression; but it was, in any case, congenial to his own thought. It is his constant contention that they who inherit the blessing promised to Abraham must do so on the same basis on which he was blessed, viz., faith, and in that sense "with" him. A reference to the fact that all who should afterwards exercise faith were in the blessing of Abraham proleptically blessed, εὐλογοῦνται being in that case a historical present, is less probable because εὐλογ. seems obviously to refer to the same fact as ἐνευλογ. of the quotation, and because to express this thought unambiguously would have required an aorist.

The adjective πιστῷ is manifestly to be taken in its active sense, as is required by ἐπίστευσεν of v. [6]. See Th. s. v. 2 and esp. Eph. 1[1]. The English word "believing" would more exactly express its meaning, but would obscure the relation between this word and ἐκ πίστεως. The translation, "Those that believe are blessed with believing Abraham," is in some respects better but does not do full justice to οἱ ἐκ πίστεως. See note on v.[7].

3. *Counter-argument that those whose standing is fixed by works of law are by the logic of the legalists under a curse, the curse of the law; yet that their logic is perverse, for O. T. teaches that men are justified by faith, and from the curse of the law Christ redeemed us when he died on the cross (3¹⁰⁻¹⁴).*

The apostle now carries his attack directly into the camp of the enemy, contending on the basis of passages from Deut. and Lev. that those who claim on the basis of scripture that justification is by law must on the same basis admit that the actual sentence of law is one of condemnation; but maintaining that their contention is unjustified, since the scripture itself affirms that the righteous man shall live by faith, and declaring that Christ redeemed us from the curse of the law, in order that on the Gentiles might come the blessing of Abraham (not by law but by faith).

¹⁰*For as many as are of works of law are under a curse. For it is written, "Cursed is every one that continueth not in all the things that are written in the book of the law to do them." ¹¹And that no man is justified in law before God, is evident, because, "The righteous man shall live by faith"; ¹²and the law is not of faith; but, "He that doeth them shall live in them." ¹³Christ delivered us from the curse of the law, becoming a curse for us, because it is written, "Cursed is every one that hangeth on a tree"; ¹⁴that upon the Gentiles might come the blessing of Abraham in Jesus Christ; that we might receive the promise of the Spirit through faith.*

10. Ὅσοι γὰρ ἐξ ἔργων νόμου εἰσὶν ὑπὸ κατάραν εἰσίν, "For as many as are of works of law are under a curse." By this sentence the apostle introduces a new weapon for the refutation of his opponents, an argument *e contrario* by which he seeks to prove that instead of men being blessed by coming under law they must, according to their own premises, come under a curse. There might have been prefixed to it the words of 4²¹: "Tell me, ye that desire to be under law, do ye not hear the law?" The word νόμου is, as always in the phrase ἔργα νόμου, used in its legalistic sense (see on 2¹⁶), and ὅσοι ἐξ ἔργων νόμου are not οἱ ποιηταὶ νόμου, of whom Paul says in Rom. 2¹³ that they will be justified, but men whose standing and character proceed from (ἐκ) works of legalistic obedience to statutes. ὑπὸ κατάραν is a qualitative phrase, equivalent to [ἐπι]κατάρατος. While this sentence undoubtedly represents the apostle's real conviction, in the sense that a man who has only works of law and not faith to commend him to God will actually fail of the divine approval (cf. 2¹⁶), yet it is most important for the purposes of its interpretation to notice that this is not what it is intended to affirm, but rather that the principle of legalism (which he contends is not the basis of God's actual judgment of men) leads logically to universal condemnation, by bringing all under the condemnation of the law. This appears clearly from the fact that the sentence by which he supports the assertion (see below) is one which does not express the apostle's own conviction as to the basis of God's judgment of men, but the verdict of the law. The curse of which the verse speaks is not the curse of God, but as Paul expressly calls it in v.¹³, the curse of the law.

γέγραπται γὰρ ὅτι "'Επικατάρατος πᾶς ὃς οὐκ ἐμμένει πᾶσιν τοῖς γεγραμμένοις ἐν τῷ βιβλίῳ τοῦ νόμου τοῦ ποιῆσαι αὐτά." "For it is written, Cursed is every one that continueth not in all the things that are written in the book of the law to do them." The quotation is from Deut. 27²⁶, with variations that do not materially affect the sense, viz., the omission of ἄνθρωπος after πᾶς, and of ἐν (which, however, many Western and Syrian authorities insert) before πᾶσιν and the substitution of γεγραμμένοις ἐν τῷ βιβλίῳ τοῦ νόμου for λόγοις τοῦ νόμου τούτου, and of αὐτά for αὐτούς. The unexpressed premise of the argument, necessary to make this passage prove the preceding proposition, is that no one does, in fact, continue in all the things that are written in the book of the law to do them. This is not quite identical with the expressed proposition of Rom. 3⁹, this being a legalistic, that an ethical, affirmation; but the failure which the apostle here assumes may nevertheless be precisely in the moral requirements of the law.

It is of capital importance for the understanding of the apostle's argument to observe that the sentence which he here quotes does not at all express his own conception of the basis of God's judgment, but a verdict of law. This sentence, though stated negatively, implies the corresponding affirmative, viz., that he who faithfully performs all the things written in the book of the law lives thereby, and this is actually so stated as the principle of law in v.[12]: "He that doeth them shall live in them." That this is the principle of God's action towards men, Paul expressly denies both directly and indirectly: directly in the immediately following v., as also before in 2[16]; indirectly in that he declares in vv. [15-18] that the principle of faith established under Abraham was not displaced by the subsequent incoming of law, law having for its function not to justify men, but to increase transgression. It is necessary, therefore, throughout the passage, to distinguish between the verdicts of law and the judgments of God, and to recognise that the former are, for Paul, not judgments which reflect God's attitude now or at any time or under any circumstances, but those which the legalist must, to his own undoing, recognise as those of the law interpreted as he interprets it, and which on the basis of his legalism he must impute to God. Those that are of works of law are under the curse of the law, which falls on all who do not fully satisfy its requirements. This being so, Paul argues, the assumption of the legalist that the law is the basis of the divine judgment involves the conclusion that all men are accursed, and must be false. On the harmony of this position with the apostle's belief that the law is of God, see in detached note on Νόμος, pp. 451 ff., and comment on v. [22b] below.

11. ὅτι δὲ ἐν νόμῳ οὐδεὶς δικαιοῦται παρὰ τῷ θεῷ δῆλον, "And that no one is justified in law before God is evident." δέ introduces an additional argument for the position maintained in v.[10]. νόμῳ is manifestly in the legalistic sense; on the force of ἐν, see on 2[17]. παρὰ τῷ θεῷ is a most significant element of the sentence. By it the apostle makes clear that as over against the verdict of law set forth in the preceding sentence he is now speaking of the actual attitude of God. Cf. notes on v.[10].

That the clause preceding δῆλον is the subject of the proposition δῆλόν ἐστι, and the following clause the proof of it, rather than the reverse, which is grammatically possible, is proved by the fact that the following clause is a quotation from O. T., and, therefore, valuable for proof of the apostle's assertion while not itself requiring to be proved.

ὅτι "Ὁ δίκαιος ἐκ πίστεως ζήσεται," "because, The righteous man shall live by faith." On the use of ὅτι, see on ὅτι . . . δῆλον above. In the quotation from Hab. 2⁴ the apostle finds an affirmation of his own doctrine of justification by faith. The particular sense which the words bore for Paul and which he intended them to convey to his readers is undoubtedly to be determined rather by Pauline usage in general, and by the part which the sentence plays in the apostle's argument, than by the meaning which the original Heb. had for the prophet. By these considerations ὁ δίκαιος is shown to be a forensic rather than an ethical term, the man approved of God, rather than the morally righteous; πίστεως bears its usual active sense, required by the context, "faith." ζήσεται, "shall live," refers either to the obtaining of eternal life (cf. Rom. 8⁶, ¹⁰, ¹¹, ¹³) as the highest good and goal to which justification looks, or, by metonymy, to justification itself. It is justification, in any case, that is chiefly in mind. Cf. the other instances of quotation from O. T., in which the word occurs (v.¹² Rom. 1¹⁷ 10⁵). The terms δίκαιος and ζήσεται thus combine to express the idea of divine approval, and the sentence in effect means, "It is by faith that he who is approved of God is approved (and saved)." Cf. Rom. 1¹⁷, where the same passage is quoted and the context requires the same meaning. On the relation of this meaning to the original sense of Hab. 2⁴, see below.

For defence of the view that ξήσεται refers to "life," but, as always when Paul speaks of life, to physical life, see Kabisch, *Eschatologie des Paulus*, pp. 52 ff.

The Hebrew of Hab. 2⁴ reads: וְצַדִּיק בֶּאֱמוּנָתוֹ יִחְיֶה. The Lxx read: ὁ δὲ δίκαιος ἐκ πίστεώς μου ξήσεται. אֱמוּנָה signifies "faithfulness," "steadfastness," "integrity." The prophet confronted by the apparent triumph of the wicked Babylonian nation over Israel affirms his conviction that in the end righteous Israel will for her steadfastness prosper. The use of the passage with the active sense of πίστις involves no radical perversion of its meaning, since faith in this sense might easily be conceived to be an ingredient or basis of faithfulness. Yet there is no definite evidence that Paul arrived at the active meaning by such an inferential process. It is, perhaps, quite as likely that he took the passage at what was for him the face value of the Lxx translation.

12. ὁ δὲ νόμος οὐκ ἔστιν ἐκ πίστεως, "and the law is not of faith." That is, the principles of legalism and of faith are mutually exclusive as bases of justification. It would have been formally more exact to have used ὁ νόμος and ἡ πίστις or ἐξ ἔργων νόμου and ἐκ πίστεως. But with essential clearness the apostle employs in the predicate the prepositional phrase that was the watchword of the one doctrine, though for the other he had used in the subject a nominative in preference to the grammatically harsh prepositional expression. By this assertion the apostle excludes the thought of compromise between the two principles. Faith is one thing, legalism another, and as bases of justification they can not be combined. No doubt there were those who sought to combine them, admitting that justification was by faith, but claiming that obedience to law was nevertheless requisite to salvation; as a modern Christian will affirm that religion is wholly a spiritual matter, yet feel that he is surer of salvation if he has been baptised.

ἀλλ' "Ὁ ποιήσας αὐτὰ ζήσεται ἐν αὐτοῖς." "but, He that doeth them shall live in them." The ἀλλά marks the antithesis between this statement of O. T. (Lev. 18⁵), which the apostle takes as a statement of the principle of legalism, and the possibility just denied that this principle and that of faith might somehow be reconciled or reduced to one. One must mentally supply after ἀλλ' "the law says." Thus to the principle of legalism stated in its negative form in v.¹⁰ and set over against the quotation from Habakkuk with its affirmation of the principle of faith, the apostle adds an assertion of the principle of legalism in its positive form, also taken like that in v.¹⁰ from O. T. On the point of view from which the apostle thus quotes

O. T. for both doctrines, see on v.[10], and more fully in fine print below.

13. Χριστὸς ἡμᾶς ἐξηγόρασεν ἐκ τῆς κατάρας τοῦ νόμου "Christ delivered us from the curse of the law." "The curse of the law" here spoken of can consistently with the context be none other than that which is spoken of in v.[10], viz., the curse which the legalistic passages of O. T. pronounce on those who do not perfectly obey its statutes. As pointed out above on v.[10], this is not the judgment of God. To miss this fact is wholly to misunderstand Paul. But if the curse is not an expression of God's attitude towards men, neither is the deliverance from it a judicial act in the sense of release from penalty, but a release from a false conception of God's attitude, viz., from the belief that God actually deals with men on a legalistic basis. The work here ascribed to Christ is, therefore, of the same nature as that spoken of in Rom. 3[21ff.], and there said to be accomplished by Christ in his death, viz., a revelation of the way of achieving acceptance with God, a demonstration of the divine character and attitude towards men.

The verb ἐξαγοράζω, found in late writers only from the Lxx (Dan. 2[8] only) down, is used in two senses: (1) "to buy up," or, figuratively, "to secure" (by adroitness): Diod. Sic. 36. 2[2]; and (2) "to redeem, to deliver at cost of some sort to the deliverer." The middle occurs once in Eph. and once in Col. in the former sense in the phrase ἐξαγοράζεσθαι τὸν καιρόν. The active occurs in the same sense in Dan. 2[8]. The active is found in the second sense in Gal. 4[5], ἵνα τοὺς ὑπὸ νόμου ἐξαγοράσῃ. The meaning here is evidently the same as in 4[5], "to deliver, to secure release for one," probably with the implication conveyed in the etymological sense of the word (the simple verb ἀγοράζω means "to buy," and is frequently used in this sense in the Lxx) that such deliverance involves cost of some kind (effort, suffering, or loss) to him who effects it. The question to whom the price is paid is irrelevant, unless demanded by the context, intruding into later usage of the word an idea left behind in its earlier development.

It requires no argument to show that in the phrase ἐκ τῆς κατάρας τοῦ νόμου the apostle has in mind some phase, aspect, or conception of the law of God, not civil law or law in an inclusive sense of the word. It has been maintained above that he refers to law legalistically understood, and to deliverance from the curse which God is falsely supposed to pronounce upon men on the basis of such a law.

In support of this interpretation and against the view, that the law here spoken of is law in any other sense of the word (see detached note on Νόμος, esp. V 2a, b, c, d), or that the deliverance is the forgiveness of the individual, are the following considerations.

(a) Throughout this passage Paul is speaking of law legalistically understood, law as a body of statutes for failure to obey any of which men are under a curse. This is especially clear in vv.¹⁰⁻¹² (q. v.). In the phrase κατάρα τοῦ νόμου itself there is, indeed, no insuperable obstacle to taking νόμος in the abstract-historical sense (cf. Rom. 2¹³, and detached note on Νόμος V 2 b), and understanding by it the condemnation which God actually pronounces upon those who not simply fall short of perfect obedience to the statutes of the law, but hold down the truth in iniquity (Rom. 1¹⁸), who disobey the truth and obey iniquity (2⁸), who though they may be hearers of the law are not doers of it (2¹³). κατάρα would in that case represent substantially the idea expressed by ὀργή in Rom. 1¹⁸ 2⁸, to which it is practically equivalent. Nor is an abrupt change to law in another sense in itself impossible. It might easily occur if the change of sense were made evident, as it is in Rom. 3²¹ and in various other passages, or if the argument were such and the two meanings so related that the logic of the passage would be but little affected, whether the meaning be retained or changed, as in Rom. 2¹², ¹³. But in the present passage these conditions do not exist. The continuity and validity of the argument depend on the word in the present verse meaning the same as in the preceding verses. Indeed, there is no place in the whole chapter for a change in the meaning or reference of the word νόμος. Yet, it must also be recognised that the law of which the apostle speaks is not legalism in the abstract, but a concrete historical reality. It came four hundred and thirty years after Moses (v.¹⁷); its fundamental principle is expressed in a definite passage of O. T. (v.¹⁰).

(b) The tense of the verb ἐξηγόρασεν is itself an argument for taking the deliverance referred to not as an often repeated individual experience but as an epochal event. But there are other more decisive considerations. Thus (i) it is achieved by Christ on the cross; (ii) its primary effect is in relation to the Jews; for the use of the article with νόμου in v. ¹³, excluding a qualitative use of the noun, and the antithesis of ἡμᾶς in v. ¹³ to τὰ ἔθνη in v. ¹⁴, necessitate referring the former primarily to the Jews; and (iii) the purpose of the redemptive act is to achieve a certain result affecting the Gentiles as a class. These facts combine to indicate that the apostle is speaking not, e. g., of the forgiveness of the individual, his release from the penalty of his sins, but of a result once for all achieved in the death of Christ on the cross. It is, therefore, of the nature of the ἀπολύτρωσις of Rom. 3²⁴ rather than of the λύτρωσις of 1 Pet. 1¹⁸.

But the fact that the deliverance is an epochal event confirms our judgment that it is law in a legalistic sense that is here referred to. Condemnation for failure to fulfil law in the ethical sense is not abolished by the death of Christ. *Cf.* chap. 5[13ff.] Rom. 2[1-16] 8[1-4]. Nor can the reference be to the law as a historic régime, the Mosaic system as such. For though Rom. 10[4] might be interpreted as meaning that Christ is the end of the law in this sense, and though the apostle undoubtedly held that those who believe in Christ are not under obligation to keep the statutes of the Law of Moses as such, yet (i) release from obligation to obey statutes is not naturally spoken of as release from the *curse* of the law, and (ii) the idea of the abolition of statutes is foreign to this context. It remains, therefore, to take the term in its legalistic sense, yet as referring to an actual historically existent system.

Yet the release from the curse of the law can not be the abolition of legalism in the sense that the divine government before Christ having been on a legalistic basis is henceforth of a different character   Against any interpretation that makes the curse of the law a divine condemnation of men on grounds of legalism, in force from Moses to Christ, it is a decisive objection that the apostle both elsewhere and in this very chapter insists that God had never so dealt with men, but that the principle of faith established before law was not set aside by it (see esp. v.[17]).

Neither can we suppose that Paul, though admitting that legalism had historic existence in the O. T. period and concrete expression in O. T., denied to it all value and authority, as if, *e. g.*, it were a work of the devil. For he elsewhere declares that the law is holy and righteous and good (Rom. 7[12]) and in this chap. (vv.[19f.]) implies that it had its legitimate divinely appointed function. Exalting the older principle of faith above the later law, the apostle yet sees value and legitimacy in both.

The only explanation that meets these conditions is that in the historic legalism of O. T. Paul saw a real but not an adequate disclosure of the divine thought and will, one which when taken by itself and assumed to be complete gave a false notion of God's attitude towards men.

The curse of the law is the verdict of a reality, of the law isolated from the rest of the O. T. revelation. But so isolated it expressed, according to Paul, not the truth but a fraction of it; for the law, he held, was never given full possession of the field, never set aside the previously revealed principle of faith (3[17]). Its function was never that of determining the standing of men with God. The curse of the law was, therefore, an actual curse in the sense that it expressed the verdict of legalism, but not in the sense that he on whom it fell was ac-

cursed of God. It was a disclosure of the status of a man on a basis
of merit estimated by actual achievement, not of God's attitude towards
him. The latter, Paul maintained, was determined by other than
legalistic considerations, by his faith (v.⁶), by his aspiration, his striv-
ing, the fundamental character of his life and conduct (Rom. 2⁶⁻¹¹).

But if this is the meaning of the phrase, "the curse of the law," and
if deliverance from it was an epochal event accomplished by the death
of Christ on the cross, it must have been achieved through the reve-
latory value of the event, by that which God through that event
revealed; and this either in the sense that God thereby announced the
end of that system of legalism which in the time of Moses came in to
achieve a temporary purpose, or in that he thereby revealed his own
attitude towards men, and so gave evidence that legalism never was
the basis of his judgment of men. It is the first of these thoughts that
Paul has apparently expressed in Rom. 10⁴, and it is not impossible
here. Yet it is more consonant both with the fact that Paul speaks
of deliverance from the curse of the law rather than from the law, and
with what follows (see below on γενόμενος . . . κατάρα, etc.) to suppose that, as in Rom. 3²⁵, ²⁶ 5⁸, he is speaking of a disclosure of the unchanged and unchangeable attitude of God.

If, indeed, and in so far as the law is thought of as brought to an
end, it is probably in the sense that this results from the revelation
of God's character rather than by anything like a decree in terms abolish-
ing it. This is also not improbably the thought that underlies Rom. 10⁴.

γενόμενος ὑπὲρ ἡμῶν κατάρα, "becoming a curse for us."
κατάρα, literally "a curse," "an execration," "an expression or
sentence of reprobation" (as in the preceding clause and v.¹⁰),
is evidently here used by metonymy, since a person can not
become a curse in a literal sense. Such metonymy is common
in Paul. Cf. the use of περιτομή for the circumcised, and
ἀκροβυστία for Gentiles in 2⁷, ⁹ and Rom. 3³⁰. Cf. also 1 Cor. 1³⁰,
"who became wisdom to us from God, and righteousness and
sanctification and redemption"; but esp. 2 Cor. 5²¹: "Him who
knew no sin he made to be sin on our behalf (ὑπὲρ ἡμῶν), that
we might become righteousness of God in him." As there
ἁμαρτία stands in a sense for ἁμάρτωλος and δικαιοσύνη for
δίκαιος, so doubtless here κατάρα stands for [ἐπι]κατάρατος
as the ἐπικατάρατος in the following quotation also suggests.
More important is the fact, which the close connection with the
phrase ἐκ τῆς κατάρας τοῦ νόμου indicates, that κατάρα here

refers to a curse *of the law*, which, as we have seen above, is not to be understood as a curse of God. γενόμενος is probably a participle of means, the whole phrase expressing the method by which Christ redeemed us from the curse. ὑπὲρ ἡμῶν means "on our behalf." It can not be pressed to mean "in our place" (ἀντί). See further on 1³, ὑπὲρ τῶν ἁμαρτιῶν ἡμῶν. Precisely in what sense and how Christ came under the curse of the law, and how this availed to deliver us from that curse, must appear from a consideration of the quotation by which Paul supports his affirmation.

The following are conceivable meanings of the phrase γενόμενος . . . κατάρα, taken by itself: (1) Christ became a curse in that he was the object of divine reprobation, personally an object of divine disapproval. (2) He became the actual object of divine reprobation vicariously, enduring the penalty of others' sins. (3) He experienced in himself God's wrath against sinners, not as himself the object of divine wrath, but vicariously and by reason of his relation to men. (4) He was the object of human execration—cursed by men. In this case γενόμενος would be a participle not of means, but of accompanying circumstance, the phrase suggesting the cost at which Jesus redeemed us from the curse of the law. How he did so would be left entirely unsaid. (5) He fell under the curse *of the law*, not of God or of men. The first of these five interpretations is easily excluded by its utter contrariety to Paul's thought about God's attitude towards Christ and the righteousness of his judgments. The second, though often affirmed, is not sustained by any unambiguous language of the apostle. The third is probably quite consistent with the apostle's thought. As in 2 Cor. 5²¹ he says that "him who knew no sin he made to be sin for us, that we might become righteousness of God in him," not meaning that Christ actually became sinful, but that by reason of his relation to men he experienced in himself the consequences of sin. so by this language he might mean that Jesus by reason of his sympathetic relation with men experienced in himself the curse of God upon men for their sin. But there is no expression of this thought in the context, and it is, on the whole, inharmonious with the meaning of the word κατάρα throughout the passage. The fourth is equally possible in itself, but, like all the preceding, is open to the objection that it does not, as the context suggests, make the curse that of the law. The fifth, though without support in any other passage of the apostle's writings, is most consonant with the context, if not actually required by it.

ὅτι γέγραπται, "'Ἐπικατάρατος πᾶς ὁ κρεμάμενος ἐπὶ ξύλου," "because it is written, Cursed is every one that hangeth on a tree." The quotation, from Deut. 21²³, is introduced to support the statement that Christ became a curse, not that he thereby "delivered us from the curse of the law," or that it was "for us." The original passage refers to the body of a criminal which, after the man had been put to death, was hanged upon a tree. In such a case it is said, "Thou shalt surely bury him the same day; for he that is hanged is the curse of God, that thou defile not thy land which the Lord thy God giveth thee for an inheritance." Between this passage and the fact of which the apostle is speaking there seems to be only a superficial connection. On the question whether the apostle found a more real connection, see below.

Deut. 21²³, which in the Lxx reads ὅτι κεκατηραμένος ὑπὸ θεοῦ πᾶς κρεμάμενος ἐπὶ ξύλου, may be supposed to furnish support to Paul's previous statement that Christ became a curse for us in several ways: (1) γενόμενος κατάρα being understood to have any of the first three meanings suggested above, the O. T. passage may be quoted purely for its verbal resemblance to the assertion which the apostle has made; there is manifestly nothing in its real meaning to support the assertion that Christ, who died not for his own sins but as an innocent man, came in any sense under the curse of God. Its use for this purpose would be verbalism pure and simple. (2) If γενόμενος κατάρα be supposed to refer to the reprobation of men, the passage may be used to explain that reprobation, men naturally looking upon one who died the death of a criminal as actually such and under the curse of God. (3) If κατάρα refers to the curse of the law, then the quotation may be understood to define precisely how and in what sense he became a curse of the law. Inasmuch as the law affirms that whoever is hanged on a tree is accursed, and Jesus died on the cross, he falls under this verdict and the curse of the law. But inasmuch as this verdict is manifestly false and monstrous, in it the law does not so much condemn Christ as itself, and thereby, since false in one it may be so in all, it emancipates us from the fear of its curse. Or, (4), with somewhat less of literalism κατάρα may be supposed to refer to the curse of the law, the O. T. quotation, however, being cited not solely with reference to the fact of hanging on the tree, but to all that the crucifixion represents. Law and he who takes his stand on law, must say that Christ, having died on the cross, is a sinner—i. e., that under law no one could come to such a death who was not himself guilty of sin—as vividly the law says in the words of the quotation. But in that verdict of legalism it condemns itself, and in the fact that Christ the righteous died the death of the cross it is evident that the government of God is not one of legalism, but of love and of vicarious suffering, the righteous for the wicked.

Of these various interpretations the last two alone comport with the fact that it is the curse of the law of which Paul is speaking throughout the passage, and the last is preferable because more consonant with the fact that for Paul generally the cross signifies not the outward fact that Jesus died by crucifixion or on a tree, but all that the fact stood for as a revelation of God and the principles of his dealings with men. See 1 Cor. 1[17, 18, 23]. So understood, the quotation serves the same purpose as those in vv.[10, 12], viz., to show the impossible position in which the logic of legalism lands its advocates. The argument is akin, also, to that of 2[21], in that it uses the fact of the death of Christ to refute the legalist, Paul there saying that legalism makes that death needless, here that it proves Christ accursed. The omission of ὑπὸ θεοῦ is probably due, as Ltft. suggests, to a shrinking of the apostle from the suggestion that Christ was the object of God's reprobation.

If both the latter interpretations be rejected because it seems impossible that under these words there lies so much thought not directly expressed (though this objection will hold against any interpretation that seeks to ascertain the real thought of the apostle) our choice of a substitute would probably be among the following combinations of views already separately objected to: (1) The curse of the law may be supposed to be a real curse, the death on the cross a penal expiation of it, and the O. T. passage a proof of its penal character. The serious objection to this interpretation is not that the O. T. passage is related to the fact which it is supposed to sustain in a purely verbal and external way, for in view of 3[16, 20] and 4[24] (on which, however, see the possibility that these are early scribal glosses) it can not be assumed that Paul was incapable of such a use of scripture, but that in making the curse of the law a real curse (of God) this interpretation makes the apostle directly contradict the very proposition which he is maintaining in this chapter, viz., that men are not judged by God on a basis of legalism. Or (2) we may suppose that the phrase "the curse of the law" bears the meaning required by the context, but that after the first clause of v.[13] the apostle abandons thought for words, and seeks to substantiate his assertion that Christ redeemed us from the curse of the law by affirming that Christ took upon him the curse of our sin, and that he sustains this statement by an O. T. passage which supports it in sound but not in sense. As in the preceding case, the real difficulty of the interpretation lies in the method of reasoning which it imputes to Paul. Having in Χριστός . . . νόμου affirmed our release from the curse of the law, according to this interpretation he substantiates this statement by affirming that Christ became a curse in a quite different sense of the words, and one really remote from the context. That the scripture that he quotes supports this statement only in appearance is a secondary matter. It remains to consider as a final possibility (3) the view that the apostle follows up his affirmation that Christ redeemed us from the curse of the law, not with proof or explanation, but with a statement intended to suggest the cost at which he achieved the deliverance of men from the curse of the law, γενόμενος . . . κατάρα, referring to the reprobation of Christ by men. Cf. Heb. 12²; see (4) on p. 172. The O. T. passage then explains why the death on the cross led men to look on him with reprobation as one accursed. To this interpretation the only serious objection is that the transition from the idea "cursed by the law" to "cursed by men" is expressed only negatively, and it would seem inadequately, by the absence of any limiting phrase after κατάρα; the omission of the ὑπὸ θεοῦ of the Lxx naturally implies the carrying forward of a reference to the law. In order of probability this view stands next after the fourth in the preceding list.

The choice between interpretations must be made, not on the ground that one does and the other does not supply unexpressed elements of thought, or that one does and the other does not take O. T. scripture in its historic sense, but on the answer to the question whether it is more consistent with the apostle's usual methods of thinking to argue illogically, dealing in words rather than thoughts, or to express reasonably consistent thought in brief and obscure language.

14. ἵνα εἰς τὰ ἔθνη ἡ εὐλογία τοῦ Ἀβραὰμ γένηται ἐν Ἰησοῦ Χριστῷ, "that upon the Gentiles might come the blessing of Abraham in Jesus Christ." In this clause and the following one the apostle states the purpose not of any of the subordinate elements of v.¹³, but of the whole fact, especially the principal element, ἐξηγόρασεν . . . τοῦ νόμου. By ἡ εὐλογία τοῦ Ἀβραάμ must be understood, in the light of vv.⁸, ⁹, the blessing of justification by faith, which, according to Paul's interpretation of Gen. 12³ (cf. Gen. 28⁴), was promised beforehand to the Gentiles, and which they shared with him. This blessing came to the Gentiles in Jesus Christ in that it was through him that the purpose of God to accept men by faith was revealed, and that through faith in him they enter into actual participation in the blessing.

εἰς is probably to be taken as marking its object as the destination of a movement. *Cf.* 1 Thes. 1⁵. In ἐν 'Ιησοῦ Χριστῷ the preposition is doubtless used in its basal sense; *cf.* on 2¹⁷.

'Εν 'Ιησοῦ Χριστῷ is the reading of אB Syr. (psh.) Aeth., most authorities reading ἐν X. 'I. The facts stated in the textual note on 2¹⁴ with reference to the tendency of the mss., together with the high authority of אB, leave no room for doubt that ἐν Χριστῷ 'Ιησοῦ is a corruption due to assimilation of the text to the usual form. *Cf.* the other instances of אB and secondary authorities against the other uncials in 3⁷· ¹⁰ 4¹⁰· ·⁹ 5²¹ 6¹⁰.

ἵνα τὴν ἐπαγγελίαν τοῦ πνεύματος λάβωμεν διὰ τῆς πίστεως. "that we might receive the promise of the Spirit through faith." τὴν ἐπαγγελίαν τοῦ πνεύματος is a metonymic phrase meaning the promised Spirit. *Cf.* Lk. 24⁴⁹ Acts 1⁴ 26⁶ Heb. 9¹⁵ and especially Acts 2³³. See also the similar cases of ἐλπίς meaning "that which is hoped for," chap. 5⁵ Col. 1⁵. This second ἵνα-clause is probably to be taken, not as dependent on the first, but as co-ordinate with it, and the implied subject ἡμεῖς as referring to Christians as such, rather than to believing Jews, as is probably the case in v.¹³; for it is difficult to see how the reception of the Spirit by the Jews could be conditioned upon the Gentiles obtaining the blessing of Abraham; and if the two clauses referred to Gentiles and Jews respectively this antithesis would probably have been indicated by an expressed ἡμεῖς in the second clause. Obviously the latter can not refer to the Gentiles only. Christ's redemption of us from the curse of the law had then as co-ordinate ends the opening of the door of faith and justification through faith apart from works of law, to the Gentile, and the bestowment of the promised Spirit on those that have faith. The adaptation of means to end as respects this second clause seems obviously to lie in the fact that the redemption of men from the curse of the law by their enlightenment as to God's true attitude to them carries with it the revelation of faith as the means by which men become acceptable to God, and that through such faith they receive the Spirit. *Cf.* v.²; also vv.²⁴⁻²⁶ and 4⁶. These final clauses, therefore, with their double statement of the purpose of Christ's redemptive work, confirm the

conclusion already reached that the redemption from the curse
of the law was an epochal event, having its significance and its
redemptive power in the revelation which it conveys of the true
attitude of God towards men.

> Whether in speaking of the promise of the Spirit the apostle has in
> mind the prophecy of Joel. 2²⁸ Ezek. 36²⁷, or, being acquainted with
> the tradition underlying Acts 1⁵, refers to a promise of Jesus can not
> be stated with certainty. It is possible that the second final clause
> is to be taken as, to this extent, epexegetic of the first that the Holy
> Spirit is a definition of the blessing of Abraham. In that case the
> apostle refers to the promise to Abraham and has learned to interpret
> this as having reference to the gift of the Spirit. This possibility is
> in a measure favoured by the use of ἐπαγγελία in vv. ¹⁶, ¹⁷ of the promise
> to Abraham.

> ### 4. Argument from the irrevocableness of a covenant and the priority of the covenant made with Abraham to the law, to the effect that the covenant is still in force (3¹⁵⁻¹⁸).

Drawing his argument from the common knowledge of men
that contracts once agreed to can not be modified (except by
mutual consent), the apostle applies this thought to the covenant with Abraham, contending that the law coming centuries afterwards can not modify it.

¹⁵*Brethren, I speak from the point of view of men. Though it
be man's, yet a covenant once established no one annuls or adds
to.* (¹⁶*Now to Abraham were the promises spoken, "and to his
seed." He saith not, "And to the seeds," as of many, but as of
one, "And to thy seed," which is Christ.*) ¹⁷*Now this I mean:
A covenant previously established by God, the law, which came four
hundred and thirty years afterwards, does not annul so as to make
inoperative the promise.* ¹⁸*For if the inheritance is of law, it is
no longer of promise; but to Abraham God granted it by promise.*

15. Ἀδελφοί, κατὰ ἄνθρωπον λέγω. "Brethren, I speak from
the point of view of men." On the use of ἀδελφοί, see on 1².
Its use here is probably due to the apostle's feeling that he is
now addressing the Galatians more directly than in the preceding paragraph, in which he was really speaking to the judaisers

whose argument he was refuting, and to his desire to secure their friendly attention. On κατὰ ἄνθρωπον, see on 1[11]. The regular meaning of the phrase after a verb is, "as men do," the specific point of resemblance being indicated in the context. Here this general meaning naturally becomes, "I speak as men do about their affairs" (*cf.* 1 Cor. 9[8]), *i. e.*, "I draw an illustration from common human practice." A reference to human authority such as is suggested in 1 Cor. 9[8] is improbable here, both because there is no suggestion of it in the context and because the depreciation of the value of the argument which such a reference would imply is uncalled for and without value for the apostle's purpose.

ὅμως ἀνθρώπου κεκυρωμένην διαθήκην οὐδεὶς ἀθετεῖ ἢ ἐπιδιατάσσεται. "Though it be man's, yet a covenant once established no one annuls or adds to." Of the force of ὅμως two views are possible: (1) It may mark an antithesis between κατὰ ἄνθρωπον λέγω and what follows. In this case, since ἀνθρώπου, etc., is not directly adversative to κατὰ . . . λέγω, the second member of the antithesis must be supposed to be suggested by, rather than expressed in, the words that follow; most probably by the whole argument of vv. [15b, 17]. The thought will then be, "Though I speak from the point of view of men's affairs, yet what may be so said is not without force: a man's ratified covenant," etc. (So substantially Rück. Olsh., cited by Wies.) (2) The antithesis may be between ἀνθρώπου and what follows. This involves a trajection by which ὅμως stands not in its natural place before the second member of the antithesis, but before the first. *Cf.* 1 Cor. 14[7]: ὅμως τὰ ἄψυχα φωνὴν διδόντα . . . ἐὰν διαστολὴν τοῖς φθόγγοις μὴ δῷ . . . where ὅμως indicates an antithesis between ἄψυχα and φωνὴν διδόντα, or more probably between φωνὴν διδόντα and ἐὰν διαστολὴν . . . μὴ δῷ. With this passage have been compared also Plat. *Phaed.* 91C (φοβεῖται μὴ ἡ ψυχὴ ὅμως καὶ θειότερον καὶ κάλλιον ὂν τοῦ σώματος προαπολλύηται ἐν ἁρμονίας εἴδει οὖσα), Thuc. 7.77[3], and Xen. *Cyr.* 5. 1[26] (νῦν δ' αὖ οὕτως ἔχομεν ὡς σὺν μὲν σοὶ ὅμως καὶ ἐν τῇ πολεμίᾳ ὄντες θαρροῦμεν). *Cf.* WM. p. 693, Kühner-Gerth,

II 2, p. 85. In this case the contrast is between the διαθήκη as man-made and its irrevocability after its ratification. The first view has the advantage of grammatical simplicity. But in view of the instances of trajection, including the only other instance of ὅμως in Paul, and of the greater logical simplicity of the second view, it is probably to be preferred. κεκυρωμένην, characterising the supposed covenant as having been executed and hence actually in force, expresses a thought which is implied in διαθήκην, but adds to the clearness of the sentence. It clearly belongs to the second element of the antithesis, with οὐδεὶς ἀθετεῖ. The validation of the covenant is evidently in the apostle's mind not, like ἀνθρώπου, a fact in spite of which no one annuls it or adds to it, but the ground of the irrevocability, as is implied in the re-expression of the idea in the word προκεκυρωμένην in v.¹⁷. By διαθήκη must be understood not "testament" (as Th. Cremer, Sief. Ram. Zahn, ERV.mg. Behm, Lohmeyer, et al.) nor "stipulation," "arrangement," in a sense broad enough to cover both will and covenant (Hauck in *Th. St. u. Kr.*, 1862, pp. 514 ff., Segond, and Bous.), but as the usage of N. T. in general and of Paul in particular and the context here require, "covenant" in the sense of the O. T. בְּרִית (so Mey. Alf. Ell. Ltft. ERV.text, ARV. Beet). *Cf.* on v.¹⁷, and for fuller statement of the evidence, see detached note on Διαθήκη, pp. 496 ff.

Ἀνθρώπου. The singular number of this noun furnishes no argument against the meaning "covenant" (a) because, as will appear below, the covenant as conceived of in Hebrew thought, though constituting a relation between two persons often proceeds from one, and (b) because the noun is here most naturally understood as qualitative as in the phrase κατὰ ἄνθρωπον. *Cf.* 1¹ δι' ἀνθρώπου and other examples given there.

Κεκυρωμένην from κυρόω, cognate with κύριος (*cf.* the adjectival use in 1 Mac. 8³⁰ in the sense "established") means "validated," "effected," "executed," referring neither to the drafting of an agreement or will preceding its execution nor to a confirmation which follows the actual execution (the latter sense though occurring is infrequent; see Æsch. *Pers.* 521, and 4 Mac. 7⁹; Plut. *Orat. vit. Lys.*), but to the execution itself, that without which it would not be in force at all. The prefixing of the participle to διαθήκην, therefore, simply emphasises what is

implied in the word itself, pointing out that what is referred to is a
διαθήκη actually in force, not simply under consideration or written out
but not yet agreed to and therefore still subject to modification. *Cf.*
Thuc. 8. 6⁹: ἡ ἐκκλησία . . . κυρώσασα ταῦτα διελύθη. Polyb. 1. 11¹:
καὶ τὸ μὲν συνέδριον οὐδ' εἰς τέλος ἐκύρωσε τὴν γνωμήν . . . Boeckh.
C.I.G. 1570 a. 45. τὸ ψήφισμα τὸ κυρωθέν. Gen. 23²⁰: καὶ ἐκυρώθη ὁ ἀγρὸς
. . . τῷ Ἀβραὰμ εἰς κτῆσιν τάφου παρὰ τῶν υἱῶν Χέτ. (Aq. uses the same
word in v.¹⁷). Dan. 6⁹ (Lxx): καὶ οὕτως ὁ βασιλεὺς Δαρεῖος ἔστησε καὶ
ἐκύρωσεν. Plut. *Alcib.* 33¹: τὸ μὲν οὖν ψήφισμα τῆς καθόδου πρότερον ἐκε-
κύρωτο. See also Plut. *Sol.* 30⁵; *Peric.* 32³; *Pomp.* 48³.

οὐδεὶς ἀθετεῖ ἢ ἐπιδιατάσσεται is to be taken without
qualification, least of all with the qualification, "except the
contractor" (so Schm., *Encyc. Bib.* II 1611; *cf.* Zahn, Bous.
ad loc.). That a compact may be modified by common consent
of both the parties to it is, of course, not denied, but simply
assumed and ignored. But to assume that either party alone is
excepted is to deprive the statement of all meaning. For evidence that this assertion itself shows that the διαθήκη ἀνθρώπου, which Paul uses, κατὰ ἄνθρωπον, to prove the unchangeableness of the διαθήκη of God is a covenant, not a
will, see detached note on Διαθήκη, pp. 496 *ff.*

Ἀθετέω, "to render ἄθετος" (= without place or standing, invalid),
occurs from Lxx and Polybius down, signifying in respect to laws and
the like "to disregard," "to violate" (Polyb. 8. 2⁵; Mk. 7⁹ Heb. 10²⁸),
or "to annul," "to abrogate" (1 Mac. 11³⁶ 2 Mac. 13²⁵); of persons "to
set at nought," "to reject," "to rebel against" (Deut. 21¹⁴ Isa. 1²).
Cf. also M. and M. *Voc. s.v.* "To annul" is clearly the meaning here.

Ἐπιδιατάσσεται furnishes the only extant instance of this word,
but διατάσσω is frequent both in Greek writers and N. T. in the sense
"to arrange," "to prescribe"; the middle occurring in Plut. in the
sense "to make a will," "to order by will." The compound ἐπιδιατάσσω
evidently signifies "to make additional prescriptions" (*cf.* ἐπιδιατίθημι,
Dio Cass. 62¹⁵ and ἐπιδιαθήκη, "codicil," Jos. *Ant.* 17. 226 (9⁴) and examples cited by Norton, *A Lexicographical and Historical Study of
Διαθήκη* . . . Chicago, 1908). Whether such prescriptions are contrary
to the original compact (they of course modify it or they would not be
added) is beside the mark; a compact once executed can not be changed.

16. τῷ δὲ Ἀβραὰμ ἐρρέθησαν αἱ ἐπαγγελίαι "καὶ τῷ σπέρματι" αὐτοῦ· "Now to Abraham were the promises spoken,
'and to his seed.'" For the evidence that this proposition and

the next (v.[16]) are parenthetical, see on τοῦτο δὲ λέγω, v.[17]. The promises here spoken of are those which accompanied the covenant and which constituted it on the side of divine grace. On the relation of promise and covenant, see detached note on Διαθήκη, p. 497, and *cf.* Gen. 9[12ff.]; but esp. Gen. 17[1-8]. See also Cremer[10], p. 1062. The apostle more commonly uses the singular ἐπαγγελία (see vv.[17, 18, 22, 29] Rom. 4[13, 14, 16, 20]), but also without marked difference of thought employs the plural (see v.[21] and Rom. 9[4]), the basis for which is in the repeated occasions on which the promise was made to Abraham, and the various forms in which it was expressed. See Gen. 12[2ff.] 13[14-17] 15[1, 5, 18] 17[2-8]. On Paul's definition of the content of the promise as interpreted in the light of subsequent events, see on κληρονομία, v.[18]. From a strictly grammatical point of view τῷ σπέρματι is a dative of indirect object after ἐρρέθησαν. But it is only by a rhetorical figure that the promises are said to be uttered to the seed. In the original passage, Gen. 13[15] 17[7, 8], and in this sentence by intent the seed are included with Abraham in those to whom the promises are to be fulfilled.

οὐ λέγει " Καὶ τοῖς σπέρμασιν," ὡς ἐπὶ πολλῶν, ἀλλ' ὡς ἐφ' ἑνός "Καὶ τῷ σπέρματί σου," ὅς ἐστιν Χριστός. "He saith not, And to the seeds, as of many, but as of one, And to thy seed, which is Christ." The subject of λέγει to be supplied in thought is doubtless ὁ θεός as implied in ὑπὸ τοῦ θεοῦ (v.[17]). ὡς indicates that the following expressions refer to the point of view of the speaker, ὁ θεός, so that it is equivalent to "meaning this." *Cf.* Th. *s. v.* 3. ἐπί with the genitive in the sense "in respect to," apparently occurs here only in N. T., but is found in classical writers. *Cf.* Th. *s. v.* A I. 1. e. If these words are from the apostle it must be supposed that for the purpose of heightening the impression of the dignity and inviolability of the covenant and suggesting the impossibility of its having already received its fulfilment before the law came in, he avails himself of an unusual use of σπέρμα in the singular as meaning, or applied to, an individual descendant, and founds on this fact an argument for referring the O. T. passage to Christ; yet probably to him not as an individual, but as the head of a spiritual race; *cf.* the use of Israel as meaning the race of Israel, Rom. 9⁶, ³¹, but especially 9²⁸ and 1 Cor. 12¹². This is, of course, not the meaning of the original passage referred to (Gen. 13¹⁵, or 17⁷ or ⁸). But neither is there any other interpretation which will satisfy the requirements both of the Gen. passages and of the context here. The latter must, therefore, decide the apostle's meaning; *cf.* on v.¹¹. It is not probable, indeed, that the apostle derived the meaning of the promise from the use of the singular σπέρματι. He is well aware of the collective sense of the word σπέρμα in the Gen. passage (see v.²⁹ and Rom. 4¹³⁻¹⁸). He doubtless arrived at his thought, not by exegesis of scripture, but from an interpretation of history, and then availed himself of the singular noun to express his thought briefly. It should be observed that ὅς ἐστιν Χριστός is in any case an assertion of the apostle, for which he claims no evidence in O. T. beyond the fact that the promise refers to one person. On the possibility that the words οὐ λέγει . . . Χριστός are the work of an early editor of the epistles of Paul, see end of detached note on Σπέρματι and Σπέρμασιν, p. 509.

17. τοῦτο δὲ λέγω· "Now this I mean." The function of this phrase is to take up for further argument or explanation a thought already expressed. *Cf.* 1 Cor. 1¹² and similar phrases in 1 Cor. 7²⁹ 10²⁹ 16⁵⁰. The following phrase, διαθήκην προκεκυρωμένην ὑπὸ τοῦ θεοῦ, shows that the reversion of thought here intended is to the ὅμως ἀνθρώπου κεκυρωμένην διαθήκην of v.¹⁵. V.¹⁶ is, therefore, parenthetical.

διαθήκην προκεκυρωμένην ὑπὸ τοῦ θεοῦ ὁ μετὰ τετρακόσια καὶ τριάκοντα ἔτη γεγονὼς νόμος οὐκ ἀκυροῖ, εἰς τὸ καταργῆσαι τὴν ἐπαγγελίαν. "A covenant previously established by God, the law which came four hundred and thirty years afterwards does not annul so as to make inoperative the promise." The word διαθήκη is itself ambiguous, meaning either (a) "covenant," "agreement," or (b) "will," "testament." But the διαθήκη here referred to is manifestly that spoken of in Gen., chap. 17, and this alike in the thought of the O. T. writer, of the Lxx translators, and of Paul was essentially a covenant. Its fulfilment lay, indeed, in part in the distant future, pertaining even to generations yet unborn. In it God took the initiative, and it was primarily an expression of his grace and authority, not a bargain between equals. Yet none of these things contravene the character of a covenant, while its mutuality, its irrevocability (see v.¹⁵), and the practical exclusion of the idea of the death of the testator, mark it as essentially a covenant and not a will. See on διαθήκη in v.¹⁵ and detached note on Διαθήκη, p. 502. The emphatic elements of the sentence on which the argument turns are the προ- in προκεκυρωμένην, the phrase ὑπὸ τοῦ θεοῦ, and μετά. The major premise of the argument is in κεκυρωμένην διαθήκην οὐδεὶς . . . ἐπιδιατάσσεται of v.¹⁵; the minor premise is in the ὁ μετὰ . . . νόμος of this verse, while ὑπὸ τοῦ θεοῦ over against the ἀνθρώπου of v.¹⁵ heightens the force of the argument, giving it an *a minori ad majus* effect. If a covenant once in force can not be modified or annulled by any subsequent action, the covenant with Abraham can not be set aside by the subsequent law. If this is true of a man's covenant, much more is it true of a covenant made by God with Abraham, since God must be more certainly true to his promises than man. *Cf.* Rom. 3⁴. The apostle is especially fond of arguments of this type. See the several illustrations in Rom., chap. 5.

The words εἰς Χριστόν after θεοῦ, found in the leading Western mss., and adopted by most Syrian authorities, are an interpretative addition, akin to and doubtless derived from v.¹⁶.

The verb προκυρόω occurs elsewhere only in much later writers (Eus. *Præp. Evang.* X 4, etc.). The προ- is temporal, and in this context means "before the law." On the use of γίνομαι in the sense "to come," "to appear in history," see Mk. 1⁴ Jn. 1⁶, ¹⁷ 1 Jn. 2¹⁸. The perfect tense marks the coming of the law as something of which an existing result remains, in this case evidently the law itself. B*MT* 154. This phase of the meaning can not well be expressed in English. *Cf.* B*MT* 82.

The number four hundred and thirty is evidently derived by the apostle from Exod. 12⁴⁰, where, though according to the Hebrew text, "the time that the children of Israel dwelt in Egypt was four hundred and thirty years," the Vatican ms. of the Lxx, with which agrees, also the Samaritan Pentateuch, reads: ἡ δὲ κατοίκησις τῶν υἱῶν

Ἰσραὴλ ἦν κατῴκησαν ἐν γῇ Αἰγύπτῳ καὶ ἐν γῇ Χανάαν ἔτη τετρακοσία τριάκοντα πέντε, but AF, perhaps also the second hand of B, omit πέντε (so Tdf.), and A adds αὐτοὶ καὶ οἱ πατέρες αὐτῶν. The expression καὶ ἐν γῇ Χανάαν, for which there is no equivalent in Hebrew, evidently refers to the residence in Canaan previous to that in Egypt, so that the whole period covered is, roughly speaking, from Abraham to Moses. On the comparison between this datum and Gen. 15¹³, quoted in the speech of Stephen, cf. Alf. on Gal. ad loc. For the apostle's argument the length of the period has, of course, no significance, save that the longer the covenant had been in force, the more impressive is his statement.

That ὁ νόμος is the law promulgated by Moses, the participial phrase clearly shows; yet the presumption is that the apostle is still thinking of that law in the same light, or of the same aspect of it, as in 3¹³ (q. v.); and there is the less reason to depart from that presumption because it is the supreme place which Paul's opponents had given, in their doctrine of the basis of acceptance with God, to the legalistic element of the law that leads Paul to make the affirmation οὐκ ἀκυροῖ. The legalistic aspect is, therefore, though less in the foreground than in vv.¹⁰, ¹², ¹³, still present. See detached note on Νόμος, p. 457.

Ἀκυρόω, a late Greek word (1 Esd. 6²³; Dion. Hal. Antiq. 2. 72⁴³; Mt. 15⁶ Mk. 7¹³ 4. Mac. 2¹ 5¹⁸ 7¹⁴ 17²; Plut. Dio, 48²; Apoph. lacon. 3), signifying "to make invalid," whether by rescinding or by overriding, or otherwise (in Plut. Cic. 49³, apparently in a more material sense, "to destroy"), is here used in the first sense. Cf. ἀθετεῖ, v.¹⁵; M. and M. Voc. on ἀκυρόω and ἀθέτησις; and De.BS. p. 228, quoting from papyri the phrase εἰς ἀθέτησιν καὶ ἀκύρωσιν. Paul would not have denied that in the thought and practice of men law had displaced the covenant, but that law legitimately did so (as a new law may specifically repeal previous legislation). εἰς τό with the infinitive expresses the measure of effect or conceived result of ἀκυροῖ (BMT 411). καταργέω (of rare occurrence in Greek authors, in Lxx only 2 Esd. 4²¹, ²³ 5⁵ 6⁸; in N. T. frequent in Paul, elsewhere only in Lk. 13⁷ Heb. 2¹⁴) means "to make ineffective, inoperative" (α-εργον). τὴν ἐπαγγελίαν signifies the same as αἱ ἐπαγγελίαι in v.¹⁶, the singular here reflecting the substantial identity of the promises made on the several occasions, as the plural there recalls the various occasions and utterances.

18. εἰ γὰρ ἐκ νόμου ἡ κληρονομία, οὐκέτι ἐξ ἐπαγγελίας· "For if the inheritance is of law, it is no longer of promise." As in v.¹², the apostle excludes the possibility of a compromise between the two principles, and so justifies the use of the strong terms ἀκυροῖ and καταργῆσαι. I say "annul" and "make of no account," for if the law affects the promise at all, it annuls it. It can not be added to it; it destroys it. The previous reference to the διαθήκη and the ἐπαγγελία make it clear that ἡ κληρο-νομία—note the restrictive article—refers to the possession promised in the covenant (Gen. 13¹⁵ 15⁷ 17⁸; cf. Rom. 4¹³, ¹⁴), which was with Abraham and his seed. This promised posses-sion, while consisting materially in the promised land, was the expression of God's favour and blessing (cf., e. g., 2 Chron. 6²⁷ Ps. Sol. 7² 9² 14³, ὅτι ἡ μέρις καὶ ἡ κληρονομία τοῦ θεοῦ ἐστιν Ἰσραήλ, 17²⁶), and the term easily becomes in the Chris-tian vocabulary a designation of the blessing of God which they shall obtain who through faith become acceptable to God (see Acts 20³² 1 Cor. 6⁹, ¹⁰ 15⁵⁰ Gal. 5²¹ Eph. 5⁵ Col. 3²⁴), of which blessing the Spirit, as the initial gift of the new life (v.²) is the earnest (2 Cor. 1²² 5⁵ Eph. 1¹³, ¹⁴ 4³⁰), and so the fulfilment of the promise (v.¹⁴). Such a spiritualised conception in general doubtless underlies the apostle's use of it here. Cf. Rom. 4¹⁴ and the suggestion of v.¹⁴ above, that he thought of the promise to Abraham as a promise of the Spirit. But for the purposes of his argument at this point, the content of the κληρονομία is not emphasised. It was whatever the covenant promised to Abraham and to his seed. His opponents would concede that this was a spiritual, not simply a material, blessing.

Κληρονομία (κλῆρος, "a share," νέμω, "to distribute"), found in Isocrates, Demosthenes, and other classical writers, is in their writings usually a possession obtained by inheritance, but sometimes possession without the idea of inheritance (Aristot. Nic. Eth. 7. 14⁶ [1153 b¹¹]). In the papyri it is used either of one's estate, which is to pass to one's heirs, or of that which one receives by inheritance: Pap. Amh. II 72⁶, ⁸; BGU. I 19, II 3, 350 ⁴, ⁵; Pap. Tebt. II 319⁵, ²⁹, et freq. It occurs very often in the Lxx, in the great majority of cases as the translation of נַחֲלָה. This Hebrew word, originally signifying "gift," then "possession," or "share," often refers to the possession given to Israel in Canaan (Deut. 12⁹ 19¹⁴ Judg. 20⁶ Isa. 58¹⁴ 1 Chr. 16¹⁶⁻¹⁸; cf. Gen. 17⁷, ⁸, where, however, the Heb. has אֲחֻזָּה and the Lxx κατάσχεσις); or to the share of a particular tribe (Josh. chap. 19); or to Israel, or the land of Israel, as the possession of God (Deut. 4²⁰ Ps. 78 [79]¹). Sometimes it denotes an inheritance, usually, however, not in the sense of property received by inheritance, but of property which is left by one at death, or which will by usage pass to one's descendants (Num. 27⁷⁻¹¹ 36²⁻⁴, ⁷, ⁸). Rarely, if ever, does it refer to property transmitted by will; but see Job 42¹⁵. κληρονομία in the Lxx has the same range of meaning. See also Sir. 44¹⁹⁻²³ Ps. Sol. 7² 9² 14³, ⁶ 15¹² 17²⁶. In N. T., though always translated "inheritance" in E. V., only in Lk. 12¹³ does it refer strictly to property received or transmitted by inheritance. In Mt. 21³⁸ Mk. 12⁷ Lk. 20¹⁴ Acts 7⁵ Heb. 11⁸ it means "property," "possessions" in the material sense. In Acts 20³² Eph. 1¹⁴, ¹⁸ 5⁵ Col. 3²⁴ Heb. 9¹⁵ 1 Pet. 1⁴, it is used figuratively of a spiritual blessing which men are to receive from God. It is in this sense of "promised possession" that it is doubtless to be taken here, consistently with the use of διαθήκη in the sense of "covenant." Nor is there anything in the usage of κληρονομία to combat this sense of διαθήκη.

The anarthrous nouns νόμου and ἐπαγγελίας are both to be taken qualitatively: the actual things referred to are ὁ νόμος and ἡ ἐπαγγελία (see on v.¹⁷), but are by these phrases presented not individually as the law and the promise, but qualitatively as law and promise. The legalistic aspect of the law is a shade more in thought here than in v. ¹⁷. ἐκ denotes source, specifically that on which something depends (Th. s. v. II 6), and ἐκ νόμου is substantially equivalent to ἐν νόμῳ in v.¹¹. οὐκέτι is to be taken not temporally but logically, as in Rom. 7¹⁷, ²⁰ 11⁶ (Gal. 2²⁰, cited as an example of this usage by Grimm, is probably not such, but suggests how the logical use might grow out of the temporal). The conditional clause, as in chap. 2²¹, sets forth as a simple supposition what the apostle in fact regards as a condition contrary to fact. See BMT 243.

τῷ δὲ Ἀβραὰμ δι' ἐπαγγελίας κεχάρισται ὁ θεός. "but to Abraham God granted it by promise." The implied object of the verb is evidently τὴν κληρονομίαν. κεχάρισται emphasises the gracious, uncommercial, character of the grant, and the perfect tense marks the grant as one still in force, thus recalling the argument of vv.¹⁵⁻¹⁷. The statement as a whole constitutes the minor premise of which the preceding sentence is the major premise. If the inheritance is by law, it is not by promise; but it is by promise; therefore it is not by law.

Χαρίζομαι is used from Homer down in the general sense "to do something pleasant or agreeable" (to another), "to do one a favour"; in N. T. with the meanings (a) "to forgive" and (b) "to grant graciously"; cf. Rom. 8³², etc.

5. Answer to the objection that the preceding argument leaves the law without a reason for being (3¹⁹⁻²²).

The apostle's strong and repeated insistence on the inferiority of law to the promise, and its inability to justify, naturally raises the question, weighty for one who was not prepared to deny to the law all divine authority, What, then, is the law for? This Paul answers by ascribing to it the function of producing transgressions, denying to it power to give life, and making it simply temporary and preparatory to the gospel.

¹⁹*What then is the significance of the law? For the sake of the transgressions it was added, to continue until the seed should come to whom the promise still in force was made, being enacted through the agency of angels in the hand of a mediator.* ²⁰*But the mediator is not of one; but God is one.* ²¹*Is the law, then, contrary to the promises of God? By no means. For if there had been given a law that could give life, righteousness would indeed be by law.* ²²*But the scripture shut up all things under sin that, on ground of faith in Jesus Christ, the promise might be given to those who believe.*

19. τί οὖν ὁ νόμος; "What then is the significance of the law?" A question obviously raised by the argument advanced in vv.¹⁵⁻¹⁸, which seemed to leave the law without function. ὁ νόμος is, of course, the same law there spoken of; see on v.¹⁷ and on v.¹³.

> There is no perfectly decisive consideration to enable us to choose between the translations "why is" and "what is," "what signifies." Paul frequently uses τί adverbially (Rom. 3⁷ 14¹⁰ 1 Cor. 4⁷ Gal. 5¹¹, etc.), yet never elsewhere in the phrase τί οὖν. On the other hand, while τί οὖν elsewhere signifies "what then," not "why then" (Rom. 3¹, ⁹ 4¹ 6¹, ¹⁵, etc.), yet when the thought "what signifies" is to be expressed, the copula is usually inserted, not left to be supplied. See 1 Cor. 3⁵: τί οὖν ἐστιν Ἀπολλώς; τί δέ ἐστιν Παῦλος; Jn. 6⁹: ταῦτα δὲ τί ἐστιν; but cf. other examples of a similar sense, without copula in Bernhardy, *Syntax*, p. 336. The difference of meaning is not great; the question, "Why the law?" is included in the more general question "What signifies the law, how is it with the law?" and this, as the context shows, is in any case the most prominent element of the thought in the apostle's mind. οὖν connects this question with what precedes, signifying "in view, then, of these statements."

τῶν παραβάσεων χάριν προσετέθη, "For the sake of the transgressions it was added." προσετέθη marks the law as supplementary, and hence subordinate to the covenant. The statement is not in contradiction with vv.[15ff.], because the law in the apostle's thought forms no part of the covenant, is a thing distinct from it, in no way modifying its provisions. It is the apparent contradiction that probably gave rise to the reading ἐτέθη, which occurs in this v. in D*FG and other Western authorities.

In itself χάριν may be either telic as in Tit. 1[5, 11] Jude[16] Prov. 17[17], perhaps also Eph. 3[1, 14], or causal as in Lk. 7[47] 1 Jn. 3[12]; Clem. Hom. 11[16]: τῶν παραπτωμάτων χάριν ἡ τιμωρία ἔπεται (cited by Ell. and Ltft). The context and Paul's usual conception of the functions of the law are both in favour of the telic force. For, since it is clearly the apostle's usual thought that where there is no law, though there may be sin, there is no transgression (παράβασις, see Rom. 4[15] 5[13]), his choice of the word παραβάσεων here must be taken to indicate that he is speaking not of that which is antecedent but of that which is subsequent to the coming of law. The phrase is, therefore, by no means the equivalent of ἁμαρτιῶν χάριν, and since the distinguishing feature of παράβασις is that it is not simply the following of evil impulse, but violation of explicit law, it naturally suggests, as involved in the παραβάσεων, the recognition of the sinfulness of the deeds, which otherwise might have passed without recognition. Nor can it be justly said that this interpretation involves the supplying of the phrase, "knowledge of" (cf. Sief. "so hätte doch Paulus, um verstanden zu werden, schreiben müssen τῆς ἐπιγνώσεως τῶν παραβάσεων χάριν"), but only the discovery in the expression τῶν παραβάσεων of its implicate, τῆς ἐπιγνώσεως τῆς ἁμαρτίας. For the evidence that the latter was in Paul's thought a function of the law and that he probably conceived of it as brought about through the conversion of sin into transgression, see Rom. 3[20] 4[15] 5[13, 14, 20] 7[7-12]. The article before παραβάσεων is restrictive, but not retrospective. The thought probably is, "the transgressions which will thereby be produced."

ἄχρις ἂν ἔλθῃ τὸ σπέρμα ᾧ ἐπήγγελται, "to continue until the seed should come to whom the promise still in force was made." τὸ σπέρμα is, doubtless, to be taken in the same sense as in v.[16b], viz., Christ, if v.[16b] is from Paul (cf. p. 182); otherwise as in v.[29], those who are Christ's. ἐπήγγελται, perfect tense, referring to a past fact and its existing result, marks the promise as being still in force. The whole clause, ἄχρις, etc., sets the limit to the period during which the law continues. Thus the covenant of promise is presented to the mind as of permanent validity, both beginning before and continuing through the period of the law and afterwards, the law on the other hand as temporary, added to the permanent covenant for a period limited in both directions. That the relation of men to God was different after the period of law was ended from what it had been under the law is implied in v.[23]. But that the promise with its principle of faith was in no way abrogated or suspended in or after the period of the law is the unequivocal affirmation of vv.[15-18], and clearly implied in the quotation in v.[11] of Hab. 2[4], which the apostle doubtless ascribed to this period.

Ἄχρις ἄν is the reading of B33, 1912 Clem. Eus. All others apparently read ἄχρις οὗ. Both ἄχρις ἄν and ἄχρι οὗ are current forms in the first century (M. and M. *Voc. s. v.*), but Paul elsewhere reads ἄχρι[ς] οὗ (Rom. 11[25] 1 Cor. 11[26] 15[25]). In Rom. 11[25] and 1 Cor. 15[25] mss. vary between ἄχρι and ἄχρις before οὗ and in 1 Cor. 11[26] 15[25] a considerable group add ἄν after οὗ, yet none apparently read ἄχρις ἄν. It is improbable, therefore, that this reading is the work of the scribes.

διαταγεὶς δι' ἀγγέλων ἐν χειρὶ μεσίτου· "being enacted through the agency of angels in the hand of a mediator." The mediator is self-evidently Moses; the expression ἐν χειρί is probably, as Sief. suggests, intended literally; see Exod. 31[18] 32[19]. Concerning the tradition that angels were concerned in the giving of the law, see Deut. 33[2] (Lxx not Heb.), ἐκ δεξιῶν αὐτοῦ ἄγγελοι μετ' αὐτοῦ. Jos. *Ant.* 15. 136 (5[3]); Test. XII Pat. Dan. 6; Jub. 1[29]; Heb. 2[2] Acts 7[38, 52] and Talmudic passages cited by Dib.*Gwt.* p. 27. The intent of the whole phrase is to depreciate the law as not given directly by God.

On διατάσσω, with reference to the enactment of a law, cf. Hes. Op. 276; Plato, Legg. XI 931 E. The participle is an aor. of identical action, describing one phase of the fact denoted by προσετέθη (BMT 139f.).

Μεσίτης, "mediator," belongs to late Greek. Job 9³³: εἴθε ἦν ὁ μεσίτης ἡμῶν καὶ ἐλέγχων καὶ διακούων ἀνὰ μέσον ἀμφοτέρων. Polyb. 28. 15 (17)⁸: ἐβούλετο τοὺς 'Ροδίους προνύξας μεσίτας ἀποδεῖξαι. Diod. Sic. 4. 54, τοῦτον γὰρ μεσίτην γεγονότα τῶν ὁμολογιῶν. Cremer, s. v., and Riggenbach, "Der Begriff der Διαθήκη im Hebräerbrief," in Theologische Studien Th. Zahn . . . dargebracht, p. 307, interpret the word in this passage and in Jos. Ant. 4. 133 (6⁷)—see below—as meaning "surety," "guarantor." But while this meaning would give reasonable sense to the passages, there is nothing in the context to require it, and these passages can not, therefore, be regarded as vouchers for it. Philo De Somn. I 142 (22); Vita Mosis, III 163 (19): Μωυσῆς . . . μεσίτης καὶ διαλλάκτης . . . Assumpt. Mos. 1¹⁴ (quoted by Gelasius): καὶ προεθεάσατό με (Μωυσὴν) ὁ θεὸς πρὸ καταβολῆς κόσμου εἶναί με τῆς διαθήκης αὐτοῦ μεσίτην. See Charles, Apoc. and Pseud., ad loc. (cf. 3¹²): itaque excogitavit et invenit me, qui ab initio orbis terrarum præparatus sum, ut sim arbiter testamenti illius; Test. XII Pat. Dan. 6, μεσίτης θεοῦ καὶ ἀνθρώπου (cf. Charles on Jub. 1²⁹); Jos. Ant 4. 133 (6⁷), ταῦτα δὲ ὀμνύντες ἔλεγον καὶ θεὸν μεσίτην ὧν ὑπισχνοῦντο. Ant. 16. 24 (2²). Pap. Gd. Cairo, p. 30: ἐάν σοι δόξῃ μεσείτην ἡμεῖν δός (the passage is from the second century A. D. ἡμεῖν refers to two rival claimants for an estate between whom the μεσίτης was to be arbiter). Plut. De Is. et Osir. 46: διὸ καὶ Μίθρην Πέρσαι τὸν μεσίτην ὀνομάζουσιν. See other reff. in Th. s. v. In N. T., besides the present passage, the word occurs in Heb. 8⁶ 9¹⁵ 12²⁴ 1 Tim. 2⁵, in all of which it is a title of Jesus, though in Heb. 8⁶ there is also a suggestion of Moses as the mediator of the old covenant, meaning the law.

20. ὁ δὲ μεσίτης ἑνὸς οὐκ ἔστιν, ὁ δὲ θεὸς εἷς ἐστίν. "But the mediator is not of one; but God is one." This is a part of the argument in depreciation of the law as compared with the covenant of promise, reiterating in part what has already been said in v.¹⁹. The first clause is a general statement deduced from the very definition of a mediator. From the duality of the persons between whom the mediator acts and the fact that God is but one person, the inference intended to be drawn is that the law, being given through a mediator, came from God indirectly. That the promise came directly is not affirmed, but assumed to be in mind. To find here the thought that the law is conditional while the promise is unconditional, or a reference to the unchangeableness of God, is to go beyond the implication of the words or the context.

For the interpretation of this perplexing verse, of which, according to Fricke, *Das exegetische Problem Gal.* 3²⁰, Leipzig, 1879, about three hundred interpretations have been proposed, the following data seem determinative. 1. ὁ μεσίτης is in this clause generic, lit., "The mediator of one does not exist," or "the mediator is not [a mediator] of one." To make it refer directly and exclusively to a specific mediator is to make the whole sentence simply assertion, lacking even the appearance of argument, and to render the second half of the sentence superfluous. It would, indeed, come to the same thing to make ὁ μεσίτης refer to the mediator of v.¹⁹, if the assertion of v.²⁰ be understood to be true of the mediator of v.¹⁹ because true of the mediator as such. But this is unnecessarily to complicate the thought. 2. This generic statement of v.²⁰: ὁ δὲ μεσίτης ἑνὸς οὐκ ἔστιν, is intended to be applied to Moses, the mediator, referred to in v.¹⁹. To introduce the conception of some other mediator, as, *e. g.*, Christ (Jerome Chrys. *et al.*), or the law itself (Holsten), is to exceed the indications of the context without warrant. 3. ἑνός must be taken as masculine, and, accordingly, as personal, the plurality affirmed in ἑνὸς οὐκ ἔστιν referring to the contracting parties to a transaction effected through a mediator; no other interpretation is consistent with the use of εἷς in the clause ὁ δὲ θεὸς εἷς ἐστίν. 4. The plurality affirmed in ἑνὸς οὐκ is not a plurality of persons constituting one party to the transaction effected through a mediator, but a duality of parties: in other words, ὁ μεσίτης ἑνὸς οὐκ ἔστιν affirms not that the party for whom the mediator acts must consist of a plurality of persons, but that there must be two parties to the transaction between whom the mediator acts as go-between. However attractive the interpretation which is built upon this definition of μεσίτης as the single person acting as the representative of a group, Paul being thus made to say that since a mediator can not be the representative of one, and God is one, Moses as mediator was not the representative of God, but of the angels (Vogel in *Stud. u. Krit.* 1865, pp. 524–38) or of the people (B. Weiss, *Die paul. Briefe im berichtigten Text, ad loc.*), it must be rejected on the clear evidence of usage (see the passages above): a μεσίτης by no means uniformly acted for a plurality of persons (constituting one party), but always, however, he may be thought of as specially representing the interests of one party, stood, as both the term itself and usage show, as the middleman between two parties, the latter consisting each of one person or of more, as the case might be. 5. ὁ δὲ θεὸς εἷς ἐστίν is most naturally taken as the minor premise to ὁ δὲ μεσίτης ἑνὸς οὐκ ἔστιν. The unexpressed but self-evident conclusion from these premises applied to the concrete case referred to in v.¹⁹ is that to the giving of the law, in which Moses was mediator, there was, besides God, a second party. This in itself serves to emphasise the statement of v.¹⁹, that the law was given through a mediator and to intimate that the covenant, in which God acted alone, without a mediator, is in this particular different from the law and superior to it.* So in the main, Fricke, *op. cit.* The reasoning is not indeed characteristically Pauline; like that of v.¹⁶ᵇ it reads more like the gloss of a later commentator than a part of the original argument; and such it quite possibly is. Yet we have no decisive proof that Paul himself could not have added such a rabbinic re-enforcement of his own argument.

Ell.'s view, which while supplying "in the promise" makes the clause ὁ δὲ θεὸς εἷς ἐστίν, thus supplemented, a minor premise, the argument then running, A mediator is not of one party, but in the promise God is one; therefore, in the promise there is no mediator, only arrives by a laboured process at the point from which it started. Rendall's view, *Expositor's Grk. Test.*: The mediator, Moses, is not of one seed, but many (= the law was not like the promise for a single chosen family, but to many families of Abraham's children after the flesh), but God is nevertheless one (= the God of Sinai is one with the God of promise), is singularly regardless of the requirements alike of the language itself and of the context.

21. ὁ οὖν νόμος κατὰ τῶν ἐπαγγελιῶν τοῦ θεοῦ; μὴ γένοιτο. "Is the law, then, contrary to the promises of God? By no means." The question is suggested by the whole argument from v.¹⁰, esp. v.¹⁵ on, which obviously suggests an affirmative answer. That Paul returns a negative answer signifies, however, not that he has forgotten and is now denying what he has up to this time affirmed, nor probably that he is using the word "law" in a different sense. It would, indeed, resolve the seeming contradiction and take the words in a sense not improbable in itself to suppose that he here means the law simply

---

* It comes to nearly the same result to take ὁ δὲ θεὸς εἷς ἐστίν as referring directly to the promise, meaning, in effect: "But God, who gave the promise, is one, acted without a mediator"; in which fact the inferiority of the law to the promise is evident. So Ltft. But if this were the thought intended to be directly conveyed by this clause, it could hardly have failed to be expressed. It seems more reasonable to take the words ὁ δὲ θεὸς εἷς ἐστίν as in themselves expressing only what they directly say, and to assume that the thought to be supplied is the conclusion which the expressed premises support.

It may be objected to the view advocated above and equally to that of Ltft. that on the supposition that διαθήκην is a covenant, Paul's argument in v.¹⁷ turns on the fact of the two parties to it, and thus that the law and the covenant are in that fact placed on the same basis. But this ignores the fact that the argument concerning the mediator is in reality to the effect that the mediator stands between the two parties, making a third, separating as well as joining them, while in the covenant, God, the one, comes into direct relation with man. Moreover if, as is probably the case, and as is indicated by his use of ἐπαγγελία for what he also calls the διαθήκη, he shared the O. T. thought of the covenant as predominantly one-sided, God taking the initiative, this fact would still further tend in his mind to depreciate the law as compared with the covenant.

as a historical fact. But it is more likely that as he means here by the promises those of the covenant (vv.[16, 17, 18]), so he uses law in the same sense as throughout the passage, and that he affirms that they are not in conflict (on κατά, cf. chap. 5[16, 17] 2 Cor. 13[8] Rom. 8[31]), because they have distinct functions. Notice that it is this of which the next clause speaks. Paul admits, even affirms, that the law judges a man on a basis of works of law, and the promises on a basis of faith—in this they are different the one from the other, but he contends, as against his opponents who hold that men are actually justified by law, that the law, whose sentence is always one of condemnation, was not intended to express God's attitude towards men, is not the basis of God's actual judgment of men, but is a revelation of a man's legal standing only. He will presently add that it is thus a means of bringing us to Christ (v.[24]). At present he is content to affirm that they are not in conflict, because they operate in different spheres. Thus one may rightly say that the courts are not in conflict with the pardoning power; for though one sentences and the other releases, each is operative in its own sphere, the one saying whether the accused is guilty, the other whether he shall be punished; or that a father who first ascertains by careful inquiry whether his child has disobeyed his commands, and pronounces him guilty, and then using this very sentence of guilty to bring him to repentance, and discovering that he is repentant assures him of forgiveness and fellowship, is in no conflict with himself.

Τοῦ θεοῦ is omitted by B d e Victorin. Ephrem. (?) Ambrst. only. Despite the intrinsic improbability of the reading τοῦ θεοῦ (the sentence is equally clear, more terse, and more in Paul's usual style without the words), the evidence for the insertion of the words and the possibility that the omission by the few witnesses on this side is an accidental coincidence, is too strong to permit rejection of the words.

εἰ γὰρ ἐδόθη νόμος ὁ δυνάμενος ζωοποιῆσαι, ὄντως ἐκ νόμου ἂν ἦν ἡ δικαιοσύνη. "For if there had been given a law that could give life, righteousness would indeed be by law." νόμος, without the article, is a law, and undoubtedly, as the context

shows, a divine law, which the participial phrase ὁ δυνάμενος
ζωοποιῆσαι further describes as "a law that could give life."
The form of the sentence marks it as a supposition contrary to
fact (BMT 248). Such a sentence is often used to prove the
falsity of the hypothesis from the unreality of the apodosis.
Cf. chap. 1¹⁰ 1 Cor. 2⁸ 1 Jn. 2¹⁹. In this case the unreality of the
apodosis, righteousness by law, is for the present assumed, to
be proved later, in v.²². The fact thus established, that no law
had been given that could give life, hence that this was not
the purpose of the law of Moses, is adduced as proof (γάρ is
argumentative) that μὴ γένοιτο is the right answer to the
question just asked, i. e., that the law is not against the promises. The validity of this proof for its purpose lies in the
implication, not that the two are in agreement, being of the
same intent and significance, but that they are in separate
realms, established for different purposes, hence not conflicting.

Ἐκ νόμου is attested by all authorities except B and Cyr., who read
ἐν νόμῳ; ἦν is attested by all authorities except FG 429, 206; ἄν is read
by ABC Cyr. before ἦν; by ℵ33, 218, 1912, 436, 462 after ἦν; by
429, 206 without ἦν; by Dᵇᵉᵗ ᶜKLP al. pler. Chr. Thdrt. before ἐκ νόμου;
it is omitted by D* 88, 442, 1952 al. Dam. and, together with ἦν, by
FG. Alike external evidence and intrinsic and transcriptional probability point to ἐκ νόμου ἄν ἦν as the original reading. While 4¹⁵ shows
that Paul might omit ἄν, yet he more commonly inserts it, and when in-
serting it, places it before the verb; cf. chap. 1¹⁰ 1 Cor. 2⁸ 11³¹. Out of this
reading arise in transcription that of ℵ, etc., and that of the Syrian
authorities KLP, etc., by transposition of ἄν; that of the Western
authorities D*, etc., by the omission of ἄν (cf. the evidence on 4¹⁵); that
of B Cyr. by the substitution for ἐκ νόμου of the equally familiar
ἐν νόμῳ; and that of FG 429, 206 by the accidental omission of ἦν, the
two former from the Western reading, the two latter from the original
reading. It will be observed that the insertion of ἄν in some position
is attested by all non-Western authorities, and ἐκ νόμου by all authorities except B Cyr. The assumption of ἐν νόμῳ as original (WH.), neces-
sitating the derivation of the reading of AC from this original and then
the derivation of all other variants from this secondary form, involves
a genealogical relationship distinctly more difficult than that above
proposed, as well as the adoption of a sub-singular reading of B against
all other pre-Syrian authorities.

On an attributive with the article after an indefinite substantive, see

W. XX 4 (WM. p. 174); Rad. p. 93; Gild. *Syn.* p. 283; Rob. p. 777; *BMT* 424. *Cf.* chap. 1⁷ 2²⁰ Acts 4¹², etc.

Ζωοποιέω occurs in the Lxx in the sense, "to cause to live," "to give life": Neh. 9⁶: σὺ (θεός) ζωοποιεῖς τὰ πάντα. 2 Kgs. 5⁷; "to save alive": Jdg. 21¹⁴ Ps. 71²⁰. In N. T. it means "to cause to live," "to germinate" (of a seed): 1 Cor. 15³⁶; ' :o bring to life" (the dead): Rom. 8¹¹ 1 Cor. 15²²; "to give spiritual life": Jn. 6⁶³ 2 Cor. 3⁶. In the last passage it stands in antithesis to the death sentence of the law, and thus acquires a certain forensic sense. It is probable that this is the prominent element in the thought of the word here; that it is, in fact, the causative of ζάω as used in v.¹² (see note on ζήσεται there) and in effect means "to justify." That there is an associated idea of the ethical life which is imparted by the Spirit of God, as in 2²⁰ 5²⁵ (*cf.* 5¹⁶, ¹⁸) and Rom. 8²⁻⁹, or of the eternal life after death, as in Rom. 8¹⁰, ¹¹ (note esp. ¹¹), is not improbable. Ell. and Sief. make the reference exclusively to the latter, and interpret the argument as one from effect to cause: If there were a law that could give eternal life, then justification, which is the condition precedent of such life, would be in law. This, also, is possible, but less probable than a more direct reference to justification in ζωοποιῆσαι. ἐκ νόμου (*cf.* textual note above), here as in v.¹⁸ (*q. v.*), expresses source—righteousness would have proceeded from law, had its origin in law. It is a qualitative phrase, but that which is referred to is the Mosaic law as a legalistic system. The emphasis of ἡ δικαιοσύνη is doubtless upon the forensic element in the meaning of the word (see detached note on Δικαιοσύνη VI B 2, and *cf.* esp. 2²¹). The article reflects the thought that there is but one way of acceptance with God, the sentence meaning not, "there would be a way of acceptance with God on a basis of legalism" (*cf.* 2²¹), but "the way of acceptance would be," etc.

22. ἀλλὰ συνέκλεισεν ἡ γραφὴ τὰ πάντα ὑπὸ ἁμαρτίαν "But the scripture shut up all things under sin." ἀλλὰ marks the contrast between the unreal hypothesis of v.²¹ and the actual fact as here stated, which furnishes the proof that the apodosis of v.²¹ᵇ, "righteousness would have been of law," and hence also the protasis, "if a law had been given that could give life," which that verse by its form implies to be contrary to fact, are actually such. That the proof is drawn from the O. T. law implies that the latter is the only law actually in question, or that if the O. T. law could not justify no law could. The scripture is probably Deut. 27²⁶, referred to in v.¹⁰—a passage from the law, and cited here as embodying the verdict of the

law. The reference to v.¹⁰ and the context in general give to
ὑπὸ ἁμαρτίαν the meaning "under condemnation of sin,"
equivalent to ὑπὸ κατάραν in v.¹⁰. All this refers, it must be
noted, not to God's sentence against men, but to the verdict
of law. Paul is still arguing that from law comes no righteousness, no justification; that for this one must come to God in
faith. See the next clause.

Συνκλείω is found in Greek writers from Herodotus down in various
senses, but primarily with the meaning "to shut up," "to confine,"
either inceptive, "to put in confinement," or continuative, "to hold
confined." So also in the Lxx, Ps. 30⁸ (31⁸): οὐ συνέκλεισάς με εἰς
χεῖρας ἐχθροῦ. 77 (78)⁵⁰; likewise in N. T., Lk. 5⁶ Rom. 11³².

In the usage of the N. T. writers in general and of Paul in particular
the singular γραφή refers to a particular passage of the O. T. Note
the expressions ἡ γραφὴ αὕτη (Acts 8³⁵), ἑτέρα γραφή (Jn. 19³⁷) πᾶσα
γραφή (2 Tim. 3¹⁶), and the fact that elsewhere in the Pauline epistles
the singular is uniformly accompanied by a quotation (chap. 3⁸ 4³⁰ Rom.
4³ 9¹⁷ 10¹¹ 11²). See also 1 Tim. 5¹⁸. In 2 Tim. 3¹⁶, πᾶσα γραφή, a
specific passage is, of course, out of the question. Deut. 27²⁶, quoted
in v.¹⁰, and Ps. 143², quoted in 2¹⁶, would both be appropriate to the
apostle's purpose in this v., but the remoteness of the latter passage
makes against its being the one here meant. A reference to a passage
itself in the law is, moreover, more probable in view of the fact that
it is the function of this law that is under discussion.

Τὰ πάντα, equivalent to τοὺς πάντας in Rom. 11³², refers to all who
were under ὁ νόμος (v.²¹), i. e., the Jews, since at this point the question pertains simply to the function or reason for existence of the law.
On the neuter used of persons, the rhetorical effect being somewhat to
obliterate the thought of individuals and to present those referred to
as a solidarity, see 1 Cor. 1²⁷ Col. 1²⁰ Eph. 1¹⁰ Jn. 17¹⁰. ὑπὸ ἁμαρτίαν
in Rom. 7¹⁴ (cf. 6¹⁴, ¹⁵) means "under the power of sin" and in Rom. 3⁹
"sinful" (though some interpreters take it in the sense of "under
condemnation"). But these single instances of the phrase in different
specific senses are not sufficient to set aside the clear evidence of the
context in favour of the meaning, "under condemnation for sin,"
which is in itself equally possible.

ἵνα ἡ ἐπαγγελία ἐκ πίστεως Ἰησοῦ Χριστοῦ δοθῇ τοῖς
πιστεύουσιν. "that, on ground of faith in Jesus Christ, the promise might be given to those who believe." This clause expresses the purpose of the shutting up, referred to in the preceding clause: a purpose which, as the mention of Jesus Christ

as the object of faith shows, is to be achieved not for each individual in the period of law as he learns the lesson that law
teaches, but in the historic establishment of the new principle;
and a purpose of God, as is shown by the fact that the result
described is that which is achieved in the gospel, which is for
Paul the gospel of God. But this, in turn, implies that the
shutting up was itself an act of God, or, more exactly, that the
declaration of the scripture expressed something which God
desired men to learn from the experience under law.   In other
words, though to isolate the law and understand it as defining
the way of salvation is wholly to misunderstand God's attitude
towards men, yet the law was given by God to accomplish a
certain work preparatory to the giving of the gospel, viz., to
demonstrate that men can not be justified on grounds of merit.
Thus it is that Paul finds a way to reconcile his rejection of the
legalism which he found in the law, with the divine origin of
the law; instead of denying the latter, as Marcion later in effect
did (Iren. *Haer.* 1. 27²).

'Η ἐπαγγελία is manifestly, as in vv.¹⁴, ¹⁸, the promise to Abraham,
involved in the covenant, and, as in v.¹⁴, is used by metonymy for the
thing promised. See reff. there. Whether the reference is as in v.¹⁴
specifically to the Spirit, or more generally to acceptance with God
with all that this involves, is impossible to say with certainty.   On
ἐκ πίστεως *cf.* 2¹⁶, and notes and reff. there. It here expresses the
ground on which the giving (δοθῇ) takes place. 'Ιησοῦ Χριστοῦ is, as
always after πίστις, an objective genitive.   See notes on διὰ πίστεως
Χριστοῦ 'Ιησοῦ, 2¹⁶.   τοῖς πιστεύουσιν, a general present participle
(*BMT* 123) with generic article—to believers—is the indirect object
of δοθῇ. It is necessary to complete the sense, though the thought
has been in effect expressed by ἐκ πίστεως.   The repetition emphasises
the fact that only through faith could the promise be fulfilled.

6. *Characterisation of the condition under law, and, in
contrast with it, the condition since faith came;
then we were held in custody under law, now we
are all sons of God, heirs of the promise* (3²³⁻²⁹).

In further confirmation of the temporariness of the law and
the inferiority of the condition under it the apostle describes

the latter as one of custody, and that of a child under a pedagogue. Now, however, that that period is over and the full Christian experience of faith has come, we are no longer in subjection. Ye are sons of God, and all alike, without distinction of race, status, or sex, one in Christ Jesus; but if in him, and his, then also seed of Abraham. Thus the argument returns to its starting point in v.[7].

[23]*But before the faith came, we were kept guarded under law, shut up for the obtaining of the faith that was to be revealed.* [24]*So that the law has been for us a pedagogue to bring us to Christ, that we might be justified by faith.* [25]*But the faith having come we are no longer under a pedagogue.* [26]*For ye are all sons of God, through your faith, in Christ Jesus.* [27]*For as many of you as were baptised unto Christ did put on Christ.* [28]*There is no Jew nor Greek, no slave nor free, no male and female; for ye are all one in Christ Jesus.* [29]*And if ye are Christ's, then are ye seed of Abraham, heirs according to promise.*

23. πρὸ τοῦ δὲ ἐλθεῖν τὴν πίστιν ὑπὸ νόμον ἐφρουρούμεθα "But before the faith came, we were kept guarded under law." By τὴν πίστιν is meant not faith qualitatively; the article excludes this; not generically; Paul could not speak of this as having recently come, since, as he has maintained, it was at least as old as Abraham; nor the faith in the sense "that which is believed" (*cf.* on 1[23]); but the faith in Christ just spoken of in v.[22]. That this was, in the apostle's view, fundamentally alike in kind with the faith of Abraham is clear not chiefly from the use of the same word, but from the apostle's definite defence of the Christian faith on the ground that the principle was established in the case of Abraham. That it was specifically different is indicated by the use of the definite article, the frequent addition of Ἰησοῦ Χριστοῦ, and by the assertion of this verse that the faith came at the end of the reign of the law. The phrase ὑπὸ νόμον is a qualitative phrase, "under law," but the law referred to is, of course, that spoken of in v.[19], and this in turn the same as in v.[13] (*q. v.*). That the subjection referred to in this phrase was not absolute, excluding the possibility or privilege of faith, or justification by it,

is shown by v.[11], and the argument of vv.[15ff.]. The law has a
real function, but that function is not the displacement of faith.
Cf. on v.[22b]. That the apostle has so far modified his thought
of that function since v.[19] as to be speaking here in ἐφρουρούμεθα
of protection against transgressions is wholly improbable, for
though φρουρέω in itself may be used of a protective guarding
(2 Cor. 11[32] Phil. 4[7] 1 Pet. 1[5], and examples in classical writers)
yet the proximity of v.[19] and the participle συνκλειόμενοι
compel us to understand it here of a restrictive guarding.

συνκλειόμενοι εἰς τὴν μέλλουσαν πίστιν ἀποκαλυφθῆναι.
"shut up for the obtaining of the faith that was to be
revealed." On the meaning of συνκλειόμενοι, see συνέκλεισεν,
v.[22]. It is here a present participle of identical action, hence
used in its continuative sense, "to hold in confinement," as in
Aristot. *Part. Animal. II* 9. 8 (654 b[35]): αἱ συνκλείουσαι πλευ-
ραὶ τὸ στῆθος. The sense "having been put into confinement" would demand an aor. or perfect participle, the latter
of which some mss., most of them late, have. The participle
μέλλουσαν, limiting πίστιν, marks the latter as future from
the point of view of the verb ἐφρουρούμεθα (B*MT* 142); the
revelation is at the time of the writing already past. εἰς may
be either temporal, as in Phil. 1[10] 2[16], or telic, "in order to
produce, give, or obtain" (in this case the latter), as in 1 Cor.
5[5] Rom. 3[25] Col. 1[29] Acts 2[38] 1 Pet. 1[3, 4]. So Th. for this passage,
interpreting it "that we might the more readily embrace the
faith when its time should come." Of similar ambiguity and
interestingly parallel to this passage is 1 Pet. 1[5], φρουρουμένους
διὰ πίστεως εἰς σωτηρίαν ἑτοίμην ἀποκαλυφθῆναι ἐν καιρῷ ἐσ-
χάτῳ (*cf.* vv.[3, 4]), which may mean "guarded until (we obtain)
a salvation," etc., or "that we may obtain." The temporal
meaning is the simpler, finding in the phrase less that is not
certainly expressed by it, but in view of the fact that εἰς with
temporal force is usually followed by a term of time, and that
the thought which the telic sense implies is expressed both in
v.[20] above and v.[24] below, it is probably best to suppose it to
be intended here also. On ἀποκαλυφθῆναι, see detached note,
p. 433, and *cf.* esp. Rom. 1[17] 8[18] 1 Cor. 2[10] Eph. 3[5] 1 Pet. 1[5].

24. ὥστε ὁ νόμος παιδαγωγὸς ἡμῶν γέγονεν εἰς Χριστόν, "So that the law has been for us a pedagogue to bring us to Christ." ὁ νόμος has the same significance as in v.²³, except that it is here definitely instead of qualitatively spoken of. A παιδαγωγός was a slave employed in Greek and Roman families to have general charge of a boy in the years from about six to sixteen, watching over his outward behaviour and attending him whenever he went from home, as e. g. to school. See exx. below. By describing the law as having the functions of a παιδαγωγός Paul emphasises both the inferiority of the condition of those under it, analogous to that of a child who has not yet arrived at the freedom of a mature person, and its temporariness (cf. v.²⁵). εἰς Χριστόν may be temporal (cf. on εἰς τὴν . . . πίστιν, v.²³) or may be pregnantly used. For exx. of a somewhat similar though not identical pregnant force, see Rom. 8¹⁸, ²¹ Mt. 20¹ 1 Pet. 1¹¹, τὰ εἰς Χριστὸν παθήματα. In view of the fact that εἰς temporal usually takes a temporal object, and of the final clause, ἵνα . . . δικαιωθῶμεν, the pregnant use is here the more probable. Yet it does not follow, nor is it probable that it is to Christ as a teacher that men are thought of as coming; the functions of the παιδαγωγός were not so exclusively to take the boy to school as to suggest this, and the apostle's thought of Christ both in general and in this passage is not of him as a teacher but as one through faith in whom men were to be saved. Nor is the reference to the individual experience under law as bringing men individually to faith in Christ. For the context makes it clear that the apostle is speaking, rather, of the historic succession of one period of revelation upon another and the displacement of the law by Christ. See esp. vv.²³ᵃ, ²⁵ᵃ. How the law accomplished its task is in no way intimated in this word or phrase, but appears in the final clause following, and the repeated intimations of the entire context. See esp. v.¹⁹. Cf. Th. s. v. παιδαγωγός.

On the use of the word παιδαγωγός, see Hdt. 8⁷⁵: Σίκιννος, οἰκέτης δὲ καὶ παιδαγωγὸς ἦν τῶν Θεμιστοκλέος παίδων. Eur. Ion, 725, ὦ πρέσβυ παιδαγώγ' Ἐρεχθέως πατρός τοὐμοῦ ποτ' ὄντος, and esp. the following passage quoted by Ltft. ad loc. from Plato, Lysis, 208 C: σὲ αὐτὸν ἐῶσιν ἄρχειν σεαυτοῦ, ἢ οὐδὲ τοῦτο ἐπιτρέπουσί σοι; Πῶς γάρ, ἔφη, ἐπιτρέπουσιν; 'Αλλ' ἄρχει τίς σου; "Οδε παιδαγωγός, ἔφη. Μῶν δοῦλος ὤν; 'Αλλὰ τί μήν; ἡμέτερός γε, ἔφη. 'Η δεινόν, ἦν δ' ἐγώ, ἐλεύθερον ὄντα ὑπὸ δούλου ἄρχεσθαι. τί δὲ ποιῶν αὖ οὗτος ὁ παιδαγωγός σου ἄρχει; "Αγων δήπου, ἔφη, εἰς διδασκάλου. See also Xen. *Laced.* 3¹: ὅταν γε μὴν ἐκ παίδων εἰς τὸ μειρακιοῦσθαι ἐκβαίνωσι, τηνικαῦτα οἱ μὲν ἄλλοι παύουσι μὲν ἀπὸ παι-δαγωγῶν, παύουσι δὲ καὶ ἀπὸ διδασκάλων, ἄρχουσι δὲ οὐδένες ἔτι αὐτῶν, ἀλλ' αὐτονόμους ἀφιᾶσιν. Plut. *Fab.* 5⁴: οἱ τὸν μὲν Φάβιον σκώπτοντες καὶ καταφρονοῦντες 'Αννίβου παιδαγωγὸν ἀπεκάλουν. The word is frequent in Plutarch's *Lives.* With the παιδαγωγία of Plut. *Numa,* 15¹ (*cf.* Ltft.) in the sense of "moral education" this passage has little or no connection. For further treatment and references, see Becker, *Charicles,* E. T. 4th ed., pp. 226*f.*; Becker and Marquardt, *Röm. Alt.* vol. I, pp. 114, 122, 164; Girard, *L'Education Athénienne,* pp. 114*ff.*; Cramer, *De Educatione Pue-rorum apud Athenienses,* Marburg, 1823. *Harper's Dictionary of Clas-sical Lit. and Antiq.,* art. "Education"; HDB, art. "Schoolmaster"; further references to sources in L. & S. *s. v.*

ἵνα ἐκ πίστεως δικαιωθῶμεν· "that we might be justified by faith." The clause expresses the ultimate purpose of the law in its function as παιδαγωγός, as v.¹⁹ expresses the imme-diate intended result. The emphasis of the expression is on δικαιωθῶμεν, not on ἐκ πίστεως, as if there were different ways of justification, and the purpose of the law was that we might be justified in this rather than in some other way; for the apostle maintains that there is no other way. *Cf. ἐκ πίστεως Χριστοῦ* in 2¹⁶ᵇ, which is similarly added for complete-ness, and with descriptive rather than restrictive force. On the meaning of ἐκ πίστεως, *cf.* also on 2¹⁶ᵇ (pp. 121, 123), and on δικαιωθῶμεν see detached note on Δίκαιος, etc., p. 473.

25. ἐλθούσης δὲ τῆς πίστεως οὐκέτι ὑπὸ παιδαγωγόν ἐσμεν. "But the faith having come we are no longer under a peda-gogue." The article with πίστεως is restrictive, and the refer-ence is as in v.²⁴ (*q. v.*) to the faith in Christ. οὐκέτι is tem-poral, contrasting the two periods of time, with possibly a suggestion of consequence, the *post hoc* being also a *propter hoc.* *Cf.* on 3¹⁸. The phrase ὑπὸ παιδαγωγόν is equivalent, as con-cerns the fact referred to, to ὑπὸ νόμον, the epithet being sub-stituted for the name; but conveys more clearly than ὑπὸ νόμον the idea of subjection and inferior standing. The coming of the faith is a historic event, identical with the giving of the gospel (see 4⁴, ⁵ Rom. 1¹⁶, ¹⁷), not an experience of successive individuals. *Cf.* on v.²⁴. How far this historic event was itself conditioned on personal experience, or how far it repeats itself in the experience of each believer is remote from the apostle's thought here.

26. Πάντες γὰρ υἱοὶ θεοῦ ἐστὲ διὰ τῆς πίστεως ἐν Χριστῷ Ἰησοῦ. "For ye are all sons of God, through your faith, in Christ Jesus." By the change from the first person of v.²⁵, with its reference to the Jewish Christians, to the second person in this v. the apostle applies the thought of that v. directly to his readers. One must supply as the connecting thought to which γάρ is, as often, directly related, some such phrase as, "And this applies to all of you." That πάντες is emphatic is indicated by its position, but esp. by the continuation of the thought of universality in v.²⁸. It may then mean "all you Gentiles," so including the Galatians; or if, as is possible, there were some Jews in the Galatian churches, it may mean "all you Galatians," emphasising the fact that the statements of v.²⁵ apply to all the Christians of Galatia, Gentiles as well as Jews. In either case υἱοὶ θεοῦ, a qualitative expression without the article, repeats and explicates the idea of οὐκέτι ὑπὸ παιδαγωγόν (*cf.* the use of various phrases for the related idea "sons of Abraham" in vv.⁷, ⁹, ²⁹). The emphasis of the expression is, therefore, upon "sons of God" as objects of God's favour, men in filial favour with God. See detached note on *Titles and Predicates of Jesus*, V, p. 404. *Cf.* 4⁴, ⁵ for the expression of the thought that subjection to law and sonship to God are mutually exclusive. That ἐν Χριστῷ Ἰησοῦ does not limit πίστεως is evident because Paul rarely employs ἐν after πίστις (see, however, Col. 1⁴ Eph. 1¹⁵), and in this letter always uses the genitive (2¹⁶, ²⁰ 3²²), but especially because vv.²⁷, ²⁸ take up and dwell upon the fact that the Galatians are in Christ Jesus. And this fact in turn shows that, unless Paul shifts his thought of the meaning of ἐν after he has used it before Χριστῷ Ἰησοῦ, it has here its metaphorical spatial sense, marking Christ as one in whom the believers live, with

whom they are in fellowship. This does not of necessity exclude
the thought that Christ is the basis of their sonship to God,
but makes this a secondary and suggested thought. For a
similar instance of a phrase introduced by ἐν standing after
πίστις but limiting an earlier element of the sentence, see
ἐν . . . αἵματι Rom. 3²⁵. τῆς πίστεως, standing then without limitation, the article may refer specifically to the Christian type of faith, as in vv.²³, ²⁵, or to the faith of the Galatians,
meaning "your faith"; cf. 2 Cor. 1²⁴. The latter is more probable because of the personal character of the statement as
against the impersonal, historical, character of vv.²³, ²⁵.

On θεός without the article in υἱοὶ θεοῦ, see on chap. 4⁸.

27. ὅσοι γὰρ εἰς Χριστὸν ἐβαπτίσθητε, Χριστὸν ἐνεδύσασθε·
"For as many of you as were baptised unto Christ did put on
Christ." The fact that the verbs are in the second person,
requires the insertion of the words "of you" into the translation, though they are not in the Greek. But it must not be
supposed that ὅσοι includes only a part of the πάντες; for this
would be itself in effect to contradict the preceding v. By
ἐβαπτίσθητε the apostle undoubtedly refers to Christian baptism, immersion in water. See Th. *s. v.* II; Preusch. *s. v.*;
M. and M. *Voc. s. v.* This is the uniform meaning and application of the term in Paul (1 Cor. 1¹³⁻¹⁷ 12¹³ 15²⁹ Rom. 6³), with
the single exception of 1 Cor. 10², where he speaks of the baptism of the Israelites into Moses in the cloud and in the sea
as a thing of similar character and significance with Christian
baptism. Nowhere does he use the term in a figurative sense
as in Mk. 1⁸ᵇ 10³⁸, ³⁹ Jn. 1³³ᵇ Acts 1⁵ᵇ. εἰς Χριστόν is probably
to be taken here and in Rom. 6³ in the sense "with reference to
Christ" (on this use of εἰς see Th. B II 2 a), and as equivalent to εἰς τὸ ὄνομα Χριστοῦ. See more fully in fine print
below. "To put on Christ" is to become as Christ, to have
his standing; in this context to become objects of the divine
favour, sons of God, as he is the Son of God. *Cf.* 4⁶, ⁷. By
the whole sentence the apostle reminds his readers that they,
who have been baptised, in confession of their acceptance of

Christ, already possess all that it is claimed that circumcision and works of law could give them, viz., the divine favour, a relation to God like that which Christ sustains to God. It is a substantiation (γάρ) of the assertion of v.²⁶, that they are sons of God, drawn from an interpretation of the significance of their baptism.

The idiom ἐνδύεσθαι with a personal object is found in late Greek writers. Thus in Dion. Hal. *Antiq*. 11. 5², τὸν Ταρκύνιον ἐκεῖνον ἐνδυόμενοι, "playing the part of that Tarquinius"; Libanius, *Ep*. 968 (350 A. D.), ῥίψας τὸν στρατιώτην ἐνέδυ τὸν σοφιστήν: "He laid aside the character of the soldier, and put on that of the sophist." It occurs once in the Lxx with a somewhat different force: Isa. 49¹⁸: πάντας αὐτοὺς ὡς κόσμον ἐνδύσῃ, καὶ περιθήσεις αὐτοὺς ὡς κόσμον, ὡς νύμφη, and several times in N. T.: Rom. 13¹⁴: ἀλλὰ ἐνδύσασθε τὸν κύριον Ἰησοῦν Χριστόν. Col. 3⁹⁻¹⁰, ἀπεκδυσάμενοι τὸν παλαιὸν ἄνθρωπον σὺν ταῖς πράξεσιν αὐτοῦ, καὶ ἐνδυσάμενοι τὸν νέον τὸν ἀνακαινούμενον. Eph. 4²²⁻²⁴, ἀποθέσθαι . . . τὸν παλαιὸν ἄνθρωπον . . . καὶ ἐνδύσασθαι τὸν καινὸν ἄνθρωπον. The related figure of clothing one's self with strength, righteousness, glory, salvation, occurs frequently in O. T.: Prov. 31²⁵ Job 8²² 29¹⁴ 39¹⁹ Ps. 92¹ 103 (104)¹ 131 (132)⁹, ¹⁶, ¹⁸ Isa. 51⁹ 52¹ 61¹⁰ 1 Mac. 1²⁸; and a similar figure with a variety of objective limitations in N. T.: Rom. 13¹²: ἐνδυσώμεθα τὰ ὅπλα τοῦ φωτός. 1 Cor. 15⁵³: ἐνδύσασθαι ἀφθαρσίαν . . . ἐνδύσασθαι ἀθανασίαν. 15⁵⁴: ἐνδύσηται ἀθανασίαν. Eph. 6¹¹: ἐνδύσασθε τὴν πανοπλίαν τοῦ θεοῦ. 6¹⁴, ἐνδυσάμενοι τὸν θώρακα τῆς δικαιοσύνης. Col. 3¹²: ἐνδύσασθε . . . σπλάγχνα οἰκτιρμοῦ. 1 Th. 5⁸, ἐνδυσάμενοι θώρακα πίστεως καὶ ἀγάπης. These passages show that the idiom conveyed no suggestion of putting on a mask, but referred to an act in which one entered into actual relations. Used with an impersonal object, it means "to acquire," "to make a part of one's character or possessions" (1 Thes. 5⁸ 1 Cor. 15⁵³, ⁵⁴ Rom. 13¹² Col. 3¹²); with a personal object it signifies "to take on the character or standing" of the person referred to, "to become," or "to become as." See Rom. 13¹⁴ Col. 3¹⁰; note in each case the adjacent example of the impersonal object and *cf*. the exx. from Dion. Hal. (where the context makes it clear that τὸν Ταρ. ἐκ. ἐνδυόμενοι means "acting the part of Tarquinius," "standing in his shoes,") and Libanius. This meaning is appropriate to the present passage. The fact that the Galatians have put on Christ is cited as proof that they are sons of God as Christ is the Son of God.

The preposition εἰς with βαπτίζω signifies (a) literally and spatially "into," followed by the element into which one is plunged: Mk. 1⁹; *cf*. 1⁸ᵃ; (b) "unto" in the telic sense, "in order to obtain": Acts 2³⁸; (c) followed by ὄνομα, "with respect to," specifically, "with mention or

confession of": 1 Cor. 1¹³, ¹⁵ Mt. 28¹⁹ Acts 8¹⁶ 19⁵; with similar force
but without the use of ὄνομα: Acts 19². It was formerly much discussed whether here and in Rom. 6³ the meaning is the same as in
1 Cor. 1¹³, ¹⁵, etc., or whether εἰς signifies "into fellowship with," Th.
(*cf.* βαπτίζω, II b. *aa*) Ell., S. and H. on Rom., *et al.* hold; Sief. combines
the two views. As between the two the former is to be preferred, for,
though the conception of fellowship with Christ in his death is expressed in the context of Rom. 6³, neither general usage of the phrase
nor that passage in particular warrant interpreting βαπτίζω εἰς as
having other than its usual meaning, "to baptise with reference to."
But if this is the case with Rom. 6³, then usage brings to the present
passage no warrant for finding in it any other than the regular meaning
of the phrase, and the context furnishing none, there is no ground for
discovering it here. More recent discussion, however, has turned upon
the question whether in both groups of passages (1 Cor. 1¹³, ¹⁵ Acts 8¹⁶
19⁵, as well as Rom. 6³ and here) there is a reference to the use of the
name in baptism with supposed magical effect, as in the mystery religions. See Preusch. *s. v.* βαπτίζω and literature there referred to, esp.
Heitmüller, *Taufe und Abendmahl;* also Lake, *The Earlier Epistles of
St. Paul*, pp. 383–391; Case, *The Evolution of Early Christianity*, pp.
347 *f*. For the purposes of this commentary it must suffice to point
out the following outstanding facts affecting the interpretation of
Paul's thought: (a) The use of βαπτίζω εἰς τὸ ὄνομα was in all probability derived from the usage of the mystery religions, and to one
familiar with that usage would suggest the ideas associated with such
phraseology. (b) The apostle constantly lays emphasis on faith and
the Spirit of God (see, *e. g.*, 5⁶, ¹⁶, ¹⁸, ²²) as the characteristic factors of
the Christian experience. It would seem that if, denying all spiritual
value to such a physical rite as circumcision, he ascribed effective force
to baptism, his arguments should have turned, as they nowhere do, on
the superiority of baptism to circumcision. (c) 1 Cor. 10¹⁻¹² makes it
probable that the Corinthians were putting upon their Christian baptism the interpretation suggested by the mystery religions, viz., that
it secured their salvation. Against this view Paul protests, using the
case of the Israelites passing through the Red Sea, which he calls a
baptism into Moses, to show that baptism without righteousness does
not render one acceptable to God. This may, of course, signify only
that he conceived that the effect of baptism was not necessarily permanent, or that to baptism it is necessary to add a righteous life. But
it is most naturally interpreted as a protest against precisely that doctrine of the magical efficiency of physical rites which the mystery
religions had made current. If this is the case and if the thought of
the apostle here is consistent with that in 1 Cor. 10, the relation between
the fact referred to in the relative clause and that of the principal

clause is not (as in 3⁷ Rom. 8¹⁴) causal, but that of symbol and symbolised fact. The requirement of the passage that there shall be a natural
connection of thought both between this v. and the preceding, and
between the two clauses of this, is met by supposing (1) that the
exceptional mention of baptism in this passage (as, *e. g.*, instead of faith)
was suggested by its relation as the initiatory Christian rite to circumcision (*cf.* Col. 2¹¹, ¹²) which the Galatians were being urged to accept,
and (2) that there was something in the act of baptism as thought of
by the apostle which suggested the figure of being clothed with Christ.
This may have been that in baptism one was, as it were, clothed with
the water, or, possibly, that the initiate was accustomed to wear a
special garment. To such a relation in thought between fact and outward symbol there can be, despite Lake's statement that such a thought
was almost unknown to the ancients, no serious objection in view of
Gal. 2²⁰ Rom. 5¹⁴ 1 Cor. 11²⁶. If, indeed, the relation is causal, the
apostle must have changed his conception of the matter between the
writing of Gal. and 1 Cor., or he conceived of the rite as having no
necessarily permanent effect and its value as conditioned upon the
maintenance of a morally pure life.

28. οὐκ ἔνι Ἰουδαῖος οὐδὲ Ἕλλην, οὐκ ἔνι δοῦλος οὐδὲ
ἐλεύθερος, οὐκ ἔνι ἄρσεν καὶ θῆλυ· "There is no Jew nor
Greek, no slave nor free, no male and female." Following the
previous sentence without connective either causal or illative,
these words do not demand to be closely joined in thought to
any specific element of what immediately precedes. With the
thought of the basis of acceptance with God in mind, expressed
in v.²⁶ in the form that through faith men become sons of God,
and in v.²⁷ in a different form, the sweep of his thought carries
him beyond the strict limits of the question at issue in Galatia
to affirm that all distinctions are abolished, and to present an
inspiring picture of the world under one universal religion.
ἐν Χριστῷ, expressed in the similar passage 5⁶, and implied in
Col. 3¹¹, is doubtless to be mentally supplied here also. It is
only in the religion of Christ that Paul conceives that men can
thus be brought together. That he is speaking of these distinctions from the point of view of religion is evident from the
context in general, but especially from his inclusion of the
ineradicable distinction of sex. The passage has nothing to do
directly with the merging of nationalities or the abolition of

slavery. *Cf.* 1 Cor. 7^17-24^. Nor are the passages from ancient
writers, quoted, *e. g.*, by Zahn *ad loc.* (p. 187), in which these
distinctions are emphasised, directly antithetical to this affirmation of the apostle. Yet that the principle had its indirect
social significance is shown in the implications of the Antioch
incident 2^11-14^, and in Phm. ^15, 16^ Col. 4^1^.

On Ἕλλην, meaning Gentile, not specifically Greek, see on 2^4^. ἔνι,
not a contracted form of ἔνεστι, but a lengthened form of ἐν, ἐνί with
recessive accent, but having the force of ἔνεστι or ἔνεισι, as παρά and
ἐπί are used with the force of ἔπεστι and πάρεστι, may, like the form
ἔνεστι itself, mean either "it is present," "there is," or "it is possible."
See W. § XIV 1 (older eds. 2); Bl.-D. 98; Hatzidakis, *Einleitung in die
neugriechische Grammatik*, 207, and the examples of both meanings
given in L. & S. Ltft., without assigning reasons, maintains that οὐκ
ἔνι must here negative "not the fact only but the possibility," and
RV. adopts this interpretation in all the N. T. instances: Jas. 1^17^
1 Cor. 6^5^ Col. 3^11^, and the present passage. But in none of these passages does the context demand this meaning, and in 1 Cor. 6^5^ it is a distinctly difficult meaning. In 4 Mac. 4^12^ the meaning is clearly "it is
possible," but in Sir. 37^2^ as clearly "there is (in it)." It seems necessary therefore to make choice between the two meanings for the
present passage solely by the context. And this favours the meaning
"there is" (so Sief. Bous.) rather than "there can be." There is
nothing in the sentence to suggest that Paul has passed from the statement of fact to that of possibilities. On the other hand, it is apparently
true that the word never quite loses the force derived from ἐν as a
preposition of place, and that one must mentally supply after it a
prepositional phrase introduced by ἐν, or the like: in this case not
ἐν ὑμῖν, for which the context furnishes no basis, but ἐν Χριστῷ, as
suggested by Χριστὸν ἐνεδύνασθε and 5^6^.

πάντες γὰρ ὑμεῖς εἷς ἐστὲ ἐν Χριστῷ Ἰησοῦ. "for ye are
all one in Christ Jesus." These words confirm, by repeating
it in another form, the thought of the preceding sentence. εἷς
may be taken distributively and qualitatively, or inclusively
and numerically. In the former case the meaning is: once in
Christ Jesus, whether you be Jew or Gentile, slave or master,
man or woman, all these distinctions vanish (there is no respect
of persons with God); it is as if it were always the same person
reappearing before him. *Cf.* 1 Cor. 3^8^. In the latter case the

thought is that all those in Jesus Christ merge into one personality. *Cf.* 1 Cor. 10¹⁷ 12¹², ¹³ Rom. 12⁴, ⁵ Col. 3¹⁵. There is
little ground for a choice between the two ideas. Both are
equally Pauline and equally suitable to the immediate context.
Only in the fact that the second interpretation furnishes a
sort of middle term between the assertion of v.¹⁶ᵇ that Christ
is the seed, and that of v.²⁹ that those who are Christ's are seed
of Abraham is there a ground of preference for the second interpretation, and this only in case ¹⁶ᵇ is from Paul. ἐν Χριστῷ
Ἰησοῦ is doubtless to be understood substantially as in v.²⁶,
describing Jesus Christ as the one in whom they live, by whom
their lives are controlled. with the added suggestion that by
this fact their standing before God is also determined.

εἷς ἐστὲ ἐν Χριστῷ Ἰησοῦ: so אᶜBCDKLP al. pler. Syr. (psh.) Boh. (but
some mss. omit Ἰησοῦ) Clem. Athan. Chrys. Euthal. Thdrt. al.; ἓν ἐστέ: FG
33, d e f g Vg. Or. Athan Bas. al.; ἐστὲ Χριστοῦ Ἰησοῦ, omitting εἷς: אA,
but A has ἐν deleted after ἐστέ. א is thus a witness to ἐν X. I. as well as
to the genitive. With practically all the witnesses, except A, attesting ἐν X.
I. against אA for the genitive there can be no doubt that the reading of the
latter is derivative, due to assimilation to v.²⁹. Before ἐστέ, εἷς is clearly the
original reading, changed by Western authorities to ἓν, as in 3¹⁶ ὅς is changed
to ὅ by a part of the Western documents.

29. εἰ δὲ ὑμεῖς Χριστοῦ, ἄρα τοῦ Ἀβραὰμ σπέρμα ἐστέ, κατ'
ἐπαγγελίαν κληρονόμοι. "And if ye are Christ's, then are
ye seed of Abraham, heirs according to promise." δέ is continuative, the new sentence adding fresh inferences from what
has already been said. The conditional clause, expressing in
itself a simple supposition, refers, as is frequently the case, to
something assumed to be true. *BMT* 244. ὑμεῖς Χριστοῦ is
assumed to have been previously affirmed or implied, and
doubtless in εἷς ἐν Χριστῷ Ἰησοῦ or in ἐν Χριστῷ Ἰησοῦ alone.
Of these latter alternatives the second is more probable, since
there is nothing to indicate that in this v. the apostle is intending to carry forward the idea of the unity of believers in one
body, or their equal standing before God. Had this been his
purpose, he must have employed some such phraseology as
that of 1 Cor. 12¹², ²⁷, or Rom. 12⁵, *e. g.*, εἷς [or ἓν σῶμα] ἐν

Χριστῷ, or τὸ σῶμα Χριστοῦ. More probably, therefore, the genitive is to be taken, as in 1 Cor. 3²³; *cf.* vv.²¹, ²²; also Rom. 8⁸, ⁹, with its implication that those who have the spirit of Christ are pleasing to God, and Rom. 8¹⁷, ³², with the suggestion that believers are sharers in the possessions of Christ, objects of God's love. In the words τοῦ Ἀβραὰμ σπέρμα the apostle reverts abruptly to the thought first expressed in v.⁷ but repeated in variant phraseology in vv.⁹, ¹³. The prize which the opponents of Paul had held before the eyes of the Galatians, and by which they hoped to persuade them to accept circumcision and become subjects of the law, was the privilege of becoming seed of Abraham, and so heirs of the promise to him and to his seed. This prize, the apostle now assures the Galatians, belongs to them by virtue of the fact that they are Christ's, as in v.⁷ he had said it belongs to those who are of faith. In the phrase κατ᾽ ἐπαγγελίαν κληρονόμοι both nouns are qualitative, but the substance of the thought recalls the previous mention of the promise and the inheritance in vv.¹⁴, ¹⁶, ¹⁷, ¹⁸, ¹⁹, ²¹, ²², and emphasises the aspect of Abrahamic sonship that is important to the apostle's present purpose. On the use of κληρονόμος, see detached note on Διαθήκη, p. 503. The κληρονομία is, doubtless, as in v.¹⁸ (*q. v.* and *cf.* v.¹⁴), the blessing of justification. The absence of the article before σπέρμα is significant. Paul does not say to his readers, "Ye are the seed of Abraham," as he might perhaps have done if, having written v.¹⁶ᵇ, he wished now to identify the followers of Christ with Christ as the seed of Abraham. Observe, also, that in the preceding clause he has not said, "ye are Christ," but "ye are Christ's." Though the article before Ἀβραάμ is restrictive, as in Rom. 4¹³, directing the thought to a preceding mention of him and probably to vv.⁷, ⁹, ¹⁶ᵃ, yet σπέρμα, being without the article, is indefinite or qualitative. It may designate its subject as included in the seed (as distinguished from constituting it, which would have required the article) or, like υἱοὶ Ἀβραάμ in v.⁷, ascribe to them the standing and privilege of Abrahamic seed. *Cf.* Ἰουδαῖος Rom. 2²⁸, ²⁹. If we suppose that Paul wrote v.¹⁶ᵇ, the reasoning is probably to this effect:

"If you belong to Christ, who is the seed of Abraham, you share his standing as such." If v.[16b] is not from him the thought may be more akin to that of the passages cited above (1 Cor. 3[21-23] Rom. 8[17, 32]): "If ye are Christ's then by virtue of that fact you are objects of God's approval," which for the purposes of argument against his opponents he translates into "seed of Abraham," since in their vocabulary that phrase really means "acceptable to God." In either case the phrase "seed of Abraham" is a synonym for objects of God's approval; the occasion of its employment was its use by those whose views and arguments Paul is opposing; and the ground of its application to the Gentiles is in their relation to Christ. The matter of doubt is whether a previous designation of Christ as *the* seed of Abraham (v.[16b]) furnished the ground for applying the term qualitatively to those who being in Christ are Christ's, or the reasoning is independent of a previous application of the phrase to Christ.

7. *Continuation of the argument for the inferiority of the condition under law, with the use of the illustration of guardianship* (4[1-7]).

Still pursuing his purpose of persuading the Galatians that they would lose, not gain, by putting themselves under the law, Paul compares the condition under law to that of an heir who is placed under a guardian for a period fixed by the father and in that time has no freedom of action, and describes it as a bondage under the elements of the world. Over against this he sets forth the condition into which they are brought by Christ as that of sons of God, living in filial and joyous fellowship with God.

[1]*Now I say, so long as the heir is a child, he differs in no way from a slave, though he is lord of all,* [2]*but is under guardians and stewards until the time set by the father.* [3]*So also we, when we were children, were enslaved under the elements of the world.* [4]*But when the fulness of the time came, God sent forth his Son, born of woman, made subject to law,* [5]*that he might deliver those that were*

under law, that we might receive the adoption. ⁶*And because ye are sons, God sent forth the Spirit of his Son into your hearts, crying, Abba, Father.* ⁷*So that thou art no longer a slave but a son, and if son, then heir through God.*

1. Λέγω δέ, 'εφ' ὅσον χρόνον ὁ κληρονόμος νήπιός ἐστιν, οὐδὲν διαφέρει δούλου κύριος πάντων ὤν, 2. ἀλλὰ ὑπὸ ἐπι-τρόπους ἐστὶ καὶ οἰκονόμους ἄχρι τῆς προθεσμίας τοῦ πατρός. "Now I say, so long as the heir is a child, he differs in no way from a slave, though he is lord of all, but is under guardians and stewards until the time set by the father." Though the argument introduced in 3²³ was brought to a conclusion in v.²⁹ with a reversion to the thought of 3⁷, the apostle now takes up again the thought of the inferiority of the condition under law (note the resumptive λέγω δέ; *cf.* on 3¹⁷ and 5¹⁶); availing himself of the familiar custom of guardianship and of current laws or usages concerning it, he compares the condition of those under law to that of an heir who in his youth and till a time appointed by his father, though prospective owner of the whole estate, is subject to guardians, and characterises it as practical slavery. The sting of the argument is in νήπιος, δοῦλος, and ὑπὸ ἐπιτρόπους καὶ οἰκονόμους, which he employs to describe the condition of those under law; its persuasive element is in ἄχρι... πατρός which suggests that the time of slavery has gone by, and men ought now to be free.

The term κληρονόμος, "heir," suggests that the illustration is taken from the law or custom of inheritance, the son inheriting from a deceased father (πατρός) under the will of the latter. Nor does this element of the illustration create serious incongruity between illustration and thing illustrated. For an illustration is not necessarily perfect at every point, and there is no decisive reason why the apostle should not illustrate the condition of the Jewish nation or of the human race in the period of law by that of a son who is under guardians awaiting an appointed time to take possession of the property left him by his father's will; the point of the illustration lying not in the condition of the father, but in the relation of the son to his guardians. But neither does κληρονόμος necessarily imply that in the illustration, still less in the thing illustrated, the father is dead in the period of the guardianship; since a guardianship may be created during the lifetime of the father, and the term κληρονόμος may be used proleptically simply to describe the son as the one who is eventually to possess the property. *Cf.* κύριος πάντων ὤν, and see detached note on Διαθήκη, p. 496.

Νήπιος, properly "one without understanding," is used by Greek writers and in the Lxx both in this sense and with the meaning "child"; in N. T. apparently in the latter sense (1 Cor. 13¹¹ Eph. 4¹⁴) with the added implication of immaturity, intellectual or moral. No instance has been pointed out of its use as a technical term for a minor, a child not possessed of manhood's rights, but it is evidently this characteristic of a child that the apostle here has specially in mind. κύριος is used in the sense, rather infrequent in N. T., of "owner," with the added idea of control. *Cf.* Mt. 20⁸ 21⁴⁰. The participle ὤν is, of course, concessive. See B*MT* 437.8.

The phrase ἐπιτρόπους καὶ οἰκονόμους has given rise to much discussion as to the precise meaning of the words and the law which the apostle has in mind. The difficulty, however, pertains not to ἐπίτροπος. This is a frequent word for the guardian of a minor orphan. See Plato, *Legg.* VI 766 C: καὶ ἐὰν ὀρφανῶν ἐπίτροπος τελευτήσῃ τις. Dem. 988²: τούτων Ἀρίσταιχμος ἐπίτροπος καὶ κηδεμὼν ἐγένεθ᾽ ἑκκαίδεκα ἔτη. Xen. *Mem.* I. 2⁴⁰: λέγεται γὰρ Ἀλκιβιάδην, πρὶν εἴκοσιν ἐτῶν εἶναι, Περικλεῖ ἐπιτρόπῳ μὲν ὄντι ἑαυτοῦ προστάτῃ δὲ τῆς πόλεως τοιάδε διαλεχθῆναι περὶ νόμων. Arius Did. quoted in Mullach, *Frag. Phil. Gr.* II 87²·⁶: ἀπὸ ταύτης γοῦν τῆς φιλοστοργίας καὶ διαθήκας τελευτᾶν μέλλοντας διατίθεσθαι, καὶ τῶν ἔτι κυοφορουμένων φροντίζειν, ἐπιτρόπους ἀπολιπόντας καὶ κηδεμόνας, καὶ τοῖς φιλτάτοις παρατιθεμένους, καὶ παρακαλοῦντας ἐπικουρεῖν αὐτοῖς. οἰκονόμος, on the other hand, usually denotes a slave acting as house-steward for his master, or an employed steward acting as agent for his principal, or a treasurer. See 1 Ki. 4⁶ 18³ 1 Esd. 4⁴⁷ Lk. 12⁴² 16¹ Rom. 16²³. Paul also uses it in a figurative sense of those to whom the gospel is entrusted, 1 Cor. 4¹·². There is no clear instance of its use with reference to one who has charge of the person or estate of a minor heir, and in particular no other instance of the use of the two terms ἐπίτροπος and οἰκονόμος together.

Under Roman law indeed (of a period a little later than that of Paul —see Sief. *ad loc.*, p. 234) the minor was under a *tutor* till his fourteenth year, and thereafter under a *curator* until his twenty-fifth year. But against the supposition that it was this usage that Paul had in mind is the fact that he adds ἄχρι τῆς προθεσμίας τοῦ πατρός, whereas Roman law itself fixed the time during which the child was under the tutor and curator respectively. On προθεσμίας, a frequent legal term, see Dem. 952¹⁹; Plato, *Legg.* XII 954 D,* etc. *Cf.* Job 28³ Dan. 9²⁶ (Sym.). It is not found in Lxx and occurs here only in N. T.

* Dem. 952¹⁹: λάβε δή μοι καὶ τὸν τῆς προθεσμίας νόμον. Plato, *Legg.* XII 954 D: ἐὰν δὲ κατ᾽ οἰκίας ἐν ἄστει τέ τις χρῆται, τριετῆ τὴν προθεσμίαν εἶναι, ἐὰν δὲ κατ᾽ ἀγροὺς ἐν ἀφανεῖ κέκτηται, δέκα ἐτῶν, ἐὰν δ᾽ ἐν ἀλλοδημίᾳ, τοῦ παντὸς χρόνου, οταν ανευρῃ που, μηδεμίαν εἶναι προθεσμίαν τῆς ἐπιλήψεως.

Ramsay holds that Paul refers to the law followed in Greco-Phrygian cities, and cites the Syrian law book of the fifth century A. D., according to which the practice was the same as under the Roman law except that whereas under Roman law the father appointed only the tutor, and could not appoint the curator, under the Syrian law the father appointed both the ἐπίτροπος who, like the Roman tutor, had charge of the child till he reached the age of fourteen, and the curator who had the management of the property till the son was twenty-five years old.*

But aside from the fact that it is precarious to assume that the law found in a Syrian law book of the fifth century was in force in Phrygian cities in the first century, Ram. overlooks the fact that this usage is equally at variance with the language of Paul, who says nothing about who appoints the ἐπίτροπος and οἰκονόμος but does indicate that the father fixes the time at which the son passes from under their control.

In Greek, e. g., Athenian, law there was, so far as has been pointed out, no such distinction between tutor and curator or ἐπίτροπος and οἰκονόμος.

But the use of ἐπίτροπος καὶ κηδεμών in Dem. 988² as a double title of one person (see the passage above) suggests that we should not seek to distinguish between the functions of the ἐπίτροπος and those of the οἰκονόμος, but regard οἰκονόμος as Paul's synonym for κηδεμών and, like that word, a further description of the ἐπίτροπος. *Cf.*, also, Seneca, *De Beneficiis*, Lib. IV, chap. XXVII, *ad fin.*: *quomodo dementissime testabitur, qui tutorem filio reliquerit pupillorum spoliatorem:* "As he makes a most mad will who leaves as tutor to his son one who has been a spoiler of orphans." There remains, however, the difficulty

---

*Bruno und Sachau, *Syr.-röm. Rechtsbuch*, Leipzig, 1880. In the following translation courteously made from the Syriac text for this work by Professor Martin Sprengling, Ph.D., of the University of Chicago, ἐπίτροπος and curator, have been retained as they stand transliterated in the Syriac text. The Syriac terms have been rendered literally because the English has but one term covering the functions of both classes of officers, viz., "guardian," the use of which for both Syriac words would be confusing. "The law (νόμος) is asked: Can minors make a will (διαθήκας), and at what age can they do it? A girl up to twelve years is subject to the ἐπίτροπος, which, being translated, is the one in command, and can not write a will (διαθήκη). But when she has passed twelve years, she passes from subordination to the ἐπίτροπος and comes to be under that of the curator, which, being translated, is examiner. And from the time when the girl is subject to the curator, she has authority to make a will (διαθηκη). Thus also a boy, until fourteen years, is under the authority of the ἐπίτροπος, and can not write a will (διαθήκη). But from fourteen years and upward he is under the authority of the curator and may write a will (διαθήκη), if he choose. But minors are under the authority of the curator up to twenty-five years; and from twenty-five years the boy is a perfect man and the girl a full woman. If a man die and leave children orphans, and make a will (διαθήκη) and appoint therein an ἐπίτροπος [or curator] for the orphans, they do not give security.

"Those who by will (διαθήκας) are appointed curators, the law (νόμος) provides that they shall not give security, because the owners of the property chose to establish them administrators."

hat we have no knowledge of a guardianship the period of which is fixed by the father. If, therefore, the apostle is speaking of inheritance of property from a deceased father, dying while the son is still a child, he must apparently be speaking in terms of some usage not otherwise definitely known to us.

In view of this fact, recourse may be had to a guardianship established for special reasons during the lifetime of the father, such as is illustrated in the case of Antiochus Epiphanes and his son, Antiochus Eupator. In 1 Mac. 3[32, 33] it is stated that Antiochus Epiphanes, being about to go on a military expedition into Persia, left Lysias ἐπὶ τῶν πραγμάτων τοῦ βασιλέως . . . καὶ τρέφειν 'Αντίοχον τὸν υἱὸν αὐτοῦ ἕως τοῦ ἐπιστρέψαι αὐτόν. In 1 Mac. 6[17] it is said that when Lysias knew that the king was dead he set up Antiochus, his son, to reign in his stead, whom he had brought up (ἔτρεψεν). From these two passages it appears that Antiochus, the father, appointed Lysias to be steward of the affairs of the kingdom and guardian of his son until a specified time, in effect directing that such stewardship and guardianship terminate by the resumption of authority by the father on his return, or by succession of his son on the father's death. While, therefore, the precise terms used by Paul do not occur, equivalents of all three of them (ἐπίτροπος, οἰκονόμος, προθεσμίας τοῦ πατρός) are found in the passage in 1 Mac. This equivalence is, moreover, somewhat confirmed by certain passages in 2 Mac. In 10[11] it is stated that Antiochus Eupator, παραλαβὼν τὴν βασιλείαν, ἀνέδειξεν ἐπὶ τῶν πραγμάτων Λυσίαν, and thereafter, in 2 Mac. 11[1] and 13[2] (cf. also 14[2]), Lysias is referred to as ἐπίτροπος τοῦ βασιλέως καὶ ἐπὶ τῶν πραγμάτων, "guardian of the king and chancellor or steward." Thus the son, on acquiring his throne, re-established for himself the relation which his father had created, and the author of 2 Mac. employs to designate the office of Lysias ἐπίτροπος καὶ ἐπὶ τῶν πραγμάτων, which are evidently nearly or quite the equivalent of Paul's ἐπίτροπος καὶ οἰκονόμος. If it may be supposed that these passages were before the apostle's mind, or that he had in mind such a case as that of Antiochus Ep phanes and his son, his language would become entirely clear, as referring to the case of a father who during his life placed his son for special reasons under the care of one who was at the same time ἐπίτροπος and οἰκονόμος and who was to hold that office for a period the limit of which was indicated by the father. The two terms would not then designate different persons, but two functions of one person, and the plural would be a qualitative plural. It is, perhaps, also in favour of this understanding of the passage that the situations compared are alike even in the fact that the father, corresponding to God, is still alive in the period of the stewardship. Yet reference to an ordinary guardianship of a minor orphan, in the terms of some existing legal usage not definitely

known to us, remains a possibility. Fortunately the application of
the illustration to the condition of men under law is but little affected
by any uncertainty respecting the source of the illustration

3. οὕτως καὶ ἡμεῖς, ὅτε ἦμεν νήπιοι, ὑπὸ τὰ στοιχεῖα τοῦ
κόσμου ἤμεθα δεδουλωμένοι· "So also we, when we were
children, were enslaved under the elements of the world."
ἡμεῖς is best understood as referring to Christians generally,
the predicates of the sentence describing their pre-Christian
condition. For, though the language of vv.[3-5] is specially
appropriate to Jewish Christians and was probably written
with them specially in mind, as that in v.[6] was probably written
with the Gentile Galatians especially in mind, yet the use of
the same or the equivalent expressions with reference to those
who are included under the first person, ἡμεῖς, and those who
are addressed (in the second person), together with the change
in pronoun or the person of the verb when there is no antithesis but, on the contrary, continuity of reference is required
by the argument, shows that these grammatical changes do
not mark a substantial change of persons denoted. *Cf.* ἡμεῖς
. . . δεδουλωμένοι of v.[3] with οὐκέτι εἶ δοῦλος of v.[6] (notice
especially the implication of οὐκέτι that the persons addressed
—the Galatians—had previously been in bondage), and observe
that in v.[5] τοὺς ὑπὸ νόμον (third person) are evidently the same
who constitute the subject of ὑπολάβωμεν, that in v.[6] ἡμῶν is
used of those who are the subject of the verb ἐστέ, and that it
is scarcely less clear from the nature of the argument that there
is no real change of persons referred to (other than the change
of emphasis above mentioned) in passing from v.[5] to v.[6]. A
comparison of ὑπὸ τὰ στοιχεῖα τοῦ κόσμου ἤμεθα δεδουλωμένοι
of this verse with πῶς ἐπιστρέφετε πάλιν ἐπὶ τὰ . . . στοιχεῖα
οἷς πάλιν ἄνωθεν δουλεύειν θέλετε of v.[9] points in the same
direction, v.[9] clearly implying that the previous condition of
the Galatians, as well as that to which they are now in danger
of turning, was a bondage to the στοιχεῖα, while v.[8] as distinctly marks them as having previously been worshippers of
idols, and 3[1-6] shows that they had come to faith in Christ not
through judaism as proselytes, but directly from their worship

of idols. On the bearing of the phrase ὑπὸ νόμον on the inclusiveness of ἡμεῖς, see on v. ⁴. For a change of person similar to that which takes place in passing from v.⁵ to v.⁶, cf. 3²⁶ and notes there. Jews and Gentiles are therefore classed together as being before the coming of Christ in the childhood of the race, and in bondage, and the knowledge of religion which the Jews possessed in the law is classed with that which the Gentiles possessed without it under the common title, "the elements of the world," τὰ στοιχεῖα τοῦ κόσμου. On the meaning of this phrase, see detached note, p. 510. For a direct assertion of what is here implied as to the common standing of Jews and Gentiles as concerns possession of truth (but without reference to its inferiority to the Christian revelation), see Rom. 2¹⁴, ¹⁵.

אD*FG. 33, 44², 463 read ἤμεθα δεδουλ.; ABCDᵇ ᵉᵗ ᶜKL. most cursives Clem. Chrys. Euthal. Thdrt. read ἦμεν. Despite the weightier external evidence for ἦμεν the strong improbability that for the common ἦμεν the unusual ἤμεθα would be substituted is decisive for the latter.

4. ὅτε δὲ ἦλθεν τὸ πλήρωμα τοῦ χρόνου, ἐξαπέστειλεν ὁ θεὸς τὸν υἱὸν αὐτοῦ, γενόμενον ἐκ γυναικός, γενόμενον ὑπὸ νόμον, "But when the fulness of the time came, God sent forth his Son, born of woman, made subject to law." That the time of all important events, and so pre-eminently that of the coming of the Christ, was fixed in the purpose of God, was probably a common thought of early Christianity (Mk. 1¹⁴ Jn. 2⁴ 7⁸, ³⁰, etc. Acts 17²⁶ Eph. 1¹⁰; cf. Tob. 14⁵). It was evidently shared by the apostle (Rom. 3²⁶ 5⁶). Whether he thought of the time as fixed by the necessity that certain things must first be accomplished, or that the world reach a certain condition (cf. 2 Thes. 2³ᵈᶠ·), or as appointed to occur after the lapse of a certain definite period (cf. Dan. 9²⁴ᵈᶠ·) is not here or elsewhere in the epistles clearly indicated. Cf. Bous. Rel. d. Jud.², pp. 278 ff. That it was associated in his mind with the two ages (cf. on 1⁴) is probable, yet the fulness of the time did not mark the beginning of the new age, since the former was past, the latter still future. The words ἐξαπέστειλεν ὁ θεὸς τὸν υἱὸν αὐτοῦ, though in themselves capable of refer-

ring to the sending of Jesus as God's Son out among men from
the seclusion of his private life (*cf.* Acts 9³⁰ 11²² Jn. 1⁶) must
yet, in view of the apostle's belief in the pre-existence of
Jesus, as set forth in 1 Cor. 8⁶ Phil. 2⁶ᶠᶠ· Col. 1¹⁵, ¹⁶, and of the
parallelism of v.⁶, be interpreted as having reference to the
sending of the Son from his pre-existent state (ἐν μορφῇ θεοῦ,
Phil. 2⁶) into the world. This is also confirmed by the two
expressions that follow, both of which (see below) are evidently added to indicate the humiliation (*cf.* Phil. 2⁷, ⁸) to
which the Son was in the sending forth subjected, the descent
to the level of those whom he came to redeem. For if
ἐξαπέστειλεν referred simply to a sending forth among men,
as a prophet is sent forth under divine commission, these expressions would mark his condition previous to that sending
forth, and there would be no suggestion of humiliation, but,
rather, the contrary. Yet on the other hand, ἐξαπέστειλεν
need not, probably should not, be limited to the entrance into
the world by and at birth, but should rather be understood
as extending to, and including, the appearance of Jesus among
men as one sent from God. On the expression τὸν υἱὸν αὐτοῦ,
equivalent to τὸν υἱὸν τοῦ θεοῦ, see detached note on *Titles
and Predicates of Jesus*, V D, p. 408, for discussion of the
evidence that the phrase here refers to the pre-existent Son and
that it has special reference to the Son as the object of
divine love, in the enjoyment of filial fellowship with God.
Cf. also vv. ⁶, ⁷. The phrase γενόμενον ἐκ γυναικός can
not be interpreted as excluding human paternity, as some
interpreters, both ancient and modern, have maintained (*cf.*
Sief. and Zahn *ad loc.*). See, *e. g.*, Job 14¹, βροτὸς γεννητὸς
γυναικός. Mt. 11¹¹, ἐν γεννητοῖς γυναικῶν. It could be reasonably supposed to imply birth from a virgin only in case it
were otherwise established that the apostle knew and accepted
the dogma or narrative that Jesus was so born, and not even
then would it be certain that this phrase was intended to refer
to this aspect of Jesus' birth. But of such knowledge or
acceptance the writings of the apostle give no hint. γυναικός
is probably, like νόμου in the following phrase, not indefinite,

but qualitative, and the phrase is best translated "born of
woman." On ὑπὸ νόμον, cf. 3²³. There is no occasion to take
it here in any other sense than that which it has there, "under
law as a system of legalism." See note on 3¹³. It was from
this subjection that Christ came to deliver men. See 5¹⁸ and
cf. 5¹³, ¹⁴, as showing that those who are in Christ still remain
under law as an ethical principle. Cf. also 1 Cor. 9²⁰ Rom. 6¹⁴, ¹⁵.
In applying this phrase to Jesus the passage resembles Phil. 2⁸,
but differs in that there it is to God and here to law that he is
said to be subject. That Paul carried his conception of Jesus'
subjection to law to the point of supposing that he was in his
own thinking a legalist is wholly improbable; the subjection to
law was, doubtless, rather in the fact of his living under legalistic judaism, obliged to keep its rules and conform to its usages.
The motive for the insertion of the phrase is doubtless to emphasise the cost at which the Son effected his redemptive work;
cf. 2 Cor. 8⁹.

Τὸ πλήρωμα is evidently used in the active sense, "that which fills,"
τοῦ χρόνου being an objective genitive; the whole period which must
elapse before the event being incomplete till its last increment is
added, the last moment, which fills it, is called πλήρωμα. It is, in the
language of the illustration, ἡ προθεσμία τοῦ πατρός (v.²).

The words γενόμενον ὑπὸ νόμον should probably be taken in the
sense "made subject to law" rather than "born under law," for,
though γενόμενον ἐκ γυναικός evidently refers to birth, that reference is neither conveyed by, nor imparted to, the participle, but lies
wholly in the limiting phrase. This idea is, therefore, not of necessity
carried over into the second phrase. Had the apostle desired to express the idea "born" in both phrases, he could have done so unambiguously by the use of γεννηθέντα. Concerning the time of the
subjection to law, whether at birth or subsequently, γενόμενον says
nothing decisive. Both participles are best understood as attributive
participles used substantively (BMT 423) in apposition, therefore,
with τὸν υἱὸν αὐτοῦ, the omission of the article giving to each phrase a
qualitative force which may be expressed in English by translating
"his Son, one born of woman, one made subject to law." The employment of the aorist presents the birth and the subjection to law as in
each case a simple fact, and leaves the temporal relation to ἐξαπέστειλεν
to be inferred solely from the nature of the facts referred to (BMT 142,
143). The thought is not very different if the participles be taken as

adverbial participles of attendant circumstances (BMT 449, 450). But the phrases are best accounted for as intended not so much to express the accompaniments of the sending as directly to characterise the Son, describing the relation to humanity and the law in which he performed his mission.

5. ἵνα τοὺς ὑπο νόμον ἐξαγοράσῃ, "that he might deliver those that were under law." The phrase ὑπὸ νόμον is, doubt-less, to be taken in the same sense as in v.[4] and 3[23], viz.: "under law" legalistically understood. But while in those cases the context shows that the law actually referred to is the O. T. law, the context here (see above on the inclusiveness of ἡμεῖς in v.[3] and note the second person in v.[6], with its unambiguous inclusion of the Galatian Gentiles) implies that τοὺς ὑπὸ νόμον includes both Jews and Gentiles. That Paul conceived the Gentiles to possess a law, and that of divine origin, appears from Rom. 2[14, 15] (cf. 1[19, 20]); and though the phrase ὑπὸ νόμον is usually employed with reference to the legalism that grew up on Jewish soil, yet that Paul was aware that the law whose work is written in the heart might also be externalised and made legalistic is intrinsically probable and is confirmed by 1 Cor. 9[20], where τοῖς ὑπὸ νόμον, standing as a middle term between Ἰουδαίοις and τοῖς ἀνόμοις, seems to designate those, whether Jew or Gentile, who were living under a system of legalism. On the use of ἐξαγοράζω, see on 3[13], p. 168. That the deliverance referred to is from the law, is implied in τοὺς ὑπὸ νόμον and the absence of any other phrase to suggest another enslaving power. That it is from subjection to law, i. e., (a) from the obligation to obey legal ordinances, and (b) from the conception of God which legalism implies, is shown as respects the former (a) by v.[10] and 5[1-4], and as respects the latter (b) by the following clause and vv.[6, 7]. The whole clause expresses the purpose not of the participle γενόμενον only and probably not of ἐξαπέστειλεν only, but of the whole assertion ἐξαπέστειλεν, with its modifiers, wherein is implied that his human birth and subjection to law were contributory to the achievement of the redemption.

And this in turn conveys an intimation that Paul already had a thought akin to that expressed in Heb. 5⁷⁻⁹ with reference to the relation between the limitations of the earthly life of Jesus and his redemptive work. Yet how he conceived that the deliverance was accomplished, whether as in 3¹³ through his death, or through his life experience reaching its climax in his death (*cf.* Phil. 2⁷, ⁸), this verse in no way decides. That the apostle conceived that Jesus himself had passed through an experience like that of Paul, referred to by him in 2¹⁹, in that he also had discovered that one does not come into the enjoyment of a filial relation to God through obedience to statutes, and that this was embodied in the teaching of Jesus, is not in itself improbable, but is not intimated either here or elsewhere in his letters.

ἵνα τὴν υἱοθεσίαν ἀπολάβωμεν. "that we might receive the adoption." υἱοθεσία, found in inscriptions in the phrase καθ᾽ υἱοθεσίαν and rarely in Greek literature (Diog. Laert. IV 9 (53), νεανίσκων τινῶν υἱοθεσίας ποιεῖσθαι), does not occur in the Lxx and appears in N. T. only in the Pauline epistles. In Rom. 9⁴ it denotes the choice of Israel to be sons of God (*cf.* Exod. 4²² Deut. 14¹, ² Hos. 11¹). In Rom. 8¹⁴, ¹⁵ they are said to be υἱοὶ θεοῦ who are led by God's Spirit, and it is added: "For ye have not received a spirit of bondage again to fear, but ye have received a spirit of adoption (πνεῦμα υἱοθεσίας) whereby we cry, Abba, Father." In Rom. 8²³ ἡ υἱοθεσία is defined as consisting in the redemption of the body, doubtless because in Paul's thought only through the resurrection and the clothing of the spirit in the spiritual body does man enter into the fulness of fellowship with God (*cf.* 1 Cor. 15¹³, ¹⁴, ⁴⁴). In Eph. 1⁵ adoption is spoken of as that which men are foreordained of God to obtain through Jesus Christ. ἡ υἱοθεσία is, therefore, for Paul, God's reception of men into the relation to him of sons, objects of his love and enjoying his fellowship, the ultimate issue of which is the future life wherein they are reclothed with a spiritual body; but the word may be used of different stages and aspects of this one inclusive experience. The article τήν is, doubtless, restrictive, pointing to the thought of vv.¹, ² that at the time appointed of the father the child is released from subjection to tutors and governors, and comes into direct relation to the

father as a mature son—an intimation more fully developed
in v.⁶.

The meaning "sonship" would satisfy most of the passages in which
υἱοθεσία occurs, but there is no occasion to depart from the etymological sense, "installation as a son." This does not, however, justify
reading back into v.¹ the idea of adoption, and from this again carrying
it back through κληρονόμος into the διαθήκη of 3¹⁵, for Paul is not
careful to maintain the consistency of his illustrations. He employs
here his usual term because he is speaking of the establishment of
those who have previously not had the privileges of a son in the full
enjoyment of them.

Whether ἵνα . . . ἀπολάβ. expresses the purpose of ἐξαγοράσῃ, or,
co-ordinately with that clause, expresses the purpose of ἐξαπέστειλεν
is impossible to say with certainty; nor is the distinction important.

6. Ὅτι δέ ἐστε υἱοί, ἐξαπέστειλεν ὁ θεὸς τὸ πνεῦμα τοῦ
υἱοῦ αὐτοῦ εἰς τὰς καρδίας ἡμῶν, "And because ye are sons,
God sent forth the Spirit of his Son into your hearts." The
clause ὅτι . . . υἱοί is naturally interpreted as causal, giving
the reason in the divine mind for the act ἐξαπέστειλεν . . .
ἡμῶν, there being no verb of saying or the like for it to depend
upon as an object clause. Nor is there any sufficient reason
for departing from this obvious interpretation. It follows,
however, that the sonship here spoken of being antecedent to
and the ground of the bestowal of the Spirit is not the full,
achieved fact, nor the consciousness of a filial relation, but the
first and objective stage which the preceding context has emphasised, viz.: release from bondage to law, figuratively described as a pedagogue or guardians and stewards. It is involved in this relation of sonship and the possession of the
Spirit that from the consciousness of the latter one may infer
the former, and it is doubtless to induce the Galatians to draw
this inference from their consciousness of possessing the Spirit
(cf. 3³⁻⁵) that this sentence was written. But the direct affirmation of the sentence is that the sonship is the cause of the
experience of the Spirit.

To take ὅτι as meaning "that," making ὅτι . . . υἱοί the proposition to be established, and then to supply after it "is proved by the

fact" (Philippi, following ancient interpreters), or to take ὅτι in the sense of *quod*, "as respects the fact that" (Wies.), introduces unwarranted complication into a sentence which is on its face complete and simple. That in Rom. 8¹⁴, ¹⁵ sonship is apparently proved by possession of the Spirit does not forbid our interpreting this passage as making the sonship the ground of the bestowal of the Spirit; for not only is the language of Rom. 8¹⁴, ¹⁵ open to interpretation as an argument from effect to cause, in which case there also adoption precedes possession of the Spirit, but if the reverse is true there, antecedence of sonship to the bestowal of the Spirit, clearly indicated in this passage, is explicable by the fact that υἱοθεσία (see on v.⁵) is used by the apostle of different stages of the process by which men come to the full possession of the relationship of sons to God, and that the context implies that it is the first and objective stage of which he is here speaking.

Precisely the phrase τὸ πνεῦμα τοῦ υἱοῦ αὐτοῦ does not occur elsewhere in N. T., but in Phil. 1¹⁹ Paul uses τὸ πνεῦμα Ἰησοῦ Χριστοῦ and in Rom. 8⁹ᶜ πνεῦμα Χριστοῦ (*cf.* also 2 Cor. 3¹⁷ Acts 16⁷ 1 Pet. 1¹¹ Heb. 9¹⁴ Rev. 19¹⁰). Particularly instructive is Rom. 8⁹, ¹⁰, where (a) πνεῦμα θεοῦ ἐν ὑμῖν, (b) πνεῦμα Χριστοῦ ἔχειν, and (c) Χριστὸς ἐν ὑμῖν all express the same fact of experience. It is manifestly also the same experience for which Paul employs in Gal. 2²⁰ the phrase ζῇ ἐν ἐμοὶ Χριστός and in 5²⁵ ζῶμεν πνεύματι. Historically speaking, the sending of the Son and the sending of the Spirit are distinguished in early Christian thought, most markedly so in the fourth gospel (Jn. 3¹⁷ 7³⁹ 16⁷; but note also that the coming of the Spirit is practically identified with the return of the Son), but also in Paul (*cf.* the ἐξαπέστειλεν of v.⁴ with the same verb in this v.). The two terminologies, that of the Christ and that of the Spirit, have also a different origin, both, indeed, having their roots largely in O. T., but being there and in later Jewish thought quite distinct. But in the experience of the early Christians the Christ who by his resurrection had become a spirit active in their lives, and the Spirit of God similarly active, could not be distinguished. *Cf.* Burton, *Spirit, Soul, and Flesh*, p. 189. Precisely to what extent this experiential identification of the heavenly Christ and the Spirit of God has caused a numerical identification of them as personalities is difficult to say. Apparently the apostle Paul, while clearly distinguishing Christ from God the Father (see 1 Cor. 8⁶ Phil. 2⁶⁻⁸, etc.) and less sharply distinguishing the Spirit from God (Rom. 5⁵ 8⁷, ⁸, ⁹, ¹⁴, ¹⁵), is not careful to distinguish the Spirit and Christ, yet never explicitly identifies them. *Cf.* Wood, *The Spirit of God in Biblical Literature*, pp. 229–231. The choice of τὸ πνεῦμα τοῦ υἱοῦ αὐτοῦ for this passage in preference to any of its equivalents is due, on the one side to the necessity of distinguishing the fact referred to from the historic coming of the Christ (4⁴), which excludes τὸν υἱὸν αὐτοῦ and Χριστόν, and on the other to the desire to connect this experience closely with the gift of Christ, which excludes τὸ πνεῦμα or τὸ πνεῦμα τοῦ θεοῦ.

On εἰς τὰς καρδίας ἡμῶν, added to emphasise the transition from the objective sonship to the subjective experience, see Rom. 5⁵ 1 Cor. 2²² Eph. 3¹⁷. It is in the heart, as the seat of intellectual and spiritual life in general (1 Cor. 2⁹ Rom. 9² 10¹, etc.) and in particular of the moral and spiritual life (2 Cor. 4⁶ Rom. 1¹². ²⁴), that the Spirit of God operates. The use of the expression here shows that ἐξαπέστειλεν refers (not as the same word in v.⁴ does) to a single historic fact (the day of Pentecost, e. g.), but to the successive bestowals of the Spirit on individuals (cf. 3³), the aor. being, therefore, a collective historical aor. (BMT 39). On the translation of an aor. in such a case, see BMT 46, 52. On ἡμῶν, undoubtedly to be preferred to ὑμῶν, a Western and Syrian reading, see on v.³.

κράζον Ἀββά ὁ πατήρ. "crying, Abba, Father." The recognition of God as Father is the distinguishing mark of the filial spirit. The participle κράζον agreeing with πνεῦμα ascribes the cry to the Spirit of God's Son; yet it is undoubtedly the apostle's thought that it is the expression of the believer's attitude also. For the Spirit that dwells in us dominates our lives. See chap. 2²⁰ 5²⁵, and cf. Rom. 8¹⁵: ἐλάβετε πνεῦμα υἱοθεσίας, ἐν ᾧ κράζομεν Ἀββά ὁ πατήρ. The use of κράζον, usually employed of a loud or earnest cry (Mt. 9²⁷ Acts 14¹⁴ Rom. 9²⁷) or of a public announcement (Jn. 7²⁸, ³⁷), in the Lxx often of prayer addressed to God (Ps. 3⁵ 107¹³), emphasises the earnestness and intensity of the utterance of the Spirit within us. Though the word κράζον itself conveys no suggestion of joy, it can hardly be doubted that the intensity which the word reflects is in this case to be conceived of as the intensity of joy. Though to be free from law is to obtain adoption, sonship in its full realisation is more than mere freedom from law. The significance of such freedom lies, indeed, precisely in the fact that it makes it possible that a truly filial relation and attitude of man to God shall displace the legal relation that law creates, that instead of our looking upon God as lawgiver in the spirit of bondage and fear (Rom. 8¹⁵) he becomes to us Father with whom we live in fellowship as his sons. See detached note on Πατήρ as applied to God, p. 391.

Ὁ πατήρ, Greek equivalent of the Aramaic Ἀββά, אַבָּא, is a nominative form with vocative force. *Cf.* Rom. 8¹⁵ Mk. 14³⁶ Mt. 11²⁶ Jn.
20²⁸; Bl. D. 147.3. The repetition of the idea in Aramaic and Greek
form gives added solemnity to the expression, and doubtless reflects a
more or less common usage of the early church (see Mk. 14³⁶ Rom. 8¹⁵).
On the origin of this usage, see Th. *s. v.* Ἀββά, Ltft. *ad loc.*, Sief. *ad loc.*
It is quite likely that the use of the Aramaic word was derived from
Jesus, being taken up into the vocabulary of Greek-speaking Christians
through the medium of those who, knowing both Aramaic and Greek,
in reporting in Greek the words of Jesus used this word with a sort of
affectionate fondness for the very term that Jesus himself had used to
express an idea of capital importance in his teaching. This is more
probable than that it was taken over into the Christian vocabulary
from that of the Jewish synagogue in which the idea of God as Father
had so much less prominent place than in the thought and teaching of
Jesus. See Bous. *Rel. d. Jud.*² pp. 432–3, 434; Dal. *WJ.* p. 192.
The attachment of the Greek translation ὁ πατήρ to the Aramaic word
would naturally take place on the passage of the term into Greek-
speaking circles.

7. ὥστε οὐκέτι εἶ δοῦλος ἀλλὰ υἱός· "So that thou art no
longer a slave, but a son." In the possession of the Spirit
of God's Son, assumed to be known as a fact of the experience
of the readers (*cf.* 3²), the apostle finds confirmation of the
ἐστὲ υἱοί of v.⁶, as there the sonship is said to be the ground
for the bestowal of the Spirit. That the emphasis of sonship
is still upon the fact of freedom from bondage to law is shown
in the insertion of the negative οὐκέτι δοῦλος, and that those
addressed were formerly in this bondage is implied in οὐκέτι.
The change from plural to singular has the effect of bringing
the matter home to each individual reader; the persons designated remaining, of course, unchanged. *Cf.* 6¹, and for classical
examples, see Kühner-Gerth, 371.5, b.

εἰ δὲ υἱός, καὶ κληρονόμος διὰ θεοῦ, "and if son, then heir
through God." That here as throughout the passage υἱός
means υἱὸς θεοῦ needs no specific proof; it is sufficiently indicated in the expression τοῦ υἱοῦ αὐτοῦ in vv. ⁴, ⁶, and the relation of this expression to υἱός. This obviously suggests that
κληρονόμος means κληρονόμος θεοῦ. *Cf.* Rom. 8¹⁷: εἰ δὲ τέκνα,
καὶ κληρονόμοι· κληρονόμοι μὲν θεοῦ, συνκληρονόμοι δὲ Χριστοῦ.

To this conception the phrase διὰ θεοῦ adds the thought, "made so by God," thus equivalent to κατὰ θέλημα θεοῦ; cf. 3²⁹, κληρονόμοι κατ' ἐπαγγελίαν. The purpose of the addition is perhaps to remind the Galatians that their position as heirs is due to divine grace, not one of right or desert, but more probably to emphasise the certainty of their possession of it. The absence of the article before θεοῦ makes the noun not indefinite but qualitative, emphasising the divineness of the one through whom they were made heir. Cf. on θεόν, v.⁷. The reversion to the thought of the κληρονομία expressed in 3¹⁸, ²⁹ shows that the apostle has not lost sight of his main purpose throughout this and the preceding chapter, viz., to convince the Galatians that it was not through law but through the retention of their freedom from it that they could obtain the blessings promised to the sons of Abraham, which the judaisers had held before their eyes as a prize greatly to be desired but obtainable only through circumcision. The appeal of the apostle is to retain the status they already possess. Cf. v.⁶, "ye are sons," and v.⁹, "how turn ye back?" That he should not here employ the term υἱοὶ Ἀβραάμ, as in 3⁷, but κληρονόμοι, as in 3²⁹, is natural, not only because κληρονόμοι more distinctly suggests the idea of the blessing to be received, but also because after υἱοί, meaning sons of God, sons of Abraham would have the effect of an anticlimax. κληρονόμοι should, therefore, be taken here in the sense, heirs of God, and as such recipients of the blessing promised to Abraham's seed; this blessing has already been defined as justification, acceptance with God, possession of the Spirit. Cf. 3⁷⁻¹⁴. It is, moreover, as present possessors of the κληρονομία that they are κληρονόμοι. That other blessings are in store for them is undoubtedly a Pauline thought (Rom. 5¹¹ 8¹⁷⁻²³), and that the conception of the κληρονόμος easily lends itself to the presentation of this phase of the matter, that which has been received being thought of as simply the earnest and first-fruit of the full blessing (see Rom. 8¹⁷⁻²³ Eph. 1¹⁴) is also true. But the Galatians already possess the promised Spirit, and the emphasis in this context is upon that which is already possessed, with no clear indication that the thought goes beyond that.

Against the supposition—at first sight most natural—that the term as here used is intended to carry the thought back specifically to κληρονόμος in v.¹, is the fact that κληρονόμος is there applied to one who not having yet entered into possession of his κληρονομία is in the position of νήπιος and δοῦλος, precisely that position, therefore, which it is the purpose of this v. to deny; and, though the title κληρονόμος carries with it the idea of future release from the status of δοῦλος, the contention of the apostle is here not that the Galatians will be, but already are, sons and no longer slaves.   It is more probable, therefore, that by this word he reverts for the moment to the idea of κληρονόμοι in 3²⁹ (cf., also, 3¹⁸), heirs according to the promise made to Abraham, i. e., possessors of the blessing promised to Abraham and to his seed. This is not to take κληρονόμος as meaning heir of Abraham, a predicate which the apostle never applies to Christians.   They are indeed called "sons of Abraham," because it is to the seed of Abraham that the promise applies, but it is God who established the διαθήκη and makes the ἐπαγγελία, and they to whom the promise is fulfilled are his κληρονόμοι.   Cf. on 3¹⁸ and detached note on Διαθήκη, p. 496.   This also makes it evident that the term κληρονόμος is not used in its strict sense of heir, i. e., recipient of the property of another who has died, or prospective recipient of the property of another when he shall have died, but, tropically, possessor of a promised possession.

The fact that κληρονόμοι here means heirs of God, and the deduction of heirship from sonship, itself inferred from an act of adoption, υἱοθεσία, gives a certain colour of support to Ramsay's view that the διαθήκη of 3¹⁵ᶠᶠ· is not a covenant but a will, and specifically a will involving the adoption of a son.   If the language of 3¹⁵ᶠᶠ· were harmonious with these suggestions of the present passage, the latter would fall in with that passage as part of an illustration consistently carried through the whole passage.   But (1) the possibility of interpreting this phrase in the way above suggested is not sufficient ground for setting aside the strong counter-evidence that by διαθήκη he means not a will, but a covenant.   Even if the expression here employed could be shown to involve the idea of adoption by will and inheritance as an adopted son, this would only show that the apostle is now illustrating the spiritual relations which are the real subject of his thought by a different group of facts of common life from those which he employed in 3¹⁵ᶠᶠ·   But (2) it is improbable that it is specifically an adoptive sonship that the apostle has in mind in εἰ δὲ υἱός.   For, though he represents the sonship of the Galatians in common with other believers as acquired by adoption, yet the fact of adoption is nowhere emphasised, and in the actual spiritual realm that which is illustratively called adoption carries with it, as a consequence, the bestowal of the Spirit of God's Son, by which, it is implied, those who are sons come into like relation to

God with that which the Son himself sustains. The conception of adoption, accordingly, falls into the background, leaving simply that of sonship.

8. *Description of the former condition of the Galatians as one of bondage to gods not really such, and exhortation to them not to return to that state* (4⁸⁻¹¹).

Again directly addressing the Galatians as in 3¹, and as in v.¹ characterising their former condition as one of enslavement, the apostle describes them as in bondage to gods that were not in reality such, and appeals to them, now that they have come into fellowship with God, not, as they threaten to do by their adoption of the Jewish cycle of feasts and fasts, to return to those weak and beggarly rudimentary teachings under which they formerly were, and expresses his fear that he has laboured over them to no purpose.

⁸*But at that time, not knowing God, ye were in bondage to the gods that are not such by nature.* ⁹*But now having come to know God, or rather having become known by God, how is it that ye are turning back again to the weak and beggarly rudiments, to which ye wish to be in bondage again?* ¹⁰*Ye are observing days and months and seasons and years.* ¹¹*I fear that in vain have I spent my labour on you.*

8. Ἀλλὰ τότε μὲν οὐκ εἰδότες θεὸν ἐδουλεύσατε τοῖς φύσει μὴ οὖσι θεοῖς· "But at that time, not knowing God, ye were in bondage to the gods that are not such by nature." Doubling, so to speak, upon his course, the apostle reverts to the condition of the Galatians before they received his message, and in antithesis (ἀλλά) to the description of them in v.⁷ as heirs through God, describes them as having been in that former time ignorant of God who is in reality such, and in bondage to the gods that by nature are not gods. The purpose of this v. appears in v.⁹, where he again dissuades them from returning to the state of bondage. That Paul conceived of the deities whom the Galatians formerly worshipped as real existences, is neither proved nor disproved by this sentence, in which he denies to them deity, θειότης, but neither affirms nor denies

existence; nor by the phrase ἐπιτρόποις καὶ οἰκονόμοις in v. ²,
since that may be used only by way of rhetorical personification
of the law and have no reference to the gods of the Gentiles
(*cf.* on τὰ στοιχεῖα τοῦ κόσμου, v.³); but that he did so conceive
of them is rendered probable by the evidence of 1 Cor. 8⁵, ⁶
10¹⁹, ²⁰ Col. 2¹⁵. *Cf.* also Deut. 4¹⁹ and see literature cited in
special note on Τὰ στοιχεῖα τοῦ κόσμου, p. 510.

Τότε refers to the past time implied in οὐκέτι (v.⁷), when the Galatian Christians were still δοῦλοι; note the ἐδουλεύσατε of this sentence.

Εἰδότες is a perfect participle of existing state, μὴ εἰδότες meaning
"not possessing knowledge." How this state of ignorance came about
is not here discussed, or whether it was partial or absolute. *Cf.* Rom.
1¹⁸ᶠᶠ.

The omission of the article with θεόν makes the word not indefinite (as in Acts 12²² 1 Cor. 8⁴), but, as in v.⁷ and very often, qualitative, referring definitely to the one God, but with an emphasis on
his attributes as God, which is lacking when he is called ὁ θεός.
For a similar use of θεός, with strong emphasis on the qualities of
deity, see Jn. 1¹⁸, θεὸν οὐδεὶς ἑώρακεν πώποτε, where the contrast,
however, is not between one in reality God, as compared with those
not really such, but between God in the absolute sense, incapable of
being directly known, and God as revealed in the person of the Son.
For other examples of this indubitable, though often overlooked,
qualitative use of personal appellations without the article, see Rom.
1²¹: γνόντες τὸν θεὸν οὐχ ὡς θεὸν ἐδόξαξαν. Rom. 8³³ Gal. 3²⁸ 4¹⁴ 5¹¹
Phil. 2¹³ 1 Thes. 1⁹: ἐπεστρέψατε πρὸς τὸν θεὸν ἀπὸ τῶν εἰδώλων δουλεύειν
θεῷ ζῶντι καὶ ἀληθινῷ. 2 Thes. 2⁴. Other examples more or less clear,
but together clearly establishing the usage, are very numerous. See
note on chap. 2⁶, pp. 88 *ff.*, detached note on Πατήρ *as applied to God*,
p. 384, and Slaten, *Qualitative Nouns in the Pauline Epistles*, pp. 64–68.

Ἐδουλεύσατε is a simple historical aorist, not inceptive, referring not
to a point of time but to a period, *BMT* 38, 39, 41 Rem.

Φύσις, from φύω, is properly that which belongs to a person or thing
by virtue of its origin; then its essential character; used thus even of
the divine nature, which is without origin, 2 Pet. 1⁴. φύσει μὴ οὖσι
may be an adjective element limiting θεοῖς, or οὖσι may be an adjective participle used substantively, with θεοῖς as a predicate after it.
In the former case the beings referred to are characterised as gods,
but with the qualification that they are not so by nature, i. e., in reality; in the latter case they are not called θεοί at all, but are characterised negatively only, as beings that by nature are not gods. Gram-

matically and contextually there is no ground of decisive choice
between these, but 1 Cor. 8⁵, showing that Paul could apply the term
θεοί to the gods of the Gentiles, though denying that it really belonged
to them, favours the first interpretation. The comparison of Plato,
Legg. X 904 A, οἱ κατὰ νόμον ὄντες θεοί, perhaps suggests what the
positive element of the apostle's thought was. He was speaking of
"the gods of popular opinion," as Jowett translates Plato's phrase,
Cf. 1 Cor. 8⁵, λεγόμενοι θεοί.

On οὐ with εἰδότες and μή with οὖσι, see BMT 485; the choice of
negatives, though doubtless unconscious, probably reflects the feeling
that οὐκ εἰδότες expressed a fact, τοῖς φύσει μὴ οὖσιν θεοῖς a conception,
a description of a class, but without implication of its existence or non-
existence. The few instances in which Paul uses οὐ with an attributive
participle are quotations from the Lxx, his otherwise regular habit
being to use μή with such participles and with adverbial participles
not involving a direct assertion (Rom. 1²⁸ 2¹⁴ 4¹⁷ Gal. 6⁹). οὐ, with the
possible exception of Col. 2¹⁹, in effect negatives an assertion (1 Cor.
4¹⁴ 9²⁶ 2 Cor. 4⁸ 12⁴).

9. νῦν δὲ γνόντες θεόν, μᾶλλον δὲ γνωσθέντες ὑπὸ θεοῦ,
"But now having come to know God, or rather to be known
by God." Their coming to know God is manifestly through
the apostle's preaching. Cf. 1 Thes. 1⁹: πῶς ἐπεστρέψατε πρὸς
τὸν θεὸν ἀπὸ τῶν εἰδώλων δουλεύειν θεῷ ζῶντι, language
which, as the evidence of this epistle shows, might have been
addressed to the Galatians also. That γνωσθέντες as here
used can not refer simply to knowledge in a purely theoretic or
intellectual sense is evident, since the apostle must have regarded
such knowledge as always, not simply now (νῦν in contrast with
τότε), possessed by God. For the meaning required here, "having become objects of his favourable attention," cf. Ps. 1⁶
Nah. 1⁷ 1 Cor. 8³ Mt. 7²³, and on the thought of God receiving
the Gentiles into a favour not previously enjoyed by them, see
Rom. 9²⁵ᶠ· 11³⁰. This fact respecting Gentiles in general the
apostle conceived to be realised in respect to the Galatians in
particular through his preaching the gospel to them in accordance with his commission as apostle to the Gentiles. The purpose of this added phrase, in a sense displacing the previous
γνόντες, etc., is doubtless to remind the Galatians that it is
not to themselves but to God that they owe their knowledge of

him and escape from idolatry (*cf.* chap. 1⁶: μετατίθεσθε ἀπὸ τοῦ καλέσαντος ὑμᾶς ἐν χάριτι Χριστοῦ, and Eph. 2⁸), and so to emphasise the folly and wrong of abandoning this advantage through another ἐπιστρέφειν.

Though γινώσκω does not always retain its inchoative force (see Th. *s. v.*) even in the aorist, yet this is often clearly discernible (*cf.* Lk. 24¹⁸ 1 Cor. 1²¹), and the aorist participle in particular always, apparently, retains this meaning, signifying either "having learned, having come to know," or "knowing" (result of having come to know), not "having known." See Mt. 16⁸ 22¹⁸ 26¹⁰ Mk. 6³⁸ 15⁴⁵ Lk. 9¹¹ Jn. 5⁶ Acts 23⁶ Rom. 1²¹ 2 Cor. 5²¹ Gal. 2⁹. By γνόντες there is, therefore, affirmed the acquisition of that knowledge the former possession of which is denied in οὐκ εἰδότες. Of any other distinction between εἰδότες and γνόντες, as, *e. g.*, that the former denotes an external knowledge that God is, the latter an inner recognition of God, there is no basis in usage or warrant in the context. The absence of the article with θεόν is not without significance (*cf.* Rom. 1²¹, γνόντες τὸν θεόν. 1 Cor. 1²¹: οὐκ ἔγνω ὁ κόσμος . . . τὸν θεόν), being doubtless due to the same cause that led to the omission of the article in v.⁸ (*q. v.*), viz., emphasis upon the qualities of deity in antithesis to the φύσει μὴ ὄντες θεοί. *Cf.* 1 Thes. 1⁹ quoted above, noting τὸν θεόν in the first mention of God, and θεῷ without the article when the word follows the mention of the idcls and with emphasis on the qualities of true deity. One might imperfectly reproduce the effect in English by reading with strong emphasis on the word God. But now having come to know [a] *God* (not those that are no real gods).

Μᾶλλον δέ, following a negative phrase, introduces and emphasises its positive correlate (Eph. 4²⁸ 5¹¹); following a positive expression it introduces an additional and more important fact or aspect of the matter, not thereby retracting what precedes (probably not even in Wisd. 8²⁰, certainly not in Rom. 8³⁴ 1 Cor. 14¹⋅ ⁵ 2 Mac. 6²³), but so transferring the emphasis to the added fact or aspect as being of superior significance as in effect to displace the preceding thought. So clearly here, as in Rom. 8³⁴, etc.

πῶς ἐπιστρέφετε πάλιν ἐπὶ τὰ ἀσθενῆ καὶ πτωχὰ στοιχεῖα, οἷς πάλιν ἄνωθεν δουλεύειν θελετε; "how is it that ye are turning back again to the weak and beggarly rudiments, to which ye wish to be in bondage again?" The question is rhetorical, intended to set forth the absurdity of the action referred to. On the use of πῶς in such questions, meaning "how is it possible that," see chap. 2¹⁴ Rom. 3⁶ 6² Mt. 7⁴ 12²⁶, ²⁹, *et freq.* The present tense presents the action as already in progress. (Observe that in the examples cited, when a theoretical possibility is spoken of the tense is a future or a form referring to the future, but in chap. 2¹⁴ it is a present, referring, as in this case, to something in progress.) This corresponds with the representation of the situation in Galatia given in 1⁶: θαυμάζω ὅτι ... μετατίθεσθε. *Cf.* also θέλετε in next clause. The phrase τὰ ἀσθενῆ καὶ πτωχὰ στοιχεῖα manifestly refers to what v.³ calls τὰ στοιχεῖα τοῦ κόσμου; see on that v., and detached note, p. 510. The present expression emphasises the ineffectualness and poverty of the old religious systems in contrast with the power and richness of the gospel. See chap. 5⁶, ¹⁶⁻²⁴ Rom. 1¹⁷ 8³, ⁴. It is, of course, that to which they were now turning that is specially in mind, yet the former heathenism, included under the στοιχεῖα by implication of the repeated πάλιν, is also thereby stigmatised as ἀσθενῆ καὶ πτωχά. Both were at bottom legalistic, without clear perception of ethical principles and destitute of dynamic to make possible the realisation of them in life. What the apostle says in Rom. 8³ of *the* law, ὁ νόμος, is affirmed of it, not because of anything peculiar to it as distinguished from the still more imperfect ethnic systems, but because of that which was common to them both, and his usual term for the displaced system is not ὁ νόμος, but νόμος (see, *e. g.*, chap. 3², ¹⁰, ¹¹, Rom. 3²⁰, ²¹ᵃ. etc.). The word θέλετε in the appended relative clause expresses forcibly the inclination of the Galatians to abandon the Pauline gospel. *Cf.* θέλοντες, v.²¹.

Δουλεῦσαι is attested by אB only; all other authorities apparently read δουλεύειν. The former is quite certainly a modification of the original text under the influence of πάλιν ἄνωθεν, which naturally calls for an inceptive form. The scribe missing the reference of the present to a second *period* of enslavement, substitutes the aorist to express the idea of a return to bondage. πάλιν ἄνωθεν δουλεῦσαι would have furnished no temptation to change it.

Πάλιν originally meaning "back" (return to a previous position; *cf.* L. & S. and Th. *s. v.* and reff. there) but more commonly, in later Greek, "again" (repetition of a previous action) is often used when the repetition involves return to a previous state or position (Mk. 2¹ 3¹); but also (like the English "again") when the action is a return to a previous state through reversal, not, strictly speaking, repetition. So in chap. 1¹⁷ Jn. 10¹⁸ Rom. 11²³. So also here, since there had been̄no previous ἐπιστρέφειν ἐπὶ τὰ . . . στοιχεῖα, but only an εἶναι ὑπὸ τὰ στοιχεῖα, and the contemplated ἐπιστρέφειν was not a repetition of a previous act but a reversal of the ἐπιστρέφειν πρὸς τὸν θεόν (cf. 1 Thes. 1⁹), here described in γνόντες θεόν. Wieseler's statement, "Das πάλιν, welches hier wiederum, nicht rückwärts, heisst, weist auf eine frühere Bekehrung (ἐπιστροφή) hin, nämlich auf die ihrem, v.⁸ erwähnten Heidenthume gegenüber in dem νῦν δέ u. s. w. angedeutete Bekehrung von den Götzen (ἐπιστροφὴ ἀπὸ τῶν εἰδώλων) zu Gott in Christo," escapes self-contradiction only by the expedient of supposing πάλιν to apply to ἐπιστρέφετε only, not to ἐπιστρέφετε ἐπὶ . . . στοιχεῖα, an interpretation which would require us to read: "How turn ye again, this time to the weak and beggarly rudiments?" The view, moreover, in support of which he resorts to this difficult expedient, viz., that Paul does not include the former heathenism of the Galatians under τὰ . . . στοιχεῖα compels him further to limit the effect of πάλιν ἄνωθεν in the next clause to δουλεύειν, reading in effect, "to which ye desire to be in bondage, this constituting for you a second bondage." Such a harsh severance of verb and adverb in two successive clauses is not demanded by the usage of πάλιν and is, in fact, self-refuting. The obvious and unescapable implication of the language is that the conversion to τὰ . . . στοιχεῖα is a return to a state generically the same as the idol-worship under which they formerly were. Against this it is irrelevant to point out that ἐπιστρέφειν does not mean "return" but only "turn," since the idea of reversal is expressed in the adverb. The expression πάλιν ἄνωθεν δουλεύειν is pregnant, the adverb suggesting a renewed enslavement and the present tense of the infinitive a continued state; hence in effect again to become enslaved and to continue so, or to endure a second period of enslavement. δουλεῦσαι would probably be inceptive. πάλιν, then, in this case expresses repetition rather than, as in the preceding clause, reversal, though, as in many other cases (Mk. 2¹ 3¹, etc.), the repetition involves also return to a former position. Cf. 5¹. It is enforced by the nearly synonymous ἄνωθεν "anew." It is probably an overrefinement to find in this use of the two words (cf. Wisd. 19⁶) anything more than emphasis, such as is often expressed in Greek writers by αὖθις, ἄνωθεν, etc.

10. ἡμέρας παρατηρεῖσθε καὶ μῆνας καὶ καιροὺς καὶ ἐνιαυτούς. "Ye are observing days and months and seasons and years." That the days, etc., referred to are those which the Jewish law required to be observed is made certain by the unquestioned character of the influence to which the Galatians were yielding. See esp. v.[21]. Compared with 5[1ᵈ⁻], in which it appears that the question of adopting circumcision was still pending, and 5[3], which indicates that the Galatians had not yet been asked to adopt the whole law, this sentence indicates that the judaisers had pursued the adroit course of presenting to them at first a part only of the requirements of the Jewish law and had begun with those things that would be least repulsive. Having secured the adoption of the festivals, and perhaps the fast-days, of the Jewish cycle, they were now urging circumcision. Whether, however, the feasts and fasts were all that the Galatians had adopted as yet, is not made clear, since the apostle may have mentioned these only as examples of their subjection to the law. But the silence of the letter about any statute of the law except circumcision, which they had not yet adopted, and the fasts and feasts, which they had, there being, for example, no mention in connection with the situation in Galatia of the law of foods, leaves no positive ground for supposing that any points except these had been raised.

On παρατηρεῖσθε, "ye observe, keep religiously," cf. Jos. Ant. 3. 91 (5[8]): παρατηρεῖν τὰς ἑβδομάδας. 14. 264 (10[25]), παρατηρεῖν τὴν τῶν σαββάτων ἡμέραν. Contra Ap. 2. 282 (39, Whiston 40): οὐδὲ ἓν ἔθνος ἔνθα . . . πολλὰ τῶν εἰς βρῶσιν ἡμῖν οὐ νενομισμένων παρατετήρηται. Nowhere in the Lxx does the word appear with this meaning, and in non-biblical writers instances have been observed only in Dion Cassius, 38. 13, τὰ ἐκ τοῦ οὐρανοῦ γιγνόμενα παρατηρεῖν. It occurs here only in N. T. in this sense, τηρεῖν being used in Mt. 19[17] Jn. 8[51] Acts 15[5], etc.; φυλάσσειν in Mt. 19[20] Lk. 11[28] Acts 7[53] Rom. 2[26] Gal. 6[13], etc.

'Ημέρας probably refers primarily to the sabbath days, but includes also the feasts, which are observed each on a single day.

Μῆνας, strictly "months," may be used by metonymy for monthly recurring events (cf. Isa. 66[23]). If used in the strict sense, the word probably refers to the seventh month (see Num., chap. 29), for, though there were feasts in other months, no other month was so occupied with celebrations that it itself could be said to be observed. But it is more likely that the reference is to the celebration of the appearance of the new moon which marked the beginning of the month, this being in a sense an observance of the month. See Num. 10[10] 28[11]; cf. 1 Chron. 23[31] Col. 2[16].

Καιρούς, in itself indefinite as to either length or frequency of cele-

bration, probably here refers to a class of celebrations not limited to a
single day, thus to the great feasts, Passover, Tabernacles, etc. (see
2 Chron. 8¹³, ἐν τοῖς σαββάτοις καὶ ἐν τοῖς μησὶν καὶ ἐν ταῖς ἑορταῖς, τρεῖς
καιροὺς τοῦ ἐνιαυτοῦ, ἐν τῇ ἑορτῇ τῶν ἀζύμων, ἐν τῇ ἑορτῇ τῶν ἑβδομάδων,
ἐν τῇ ἑορτῇ τῶν σκηνῶν), or to these and the fasts of the fourth and fifth
and seventh and tenth months. See Zech. 8¹⁹.

Ἐνιαυτούς, "years," may refer to the year of Jubilee or the sabbatical year. So Ell. Ltft. *et al.*, esp. Barton (*JBL*. XXXIII, 118 *ff*.), who,
referring it to the sabbatical year, founds on this interpretation an
argument for the dating of the epistle in the year 54 or 55 A. D., this in
turn carrying with it the conclusion that the letter was written to
churches in North Galatia, so called. The doubt of Benzinger (*Encyc.
Bib.* II 1514) whether these year-long celebrations were ever actually
observed is perhaps scarcely justified in view of 1 Mac. 6⁴⁹⁻⁵³; Jos. *Ant.*
13. 234 (8¹), 14. 475 (16²); *Bell.* 1. 60 (2⁴). But in view of the fact
which the epistle clearly shows, that the Galatians had not yet undertaken to keep the whole law, not even having at all generally accepted
circumcision (*cf.* on 4¹ 5³), it must be regarded as very improbable that
among the requirements of the law already adopted was a custom eco-
nomically so burdensome and socially so difficult as the sabbatical
year. It is, therefore, much more probable that, as he speaks of the
observance of the new moon as an observance of months, so by the
observance of years he means the celebration of the beginning of the
year, probably on the first of the month Tishri. Against this view
Barton urges it as a fatal objection that since the Talmud includes
New Year's Day among the great festivals and calls these by a word
equivalent to καιροί, therefore Paul's ἐνιαυτούς, if it refers to New
Year's Day, has already been included in καιρούς (see Barton, *op. cit.*,
p. 120). But it is quite unsafe to argue that because the Talmud includes New Year's Day among the great feasts, therefore Paul included
it in the καιροί. Moreover, non-exclusiveness of his terms is in itself
not improbable. Formal exactness in such matters is not characteristic of Paul. It is, indeed, most likely that, as used here, μῆνας is
included in ἡμέρας, and ἐνιαυτούς in καιρούς or ἡμέρας, the four terms
without mutual exclusiveness covering all kinds of celebrations of days
and periods observed by the Jews.

11. φοβοῦμαι ὑμᾶς μή πως εἰκῇ κεκοπίακα εἰς ὑμᾶς. "I fear
that in vain have I spent my labour upon you," *i. e.*, that the
labour which I bestowed on you is to result in nothing. A
paratactically added expression of the apostle's feeling in view
of the tendency of the Galatians to adopt legalistic practices,
which clearly indicates his estimate of the deadly character of

legalism. Should they really come under its dominion, his
labour would have been for naught.   For the expression of the
more hopeful feeling, between which and that of fear of the outcome expressed here the letter swings, see 5¹⁰.

Ὑμᾶς is best regarded as proleptically employed, not properly an
object of φοβοῦμαι, but anticipating the ὑμᾶς in the subordinate
clause. Cf. W. LXVI 5, and such N. T. examples as Mk. 12³⁴ Acts 13³²
Gal. 1¹¹. It is true that as a rule the object accusative anticipates
the subject of the subordinate clause. But that this is not uniformly
the case, see Krüger, Gr. Sprachl. 61. 6⁶, and the example there cited:
τὴν νῆσον ταύτην ἐφοβοῦντο μὴ ἐξ αὐτῆς τὸν πόλεμον σφίσι ποιῶνται,
Thuc. 4. 8⁵. μὴ κεκοπίακα is then an object clause after a verb of
fearing. The indicative is employed because the fact spoken of is, as
an event, already past, though the result is undecided or not yet
known to the writer. See BMT 227, and cf. on chap. 2². On εἰκῇ
cf. 3⁴. The meaning here is evidently "without effect." The perfect
κεκοπίακα, referring to a past action and its existing result, is appropriately employed, since it is precisely the result of his action that the
apostle has chiefly in mind. εἰς ὑμᾶς is equivalent to a strengthened
dative of advantage, "for you."

9. *An affectionate appeal to the Galatians to enter fully
into their freedom from law, referring to their former
enthusiastic reception of the apostle and affection
for him, and expressing the wish that he were now
with them and could speak to them in more persuasive language than he had formerly used* (4¹²⁻²⁰).

Dropping argument, the resumption of which in vv.²¹⁻³¹ is
probably an after-thought, the apostle turns to appeal, begging
the Galatians to take his attitude towards the law, referring to
the circumstances under which he had preached the gospel to
them, and the enthusiasm and personal affection with which,
despite an illness which made him unattractive to them, they
had received him and his message. He compares his own
zealous pursuit of them with that of his opponents, justifying
his by its motive, but expresses, also, the wish that he could be
present with them right now and speak in a different tone
from that, by implication harsher one, which he had employed
on some previous occasion when he had "told them the truth."

¹²*Become as I am (or have become), because I am as ye are, I beseech you, brethren.* ¹³*Ye did me no wrong, but ye know that because of an infirmity of the flesh I preached the gospel to you on that former occasion;* ¹⁴*and that which was a temptation to you in my flesh, ye did not reject or despise, but ye received me as an angel of God, as Christ Jesus.* ¹⁵*Where, then, is that gratulation of yourselves? For I bear you witness that ye would, if possible, have plucked out your eyes and given them to me.* ¹⁶*So that I have become your enemy by telling you the truth!* ¹⁷*They zealously seek you, not honestly, but wish to shut you out that ye may seek them.* ¹⁸*But it is good to be zealously sought after in a good thing, always, and not only when I am present with you,* ¹⁹*oh, my children, with whom I travail again in birth pangs till Christ be formed in you.* ²⁰*But I could wish to be present with you now, and to change my tone ; because I am in perplexity in reference to you.*

12. Γίνεσθε ὡς ἐγώ, ὅτι κἀγὼ ὡς ὑμεῖς, ἀδελφοί, δέομαι ὑμῶν. "Become as I am (or have become), because I am as ye are, I beseech you, brethren." With this sentence the apostle, under the influence, probably, of the fear expressed in v.¹¹, turns from argument to entreaty and appeals to the feelings of the Galatians. *Cf.* the similar manner of approach in 3¹⁻³, and notice here the affectionate ἀδελφοί (*cf.* on 1¹¹) and the use of δέομαι, "I entreat." The entreaty itself is enigmatical and paradoxical. Yet its meaning can scarcely be doubtful. The apostle desires the Galatians to emancipate themselves from bondage to law, as he had done, and appeals to them to do this on the ground that he, who possessed the advantages of the law, had foregone them and put himself on the same level, in relation to law, with them. Thus while γίνεσθε ὡς ἐγώ addresses them as subject to law, or on the point of becoming so, ὡς ὑμεῖς looks at them as Gentiles without the advantages of law. A similar thought is expressed less enigmatically in 2¹⁵, ¹⁶ (*cf.* v.⁹) and in Phil. 3⁴ᶠ·, esp. v.⁸. *Cf.* also 1 Cor. 9²¹.

It affects the sense but little whether with κἀγώ we supply εἰμί or γέγονα (or ἐγενόμην); γέγονα corresponds best with γίνεσθε and the actual facts, since the apostle's freedom from law was the result of a becoming, a change of relations. On the other hand, εἰμί corresponds best with εστε, which must be supplied with ὑμεῖς and better fits the parallelism, which is evidently intended to be paradoxical. The interpretation of Chrys. *et al.*, according to which ἤμην is supplied after κἀγώ, giving the meaning, "because I was formerly under law as ye now are," is open to the two objections: (a) that, the reference to past time being essential to the thought, ἤμην could hardly have been left to be supplied, and (b) that the appeal, to be effective, must be not simply to the apostle's former state, which he has now abandoned, but to his present state or his abandonment of the former state.

οὐδέν με ἠδικήσατε· **13.** οἴδατε δὲ ὅτι δι' ἀσθένειαν τῆς σαρκὸς εὐηγγελισάμην ὑμῖν τὸ πρότερον, "Ye did me no wrong, but ye know that because of an infirmity of the flesh I preached the gospel to you on that former occasion." οὐδέν με ἠδικήσατε is in all probability an allusion to an assertion of the Galatians that they had done the apostle no wrong, it being equally their right to accept his message when he came and that of the later Christian teachers when they came; to which the apostle adroitly replies conceding that they did him no wrong in the first instance, and going on to remind them of their former generous and affectionate treatment of him. In v.[16] he follows this up with the intimation that they are now doing him a wrong in counting him their enemy. The reference to the bodily weakness which was the occasion of his preaching to them had for its purpose in Paul's mind to remind them of their affectionate attitude towards him and to renew it. For the modern reader it has the added value of furnishing an interesting and valuable detail concerning the circumstances under which Paul first preached in Galatia. On this aspect of the matter, see the *Introd.*, p. xxix. On the nature of the illness, see fine print below. Whether τὸ πρότερον referred to the former of two occasions on which he had preached the gospel to them orally, hence of two visits to Galatia, was, of course, perfectly clear to the Galatians. For the modern reader this can only be definitely decided by proving, if it can be done, from sources outside this passage whether Paul had already been in Galatia once or twice. See below on τὸ πρότερον.

Οὐδέν με ἠδίκησατε is open to several interpretations according as (a) ἠδικήσατε is taken in the sense (i) "to wrong," "to do injustice to one," or (ii) "to harm," "to injure"; (b) the aorist is understood to refer to a distinctly past time, in contrast with the recent past or present, equivalent to the English past, or as covering the period up to the present, and so equivalent to the English perfect; (c) μέ is understood to be emphatic or not, and if emphatic, as standing in implied antithesis, e. g., to ὑμᾶς or Χριστόν; (d) according as the sentence is or is not supposed to refer to a claim of the Galatians to the effect that they had not wronged or harmed him. Of the different views thus resulting, those that are at all probable may be stated as follows: (1) Ye did me (at that time) no injustice; it is now that you are unjust in regarding me as your enemy (cf. v.¹⁶). The occasion of the statement is in this case not in anything that the Galatians have said, but in the apostle's own sense of having been wronged. (2) I grant that ye did me (at that time) no injustice. In this you are right. I can not grant that ye are not now wronging me in regarding me as your enemy. (3) Ye have not wronged me; it is Christ that ye have wronged. (4) Ye have not harmed me; it is yourselves that ye have harmed. Of these several views the second best accords with the context, and best accounts for the introduction of these otherwise enigmatic words. The context says nothing of their wronging Christ or injuring themselves, but does imply that they are now regarding Paul as their enemy, which would, of course, be felt by Paul as an injustice. The sentence is, moreover, more likely to have found its occasion in some word of theirs than to have originated with Paul himself. Had the latter been the case, he would probably have added some adverb or phrase of past time (cf. v.⁸); δέ is slightly adversative: Ye did me no wrong, but rather when I preached, etc., ye received me, etc.

Δι' ἀσθένειαν (cf. οὐ δυνάμενος δι' ἀσθένειαν πλεῦσαι, quoted by M. and M. Voc. s. v., from a papyrus of 135 A. D.) expresses the occasioning cause of the εὐηγγελισάμην, not the means (δι' ἀσθενείας) or limiting condition (ἐν ἀσθενείᾳ). It was a bodily weakness that gave occasion to his preaching to the Galatians, either by detaining him in Galatia longer than he had intended, or by leading him to go there contrary to his previous plan. Both here and in v.¹⁴ σάρξ is obviously to be taken in its physical sense, equivalent to σῶμα; see on 3⁵, and detached note on Πνεῦμα and Σάρξ, II 2, p. 492. Other senses of the word are plainly inappropriate to the context. The factors to be taken into account in considering what was the nature of the weakness are: (a) the phrase πειρασμὸν ὑμῖν ἐν τῇ σαρκί μου (see below), which undoubtedly refers to the same thing here designated as ἀσθένειαν τῆς σαρκός, tends to show that the latter was in some way offensive to the Galatians or calculated to lead to the rejection of his message. (b) v.¹⁵ suggests that Paul's sickness was a disease of the eyes, obstruct-

ing his sight. (c) 2 Cor. 12⁷, ἐδόθη μοι σκόλοψ τῇ σαρκί, may not improbably be understood to refer to the same fact. But neither of
these latter identifications are certain. Of the many explanations
proposed, persecution, temptation to sensuality, spiritual trials, such
as temptation to despair and doubt, wholly fail to meet the conditions.
The language can refer only to some physical ailment hard to bear,
and calculated to keep him humble and, in some measure, to repel
those to whom he preached. Ltft. Lip. Dib. *Gwt.* pp. 46*ff.*, *et al.*,
favour epilepsy, Rückert *et al.* some affection of the eyes; Ramsay,
reviving in part an ancient opinion, thinks it was fever with accompanying severe headache (*St. Paul*, pp. 94 *ff.*, and *Com. on Gal.*,
pp. 422 *ff.*). For fuller list of conjectures, see Ltft. pp. 186 *ff.*, Stanley,
Com. on Cor., pp. 547 *ff.* Ramsay's view could be sustained only by
showing that fever was, in Galatia, regarded as an infliction of the
gods, showing the sufferers to be under their special disapprobation.
But that this was in any peculiar sense true of fevers is scarcely shown
by anything that Ramsay advances. *Cf. ut supra.* The reference to
a disease of the eyes, though favoured by v.¹⁵, is weakened by the lack
of any emphasis upon ὑμῶν indicated by position or otherwise. Epilepsy fulfils the conditions, but no better, perhaps, than many other
diseases. The precise nature of the apostle's suffering must be left
undecided. No decisive inference can be drawn from this illness concerning the location of the Galatian churches. εὐηγγελισάμην is used
here, as everywhere else in the epistle (1⁸, ⁹, ¹¹, ¹⁶, ²³) in the specific
sense, to preach the gospel, to bring the good news of salvation in
Christ.

Πρότερος is a comparative adjective in frequent use from Homer
down. πρότερον is employed as a temporal adverb from Pindar and,
with the article, from Herodotus down. In the latter use it is usually
the case that an event having happened twice (*e. g.*, a place visited or
a battle fought) or two periods of time being brought into comparison,
and the latter having been specifically mentioned, τὸ πρότερον designates the earlier one. The two occasions or periods may both be in
the past: Hdt. 2¹⁴⁴; Thuc. 1. 59², 3. 87², ¹¹⁶, 5. 65⁵; Xen. *Mem.* 3. 8¹;
Hell. 5. 3.¹⁵; Isoc. 59 c (4⁹¹), 151 d (7⁵⁸); Gen. 13² 28¹⁹ Deut. 9¹⁸ Josh. 10¹⁴
11¹⁰ 1 Kgs. 13⁶ Dan. 3²² 1 Mac. 3⁴⁶ 4⁶⁰ 5¹ 6⁷. Or one may be past
and the other present: Thuc. 6. 86¹; Plato, *Crat.* 436 E; *Rep.* 522 A; Dem.
43⁷, ³⁸, ⁴², ⁴⁷ 48²⁹; Deut. 2²⁰ Josh. 14¹⁵ 15¹⁵ Judg. 1¹⁰ 18²⁹. Or one may
be past and the other future: Isa. 1²⁶ Jer. 37 (30)²⁰ 40 (33)⁷, ¹¹ 1 Mac.
6⁵⁹. Occasionally the two events are not similar but contrasted. See
exx. of this usage in Xen. *An.* 4. 4¹⁴; Neh. 13⁵ Job 42⁵ 1 Tim. 1¹³.
πρότερον without the article signifies in enumerations "first," implying also a second in the series (Heb. 7²⁷); or "on a former occasion,"
without implying either repetition or contrast, though the context

sometimes suggests that what was πρότερον, "formerly," no longer existed at the time denoted by the principal verb. Isa. 41²² Jn. 7⁵⁰ 2 Cor. 1¹⁵ Heb. 4⁶. In a few cases τὸ πρότερον seems also to be employed in this way: Isoc. 70 (15¹¹³), 354 c (16³⁷); Isa. 52⁴; Sus. 52; Jn. 6⁶² 9⁸. It is important to notice that when τὸ πρότερον designates the former of two occasions or periods, the later one is always one which is distinctly referred to or implied in the context, never, so far at least as the above examples or any others that have been cited show, one which is itself implied only in that an earlier one is called τὸ πρότερον, the former. In other words, in observed instances it implies no duality except that of an occasion mentioned in the context (which may be past, present, or future), and of the event to which τὸ πρότερον itself applies. Yet it is obvious that the knowledge of the readers might supply what is lacking in the context. While, therefore, τὸ πρότερον in this passage does not imply two previous visits, it does not exclude the possibility of them, despite the fact that we have no extant example of πρότερον referring to the former of two occasions neither of which is otherwise referred to in the context. To this should be added the evidence of vv.¹⁶ and ²⁰ (q. v.), slightly confirmed by 1⁹, that between his first visit to Galatia and the writing of the present letter Paul had communicated with the Galatians, either in person or by letter. There are, accordingly, three possibilities: (a) τὸ πρότερον implies no comparison of occasions of preaching, but means simply "formerly." Against this is the apparent needlessness of the phrase, if this is all that it means. It is so self-evident that his preaching in Galatia was formerly, that the inclusion of the word in this sense is seemingly motiveless. (b) The apostle regarded the present letter as a reiteration of the gospel in its distinctive features, and referred to the one and only oral proclamation of the gospel as on the former occasion, as compared with the letter. Against this is the fact that on the hypothesis that this letter is considered a preaching of the gospel, and in view of the evidence of an intervening communication cited above, the present preaching was the third, which renders it improbable that the first would be said to be τὸ πρότερον. Against it is also the fact that Paul and N. T. writers generally use εὐαγγελίζομαι of oral preaching only. Yet there is nothing in the word itself to exclude a reference to publication in writing, and ἡ γραφὴ . . . προευηγγελίσατο of 3⁸ is perhaps some evidence that Paul might use the simple verb in the same way. (c) It being known to the Galatians that Paul had preached to them orally twice, τὸ πρότερον self-evidently meant for them on the former of these two occasions. This takes the verb and τὸ πρότερον in their usual sense, and though involving a use of τὸ πρότερον with reference to the former of two events, knowledge of the second of which is supplied by the readers, not by the context—

a usage which is without observed parallel—is, on the whole, the most probable. Parallels would in the nature of the case be difficult to discover, since they could be recognised only by evidence not furnished in the context. It remains, however, that the significance of τὸ πρότερον depends on the question of fact whether Paul had actually preached twice in Galatia before writing this letter; τὸ πρότερον itself does not prove him to have done so. See further in *Introd.* p. xlv.

That τὸ πρότερον implies two visits to Galatia is the view of Alf. Ltft. Sief. (Zahn, two or more) Bous., and many other modern interpreters from Luther down. Sief. quotes Grot. and Keil for the second of the views stated above. Vernon Bartlet, in *Expositor*, Series V, vol. 10 (1899), p. 275, explains τὸ πρότερον as meaning "at the beginning," in the earlier part of his evangelising visit, and as suggesting that it was only the initiation of his work that was occasioned by his illness, the continuance of it being for other reasons. He supports this view by the contention that εὐαγγελίζομαι refers to the presentation of the gospel to a people who have not received it, and, therefore, can not be used to cover two visits (a statement sufficiently refuted by Rom. 1¹⁵ 15²⁰). No instances of τὸ πρότερον in this sense are cited, nor does it seem to be justified by usage. The view of McGiffert, *Apostolic Age*, p. 228, that τὸ πρότερον refers to the eastward journey from Antioch to Derbe, the later, implied, journey being the return westward, does less violence to the usage of τὸ πρότερον and εὐαγγελίζομαι. But inasmuch as the letter is addressed to all the churches of the group, and the most eastern would on this theory have been visited but once, it is improbable that the apostle would have spoken of the journey up and back as involving two evangelisations of them.

14. καὶ τὸν πειρασμὸν ὑμῶν ἐν τῇ σαρκί μου οὐκ ἐξουθενήσατε, οὐδὲ ἐξεπτύσατε, "and that which was a temptation to you in my flesh, ye did not reject or despise." On ὑμῶν as objective genitive after πειρασμόν cf. Lk. 22²⁸. The whole phrase, τὸν πειρασμὸν ὑμῶν ἐν τῇ σαρκί μου, stands, as the following verbs show, by metonymy for some such expression as ἐμὲ πειράζοντα ὑμᾶς διὰ τὴν ἀσθένειαν τῆς σαρκός μου. For similar metonymy, see Ps. 22²⁴ (²⁵). πειρασμόν is probably temptation rather than simply trial; there was something in the apostle's physical condition which tempted them to reject him and his message. ἐξεπτύσατε, not found in the Lxx and here only in N. T., is found in Greek writers from Homer down.

Sief.'s attempt, following Lach. and Butt., to escape the difficulty
that πειρασμόν is not logically the object of ἐξουθενήσατε and ἐξεπτύσατε by placing a colon after σαρκί μου, thus making πειρασμόν the
object of οἴδατε, and ἐξουθενήσατε the beginning of a new sentence,
is extremely forced, and in view of Ps. 22²⁴ (²⁵) is quite unnecessary.

Though in all other extant instances ἐκπτύω is used of a physical act,
"to spit out," the impossibility of such a sense here and the fact that
the similar compounds of πτύειν (cf. ἀποπτ. Aesch. Eum. 303: ἀποπτύεις
λόγους. Aesch. Ag. 1192: ἀπέπτυσαν εὐνὰς ἀδελφοῦ) and other words
of similar meaning (cf. Rev. 3¹⁶: μέλλω σε ἐμέσαι ἐκ τοῦ στόματός μου)
are used in the tropical sense, make it unnecessary to question the
tropical meaning, "to reject," here.

ἀλλὰ ὡς ἄγγελον θεοῦ ἐδέξασθέ με, ὡς Χριστὸν Ἰησοῦν, "but
ye received me as an angel of God, as Christ Jesus." ἄγγελος is
commonly used by Paul not in its general sense of "messenger"
(Mt. 11¹⁰ Lk. 7²⁴,²⁷ 9⁵² Mk. 1² Jas. 2²⁵), for which he uses ἀπόστολος (2 Cor. 8²³ Phil. 2²⁵), but an "angel," a superhuman being.
Cf. 1⁸ 3¹⁹ 1 Cor. 4⁹ 13¹; M. and M. Voc. s. v. This is doubtless
its sense here. That Paul was God's "messenger" is implied
by the context, not the word. The use of θεοῦ without the
article emphasises the qualitative character of the phrase, and
brings out more strongly the dignity ascribed to Paul as God's
representative. Cf. on v.⁸. The sentence, however, means
not that they supposed him actually to be superhuman, but
that they accorded him such credence and honour as they would
have given to an angel of God. Note ὡς Χριστὸν Ἰησοῦν and
cf. Phm. ¹⁷. ἐδέξασθε suggests the idea of welcome more distinctly than would have been done by ἐλάβετε or παρελάβετε.
Cf. chap. 1⁹, ¹² 3²; yet see also 2 Cor. 11⁴, where both verbs occur.
ὡς Χριστὸν Ἰησοῦν is a climactic addition. Cf. Rom. 8³⁸ Col.
1¹⁵, ¹⁶. The force of ὡς is the same as with ἄγγελον. As to
the relation of the apostle to Christ Jesus which makes such
reception possible, see 2 Cor. 5²⁰.

The meaning of the sentence would not be materially different if
ἄγγελον were taken in the not impossible sense of "messenger." Cf.
2 Cor. 12⁷, where ἄγγελος Σατανᾶ is similarly ambiguous, the phrase
referring figuratively to a bodily affliction of some kind. Yet, that in

both cases the word itself denotes a superhuman being is rendered probable by Paul's evident belief in such beings and his usual use of the word. See Everling, *Die paulinische Angelologie und Dämonologie*, pp. 59 *ff.* Dib. *Gwt.* pp. 45 *ff.*

15. ποῦ οὖν ὁ μακαρισμὸς ὑμῶν· "Where, then, is that gratulation of yourselves?" The question is rhetorical, implying that the gratulation has ceased, but without good reason. *Cf.* Lk. 8²⁵: ποῦ ἡ πίστις ὑμῶν; and for instances with different implication, see Rom. 3²⁷ 1 Cor. 1²⁰ 12¹⁷, ¹⁹. οὖν has the force of *quae cum ita sint*, referring to the facts stated in vv.¹³, ¹⁴. ὑμῶν is probably objective genitive after μακαρισμός, "declaration of blessedness," as is τοῦ ἀνθρώπου in Rom. 4⁶. Even if ὑμῶν be taken as subjective genitive (Sief.), it would be necessary to understand it as referring to a gratulation of themselves, not of others, as is shown clearly by the following sentence introduced by γάρ and referring to the enthusiasm of the Galatians in receiving Paul. On the use of the simple pronoun for the reflexive, see Rob. p. 681, and the examples in the immediately preceding and following sentences, πειρασμὸν ὑμῶν and ὀφθαλμοὺς ὑμῶν.

Ποῦ is the reading of ℵABCFGP 33, 104, 424**, 442, 1912 f g Vg. Syr. (psh. harcl. mg.), Boh. Arm. Euthal. Dam. Hier. Pelag. Of these f Vg. Boh. (?) Arm. Hier. al. add ἐστίν after οὖν. DKL al. pler. d Goth. Syr. (harcl. txt.) Thdr. Mop. Sever. Chr. Thdrt. Thphyl. Oec. Victorin. Aug. Ambrst. al. read τίς instead of ποῦ. DFGK al. pler. d e Goth. Chr. Thdrt. Aug. Ambrst. add ἦν after οὖν. The choice is between ποῦ οὖν and τίς οὖν ἦν, the other readings being corruptions or conflations of these. Internal evidence is indecisive. Mey. and, following him, Zahn prefer τίς οὖν ἦν. But the strong preponderance of external evidence requires the adoption of ποῦ οὖν. The alternative reading is probably an unintentional clerical corruption, ΠΟ being converted into ΤΙΣ, and Υ omitted to make sense.

μαρτυρῶ γὰρ ὑμῖν ὅτι εἰ δυνατὸν τοὺς ὀφθαλμοὺς ὑμῶν ἐξορύξαντες ἐδώκατέ μοι. "For I bear you witness that ye would, if possible, have plucked out your eyes and given them to me." A confirmation immediately of the assertion implied in ὁ μακαρισμὸς ὑμῶν but indirectly of the affirmation of their former favourable attitude, which began with οὐδὲν ἠδικήσατέ με, v.[13]. That he dwells on this matter at such length and states it so strongly shows the apostle's strong desire to reinstate himself in the affections of the Galatians. The language escapes hyperbole only by the expression εἰ δυνατόν. The inference from the reference to the eyes that Paul's weakness of the flesh was a disease of the eyes, though slightly favoured by εἰ δυνατόν in preference, e. g., to εἰ ἀναγκαῖον is very precarious.

Ὑμῖν is not an indirect object denoting the person who receives the testimony (cf. Acts 15[8]), but dative of advantage, denoting the one to whose credit witness is borne (cf. Acts 22[5] Rom. 10[2] Col. 4[13]). εἰ δυνατὸν . . . ἐδώκατέ μοι is evidently a hypothesis contrary to fact, ἄν being omitted. Cf. BMT 249 and Mt. 26[24] Jn. 9[33] 15[22] 19[11]. On the mention of the eyes as the most precious members of the body, cf. Deut. 32[10] Ps. 17[8] Zach. 2[8], and on ἐξορύσσω of the plucking out of the eyes, see Hdt. 8[116]: ἐξώρυξε αὐτῶν ὁ πατὴρ τοὺς ὀφθαλμοὺς διὰ τὴν αἰτίην ταύτην (viz., for going to war against his command), and other exx. cited by Wetst., ad loc., also Lxx, Judg. 16[21] (A; B reads ἐκκόπτω); 1 Sam. 11[2]. Jos. Ant. 6. 69 (5[1]) uses ἐκκόπτω; Mt. 5[30] 18[9], ἐξαιρέω. Of mention of the plucking out of one's eyes as an act of self-sacrifice no example other than the present has been pointed out.

16. ὥστε ἐχθρὸς ὑμῶν γέγονα ἀληθεύων ὑμῖν. "So that I have become your enemy by telling you the truth!" ἐχθρός must doubtless be taken not in the passive sense, "hated by" (so from Homer down; and probably in Rom. 5[10] 11[28]), but in the active sense, "hostile to," "hater of," since in N. T. (Mt. 5[43] Rom. 12[20], et freq.) and (according to Sief. ad loc., citing Dem. 439[19] 1121[12]; Xen. An. 3. 2[5]; Soph. Aj. 554) in classical writers also, ἐχθρός with the genitive regularly has this active sense. The passive sense requires a dative expressed or understood. Xen. Cyr. 5. 4[50], etc. It follows that the phrase ἐχθρὸς ὑμῶν expresses not the fact as Paul looked at it, but the view which the Galatians were taking or disposed to take; and the sentence is either a question asking (indignantly) whether [they hold that] he has indeed become hostile to them by telling the truth, or an exclamation expressing in ἐχθρὸς ὑμῶν γέγονα the view which the apostle sadly recognises the Galatians are taking of him, and in ἀληθεύων ὑμῖν the cause to which he ascribes their hostility. The latter explanation is the more probable, for ὥστε does not elsewhere, in N. T. at least, introduce a question nor bear the weak sense (= οὖν) which the interrogative interpretation requires. ὥστε . . . ὑμῖν is, then, an inference from the facts stated in vv.[14, 15], and the further premise supplied by the apostle's conscience, that he has done nothing to produce this effect except to tell them the truth. "Since you, then, regarded me with such affection and now count me your enemy, this can only have come about through my telling you the truth." The appropriate punctuation is, therefore, an exclamation point.

The question when the truth-speaking referred to in ἀληθεύων took place is of considerable interest for the chronology of Paul's relations to the Galatians. That it can not have been on the occasion referred to in vv.[14, 15] is plain from the force of γέγονα, which, denoting a present state the result of a past act of becoming, describes a change from a former condition, as well as by the manifest contrariety between the enmity expressed in ἐχθρός and the friendly relations described in vv.[13-15]. Had it been alleged that Paul had really been on that first visit not their friend but their enemy in that he had taught them things which he affirms to be true, but which his opponents called false, which enmity they had only discovered through the subsequent teachings of the judaisers, that thought must have been expressed by some such phrase as ἐγενόμην ἐχθρὸς ὑμῶν τῷ ἀληθεύειν, or εὕρημαι (or εἰμί) ἐχθρὸς ὑμῶν διὰ τὸ ἀληθεύειν (or ἀληθεῦσαι). Nor can the truth-speaking be that of this letter, since γέγονα implies a result already existing, and the Galatians had not yet read the letter. Zahn, indeed, proposes to take it as an epistolary perfect, referring to what the Galatians will say when the letter is read. But aside from the improbability that Paul would intimate to the Galatians that the effect of his letter would be to make them call him their enemy, the very existence of the epistolary perfect is doubtful (the usage described in Kühner-Gerth, 384⁵, Gild. *Syntax*, 234 is not precisely this), and, if one may judge from the analogy of the epistolary aorist (*BMT* 44), would be confined to verbs of writing and sending. The natural inference, therefore, is that the reference is to things said at a second visit or in a letter previous to this one. That the utterances here referred to were those spoken of in 1⁹, or utterances made at the same time, is an obvious suggestion in view of the somewhat minatory tone of 1⁹.

This, however, if accepted, would not decide whether the utterance
was in person or letter (since προειρήκαμεν in 1⁹ can, just as well as
λέγω, refer to a written statement), and the present verse contributes
to the question whether Paul had made a second visit to Galatia only
the probability that there had been some communication from Paul
to the Galatians between the evangelising visit and this letter. *Cf.*
above on v.¹⁴ and below on v.²⁰.

17. ζηλοῦσιν ὑμᾶς οὐ καλῶς, ἀλλὰ ἐκκλεῖσαι ὑμᾶς θέλουσιν,
ἵνα αὐτοὺς ζηλοῦτε.   "They zealously seek you, not honestly,
but wish to shut you out that ye may seek them."   In contrast
with his own frank truthfulness by which he risked incurring
and actually incurred the suspicion of hostility to the Galatians,
the apostle declares that they—his opponents, unnamed by so
much as a pronoun but clearly enough referred to—are courting
the favour of the Galatians, not honourably (*cf.* Heb. 13¹⁸), *i. e.*,
not sincerely and unselfishly, but with selfish motive.   That
from which these opponents of Paul wish to exclude the Galatians is not stated; the context implies either (a) the privilege
of the gospel, *i. e.*, the sense of acceptance with God which
those have who believe themselves to have fulfilled the divine
requirements, or (b) the circle of those who hold the broader
view, Paul and his companions and converts, who maintain
that the Gentiles are accepted if they have faith and without
fulfilling the requirements of the law.   In either case, the effect
of such exclusion would be that the Galatians would turn
to the Jewish Christians for guidance and association, and
the latter would be in the position of being sought after
(ζηλοῦτε).   The verb ἐκκλεῖσαι rather favours the former
interpretation, since it is not natural to speak of one group of
persons as shutting others out from another group; a verb meaning to alienate, or to cause separation from, would be more
probable.   On ζηλοῦτε, see Bl.-D. 93; *BMT* 198.   Whether we
have here an irregularity of form (ζηλοῦτε being thought of as
subjunctive) or of syntax (ζηλοῦτε being an indicative after
ἵνα) is not possible to determine with certainty.

18. καλὸν δὲ ζηλοῦσθαι ἐν καλῷ πάντοτε, καὶ μὴ μόνον ἐν τῷ
παρεῖναί με πρὸς ὑμᾶς, "But it is good to be zealously sought

after in a good thing, always, and not only when I am present with you." Most probably a reference to his own persistent seeking after the Galatians, which he by implication characterises as ἐν καλῷ in contrast with that of the judaisers, which was οὐ καλῶς, and for the continuance of which, even while absent, he justifies himself by this statement, enforced by v.[19]. This interpretation retains as the implied subject of the passive ζηλοῦσθαι the object of the active ζηλοῦτε in v. [17b], and best comports with the tone of v.[19] into which he passes from this v. apparently without break in thought.

Ζηλοῦσθαι must be taken as a passive, no instance of the middle being found elsewhere, and there being no occasion for change from active to middle form. ἐν καλῷ defines the sphere in which alone καλὸν ζηλοῦσθαι is true. πάντοτε is in evident antithesis to the following phrase, καὶ μὴ . . . πρὸς ὑμᾶς. The addition of this phrase, with its definite personal pronoun shows that καλὸν . . . καλῷ, though in form simply a general maxim, had in the apostle's mind specific reference to the existing situation, the relations of the Galatians to Paul and his opponents. The words might therefore mean, "I do not object to others as well as myself seeking to gain your friendship, so only they do it in a good thing, in the realm of that which is for your good." It is an objection to this interpretation that μὴ μόνον . . . ὑμᾶς awkwardly expresses the idea "by others as well as myself," and that such a disclaimer of desire on the apostle's part to monopolise the interest and affection of the Galatians does not lead naturally to v.[19]. The words may also be explained by taking Paul as the implied subject of ζηλοῦσθαι. "It is a fine thing—I myself could desire—to be sought after, in a good thing—always, when I am away from you as well as when I am present." In this case the sentence is a thinly veiled reproach of the Galatians for their fickleness in changing their attitude towards him, now that he is no longer with them. The change in implied subject of ζηλοῦσθαι without indication that the reference is now to the apostle himself is an objection to this interpretation, though not a decisive one; the apostle may have preferred to leave the reference somewhat veiled. But it is difficult on this interpretation to account for ἐν καλῷ, no such qualification being called for if the apostle is thinking of the Galatians seeking after him. Probably, therefore, the interpretation first proposed is the true one. δέ is in that case adversative, marking an antithesis between the ζηλοῦν of the judaisers, which he disapproves, and his own, which he justifies.

19. τέκνα μου, οὓς πάλιν ὠδίνω μέχρις οὗ μορφωθῇ Χριστὸς ἐν ὑμῖν. "oh, my children with whom I travail again in birth pangs till Christ be formed in you." Language of deep affection and emotion, called forth by the previous words defending his right to continue his zealous efforts to hold the affection of his readers, and probably to be attached to the preceding v. The figure is after the fashion of the apostle, and extremely bold; τέκνα addresses them in affectionate tone as his children, *i. e.*, as those whom he has already begotten or borne; οὓς πάλιν ὠδίνω represents them as again in the womb, needing a second (spiritual) birth, and himself as a mother suffering again the birth pangs, which must continue till Christ be formed in them, *i. e.*, until it be true of them as of him that Christ lives in them (2²⁰).

Were it not for the δέ at the beginning of v.²⁰, v.¹⁹ would naturally be taken as the beginning of a sentence and v.²⁰ as its completion. The occurrence of δέ, however, necessitates either connecting v.¹⁹ with v.¹⁸, as in WH., or assuming an anacoluthon at the beginning of v.²⁰, as in RV. The recurrence in v.²⁰ of the expression παρεῖναι πρὸς ὑμᾶς, used also in v.¹⁸, implies a close connection between these vv. and makes it improbable that v.¹⁹ begins a new line of thought, which is broken off at v.²⁰. The punctuation of WH. is therefore more probably correct than that of RV.

The figure of speech involved in ὠδίνω, though startling to modern ears, is unambiguously clear. The precise form of the thought expressed in μορφωθῇ is less certain. There are three possibilities: (a) In themselves the words not unnaturally suggest a reversal of the preceding figure, those who were just spoken of as babes in the womb, now being pictured as pregnant mothers, awaiting the full development of the Christ begotten in them. Such abrupt change of figure is not uncharacteristic of the apostle. In Rom. 7⁴, illustrating the relation of the believer to the law and to Christ by remarriage, following death, he makes the deceased one remarry, sacrificing illustration to the thing illustrated. In 1 Thes. 2⁷, if, as is probable, the true text is νήπιοι, the apostle in the same sentence calls himself a child, and a mother, and a nurse, each term expressing a part of his thought, and in v.¹¹ compares himself to a father. Nor is it a serious objection to this view of the present passage that the apostle has not elsewhere employed the figure of Christ being begotten in the believers. It would be easy to give examples of figures of speech employed by him but once, as, *e. g.*, in this very verse the comparison of himself to a mother in birth pangs. Nor does he shrink from the employment of equally bold figures taken from the same general sphere. See Rom. 7⁴, where he speaks of the believer as married to Christ and as bringing forth fruit (children) to God, and 1 Cor. 4¹⁵ and Phm. ¹⁰, where he speaks of himself as the begetting father of his converts. The word μορφωθῆ (occurring nowhere else in Lxx or N. T.) is more consonant with this view than with any other. *Cf.* the use of the synonyms πλάσσω in Jer. 1⁵, πρὸ τοῦ με πλάσαι σε ἐν κοιλίᾳ, Rom. 9²⁰ 1 Tim. 2¹³. The only weighty objection to this understanding of the figure is that it is not in itself strikingly appropriate for the spiritual fact to which the apostle evidently refers, and that when elsewhere Paul speaks of Christ in the believer (chap. 2²⁰ Col. 1²⁷ *et freq.*) the language conveys no suggestion of pregnancy, but in less materialistic fashion denotes the indwelling presence of Christ. Yet over against this objection is to be set the fact that this passage contains, what all the others lack, the word μορφωθῆ, suggesting if not requiring the view that here the thought of the apostle takes on a different form from that which it has elsewhere. (b) It is perhaps not impossible that without reversal of figure the apostle thinks of his birth pangs as continuing till the child in the womb takes on the form of the begetting father, who is now thought of as being not Paul but Christ. The choice of μορφωθῆ Χριστὸς ἐν ὑμῖν rather than, *e. g.*, ὑμεῖς ἐν ὁμοιώματι Χριστοῦ μορφωθῆτε might in this case be due to the influence of the apostle's favourite form of thought expressed in the formula Χριστὸς ἐν ὑμῖν or the like. (c) The figure suggested by ὠδίνω may be dropped altogether, μέχρις οὗ μορφωθῆ referring figuratively, of course, but without specific thought of the birth process, to that spiritual process, the full achievement of which is elsewhere expressed by Χριστὸς ἐν ὑμῖν and like phrases. Of these three conceptions of the apostle's figure of speech the first seems somewhat the most probable; yet there is no perfectly decisive evidence for either as against the others. The spiritual fact for which the figure stands is substantially the same in any case. The reactionary step which the Galatians are in danger of taking, forces upon the apostle the painful repetition of that process by which he first brought them into the world of faith in Christ, and his pain, he declares, must continue till they have really entered into vital fellowship with Christ.

Against the strong external evidence for τέκνα, ℵ*BD*FG Eus., there is no clearly pre-Syrian witness for τεκνία except Clem. Alex.; For ℵᶜACDᵇ ᵉᵗ ᶜKLP al. pler. are predominantly Syrian. But combined with Clem. they probably mark the reading as of Alexandrian origin. The adoption of τεκνία by WH. txt. (mg. τέκνα) is a departure from their usual practice (*cf.* WH. II p. 342), for which there seems no sufficient warrant in the evidence.

20. ἤθελον δὲ παρεῖναι πρὸς ὑμᾶς ἄρτι, καὶ ἀλλάξαι τὴν φωνήν μου, ὅτι ἀποροῦμαι ἐν ὑμῖν. "But I could wish to be present with you now, and to change my tone; because I am in perplexity in reference to you." Moved by his deep sense of the unhappy situation in Galatia (v.¹¹), stirred by his strong affection for the Galatians (v.¹⁹) and in doubt as to what the outcome might be (ὅτι ἀποροῦμαι ἐν ὑμῖν), the apostle regrets for the moment the strong language which he had used when he told them the truth, and so gave occasion for its being subsequently said that he had become their enemy (v.¹⁶), and expresses the fervent wish, evidently regarded as impossible to be carried out, that he were even now (ἄρτι) with them and could speak in a different tone from that which he had used on that other occasion. For an entirely similar instance of strong language subsequently for a time regretted, see 2 Cor. 7⁸, and for the letter to which he there refers, 2 Cor., chaps. 11–13.

On ἤθελον, cf. BMT 33; Rob. 885 f. The wish is evidently regarded as impracticable, though not distinctly characterised as such by the language. ἄρτι with more sharply defined reference to the present moment than νῦν means "at this very moment." The clause ὅτι . . . ἐν ὑμῖν suggests for ἀλλάξαι τὴν φωνήν μου the meaning "to change my tone according to the situation." But the absence of a limiting phrase such as κατ' ἀναγκαῖον is against this and necessitates understanding it to mean, "to modify my tone," i. e., to adopt a different one; yet certainly not different from the immediately preceding language of strong affection: to express this wish would be unaccountably harsh. The reference can only be to a tone different from that, doubtless less considerate, manner of speech which he had used when he told them the truth (v.¹⁶; cf. note on that v. and reference to 1⁹). ὅτι ἀποροῦμαι, giving the reason for ἤθελον. etc., probably has chief reference to παρεῖναι πρὸς ὑμᾶς; because of his perplexity about them, he wishes he were even now present with them. δέ is slightly adversative. Though justifying his attitude towards the Galatians when he was present with them as having been ἐν καλῷ (v.¹⁸), he yet wishes that he could now speak in a different tone. ἀποροῦμαι is middle (the middle and passive forms are thus used with nearly the same meaning as the active in Dem. 830³, etc.; Sir. 18⁷ Lk. 24⁴ Jn. 13²² Acts 25²⁰ 2 Cor. 4⁸). ἐν ὑμῖν means "in respect to you," as in 2 Cor. 7¹⁶.

10. *A supplementary argument based on an allegorical use of the story of the two sons of Abraham, and intended to induce the Galatians to see that they are joining the wrong branch of the family* (4^{21-31}).

Before leaving the subject of the seed of Abraham it occurs to the apostle, apparently as an after-thought, that he might make his thought clearer and more persuasive by an allegorical interpretation of the story of Abraham and his two sons, Ishmael and Isaac, the one born in course of nature only, the other in fulfilment of divine promise. The two mothers he interprets as representing the two covenants, that of law and that of promise, and the two communities, that of the lineal descendants of Abraham, and that of those who walked in the footsteps of his faith. In the antagonism between the two sons, or their descendants, he finds a parallel to the persecution to which the Gentile Christians have been subjected at the hands of the Jewish Christians, and cites scripture to show that the former are rejected of God. The argument is in effect this: Would you be, as the judaisers have been exhorting you to be, sons of Abraham? Be so, but observe that of the Abrahamic family there are two branches, the slave and the free. We, brethren, whose relation to Abraham is spiritual, not physical, we are the sons not of the slave, but of the free.

^{21}*Tell me, ye that wish to be under law, do ye not hear the law?* ^{22}*For it is written that Abraham had two sons, one by the maid servant, and one by the freewoman.* ^{23}*But the son of the maid servant was born according to the flesh; the son of the freewoman through promise.* ^{24}*Which things are allegorical utterances. For these women are two covenants, one proceeding from Mount Sinai, bringing forth children unto bondage, which is Hagar* ^{25}(*now Hagar is Mount Sinai in Arabia) and corresponds to the Jerusalem that now is. For she is in bondage with her children.* ^{26}*But the Jerusalem above is free, which is our mother.* ^{27}*For it is written, Rejoice thou barren woman that bearest not, break forth and shout, thou that travailest not. For more are the children of the desolate than of her that hath the husband.* ^{28}*And ye, brethren, like Isaac, are children of promise.* ^{29}*But as then he that was born*

*according to the flesh persecuted him that was born according to
the Spirit, so also now.* ³⁰*But what saith the scripture? Cast out
the maid servant and her son. For the son of the maid servant
shall not inherit with the son of the freewoman.* ³¹*Therefore,
brethren, we are children, not of a maid servant, but of the freewoman.*

21. Λέγετέ μοι, οἱ ὑπὸ νόμον θέλοντες εἶναι, τὸν νόμον οὐκ
ἀκούετε; "Tell me, ye that wish to be under law, do ye not hear
the law?" The abrupt beginning reflects excited feeling, and is
calculated to arrest attention. *Cf.* chap. 3²: τοῦτο μόνον θέλω
μαθεῖν ἀφ' ὑμῶν. It had apparently only just occurred to the
apostle that he might reach his readers by such an argument as
that which follows. The address οἱ ὑπὸ νόμον θέλοντες εἶναι
implies, as is indicated throughout the letter, that the Galatians
have not adopted, but are on the point of adopting, the legalistic principle and practices. *Cf.* 1⁶ 3³ 4¹¹, ¹⁷. The Galatians are
not ὑπὸ νόμον but ὑπὸ νόμον θέλοντες εἶναι. ὑπὸ νόμον evidently has the same meaning as in 3²³, v.⁴, and in Rom. 6¹⁴, ¹⁵;
the word νόμος thus bearing the same sense which it has constantly in this and the preceding chapter, divine law viewed by
itself as a legalistic system. See note on 3¹³ and detached note
on Νόμος, V 2. c. On the other hand, τὸν νόμον in itself
probably refers, as is indicated by 4²², etc., to the O. T. scriptures (detached note, V 3), which, they had been taught, contained that legalistic system which they were urged to accept.

22. γέγραπται γὰρ ὅτι Ἀβραὰμ δύο υἱοὺς ἔσχεν, ἕνα ἐκ
τῆς παιδίσκης καὶ ἕνα ἐκ τῆς ἐλευθέρας· "For it is written that
Abraham had two sons, one by the maid servant, and one by
the freewoman." See Gen., chaps. 16, 17. παιδίσκη, properly
referring to a young woman, and denoting age, not status, became among the Greeks a term for a female slave (see L. & S.)
and is frequently so used in the Lxx.

23. ἀλλ' ὁ μὲν ἐκ τῆς παιδίσκης κατὰ σάρκα γεγέννηται, ὁ
δὲ ἐκ τῆς ἐλευθέρας δι' ἐπαγγελίας. "But the son of the
maid servant was born according to the flesh; the son of the
freewoman through promise." κατὰ σάρκα, "by natural generation," in the ordinary course of nature (*cf.* Rom. 1³ 9⁵ and

detached note on Πνεῦμα and Σάρξ, p. 492, 3 (a) under σάρξ), and δι' ἐπαγγελίας, "through promise," are antithetical, not by mutual exclusion, but in the fact that, though Isaac was begotten and born κατὰ σάρκα, his birth was also δι' ἐπαγγελίας, and was significant because of this, while the birth of Ishmael was simply κατὰ σάρκα. On the ἐπαγγελία here referred to, see Gen. 15⁴ 17¹⁹, and *cf.* chap. 3¹⁸. The perfect γεγέννηται is used in preference to the aorist ἐγεννήθη, because the writer is thinking not simply of the historical fact but of the existing result of that fact, in the race of Ishmael's descendants and especially (for γεγέννηται belongs in thought to both members of the sentence) in Isaac's descendants.

WH. bracket μέν, omitted by B f Vg. Tert. Hil. Hier. Yet the concurrent omission of such a word by one Grk. ms. and a small group of Latin authorities seems to raise no serious question of its belonging to the text. Between δι' ἐπαγγελίας (אAC 33, 442 al.) and διὰ τῆς ἐπαγγελίας (BDFGKLP al. pler. Or.) it is impossible to choose with confidence. Both readings are supported by good pre-Syrian groups. But the probability that Paul would have opposed to κατὰ σάρκα a qualitative δι' ἐπαγγελίας rather than used the article in referring to a promise not previously mentioned seems to turn the scale in favour of δι' ἐπ.

24. ἅτινά ἐστιν ἀλληγορούμενα· "Which things are allegorical utterances." The present tense of the participle, the meaning of the verb as established by usage, and the facts respecting current views, combine to make the above the only tenable translation, the participle being interpreted as an adjective participle used substantively in the predicate. BMT 432. The assertion pertains not to the original sense of the passage, what the writer meant when he wrote it, nor to the current or proper interpretation of the words, but to the character of the utterances as they stand in the scripture. Substantially the same thought might have been expressed by ἅτινα ἡ γραφὴ ἀλληγορεῖ in the sense, "which things the scripture says allegorically," the scripture being conceived of apart from the author of the scripture and as now speaking.

The verb ἀλληγορέω, a late Greek word not found in the Lxx, and here only in N. T., occurs first in Strabo 1. 2⁷, though ἀλληγορία occurs as early as Demosthenes. Classical writers used αἰνίττομαι, in the sense, "to speak in riddles" (cf. Jos. Ant. Proem. 24 (4), where αἰνίττομαι and ἀλληγορέω occur together), and ὑπόνοια of an underlying figurative or allegorical meaning: Xen. Symp. 3⁶; Plato. Rep. 378 D; cf. Philo, Vita contempl. 28 (3). The meanings of ἀλληγορέω are as follows:

1. To speak allegorically, to utter something which has another meaning than that of the words taken literally—the object of the verb or subject in the passive being the words uttered: Philo, Leg. alleg. II 5 (2): ἀλλὰ καὶ ταῦτα φυσικῶς ἀλληγορεῖ. Mut. nom. 67 (9); Jos. Ant. Proem. 24 (4); Clem. Alex. Paed. I 45 (chap. vi); Porphyr. Antr. Nymph. 4. In the passive, to be spoken allegorically: Porphyr. Vita Pythag. 12; Origen, Cels. 4³⁸: Ἡσιόδῳ εἰρημένα ἐν μύθου σχήματι περὶ τῆς γυναικὸς ἀλληγορεῖται. Philo, Vita contempl. 29 (3 b) πολλὰ μνημεῖα τῆς ἐν τοῖς ἀλληγορουμένοις ἰδέας ἀπέλιπον. Execrat. 159 (7)

2. To speak of allegorically, the object being not the words uttered or the thing actually mentioned, but that to which there is underlying reference. Philo, Leg. alleg. II 10 (4); Plut. Es. carn. Orat. 1. 7⁴. In the passive, Philo, Cherub. 25 (8): τὰ μὲν δὴ χερουβὶμ καθ' ἕνα τρόπον οὕτως ἀλληγορεῖται. Clem. Paed. I 47 (chap. vi): οὕτως πολλαχῶς ἀλληγορεῖται ὁ λόγος. Paed. I 46 (chap. vi). With a double object, to call (a thing something) allegorically: Clem. Paed. I 43 (chap. vi): σάρκα ἡμῖν τὸ πνεῦμα τὸ ἅγιον ἀλληγορεῖ. In the passive, Clem. Paed. II 62 (chap. viii): οἱ . . . ἀπόστολοι . . . πόδες ἀλληγοροῦνται κυρίου. Paed. I 47 (chap. vi) bis.

3. To interpret allegorically, i. e., to draw out the spiritual meaning supposed to underlie the words in their literal sense: Philo, Leg. alleg. III 238. (85): ἵνα . . . ἀλληγορῆς—"ποιεῖν τὰ ἔργα αὐτοῦ." Origen, Cels. 1¹⁷: αἰτιᾶται τοὺς τροπολογοῦντας καὶ ἀλληγοροῦντας αὐτήν. Philo, Vita contempl. 28 (3 a); Origen, Com. in Joan. 20¹⁰. Cels. 1¹⁸; 4⁴⁸; 4⁸⁷; 7³⁰; 8⁶⁸.

For ἀλληγορία in the sense "an allegory," "a thing to be understood allegorically," see Philo, Leg. alleg. III 236 (84).

The second of these meanings of the verb is excluded for the present passage by the fact that ἅτινα evidently refers either to the persons and events just named or to the statements concerning them, not to their spiritual significates, which have not yet been named; whereas this meaning occurs only in reference to the spiritual significates. If, then, we take into consideration the two remaining and for this passage only possible significations and the possible usages of the present participle in predicate, there result the following possible interpretations of ἐστιν ἀλλ., those that are too improbable to deserve consideration being ignored: (1) ἔστιν ἀλληγορούμενα may be, so far as usage is concerned, a periphrastic present of customary action, and mean (a) "are wont to be spoken allegorically"; but this is excluded by the fact that the subject refers to statements taken for substance from scripture, of which it might be said that they were spoken allegorically, but not that they are wont to be so spoken; or (b) "are wont to be interpreted allegorically"; but this is excluded by the context, for with this meaning the following clause introduced by γάρ must be understood as containing the interpretation thus referred to; but this interpretation was certainly not the current Jewish one, and it is very improbable that a current Christian interpretation had yet sprung up, or, even if it had, that it would be such as that which follows; this is adapted to express and sustain Paul's own conception of things, and must be ascribed to him rather than supposed to be borrowed by him from a current view. The tempting modification of this, "are to be interpreted allegorically," would give excellent sense, but is not sustained by Greek usage, which would have required ἀλληγορητέα; cf. Origen, Lam. Jer. 1¹⁰. Such cases as Acts 15²⁷ 21³ 2 Pet. 3¹¹ are only apparently vouchers for such a use of the participle, since, though they may be translated into English by "to be," etc., they really denote not propriety, but impending futurity. To the same effect is the interpretation of Mey. Sief., "which things have an allegorical sense"; which is sustained neither by any recognised force of the participle nor by specific instances of such a meaning of the passive of this verb. (2) ἔστιν ἀλληγορούμενα may be supposed to be a periphrastic present indicative, meaning "are spoken allegorically," equivalent to ἡ γραφὴ ἀλληγορεῖ, the utterance being thought of as present because made by the ever-present scripture. Cf. Rom. 4³: τί γὰρ ἡ γραφὴ λέγει; Rom. 10⁵; v.²⁸ below, et freq., and in the passive, Heb. 7¹³, ἐφ' ὃν γὰρ λέγεται ταῦτα. But for this idea a periphrastic present would scarcely be used, the expression being, indeed, approximately "aoristic," neither progression nor customariness being distinctly suggested. (3) The participle may be a present participle for the imperfect, referring to an action, strictly speaking, antecedent in time to that of the principal verb (BMT 127; Mt. 2²⁰, etc.). But the pres. part. is apparently never used in this way when the fact referred to belongs definitely to time distinctly past in reference to the principal verb, as must be the case here if the utterance is thought of as past at all. (4) It may be a general present participle equivalent to a noun, and meaning "allegorical utterances" (BMT 123. 432 (a); MGNTG. p. 127); cf. Jn. 12⁶, τὰ βαλλόμενα "the deposits"; Rom. 10²¹ 1 Cor. 15²⁹ 1 Thes. 2¹² 5²⁴ 2 Thes. 1⁶ Gal. 5³, περιτεμνόμενος, "one who receives circumcision"; 6ᵃ. ¹³ Eph. 4²⁸ Rom. 11²⁶ 1 Thes. 1¹⁰, ὁ ῥυόμενος, "the deliverer"; Philo, Leg. alleg. III 239 (85), ἵνα τὸ λεγόμενον . . . γένηται. It is true that N. T. furnishes no example of a present participle applied in just this way to utterances of scripture, such utterances, when designated by a participle used substantively, being always elsewhere expressed by a perfect participle (τὸ εἰρημένον: Lk. 2²⁴ Acts 2¹⁶ 13⁴⁰ Rom. 4¹⁸; τὸ γεγραμμένον: Acts 13²⁹ 24¹⁴ 2 Cor. 4¹³ Gal. 3¹⁰ Rev. 1³) or by an aorist participle (τὸ ῥηθέν: Mt. 1²² and ten other passages in Mt.). Yet in view of the frequent occurrence of the present participle of other verbs with substantive force (see exx. above) and of such expressions as ἡ γραφὴ λέγει (Rom. 4³, etc.), λέγεται ταῦτα (Heb. 7¹¹; sc. ἐν γραφῇ), and ἡ γραφὴ ἡ λέγουσα (Jas. 2²³), and the apparent use of ἀλληγορούμενα with substantive force, meaning "allegorical sayings," in Philo, Vita contempl. 29 (3 b) cited above, such a use here is not improbable, and, though grammatically more difficult than interpretation (1), must because of the contextual difficulties of the former be preferred to it. It is substantially identical with (2), but grammatically more defensible; and is in substance the interpretation of the ancient versions and of the Greek interpreters. See Zahn, ad loc. The apostle is then speaking not of what the passage meant as uttered by the original writer, but of the meaning conveyed by the passage as it stands. In common with Philo before him, and the author of the Epistle to the Hebrews and Origen after him, he conceived of the scriptures as speaking in his own day; and since Paul elsewhere in this epistle and in Romans speaks without qualification of Abraham as a historical character, it is apparent that in this passage at least he ascribes to the scripture as now speaking a meaning distinct from that which it bore as originally written, regarding the latter as representing historic truth,* the latter as conveying spiritual truth. The only question can be whether in this case he regarded the spiritual truth as really conveyed and vouched for by scripture, or only for the purposes of appeal to the Galatians adopted a current method of using scripture. The unusualness of this method of argument on his part perhaps favours the latter view; but the absence of anything in the language of this passage (e. g., κατ' ἄνθρωπον λέγω) to indicate that he is speaking otherwise than in accordance with his own convictions, together with such other instances as 1 Côr. 9⁸ ¹⁰ 10⁴, favours the former.

* Against the strong evidence that Paul ascribed historicity to the O. T. narratives, including those here referred to, the word ἀλληγορούμενα can not be cited as valid evidence to the contrary. For though the word may often be used when the statements literally understood are regarded as not historically true, yet this is not involved in the meaning of the word. Cf. e. g., Origen. Cels. 4⁴⁴, where Origen, going beyond Paul and saying that the statements as originally uttered were allegorically spoken (ἠλληγόρηται), yet implies also their historicity in their literal sense. Philo, also, though he often rejects the literal meaning as absurd and false (Somn. I 102 [17]), yet in other instances clearly accepts as historically true in their literal sense passages which he also interprets allegorically. (Mut. nom. 81 [12]). Cf. Bous. Rel. d. Judent.³, p. 185, "Er [der tiefere. allegorische Sinn] tritt neben den andern [den Sinn des Wortlauts], nur in den selteneren Fällen hebt er ihn auf."

It is doubtful whether any stress can be laid on the fact that Paul uses the compound relative ἅτινα rather than the simple ἅ. The generic force of ἅτινα, "which as other like things" (cf. Th. s. v. 2; MGNTG. p. 91 ff.; Ell. ad loc.) is appropriate enough in this place, conveying the thought that the predicate ἀλληγορούμενα applies not simply to the passage or events just mentioned, but to others of like character in O. T. But the use of the relatives in the Pauline letters seems to indicate both a preference for the longer form in the nom. plur. and an ignoring of the distinction between these and the shorter forms. Thus οἵτινες occurs in Rom. 1²⁵, ³² 2¹⁵ 6² 9⁴ 11⁴ 16⁴, ⁷ 1 Cor. 3¹⁷ 2 Cor. 8¹⁰ Gal. 2⁴ 5⁴ Eph. 4¹⁹ Col. 4¹¹ 2 Tim. 2², ¹⁸ Tit. 1¹¹, while οἵ occurs in Rom. 16⁷ only; αἵτινες occurs in Phil. 4³ 1 Tim. 1⁴ 6⁹, with no instance of αἵ; ἅτινα occurs, besides the present passage, in Gal. 5¹⁹ Phil. 3⁷ Col. 2²³; the only certain instance of ἅ in nom. is Col. 2²²; in 1 Cor. 4⁶ and Tit. 2¹ it was probably felt to be accus.; in Col. 2¹⁷ the reading is uncertain; in Eph. 5⁴ it is possibly an accus., but more probably a nom. If, then, the three cases of ἅ in the nom. (probably or certainly such), viz. Col. 2¹⁷, ²² Tit. 2¹, be compared with the instances of ἅτινα, it will be impossible to discover any difference in the relation of the relative clause to the antecedent that will account for the use of ἅτινα in one group and ἅ in the other. This is especially clear in Col. 2²², ²³, where of successive clauses in entirely similar relation to what precedes the former uses ἅ and the latter ἅτινα. There is even less reason for ascribing to ἥτις in vv.²⁵, ²⁶ any force different from that of the simple relative than in the case of ἅτινα here; for not only is it difficult to discover any of the logical relations sometimes intimated by the use of the compound relative, but Paul's uniform employment of ἥτις for the fem. sing. nom. forbids any argument based on his use of it here in preference to ἥ.

αὗται γάρ εἰσιν δύο διαθῆκαι, μία μὲν ἀπὸ ὄρους Σινά, "For these women are two covenants, one proceeding from Mount Sinai." With these words the apostle proceeds to give the allegorical interpretation of the persons and events referred to in vv.²², ²³, i. e., to point out what they mean when they are taken as allegorical utterances. From this point of view εἰσίν is to be interpreted as meaning in effect "represent," "stand for." Cf. Mt. 13³⁸ Mk. 14²⁴; Philo, Cherub. 23 (7): γίνεται οὖν τὸ μὲν ἕτερον τῶν χερουβὶμ ἡ ἐξωτάτω (σφαίρα). On διαθῆκαι, here meaning "covenants," not "testaments," see detached note on Διαθήκη, p. 496. Of the two covenants here referred to, the first only is named, the phrase μία . . . Σινά identifying it

as the covenant involved in the giving of the law, a familiar
idea, as is shown by Heb. 8⁹ (quoting Jer. 31³²) 9⁴ 2 Cor. 3⁶, ¹⁴
Sir. 24²³ Ps. Sol. 10⁵. The ἑτέρα διαθήκη implied in δύο διαθῆκαι and μία is left unnamed, but is evidently that of
which faith is the basal principle and which is referred to in
3¹⁵⁻¹⁷ as a covenant in contrast with the law, which is not there
designated as a covenant.

εἰς δουλείαν γεννῶσα, "bringing forth children unto bondage," i. e., bearing children destined to be slaves. The participle is adjective in force and timeless (BMT 123, 420). Applied to Hagar the phrase designates her as one who, being a
slave woman, bears children who share her status of slavery.
As applied to the Sinai covenant it refers to the fact that they
who came under this covenant were in the position of slaves as
being in bondage to the law. Cf. 4¹. The form of the expression, γεννῶσα, etc., is, of course, determined by the fact literally taken; there is nothing in the spiritual experience exactly
corresponding to the child-bearing.

> It is assumed in O. T. that in general the offspring of a man's slaves
> were also his slaves. See Gen. 14¹⁴ 17¹², ¹³. The status of the children
> which a slave concubine bore to her master is not definitely defined.
> The Genesis story of Hagar and Ishmael indicates that the slave mother
> remained a slave at least in cases in which she had been a slave before
> becoming her master's concubine, and that her son was not *ipso facto*
> the heir of his father (Gen. 21¹⁰), but suggests that the status of the
> son was at the option of the father.

ἥτις ἐστὶν Ἄγαρ, "which is Hagar." The clause is best
taken as identifying. On the force of ἥτις, see above on ἅτινα
and on that of ἐστίν, see εἰσίν, above. This clause simply
states that of the two women named above, Hagar represents
in the allegory the covenant that proceeded from Sinai.

25. τὸ δὲ Ἄγαρ Σινὰ ὄρος ἐστὶν ἐν τῇ Ἀραβίᾳ, "Now Hagar is
Mount Sinai in Arabia." It is not the woman Hagar (ἡ Ἄγαρ)
of whom the statement is made, either as a historical person or
as a character in the narrative to which he is giving an allegorical interpretation, but either the word, in which case ἐστίν
affirms the equivalence of the two expressions Ἄγαρ and Σινὰ

ὄρος (note the neuter article; *cf.* W. XVIII 3; Rob. 766), or, by association of ὄρος after Σινά with both Ἄγαρ and Σινά, the mountain (*cf.* WH. vol. II, *ad loc.*, citing as parallel cases Rom. 2²⁸ff. 3²⁹). The clause accordingly implies that Mount Sinai was sometimes, directly or by implication, called Hagar or something sufficiently similar in sound to be so represented in Greek. Whether the statement is from the apostle or, as is on the whole more probable, a gloss from the hand of a scribe (see below, in discussion of the text), its intent is to confirm the previously affirmed identification of Hagar with the covenant proceeding from Sinai. Such a double name of the mountain has from the historical point of view no real value, of course, as proving a relation between Hagar and the Mount Sinai covenant; still less as proving that the favour of God rests on the spiritual followers of Abraham's faith rather than on his physical descendants. But the statement is consonant with the allegorical method of interpretation which the whole paragraph illustrates. If it is a gloss, it is by that fact a parenthesis, and is probably so in any case. The use of δέ (rather than γάρ) is probably due to the fact that as a parenthesis it is felt to be additional and incidental rather than a part of the main argument. *Cf.* Th. *s. v.* 6, and, as illustrating the approximation of δέ and γάρ in meaning which led to their interchange, see 1¹¹.

The following are the readings of the first clause attested by ancient evidence:

(a) τὸ γὰρ Σινὰ ὄρος ἐστίν: ℵCFG 33 (but 33* app. τὸ δέ) f g Vg. Arm. Aeth. Orig. (both Lat. tr. and Gr. as testified by Athan.; see Zahn, p. 296, citing Goltz.). Sah. reads: quae vero mons Sina est. Goth. omits γάρ. It is important to note, however, that ℵ adds ὄν, reading: τὸ γὰρ Σινὰ ὄρος ἐστὶν ὄν ἐν τῇ Ἀραβίᾳ, "For Sinai is a mountain, being in Arabia." But since without Ἄγαρ there would be no occasion to insert ὄν, the probability is that Ἄγαρ has fallen out, and that the testimony of ℵ is really in favour of the presence of Ἄγαρ in the text. (b) τὸ γὰρ Ἄγαρ Σινὰ ὄρος ἐστίν: KLP 33** al. pler. Syr. (psh. et harcl. txt.) Arm. Chrys. Theod. Mops. Thdrt. Thphyl. (c) τὸ γὰρ Ἄγαρ ὄρος ἐστίν: d. (d) τὸ δὲ Ἄγαρ Σινὰ ὄρος ἐστίν: ABD 31, 442, 436, 40 lect. Syr. (harcl. mg.). Boh.: Ἄγαρ δὲ Σινά etc., some mss. omitting δέ.

Of these readings both the character of the witnesses to (b) and its apparently conflate character indicate that it is derivative; (c) is too slightly attested to be considered. Modern editors are divided between (a) and (d), Westcott, Ltft., Zahn adopting (a), Hort, Ws. Sief. (d). The latter seems, on the whole, best supported. If the presence of ὄν in ℵ in effect makes that ms. a witness not against but for a text containing Ἁγαρ (cf. Sief. ad loc.), the external evidence is distinctly more favourable to (d) than to (a); and transcriptional probability is likewise in favour of (d), since whether through the accidental omission of ΔΕΑ, or through a feeling of the difficulty of this reading, (d) is easily susceptible of modification into (a) while there is nothing in the form or meaning of (a) to make its conversion into (d) likely.

The difficulty of interpretation, especially the absence of definite evidence of any usage that would account for the identification of Hagar and Sinai, either as names or places suggests the possibility of an interpolation at this point. Bentley (Letter to Mill, p. 45; according to Ellis, Bentleii Crit. Sac., he afterwards changed his mind and adopted reading (a)) suggested that the words Σινὰ ὄρος ἐστὶν ἐν τῇ Ἀραβίᾳ were a marginal gloss afterwards introduced into the text; and Holsten, Das Evangelium des Paulus, I. 1, p. 171, et al., conjecture that the whole sentence τὸ δὲ . . . Ἀραβίᾳ is an interpolation. Cf. Clemen, Einheitlichkeit der Paulinischen Briefe, pp. 118 f.

Either of these conjectural emendations would remove the obscurity of the passage as representing the thought of Paul, and transfer the words to another writer who would perhaps feel no necessity for a better basis for this additional piece of allegorising than his own imagination, or who may have heard Mount Sinai called Ἁγαρ or the like. Of the two suggestions that of Holsten is the simpler and more probable, and, in view of the process bv which the Pauline epistles were collected and transmitted, not in itself improbable. See notes on 3[16b] and 3[20].

Precisely what the fact was of which the apostle thus avails himself (if he wrote the sentence) we do not with certainty know. It may have been that he was aware that the Arabians or certain tribes of them were called sons of Hagar (הַגְרִים, Ἀγγαρηνοί, Ps. 83[7]; הַגְרִיאִים, Ἀγαρηνοί, 1 Chron. 5[19], cf. Ltft. ad loc.). Or he may have had in mind that there is an Arabic word, ḥagar, which may be reproduced in Hebrew as חגר and signifies "cliff, rock"; it is possible that the word may have been applied by the Arabs to that particular mountain which in Paul's day was regarded as the scene of the giving of the law. To this it is no serious objection that the name of the mountain was on this theory חגר, while that of the woman was הגר, for scientific exactness in such a matter is not to be expected of an ancient writer. In the absence of definite evidence, however, that the word Ἁγαρ, or anything closely resembling it, was applied to a mountain also known as Σινά, all such suggestions must remain conjectures only. See Ltft., detached note, pp. 197 ff. This fact has influenced Ltft. Wies. Zahn, et al., to adopt the otherwise inferiorly attested reading τὸ γὰρ Σινὰ ὄρος ἐστὶν ἐν τῇ Ἀραβίᾳ, interpreting it, however, variously. Ltft. translates: "For Sinai is a mountain in Arabia," i. e., in the land of bondsmen themselves descended from Hagar, and finds in this statement a confirmation not of ἥτις ἐστὶν Ἄγαρ, but of εἰς δουλείαν γεννῶσα. Zahn interprets "For Mount Sinai is in Arabia," i. e., not in the promised land, the possession of which is the central element of the divine promise; from which it follows that the Sinai covenant does not involve the fulfilment of the promise, but, on the contrary, the enslavement of those to whom it is given. Both interpretations perhaps involve Paul's assuming a knowledge on the part of the Galatians hardly likely to be possessed by them; but the decisive reasons are against the text rather than against the interpretation. See textual note. Ell. and Sief. reading τὸ δὲ Ἄγαρ understand the words ἐν τῇ Ἀραβίᾳ as defining not the location of Mount Sinai, but the region in which the name Hagar is applied to Sinai. This would be entirely possible if, instead of ἐστίν, Paul had written καλεῖται (with the necessary change in the order of the words preceding ὄρος), but of such a geographical expression used in this sense in such a sentence as this no example is cited.

συνστοιχεῖ δὲ τῇ νῦν Ἰερουσαλήμ, "and corresponds to the Jerusalem that now is." Best understood as continuing ἥτις ἐστὶν Ἄγαρ after the parenthetical τὸ δὲ Ἄγαρ ... Ἀραβίᾳ. Yet the logical subject of συνστοιχεῖ is rather Ἄγαρ than ἥτις (= μία διαθήκη), as δουλεύει γάρ indicates. The words continue the allegorical explanation of the O. T. passage, point by point. "The Jerusalem that now is" is manifestly used by metonymy for that Judaism of which Jerusalem was the centre.

The military use of συνστοιχεῖν, "to stand in the same file" (Polyb. 10. 23 (21)⁷) suggests that the two terms referred to are in the same column, on the same side of the parallelism. Thus Ltft., who represents the thought thus:

Hagar, the bond woman.	Sarah, the freewoman.
Ishmael, the child after the flesh.	Isaac, the child of promise.
The old covenant.	The new covenant.
The earthly Jerusalem.	The heavenly Jerusalem.

But the language of the apostle (note the use of the singular number and the term-by-term parallelism) indicates that he is not simply putting things into two columns, one containing all that falls on the side of the bond and the other all that belongs to the free, but is pointing out the equivalents of the several elements of the narrative allegorically treated. If, then, it is necessary to take the word in the precise sense suggested by Polybius, the following would seem to be the diagram that would represent the thought, the items 1, 2, 3, 4, at the head of the several columns representing the four elements of the narrative on which the apostle puts an allegorical interpretation, and the items below each of these representing the things for which they stand.

(1)	(2)	(3)	(4)
Hagar, the bond woman, bearing children unto bondage.	Ishmael, born after the flesh, born unto bondage.	Sarah, the freewoman (bearing free children).	Isaac, born according to promise.
(a)		(a)	
The covenant from Sinai.		The new covenant.	
(b)		(b)	
The Jerusalem that now is.	The children of Jerusalem in bondage to legalism.	Jerusalem that is above.	The children of Jerusalem above, according to promise, free.

Yet it is doubtful whether our interpretation should be so strictly governed by the Polybius passage (which is itself not perfectly clear, and to which no parallel has been cited). The use of the verb in Musonius (*cf.* L. & S.) in a less technical sense, and the use of συστοιχία in Aristotle (*Metaph.* 1. 5, 6 (986a²²), *et al.*,) to denote the relation of the members of a correlative pair, such as "odd and even," "right and left," suggests that Paul here meant simply "is correlative to," "in the parallelism between narrative and its allegorical significance is the corresponding term." The statement of Sief. that this sense would require ἀντιστοιχεῖ is true only in the sense that if the apostle had had in mind two columns in one of which stood the terms of the narrative itself and in the other antithetically term for term their spiritual significates, he would probably have used ἀντιστοιχεῖ. But the idea of correspondence, equivalence, calls not for ἀντιστοιχεῖ but συνστοιχεῖ.

δουλεύει γὰρ μετὰ τῶν τέκνων αὐτῆς· "for she is in bondage with her children": justification of the parallelism just affirmed between Hagar and Jerusalem. As Hagar, a slave, bore children that by that birth passed into slavery, so the Jerusalem that now is and her children, viz., all the adherents of legalistic Judaism which has its centre in Jersualem, are in bondage to law.

26. ἡ δὲ ἄνω Ἰερουσαλὴμ ἐλευθέρα ἐστίν, "But the Jerusalem above is free." Instead of a formally perfect antithesis, either the Jerusalem that now is, and the Jerusalem that is to be, or the Jerusalem on earth and the Jerusalem above, the apostle mingles the two forms. The same point of view from which the seed of Abraham are, not the Jews, but believers in Christ, makes the new Jerusalem not the Jewish capital, but the community of believers in Jesus the Christ, and the conception of that community as destined soon to take up its abode in heaven (1 Thes. 4¹⁵ᶠ·) and as already living the heavenly life (*cf.* Phil. 3²⁰ᶠ· Col. 3¹⁻³) converts the Jerusalem that is to be, which would be the strict antithesis to the Jerusalem that now is, into the Jerusalem above (already existent). Heb. 12¹⁸ᶠᶠ· (see esp. v.²²) presents a similar contrast between Mount Sinai as the place and symbol of the giving of the law, and the heavenly Jerusalem as representing the community of believers (*cf.* v.²³), probably independently developed from the same root, not, of course, the source of Paul's expression here. The freedom referred to in ἐλευθέρα is manifestly the same that is spoken of in 2⁴ 5¹, and implied in antithesis to the δουλεία spoken of in 4¹⁻¹¹.

The conception of a restored and beautiful Jerusalem appears even in the O. T., Ezek., chaps. 40 *ff.* Zech., chap. 2 Hag. 2⁶⁻⁹, and in other pre-Christian Jewish writings: Sir. 36¹³ᶠ· Tob. 13⁹⁻¹⁸ 14⁵ Ps. Sol. 17³³. In I Enoch 90²⁸, ²⁹ the displacement of the old house by a new one is predicted (*cf.* Hag. 2⁹). See Bous., *Rel. d. Jud.*², p. 273; Charles, *The Book of Enoch*, note on 90²⁵. This conception of a new Jerusalem (though the precise phrase is apparently found first in Rev. 3¹² 21², *cf.* 4 Ezr. 7²⁶ 13³⁶; Apoc. Bar. 32², which, like the Apocalypse of John, were written after the destruction of Jerusalem in 70 A. D.) doubtless furnished the apostle with the basis of his conception here expressed.

ἥτις ἐστὶν μήτηρ ἡμῶν· "which is our mother." The form of expression is derived from the allegory of Hagar and Sarah; ἡμῶν refers to believers in Christ in general; the idea literally expressed would be, of which (community) we are members. The addition of πάντων by TR. may perhaps be traced to Polyc. Phil., chap. 3, or to the influence of Rom. 4¹⁶. On the force of ἥτις, see note on ἅτινα (v.²⁴).

27. γέγραπται γὰρ " Εὐφράνθητι, στεῖρα ἡ οὐ τίκτουσα· ῥῆξον καὶ βόησον, ἡ οὐκ ὠδίνουσα· ὅτι πολλὰ τὰ τέκνα τῆς ἐρήμου μᾶλλον ἢ τῆς ἐχούσης τὸν ἄνδρα." "For it is written, Rejoice thou barren woman that bearest not, break forth and shout, thou that travailest not. For more are the children of the desolate than of her that hath the husband." The quotation is from Isa. 54¹, and follows exactly the text of the Lxx (BℵAQ), which neglects to translate the רָנִּי, "rejoicing," "singing," of the Hebrew. In the prophet the words are probably to be joined with 52¹²; they are conceived of as addressed to the ideal Zion, bidding her rejoice in the return of the exiles, Yahweh leading (cf. 52⁷⁻¹²). The barren woman is Jerusalem in the absence of the exiles, the woman that hath a husband is Jerusalem before the exile; and the comparison signifies that her prosperity after the return from exile was to exceed that which she had enjoyed before the captivity. There may possibly underlie the words of the prophet a reference to Sarah and Hagar as suggesting the symbolism of the passage (cf. 51²), but there is no clear indication of this. The apostle, also, in quoting them may have thought of the barren woman as corresponding to Sarah, who till late in life had no child, and the woman that hath a husband to Hagar. But his chief thought is of the O. T. passage as justifying or illustrating his conception of a new redeemed Jerusalem whose glory is to surpass that of the old, the language being all the more appropriate for his purpose because it involved the same figure of Jerusalem as a mother, which he had himself just employed, unless, indeed, v.²⁶ is itself suggested by the passage which was about to be quoted. There is a possible further basis for the apostle's use of the passage in the fact that its context expresses the thought that God is the redeemer not of Israel after the flesh, but of those in whose heart is his law (cf. 51¹⁻⁸, esp. v.⁷). But whether the apostle had this context in mind is not indicated. The γάρ is doubtless confirmatory, and connects the whole statement with ἥτις ἐστὶν μήτηρ ἡμῶν.

28. ὑμεῖς δέ, ἀδελφοί, κατὰ Ἰσαὰκ ἐπαγγελίας τέκνα ἐστέ· "And ye, brethren, like Isaac, are children of promise." With

this sentence the apostle takes up his allegorical development
of the O. T. narrative at a new point. Having in vv.²², ²³
developed it with reference to the two women, which he has
made to represent the two communities, and incidentally enforced his thought by a quotation from the prophets, he now
makes use of the sons, Isaac and Ishmael, and more pointedly
applies his allegory to his readers. Note the address ὑμεῖς δέ,
ἀδελφοί. As Isaac was born in fulfilment of a promise, not in
the usual course of nature, so Paul assures the Galatians, they
also are children of promise, whose standing with God rests
not on physical descent, but on the promise made to Abraham,
which has already been interpreted as applying to all who have
faith (3⁷, ⁸, ¹⁰). δέ is continuative, introducing this element of
the allegorical interpretation of the O. T. passage as an addition to that of vv.²⁴⁻²⁷.

As in 4²³, evidence is very evenly divided between ὑμεῖς . . . ἐστέ
and ἡμεῖς . . . ἐσμέν. The former is attested by the group BDG,
supported by 33, 424** Sah., the latter by אAC with the concurrence
of LP f Boh. and Cyr. and the great body of the Syrian authorities.
Transcriptional probability favours ὑμεῖς . . . ἐστέ, the change of
this form to the first person being more easily explicable as due to
assimilation to vv. ²⁷, ³¹ than the reverse. ὑμεῖς is unobjectionable on
grounds of intrinsic probability, such changes of person being characteristic of Paul; cf. 4²³⁻²⁹.

Κατά in the sense "like," "after the manner of," occurs not infrequently in classic writers (L. & S. s. v. B. III 3) and in N. T. Cf.
Eph. 4²⁴ 1 Pet. 1¹⁵ 4⁶ Heb. 8⁹. The position of ἐπαγγελίας (gen. of
characteristic) is emphatic. The term is qualitative, but the reference
is undoubtedly to the promise already repeatedly referred to in the
epistle (3¹⁶, ¹⁸, ²¹, ²²). Whose children they are, whether sons of God
or sons of Abraham is not emphasised; but the context as a whole
implies the latter. To take τέκνα as meaning children of the Jerusalem
above (Sief.) is to insist upon a closeness of connection with v.²⁷ which
is not only not justified by anything in this v. but is practically excluded
by the phrase κατὰ Ἰσαάκ and vv.²⁹ff.

29. ἀλλ' ὥσπερ τότε ὁ κατὰ σάρκα γεννηθεὶς ἐδίωκε τὸν
κατὰ πνεῦμα, οὕτως καὶ νῦν. "But as then he that was born
according to the flesh persecuted him that was born according
to the Spirit, so also now." The persecution which the Gentile

Christians had suffered at the hands of the descendants of Abraham according to the flesh, the apostle adroitly converts to the purposes of his allegorical argument by pointing out that this fact had its analogue in the relations of Ishmael and Isaac. In speaking of the persecution of those who are according to the Spirit the apostle probably has in mind chiefly the persistent efforts of the judaisers to induce the Galatians to take on the burden of the law. Cf. v.[17] 1[7] 5[10]. Cf. also 3[4], though as shown there that passage does not necessarily refer to persecutions. That persecutions of a more violent nature and at the hands of Jews (cf. 1 Thes. 2[15, 16]) are also in mind is possible but not probable. The persecution of Isaac probably refers to Gen. 21[9], and the traditions that had gathered about it, but the apostle may also have had in mind the mutual hostility of the nations supposed to have descended from the two brothers.

The adversative ἀλλά introduces a fact which is on the face of it in contrast with the preceding statement. ὁ κατὰ σάρκα is, of course, in the literal sense Ishmael. Cf. on v.[23] In the allegorical interpretation it stands for those who are descendants of Abraham, but do not walk in the footsteps of his faith. The Lxx of Gen. 21[9] reads παίζοντα μετὰ Ἰσαὰκ τοῦ υἱοῦ ἑαυτῆς. On the possibility that this represents an original Hebrew different from our present Hebrew, and on the rabbinic expansion of the incident, see Ltft. ad loc. The Talmud (Beresch. Rabb. 53[15]) says: "Dixit Ismael Isaaco: Eamus et videamus portionem nostram in agro; et tulit Ismael arcum et sagittas, et jaculatus est Isaacum et prae se tulit, ac si luderet." (Quoted by Wies. ad loc.) For κατὰ πνεῦμα we should naturally expect κατ' ἐπαγγελίαν (3[29]) or δι' ἐπαγγελίας (v.[23]). The introduction of πνεῦμα might naturally be explained as a substitution of the giver of the promise for the promise. But while Paul speaks of the Spirit as the content of the promise (3[14]), he is not wont to speak of the promises or prophecies as given by the Spirit (cf. Mk. 12[36]), and in the absence of such usage it seems necessary to suppose that the phrase stands in the clause by a species of trajection from the clause which expresses the second element of the comparison, οὕτως καὶ νῦν. The full sentence would have read ὥσπερ γὰρ . . . ἐδίωκε τὸν κατὰ ἐπαγγελίαν, οὕτως καὶ νῦν ὁ κατὰ σάρκα τὸν κατὰ πνεῦμα. Cf. Rom. 8[5]. That πνεῦμα is in the apostle's vocabulary the usual antithesis to σάρξ (cf. 3[3] 5[16, 17] 6[8] Rom. 8[4ff.]) may also have had some influence. If the phrase be thought of strictly with reference to Isaac it must be explained by the fact that the promise pertaining to Isaac involved also the ultimate bestowal of the Spirit. *Cf.* 3¹⁴. But see also Philo, *Leg. alleg.* III 219 (77): 'Ισαὰκ ἐγέννησεν ὁ κύριος.

30. ἀλλὰ τί λέγει ἡ γραφή; "῎Εκβαλε τὴν παιδίσκην καὶ τὸν υἱὸν αὐτῆς, οὐ γὰρ μὴ κληρονομήσει ὁ υἱὸς τῆς παιδίσκης μετὰ τοῦ υἱοῦ τῆς ἐλευθέρας." "But what saith the scripture? Cast out the maid servant and her son: for the son of the maid servant shall not inherit with the son of the freewoman." As over against the fact that the Gentile Christians are children of promise he set in contrast the fact of their persecution, so over against this last he introduces with ἀλλά the language of scripture concerning the persecutor. The quotation is from Gen. 21¹⁰, and follows the Lxx except that it omits ταύτην after παιδίσκην and substitutes τῆς ἐλευθέρας for μου Ἰσαάκ at the end. The language is that of Sarah to Abraham, but probably neither this fact nor the statement of v.¹² that God said to Abraham, "In all that Sarah saith unto thee, hearken unto her voice," has anything to do with Paul's use of this passage here. From the point of view of the allegorical interpretation every scripture is significant; *cf.* under v.²⁴. Allegorically interpreted the expulsion of Ishmael points to a rejection of the children of Abraham according to the flesh in favour of the sons of Abraham by faith.

31. διό, ἀδελφοί, οὐκ ἐσμὲν παιδίσκης τέκνα ἀλλὰ τῆς ἐλευθέρας. "Therefore, brethren, we are children not of a maid servant, but of the freewoman." The omission of the article before παιδίσκης gives to the term a qualitative emphasis: "not of a slave woman"; while the article inserted before ἐλευθέρας makes this expression refer specifically to the free mother Sarah, and to that which in the allegorical interpretation corresponds to Sarah, the Christian community or church. Translated into terms more directly expressing the spiritual fact the sentence means that we who have faith belong not to a community or nation that is in bondage to the legal statutes (*cf.* vv.¹⁻¹⁰), but to that community of believers whose relation to God is that of sons, having the spirit of sonship, not of bond-

age (vv.[6, 7]). Taken in its connection it constitutes a brief
statement of the doctrine of the rejection of Israel according to
the flesh which is expounded at length in Rom., chaps. 9–11.
That the conclusion is derived from an allegorical argument in
no way diminishes its value as a disclosure of Paul's thought,
the allegory being itself resorted to for the very purpose of presenting his thought more convincingly to his readers. *Cf.* on
v.[21]. The validity of the argument itself as a piece of exegesis
depends, of course, upon the validity of the allegorical method
in general and its applicability to this passage in particular.
Its postulates are that the O. T. story of Isaac and Ishmael
bears a meaning which is to be derived from it by reading it as
an allegory, and that Isaac represents the spiritual seed of
Abraham, viz., those who, by faith like Abraham's, come into
filial relation to God like that of free sons to a father, Ishmael
standing for those whose relation to Abraham is simply that of
natural descent. Whether Paul himself accepted these premises and ascribed a corresponding validity to his argument, or
only meant by such an argument to bring his thought before
his readers in a form which would appeal to them, is, as said
above, not wholly clear. Presumably he did conceive that the
argument had some real value; though in view of his use of
scripture in general it can scarcely be doubted that it was for
him not determinative of his view, but only confirmatory of an
opinion reached in some other way. On παιδίσκη, *cf.* v.[22].

This verse is so evidently by its very terms—note παιδίσκης,
ἐλευθέρας, etc., occurring in the preceding verses but not after
this point—the conclusion of the allegorical argument introduced in v.[21], that it is surprising that it should ever have been
thought of otherwise. So, *e. g.*, Meyer. It is a matter of less
consequence whether v.[31] is an inference from v.[30] or the summary of [21-30]. But since from v.[30], even if the premise, "we
as Christians correspond to Isaac" (*cf.* Sief.), be supplied, the
natural conclusion is not "we are children of the free," but, "we
as children of the freewoman are heirs of the promise"; it is
more probable that we should take this sentence as the summa-
tion of the whole allegorical argument (*cf.* the use of διό in

2 Cor. 12^{10} 1 Thes. 5^{11}) and as expressing the thought which the apostle wished by this whole paragraph to impress upon the minds of the Galatians.

IV. HORTATORY PORTION OF THE LETTER (5^1-6^{10})

1. *Exhortations directly connected with the doctrine of the letter* (5^1-6^5).

(*a*) Appeal to the Galatians to stand fast in their freedom in Christ (5$^{1-12}$).

Having in 1^{11}-2^{21} defended his own independent right to preach the gospel to the Gentiles uncontrolled by any others, even those who were apostles before him, and in chaps. 3, 4 having answered the arguments of his opponents in favour of the imposition of legalism upon Gentile Christians, the apostle now passes to fervent exhortation of his readers not to surrender the freedom which they have in Christ Jesus.

¹With this freedom Christ set us free: stand, therefore, and be not entangled again in a yoke of bondage. ²Behold, I, Paul, say to you that if ye shall be circumcised, Christ will be of no advantage to you. ³And I protest again to every man that receiveth circumcision that he is bound to do the whole law. ⁴Ye have severed your relation to Christ, ye who are seeking to be justified in law. Ye have fallen away from grace. ⁵For we, by the Spirit, by faith, wait for a hoped-for righteousness. ⁶For in Christ Jesus neither circumcision availeth anything nor uncircumcision, but faith working through love. ⁷Ye were running well; who hindered you from obeying truth ? ⁸This persuasion is not from him that calleth you. ⁹A little leaven is leavening the whole lump. ¹⁰I have confidence, in the Lord, respecting you that ye will take no other view than this; but he that troubleth you shall bear his judgment, whoever he may be. ¹¹And I, brethren, if I am still preaching circumcision, why am I still being persecuted ? Then is the stumbling-block of the cross done away with. ¹²I would that they who are disturbing you would even have themselves mutilated.

1. τῇ ἐλευθερίᾳ ἡμᾶς Χριστὸς ἠλευθέρωσεν· στήκετε οὖν καὶ μὴ πάλιν ζυγῷ δουλείας ἐνέχεσθε. "With this freedom Christ set us free: stand, therefore, and be not entangled again in a yoke of bondage." With this reading of the text (see textual note below) these words are not to be attached to 4³¹ (so Zahn, e. g., reading ᾗ ἐλευθερίᾳ), but constitute an independent sentence in which, the allegory of 4²¹⁻³¹ being left behind, the apostle expresses himself in language akin to that of 4⁴⁻¹¹. The sentence, without connective particle οὖν or γάρ to mark its relation to what precedes, constitutes a transition paragraph of itself, on the one side a summary of 4²¹⁻³¹ (but without its allegorical terminology) if not also of chaps. 3, 4 as a whole, and on the other an introduction to the exhortations of chap. 5. The article before ἐλευθερίᾳ is restrictive, referring to that freedom from the law with which the whole epistle from 2¹ on has dealt; see esp. 3²³⁻²⁵ 4⁹, ³¹. On Χριστὸς ἠλευθέρωσεν cf. for substance of thought 3¹³ 4⁴. The sentence is, in fact, an epitome of the contention of the whole letter.

The variations of the textual evidence are so complex as to make clear exposition of them difficult. The chief variations may be set forth as follows:

I. Respecting the words immediately accompanying ἐλευθερίᾳ:
   1. τῇ ἐλευθερίᾳ (without ᾗ following): אABCD*HP 31, 33, 442, al. Sah. Arm. Syr. (harcl.) Euthal. Thrdt. Dam.; τῇ γὰρ ἐλ.: Boh.; ἐν τῇ: Chr.
   2. τῇ ἐλευθερίᾳ ᾗ: Dᵇ ᵉᵗ ᶜKL, the great body of cursives, Syr. (psh. et harcl.) Marc. Chr. Cyr. Thdrt. Thphyl. Oec. al.
   3. ᾗ ἐλευθερίᾳ: FG d f g Vg. Goth. Tert. Or. Victorin. Hier. Ambrst. Aug.

II. Respecting the position of ἡμᾶς:
   1. ἐλευθερ. ἡμᾶς Χρ.: א*ABDFGP 31, 33, 327, 2125, some mss. of the Vulg. Goth. Cyr. Dam.
   2. ἐλευθερ. Χρ. ἡμᾶς: אᶜCKL, most of the cursives, Chr. Thrdt. Tert. Victorin. Hier.
   3. Χρ. ἠλευθέρωσεν ἡμᾶς: Thphyl. (so Ltft.).

III. Respecting οὖν :
   1. After ἐλευθερίᾳ: CᶜKL and many cursives, Marc. Dam. Thphyl. Oec.
   2. After στήχετε: אABCFGP 33, 104, 336, 424**, 442, 1912, f g Goth. Boh. Sah. Eth. Arm. Bas. Cyr. Or ⁱⁿᵗ·Victorin. Aug.

3. Omit in both places: D d 263, 1908, Vg. Syr. (harcl.) Thdrt. Chr. Dam.

The weight of external evidence thus strongly favours τῇ ἐλευθερίᾳ ἡμᾶς Χριστὸς ἠλευθέρωσεν· στήκετε οὖν, and the originality of this reading is confirmed by the fact that it accounts for all the rest. It is adopted by Ln. Tdf. Alf. WH. Sief. Those who have preferred another reading (Ell. Ltft.: τῇ ἐλευθερίᾳ ᾗ; Zahn: ᾗ ἐλευθερίᾳ) have done so on the ground of the syntactical difficulty of τῇ ἐλευθερίᾳ as a limitation of ἠλευθέρωσεν. But this construction, though unusual, does not seem to be impossible (see exegetical notes). On the other hand, Hort's suggestion that τῇ is a primitive error for ἐπ' (cf. v. ¹³, ἐπ' ἐλευθερίᾳ ἐκλήθητε) has much to commend it. The only choice is between τῇ ἐλ. ἡμ., etc., which is undoubtedly the parent of all the other existing readings, and ἐπ' ἐλ. ἡμ. as the unattested original of the former.

The dative τῇ ἐλευθερίᾳ is to be explained as a dative of instrument (not intensive as in Lk. 22¹⁵, ἐπιθυμίᾳ ἐπεθύμησα, and Jas. 5¹⁷, προσευχῇ προσεύξατο, in which case the noun, being qualitative, would be without the article), but descriptive, "by (bestowing) the freedom (spoken of above) Christ made us free"; cf. Jn. 12³³, ποίῳ θανάτῳ ἤμελλεν ἀποθνήσκειν. To this view the article is no objection: cf. 1 Thes. 3⁹, πάσῃ τῇ χαρᾷ ᾗ χαίρομεν, where the relative ᾗ limiting χαίρομεν has all the definiteness of τῇ χαρᾷ. Or it may be a dative of destination (cf. Acts 22²⁵: προέτειναν αὐτὸν τοῖς ἱμᾶσιν: "They stretched him out for the thongs" with which he was to be scourged). The meaning would then be: "For the freedom (above spoken of) Christ set us free." The latter interpretation is favoured somewhat by v.¹³, and perhaps by the absence of any exact parallel to such a use of verb and cognate noun with the article as the former view supposes; while against it is the unusualness of such a dative as it supposes (even Acts 22²⁵ is not quite certain) and the probability that Paul would have expressed this idea by εἰς ἐλευθερίαν (cf. Rom. 5²). On the whole the former construction is the more probable, if τῇ be the correct reading. It is, perhaps, still more likely that Paul wrote ἐπ' (see textual note above), in which case the meaning would be substantially that of the dative denoting destination.

Στήκω, a post-classical word, derived from ἕστηκα, has with Paul the meaning not simply "to stand" (as in the gospels), but with intensive force, "to stand firm." Cf. 1 Cor. 16¹³ Phil. 1²⁷ 4¹, etc. πάλιν recalls the fact that as Gentiles they had been in slavery, and classes the burden of Jewish legalism with that of heathenism. Cf. 4⁹ and notes there. The omission of the article with ζυγῷ δουλείας gives to the phrase a qualitative force, and though the reference is clearly to the yoke of legalism, is appropriate after πάλιν because the new yoke which he would have them avoid is not identical with that previously borne.

'Ενέχεσθε—a frequent classical word, "to be held in," "to be ensnared," is in the present tense, denoting action in progress, not probably because Paul thinks of them as already entangled (so that the expression would mean "cease to be entangled"), but because he is thinking about and warning them against not only the putting of their necks into the yoke, but the continuous state of subjection which would result therefrom.

2. Ἴδε ἐγὼ Παῦλος λέγω ὑμῖν ὅτι ἐὰν περιτέμνησθε Χριστὸς ὑμᾶς οὐδὲν ὠφελήσει. "Behold, I, Paul, say to you that if ye shall be circumcised, Christ will be of no advantage to you." The acceptance of circumcision is, under the circumstances then existing in the Galatian churches, the acceptance of the principle of legalism, the committal of the Galatians to a relation to God wholly determined by conformity to statutes and leaving no place for Christ or the development of spiritual life through faith in him and spiritual fellowship with him. This is the position which the apostle has taken throughout the letter (cf. $2^{18ff.}$ 3^{12}). The possibility of any compromise between the two conceptions of religion he does not consider, but points out the logical outcome of the adoption of the principle of legalism, which he conceives to be involved in the acceptance of circumcision. Though circumcision is mentioned here for the first time in direct relation to the Galatians, the manner in which it is spoken of in this paragraph and in 6^{11-13} (confirmed by the implications of chap. 3) makes it certain that it was this rite especially that the opponents of Paul were urging the Galatians to adopt, or at least that on this the contest was at this moment concentrated. Though the sentence is introduced without γάρ, the purpose of it is evidently to enforce the exhortation of v.¹. Its separation from that v. in a distinct paragraph is justified only by the double relation which it sustains on the one hand to $4^{21, 31}$, and on the other to this and the following sentences.

The first three words of this sentence, none of them strictly necessary to the thought, serve to give emphasis to the whole statement that follows. As an exclamation Paul elsewhere employs not ἴδε, but ἰδού; see 1 Cor. 15⁵¹ Gal. 1²⁰, *et al.*; ἴδε in Rom. 11²² and ἴδετε in Gal. 6¹¹ are proper imperatives with limiting object. For other instances of ἐγώ, emphatic, see 1¹² 2¹⁹⋅ ²⁰ 4¹² 5¹⁰⋅ ¹¹ 6¹⁷ *et freq.* For ἐγὼ Παῦλος, see 1 Thes. 2¹⁸ 2 Cor. 10¹ Eph. 3¹ Col. 1²³; see also Col. 4¹⁸ 2 Thes. 3¹⁷. The intent of the words here is doubtless, as in most of the above instances, to give to what he is about to say all the weight of his personal influence.

The form of the conditional clause ἐὰν περιτέμνησθε, referring to a future possibility, reflects the fact that the question whether they will be circumcised is still pending. *Cf.* 1⁶. The use of the present tense, at first thought surprising, indicates that the apostle is not thinking of circumcision as a simple (possible future) fact, or result accomplished, but of the attempt or decision to be circumcised, the verb being substantially conative in force; see note on ἤρεσκον in 1¹⁰. What the apostle says is not that to be or to have been, as a matter of fact, circumcised would render Christ of no avail to them (see the contrary stated in v.⁶), but that their seeking or receiving circumcision under the circumstances under which it is being urged upon them would do so. Observe the use of the present tense, also, in v.³ 6¹²⋅ ¹³ 1 Cor. 7¹⁸. The aorist in 2³, on the other hand, was necessary because of the resultative force of the whole phrase. The view of Alford, that the present tense "implies the continuance of a habit, 'if you will go on being circumcised,'" though grammatically unobjectionable, is excluded by the fact that circumcision could be thought of as a habit, not in respect to individuals, but only as concerns the community; in which case it would follow that Paul's thought was that if the community continued the already existing practice of circumcision, the community would have no benefit from Christ; whereas, on the contrary, v ³³, confirmed by the apostle's constant teaching concerning justification, shows that relation to Christ pertains to the individual, not to the community. Alford's explanation, moreover, fails to account for the present tense in περιτεμνομένῳ, and is, therefore, probably not applicable to περιτέμνησθε. The language, therefore, furnishes no basis for the conclusion that the Galatians had already begun the practice of circumcision.

On οὐδὲν ὠφελήσει, *cf.* Jn. 6⁶³ Rom. 2²⁵ 1 Cor. 13³. There is no ground for assuming an exclusive reference to any specific point of future time, as to the parousia or the judgment. The absence of any specific reference to these events, such as is expressed in Rom. 2¹³⋅ ¹⁶, or implied in Rom. 14¹⁰⁻¹², makes it natural to assume that the future dates from the time indicated in the subordinate clause; and this is confirmed by the use of the aorists κατηργήθητε and ἐξεπέσατε in v.⁴, which see.

3. μαρτύρομαι δὲ πάλιν παντὶ ἀνθρώπῳ περιτεμνομένῳ ὅτι
ὀφειλέτης ἐστὶν ὅλον τὸν νόμον ποιῆσαι. "And I protest
again to every man that receiveth circumcision that he is bound
to do the whole law." Joined to v.² by δέ, this sentence sup-
plements that one by a further reason why the Galatians should
not receive circumcision. Not only do they thereby lose any
advantage which the relation to Christ would confer, but they
assume a heavy burden. The acceptance of circumcision is in
principle the acceptance of the whole legalistic scheme. The reasons that can be urged in favour of circumcision apply equally
to every statute of the law. That Paul points out this logical
consequence of circumcision implies that the judaisers had not
done so. They were now urging the Galatians to accept circumcision as the rite by which they could become sons of Abraham and participators in the blessings of the Abrahamic covenant (cf. chap. 3 passim); they had already persuaded them to
adopt the cycle of Jewish festivals (4¹⁰), perhaps as serving to
mark them off from their heathen compatriots, perhaps because
of the appeal which these observances would make to the Galatians. On the question whether the judaisers had imposed or
endeavoured to impose upon their consciences any other requirements of the law, see on 4¹⁰. It is certain only that the Galatians had adopted the festival cycle, that they were undecided
concerning circumcision, and that the judaisers had not proposed to them to undertake to keep the whole law.

Μαρτύρομαι without obj. acc. signifies, not "to call to witness" (so
with obj. acc. in Soph. Eur. et al.), but "to affirm," "to protest"
(Plato, *Phil*. 47C.; Jos. *Bell*. 3. 354 (8³); Acts 20²⁶ 26²² Eph. 4¹⁷),
differing from μαρτυρέω in that it denotes a strong asseveration, not
simple testimony.

Πάλιν, "again," can not be understood as referring either to the
content of v.², of which this is regarded as a repetition (Ltft.), for the
two verses, though related, are not identical in thought; or to any
previous passage in this epistle, since there is none in which this statement is made; nor can it be taken as marking this verse as a second
μαρτυρία, of different content from the former one, for in that case it
would have preceded the verb, as in Mt. 4⁷ 5³³ Rom. 15¹⁰, ¹². It must,
therefore, refer to a statement previously made to the Galatians, and
in that case probably to a statement made on the occasion referred to

in 4¹⁶ (ἀληθεύων) and 1⁹. *Cf.* notes on these passages and 5²¹. The present passage thus furnishes some confirmatory evidence that Paul had either visited the Galatian⁀ or written to them since the visit spoken of in 4¹³; since definitely anti-legalistic instruction at that time before the legalistic influence had been exerted among them is improbable, though not, indeed, impossible.

The words παντὶ ἀνθρώπῳ περιτεμνομένῳ mean not, "to every one who has been circumcised" (which would call for the perfect περιτετμημένῳ or aorist περιτμηθέντι), but "to every man that receives circumcision." *Cf.* BMT 124. The warning is addressed not to the man who has already been circumcised but (like ἐὰν περιτέμνησθε, v.²) to the one who is contemplating circumcision.

'Οφειλέτης is one who is under obligation, one who is bound, ὀφείλει, to do a certain thing; here in effect one who binds himself; for the obligation is, as the context shows, one which he ought not to assume. *Cf. contra* Rom. 1¹⁴.

Ὅλον τὸν νόμον refers to the whole body of O. T. statutes, legalistically interpreted. See detached note on Νόμος, V 2. (c), p. 457. For a Gentile to receive circumcision is to commit himself logically to the whole legalistic system. The clear implication of the sentence is that the believer in Christ is under no such obligation. The freedom of the believer in Christ is not simply from the law's condemnation of him who does not obey its statutes, or from the law as a means of justification, but from the obligation to render obedience to these statutes. The Galatians are not simply not to seek justification by circumcision; they are not to be circumcised; they are not to do the whole law.

4. κατηργήθητε ἀπὸ Χριστοῦ οἵτινες ἐν νόμῳ δικαιοῦσθε, "Ye have severed your relation to Christ, ye who are seeking to be justified in law." κατηργήθητε ἀπὸ Χριστοῦ repeats in effect the Χριστὸς ὑμᾶς οὐδὲν ὠφελήσει of v.², and like that verse expresses forcibly the apostle's thought that the adoption of legalism is the repudiation of Christ. The two methods of obtaining righteousness are incompatible. He who turns to one foregoes the other. Notice the direct address to the Galatians, much more impressive than a statement of a general principle.

Some Syrian authorities and Boh. read τοῦ Χριστοῦ, but Χριστοῦ is sustained by practically all pre-Syrian evidence, ℵBCD al. On Paul's usage of Χριστός and ὁ Χριστός, *cf.* detached note on *The Titles and Predicates of Jesus*, p. 395.

'Εν νόμῳ evidently has the same meaning as in 3¹¹ (q. v.), "in the sphere of" (more specifically, "on the basis of") "legal obedience to statutes," thus equivalent to ἐξ ἔργων νόμου in 2¹⁶, etc. δικαιοῦσθε is conative. The present can not mean "are (i. e., have been) justified"; and a progressive present proper, "are in the process of being justified" is excluded by the fact that Paul thinks of justification not as a process but an act, and more decisively by his repeated assertion that no man is actually justified in law (chap. 3¹¹ Rom. 3²⁰).

There is no reason to regard the assertion of this sentence as hypothetical; it must rather be understood as referring to persons among the Galatians who, having accepted the legalistic principle, were seeking justification in law (cf. 4¹⁰). Only, in view of 1⁶ 5¹, ¹⁰, etc., it can not be supposed to designate the Galatians as a whole, or in view of v.², be understood as necessarily implying that they have carried their legalism to the extent of being circumcised. Wherever in the epistle the apostle speaks of circumcision, it is as of a future possibility to be prevented. This excludes not the possibility of some having already been circumcised, but the general adoption of circumcision; but there is no positive indication that any have accepted it.

Καταργέω, properly meaning "to make ineffective," is used in Rom. 7², ⁶, and here in the passive with ἀπό, meaning "to be without effect from," "to be unaffected by," "to be without effective relation to." The explanation of the idiom as a brachylogical expression for κατηργήθητε καὶ ἐχωρίσθητε (Ltft., Sief., et al.), and the comparison of Rom. 9³ and 2 Cor. 11³ as analogous examples, are scarcely defensible; for while in these latter instances the expressed predicate applies to the subject independently of the phrase introduced by ἀπό, and the verb denoting separation is simply left to be supplied in thought, this is not the case with καταργεῖσθαι ἀπό. The idiom is rather to be explained as a case of rhetorical inversion, such as occurs in Rom. 7⁴, ἐθανατώθητε τῷ νόμῳ, where consistency with both preceding and following context would require ὁ νόμος ἐθανατώθη ὑμῖν. Cf. the English expression, "He was presented with a gift," for "A gift was presented to him." The use of the aorist tense, denoting a past event viewed as a simple fact, has, in contrast with the present δικαιοῦσθε a certain rhetorical force; as if the apostle would say: "Your justification in law, which is but an attempt, has already resulted in separation from Christ as a fact." The English perfect best expresses the force of an aorist in such cases as this, when the event belongs to the immediate past (cf. BMT 46, 52).

τῆς χάριτος ἐξεπέσατε. "Ye have fallen away from grace." The article with χάριτος marks the word as referring specifically to that grace of God or of Christ which was the distinctive element of the gospel which Paul had preached to the Gala-tians. *Cf.* 1⁶, and special note on Χάρις. Grace, by virtue of which God accepts as righteous those who have faith, itself ex-cludes, and is excluded by, the principle of legalism, according to which the deeds of righteousness which one has performed are accredited to him as something which he has earned. *Cf.* 3¹² Rom. 4⁵ 11⁶. They, therefore, who are seeking justification by the way of legalism have fallen away from, abandoned, the divine grace. Logically viewed, the one conception excludes the other; experientially the one experience destroys the other. One can not with intellectual consistency conceive of God as the bookkeeping God of legalism and at the same time the gracious God of the Pauline gospel, who accepts men because of their faith. One can not live the life of devotion to the keep-ing of statutes, which legalism calls for, and at the same time a life of faith in Jesus Christ and filial trust in the God of grace. This strong conviction of the incompatibility of the two con-ceptions, experientially as well as logically, is doubtless grounded in the apostle's own experience. *Cf.* 2¹⁹.

The verb ἐκπίπτω in classical writers from Homer down, signifying "to fall out of," with various derived significations, is probably used here, as usually when limited by a genitive without a preposition, with the meaning, "to fail of," "to lose one's hold upon" (τῆς χάριτος being a genitive of separation), not, however, here in the sense that the divine grace has been taken from them (as in Jos. *Antiq.* 7. 203 (9²), ὡς ἂν βασιλείας ἐκπεσών), but that they have abandoned it. *Cf.* 2 Pet. 3¹⁷: φυλάσσεσθε ἵνα μὴ . . . ἐκπέσητε τοῦ ἰδίου στηριγμοῦ. For to affirm that their seeking justification in law involved as an immediate consequence the penal withdrawal of the divine grace (note the force of the aorist in relation to the present δικαιοῦσθε; *cf.* above on κατηργήθητε) involves a wholly improbable harshness of concep-tion. On the form ἐξεπέσατε *cf.* Win.-Schm. XIII 12.

5. ἡμεῖς γὰρ πνεύματι ἐκ πίστεως ἐλπίδα δικαιοσύνης ἀπεκ-δεχόμεθα. "For we by the Spirit, by faith, wait for a hoped-for righteousness." ἡμεῖς is emphatic, we in contrast with all who hold to legalism. πνεύματι is used without the article, hence qualitatively, but undoubtedly with reference to the Spirit of God. *Cf.* the similar usage in 3³ 5¹⁶, ¹⁸, ²⁵, and see

special note on Πνεῦμα and Σάρξ, p. 491. The contrast with
the flesh which in 5¹⁶, ¹⁸, ²⁵ is expressed is probably here latent.
He who seeks divine acceptance by law is in reality relying
upon the flesh. See Rom. 7¹⁸–8⁹. *We*, on the other hand,
depend not on flesh but on the Spirit. The word δικαιοσύνη
is best understood in its inclusive sense, having reference both
to ethical character and to forensic standing. It is this which
is the object of the Christian's hope and expectation (Phil. 3⁹, ¹⁰).
Cf. detached note on Δίκαιος, etc., VI B. 2, p. 471, and the
discussion there of this passage. Observe also the expression
δι' ἀγάπης ἐνεργουμένη in v.⁶ as indicating that the apostle is
here including the ethical aspect of righteousness. The whole
sentence introduced by γάρ is an argument *e contrario*, confirming the assertion of v.⁴ by pointing out that we, *i. e.*, we who
hold the gospel of grace, look for the realisation of our hope of
righteousness, not in law, ἐν νόμῳ, but on the one side by the
Spirit of God and on the other through faith.

Πνεύματι is probably a dative of means, limiting ἀπεκδεχόμεθα, or,
to speak more exactly, the verb of attaining implied in ἀπεκδεχόμεθα,
the thought being, "By the Spirit we expect to attain," etc. ἐκ
πίστεως also denotes means, the phrase being complementary to
πνεύματι, and expressing the subjective condition of attaining ἐλπ.
δικ., as πνεύματι denotes the objective power by which it is achieved.

Ἀπεκδέχομαι, used only in N. T. (Paul, Heb. and 1 Pet.) and in
considerably later writers (*cf.* Nägeli, *Wortschatz*, p. 43; M. and M.
Voc., s. v.) signifies "to await with eagerness," ἀπό apparently inten-
sifying the force given to the simple verb by ἐκ, "to be receiving from
a distance," hence "to be intently awaiting."

The interpretation, "by a Spirit which is received by faith," the
phrase πνεύματι ἐκ πίστεως thus qualitatively designating the Spirit
of God, is neither grammatically impossible (*cf.* Rom. 8¹⁵, πνεῦμα
υἱοθεσίας. Eph. 1¹⁷, πνεῦμα σοφίας καὶ ἀποκαλύψεως. Rom. 3²⁵,
ἱλαστήριον διὰ πίστεως, none of which are, however, quite parallel
cases), nor un-Pauline in thought (*cf.* 3¹⁴: ἵνα τὴν ἐπαγγελίαν τοῦ
πνεύματος λάβωμεν διὰ τῆς πίστεως). Yet the nature of the relation
which this interpretation assumes between πνεύματι and ἐκ πίστεως
is such as would probably call for πνεύματι τῷ ἐκ πίστεως (*cf.* 2²⁰,
πίστει . . . τῇ τοῦ υἱοῦ τοῦ θεοῦ), while, on the other hand, the succession of co-ordinate limitations is not uncharacteristic of the apostle;
cf. Rom. 3²⁵.

Ἐλπίδα, as is required by ἀπεκδεχόμεθα, is used by metonymy for that which is hoped for. *Cf.* Col. 1⁵ Tit. 2¹³ Heb. 6¹⁸. The genitive δικαιοσύνης may be considered as an objective genitive, if the whole phrase be supposed to be taken by metonymy—"a hope of righteousness," standing for "a hoped-for righteousness," or a genitive of description (appositional genitive) if the metonymy be thought of as affecting the word ἐλπίδα alone. In either case it is the righteousness which is the object both of hope and expectation. On the combination ἐλπ. ἀπεκδεχ. *cf.* Tit. 2¹³, προσδεχόμενοι τὴν μακαρίαν ἐλπίδα. Eur. *Alcest.* 130: νῦν δὲ βίου τίν' ἔτ' ἐλπίδα προσδέχωμαι. Polyb. 8. 21⁷, ταῖς προσδεχωμέναις ἐλπίσιν (cited by Alf. *ad loc.*).

6. ἐν γὰρ Χριστῷ Ἰησοῦ οὔτε περιτομή τι ἰσχύει οὔτε ἀκροβυστία, ἀλλὰ πίστις δι᾽ ἀγάπης ἐνεργουμένη. "For in Christ Jesus, neither circumcision availeth anything, nor uncircumcision, but faith working through love." For the disclosure of the apostle's fundamental idea of the nature of religion, there is no more important sentence in the whole epistle, if, indeed, in any of Paul's epistles. Each term and construction of the sentence is significant. ἐν Χριστῷ Ἰησοῦ (the bracketing of Ἰησοῦ by WH., because of its omission by B. Clem., seems scarcely justified) limits ἰσχύει. It is not precisely equivalent to τοῖς ἐν Χριστῷ Ἰησοῦ, but means, rather, "on that basis which is created by Christ Jesus"; nearly equal, therefore, in modern phrase, to "in Christianity," "on the Christian basis." With ἰσχύει (from Æschylus down, "to have strength," "to be able," "to avail") is to be supplied, not δικαιοῦν ("is able to justify"; *cf.* Acts 6¹⁰), which would be to limit the thought more narrowly than the context would warrant, but εἰς δικαιοσύνην, as suggested by the preceding sentence, and in the inclusive sense of the term as there used. By the omission of the article with περιτομή and all the following nominatives, these nouns are given a qualitative force, with emphasis upon the quality and character of the acts. This might be expressed, though also exaggerated, by some such expression as, "by their very nature circumcision," etc. The phrase δι᾽ ἀγάπης ἐνεργουμένη furnishes a most significant addition to the word πίστις, which has filled so large a place in the epistle thus far. For not only has he not previously in this epistle used the word ἀγάπη, but, though often using each alone in other epistles (for πίστις, see Rom. 1¹⁷ 3²², etc.; and for ἀγάπη, see esp. 1 Cor., chap. 13) he has nowhere else in any of his letters brought the two words into immediate connection. The relation between the two terms, which is here expressed but not perfectly defined by ἐνεργουμένη διά, "operative, effective through," "coming to effective expression in," is made clearer by a consideration of the nature of the two respectively, as Paul has indicated that nature elsewhere. Faith is for Paul, in its distinctively Christian expression, a committal of one's self to Christ, issuing in a vital fellowship with him, by which Christ becomes the controlling force in the moral life of the believer. See esp. 2²⁰ and *cf.* detached note on Πίστις and Πιστεύω, V B. 2. (e), p. 482. But the principle of Christ's life is love (see 2²⁰, τοῦ ἀγαπήσαντος, etc.; Rom. 5⁵⁻⁸ 8³⁵⁻³⁹). Faith in Christ, therefore, generates love, and through it becomes effective in conduct. See also v.²², where first among the elements which life by the Spirit (which, as v.⁵ indicates, is the life of faith) produces is love; and on the moral effect and expression of love, see especially 1 Cor., chap. 13. On the meaning of ἀγάπη, see on v.¹⁴. That the apostle added the words δι' ἀγάπης ἐνεργουμένη instead of writing πίστις or ἡ πίστις alone is probably due to his having in mind, even here, that phase of the matter which he discusses more fully in vv.¹³ ff.; *cf.* Rom. 3¹⁻⁴, and 3³⁰ for similar brief anticipations of matters to be more fully discussed later. Anticipating the objection that freedom from law leaves the life without moral dynamic, he answers in a brief phrase that faith begets love and through it becomes operative in conduct.

The whole sentence affirming the valuelessness alike of circumcision and of uncircumcision for the Christian life, and ascribing value to faith and love, shows how fully Paul had ethicised and spiritualised his conception of religion. That he says not simply περιτομὴ οὐδὲν ἰσχύει, but οὔτε περιτομὴ . . . οὔτε ἀκροβυστία naturally implies not only that he is opposed to the imposition of circumcision upon the Gentiles, but that he repudiates every conception of religion which makes physical conditions of any kind essential to it. The sentence, therefore, in no way contradicts vv.² ³, since the latter declare to the Galatians that if they accept a physical rite as religiously essential, they thereby repudiate the principle of the religion of Christ. He could have said the same thing about uncircumcision had he been addressing men who were in danger of adopting this as essential to religion. Indeed, this he does say in 1 Cor. 7¹⁸ ¹⁹: περιτετμημένος τις ἐκλήθη; μὴ ἐπισπάσθω. The doctrine of that passage as a whole is identical with the teaching in this letter. For though in v.¹⁹ τήρησις ἐντολῶν θεοῦ, "a keeping of divine commandments," fills the place occupied here by πίστις δι᾿ ἀγάπης ἐνεργουμένη, v.¹⁴ here shows that these two expressions are at bottom not antithetical but in effect equivalent.

Ἰσχύω, from Æschylus down, in the sense "to have strength," "to be able," "to avail" is rare in Paul, but not infrequent in other N. T. writers. It is used as here in the third of the above-named senses in Heb. 9¹⁷, and with similar meaning in Mt. 5¹³. Note the construction there.

Ἐνεργουμένη is to be taken, in accordance with the regular usage of ἐνεργεῖσθαι in Paul, as middle, not passive, and as meaning "operative," "effective": Rom. 7⁵ 2 Cor. 1⁶ 4¹² Eph. 3²⁰ Col. 1²⁹ 1 Thes. 2¹³ 2 Thes. 2⁷ Jas. 5¹⁶; see also Polyb. 1. 13⁵; Jos. Ant. 15. 145 (5²). The active, on the other hand, is used of persons: 1 Cor. 12⁶ ¹¹ Gal. 2⁸ 3⁵ Eph. 1¹¹ ²⁰ 2². That the preposition διά denotes not antecedent cause but mediate agency, the object of the preposition being that through which the πίστις becomes effective, is made practically certain not on grammatical grounds, but because of the nature of the two attitudes expressed by πίστις and ἀγάπη as conceived of by the apostle. See above in the larger print. See note on διά under 1¹ and cf. 2 Cor. 1⁶, where a similar relation is expressed by ἐν. Since πίστις is without the article, the participle, though anarthrous, may be attributive, "which works"; but 2²⁰ suggests that to express this thought Paul would have written πίστις ἡ ἐνεργουμένη, and makes it likely that ἐνεργουμένη is adverbial, expressing means or cause.

7. Ἐτρέχετε καλῶς· τίς ὑμᾶς ἐνέκοψεν ἀληθείᾳ μὴ πείθεσθαι; "Ye were running well; who hindered you from obeying truth?" As in 4¹², the apostle breaks off argument to make an appeal to the feelings of his readers by reminiscence of the former conduct

of the Galatians before they fell under the influence of the judaisers. It is to this time obviously that the imperfect ἐτρέχετε refers. τίς ὑμᾶς, etc., is not a question for information but of appeal.

On the use of running as a figure for effort looking to the achievement of a result, see 2² Rom. 9¹⁶ 1 Cor. 9²⁴⁻²⁶ Phil. 2¹⁶ 3¹⁴ 2 Thes. 3¹. It is probable that in all cases the apostle has in mind the figure of running a race, as expressly in 1 Cor. 9²⁴⁻²⁶. ἐνκόπτω is used by Hippocrates in the sense "to make an incision," but with the meaning "to hinder" first in Polybius. Here, if the figure is that of a race, the word suggests a breaking into the course, getting in the way, or possibly a breaking up of the road. That Paul uses the aorist (resultative) rather than the present (conative) indicates that he is thinking of what his opponents have already accomplished in their obstructive work. The present infinitive, πείθεσθαι, on the other hand, is progressive, so that the meaning of the whole expression is, "who has succeeded in preventing you from continuing to obey truth?" and the implication is that, though they have not fully adopted the views of Paul's opponents, they have ceased to hold firmly to that which Paul taught them. πείθεσθαι is difficult to render exactly into English. "Believe" expresses rather less, "obey" rather more, than its meaning. It denotes not merely intellectual assent, but acceptance which carries with it control of action; cf. Acts 5³⁶· ³⁷· ⁴⁰; Rom. 2⁸. On the construction of πείθεσθαι (inf. with μή after verbs of hindering), see BMT 402, 483; Bl.-D. 429. The omission of the article with ἀληθείᾳ gives to it a qualitative force, and shows that, though what the apostle has in mind is doubtless the same that in 2⁵ and 2¹⁴ he calls ἡ ἀλήθεια τοῦ εὐαγγελίου, he desires to emphasise the quality of his message as truth, thus conveying the implication that they are turning from something that is *true* to something that is false. Cf. for similar anarthrous use of ἀλήθεια Rom. 9¹ 2 Cor. 6⁷ Eph. 4²¹. Some authorities insert the article here (omitted by ℵ*AB). Evidently some scribe, recognising that the reference was to the truth of the gospel, stumbled at the qualitativeness of the expression.

8. ἡ πεισμονὴ οὐκ ἐκ τοῦ καλοῦντος ὑμᾶς. "This persuasion is not from him that calleth you." The restrictive article with πεισμονή makes it refer definitely to that persuasion just spoken of, viz., the persuasion no longer to hold (his message which is) truth. By τοῦ καλοῦντος Paul means God. On the meaning of the term and its reference to God, see on 1⁶; and on the omission of θεοῦ, see on 2⁸ 3⁵. The negative statement carries with it the positive intimation that the influence which is affecting them is one that is hostile to God, an intimation which is definitely expressed in v.⁹.

Πεισμονή may be either active (Chrys. on 1 Thes. 1³; Just. Mart. *Apol.* 53¹) or passive (Ign. *Rom.* 3² Iren. *Haer.* 4. 33⁷), and it is impossible to tell in which sense Paul thought of it here. The passive sense involves the thought of a persuasion actually accomplished, the active an effort. It was, of course, the latter, but ἐνέκοψεν shows that in Paul's thought it was in a sense the former, also. On the tense and modal force of καλοῦντος (general present; adjective participle used substantively), see B*MT* 123, 124, 423, and *cf.* 1 Thes. 2¹² 5²⁴.

9. μικρὰ ζύμη ὅλον τὸ φύραμα ζυμοῖ. "A little leaven is leavening the whole lump." The occurrence of exactly the same words in 1 Cor. 5⁶ and the way in which they are there used indicate that they were a proverbial saying, referring to the tendency of an influence seemingly small to spread until it dominates the whole situation. In 1 Cor. ζυμή refers to the immoral conduct and influence of the incestuous man, and φύραμα represents the Corinthian church, whose whole moral life was in danger of being corrupted. Here, over against the negative statement of v.⁸, this verse states the true explanation of the situation, viz., that the doctrine of the necessity of circumcision, insidiously presented by a few, is permeating and threatening to pervert the whole religious life of the Galatian churches. ζυμοῖ is probably not to be taken as a general present (as in 1 Cor.) but as a present of action in progress. It agrees with all the other evidence of the epistle in indicating that the anti-Pauline movement had as yet made but little, though alarming, progress.

On τὸ φύραμα ζυμοῖ, *cf.* Exod. 12³⁴, and on leaven as a symbol of an evil influence (of good, however, in Mt. 13¹³ Lk. 13²⁰, ²¹), see Ltft.

10. ἐγὼ πέποιθα εἰς ὑμᾶς ἐν κυρίῳ ὅτι οὐδὲν ἄλλο φρονήσετε· "I have confidence, in the Lord, respecting you that ye will take no other view than this." With the abruptness

284

GALATIANS

which characterises the whole passage, the apostle turns suddenly from the discouraging aspects of the situation to an expression of hopeful confidence. The use of ἐγώ emphasises the personal, subjective character of the confidence. "I, at least, whatever others think." εἰς ὑμᾶς designates the persons in reference to whom (Th. εἰς B. II 2 a) the confidence is felt; ἐν κυρίῳ defines the Lord, i. e., Christ, not precisely as the object of trust but as the one who constitutes the basis or ground of confidence (Th. ἐν, I 6 c.; cf. 2⁴ and 2¹⁷ and notes on these passages). The whole passage is marked by such abruptness of expression and sudden changes of thought that the words οὐδὲν ἄλλο may mean in general no other view of the true nature of religion or the true interpretation of the gospel than that which Paul had taught them. Most probably they refer directly to the opinion just expressed by Paul in v.⁹. In that case the sentence is an expression of confidence that the Galatians will share his conviction that the influence exerted by the judaisers is, in fact, a leaven (of evil) coming not from God but from men, and threatening the religious life of the whole community of Galatian Christians.

The constructions employed by Paul after πέποιθα are various: (a) ἐπί, with a personal object (2 Cor. 1⁹ 2³ 2 Thes. 3⁴), and ἐν with an impersonal object (Phil. 3³ˑ ⁴), designating the object of confidence, that which one trusts; (b) ἐν with a personal object (Phil. 2²⁴ 2 Thes. 3⁴ and the present passage) designating the ground on which confidence rests; (c) εἰς with the accusative occurring in the present passage, without parallel elsewhere; in accordance with the not infrequent use of εἰς in other connections, the preposition is to be explained, as above, as meaning "in respect to." To take εἰς ὑμᾶς as denoting the object of faith (Butt. p. 175) is without the support of other examples with this verb, or of the preposition as used with other verbs; for while the accusative after πιστεύω εἰς denotes the object of faith, this construction is practically restricted to use in respect to Christ (cf. detached note on Πιστεύω, p. 480), and furnishes no ground for thinking that πέποιθα εἰς would be used with similar force in respect to other persons. 2 Cor. 8²², πεποιθήσει πολλῇ τῇ εἰς ὑμᾶς, is indecisive both because it contains not the verb but the noun, and because it shares the ambiguity of the present passage.

The expression ἐν κυρίῳ occurs in the Pauline epistles approximately forty times. That it means "in Christ," not "in God," is rendered practically certain by these considerations: (a) of ἐν Χριστῷ, or ἐν τῷ Χριστῷ, or ἐν Χριστῷ Ἰησοῦ there are about eighty instances, and in many of these the connection of thought is closely similar to those in which ἐν κυρίῳ is employed. (b) In seven cases (Rom. 6²³ 14¹⁴ 1 Cor. 15³¹ 1 Thes. 1¹ 4¹ 2 Thes. 1¹ 3¹²) κυρίῳ after ἐν is defined by a preceding or following Ἰησοῦ, Χριστῷ, or both together, as referring to Christ, and in these instances, also, the connection of thought is similar to that in which ἐν κυρίῳ alone occurs. (c) ἐν θεῷ and ἐν τῷ θεῷ occur but rarely in Paul (Rom. 2¹⁷ 5¹¹ Eph. 3⁹ Col. 3³ 1 Thes. 1¹ 2² 2 Thes. 1¹), and in two of these instances (1 Thes. 1¹ 2 Thes. 1¹), with θεῷ is joined κυρίῳ in such ways as to show that ἐν κυρίῳ refers to Christ. Against these strong considerations there is only the fact that in general κύριος without the article refers to God, ὁ κύριος to Christ. But the force of this general rule is diminished by the further fact that in set phrases, especially prepositional phrases, the article is frequently omitted without modification of meaning. *Cf.* detached note on Πατήρ *as applied to God*, p. 387. On οὐδεὶς ἄλλος *cf.* Jn. 15²⁴ Acts 4¹².

ὁ δὲ ταράσσων ὑμᾶς βαστάσει τὸ κρίμα, ὅστις ἐὰν ᾖ. "but he that troubleth you shall bear his judgment, whoever he may be." In itself ὁ ταράσσων might refer to a particular individual identified or unidentified, and the troubling might be present, past, or future. But the indefinite relative clause, ὅστις ἐὰν ᾖ, referring to the future (B*MT* 303, 304; a present general supposition is excluded by the future βαστάσει, and a present particular by the subjunctive ᾖ) requires us to take ὁ ταράσσων as designating not a particular individual mentally identified, but as referring to any one who hereafter may disturb them. The article is distributive generic, as in 3¹², ¹⁴ Jn. 3¹⁸. Doubtless this is but another way of referring to those who are spoken of in 1⁶, τινές εἰσιν οἱ ταράσσοντες ὑμᾶς, καὶ θέλοντες μεταστρέψαι τὸ εὐαγγέλιον τοῦ χριστοῦ, and in v.¹² as οἱ ἀναστατοῦντες ὑμᾶς. Only their conduct is, for rhetorical effect, referred to not as a fact but as a future possibility, as in 1⁸, and an indefinite singular takes the place of a definite plural. τὸ κρίμα undoubtedly refers to the judgment of God, which carries with it by implication the consequent punishment. *Cf.* Rom. 2², ³ 3⁸, and esp. Rom. 13². How or when the punishment will be experienced the sentence does not indicate; there is nothing to show that the apostle has especially or exclusively in mind the messianic judgment (Rom. 2¹⁶).

Βαστάζω, used by classical writers from Homer down, occurs also in the Lxx, Apocr., and Pat. Ap. It is found in N. T. twenty-seven times. In all periods, apparently, it is employed both in a literal sense of bearing a burden (Mk. 14¹³ Jn. 19¹⁷) and other similar senses, and metaphorically of mental processes. In N. T. it occurs several times in the sense "to endure": Jn. 16¹² Acts 15¹⁰ Rom. 15¹. Cf. also Gal. 6², ⁵, ¹⁷. Of bearing punishment it occurs here only in N. T., but also in 2 Kgs. 18¹⁴.

11. Ἐγὼ δέ, ἀδελφοί, εἰ περιτομὴν ἔτι κηρύσσω, τί ἔτι διώκομαι; "And I, brethren, if I am still preaching circumcision, why am I still being persecuted?" Still another abrupt sentence, probably occasioned by the fact that they who were troubling the Galatians were using as one of their weapons a charge that the apostle was still, when it suited his purpose, preaching circumcision. As evidence of the falsity of the charge, Paul appeals to the fact that he is being persecuted, implying that it was for anti-legalism. The use of ἔτι with κηρύσσω implies that there was a time when he preached circumcision. The reference is doubtless to his pre-Christian life, since we have no information that he ever advocated circumcision after he became a Christian. On the reasons for holding that 1¹⁰ furnishes no evidence of a period of conformity to the views of the judaisers in the matter, see notes on that passage. What basis there was for the charge that he was still advising circumcision, and whether the charges referred to the circumcision of Gentiles or of Jews—doubtless there was something to give colour to it—may perhaps be inferred from 1 Cor. 7¹⁸, if we may assume that even before writing Galatians he had said or written things similar to that passage. On Acts 16³, see below.

The conditional clause εἰ . . . κηρύσσω, though having the form of a simple present supposition, evidently expresses an unfulfilled condition (BMT 245; cf. 2²¹ 3¹⁸ Rom. 4² Jn. 18²³), while the apodosis takes the form of a rhetorical question, meaning, "I should not be persecuted." On the possible uses of ἔτι, cf. on 1¹⁰. Despite the seeming parallelism, the two words ἔτι can hardly both be temporal. To make both mean "still as in my pre-Christian days," is forbidden by the fact that he was not in those days persecuted for preaching circumcision. To make both mean "still as in my early Christian days," is forbidden by the improbability that he was then preaching circumcision and the certainty (implied in the sentence itself) that if he had been he would not have been persecuted. If both are temporal, the meaning can only be, If I am still as in my pre-Christian days, preaching circumcision, why do they, having learned this, continue that persecution which they began supposing that I was opposed to circumcision? Simpler and more probable than this is the interpretation of the first ἔτι as temporal, and the second as denoting logical opposition; cf., e. g., Rom. 3⁷. The sentence then means: "If I am still preaching circumcision, why am I despite this fact persecuted?"

The bearing of this passage on the historicity of the statement of Acts 16³ with reference to the circumcision of Timothy belongs, rather, to the interpretation of Acts than here. If the event occurred as there narrated and became the occasion for the charge to which Paul here refers, why he made no further reply than to deny the charge, and that only by implication, can only be conjectured. Perhaps knowing that the Galatians and his critics both knew that he had never objected to the circumcision of Jews, and that the only question really at issue was the circumcision of Gentiles who accepted the gospel, he judged it unnecessary to make any reply other than an appeal to the fact that they were persecuting him.

ἄρα κατήργηται τὸ σκάνδαλον τοῦ σταυροῦ. "Then is the stumbling-block of the cross done away with." I. e., if circumcision may be maintained, the cross of Christ has ceased to be a stumbling-block. τὸ σκάνδαλον τοῦ σταυροῦ is that element or accompaniment of the death of Christ on the cross that makes it offensive (1 Cor. 1²³), viz., to the Jews, deterring them from accepting Jesus as the Christ. This offensiveness, the apostle implies, lay in the doctrine of the freedom of believers in Christ from the law. Whatever else there may have been in the fact of Jesus' death on the cross to make the doctrine of his messiahship offensive to the Jews, that which above all else made it such was the doctrine that men may obtain divine acceptance and a share in the messianic blessings through faith in Jesus, without circumcision or obedience to the statutes of Moses.*

* Cf. the words of Chrysostom quoted by Alford ad loc.: "For even the cross which was a stumbling-block to the Jews was not so much so as the failure to require obedience to the ancestral laws. For when they attacked Stephen they said not that he was worshipping the Crucified but that he was speaking against the law and the holy place."

It is natural and reasonable to suppose that this sentence reflects Paul's own pre-Christian attitude, when his own zeal for the law made him a persecutor of Christians (1¹³, ¹⁴ Phil. 3⁶). Had it been something else than its anti-legalism that chiefly made the Christian movement offensive to him, he could not have made this statement, since in that case the removal of this element would have left the doctrine of the cross offensive to those who still occupied the position which he maintained in his pre-Christian days. And this fact in turn confirms the evidence of the Acts that even in its early days the Christian movement had an anti-legalistic element. The implication of the sentence is that, in his judgment, had Christianity been content to remain Jewish-legalistic, it might have won the Jews, or at least have maintained a respected standing among Jewish sects. The conflict between the Christianity of Paul and that of the ultra-legalists, was radical. The former sought to reach the nations at the risk of becoming offensive to the Jews; the latter would win the Jews at the sacrifice of all other nations. With this view of Paul the testimony of the book of Acts is in harmony, both in its indication of the large number of Jews who attached themselves to the legalistic Christianity of James and the Jerusalem church, and in the bitter offensiveness to them of the anti-legalism of Paul. See esp. Acts, chaps. 15 and 21¹⁵⁻²².

Ltft. understands the sentence as ironical (cf. 4¹⁶), meaning: "Then I have adopted their mode of preaching, and I am silent about the cross." But this ascribes to κατήργηται an improbable meaning, and to the whole sentence a more personal reference than the language warrants.

On the use of ἄρα with the indicative without ἄν in an apodosis shown by the context to be contrary to fact, cf. 2²¹ 1 Cor. 15¹⁴, where the protasis is expressed and the condition is in form that of a simple supposition, and 1 Cor. 15¹⁸, where as here the protasis is implied in the preceding sentence.

12. Ὄφελον καὶ ἀποκόψονται οἱ ἀναστατοῦντες ὑμᾶς. "I would that they who are disturbing you would even have themselves mutilated." οἱ ἀναστατοῦντες are evidently the same who are directly referred to in 1⁶ as οἱ ταράσσοντες ὑμᾶς, and hypothetically in ὁ ταράσσων of v.¹⁰. ἀποκόψονται is clearly shown by usage (see exx. below) and the context to refer not, except quite indirectly (see below), to a withdrawal from the Christian community, or any other like act, but to bodily mutilation. In the bitterness of his feeling, the apostle expresses the wish that his opponents would not stop with cir-

cumcision, but would go on to emasculation. There is possibly
a tacit reference to the emasculation of the priests of Cybele,
with which the Galatians would doubtless be familiar and,
quite possibly, in the apostle's mind, at least, though he could
hardly have expected his Galatian readers to think of it, to the
language of Deut. 23¹ (see below). The whole expression is
most significant as showing that to Paul circumcision had become not only a purely physical act without religious significance, but a positive mutilation, like that which carried with it
exclusion from the congregation of the Lord.   It is not improbable that he has this consequence in mind: "I wish that
they who advocate this physical act would follow it out to the
logical conclusion and by a further act of mutilation exclude
themselves from the congregation of the Lord." Cf. Phil. 3²,
where he applies to circumcision as a physical act the derogatory term κατατομή, "mutilation." To get the full significance
of such language in the mouth of a Jew, or as heard by Jewish
Christians, we must imagine a modern Christian speaking of
baptism and the Lord's Supper as if they were merely physical
acts without spiritual significance; yet even this would lack the
element of deep disgust which the language of Paul suggests.

On ἀναστατόω, meaning "to disturb," see M. and M. Voc. s. v.
ὄφελον, a shortened aorist indicative for ὤφελον, "I ought," has
in N. T. the force of an interjection, "would that." Used by classical
writers generally with the infinitive, it occurs in Callimachus (260 B. C.)
with a past tense of the indicative; so also in the Lxx (Ex. 16³ Num.
14², etc.) and elsewhere in N. T. (1 Cor. 4⁸ 2 Cor. 11¹ Rev. 3¹⁵) of a
wish probably conceived of as unattainable. It occurs with the future
here only, probably with the intent of presenting the wish rhetorically
as attainable, though it can hardly have been actually thought of as
such. BMT 27. Rem. 1².

'Αποκόπτεσθαι with an accusative of specification, τὰ γεννητικά,
expressed, or unexpressed but to be supplied mentally, refers to a
form of emasculation said to be still common in the East. See Deut.
23² ⁽¹⁾: οὐκ εἰσελεύσονται θλαδίας οὐδὲ ἀποκεκομμένος εἰς ἐκκλησίαν
Κυρίου. Epict. Diss. 2. 20¹⁹: οἱ ἀποκεκομμένοι τάς γε προθυμίας τὰς
τῶν ἀνδρῶν ἀποκόψασθαι οὐ δύνανται. Philo, Sacrif. 325 (13); Leg. alleg.
III 8 (3); Dion. Cass. 79¹¹. Cf. Keil and Delitzsch on Deut. 23²:
"בְּצוּעֵי־דַכָּה [Lxx θλαδίας] literally 'wounded by crushing,' denotes one

who is mutilated in this way; Vulg. eunuchus attritis vel amputatis testiculis. כְּרוּת שָׁפְכָה [Lxx ἀποκεκομμένος] is one whose sexual member was cut off; Vulg. abscisso veretro. According to Mishnah Jebam. VI 2, 'contusus רַכָּה est omnis, cuius testiculi vulnerati sunt, vel certe unus eorum; exsectus (כְּרוּת), cuius membrum virile praecisun. est.' In the modern East emasculation is generally performed in this way. (See Tournefort, *Reise*, ii, p. 259 [*The Levant*, 1718, ii. 7] and Burckhardt, *Nubien*, pp. 450, 451.)"

> (b) Exhortation not to convert their liberty in Christ
> into an occasion for yielding to the impulse of the
> flesh (5[13-26]).

In this paragraph the apostle deals with a new phase of the subject, connected, indeed, with the main theme of the letter, but not previously touched upon. Aware that on the one side it will probably be urged against his doctrine of freedom from law that it removes the restraints that keep men from immorality, and certainly on the other that those who accept it are in danger of misinterpreting it as if this were the case, he fervently exhorts the Galatians not to fall into this error, but, instead, through love to serve one another. This exhortation he enforces by the assurance that thus they will fulfil the full requirement of the law, that they will not fulfil the desire of the flesh, nor be under law, and by impressive lists, on the one hand of the works of the flesh, and on the other of the products of the Spirit in the soul.

[13]*For ye were called for freedom, brethren. Only convert not your freedom into an opportunity for the flesh, but through love be servants one of another.* [14]*For the whole law is fulfilled in one word, even in this, Thou shalt love thy neighbour as thyself.* [15]*But if ye are biting and devouring one another, take heed lest ye be consumed by one another.* [16]*But I say, Walk by the Spirit and ye will not fulfil the desire of the flesh.* [17]*For the desire of the flesh is against that of the Spirit, and the desire of the Spirit against that of the flesh; for these are opposed to one another, that whatsoever ye will ye may not do.* [18]*But if ye are led by the Spirit, ye are not under law.* [19]*Now the works of the flesh are manifest, which are fornication, uncleanness, wantonness;* [20]*idolatry, witchcraft; enmi-*

ties, strife, jealousy, angers, self-seekings, parties, divisions, [21]*envy-ings; drunkenness, carousings, and the things like these; respect-ing which I tell you beforehand, as I have (already) told you in ad-vance,that they who do such things will not inherit the kingdom of God.* [22]*But the fruit of the Spirit is love, joy, peace, long-suffering, kindness, goodness, faithfulness,* [23]*gentleness, self-control. Against such things there is no law.* [24]*And they that belong to the Christ, Jesus, have crucified the flesh with its disposition and its desires.* [25]*If we live by the Spirit, by the Spirit also let us walk.* [26]*Let us not become vain-minded, provoking one another, envying one another.*

13. Ὑμεῖς γὰρ ἐπ' ἐλευθερίᾳ ἐκλήθητε, ἀδελφοί· "For ye were called for freedom, brethren." Like v.[1] this sentence is transitional. It belongs with what precedes in that it gives a reason (γάρ is causal) for v.[12], but even more significantly in that it is an epitome of the whole preceding argument of the epistle in behalf of the freedom of the Gentile. But it belongs with what follows in that it serves to introduce a wholly new aspect of the matter, the exposition of which begins with μόνον. ὑμεῖς, immediately following ὑμᾶς of v.[12], is emphatic. "Ye, whom they are disturbing, for freedom were called."

On ἐπί, expressing destination, see Th. B. 2 a ζ; 1 Thes. 4[7] Phil. 4[10]. ἐλευθερίᾳ manifestly refers to the same freedom that is spoken of in v.[1], but being without the article is qualitative. On ἐκλήθητε, cf. on τοῦ καλοῦντος v.[8] and more fully on 1[6]. On ἀδελφοί, see on 1[11].

μόνον μὴ τὴν ἐλευθερίαν εἰς ἀφορμὴν τῇ σαρκί, "Only con-vert not your freedom into an opportunity for the flesh." μόνον, used also in 1[23] 2[10] Phil. 1[27], to call attention not to an exception to a preceding statement, but to an important addi-tion to it, here introduces a most significant element of the apostle's teaching concerning freedom, which has not been pre-viously mentioned, and which occupies his thought throughout the remainder of this chapter. On this word, as on a hinge, the thought of the epistle turns from freedom to a sharply con-trasted aspect of the matter, the danger of abusing freedom. So far he has strenuously defended the view that the Gentile is

not under obligation to keep the statutes of the law, and though
he has not referred specifically to any statute except those that
pertain to circumcision, food, and the observance of days
and seasons, he has constantly spoken simply of law, or the
law, without indicating that his thought was limited to any
portion or aspect of it. To men who have been accustomed to
think of law as the only obstacle to free self-indulgence, or to
those who, on the other hand, have not been accustomed to
high ethical standards, such language is (despite the contrary
teaching of vv.[5, 6]) easily taken to mean that for the Christian
there is nothing to stand in the way of the unrestrained indul-
gence of his own impulses. Of this danger Paul is well aware
(cf. Rom. 6[1ff.] Phil. 3[17ff.] Col. 3[1ff.]), and beginning with this v.
addresses himself vigorously to meeting and averting it. The
word $\sigma\acute{\alpha}\rho\xi$, previously in this epistle a purely physical term, is
used here and throughout this chapter (see vv. [16, 17, 20, 24]) in a
definitely ethical sense, "that element of man's nature which
is opposed to goodness, and makes for evil," in which it appears
also in Rom., chap. 8; see detached note on $\Pi\nu\epsilon\hat{\upsilon}\mu\alpha$ and $\Sigma\acute{\alpha}\rho\xi$
II 7, p. 493, and the discussion following 7. For fuller treat-
ment, see Burton, *Spirit, Soul, and Flesh*, chap. VI, pp. 186,
191 *ff*. Of any physical association with this ethical sense of the
term there is no trace in this passage.

The article before ἐλευθερίαν is demonstrative, referring to ἐλευθερία
of the preceding clause, and through it to that of 5¹ and the implication
of the whole context. On the omission of the verb with μή, cf. μὴ
'μοίγε μύθους, Aristoph. *Vesp.* 1179; μὴ τριβὰς ἔτι, Soph. *Antig.* 575;
μή μοι μυρίους, Dem. 45¹³ (cited by Alf.); Hartung, *Partikeln* II 153;
Devarius, *De Particulis*, Ed. Klotz, II 669; W. LXIV˙6; Mk. 14². Note
also the omission of the verb after μόνον, in 2¹⁰. What verb is to be
supplied, whether ἔχετε, ποιεῖτε, τρέπετε (cf. Sief. Ell. *et al.*),
στρέφετε or μεταστρέφετε (Rev. 11⁶ Acts 2¹⁹, ²⁰), or some other, is not
wholly clear. The thought is probably not "use not this freedom for,
in the interest of," but "convert not this freedom into." On the use
of εἰς, cf. Jn. 16²⁰: ἡ λυπὴ ὑμῶν εἰς χαρὰν γενήσεται, and Acts 2¹⁹, ²⁰.
ἀφορμή, properly the place from which an attack is made (Thucydides,
Polybius), is used also figuratively by Xenophon, *et al.*, with the meaning, "incentive," "opportunity," "occasion." In N. T. it occurs in
the Pauline letters only (Rom. 7⁸ 2 Cor. 5¹² 11¹² 1 Tim. 5¹⁴) always in

this latter meaning, and in the same phrases as in Isocrates and Demosthenes: ἀφορμὴν λαβεῖν, Isoc. 53 A; Rom. 7⁸, ¹¹; ἀφορμὴν διδόναι, Dem. 546¹⁹; 2 Cor. 5¹² (cf. L. and S.). It is best taken here in the sense of "opportunity." τῇ σαρκί is a dative of advantage limiting ἀφορμήν. The article is probably generic, as clearly in v.¹⁷, and the term is at least semi-personified.

ἀλλὰ διὰ τῆς ἀγάπης δουλεύετε ἀλλήλοις· "but through love be servants one of another." This is the apostle's antidote alike to the harmful restrictions of legalism and the dangers of freedom from law: love, expressed in mutual service. On what he means by ἀγάπη, see on v.⁶ and detached note on Ἀγάπη, p. 519. The phase of love here emphasised is clearly that of benevolence, desire for the well-being of others, leading to efforts on their behalf. δουλεύω, generally meaning "to yield obedience to," "to be in subjection to" (see 4⁸, ⁹), is evidently here employed in a sense corresponding to that which δοῦλος sometimes has (cf. on 1¹⁰), and meaning "to render service to," "to do that which is for the advantage of." Having urgently dissuaded the Galatians who were formerly enslaved to gods that are not really gods from becoming enslaved to law (4⁹ 5¹), he now, perhaps with intentional paradox, bids them serve one another, yet clearly not in the sense of subjection to the will, but of voluntary devotion to the welfare, of one another. Cf. Rom. 12¹⁴⁻²¹ 14¹⁵ 1 Cor. 11²⁵⁻³³. See also Mk. 9³⁵ 10⁴³, where, however, διάκονος, not δοῦλος, is used. The present tense of δουλεύετε reflects the fact that what Paul enjoins is not a single act of service, nor an entrance into service, but a continuous attitude and activity.

Ἀλλά as often (cf. Rom. 1²¹ 2¹³, etc.) introduces the positive correlative of a preceding negative statement or command (German, sondern). The article before ἀγάπης is demonstrative, either referring to v.⁶, or, perhaps, in view of the distance of this v., to that love which is characteristic of the Christian life. Cf. 1 Cor. 13³ 14¹ Rom. 12⁹. διά, as in διὰ χάριτος, 1¹⁵, marks its object as the conditioning cause, that the possession of which makes possible the action of the verb, rather than as instrument in the strict sense. Cf. note on διά in 1¹.

14. ὁ γὰρ πᾶς νόμος ἐν ἑνὶ λόγῳ πεπλήρωται, ἐν τῷ "Ἀγαπήσεις τὸν πλησίον σου ὡς σεαυτόν." "For the whole law is fulfilled in one word, even in this, Thou shalt love thy neighbour as thyself." A striking paradox. Having devoted practically all his effort up to this point, directly or indirectly, to dissuading the Galatians from coming into bondage to the law by undertaking to obey its statutes, he now gives as the reason for their serving one another that thus they will fulfil the whole law. But the paradox is itself most instructive; for it shows that there was a sense of the word "law" according to which it was essential that its requirements be fully met by the Christian. *Cf.* Rom. 8⁴. The explanation of the paradox lies partly in the diverse senses of the word "law," and the fact that the apostle employs it here not, as heretofore in the epistle, of its legalistic element, or of law legalistically interpreted, but of divine law conceived of as consisting in an ethical principle (see detached note on Νόμος, V 2. (d), p. 458); partly, but to a less extent, in the difference between keeping statutes in slavish obedience and fulfilling law as the result of life by the Spirit. *Cf.* vv. 6, 16. The apostle's statements become intelligible and consistent only when it is recognised that he held that from the whole law as statutes, from the obligation to obey any of its statutes as such, men are released through the new revelation in Christ; and that, on the other hand, all that the law as an expression of the will of God really requires, when seen with eyes made discerning by experience, is love, and he who loves therefore fulfils the whole law. Statutes he will incidentally obey in so far as love itself requires it, but only so far, and in no case as statutes of the law. *Cf.* the apostle's bold application of this principle even to chastity in 1 Cor. 6¹², showing that in Paul's view even when things prohibited by the law were also excluded by love, it was on the latter ground, not the former, that they were to be avoided by the Christian.

The precise meaning of this sentence turns in no small part on the meaning of πεπλήρωται, on which diverse interpretations have been put. It has been interpreted above as meaning "is fully obeyed." This interpretation demands substantiation. πληρόω, a classical word, from Æschylus and Herodotus down, means properly "to fill," "to make full"; its object is, therefore, a space empty or but partly filled.

In this sense it occurs rarely in N. T.: Mt. 13⁴⁸ Lk. 3⁵ Jn. 12³. Employed tropically it signifies: 1. "to fill," "to fulfil," the object being thought of under the figure of a receptable or empty vessel. It is used (a) with a personal object and means, "to fill," "to supply abundantly": Acts 13⁵² Rom. 1²⁹; (b) with an impersonal object, originally at least pictured to the mind as a receptacle to be filled, an empty form to be filled with reality; thus of a promise, prophecy, or statement of fact, "to satisfy the purport of," "to fit the terms of": Mt. 1²² et freq. in Mt. Acts 1¹⁶ 3¹⁸, etc.; of commands and laws, "to satisfy the requirements of," "to obey fully": Rom. 8⁴ 13⁸, probably also Mt. 5¹⁷; of needs, "to satisfy": Phil. 4¹⁹. When the object is a task or course of action it means "to complete," "fully to perform": Mt. 3¹⁵ Lk. 7¹ Acts 12²⁵ 14²⁶ Col. 4¹⁷. 2. When the object is thought of as something incomplete, and requiring to be filled out to its normal or intended measure, its meaning is "to complete," "to make perfect": Mk. 1¹⁵ Jn. 7⁸ 15¹¹ 16²⁴. In Rom. 8⁴ 13⁸ Paul uses the word as here with νόμος, and quite unambiguously in the sense, "fully to obey"; this fact creates a strong presumption in favour of that meaning here. The use of the perfect tense, also, which might seem to favour the meaning "to make perfect" (the sentence in that case meaning, "the whole law stands complete, made perfect, in the one word," etc.) is sufficiently explained by πεπλήρωκεν in Rom. 13⁸: ὁ γὰρ ἀγαπῶν τὸν ἕτερον νόμον πεπλήρωκεν, "he that loveth his neighbour stands in the position of having fulfilled law, is a fulfiller of law," the tense in both sentences being a gnomic perfect (BMT 79). The present sentence then means, "The whole law stands fully obeyed in (obedience to) one word," etc. So Luther's translation (though freely expressed): "Alle Gesetze werden in einem Worte erfüllet"; Stage's German version: "Das ganze Gesetz findet seine Erfüllung in dem einen Worte"; so also Ell. Ltft. Sief., et al. The meaning (2) "is completed," though entirely possible in connection with such a word as νόμος, is practically excluded here (a) by πᾶς in ὁ πᾶς νόμος, indicating that the apostle is speaking, not of the law as incomplete, but as already complete, and (b) by the evidence of Rom. 8⁴ 13⁸ in favour of "fulfil." The meaning "is summed up" (so Weizs., "geht in ein Wort zusammen," and Stapfer, "se résume d'un seul mot") is also appropriate to the context and harmonious with πᾶς, and repeats the thought of Paul in Rom. 13⁹. But it is opposed by the evidence of Rom. 13⁸, ⁹, where Paul using both πληρόω and ἀνακεφαλαιόω clearly distinguishes them in meaning, using the latter in the sense "to sum up" and the former to mean "fulfil," "obey fully," and by the fact that πληρόω is never used in the sense which this interpretation requires either in N. T., the Lxx, or in any Greek writer so far as observed. Sief. cites thirteen of the older commentators and translators who take πεπλήρωται in the sense of ἀνακεφαλαιοῦται. An examination of nine of the ablest of these authorities shows no lexicographical basis for the position taken. The strongest, though entirely untenable, reason given is a comparison of πεπλήρωται here with ἀνακεφαλαιοῦται in Rom. 13⁹, whereas the proper comparison is with πεπλήρωκεν in Rom. 13⁸.

The position of πᾶς between the article and the noun νόμος is unusual; if a distinction is to be drawn between the more usual πᾶς ὁ νόμος and the form here employed, the latter expresses more clearly the idea of totality, without reference to parts. See Butt., p. 120; Bl.-D. 275. 7; Acts 19⁷ 20¹⁸ 27³⁷; 1 Tim. 1¹⁶. The context makes it clear that the reference is to the law of God; but clearly also to the law of God as revealed in O. T., since it is this that has been the subject of discussion throughout the epistle. See detached note on Νόμος, V 2. (d), p. 459.

Λόγος, meaning "utterance," "saying," "reason," etc., always has reference not to the outward form or sound, but to the inward content; here it evidently refers to the sentence following. Cf. Mt. 26⁴⁴ Lk. 7¹⁷, etc.

The sentence ἀγαπήσεις . . . σεαυτόν is quoted from Lev. 19¹⁸, following the Lxx. ἀγαπήσεις clearly refers specially to the love of benevolence (see detached note on Ἀγαπάω and Ἀγάπη). In the original passage, רֵעַ‎ וְאָהַבְתָּ לְרֵעֲךָ כָּמוֹךָ‎, though in itself capable of being used colourlessly to denote another person without indication of the precise relationship, doubtless derives from the context ("Thou shalt not take vengeance, nor bear any grudge against the children of thy people, but thou shalt love thy neighbour as thyself") a specific reference to fellow Israelites. This limitation of the command, as, of course, also those passages which enjoin or express a hostile attitude to non-Israelites or to personal enemies (Deut. 23³⁻⁶ 25¹⁷⁻¹⁹ Ps. 41¹⁰ 69²²⁻²⁸ 109⁶⁻¹⁵), the apostle disregards, as he does the specific statutes of the law, such, e. g., as those requiring circumcision and the observance of days, which he conceived to be no longer valuable and valid. His affirmation is to be taken not as a verdict of mere exegesis, summing up with mathematical exactness the whole teaching of O. T., and giving its precise weight to each phase of it, but as a judgment of insight and broad valuation, which, discriminating what is central, pervasive, controlling, from what is exceptional, affirms the former, not introducing the latter even as a qualification but simply ignoring it. It is improbable that he drew a sharp distinction between portions of the law, and regarded those which were contrary to the spirit of love or not demanded by it as alien elements intruded into what was otherwise good; at least he never intimates such a discrimination between good and bad parts of the law. Rather, it would seem, he looked at the law as a whole, as one might view a building many parts of which taken alone are without form or comeliness, yet which as a whole is wholly beautiful. Its total meaning was to him love; and this was the law of God; the parts as such had for him no authority.

15. εἰ δὲ ἀλλήλους δάκνετε καὶ κατεσθίετε, βλέπετε μὴ ὑπ' ἀλλήλων ἀναλωθῆτε. "But if ye are biting and devouring one another, take heed lest ye be consumed by one another." The form of the conditional clause and the tense of the verbs imply that the apostle has in mind a condition which he knows to be, or thinks may be, even now existing. It would but slightly exaggerate this suggestion to translate, "If ye continue your biting and devouring of one another." What the condition was to which he referred neither the passage nor the context discloses; most probably it was strife over the matters on which the judaisers were disturbing them.

> The verbs δάκνω, κατεσθίω, ἀναλίσκω (all of common use in classical writers, the first two from Homer down, the third from Pindar down) suggest wild animals engaged in deadly struggle. The order is climactic, the first and second by virtue of their respective meanings, the third in relation to the other two by virtue of their tenses, δάκνετε and κατεσθίετε being conative presents and ἀναλωθῆτε a resultative aorist.

16. Λέγω δέ, πνεύματι περιπατεῖτε καὶ ἐπιθυμίαν σαρκὸς οὐ μὴ τελέσητε. "But I say, Walk by the Spirit and ye will not fulfil the desire of the flesh." The use of the phrase λέγω δέ, not strictly necessary to the expression of the thought, throws emphasis upon the statement thus introduced. Cf. 3¹⁷ 4¹ 5² Rom. 10¹⁸, ¹⁹ 11¹, ¹¹ 15⁸ 1 Cor. 10²⁹ 2 Cor. 11¹⁶. By πνεύματι Paul undoubtedly refers to the Spirit of God as in v.⁵. So also σάρξ manifestly has the same ethical meaning as in v.¹³. (See detached note on Πνεῦμα, III B. 1. (c), p. 491, and Σάρξ 7, p. 493.) περιπατεῖτε is a true imperative in force, while also serving as a protasis to the apodosis οὐ μὴ τελέσητε. BMT 269. The tense of the imperative denoting action in progress is appropriately used of that which the Galatians were already doing; cf. 3³ 5⁵. Over against the danger spoken of in v.¹⁵ and the possible suggestion of the judaisers to the Gala-

tians, or the fear of the Galatians themselves, that without the
pressure of the law constraining them to do right they would
fall into sinful living, Paul enjoins them to continue to govern
their conduct by the inward impulse of the Spirit, and emphatically assures them that so doing they will not yield to the
power within them that makes for evil.   The type of life which
he thus commends to them is evidently the same which in
vv.[5, 6] he has described in the words, "For we by the Spirit, by
faith, wait for the hope of righteousness.   For in Christ Jesus
neither circumcision availeth anything nor uncircumcision, but
faith working through love"; in 2[20] in the words, "It is no
longer I that live but Christ that liveth in me, and the life that
I now live in the flesh, I live by faith, faith upon the Son of
God"; and which is described below in v.[18] in the words, "If
ye are led by the Spirit," and in v.[25], "If we live by the Spirit."
On the identity experientially of life by the Spirit, and the life
of Christ within, see p. 222.

The word περιπατέω, which Paul uses in this epistle here only, is of
frequent occurrence in his other writings.   Occurring in the synoptic
gospels exclusively, and in the Gospel of John, Revelation, and Acts
almost exclusively, in the literal sense, it appears in Paul and the
epistles of John exclusively in the figurative sense, with the meaning
"to live," "to conduct one's self."   See, e. g., Rom. 6[4] 8[4] 2 Cor. 10[3].
This idea is very frequently expressed in Hebrew by הָלַךְ and is
occasionally reproduced in the Lxx by περιπατέω (2 Kgs. 20[3] Prov.
8[20] Eccl. 11[9]), but far more commonly by πορεύω (Ps. 1[1] 26[1, 11] et freq.).
As compared with the parallel expressions in v.[18] (ἄγεσθε) and in v.[25a]
(ζῶμεν), περιπατεῖτε emphasises the outward life, conduct, as against
surrender of will to the divine guidance (v.[18]), and participation in moral
life through mystical union (v.[25]).

The absence of the article with πνεύματι and with both ἐπιθυμίαν
and σαρκός emphasises the contrast in character between the Spirit-
controlled type of life and that which is governed by impulse of the
flesh.   Cf. 3[3], though the meaning of the word σάρξ is different there.
On the different senses in which the words πνεῦμα and σάρξ are set in
antithesis to one another, see detached note on Πνεῦμα and Σάρξ, p. 494.

Τελέω, a word common in Greek writers, from Homer down, signifies, as its relation to τέλος suggests, "to bring to an end," "to complete," "to perfect"; hence of a task, promise, and the like, "to fulfil."
In N. T. it means: 1. "to finish"; 2. "to perform," "execute,"

"fulfil"; 3. "to pay." It is manifestly used here in the second sense, ἐπιθυμία σαρκός being conceived of as a demand, which, the apostle affirms, they will not fulfil. οὐ μὴ τελέσητε is equivalent to an emphatic promissory future (BMT 172) expressing, not a command, but a strong assurance that if they walk by the Spirit they will not, in fact, fulfil the flesh-lust, but will be able to resist and conquer it. For though οὐ μή with a subj. is occasionally used to express prohibition in classical writers, Lxx, and N. T. (GMT 297, BMT 167), yet both the general situation, which requires that the Galatians shall not so much be commanded as assured of the safety of the course enjoined in περιπατεῖτε, and the immediate context (vv. ¹⁷, ¹⁸) favour an assertive and predictive sense rather than the rarely occurring imperative force.

Ἐπιθυμία and ἐπιθυμέω, both occurring in classical writers from Herodotus down, properly express desire of any kind (ἐπί—θυμός, "heart for," "impulse towards"). In classical writers ἐπιθυμία means "desire," "yearning," "longing": Hdt. 1³²; Thuc. 6. 13¹; with object. gen.: Thuc. 2. 52⁷; Antipho, 115²⁹. See also Aristot. Rhet. 1.10⁸ (1369aᵇ): ὥστε πάντα ὅσα πράττουσιν ἀνάγκη πράττειν δι' αἰτίας ἑπτά, διὰ τύχην, διὰ φύσιν, διὰ βίαν, δι' ἔθος, διὰ λογισμόν, διὰ θυμόν, δι' ἐπιθυμίαν . . . (1369b), δι' ἐπιθυμίαν δὲ πράττεται ὅσα φαίνεται ἡδέα. The desires that are related to the senses (in this general sense, sensual) Plato calls αἱ κατὰ τὸ σῶμα ἐπιθυμίαι (Phaed. 82 C). Cf. Diog. Laert. VII 1⁶³ (110). In the Lxx and Apocr. ἐπιθυμία occurs frequently, being used of desire shown by the context to be good (Ps. 37¹⁰), or evil (Prov. 12¹²), or without implication of moral quality (Deut. 12¹⁵, ²⁰, ²¹). When it is employed of evil desire this is either indicated by some term of moral quality, as in Prov. 12¹², or as in Sir. 5² 18³⁰, ³¹, by such a limitation as σου or καρδίας σου, the evil lying in the element of selfishness or wilfulness; when sexual desire is referred to, this idea is not at all in the word but in the limitations of it (Sir. 20⁴). In 4 Mac. ἐπιθυμίαι is a general term for the desires, which the author says can not be eradicated, but to which reason ought not to be subjected; in 2¹ it is used of sexual desire defined as such by the limiting words; only in 1³ does it stand alone, apparently meaning evil desire, perhaps sexual, being classed with γαστριμαργία, gluttony, as one of the feelings (πάθη; cf. on πάθημα, v.²⁴) that are opposed to sobriety (σωφροσύνη). ἐπιθυμέω in classical writers is likewise a term without moral implication, signifying "to desire." In the Lxx and Apocr., also, it is a neutral term, being used of desire for that which is good (Ps. 119²⁰, ⁴⁰ Isa. 58² Wisd. 6¹¹), of desire which it is wrong to cherish (Ex. 20¹⁷ Prov. 21²⁶), and without moral implication (Gen. 31³⁰ 2 Sam. 23¹⁵). The same is true of the verb in N. T.; it is used of good (Mt. 13¹⁷ 1 Tim. 3¹) or evil desire (Rom. 7⁷ 13⁹) according to the requirements of the context. It is clearly without moral colour in the present passage. The noun also, as used in N. T., carries in itself no moral implication (Lk. 22¹⁵ 1 Thes. 2¹⁷ Phil. 1²³). When it is used of evil desire this quality is usually indicated by a limitation of the word, or by such limitation combined with the larger context (Jn. 8⁴⁴ Rom. 1²⁴ Col. 3⁵, etc.). And though there appears in N. T. a tendency (of which there are perhaps the beginnings in Sir. and 4 Mac. also) to use ἐπιθυμία for evil desire without qualifying word (see Rom. 7⁷⁻⁸ Jas. 1¹⁵), it remains for the most part a word of neutral significance without distinctly moral colour. The idea of sensuality conveyed by the word "lust" as used in modern English belongs neither to the verb ἐπιθυμέω nor to the noun ἐπιθυμία in themselves, and is, indeed, rather rarely associated with them even by the context. In the case of the noun the implication of evil (not necessarily sensuality) is beginning in N. T. times to attach itself to its use.

17. ἡ γὰρ σὰρξ ἐπιθυμεῖ κατὰ τοῦ πνεύματος, τὸ δὲ πνεῦμα κατὰ τῆς σαρκός, ταῦτα γὰρ ἀλλήλοις ἀντίκειται, ἵνα μὴ ἃ ἐὰν θέλητε ταῦτα ποιῆτε. "For the desire of the flesh is against that of the Spirit, and the desire of the Spirit against that of the flesh; for these are opposed to one another, that whatsoever ye will ye may not do." γάρ is confirmatory and the whole sentence a proof of the statement of v.¹⁶, that walking by the Spirit will not issue in subjection to the flesh. σάρξ and σαρκός evidently have the same meaning as σαρκός in v.¹⁶, but for the qualitative use of that verse the apostle substitutes a generic use of σάρξ with the article, by which the force for evil is objectified. So also πνεῦμα and πνεύματος retain the meaning of πνεύματι in v.¹⁶, save that by the use of the article they become definite, pointing directly to the Spirit of God, rather than referring to it qualitatively as in v.¹⁶. ταῦτα γὰρ . . . ἀντίκειται is probably not simply a repetition in general terms of ἡ γὰρ . . . τῆς σαρκός, in which case it adds nothing to the thought. More probably the first part of the v. having, consistently with the point of view of v.¹⁶, spoken of Spirit and flesh as mutually antagonistic forces, there is at ταῦτα γάρ a change in point of view, these and the following words referring to the conflict which takes place between these two in the soul of which neither is in full possession, as proof of their mutual antagonism. To the thought of the whole v. there is an approx-

imate parallel in the antithesis between Satan and the Spirit
in Mk. 3²³⁻²⁷. The use of ἐπιθυμεῖ with σάρξ and its antithesis
to πνεῦμα in a personal sense involves a rhetorical personification of σάρξ, but not a conception of it as actually personal.

On the question precisely what ταῦτα . . . ἀντίκειται means, and
whether ἵνα . . . ποιῆτε depends on this or the preceding clause, in
which is also involved the question whether γάρ after ταῦτα is explanatory or confirmatory, and whether the clause introduced by it is parenthetical, the following data are to be considered:

1. There is no sufficient warrant in the usage of the period for taking
ἵνα in a purely ecbatic sense, and ἵνα . . . ποιῆτε as a clause of
actual result. Nor can this clause be regarded as a clause of conceived result (BMT 218), since the principal clause refers not to a
conceived situation (denied to be actual, as in 1 Thes. 5⁴, or asked
about as in Jn. 9², or affirmed as necessary as in Heb. 10³⁶), but to one
directly and positively affirmed. Nor are any of the other sub-telic
usages of ἵνα clauses possible here; apparently it must be taken as
purely telic. This fact forbids taking ἃ ἐὰν θέλητε as referring to the
things which one naturally, by the flesh, desires, and understanding
the clause as an expression of the beneficent result of walking by the
Spirit. Cf. also Rom. 7¹⁵, where similar language is used of a state
regarded as wholly undesirable.

2. This clause also excludes understanding the whole verse as referring to a conflict between the flesh and the Spirit as forces in themselves, without reference to any experience of the reader.

3. On the other hand, to interpret the first clause, ἡ γάρ . . . σαρκός
in an experiential sense makes ταῦτα . . . ἀντίκειται a meaningless
and obstructive repetition of the preceding statement.

It seems best, therefore, to understand the sentence from ἡ γάρ to
σαρκός as referring to the essential contrariety of the two forces as
such. This contrariety the apostle adduces as proof (γάρ) of the
statement of v.¹⁶ (they will not come under the power of the flesh by
coming under the Spirit, for the two forces are of precisely opposite
tendency), and in turn substantiates it by appeal to their own experience, the reference to their experience being intimated by the use of
the second person in the telic clause. The change in point of view
from essential contrariety to that of experience is, then, at ταῦτα γάρ,
γάρ being not explanatory but confirmatory.

What condition that is in which the internal conflict described in
v.¹⁷ᵇ ensues is suggested (a) by ὑπὸ νόμον of v.¹⁸ (see notes below),
itself apparently suggested by the thought of v.¹⁷ᵇ; (b) by reference
to Rom. 6¹⁴, where, after urging his readers not to continue in sin, the
apostle abruptly introduces the expression ὑπὸ νόμον in such a way as

to show that, though he has not previously in this chapter spoken of the law, he has all the time had in mind that it is under law that one is unable to get the victory over sin; (c) by comparison of Rom. 7¹⁴–8², in which the apostle sets forth the conflict which ensues when one strives after righteousness under law, and from which escape is possible only through the law of the Spirit of life in Christ Jesus, freeing one from that other law which, though it can command the good, can not achieve it.

Ἵνα . . . ποιῆτε as a pure final clause is to be understood not as expressing the purpose of God, this conflict being represented as a thing desired by him (for neither is the subject of the sentence a word referring to God, nor is the thought thus yielded a Pauline thought), nor of the flesh alone, nor of the Spirit alone, but as the purpose of both flesh and Spirit, in the sense that the flesh opposes the Spirit that men may not do what they will in accordance with the mind of the Spirit, and the Spirit opposes the flesh that they may not do what they will after the flesh. Does the man choose evil, the Spirit opposes him; does he choose good, the flesh hinders him.

18. εἰ δὲ πνεύματι ἄγεσθε, οὐκ ἐστὲ ὑπὸ νόμον. "But if ye are led by the Spirit, ye are not under law." In this sentence the apostle harks back for a moment to the point of view of the first part of the chapter, vv.¹⁻⁶, complementing the statement of v.¹⁶, that to walk by the Spirit does not involve subjection to the flesh, by the assertion that to be led by the Spirit is not to be under law. Clearly, therefore, life by the Spirit constitutes for the apostle a third way of life distinct both on the one hand from legalism and on the other from that which is characterised by a yielding to the impulses of the flesh. It is by no means a middle course between them, but a highway above them both, a life of freedom from statutes, of faith and love. The introduction of the statement at this point may be due to a desire, even in the midst of the warning against the danger of converting freedom into an occasion to the flesh, to guard his readers against supposing that he is now really retracting what he has said before, and turning them back to legalism disguised as a life under the leading of the Spirit. This was an entirely possible danger for those to whose thought there were only the two possibilities, restraint by law or no restraint. Or perceiving that what he had said in v.¹⁷ about the contrariety of the

Spirit and the flesh and the struggle in which those find themselves in whom both Spirit and flesh are still working, might
seem to justify a doubt whether to walk by the Spirit after all
assures one the victory over the flesh, and having in mind that
it is in the case of those who are under law that the conflict is
thus indecisive, he answers the doubt by saying, "But this does
not apply to you who walk by the Spirit; for if ye are led by
the Spirit ye are not under law." There seems no decisive
ground of choice between these two explanations of the occasion of the sentence; its meaning remains the same in either
case. πνεύματι is here, as in v.¹⁶, the Holy Spirit, qualitatively spoken of. That the term is nevertheless distinctly individual is shown by the connection with the verb ἄγεσθε,
which, though practically synonymous with the περιπατεῖτε
of v.¹⁶, emphasises the voluntary subjection of the will to the
Spirit, as περιπατεῖτε on the other hand makes prominent the
conformity of conduct to the guidance of the Spirit, and ζῶμεν
in v.²⁵ the intimate and vital nature of the relation of the Christian to the Spirit. Cf. Rom. 8¹⁴: ὅσοι γὰρ πνεύματι θεοῦ
ἄγονται, οὗτοι υἱοὶ θεοῦ εἰσίν. The conditional clause expressing a present particular supposition conveys a suggestion,
as in περιπατεῖτε, of continuance of action in progress, "If ye
are continuing to be led by the Spirit." ὑπὸ νόμον is undoubtedly to be taken, as elsewhere in the epistle (cf. 3²³ 4⁴, ⁵, ²¹), as
referring to that legalistic system from which it is the apostle's
aim to keep his readers free. To understand the word in the
ethical sense in which it is used in v.¹⁴ would immediately bring
the statement into conflict with the plain implication of vv.¹³, ¹⁴.
Any other sense than one of these two is wholly foreign to the
context.

19. φανερὰ δέ ἐστιν τὰ ἔργα τῆς σαρκός, "Now the works
of the flesh are manifest." Having in v.¹⁷ affirmed the mutual
antipathy of Spirit and flesh, the apostle now reverts to that
statement (δέ is resumptive), and explicates it by enumerating
the respective manifestations of the two, doubtless having in
mind, as he writes this sentence, the content not only of vv.²⁰, ²¹,
but also of vv.²², ²³. The purpose of both enumerations is, of

course, the same as that of the whole paragraph from vv. ¹⁴⁻²⁶,
viz., to enforce the exhortation of v.¹³ᵇ, not to convert their liberty into an occasion to the flesh, but to rule their lives by love,
which is itself to be achieved by living by the Spirit. This the
repellent catalogue of vices is well calculated to do.

Φανερός (cf. 1 Cor. 3¹³ 14²⁵, etc.) signifies "open, evident," so that any
one may see, hence, "well-known." The appeal is to common knowledge. ἔργα is probably to be taken in the active sense, deeds, rather
than in the passive, products; for though the latter sense is occasionally
found, 1 Cor. 3¹⁴, ¹⁵ (sing.), Acts 7⁴¹ (plur.), yet Paul always uses ἔργα
(plur.) in the active sense. The term as here used may be associated in
his mind with the ἔργα νόμου so often spoken of in the epistle. For that
he regarded life under law as tending to produce sinful deeds is clear
from Rom. 6¹⁴ 7⁷⁻²⁵. Yet τὰ ἔργα τῆς σαρκός is not here equivalent to
ἔργα νόμου; for by the latter phrase he designates not such evil deeds
of sensuality, violence, etc., as are here enumerated, but the deeds of
obedience to statutes which fall short of righteousness because they
lack the inner spirit of faith and love. πορνεία, etc., could not be
called ἔργα νόμου in Paul's sense of this term.

ἅτινά ἐστιν πορνεία, ἀκαθαρσία, ἀσέλγεια, 20. εἰδωλολατρία, φαρμακία, ἔχθραι, ἔρις, ζῆλος, θυμοί, ἐριθίαι, διχοστασίαι, αἱρέσεις, 21. φθόνοι, μέθαι, κῶμοι, καὶ τὰ ὅμοια τούτοις,
which are fornication, uncleanness, wantonness; idolatry,
witchcraft; enmities, strife, jealousy, angers, self-seekings, parties, divisions, envyings; drunkenness, carousings, and the
things like these." The words in this list of vices fall into
four groups, indicated by the punctuation of the translation.
The first group includes three sins in which sensuality in the
narrower sense is prominent; the second includes two that are
associated with heathen religions, the third group contains eight
in which the element of conflict with others is present; the
fourth consists of drunkenness and its natural accompaniments.

After ἔχθραι, some authorities (CKL. al pler.) maintain the plural
to the end of the list, reading ἔρεις and ζῆλοι, and after φθόνοι add
φόνοι. This text Sd. adopts. The text above is that of אB, supported by other pre-Syrian authorities (varying somewhat in the case
of each word), and is clearly the original.

On ἅτινα, see note on 4²⁴, p. 257. ἅτινά ἐστιν may mean "of which
class are" (so Ell. and substantially Ltft.), but the evidence is by no

means decisive for this meaning in general, and in this passage it is the less probable because the idea "with others of the same class" supposed to be conveyed by the compound form is expressed in the words καὶ τὰ ὅμοια τούτοις in v.²¹.

Πορνεία, rarely used in the classics (the lexicons give exx. from Dem. only) but frequent in the Lxx and in N. T., probably signified originally "prostitution" (cf. πόρνη, "a prostitute," probably related to πέρνημι, "to sell [slaves]," prostitutes being commonly bought slaves), but in biblical writings, (1) "unlawful sexual intercourse" (πόρνος in the classics usually meant one guilty of unnatural vice) whether involving violation of marriage or not: Gen. 38²⁴ Hos. 1² Mt. 5³² Acts 15²⁰, ²⁹, etc., and (2) tropically, "the worshipping of other gods than Jehovah": Hos. 5⁴ Isa. 57⁹ Ezek. 16¹⁵ Jn. 8⁴¹ (?) Rev. 2²¹ 9²¹, etc. Here evidently, in the literal sense, "fornication." On the prevalence of this vice among Gentiles, and the tendency even in the Christian church to regard it as innocent, see 1 Cor. 5⁹, ¹⁰ 6¹²ff·, and commentaries on the latter passage, esp. Mey.; 1 Thes. 4³ff·.

Ἀκαθαρσία, employed in Hippocrates and Plato of the uncleanness of a sore or wound, and in Demosthenes of moral depravity, is used in the Lxx either of ceremonial impurity, Lev. 5³ et freq. (so in 2 Chron. 29⁵, ¹⁶, or perhaps in the more literal sense, "dirt"), as in Pap. Oxyr. VIII 1128²⁵, or of "moral impurity," "wickedness," with no special emphasis on sexual vice: Prov. 6¹⁶ (Lxx); 1 Esdr. 1⁴² Ezek. 9⁹, etc. In N. T. once only of physical filth, or of that which is ceremonially defiling, Mt. 23²⁷ (yet even here as a figure for wickedness); elsewhere of moral impurity. The latter instances are all in Paul (Rom. 1²⁴ 6¹⁹, etc.) and seven out of the nine stand in association with πορνεία or other word denoting sexual vice. It is probable, therefore, that in the present instance also the apostle has in mind especially sins of the flesh in the narrower sense, ἀκαθαρσία being a somewhat broader term even than πορνεία. Cf. Eph. 5³, πορνεία δὲ καὶ ἀκαθαρσία πᾶσα.

Ἀσέλγεια, of doubtful etymology, is used by Greek authors with the meaning "wantonness," "violence"; so in Plato, Isæus, Demosthenes, Aristotle. In Polyb. 37. 2⁴ the addition of the words περὶ τὰς σωματικὰς ἐπιθυμίας makes it refer especially to lewdness, yet ἀσέλγεια itself means simply "wantonness." It is not found in the Lxx (canonical books), and in the Apocr. only in Wisd. 14²⁶ and 3 Mac. 2²⁶, in the former passage with probable reference to sensuality, lewdness; in the latter without indication of such limitation. In N. T. it occurs in Mk. 7²² without restriction to sensual sin, in 1 Pet. 4³ 2 Pet. 2², ⁷, ¹⁸, without decisive indication of this limitation. Cf. Trench, Synom. § XVI, who gives further evidence that ἀσέλγεια is not exclusively "lasciviousness," but "wantonness," "unrestrained wilfulness." Yet in view of Paul's association of it elsewhere with words denoting sensuality (Rom. 13¹³ 2 Cor. 12²¹ Eph. 4¹⁹) and its grouping here with πορνεία and ἀκαθαρσία, it is probable that it refers here especially to wantonness in sexual relations. Like ἀκαθαρσία, less specific than πορνεία, and referring to any indecent conduct, whether involving violation of the person or not, ἀσέλγεια differs from ἀκαθαρσία in that the latter emphasises the grossness, the impurity of the conduct, the former its wantonness, its unrestrainedness. Lightfoot's distinction: "A man may be ἀκάθαρτος and hide his sin; he does not become ἀσελγής until he shocks public decency" seems scarcely sustained by the usage of the words. ἀσέλγεια is, indeed, unrestrained, but not necessarily public, and ἀκαθαρσία carries no more suggestion of secrecy than ἀσέλγεια. Cf. Eph. 4¹⁹.

Εἰδωλολατρία, not found in classic writers or in the Lxx, occurs in N. T. (1 Cor. 10¹⁴ Col. 3⁵ 1 Pet. 4³) and thereafter in ecclesiastical writers. Greek writers did not use εἴδωλον with specific reference to the gods of the Gentiles or their images, and the term εἰδωλολατρία apparently arose on Jewish soil. εἴδωλον, signifying in the Lxx and N. T. either the image of the god (Acts 7⁴¹ Rev. 9²⁰) or the god represented by the image (1 Cor. 8⁴, ⁷ 10¹⁹), εἰδωλολατρία doubtless shared its ambiguity, denoting worship of the image or of the god represented by it.

Φαρμακία [or -εία], a classical word occurring from Plato down, is derived from φάρμακον, which from Homer down denotes a drug, whether harmful or wholesome. φαρμακία signifies in general the use of drugs, whether helpfully by a physician, or harmfully, hence poisoning. In Demosthenes, Aristotle, Polybius, and the Lxx it is used of witchcraft (because witches employed drugs). In Isa. 47⁹ it is a synonym of ἐπαοιδή, enchantment (cf. also Philo, Migr. Abr. 83, 85 (15); 1 Enoch, chap. VIII, Syn.). In the Lxx the word is uniformly employed in a bad sense, of witchcrafts or enchantments: of the Egyptians (Exod. 7¹¹, ²²), of the Canaanites (Wisd. 12⁴), of Babylon (Isa. 47⁹, ¹²). So also in N. T. passages, Rev. 9²¹ (WH. text φαρμακῶν, mg. φαρμακιῶν, as also Tdf.); 18²³ (the latter referring, like Isa. 47⁹, ¹², to Babylon), and in the present passage, the reference is to witchcraft, sorcery, magic art of any kind, without special reference to the use of drugs. The meaning "poisoning" (Demosthenes, Polybius) is excluded here by the combined evidence of contemporary usage and the association with εἰδωλολατρία. On the prevalence of witchcraft and its various forms, see Acts 8⁹ff. 13⁸ff. 19¹³ff. 2 Tim. 3¹³; Ltft. ad loc.; Bible Dictionaries, under "Magic," and literature cited there and in Ltft.

Ἔχθραι, a classical word, from Pindar down, occurs frequently in the Lxx and N. T. Standing at the beginning of the third group it gives the key-note of that group. It is the opposite of ἀγάπη, denoting "enmity," "hostility," in whatever form manifested.

Ἔρις, a classical word, of frequent occurrence from Homer down; in Homer of "contention," "rivalry," "strife for prizes," also "fighting," "strife"; after Homer "strife," "discord," "quarrel," "wrangling," "contention." It occurs in Ps. 139²⁰ (B); Sir. 28¹¹ 40⁵· ⁹, in the latter two passages in an enumeration of the common ills of life. The nine N. T. instances are all found in the epistles ascribed to Paul.

Ζῆλος occurs in classical writers from Hesiod down; by Plato and Aristotle it is classed as a noble passion, "emulation," as opposed to φθόνος, "envy"; but in Hesiod is already used as equivalent to φθόνος. In the Lxx used for קִנְאָה, but with considerable variety of meaning. The common element in all the uses of the word is its expression of an intense feeling, usually eager desire of some kind. In the Lxx and N. T. three meanings may be recognised: (1) "intense devotion to, zeal for, persons or things" (Ps. 69¹⁰, quoted in Jn. 2¹⁷, 1 Mac. 2⁵⁸ Rom. 10² 2 Cor. 7⁷ Phil. 3⁶); (2) "anger," perhaps always with the thought that it arises out of devotion to another person or thing (Num. 25¹¹ᵇ Ezek. 23²⁵ Acts 5¹⁷ 13⁴⁵ Heb. 10²⁷, the last a quotation from the Lxx); (3) "jealousy," the unfriendly feeling excited by another's possession of good, or "envy," the eager desire for possession created by the spectacle of another's possession (Cant. 8⁶ Eccl. 4⁴ 9⁶ Rom. 13¹³ 1 Cor. 3³ Jas. 3¹⁴· ¹⁶). In the present passage it is clearly used in the last-named sense.

Θυμός, a classical word in frequent use from Homer down, signifying "breath," "soul," "spirit," "heart" (as the seat of emotion, both the gentler and the more turbulent, and as the seat of thought), "temper," "courage," "anger." It occurs very frequently in the Lxx, translating various Hebrew words, and in the Apocr. (over three hundred times in all). Its meanings are (1) "disposition" (Wisd. 7²⁰); (2) "courage" (2 Mac. 7²¹); but in the great majority of cases both in Lxx and Apocr. (3) "anger," occasionally in the expressions ἡ ὀργὴ τοῦ θυμοῦ and ὁ θυμὸς τῆς ὀργῆς; it is ascribed both to God and to men.* In N. T. the Apocalypse uses it (a) in the meaning "wrath"; with reference to the wrath of God in 14¹⁰· ¹⁹ 15¹· ⁷ 16¹· ¹⁹ 19¹⁵ (in 16¹⁹ and 19¹⁵ in the phrase ὁ θυμὸς τῆς ὀργῆς); of the rage of Satan in 12¹², and (b) with the meaning, "ardour," "passion," in the expression ὁ θυμὸς τῆς πορνείας αὐτῆς in 14⁸ 18³. Elsewhere in N. T. it means "anger": of men in Lk. 4²⁸ Acts 19²⁸ 2 Cor. 12²⁰ Gal. 5²⁰ Eph. 4³¹ Col. 3⁸ Heb. 11²⁷; of God in Rom. 2⁸ only. As compared with ὀργή, θυμός denotes an outburst of passion, ὀργή a more settled indignation; in accordance with which distinction θυμός tends to be used of the reprehensible anger of men, ὀργή of the righteous wrath of God. Yet the

---

* The apparent Lxx use of θυμός in the sense of poison (Deut. 32²⁴· ³³ Ps. 57 (58)⁴ Job 20¹⁴ Am. 6¹²) almost certainly arises from infelicitous translation of the Hebrew rather than from a usage of the Greek word in that sense.

distinction is not steadfastly maintained, as appears from the facts above stated, and especially from the occurrence of the expressions θυμὸς ὀργῆς and ὀργὴ θυμοῦ. The meaning of the word in the present passage is its most common one in biblical writers, "anger," "passionate outburst of hostile feeling."

Ἐριθία (of uncertain etymology, but having no relation to ἔρις and doubtful relation to ἔριον, wool) is cognate with ἔριθος, "a day-labourer," "a wage-earner" (from Homer down), specifically ἡ ἔριθος, "a woman weaver," Dem. 1313⁶; in this sense in the only Lxx instance, Isa. 38¹². ἐριθία first appears in Aristotle, when it means "canvassing for office" (*Pol.* 5. 2⁹ [1303 b¹⁴]) but by Hesychius and Suidas is defined as "working for hire." In Polyb. 10. 25⁹ the verb ἐριθεύομαι, used also by Aristotle in the passage just quoted, means "to seek the political co-operation of," "to inveigle into one's party," but in Tob. 2¹¹ still means "to labour for wages," or more probably "to spin." In Philo, II 555 (Mangey) ἀνερίθευτος is used in connection with ἀφιλόνεικος (ἡγεμονία δ' ἀφιλόνεικος καὶ ἀνερίθευτος ὀρθὴ μόνη), apparently meaning "without self-seeking." It is thus evident that though the extant examples of the noun are relatively few (more in N. T. than in all previous literature so far as noted), yet the word had a long history and probably bore side by side both its original meaning, "working for wages," and its derived sense, referring to office-seeking. The paucity of other examples gives to the N. T. instances a special value for lexicography. When these are examined it appears that in none of them is either the literal sense or precisely the Aristotelian sense of office-seeking possible. It remains, therefore, to seek a meaning cognate with the meanings elsewhere vouched for and consonant with the context of the N. T. passages. Examination of the passages from this point of view suggests two meanings: (1) "self-seeking," "selfishness." (2) "factiousness," "party spirit." The former of these is easily derivable from the original sense, "working for wages," and is appropriate to the context of all the examples (Rom. 2⁸ 2 Cor. 12²⁰ Phil. 1¹⁷ 2³ Jas. 3¹⁴, ¹⁶ *et h.l.*). The second is cognate with the Aristotelian sense, "office-seeking," and is appropriate to some of the passages (2 Cor. 12²⁰ Phil. 1¹⁷ 2³ *et h.l.*), less so to the other passages, and distinctly inappropriate to Rom. 2⁸. Respecting this last-named passage it should be observed (a) that there is nothing in the context to suggest the meaning "party spirit"; (b) that the term denotes what is for the apostle the very root-vice of all sin; it is certainly more probable that he found this in selfishness, the antithesis of the all-inclusive virtue, love, than in so specialised a form of selfishness as party spirit; (c) that the expression τοῖς δὲ ἐξ ἐριθίας ἀπειθοῦσι τῇ ἀληθείᾳ in effect repeats the idea of τῶν τὴν ἀλήθειαν ἐν ἀδικίᾳ κατεχόντων (Rom. 1¹⁸), and that this phrase neither in itself, nor by its further explication in the context, refers specifically to party spirit, but does by its contextual definition refer to the self-willed, self-seeking spirit. We seem, therefore, justified in deciding that ἐριθία in N. T. means "self-seeking," "selfish devotion to one's own interest"; that this is a possible meaning for all the instances; but that "party spirit" is in some passages a possible alternative. In the present passage the use of the plural might seem to favour the second meaning, or, rather, the corresponding concrete sense, factions. But there is no evidence to show that the word had such a concrete sense, and both the meaning of the word ἔργα (v.¹⁹) and the use of other abstract terms in this passage in the plural (to designate various instances or manifestations of the kind of conduct expressed by the noun) deprive this argument of any force. The position of ἐριθίαι between θυμοί and διχοστασίαι is consistent with either meaning; if ἐριθίαι means self-seekings, this is naturally followed by terms denoting those things to which such self-seekings lead, διχοστασίαι and αἱρέσεις; if it means efforts to advance one's party, actions inspired by party-spirit, it stands as the first in a group of three nearly synonymous terms. On the whole the preponderance is slightly, though only slightly, in favour of that meaning which is for the N. T. as a whole best established, "self-seeking," "selfishness."

Διχοστασία, a classical word, used by Herodotus and Solon in the sense of "dissension," by Theognis, meaning "sedition," is not found in the Lxx; occurs in Apocr. in 1 Mac. 3²⁹ only, with the meaning "dissension"; is found in N. T. here and Rom. 16¹⁷ only, in both cases in the plural and without doubt meaning "dissensions."

Αἵρεσις, in classical writers, has two general meanings, one associated with the active meaning of the cognate verb, αἱρέω, hence "a taking," "capture" (Hdt.), the other with the meaning of the middle, αἱρέομαι, hence "choice," "plan," "purpose," "preference" (Pind. Æsch. Hdt. etc.). So in the Lxx, meaning "free will," "choice." In late Greek, after Plato and Aristotle, there arises the meaning "philosophic tendency," "school," "party." So in Dion. Hal., Sext. Emp., but also in Jos. *Bell.* 2¹³⁷ (8⁷), τοῖς δὲ ζηλοῦσιν τὴν αἵρεσιν αὐτῶν (the Essenes). In Arrian's report of the teachings of Epictetus αἵρεσις and προαίρεσις are used of the soul, doubtless as that in which the power of choice lies. *Cf.* M. and M. *Voc. s. v.* In N. T. it is always associated in meaning with the middle of the verb, and usually signifies a body of people holding a chosen set of opinions; thus without reproach, of the Sadducees, Acts 5¹⁷; of the Pharisees, Acts 15⁵ 26⁵; of the Christians, spoken of as Nazarenes, Acts 24⁵. As a term of reproach, denoting a group or sect reprehensibly departing from the general body, it occurs in Acts 24¹⁴. In 1 Cor. 11¹⁹ and 2 Pet. 2¹ it seems to signify, rather, "difference of opinion," "division of sentiment," than concretely "party," "sect." The abstract meaning is also (cf. above on ἐριθίαι) more appropriate to the present passage. The meaning "heresy," a doctrine at variance with that of the general body, is not found in N. T. or in Patr. Ap. (see Ign. Trall. 6¹; Eph. 6²; cf. Zahn on the former passage) unless possibly in Herm. Sim. 9. 23⁵ and probably not here. Cf. also Kühl on 2 Pet. 2¹ in Meyer-Weiss.⁶ In Just. Mart. Apol. 26⁸; Dial. 35²; Iren. Haer. 1. 11¹, it is probably still used in the sense of "sect," or "division," as a term of reproach. It clearly means "heresy" in Mart. Pol. Epil. 1 (Ltft. 2), which is, however, of considerably later date.

Φθόνος, a classical word from Pindar and Herodotus down, means "ill-will," "malice," "envy" (cf. under ζῆλος above); not in Lxx; in Apocr., Wisd. 2²⁴ 6²³ 1 Mac. 8¹⁶ 3 Mac. 6⁷; always in a bad sense, "envy." So also in N. T. (Mt. 27¹⁸ Mk. 15¹⁰ Rom. 1²⁹, etc.) except in Jas. 4⁵, where it is used tropically, meaning "eager desire for (exclusive) possession of," and is ascribed to the Spirit of God. In the present passage it can not be sharply distinguished from ζῆλος. If the words are to be discriminated, ζῆλος would signify "jealousy," φθόνοι "envyings." The plural denotes different acts, or specific forms of envious desire.

Μέθαι and κῶμοι fall in a class by themselves. μέθη occurs in classic writers from Herodotus and Antipho down, meaning, (1) "strong drink," (2) "drunkenness," and with the same meanings in the Lxx (in Hag. 1⁶ apparently meaning "satiety" rather than "drunkenness"). In the Apocr. and N. T. it occurs in the second sense only. κῶμος (of doubtful etymology) occurs in classic writers from Homer down, meaning "revelling," "carousing," such as accompanies drinking and festal processions in honour of the gods, especially Bacchus; it is not found in the Lxx; occurs in the Apocr. in Wisd. 14²³ 2 Mac. 6⁴, and in N. T. in the same sense as in classical writers; in Rom. 13¹³ it is associated as here with μέθη, in 1 Pet. 4³, with οἰνοφλυγία, "drunkenness."

For a similar catalogue of vices, see Corpus Hermeticum XIII (XIV) 7, in Reitzenstein, Poimandres, p. 342; Mead, Thrice Greatest Hermes, Vol. II, p. 224. For a discussion of Gentile morals, see L. Friedländer, Darstellungen aus der Sittengeschichte Roms, 8th ed., 4 vols., Leipzig, 1910; E. T. from 7th ed., New York, 1909, 1910; de Pressensé, The Ancient World and Christianity, Bk. V, Chap. II, § II, pp. 424–432; Döllinger, The Gentile and the Jew, London, 1862. For the same kind of material in the form of a connected story, see Becker, Gallus; Walter Pater, Marius the Epicurean; Böttiger, Sabina. References to Gentile authors are to be found in de Pressensé and Becker, and with especial copiousness in Friedländer's great work.

ἃ προλέγω ὑμῖν καθὼς προεῖπον ὅτι οἱ τὰ τοιαῦτα πράσσοντες βασιλείαν θεοῦ οὐ κληρονομήσουσιν. "respecting

which I tell you beforehand, as I have (already) told you in
advance, that they who do such things will not inherit the
kingdom of God." To the list of the works of the flesh, calculated by their very quality to deter the Galatians from following its impulses, Paul adds the weighty statement which he
had already made to them on some previous occasion that such
things exclude one from participation in the kingdom of God.
By βασιλείαν θεοῦ the apostle doubtless means the reign of God
which is to be inaugurated on the return of Christ from the
heavens and the resurrection of the dead. *Cf.* i Cor. 15$^{50, 52}$
with i Thes. 1^{10} 4$^{16, 17}$. The phrase used without the article
with either noun is qualitative and emphasises the ethical
quality of the order of things for which the phrase stands and
the incongruity between it and οἱ τὰ τοιαῦτα πράσσοντες; thus
suggesting the reason for their exclusion. *Cf.* i Cor. 6$^{9, 10}$ 15^{50},
in all of which the phrase is as here anarthrous. This qualitative force can be imperfectly reproduced in English by the
translation, "shall not inherit a kingdom of God," but at the
cost of obscuring the definite reference of the expression.

καθώς (without καί) is the reading of ℵ*BFG f Vulg. (am. fu.
demid al.) Syr. (psh.) Eth. Goth. Tert. Cyp. Aug. al. καί is added by
ℵ^{c}ACDKLP al. omn. $^{vid.}$ d e g tol. Syr. (harcl.) Boh. Arm. Mcion.
Clem. Chr. Euthal. Thdrt. Dam. Ir$^{int.}$ Hier. Ambrst. Both readings are pre-Syrian but καί on the whole seems to be a Western corruption adopted by the Syrian text, occasioned by the natural impulse to
emphasise the comparison between προλέγω and προεῖπον. *Cf.* i Thes.
4^6.

"Α is doubtless accusative as ὅν clearly is in Jn. 8^{54}, ὅν ὑμεῖς λέγετε
ὅτι θεὸς ὑμῶν ἐστίν, but in precisely what relation Paul meant to set
it, when he wrote it, it is impossible to say, for the reason that after
καθὼς προεῖπον he has reproduced the thought of ἅ in τὰ τοιαῦτα and
given it a new construction. *Cf.* Ell. *ad loc.*

Προλέγω might consistently with the usual force of προ in composition and the classical usage of this word mean either "foretell" or
"forth tell," "tell publicly." But the fact that in all the instances in
which Paul uses it (2 Cor. 13^2 i Thes. 3^4 and here, the only N. T. instances) the object of the verb is, in fact, a prediction, and the inappropriateness of the meaning "tell publicly" (for the meaning "tell plainly"
there seems no evidence) make it quite certain that its meaning here
is "to predict."

Οἱ πράσσοντες is a general present participle with the article, meaning "those that are wont to practise."

Τὰ τοιαῦτα means either "the things previously mentioned being of such quality as they are," or "the class of things to which those named belong." *Cf.* 1 Cor. 5⁵ Rom. 1³² 2². ³ Eph. 5²⁷, and for τοιαῦτα without the article, meaning "things like those spoken of," Mk. 7¹³ Jn. 9¹⁶ Heb. 8¹. See Kühner-Gerth 465. 5; Butt. 124. 5; Bl.-D. 274.

The considerations that necessitate taking the phrase βασιλείαν θεοῦ here in its eschatological sense are the following: (1) The apostle undoubtedly looked for a personal visible return of Christ from the heavens and expected the resurrection of the righteous dead in connection therewith. 1 Thes. 1¹⁰ 4¹⁵⁻¹⁷. (2) In 1 Cor. 15⁵⁰ he speaks of inheriting the kingdom of God in connection with the resurrection of men, and in such way as to show clearly that the inheritance of the kingdom, as thought of in that passage at least, is achieved through the resurrection. It is natural to suppose that the expression has the same meaning in the other passages in the same epistle (6⁹. ¹⁰), there being nothing in the context to oppose this meaning. In 1 Thes. 2¹² the eschatological significance is most probably though not quite certainly present. There are, indeed, a number of passages in Paul in which the kingdom of God is spoken of with so distinct emphasis on its ethical quality and with such absence of eschatological suggestion that it must be questioned whether he uniformly gave to the phrase eschatological significance. See Rom. 14¹⁷ 1 Cor. 4²⁰. It is probable, therefore, that the apostle thought of the kingdom of God both as present and as future, in the latter case to be inaugurated at the return of Christ. But the considerations named above are sufficient to show clearly that it is the future kingdom that is here in mind, while it is also clear that he intended to emphasise the ethical quality of the kingdom, which is, of course, essentially the same whether present or future.

22. ὁ δὲ καρπὸς τοῦ πνεύματός ἐστιν ἀγάπη, χαρά, εἰρήνη, μακροθυμία, χρηστότης, ἀγαθωσύνη, πίστις, **23.** πραΰτης, ἐγκράτεια· "But the fruit of the Spirit is love, joy, peace, long-suffering, kindness, goodness, faithfulness, gentleness, self-control." This sentence continues the argument for the mutual contrariety of flesh and Spirit begun in v.¹⁹. By the attractiveness of the members of the series beginning with ἀγάπη, Paul appeals to the Galatians to follow the leading of the Spirit, as by the repulsiveness of the vices named in vv. ¹⁹⁻²¹ he had sought to deter them from yielding to the impulses of the flesh.

δέ is slightly adversative, introducing the fruit of the Spirit in antithesis to the works of the flesh. καρπός, used in 1 Cor. 9⁷ in its literal sense (as also 2 Tim. 2⁶), is elsewhere in the letters of Paul employed in a figurative sense only (Rom. 1¹³ Phil. 1¹¹ 4¹⁷, etc.). The choice of the word here in preference to ἔργα (v.¹⁹) is perhaps partly due to the association of the word ἔργα with the phrase ἔργα νόμου (see ἔργα alone used in this sense, Rom. 3²⁷ 4² 9¹¹ 11⁶), partly to his preference for a term which suggests that love, joy, peace, etc., are the natural product of a vital relation between the Christian and the Spirit. Observe the word ζῶμεν in v.²⁵ and cf. 2²⁰. The use of the singular serves to present all the experiences and elements of character in the ensuing list as a unity, together constituting the result of living by the Spirit. Yet too much stress can not be laid on the singular, since Paul always used it when employing the word in its figurative sense.

On the importance of the distinction in the apostle's mind between ὁ καρπὸς τοῦ πνεύματος, and τὰ χαρίσματα (τοῦ πνεύματος) or ἡ φανέρωσις τοῦ πνεύματος, see detached note on Πνεῦμα and Σάρξ, p. 489, and Gunkel, Die Wirkungen des heiligen Geistes, pp. 62–97, esp. 77 ff. The two lists, the present one and that of 1 Cor. 12⁸⁻¹¹, contain but one common term, πίστις, and this is undoubtedly used in a different sense in the two passages. Under the terms χαρίσματα πνευματικά and φανέρωσις τοῦ πνεύματος the apostle includes those extraordinary experiences and powers which were not necessarily evidential of moral character in those in whom they appeared, but because of their extraordinary character and of their association with the acceptance of the gospel message, the word of God (1 Thes. 2¹³), were regarded as effects and evidences of the presence and activity of the Spirit of God. These are all external and easily recognisable; note the term φανέρωσις in 1 Cor. 12⁷. Under the term ὁ καρπὸς τοῦ πνεύματος, on the other hand, are included those ethical qualities and spiritual experiences which were not popularly thought of as evidences of the Spirit's presence, but which, to the mind of Paul, were of far greater value than the so-called χαρίσματα. See 1 Cor.,

chaps. 12–14, esp. 12³¹, chap. 13, and 14¹.   Thus while retaining
the evidently current view, which found in the gift of tongues
and prophecy and power to heal disease evidence of the Spirit's
presence (see also Gal. 3⁵), he transferred the emphasis of his
thought, and sought to transfer that of his disciples, from these
things to the internal and ethical qualities which issue in and
control conduct.

Whether the terms listed in vv.²², ²³ fell in the apostle's mind into
definite classes is not altogether clear.   ἀγάπη, evidently meaning love
towards other men (cf. vv.¹³, ¹⁴), stands in a sense in a class by itself,
and is probably thought of as the source from which all the rest flow.
Cf. v.¹⁴ and 1 Cor., chap. 13, and note the parallelism of 1 Cor. 13⁴⁻⁸
with the list here, especially μακροθυμία with μακροθυμεῖ (v.⁴), χρηστότης with χρηστεύεται (v.⁴), πίστις with πάντα πιστεύει, πάντα ἐλπίζει,
πάντα ὑπομένει (v.⁷); πραΰτης with οὐ φυσιοῦται, οὐκ ἀσχημονεῖ (v.⁵).
Of the two terms χαρά and εἰρήνη, the first certainly, and the second
probably, refers to experiences enjoyed rather than to transitive attitudes towards others; the remaining terms, except the last, have
special reference to the relations of those who walk by the Spirit to
others, in a measure antithetical to ἔχθραι . . . θυμοί in the list of
works of the flesh; ἐγκράτεια, though belonging also in this list, seems
to stand in special antithesis to the last two terms of the preceding
list, μέθαι, κῶμοι.

Ἀγάπη, though in itself capable of denoting the adoration of and
devotion to God, is probably to be taken here in accordance with the
suggestion of v.¹⁴, and Paul's general usage (2 Thes. 3⁵ is the only
clear instance of ἀγάπη in the Pauline letters used of the love of men
towards God), as referring to that love of man for man, which resting
upon appreciation of value is chiefly characterised by desire to benefit.
See detached note on Ἀγαπάω and Ἀγάπη, p. 519.

Χαρά, in use by classical writers from Homer down, and about fifty
times in the Lxx and Apocr., is employed in the Lxx, Apocr. and
N. T. rarely of a fierce and cruel joy (3 Mac. 4¹⁶ 5²¹ 6³⁴; cf. also Jas. 4⁹),
but most frequently of joy that has a religious basis, grounded in conscious relationship to God (Ps. 30¹¹ Prov. 29⁶ Sir. 1¹² Rom. 14¹⁷ 15¹³
Phil. 1⁴, ²⁵, etc.).

On εἰρήνη, see detached note, p. 424.   Its meaning here is probably
the same as in Rom. 5¹, "tranquillity of mind" (based on the consciousness of right relation to God).   For though the idea of harmony with
God is possible here, it is an unusual meaning in Paul, and there is
nothing specially to suggest it here; the idea of spiritual well-being is
not in itself inappropriate, yet it is unlikely that the apostle would

use the word in so general a sense, standing as it does here between the more specific terms, χαρά and μακροθυμία; the meaning, "peace with men," is appropriate in connection with either χαρά (cf. Rom. 14¹⁷⋅ ¹⁹) or with μακροθυμία, but is open to the objection that, εἰρήνη in that case expressing a relation to men, as do also ἀγάπη and μακροθυμία, χαρά stands quite alone, the only non-transitive word in the group. On εἰρήνη denoting tranquillity of mind, and associated with χαρά, cf. Rom. 15¹³: ὁ δὲ θεὸς τῆς ἐλπίδος πληρῶσαι ὑμᾶς πάσης χαρᾶς καὶ εἰρήνης ἐν τῷ πιστεύειν. On peace as produced by the Spirit, cf. Rom. 1⁶, τὸ γὰρ φρόνημα τοῦ πνεύματος ζωὴ καὶ εἰρήνη, though εἰρήνη perhaps has here the more general sense of "spiritual well-being"; and Rom. 5¹⁻⁵, where hope of the glory of God, the sequel and accompaniment of peace in the sense of tranquil assurance, is the result of the love of God shed abroad in the heart by the Spirit of God.

Μακροθυμία, found first in Menander, fourth century B. C., occurs rarely in non-biblical writers, and but five times in the LXX and Apocr. It has always the same general meaning, that which its etymology suggests, viz., "steadfastness of soul under provocation to change," the specific meaning differing according as that which is endured is thought of impersonally, and the word signifies simply "endurance," "steadfastness," or personally, so that μακροθυμία includes forbearance, endurance of wrong or exasperating conduct without anger or taking vengeance. Hence (a) "patience," "persistence," "steadfastness." So in Plut. Lucull. 32⁴ 33¹; Isa. 57¹⁵ 1 Mac. 8⁴ Col. 1¹¹ 2 Tim. 3¹⁰ Heb. 6¹² Jas. 5¹⁰; (b) "forbearance," endurance of wrong without anger or avenging one's self, "long-suffering" (i) of God and of Christ towards men: Rom. 2⁴ 9²² 1 Tim. 1¹⁶ 1 Pet. 3²⁰ 2 Pet. 3¹⁵; (ii) of men towards one another: Prov. 25¹⁵ Sir. 5¹¹ 2 Cor. 6⁶ Eph. 4² Col. 3¹² 2 Tim. 3¹⁰ 4². In the present passage the word is probably, in accordance with Paul's usual usage and the context, to be taken in the last-named sense, viz., forbearance towards men whose conduct is calculated to provoke to anger.

Χρηστότης, from Euripides down, signifies in classical writers, of things, "excellence," of persons, "goodness," "honesty," "kindness." In later Greek writers, especially in Plutarch, who uses it often, it occurs sometimes in the general sense, "goodness," "excellence" of character (Plut. Phil. et Tit. 3); but more frequently in the specific sense, "kindness" (Cat. Maj. 5³: τὴν χρηστότητα τῆς δικαιοσύνης πλατύτερον τόπον ὁρῶμεν ἐπιλαμβάνουσαν. It is joined with φιλοστοργία in Agis 17², with φιλανθρωπία in Demetr. 50¹; Dem. et Cic. 3²). In the LXX it translates טוב or other forms from this root, and is used meaning "goodness," Ps. 14¹⋅ ³; "prosperity," Ps. 106⁵; but most frequently "kindness," as in Ps. 21³ 68¹⁰. In the Ps. Sol. (5¹⁵⋅ ¹⁶⋅ ¹⁷⋅ ²¹ 8³⁴ 9¹⁵ 18²) it uniformly means "kindness"; so also in Patr. Ap. (Clem. Rom. 9¹;

2 Clem. 15⁵, etc.). This is also the constant meaning in N. T. (Rom. 2⁴ 11²², etc.), except in Rom. 3¹², a quotation from Ps. 14³.

'Αγαθωσύνη appears first in the Lxx (usually translating טובָה) and like χρηστότης signifying "goodness," "righteousness" (Ps. 38²⁰ 52³), "prosperity" (Eccl. 5¹⁰, ¹⁷, etc.) and "kindness" (Judg. 8³⁵ 9¹⁶ Neh. 9²⁵, ³⁵). It is not found in Ps. Sol., which use δικαιοσύνη for "righteousness," "good character," and χρηστότης, ἔλεος, and ἐλεημοσύνη for "kindness," "mercy." In N. T. it occurs in Paul's epistles only (Rom. 15¹⁴ Eph. 5⁹ 2 Thes. 1¹¹), always apparently in the general sense, "goodness." Ltft.'s distinction between χρηστότης and ἀγαθωσύνη, that the latter is more active, differing from the former somewhat as *beneficentia* from *benevolentia*, would naturally explain the occurrence of the word in this series and at this point, but is unsustained by any other evidence. It seems necessary to choose between taking it in the wholly general sense of "goodness," and making it entirely synonymous with χρηστότης, "kindness." The few other instances of the word in N. T. and the improbability that the apostle would exactly repeat in ἀγ. the idea already expressed in χρηστ., are in favour of the meaning "goodness," even though by this interpretation the word refers less distinctly to conduct towards others than either the preceding or following term.

Πίστις is evidently not employed here as in chap. 3 to denote that attitude towards truth which is the fundamental element of religion, whether of the O. T. or N. T. type, nor as in v.⁶ of this chapter, to signify the acceptance of the gospel message concerning Jesus and the committal of one's self to him for salvation. For faith as there used is the basal principle of the life of one who lives by the Spirit (*cf.* 2²⁰ 5⁶, and the discussion under 4⁶ of the relation between Christ and the Spirit as factors in Christian experience), while the faith that is here spoken of is a product of the Spirit of God in the soul. It is, therefore, either (a) "faithfulness," "fidelity," as in Mt. 23²³ Rom. 3³ Tit. 2¹⁰; or (b) "faith" in the specific form of belief in the power and willingness of God to work through men, as in Rom. 12³, ⁶ 1 Cor. 12⁹ 13². But since the other words in this group refer to matters of distinctly ethical and religious character, and there is nothing in this context to suggest a reference to that specific form of faith that enables one to work miracles (which, indeed, Paul classifies rather with the χαρίσματα than with those distinctly ethical qualities here spoken of), it is practically certain that πίστις here means "faithfulness," "fidelity," and especially in relation to one's fellow men. So Bengel (constantia, fidelitas), Ltft. Sief. Weizs. (Treue), Segond (fidélité). The suggestion of Alf. "faith towards God and man," and that of Ell., "trustfulness, faith in God's promises and mercies and loving trust towards men," find no support in the usage of the word. On the usage of πίστις in general, see detached note on Πίστις and Πιστεύω, p. 475.

Πραότης, of which πραΰτης is a later form of identical meaning, is used by Plato, Isocrates, and Aristotle, Polybius and Plutarch. It signifies in Greek writers, "mildness," "gentleness in dealing with others": Plato, *Rep.* 558A; *Symp.* 197D.; Aristot. *Rhet.* 2. 3¹ (1380 a⁶); Plut. *Frat. am.* 18; see more fully in Cremer, on πραΰς. Unlike ταπεινός, which was frequently if not usually a term of reproach, "mean," "abject," πρᾶος and πραότης were in Greek writers terms of commendation. In the Lxx πραΰς is usually a translation of עָנָו (only rarely of עָנִי), which signifies "one who is humble in disposition and character, one who is submissive under the divine will" rather than as the English translation "meek" might suggest, submitting without resistance to the wrongs of men. See BDB, *s. v.*; Driver, article "Poor" in H*DB*, Paterson, article "Poor" in *Encyc. Bib.*, and Gray, *Com. on Numbers*, at 12³. In a few passages the Lxx translate עָנִי by πραΰς and in one of these, Zech. 9⁹, evidently use it in the meaning "gentle," "considerate." The use of πραΰτης in the Lxx (Ps. 45⁴ 132¹) adds little light, but in the Apocr. it is used both of a "submissive, teachable spirit towards God" (Sir. 1²⁷ 45⁴) and of "modesty," "consideration," "gentleness towards men" (Esth. 3¹³ Sir. 3¹⁷ 4⁸ 36²⁸), and in Sir. 10²⁸ perhaps to denote an attitude which may manifest itself towards both God and man (*cf.* Ps. 45⁴). In Patr. Ap. also the word regularly signifies gentleness towards men (Clem. Rom. 21⁷ 30⁸ 61²; Ign. *Trall.* 3² 4², etc.—the ascription of πραΰτης to God in his relation to men in Ep. ad Diogn. 7⁴ is quite exceptional). In N. T. πραΰς occurs in Mt. 11²⁹ 21⁵ (the latter from Zech. 9⁹), meaning "gentle," "considerate"; in Mt. 5⁵ (from Ps. 37¹¹) probably with the same meaning as in O. T., "submissive to God's will"; in 1 Pet. 3⁴, meaning "gentle," "modest." πραΰτης in Jas. 1²¹ is used of an attitude towards God, "teachableness," "submissiveness to his will"; elsewhere of a relation to men (1 Cor. 4²¹ 2 Cor. 10¹ Gal. 6¹ Eph. 4² Col. 3¹² 2 Tim. 2²⁵ Tit. 3² Jas. 3¹³ 1 Pet. 3¹⁵), and signifies "considerateness," "gentleness." Among N. T. writers, therefore, only James and to a limited extent Mt. show the influence of the Hebrew עָנָו, all the other instances showing simply the common Greek meaning of the word. If the two ideas were blended into one in the usage of the writers of the N. T. period, that thought must have been, negatively, the opposite of the arrogant, self-assertive spirit; positively, recognition and consideration of others: towards God, submissiveness, towards men considerateness and gentleness. But it is doubtful whether the word did not rather stand for two similar but distinct ideas, and in Paul's mind for the idea of gentleness (towards men) only. On πίστις in association with πραΰτης *cf.* Sir. 1²⁷ 45⁴; Herm. *Mand.* 12. 3¹.

Ἐγκράτεια appears in Greek literature first, so far as observed, in Plato, who uses it in the phrases ἐγκράτεια ἑαυτοῦ, *Rep.* 390B, and ἡδονῶν τινων καὶ ἐπιθυμιῶν ἐγκράτεια, *Rep.* 430E. The adjective ἐγκρατής, used in Soph., meaning "possessing power," "strong," appears in Plato and Xenophon (under influence of Socrates?) as a moral term: Plato, *Phaed.* 256B; Xen. *Mem.* 1. 2¹, etc. Neither ἐγκρατής nor ἐγκράτεια appear in the Lxx, but both are found in the Apocr.; the adjective in the sense "having mastery, possession of" (Tob. 6³ Wisd. 8²¹ Sir. 6²⁷ 15¹ 27³⁰), once absol. meaning "continent" (Sir. 26¹⁵); the noun apparently with the meaning "continence," "self-control" (Sir. 18¹⁵ 18³⁰, where it stands as a title prefixed to a series of exhortations not to follow one's lusts, ἐπιθυμίαι, or appetites, ὀρέξεις, and 4 Mac. 5³⁴). The adjective occurs in N. T. in Tit. 1⁸ only, in reference to the qualifications of a bishop. The verb ἐγκρατεύομαι is used in 1 Cor. 7⁹ of control of sexual desire, and in 9²⁵, limited by πάντα, with reference to the athlete's control of bodily appetites. In Patr. Ap. ἐγκράτεια occurs frequently, always in a moral sense, but without special reference to any class of desires or impulses. See esp. Herm. *Vis.* 3. 8⁴: ὃς ἂν οὖν ἀκολουθήσῃ αὐτῇ (ἐγκρατείᾳ), μακάριος γίνεται ἐν τῇ ζωῇ αὐτοῦ, ὅτι πάντων τῶν πονηρῶν ἔργων ἀφέξεται, πιστεύων ὅτι ἐὰν ἀφέξηται πάσης ἐπιθυμίας πονηρᾶς κληρονομήσει ζωὴν αἰώνιον. Usage thus indicates that ἐγκράτεια, signifying prop. "control," "mastery," acquired the meaning "self-control," "mastery of one's own desires and impulses," but without specific reference to any particular class of such desires. The position of the word here corresponding to that of μέθη, κῶμοι in the list of the works of the flesh, suggests a special reference in this case to control of the appetite for drink and of the consequent tendency to unrestrained and immodest hilarity. But this parallelism does not warrant the conclusion that the apostle had exclusive reference to this form of self-control.

κατὰ τῶν τοιούτων οὐκ ἔστιν νόμος. "Against such things there is no law." Without doubt an understatement of the apostle's thought for rhetorical effect. The mild assertion that there is no law against such things has the effect of an emphatic assertion that these things fully meet the requirements of the law (*cf.* v.¹⁴). The statement as it stands is true of law in every sense of the word, and νόμος is therefore to be taken in a very general sense; yet probably Paul is thinking only of divine, not of divine and human law. See special note on Νόμος, V 2 (b), p. 456, but *cf.* V 4, p. 459. The absence of the article probably marks the noun as indefinite (not, as usually in Paul, qualitative); consistently with the rhetorical figure he thinks of a conceivable plurality of divine laws and denies that there is any law against such things. This would have been expressed with emphasis by the words ἔστιν οὐδεὶς νόμος (cf. 1 Cor. 6⁵ Rom. 8¹), but it is a part of the rhetoric of the sentence not to use an emphatic form. Cf. Rom. 2¹¹ 3²². On κατά, "against," see on v.¹⁷. τῶν τοιούτων is probably generic, denoting the class of which ἀγάπη . . . ἐγκράτεια are examples as against the class denoted by τὰ τοιαῦτα in v.²¹. Cf. on that v.

24. οἱ δὲ τοῦ χριστοῦ Ἰησοῦ τὴν σάρκα ἐσταύρωσαν σὺν τοῖς παθήμασιν καὶ ταῖς ἐπιθυμίαις. "and they that belong to the Christ, Jesus, have crucified the flesh with its dispositions and its desires." τοῦ χριστοῦ Ἰησοῦ is a possessive genitive (cf. 3²⁹ 1 Cor. 3²³ 15²³), and οἱ . . . Ἰησοῦ are those who are in Christ Jesus (v.⁶), who walk by the Spirit (v.¹⁶) and are led by the Spirit (v.¹⁸; cf. Rom. 8⁹, ¹⁰). τὴν σάρκα has the same meaning as the σάρξ of vv.¹⁶, ¹⁷, ¹⁹, the force in men that makes for evil, and ἐσταύρωσαν refers to the act by which they put an end to the dominion of that force over their conduct (cf. Rom. 6¹). The addition of σὺν τοῖς . . . ἐπιθυμίαις emphasises the completeness of the extermination of this evil force, in that not only its outward fruits are destroyed, but its very dispositions and desires put to death. Combined with v.²³ to which it is joined by δέ continuative, the sentence conveys the assurance that they who are of Christ Jesus, who live by the Spirit, will not fail morally or come under condemnation, since the fruits of the Spirit fulfil the requirements of law, and the deeds of the flesh, which shut one out of the kingdom of God, they will not do, the flesh and its desires being put to death.

The unusual combination τοῦ χριστοῦ Ἰησοῦ (found elsewhere only in Eph. 3¹) is not to be regarded as the compound Χριστοῦ Ἰησοῦ with the article prefixed, there being no previous instance nearer than v.⁶ of Χριστὸς Ἰησοῦς alone, to which the demonstrative article might refer; it is, rather, the titular τοῦ χριστοῦ, the Christ, with Ἰησοῦ in apposition. It is probably otherwise in Eph. 3¹, the reference there being to the closely preceding 2²⁰. See detached Note on *Titles and Predicates of Jesus*, III 3. On the omission of Ἰησοῦ by some Western authorities, see textual note on 2¹⁶.

The aorist ἐσταύρωσαν, since it affirms crucifixion of the flesh as a past fact in the experience of all who are of the Christ, but assigns the act to no specific point of time, is best translated by the English perfect. On the use of the word, see note on σταυρός and σταυρόω, 3¹. The verb is used figuratively in N. T. here and in 6¹⁴ only; but *cf.* 2²⁰: Χριστῷ συνεσταύρωμαι. Rom. 6⁶: ὁ πάλαιος ἡμῶν ἄνθρωπος συνεσταυρώθη. Col. 3⁵: νεκρώσατε οὖν τὰ μέλη τὰ ἐπὶ τῆς γῆς, πορνείαν, etc. The choice of σταυρόω in preference to other verbs signifying "to put to death" suggests that it is the death of Jesus on the cross which has impelled us to slay the power within us that makes for unrighteousness. *Cf.* Rom. 6⁶⁻¹¹ and the notes on 2²⁰, where, however, a somewhat different use is made of the figure of crucifixion.

On the meaning of παθήμασιν, see below, and on ἐπιθυμίαις, see v.¹⁶. The article with both words is restrictive, and serves to mark the πάθημα and ἐπιθυμία as those of the σάρξ just spoken of above; for these words are in themselves of neutral significance morally, and it could not be said of the dispositions and desires generally that they that are Christ's have put them to death. On this use of the article, where the English would require a possessive, which is rather rare in N. T., see Kühner-Gerth, 461. 2; G. 949; Butt. 127. 26; Mt. 17²⁴ Gal. 6⁴ (τὸ καύχημα and τὸν ἕτερον), and the exx. of τὸν πλησίον there cited.

Πάθημα (πάσχω) occurs in classical writers from Soph. down, usually in the plural. Its meanings are: (a) "an experience in which one is passive, rather than active," distinguished therefore from ποίημα and ἔργον: Plato, *Soph.* 248C; or "experience" in general without emphasis on the element of passivity: Hdt. 1²⁰⁷: τὰ δέ μοι παθήματα ἐόντα ἀχάριτα μαθήματα γέγονε: "It is through my unpleasant experiences that I have learned"; so, probably, also, in Plato, *Rep.* 511D. (b) "a painful experience, a misfortune, disaster": Soph. *O. C.* 361; Thuc. 4. 48³; so in particular of a sickness, Plato, *Rep.* 439D. (c) "a disposition, tendency, or characteristic, in which the person himself is passive," so in contrast with μάθημα: Xen. *Cyr.* 3. 1¹⁷: πάθημα ἄρα τῆς ψυχῆς σὺ λέγεις εἶναι σωφροσύνην, ὥσπερ λύπην, οὐ μάθημα: "You maintain then that sobriety (discretion) is a passive quality of the soul, like grief, not a thing that one learns." Then, also, without special emphasis on the element of passivity; hence "disposition," "propensity," "impulse." The earliest clear instances of this usage are apparently in Aristot. *Poet.* 6² (1449 b²⁸); *Rhet.* 2. 22¹⁶ (1396 b³³); *Metaph.* 4. 14⁶ (1020 b¹⁹). (d) of material bodies, "magnitude," etc., "incident," "property," "accident": Aristot. *Metaph.* 1. 2⁸ (982 b¹⁶). Respecting the relation of πάθος and πάθημα, Bonitz maintains that in Aristotle's use there is no certain difference of meaning (*Index Arist.* 554 a⁵⁶ *sqq.*; they are apparently synonymous in *Eth. Eud.* 2³ [1221]); while Bernays, *Aristoteles über Wirkung der Tragödie*, pp. 149, 194–6, holds that πάθος is the condition of one who is πάσχων, and denotes an emotion unexpectedly breaking forth and passing away; πάθημα, on the other hand, is the condition of one who is παθητικός, and denotes an inherent quality which is liable at any time to manifest itself; in short, that πάθος is an emotion (passion), πάθημα a disposition.

Down to Aristotle, at least, πάθημα seems clearly a neutral term, morally. *Cf.* his list of forty-two πάθη (=παθήματα in *Eth. Eud.* 2³ [1220 f.]). Aristotle includes ἔλεος and φόβος under both πάθος (*Eth. Nic.* 2⁵ (4) [1105 b. *passim*]) and πάθημα (*Poet.* 6² [1449 b²⁸]), and without implying (*contra* Cremer) that these are evil.

Πάθημα is not found in the Lxx. πάθος occurs in Job 30³¹ Prov. 25²⁰ in the sense of "pain," "discomfort." It is frequent in 4 Mac., where it signifies "feeling," "emotion," of which the writer (under Stoic influence?) says the two most comprehensive classes are pleasure and pain (1²⁰), and under which he includes desire and joy, fear and sorrow, excitement (θυμός), haughtiness, love of money, love of glory, contentiousness, gluttony (1²⁴ᶠᶠ.), sexual desire (2²), yet also the love of life and fear of pain (6³¹; *cf.* preceding context, 7¹⁰), as well as the admirable love of brothers one for another (14¹) and of a mother for her children (15⁴, ¹³). All these, the writer maintains, it is the function of reason and piety not to uproot, but to control (3²⁻⁵, *et freq.*). It is clear, therefore, that πάθος is for this writer neither distinctly sensual nor utterly evil.

The three N. T. instances of πάθος (Rom. 1²⁶ Col. 3⁵ 1 Thes. 4⁵) seem to indicate that for Paul πάθος signified passion in a bad sense, and especially perhaps sensual passion, for, though always shown by the context to refer to gross sensual passion, in only one case is it felt necessary to add a defining word to indicate this limitation of meaning.

In N. T. πάθημα is used fourteen times (Rom. 8¹⁸ 2 Cor. 1⁵, etc.) with the meaning "suffering"; it refers to that of Christ and of others; and this is also the meaning in the only two passages in which it occurs in Patr. Ap.: Clem. Rom. 2¹; Ign. *Smyrn.* 5¹. In Rom. 7⁵, τὰ παθήματα τῶν ἁμαρτιῶν τὰ διὰ τοῦ νόμου, and the present passage, the meaning is evidently akin to the meaning (c) in classical usage. Nor is there any clear evidence that warrants us in going beyond the Aristotelian meaning. Apparently πάθημα means for Paul "disposition," or "propensity," rather than an outbreak of feeling, and is in itself morally neutral; the moral quality being in Rom. 7⁵ expressed by τῶν ἁμαρτιῶν and here by the article, which has the effect of an added τῆς σαρκός. The words πάθημα and πάθος are therefore further apart in N. T. than in earlier Greek, possibly under the influence of the honourable use of πάθημα in reference to the sufferings of Christ and his fellow men.

25. εἰ ζῶμεν πνεύματι, πνεύματι καὶ στοιχῶμεν. "If we live by the Spirit, by the Spirit let us also walk." The conditional clause (a present particular supposition) like that of v.¹⁸

refers to a present possibility, presumably a reality. The apostle assumes that they live or intend to live by the Spirit, and exhorts them to make this manifest in conduct. The phrase ζῆν πνεύματι, which he has not previously used, he nevertheless assumes will be understood by his readers and taken as substantially synonymous with those already employed (vv.[16, 18]; cf. v.[6] and 2[20]). The thought expressed by ζῶμεν πνεύματι is substantially the same as that of ζῇ ἐν ἐμοὶ Χριστός, πνεῦμα and Χριστός being for the apostle synonymous from the point of view of experience. See on 4[6]. Of the three expressions, πνεύματι περιπατεῖτε of v.[16], πνεύματι ἄγεσθε of v.[18], and ζῶμεν πνεύματι here, the first emphasises conduct, the second conformity of will to the Spirit's leading, and the third vital spiritual fellowship, mystical union. Assuming that they are in such fellowship, he bases on it an exhortation to the first-named, conduct, expressing this, however, by the word στοιχῶμεν (see below) instead of using περιπατεῖν as in v.[16]. That he should exhort men who live by the Spirit to do the things which it is the very nature of life by the Spirit to produce (cf. vv.[22ff.]) is not uncharacteristic of the apostle, who constantly combines the conception of morality as the product of a divine force working in men with the thought of the human will as a necessary force in producing it. Cf. Phil. 1[12, 13] Rom. 6[1-7] and 6[12ff.].

On πνεύματι cf. on v.[16]; the dative is a dative of means. The noun being anarthrous is qualitative. There is much difference of opinion on the question whether στοιχῶμεν, conveying the figure of walking (cf. περιπατεῖτε in v.[16]) in a row, refers chiefly to external conduct in contrast with inner life, ζῶμεν (so Philippi, Ell. Ltft. Sief.), or having as its basal meaning "to stand in a row," refers to conformity, agreement (so Dalmer and Cremer, following Buddeus). The lexicographical evidence is hardly decisive, but the N. T. exx. favour the view that στοιχεῖν sometimes, at least, suggested the figure of walking (Rom. 4[12]) or of walking in a straight line, and meant "to act according to a standard," "to behave properly" (Acts 21[24]). But in chap. 6[16] Phil. 3[16] either this meaning, or the meaning "to conform to," would be suitable. For the present passage this meaning, "to walk (in a straight line)," "to conduct one's self (rightly)," is distinctly more appropriate; the apostle in that case exhorting his readers who claim to live by the Spirit to give evidence of the fact by conduct controlled by the Spirit. The thought is similar to that of I Cor. 10¹² and Phil. 3¹⁵.

26. μὴ γινώμεθα κενόδοξοι, ἀλλήλους προκαλούμενοι, ἀλλήλοις φθονοῦντες. "Let us not become vain-minded, provoking one another, envying one another." This sentence, following the preceding without connective, expresses negatively one element or consequence of that which is positively expressed in πνεύματι στοιχῶμεν. Walking by the Spirit, let us not put false estimates on things, and thus, on the one side, provoke or challenge our fellows to do things they hesitate to do, or, on the other, envy our fellows who dare to do what we do not venture to do. The two parts of the exhortation doubtless have reference to two classes in the churches of the Galatians. Those who fancied that they had attained unto freedom and were in danger of converting their freedom into an occasion to the flesh (v.¹³), whose κενοδοξία took the form of pride in their fancied possession of liberty to act without restraint, would be tempted to challenge (προκαλεῖσθαι) their more timid or more scrupulous brethren, saying, e. g., "We dare do these things that the law forbids; are you afraid to do them?" On the other hand, the more scrupulous would, while not quite daring to follow in the footsteps of these, yet be tempted to regard this spurious liberty of their fellow-Christians as a thing to be desired, and to look at them with envy, wishing that they felt the same freedom. Cf. the similar, though not quite identical, situation more fully reflected in I Cor., chap. 8, where the apostle addresses especially those who with conceit of knowledge act regardless of the well-being of their more timid or more scrupulous brethren; and that set forth in Rom., chap. 14, where, however, the relation of the two parties is not as here, that one challenges and the other envies, but that one despises and the other judges. As in those cases the apostle prescribes Christian love as the corrective of the divisive evils, so here he prescribes walking by the Spirit, the fruit of which is love, joy, peace, etc.

The relation of this verse to what precedes and to what follows is similar to that of v.[1] to its context; it is the conclusion of what precedes and the introduction to what follows. Yet it is the former connection that is closest, and the greater paragraph division should be made, not as in WH., Stage, Zahn, between vv.[24] and [25], or as in Mey. Weizs. Stapfer, between vv.[25] and [26], but at the end of the chapter, as in AV. Tdf. Ell. Ltft. Segond, Sief. ERV. ARV. make a paragraph both here and at the beginning of v.[24].

The dative ἀλλήλοις before φθονοῦντες is attested by אACDFG²KL al. pler. Clem. Euthal. Thdrt. Dam. On the other hand, BG*P al. 25 Clem. Chr. Thdrt. cod. Oec. read ἀλλήλους. The latter, despite its strong support, is so contrary to known usage that it must be supposed to be a corruption under the influence of the preceding ἀλλήλους.

Κενόδοξος (like its cognates κενοδοξία and κενοδοξέω) is a word of later Greek, appearing first in Polyb. 3. 1¹; 27. 6¹², where it is associated with ἀλαζών, then in this passage, the only N. T. instance, and in Did. 3⁵, where to be φιλάργυρος or κενόδοξος is said to lead to theft: τέκνον μου, μὴ γίνου ψεύστης, ἐπειδὴ ὁδηγεῖ τὸ ψεῦσμα εἰς τὴν κλοπήν, μηδὲ φιλάργυρος μηδὲ κενόδοξος· ἐκ γὰρ τούτων ἁπάντων κλοπαὶ γεννῶνται. κενοδοξία is more frequent, occurring in Polyb. 3. 81⁹; Wisd. 14¹⁴; 4 Mac. 2¹⁵ 8¹⁹, ²⁴; Philo, Mut. nom. 96 (15); Leg. ad Gaium, 114 (16); Phil. 2³; Clem. Rom. 35⁵; Ign. Philad. 1¹; Magn. 11¹; Herm. Mand. 8⁵; Sim. 8. 9²; Galen, Tuend. valetud. 6 (quoted by Zahn, following Wetstein), φιλοτιμίας ἣν ὀνομάζουσιν οἱ νῦν Ἕλληνες κενοδοξίαν.

In several of these passages κενοδοξία is associated with ἀλαζονία, "boastfulness." Suidas defines it as μάταιά τις περὶ ἑαυτοῦ οἴησις. But usage shows that this definition is not quite comprehensive enough. The noun and the adjective are evidently closely related in meaning, and κενόδοξος means "glorying in vain things," "setting value on things not really valuable," whether possessed, or supposed to be possessed, or desired. It is the almost exact antithesis of σώφρων and σωφρονῶν, which mean "seeing things as they are, estimating them at their true value" (cf. Rom. 12³). The English word "vain" expresses the meaning of κενόδοξος approximately, but as commonly used refers more especially to pride in petty possessions and less distinctly suggests the desire for vain things not yet possessed. "Vain-minded," if we might coin an English word, would translate κενόδοξος exactly.*

Προκαλέω, though not found in the Lxx, Ps. Sol. or Patr. Ap., in the Apocr. only in a variant reading in 2 Mac. 8¹¹, and here only in N. T., occurs in classical writers from Homer down. It is evidently

---

* The verb κενοδοξέω seems to have taken on a somewhat more general meaning than the noun or the adjective, signifying to hold a baseless opinion (of any kind). See 4 Mac. 5⁸ 8⁴; Mar. Pol. 10¹.

used here in the meaning common in Greek writers, "to call forth," "to challenge."

Φθονέω, likewise not found in the Lxx, and in the Apocr. in Tob. 4⁷, ¹⁶ only, not in Ps. Sol., in Patr. Ap. 2 Clem. 15⁵ only, here only in N. T., is like προκαλ. a common classical word from Homer down. *Cf.* on φθόνος, v.²¹.

(*c*) Exhortation to restore those who fall, and to bear one another's burdens (6¹⁻⁵).

Mindful of the danger that not all those who purpose to live by the Spirit will always live thus, the apostle appends to the injunction of 5²⁵ an exhortation to those who live by the Spirit to restore any who fall, adds exhortations to mutual burden-bearing, and reminds them that each man has a burden of his own.

¹*Brethren, if a man be nevertheless overtaken in a transgression, do ye who are spiritual restore such a one in a spirit of gentleness, considering thyself lest thou also be tempted.* ²*Bear ye one another's burdens, and so fulfil the law of the Christ.* ³*For if any one thinketh himself to be something, when he is nothing, he deceiveth himself.* ⁴*And let every man prove his own work, and then shall he have his ground of glorying in respect to himself, and not in respect to his fellow.* ⁵*For each man shall bear his own burden.*

1. Ἀδελφοί, ἐὰν καὶ προλημφθῇ ἄνθρωπος ἔν τινι παραπτώματι, ὑμεῖς οἱ πνευματικοὶ καταρτίζετε τὸν τοιοῦτον ἐν πνεύματι πραΰτητος, σκοπῶν σεαυτόν, μὴ καὶ σὺ πειρασθῇς. "Brethren, if a man be nevertheless overtaken in a transgression, do ye who are spiritual restore such a one in a spirit of gentleness, considering thyself lest thou also be tempted." This sentence is closely connected with the thought of chap. 5. Recognising the possibility, too sadly proved by experience, that one who has chosen the life by the Spirit may nevertheless fall into sin, the apostle exhorts those members of the community who have not thus fallen to care for him who has. Despite the use of ἄνθρωπος instead of ἀδελφός (*cf.* 1 Cor. 5¹¹) the reference is clearly not to an outsider but to a member of the Christian community.

Zahn, following Hofmann, connects ἀδελφοί with 5²⁶. So also Ws. ἀδελφοί at the end of a sentence is not impossible (see v.¹⁸) and at the very beginning of a sentence is rather infrequent (3¹⁵ Rom. 10¹ 1 Cor. 14²⁰ Phil. 3¹³), a position near the beginning being much more common than either (1¹¹ 4¹² 5¹¹, et freq.). But a position at the end of such a sentence as 5²⁶, remote from any pronoun referring to the persons addressed (cf. 6¹⁸; Phm.⁷; also Gal. 4¹²), and after a series of distinct phrases, is extremely awkward, and unparalleled in Paul. It is safe to affirm that if ἀδελφοί had been intended to form a part of v.²⁶ it would have stood before ἀλλήλους, and that standing where it does it must be taken with what follows it, as in 3¹⁵ and other examples above.

'Εάν (or εἰ) καί may be used either (a) to introduce a concessive clause (2 Tim. 2⁵, and numerous instances of εἰ καί), i. e., a condition unfavourable to the fulfilment of the apodosis, in spite of which the apodosis is or will be fulfilled; or (b) when a second hypothesis similar to a preceding one is introduced, and καί therefore means "also"; cf. Lk. 11¹⁸ 2 Cor. 11¹⁵; or (c) when καί is intensive, putting emphasis on the immediately following word (Lk. 14³⁴), or suggesting that the hypothesis is in some sense extreme; thus in 1 Cor. 7¹¹, ²⁸ it stands in a protasis referring to a condition which the apostle has in a preceding sentence said ought never to occur; its force may be reproduced in English by an emphatic form (if she do depart, 1 Cor. 7¹¹; if thou dost marry, 7²⁸). Cf. also 1 Pet. 3¹⁴. The first use is excluded in the present case by the fact that the clause as a whole is not oppositional; without the παράπτωμα there would be no occasion for a καταρτίζειν. The second is excluded by the fact that there is no preceding similar supposition, to which this could be additional. The third possibility alone remains, and the intensive force of καί is doubtless intended to apply to the whole clause. The meaning thus yielded perfectly fits the context and constitutes an almost perfect parallel to the use of εἰ καί in 1 Cor. 7¹¹. As there the apostle, having forbidden the wife to depart from her husband, goes on to say: but if (nevertheless) she do depart (ἐὰν δὲ καὶ χωρισθῇ); so here, having in 5²⁵ bidden his readers walk by the Spirit (στοιχεῖν πνεύματι) and in 5²⁶ enforced this exhortation by negative injunctions, he now deals with the case of one who should nevertheless fail to obey this injunction, saying in effect: "If now one shall nevertheless disregard the injunction to walk by the Spirit and be overtaken in a fault, it is for those who have obeyed the injunction (πνευματικοί =στοιχοῦντες πνεύματι) to restore such a one."

Προλαμβάνω, used by classical writers from Sophocles down in a variety of meanings, does not occur in the Lxx, and in Apocr. is found only in Wisd. 17¹⁷ and as v. l. in 17¹¹. In the latter it means "to anticipate, to forecast." In 17¹⁷, εἴ τε γὰρ γεωργὸς ἦν τις . . . προλημφθεὶς [sc. αἰφνιδίῳ καὶ ἀπροσδοκήτῳ φόβῳ—cf. v.¹⁵] τὴν δυσάλυκτον ἔμενεν

ἀνάγκην, it means "to overtake," "to come upon," or "to take unawares" (not, however, "to detect"). See also Jos. *Bell.* 5.79 (2⁴): διὸ
καὶ τότε προληφθέντες οἱ Ῥωμαῖοι ταῖς ἐμβολαῖς εἶκον (cited by
Sief.), where the passive clearly means "to be taken by surprise." In
N. T. it occurs in 1 Cor. 11²¹, where it means "to take beforehand";
in Mk. 14⁸, where it means "to anticipate, to forestall" (*cf.* also Ign.
Eph. 3², the only instance in Patr. Ap.); and in the present passage, for
which no meaning is so probable as that which is vouched for Wisd.
17¹⁷; Jos. *Bell.* 5.79 (2⁴), viz., "to take by surprise," "to seize unawares"
(so *Sief.*)* If the word "overtake" be employed in translation it
should be understood in that sense. The meaning "to detect, to discover one in an act" (Ell. Alf. Ltft. Th. and not a few others), though
not an improbable derivative from the meaning "to take by surprise,"
is not attested by any observed instance and is not required by this
context. When with this interpretation of προλ. is combined the view
that καί throws its emphasis on προλ., giving the meaning, "If one be
even detected in a fault, etc.," it yields a thought wholly inharmonious
with the context. See above on εἰ καί.

Παράπτωμα, a late word meaning literally "a fall beside," but used
by Polybius, in whom the first observed instances occur, in a figurative
sense, "a false step, a blunder," is used in the Lxx for various words
meaning "sin," and with similar force in Apocr. In N. T. it is used
in the synoptic gospels in speaking of forgiveness, and in the Pauline
epistles, Rom. 4²⁵ 5¹⁵, ¹⁶, etc. Between biblical and non-biblical usage
there seems little difference, except that in the biblical writers it has
a more strictly ethical sense. The exx. in Paul show that the word
retained for him the suggestion of its etymological sense, "a falling
beside, a failure to achieve" (see esp. Rom. 11¹¹, ¹²), and it is, therefore,
probable that in the present passage there is an intended antithesis
to στοιχῶμεν "walk in a straight line, conform to a standard." ἐν is
figuratively spatial, meaning "in the midst of," "in the act of." *Cf.*
1 Thes. 2² and Th. *s. v.* I. 5.

Οἱ πνευματικοί here evidently refers to those who in obedience to the
instructions of vv.¹⁶⁻²⁶, live by the Spirit, walk by the Spirit, as against
those who, failing to do so, are still following the ἐπιθυμία τῆς σαρκός
(*cf.* 1 Cor. 3¹: οὐκ ἠδυνήθην λαλῆσαι ὑμῖν ὡς πνευματικοῖς ἀλλ' ὡς
σαρκίνοις), or as against both the latter and those who are living ὑπὸ
νόμον (*cf.* 4.¹⁸). On πνευματικός in general, see Th. *s. v.* and Burton,
Spirit, Soul, and Flesh, p. 204.

Καταρτίζω, found in classical authors from Herodotus down, and

* The passages cited for the meaning "to overtake" (as of one pursuing a fugitive) by
Meyer, do not show it. Xen. *Cyr.* 5. 19; 7. 7; Theophr. H. pl. 8. 1⁸; Polyb. 31. 23⁸; Diod. Sic.
17. 73 all show the meaning "to get the start of," "to outdistance" (used of the pursued, not
of the pursuer) quite the opposite of "overtake." In Strabo 16. 4¹⁵ *fin.* the meaning is "to
seize beforehand" or possibly "to anticipate," as in 1 Cor. 11²¹.

not infrequently in the Lxx, Apocr., and Patr. Ap., has in general three meanings: (1) "to repair," "to restore" (to a former good condition): Mk. 1¹⁹; (2) "to prepare," "to fit out": Heb. 10⁵; (3) "to perfect": Heb. 13²¹. Here evidently used in the first sense, ethically understood. On τὸν τοιοῦτον (this man, being such), *cf.* on τὰ τοιαῦτα, 5²¹.

Of the phrase ἐν πνεύματι πραΰτητος two interpretations are possible: (a) πνεῦμα may refer to the Holy Spirit qualitatively spoken of as in vv.¹⁶, ¹⁸, ²⁵; in that case πραΰτητος is a genitive of connection denoting the effect of the presence of the Spirit (*cf.* πνεῦμα υἱοθεσίας, Rom. 8¹⁵), and ἐν marks its object as the sphere in which the action takes place and by which its character is determined, as in 1 Thes. 1⁵ 1 Cor. 12³ *et freq. Cf.* 4⁶, and note that πραΰτης is named in 5²³ among those qualities which are the fruit of the Spirit. Observe, also, the connection in that case with πνευματικοί, the intimation being that those who possess the Spirit shall by virtue of that possession and the gentleness which it creates, restore the offender. (b) πνεῦμα πραΰτητος may denote a human spirit, characterised by gentleness, πραΰτητος being a genitive of characteristic, and ἐν marking its object as that with which one is furnished and under the influence of which the action takes place. See Rom. 7⁶, ἐν καινότητι πνεύματος, but esp. 1 Cor. 4²¹: ἐν ῥάβδῳ ἔλθω πρὸς ὑμᾶς ἢ ἐν ἀγάπῃ πνεύματί τε πραΰτητος; in view of these passages, the latter of which is so closely parallel to the present, the second interpretation is probably to be preferred. On the meaning of πραΰτητος, see on 5²³. The emphasis is here evidently upon the quality of considerateness.

Σκοπέω, a classical word from Homer down, signifying "to look at," "to observe," is used in N. T. in Lk. 11³⁵, meaning "to take heed," and by Paul in Rom. 16¹⁷ 2 Cor. 4¹⁸ Phil. 2⁴ 3¹⁷, always with a direct object in the accusative and in the sense "to consider," "to observe," "to give heed to"; for what purpose, whether to avoid, or to promote, or to honour, lies entirely in the context. *Cf.* Esth. 8¹³ 2 Mac. 4⁵; Clem. Rom. 51¹; Mar. Pol. 1². The change to the singular after the plural ἀδελφοί, common also in classical writers (Kühner-Gerth, 371. 5 b) serves to make the exhortation more pointed. *Cf.* the similar change of number in 4⁶, ⁷.

Μὴ καὶ σὺ πειρασθῇς may be (a) a clause of purpose after σκοπῶν σεαυτόν (Butt. p. 242), or (b) an object clause after σκοπῶν as a verb of effort (B*MT* 206), σεαυτόν being in that case proleptic and pleonastic (see 1 Cor. 16¹⁵), or (c) a clause of fear, the verb of fearing to be supplied in thought (B*MT* 225). The last is the most probable, for it is against (a) that the purpose of σκοπῶν as here referred to is manifestly not so much to avoid falling into temptation as to render one considerate in dealing with those who do so fall; and against (b) that Paul elsewhere constantly uses σκοπέω, not as a verb of effort, but in the sense "to consider, observe."

Πειράζω (from Homer down; occurring frequently in the Lxx, Apocr., and occasionally in Patr. Ap.), meaning properly "to try," "to test," in whatever way or for whatever purpose, is often used in N. T. (not so in the Lxx or Apocr.) in the sense "to solicit to sin" (note especially the title of Satan, ὁ πειράζων: Mt. 4³ 1 Thes. 3⁵; cf. 1 Cor. 7⁵), and sometimes pregnantly carrying with it the implication of yielding, also. So in 1 Cor. 7⁵, and so here also, since that which is feared is manifestly not temptation, but the sin which is likely to result from it.

2. Ἀλλήλων τὰ βάρη βαστάζετε, καὶ οὕτως ἀναπληρώσατε τὸν νόμον τοῦ χριστοῦ. "Bear ye one another's burdens, and so fulfil the law of the Christ." The reference of τὰ βάρη is clearly to that especially which is spoken of in the preceding verse, viz., the burden of temptation and possible ensuing sin. This burden they are to share, each bearing the other's. Yet the principle that underlies the injunction, and so in a sense the injunction itself, applies to burdens of any kind. The position of ἀλλήλων makes it emphatic. On the force of νόμον, see detached note Νόμος, V. 2. (d), p. 459. On τοῦ χριστοῦ, see detached note on *The Titles and Predicates of Jesus*, p. 395, and concluding discussion under B, p. 398. See also 1⁷ Col. 3¹⁶. By "the law of the Christ" Paul undoubtedly means the law of God as enunciated by the Christ; just as the law of Moses (Lk. 2²³ Acts 13³⁹) is the law of God as put forth by Moses. By the use of the official term τοῦ χριστοῦ in preference to Ἰησοῦ or even Χριστοῦ, the authoritative character of the promulgation is suggested. It is clear also that the apostle conceived of the law put forth by the Christ as consisting not in a body of statutes, but in the central and all-inclusive principle of love; though whether in his present reference to that law he had in mind its content, or thought simply of the law of God set forth by the Christ, can not be decided with certainty. Whether he is here thinking of this law as having been promulgated by Jesus while on earth and known to him, Paul, through the medium of those who followed Jesus before his death, or as communicated through his Spirit, there is likewise no wholly decisive indication. If, as seems probable, the former is the case, this is one of the few passages in which the apostle refers

to teaching of Jesus transmitted to him through the Twelve
or their companions. *Cf.* 1 Cor. 7^{10} 9^{14} 11^{23} 1 Thes. 4^{15-17} (?)
5^2 (?).

WH. read ἀναπληρώσατε with אACDKLNP al. pler. Syr. (harcl.)
Arm. Clem. Bas. Ephr. Didym. Ath. Chr. Euthal. Thdrt. Dam.
Following BFG d f g Vg. Syr. (psh.) Boh. Eth. Goth. Procl. Marc.
Thdrt. cod. Tert. Cyp. Victorin. Hier. Aug. Ambrst. al. Tdf. adopts
ἀναπληρώσετε. Neither external nor internal evidence is decisive, but
the preponderance of the latter seems in favour of —σατε. The fut. is
probably due to the natural tendency to convert the second imperative
into a promissory apodosis.

The words βάρος and βαστάζω are common, both in classical and
later Greek. βάρος is used in a great variety of applications, both
literally and metaphorically; in N. T. always metaphorically, and
either of what is desirable (2 Cor. 4^{17}), or of what is hard to be borne
(Acts 15^{28} Rev. 2^{24}), the context alone indicating the specific nature
of that which is referred to. On βαστάζω, see on 5^{10}. The reference
here is evidently not simply to endurance (enforced and reluctant, as
in 5^{10}), but to a willing, helpful, sympathetic sharing of the burden
(*cf.* Rom. 15^1), the element of willingness, etc., lying, however, in the
context rather than in the word itself.

Ἀναπληρόω, found in classical writers from Euripides down, is used
in the Lxx and N. T. as a somewhat stronger term for πληρόω, both
literally and tropical y. *Cf.* note on πληρόω, 5^{14}. Here, evidently,
with a force similar to that in Mt. 13^{14}, it means "to satisfy the requirements of." See ex. of its use with reference to a contract in M. and M.
Voc. s. v. On οὕτως, meaning "in this way, by the conduct just
enjoined," *cf.* Mt. 3^{15}. But there must be supplied in thought some
such expression as "in the matter of another's burden," since mutual
burden-bearing is evidently not the full content of the law of the
Christ.

3. εἰ γὰρ δοκεῖ τις εἶναί τι μηδὲν ὤν, φρεναπατᾷ ἑαυτόν·
"For if any one thinketh himself to be something, when he is
nothing, he deceiveth himself." Introduced by γάρ this sentence gives a reason for the injunction of v.2^b, ἀλλήλων τὰ βάρη
βαστάζετε, and implies that conceit, thinking one's self to be
something more than one really is, tends to make one unwilling
to share another's burden. Conceiving ourselves to have no
faults, we have no sympathy with those who have faults and
refuse to make their shortcomings any concern of ours.

On the expression δοκεῖν εἶναί τι, cf. on 2²·⁶. Of the two meanings
with which usage shows the expression to have been used, the context
makes it evident that it bears one in 2⁶ and the other here, meaning
there "to be esteemed of importance (by others)," here "to esteem one's
self to be of importance." Note the bearing of φρεναπατᾷ ἑαυτόν.

On the use of μηδὲν ὤν with δοκεῖν εἶναί τι, cf. Plato, Apol. 41E,
ἐὰν δοκῶσί τι εἶναι, μηδὲν ὄντες. The participle ὤν is concessive,
expressing a condition which is adverse to δοκεῖ, etc., equivalent to
εἰ μηδέν ἐστι. Otherwise stated, the conditional clause and the participial phrase together are equivalent to εἰ δοκεῖ τις εἶναί τι καὶ
μηδέν ἐστι, in which the combination of the two elements is causal-
conditional. On the combination of causal and concessive conditional
elements, see comment on 1⁸. In such cases μή is the regular negative,
both in classical and later Greek. BMT 485. Against the connection
of ὤν, as a causal participle, with the apodosis φρεναπατᾷ (Zahn) the
negative μή is not decisive, but the implied affirmation that no man is
anything and that any man who thinks himself to be something deceives himself, imports into the sentence a harshness of judgment that
is not warranted by the context or the apostle's other utterances. Cf.
esp. Rom. 12³ff· Phil. 2³ff·.

Φρεναπατάω appears here for the first time in extant Greek literature
and here only in N. T. It is not found in the Lxx, Apocr. or Patr.
Ap., but first after Paul, so far as noted, in Galen, Hesych. (L. & S.)
and eccles. and Byzant. writers (Th.). φρεναπάτης is found in Tit. 1¹⁰,
ματαιολόγοι καὶ φρεναπάται, "vain talkers and deceivers," which is
quoted in the longer recension of Ign. Trall. 6. This noun appears
also in a papyrus (Grenfell, An Alexandrian Erotic Fragment, Oxford,
1896, p. 2) said by Grenfell to be not later than 100 A. D. The Greek
of the passage is obscure,* but the word φρεναπάτης applied by a
woman to her former lover seems clearly to mean "deceiver," not as
Blass affirms (Bl.-D. 119. 2), "one who deceives his own mind," "con-
ceited." The noun is not found in the Lxx, Apocr. or Patr. Ap. On
the meaning of the verb, cf. Jas. 1²⁶, ἀπατῶν καρδίαν ἑαυτοῦ and such
compounds as φρενοθελγής (heart-charming). φρενοκλόπος† (heart-
stealing, deceiving), νομοδιδάσκαλος, ἑτεροδιδασκαλεῖν, εἰδωλολατρία,
εἰδωλολατρεῖν (Hermas, cited by Bl.-D. 119. 2), which indicate that it
means to deceive the mind, and that it differs from ἀπατάω in that it is
more intensive, as ἀπατᾷν καρδίαν ἑαυτοῦ is a stronger expression for

---

* συνοδηγὸν ἔχω τὸ πολὺ πῦρ τὸ ἐν τῇ ψυχῇ μου καιόμενον· ταῦτά με ἀδικεῖ, ταῦτά με
ὀδυνᾷ ὁ φρεναπάτης ὁ πρὸ τοῦ μέγα φρονῶν, καὶ ὁ τὴν κύπριν οὐ φάμενος εἶναι τοῦ ἐρᾶν μοι
αἰτίαν (or ποιήτριαν or μεταιτίαν), οὐκ (or ἄν) ἤνεγκε λίαν τὴν (or πάντων) τυχοῦσαν
ἀδικίαν.

† φρενοβλαβής, exceptionally among such compounds of φρήν is passive, "injured in understanding, insane."

self-deception than ἀπατῶν ἑαυτόν. There is the less reason for taking the verb as itself reflexive in that it is here accompanied by ἑαυτόν.

4. τὸ δὲ ἔργον ἑαυτοῦ δοκιμαζέτω ἕκαστος, καὶ τότε εἰς ἑαυτὸν μόνον τὸ καύχημα ἕξει καὶ οὐκ εἰς τὸν ἕτερον, "And let every man prove his own work, and then shall he have his ground of glorying in respect to himself and not in respect to his fellow." This sentence being, like v.², a command, δέ joins it not to v.³ (οὖν would in that case have been the appropriate particle), but to v.², or, better, to vv.², ³ taken together. The self-deceived man may boast of his superiority to the man who has fallen into a fault, not perceiving his own real condition. He has in reality ground of glorying only in respect to his fellow and his shortcomings. But the man who tests himself has his ground of glorying, whatever that be, in respect to himself. *Cf*. Mt. 7¹⁻⁵.

WH. bracket ἕκαστος on the basis of its omission by B Sah. But the omission is so easily explainable as in both cases a wholly inadvertent error, that even the measure of doubt expressed by the bracket seems hardly justifiable.

On the use of ἔργον, meaning "what one achieves, the result of one's effort," *cf*. 1 Cor. 3¹²⁻¹⁵. ἑαυτοῦ is here, as usually in N. T., emphatic. *Cf*. 1 Cor. 13⁵ 2 Cor. 10¹².

Δοκιμάζω, a frequent word in classical writers from Herodotus down, in the Lxx, and in N. T., occurs in Paul in the three senses: (a) "to test," "to discriminate": 1 Thes. 2⁴ᵇ 5²¹; (b) "to approve": Rom. 14²²;) "to think best": "to choose": Rom. 1²⁸ (so also Jos. *Ant*. 2. 176 [7⁴]). .Iere clearly in the first sense. *Cf*. esp. 1 Cor. 3¹³ff· 11²⁸.

Τότε, though doubtless temporal, "then, when he shall have tested his own work," has nearly the force of ἄρα, as in 5¹¹. *Cf*. 1 Cor. 4⁵. A protasis may be mentally supplied, "if his work shall be proved good," or τὸ καύχημα may mean in effect, "his ground of glorying, whatever that be," the implication in such case being that he who examines himself will not fail to find something of good in himself. On εἰς, meaning "in respect to," see Rom. 4²⁰ 2 Cor. 10¹⁶ (*cf*. vv.¹⁶, ¹⁷, where ἐν is used in a similar relation, but expressing strictly basis or ground of boasting) Phil. 1⁵. Note the emphatic position of εἰς ἑαυτὸν μόνον at the beginning of the sentence with its correlative εἰς τὸν ἕτερον.

Καύχημα, found in Pindar, but not observed elsewhere in classical writers, occurs not infrequently in the Lxx and Apocr., but not in Ps. Sol.; in N. T. in Heb. 3⁶ and ten times in Paul; in Patr. Ap. in

Clem. Rom. 34⁵ only, probably under the influence of Heb. 3⁶. It is in itself a less opprobrious term than the English word "boast," referring rather to exultation, gratulation, without the implication of the English word that it is excessive or unjustified. Though sometimes used in the active sense, "boasting, glorying" (thus in the proper sense of καύχησις, as καύχησις in turn is used in the sense of καύχημα in 2 Cor. 1¹² and probably in Rom. 15¹⁷), as, for example, in 2 Cor. 5¹², and probably in 1 Cor. 5⁶ Phil. 1²⁶ (*contra* Mey. Ell., who maintain that καύχημα never has this sense), yet in the present passage standing as the object of ἕξει, it naturally demands the more common and proper meaning, "ground of glorying." *Cf.* Rom. 4² 2 Cor. 1¹⁴, etc. The use of εἰς ἑαυτόν in preference to ἐν ἑαυτῷ (*cf.* Rom. 15¹⁷ 2 Thes. 1⁴ and note above on εἰς ἑαυτόν) favours, indeed, the meaning "glorying," since εἰς ἑαυτόν can, strictly speaking, limit only the element of glorying, καύχησις, which is involved in καύχημα, "ground of glorying." Yet such a limitation of an element of a word of complex meaning is, of course, possible, and there is, therefore, no sufficient reason for departing from the proper sense of καύχημα, especially as ἕξει also calls for the thought, "ground of glorying." The article with καύχημα is restrictive, "his ground of glorying." It emphasises the idea expressed by μόνον. He is to have, not "a ground of glorying in respect to himself," but "his (only) ground in respect to himself alone."

Τὸν ἕτερον is understood by Ell. as meaning "the other one with whom he is contrasting himself"; and this interpretation, making the article restrictive, but only as designating the individual who belongs to an imaginary situation presented to the mind, not one definitely named in the context, is not impossible (*cf.* Lk. 11¹¹ 15⁸, ⁹ Jn. 16²¹). But Rom. 2¹ 13⁸ 1 Cor. 4⁶ 6¹ 10²⁴, ²⁹ 14¹⁷ Phil. 2⁴ show clearly that ὁ ἕτερος was used in the sense of "fellow, neighbour" (*cf.* the similar use of τὸν πλησίον in Mk. 12³³ Acts 7²⁷ Rom. 13¹⁰ Jas. 4¹²). On the other hand, in quotations from the Lxx of Lev. 19¹⁸, σου is always present, Mk. 12³¹, etc., the article having the generic indefinite force, *i. e.*, making the noun refer not to the whole class (as, *e. g.*, in Mk. 2²⁷), but to any member whatever of the class. See illustrations of this latter use in the cases of τὸν πλησίον without σου cited above, and in Mt. 15¹ Acts 10³⁵ Gal. 4¹, *et freq.* The two interpretations differ only in that if the article is restrictive the reference is to the particular imagined wrong-doer with whom one compares himself; if it is generic the statement is more general; one's glorying pertains to himself, not to his (*i. e.*, any) fellow. The usage of ὁ ἕτερος and ὁ πλησίον, a synonym of ὁ ἕτερος, favours the latter view.

5. ἕκαστος γὰρ τὸ ἴδιον φορτίον βαστάσει. "For each man shall bear his own burden." Between φορτίον (used by

Greek writers from Aristotle down, in the Lxx, Apocr. and in N. T.; in Acts 27¹⁰ of a ship's cargo; elsewhere, Mt. 11³⁰ 23⁴ Lk. 11⁴⁶ and here, figuratively of a task to be accomplished or a burden borne by the mind) and $\beta \acute{a}\rho \eta$ (v.²) no sharp distinction can be drawn. Starting with the exhortation to bear one another's burdens (of sin), the apostle, having enforced this by the warning against self-deception through conceiving that it is only the other man that has such burdens to bear, and having bidden each one test himself, now argues for the necessity of such testing by the affirmation that every man has his own burden, i. e., of weakness and sin. The paradoxical antithesis to v.²ᵃ is doubtless conscious and intentional. Cf. Phil. 2¹², ¹³. It is the man who knows he has a burden of his own that is willing to bear his fellow's burden.

On ἴδιος as an emphatic possessive instead of ἑαυτοῦ or οἰκεῖος, see Bl.-D. 286; MNTG 87 ff. βαστάσει is a gnomic future; BMT 69.

2. Exhortations having a less direct relation to the principal subject of the epistle (6⁶⁻¹⁰).

Having dealt with the several aspects of the situation which the judaisers had created in Galatia by their criticism of the gospel as preached by Paul, the apostle now, as in most of his epistles, but more briefly than usually, adds exhortations having to do with the general moral and religious life of the churches. Dealing first with the support of teachers, which he urges on fundamental grounds, he exhorts them to persistence in doing good work, and specifically in doing good to their fellows, especially their fellow-Christians.

⁶*And let him that is taught in the word share with him that teacheth in all good things.* ⁷*Be not deceived; God is not mocked: for whatsoever a man soweth that shall he also reap;* ⁸*because he that soweth to his own flesh shall of the flesh reap corruption, but he that soweth to the spirit shall of the Spirit reap life eternal.* ⁹*And let us not be weary in doing that which is good; for in due season we shall reap, if we faint not.* ¹⁰*As therefore we have opportunity, let us do that which is good towards all, but especially towards those who are of the household of the faith.*

6. Κοινωνείτω δὲ ὁ κατηχούμενος τὸν λόγον τῷ κατηχοῦντι ἐν πᾶσιν ἀγαθοῖς. "And let him that is taught in the word share with him that teacheth in all good things." The thought of mutual burden bearing, more or less present throughout vv.[2-5], perhaps suggests the theme of this v., but no more than suggests it; the subject is new, having no direct relation to the topic of the epistle as a whole. *Cf.* for a similar example of passage to a new division of the subject, yet with superficial connection with what immediately precedes, Rom. 6[1ff.]. On the use of δέ at the beginning of a new division of the subject, see Rom. 11[13] 16[17, 25] 1 Cor. 7[25] 8[1]. The expressions ὁ κατηχούμενος and τῷ κατηχοῦντι, occurring in a letter so early in the apostolic age as this one, furnish interesting and instructive evidence how soon religious teaching became an element of the life of the Christian community. The fact that those who receive instruction are called upon to contribute to the support of the teacher shows that such teaching in all probability was not undertaken merely as a voluntary and relatively light avocation (comparable to the work of a modern Bible-class teacher) but occupied in preparation for it and the work itself, if not the teacher's whole time, yet enough so that it was necessary to compensate him for the loss of income which he thus sustained. In short, it is a class of paid teachers to which this verse refers. The article with both κατηχούμενος and with κατηχοῦντι is, of course, generic indefinite, designating any member of the class; *cf.* on τὸν ἕτερον, v.[4]. On the teaching class in the early church, *cf.* 1 Thes. 5[12] 1 Cor. 12[28] Eph. 4[11] 1 Tim. 5[17]. On its existence in the second century, see Dobschütz, *Christian Life in the Primitive Church*, pp. 345 *f.*; Harnack, *Expansion of Christianity*, pp. 333–366. On the subject of such teaching, see below on τὸν λόγον.

Ell. Ltft. Zahn, Tdf. Weizs. ERV. and ARV. dissociate this verse from the preceding by a paragraph at this point, and connect it with the following. Stage, Bous. and Segond put v.[6] by itself. WH. join v.[6] with what precedes, making a half paragraph at the end of v.[6]; Weymouth a full paragraph. The last-named view makes this sentence an appended remark on a subject not closely connected with what precedes; the second isolates it both from what precedes and what follows. Neither view is so probable as that which finds the suggestion of the sentence in what precedes and its further enforcement in vv.[7, 8]. Thus interpreted, the whole passage becomes continuous and intelligible. See below on vv.[7, 8].

Κοινωνέω, used by classical writers from Euripides down, in the Lxx, Apocr. N. T. and Patr. Ap., means in general "to share," i. e., "to be a partner in" (a thing) or "with" (a person). The name of the person with whom one shares is in the dative, if expressed; the thing in the genitive, in the dative, or after a preposition. See, e. g., Plato, Rep. 453A, κοινωνεῖν τινι εἰς ἄπαντα, "to be a partner with one in respect to everything"; Polyb. 31.26⁶, κοινωνεῖν τινι περί τινος. Sir. 13¹: ὁ κοινωνῶν ὑπερηφάνῳ ὁμοιωθήσεται αὐτῷ. Most commonly the emphasis is upon the receptive side of the partnership or fellowship, i. e., the subject is chiefly receptive. Thus in Rom. 15²⁷, εἰ γὰρ τοῖς πνευματικοῖς αὐτῶν ἐκοινώνησαν τὰ ἔθνη, 1 Tim. 5²² Heb. 2¹⁴ 1 Pet. 4¹³ 2 Jn. ¹¹. Yet the active aspect may also be emphasised, as in Rom. 12¹³, ταῖς χρείαις τῶν ἁγίων κοινωνοῦντες. Barn. 19⁸: κοινωνήσεις ἐν πᾶσιν τῷ πλησίον σου, καὶ οὐκ ἐρεῖς ἴδια εἶναι· εἰ γὰρ ἐν τῷ ἀφθάρτῳ κοινωνοί ἐστε, πόσῳ μᾶλλον ἐν τοῖς φθαρτοῖς, with which cf. Did. 4⁸. In Phil. 4¹⁵ the verb itself is clearly mutual or neutral in meaning, though with the emphasis on the side of giving: οὐδεμία μοι ἐκκλησία ἐκοινώνησεν εἰς λόγον δόσεως καὶ λήμψεως εἰ μὴ ὑμεῖς μόνοι. It seems probable, indeed, that the word itself is always, strictly speaking, neutral in meaning, as is the English verb, "share," and the noun, "partner." It is the context alone that indicates which aspect of the partnership is specially in mind. In the present passage the chief determinative element is the phrase ἐν πᾶσιν ἀγαθοῖς. If this referred exclusively to spiritual goods, κοινωνείτω would have reference to the receptive side, if to material goods, to impartation. Since it is apparently an inclusive term (see below) referring to both spiritual and material good, κοινωνείτω is best taken as in Phil. 4¹⁵ as referring to a mutual, reciprocal sharing, wherein he that was taught received instruction and gave of his property. Yet in view of the context, it must be supposed that here, as also in Rom. 14¹⁵; Phil. 4¹⁵; Barn. 19⁸, the emphasis is upon the impartation (of material good). See esp. the extended argument in Wies. Though taking the verb as intransitive, Ell. Alf. Ltft. suppose the reference here to be exclusively to the element of giving. Zahn takes a similar view. Mey. and after him Sief., on the other hand, suppose receiving only to be referred to.

Κατηχέω occurs first in extant literature in Philo, Leg. ad Gaium, 198 (30), κατήχηται δὲ ὅτι, "he was informed that"; then in N. T. Lk. 1⁴ Acts 18²⁵ 21²¹, ²⁴ Rom. 2¹⁸ 1 Cor. 14¹⁹ et h.l.; in Jos. Vit. 366 (65):

καὶ αὐτός σε πολλὰ κατηχήσω τῶν ἀγνοουμένων: "I will myself inform
you of many things hitherto unknown"; and in later writers, Plutarch,
Sextus Empiricus, Diogenes Laertius, Lucian, Porphyry; see Wetstein
on Lk. 1⁴. But the simple verb ἠχέω, "to sound" (intrans. and trans.),
is found in Hesiod, Herodotus, Euripides, etc.; and this fact, together
with the existence in the Philo passage of the meaning "to inform,"
which must have been developed from the literal sense "to sound
down," and the use of the noun κατήχησις in the sense of "instruction" at least as early as the third century B. C. make it probable that
κατηχέω is much older than the earliest extant example. The clue
to its meaning is found in the use of κατήχησις, which appears in
Hippocr. 28²⁵ (L. & S.) in the expression κατήχησις ἰδιωτέων, with
reference to the oral admonition of the physician to his patient (so
Cremer); and in a passage of Chrysippus (240 B. C.) preserved in Diog.
Laert. VII 1. 53 (89) (quoted by Wetstein on Lk. 1⁴): διαστρέφεσθαι
δὲ τὸ λογικὸν ζῷον, ποτὲ μὲν διὰ τὰς τῶν ἔξωθεν πραγματειῶν πιθα-
νότητας· ποτὲ δὲ διὰ τὴν κατήχησιν τῶν συνόντων: "And if a reasoning creature is astray, this is sometimes because of the allurements
of external things, sometimes because of the teaching of his companions." Here the word clearly means "instruction," or "expression of
opinion." Cicero also uses it in *ad Att.* XV 12 (quoted by Cremer): Sed
quid aetati credendum sit, quid nomini, quid hereditati, quid κατηχήσει,
magni consilii est. In N. T. the verb has the two meanings: (a) "to
inform": Acts 21²¹, ²⁴; (b) "to teach": Acts 18²⁵ Rom. 2¹⁸, etc. The
primary meaning of the word and its usage, though not wholly decisive,
suggest that it referred chiefly, if not exclusively, to oral instruction.
Cf. the derivative English words "catechism" and "catechetical."
Concerning the history of the word, especially its later ecclesiastical
usage, see v. Zezschwitz, *System der christl. Katechetik.*

Τὸν λόγον, an accusative of content, denotes the substance of the
instruction communicated by the teacher. Paul uses ὁ λόγος (absol.)
of his own message in 1 Thes. 1⁶ Col. 4³, but more commonly
characterises it as a message of God (1 Thes. 2¹³ Col. 1²⁵ Phil. 1¹⁴),
or according to its content (1 Cor. 1¹⁸ 2⁴ 2 Cor. 5¹⁹ Eph. 1¹³).
It is undoubtedly to be taken here as an inclusive term for the
Christian message. It is in the nature of the case that the instruction given by the local teachers must have been in large part
that which Paul had communicated to them. The elements that
entered into this body of teaching can not be defined accurately and
exhaustively, but probably included: (a) the doctrine of a living and
true God as against the worship of idols (see 1 Thes. 1⁹ Gal. 4⁸, ¹⁴); (b)
those narratives of the life of Jesus and those elements of his teaching which were to Paul of central significance, especially his death,
resurrection, and return (1 Cor. 11²³ff. 15¹⁻⁸ 1 Thes. 1¹⁰ 5¹ff.); with

which was joined (c) the teaching concerning the way of salvation which had its basis in these facts (see the passages cited above); (d) the fundamental principles of Christian ethics (1 Thes. 4[1ff. 9ff.]). To what extent the O. T. scriptures (in the Lxx version) were put into the hands of the converts or their teachers and made the basis of their instruction, is more difficult to determine with accuracy. That the apostle did not refer them to these scriptures as throughout an authoritative guide for the Christian life is clear from the fact that his own teaching respecting the law, in particular respecting circumcision, unclean foods, and the Sabbath, was not in accordance with the statutes of the O. T. law. Yet, on the other hand, the early acceptance of O. T. in the Christian church as sacred scripture, and the apostle's own frequent use of it and reference to it in writing to his churches (Rom. 1[2] et freq.), makes it evident that in his own day O. T. was already an important factor in the life of most of the churches founded by him. The fact that there are no express quotations from O. T. in 1 and 2 Thes. suggests the possibility that the use of O. T. in Gentile churches was due to judaising influence rather than to the apostle. Yet the evident connection between his fundamental idea of God (1 Thes. 1[9]) and O. T., and the favourable attitude which, despite his practical rejection of its authority, he assumes towards O. T. in general (cf. Rom. 7[12] 9[6], et freq.), and his frequent use of it in argument, make it probable that while his message was distinctly Christian, having its authority not in the book but in his interpretation of historical facts as learned through human experience, yet he saw in O. T. an invaluable aid to the development of religious life, and as such commended it to his converts. If, then, the λόγος of the teachers was based on that of Paul, it contained elements derived from O. T., yet was distinctly Christian in content, including historic fact, Christian doctrine, and Christian ethics.

'Ἐν πᾶσιν ἀγαθοῖς is probably to be taken as referring to both spiritual and material good. Cf. 1 Cor. 9[11] Rom. 15[27]; Barn. 19[8]; Did. 4[8]. For ἀγαθά, meaning material good, see Lk. 12[18] 16[25]; spiritual good, Mt. 12[34, 35], the latter a particularly instructive example, since it refers not precisely to good conduct but to good thoughts and words, as does the present passage if it designates that which the teacher imparts. The idea of good conduct Paul usually expressed by the singular τὸ ἀγαθόν (Rom. 2[10] 12[9, 21] 13[3b] 14[16] 16[19] 1 Thes. 5[15]; cf. the similar use of τὸ καλόν in 5[21] and in v.[9] below) or ἔργον ἀγαθόν (Rom. 2[7] 13[3] 2 Cor. 9[8] Phil. 1[6]). The neuter plural occurs in the Pauline letters in the phrase ἔργα ἀγαθά in Eph. 2[10] 1 Tim. 2[10], and without ἔργα, but with the article in Rom. 3[8] only, where it signifies things that are (spiritually) advantageous. The Pauline usage, therefore, furnishes no decisive or weighty evidence for or against either the material or the spiritual sense here; and in view of the common Greek usage illustrated in the passages from the gospels quoted above, the word πᾶσιν, and the inclusive, mutual sense of κοινωνέω, it seems probable that the phrase is intended to cover both the spiritual good which the teacher has to impart and the material good which he is to receive. The thought is then akin to that of Rom. 15²⁷, the exhortation being to those that are taught to be partners with their teachers in all goods, giving to those who teach them of that which they themselves possess, as they receive what the teachers have to impart. See esp. Wieseler's full discussion. Consistently with their respective interpretations of κοινωνείτω Ell. Alf Ltft. Zahn take it of material good only, Mey. and Sief. of spiritual good.

7. μὴ πλανᾶσθε, θεος οὐ μυκτηρίζεται· ὃ γὰρ ἐὰν σπείρῃ ἄνθρωπος, τοῦτο καὶ θερίσει. **8.** ὅτι ὁ σπείρων εἰς τὴν σάρκα ἑαυτοῦ ἐκ τῆς σαρκος θερίσει φθοράν, ὁ δὲ σπείρων εἰς το πνεῦμα ἐκ τοῦ πνεύματος θερίσει ζωὴν αἰώνιον. "Be not deceived; God is not mocked: for whatsoever a man soweth that shall he also reap; because he that soweth to his own flesh shall of the flesh reap corruption, but he that soweth to the spirit shall of the Spirit reap life eternal." With μὴ πλανᾶσθε (cf. similar use of these words in 1 Cor. 6⁹ 15³³* Jas. 1¹⁶) the apostle introduces the statement of a general principle, which serves primarily to enforce the exhortation of v.⁶ by bringing the specific matter there referred to under a great general law. To the apostle's thought the attitude of the Galatians towards their teachers is but a specific example of their attitude towards life in general. If they are unreceptive to spiritual teaching, and, undervaluing it, are unwilling to support their teachers, preferring to spend their money on themselves, they are sowing to (for the benefit of) their own fleshly natures, and the harvest will be corruption. If, on the other hand, recognising their need of teaching and its value, they are of receptive mind towards those who are able to instruct them and willingly contribute of their goods that such teaching may continue, they are sowing to (for the benefit of) the spirit, and the harvest will be eternal life. For similar instances of a seeming dis-

* It is probably only accidental coincidence that in these other Pauline instances of μὴ πλανᾶσθε the error against which he warns his readers is substantially the same as here, viz., overvaluation of the material side of life, with danger of the loss of eternal life.

parity in importance between the duty enjoined and the consideration appealed to to enforce it, see Phil. 2¹⁻¹⁰ 1 Cor. 11³¹⁻³³. Yet these verses are probably not simply for the enforcement of v.⁶. The apostle may also have desired to bring this principle before his readers for its own sake. Having in vv.¹⁻⁶. brought before his readers certain specific applications of the teaching of 5¹³⁻²⁶, thus narrowing the horizon from the general contrast between life according to the flesh and life by the Spirit, he now, reversing the process, restores the broader view with which he began.

Πλανάω, a classical word, used from Homer down in a literal sense, (a) active, "to cause to wander," passive, "to wander," "to go astray," and (b) in various figurative senses, is used in the Lxx, Apocr. and N. T. both literally and figuratively, but most commonly in an intellectual and moral sense, "to turn aside from truth," "to deceive," "to lead into sin." In Paul it always means "to deceive" (1 Cor. 6⁹ 15³³; cf. 2 Tim. 3¹³ Tit. 3³). It is somewhat frequent in Patr. Ap.: Ign. Eph. 16¹: μὴ πλανᾶσθε, ἀδελφοί μου· οἱ οἰκοφθόροι βασιλείαν θεοῦ οὐ κληρονομήσουσιν. See also Mag. 8¹; Philad. 3³.

Θεός without the article, though infrequent as subject nominative, sometimes occurs. It is always (see 2⁶ and textual note there), as in oblique cases also, qualitative, emphasising the divine attributes, and designating not simply the being God, but God as divine. This is undoubtedly the force here. God, because he is God, not man, is not mocked.

Μυκτηρίζω (cf. μυκτήρ, nose), though not found in the extant texts of classical writers, is shown by a passage in Poll. Onom. 2⁷⁸ to have been used by Lysias. μυκτηρισμός is also found in Menand. Incert. 402. Both verb and noun are frequent in the Lxx, and occur in the Apocr. In N. T. the verb alone occurs and in this passage only. If taken in its usual sense, "to turn up the nose," "to ridicule," or in the tropical meaning, "to ignore" (as perhaps in Prov. 15⁵), it is necessary to supply "with impunity" (Ell.). But even with this addition the meaning thus obtained is not appropriate to the context. That of which the apostle speaks is not a ridicule of God which he will not leave unpunished, but an outwitting of God, an evasion of his laws which men think to accomplish, but, in fact, can not. It seems necessary, therefore, to suppose here an easy metonymy (he who is outwitted being thereby made ridiculous) for "outwit, evade." Cf. for a similar, though not identical, metonymy (cited by Elsner, ad loc.), Cicero, Ep. ad Diversos, XV 19⁴: Scis quam se semper a nobis derisum putet. Vereor, ne nos rustice gladio velit ἀντιμυκτηρίσαι.

The present is gnomic, and the implication is that what does not happen can not happen. The application of the statement is in what follows: It is vain to expect to outwit God by reaping a harvest different from that which one has sown. Cf. Polyc. Phil. 5. 1: εἰδότες, οὖν, ὅτι θεὸς οὐ μυκτηρίζεται. ὀφείλομεν ἀξίως τῆς ἐντολῆς αὐτοῦ καὶ δόξης περιπατεῖν.

The figure of sowing and reaping for conduct and its results is a frequent one, occurring in Plato, Phaedr. 260C; Arist. Rhet. 3. 3⁴ (1406 b. ¹⁰); (cf also Dem. 280²⁷¹ : ὁ γὰρ τὸ σπέρμα παρασχών, οὗτος τῶν φύντων αἴτιος: "For he that furnished the seed is responsible for what grows"; Prov. 22⁸ Hos. 8⁷ 10ᴵᴵᴵ· Job. 4⁸: Sir. 7²; Test. XII Fat. Lev. 13⁶; Philo, Conf. ling. 21 (7); Lk. 19²¹ 1 Cor. 9¹¹ 2 Cor. 9⁶. Note esp. the last two passages. ὁ σπείρων is best taken as a general present participle, referring to any member of the class described by the participle. On the use of the article, cf. on τὸν ἕτερον v.⁴ and ὁ κατηχούμενος v.⁶. Though the antithesis between σάρξ and πνεῦμα recalls, probably intentionally, the same terms used antithetically in 5¹³⁻²⁴, the words are probably not used here in precisely the same sense as there. Had the apostle wished to reproduce the idea of the earlier passage, he must have written simply εἰς σάρκα or εἰς τὴν σάρκα. The addition of ἑαυτοῦ, the force of εἰς marking the σάρξ as the end, that unto which the action takes place (see below), not, as in 5¹³⁻¹⁹, that from which the tendency to evil proceeds, and the connection with v.⁶, all indicate that σάρξ is here not "that in man which makes for evil" (cf. on 5¹³), but has reference to the body, the physical element of man. Cf. chap. 3³ Rom. 2²⁸ 1 Cor. 5⁵ 2 Cor. 7¹, where σάρξ in this physical sense stands in antithesis to πνεῦμα, and chap. 4¹⁴ 2 Cor. 4¹¹ Eph. 2¹⁵ 5²⁹ Col. 1²², where limited by a possessive genitive it has this sense. He who will not share his goods with the religious teacher, withholds them, it is assumed, that he may spend the more on the gratification of bodily appetites in food, drink, and the like. Thus he sows unto his own flesh, spends effort for the (supposed) benefit or gratification of it. The position of ἑαυτοῦ is emphatic (Bl.-D. 283) and the word itself conveys an essential element of the thought; to seek the physical well-being of others would be an act of quite different moral quality and effect from devotion to the gratification of one's own physical desires. The sentence is not, then, a repetition of the self-evident proposition of v.⁷ in the specific form that if one sow evil he will reap evil, but the assertion that if one devote himself to the things of his body (which is not in itself evil) rather than to those of the spirit, if he prefer the lower to the higher, such a course issues in corruption. Ltft. interprets εἰς as meaning "into," thus making the σάρξ the soil in which one sows seed. This is not seriously to be objected to on the ground urged by Ell. that N. T. usage would in this case require ἐν or ἐπί; for all his exx. are from the gospels, and Mk. 4¹⁸, though not precisely parallel, shows the possibility of using εἰς. The real objection lies in the thought which this parabolic interpretation yields. What would be meant by casting seed into one's own flesh? What by "reaping corruption" in that literal sense which a parabolic interpretation requires as the basis of the spiritual sense? It is evident that the apostle is not constructing a condensed parable consistent throughout (like that of Mk. 4²⁶ff.), but employing individual terms "sow" and "reap" in a figurative sense, and that εἰς is not, therefore, to be taken spatially but tropically. The meaning of σάρξ in ἐκ τῆς σαρκός is doubtless the same as in εἰς τὴν σάρκα ἑαυτοῦ: the body, or, by metonymy, the bodily desires. The article may be generic, the later clause widening the horizon of the former, but is more probably restrictive, by implication carrying an αὐτοῦ with it. (On this use of the article, cf. on 5²⁴.)

Φθορά (a classical word in use from Æschylus down, meaning "decay," "destruction," "death," used also in the Lxx, Apocr. Ps. Sol. Patr. Ap.) interpreted solely by the clause in which it stands, would naturally mean "corruption," "decay" (cf. Col. 2²²) perhaps inclusive of a physical (cf. Ps. Sol. 4⁶ [?]) and a moral sense, but probably referring particularly to moral corruption (Wisd. 14¹² 2 Pet. 1⁴; 2 Clem. 6⁴; cf. the use of φθείρω in 1 Cor. 15³³ 2 Cor. 7² 11³ Eph. 4²²). Nor is it impossible that this is the apostle's meaning, for to such a thought, eternal life, ζωὴ αἰώνιος, is not an impossible antithesis. Yet in view of the Pauline use of φθορά (Rom. 8²¹ 1 Cor. 15⁴², ⁵⁰), the reference to the flesh in the immediate context, and the antithesis of eternal life in the second member of the sentence, it seems probable that by φθοράν Paul means that corruption and death of the body, from which, for those who have not lived according to the spirit, there is no rising to eternal life. See Rom. 6¹⁹⁻²³ 8⁸⁻¹⁷, esp. 13: εἰ γὰρ κατὰ σάρκα ζῆτε μέλλετε ἀποθνήσκειν, εἰ δὲ πνεύματι τὰς πράξεις τοῦ σώματος θανατοῦτε ζήσεσθε, where, to be sure, σάρξ is used in a distinctly ethical, not as here in a physical sense, but τὰς πράξεις τοῦ σώματος conveys very nearly the idea here expressed by σπείρων εἰς τὴν σάρκα ἑαυτοῦ. In other words Paul here affirms that devotion of one's self to the material, bodily side of life, brings physical death unrelieved by the Christian hope of resurrection which rests upon the indwelling of the Spirit of him that raised up Jesus from the dead.

Εἰς τὸ πνεῦμα, ἐκ τοῦ πνεύματος is in form a perfect antithesis to εἰς τὴν σάρκα, ἐκ τῆς σαρκός. Yet πνεῦμα and πνεύματος are probably not used in precisely the same sense. The πνεῦμα unto which one sows is primarily one's own πνεῦμα, the non-material, intellectual, spiritual side of man's being, which is the seat of the religious life, and that which survives the cataclysmic experience of physical death or the day of the Lord. See detached note on Πνεῦμα and Σάρξ, III A 2, p. 490, and *cf.* 1 Cor. 5⁵ 7³⁴ Rom. 1⁴ 2²⁹ 7⁶ 8⁵, ¹⁶ Phil. 4²¹ 1 Thes. 5²³. εἰς signifies, as in εἰς τὴν σάρκα ἑαυτοῦ, "unto," "for the benefit of," and the whole expression σπείρων εἰς τὸ πνεῦμα refers to devotion of energy and resources to the enrichment of the life of the spirit, in particular through the reception of the instruction of the κατηχῶν τὸν λόγον. *Cf.* Col. 1⁹. That ἑαυτοῦ is not added to πνεῦμα, as to σάρκα, signifies not that τὸ πνεῦμα refers to the spiritual life of the whole community, but that the explicit narrowing of the reference to the spirit of the individual would have been incongruous, suggesting a certain (spiritual) self-centredness. ἐκ τοῦ πνεύματος probably signifies from the Spirit of God, which dwelling in man is the cause of resurrection, and the earnest of eternal life (Rom. 8¹¹ 2 Cor. 5⁵ Eph. 1¹⁴). The transition to this meaning from πνεῦμα referring to the human spirit, is easy because it is the human spirit as engaged in the things of the Spirit of God (*cf.* 1 Cor. 2¹⁴, ¹⁵) to which τὸ πνεῦμα refers (*cf.* Rom. 8¹⁶).

Ζωὴ αἰώνιος, here for the first time in Paul, occurs in his epistles much less frequently than in the Johannine literature. See Rom. 2⁷ 5²¹ 6²², ²³; *cf.* 1 Tim. 1¹⁶ 6¹² Tit. 1³ 3⁷. The earliest appearance of this phrase is in the Greek of Dan. 12², translating עוֹלָם חַיֵּי, then in Ps. Sol. 3¹⁶: οἱ δὲ φοβούμενοι κύριον ἀναστήσονται εἰς ζωὴν αἰώνιον. 1 Enoch (Syn. and Giz.) 10¹⁰: ἐλπίζουσι ζῆσαι ζωὴν αἰώνιον, καὶ ὅτι ζήσεται ἕκαστος αὐτῶν ἔτη πεντακόσια. So doubtless in 37⁴ 40⁹, though these passages are not extant in Greek. *Cf.* also 2 Mac. 7⁹ 4 Mac. 15³. ζωή (in classical writers from Homer down) is used by Paul of (a) physical life, the antithesis of death (Rom. 8³⁸ 1 Cor. 3²² Phil. 1²⁰, etc.); accompanied by αὕτη, meaning the period of existence in the body (1 Cor. 15¹⁹, *cf.* 1 Tim. 4⁸), in contrast with that which is after the resurrection; but more commonly (b), as constantly in John, in a moral-qualitative sense, denoting "existence according to the ideal of existence for moral beings," in which ideal are included righteousness, the divine approval, blessedness (Rom. 6⁴ 7¹⁰ 8², ⁶). Such life, possessed by God (Col. 3³; *cf.* Eph. 4¹⁸) and by Christ (Rom. 5¹⁰ 2 Cor. 4¹⁰), belongs by virtue of his relation to God in Christ to the believer in Christ, both while still in the body (Rom. 6⁴ 2 Cor. 4¹⁰) and after the resurrection (2 Cor. 5⁴), and is not infrequently spoken of without limitation to either period of its possession (2 Cor. 2¹⁶ Phil. 2¹⁶). Accompanied by αἰώνιος this ζωή is characterised as "eternal." αἰώνιος appears first in Plato, meaning "perpetual" (*Rep.* 363D: ἡγησάμενοι κάλλιστον ἀρετῆς μισθὸν μέθην αἰώνιον, "esteeming perpetual drunkenness the finest reward of virtue"); "everlasting" (*Tim.* 37, 38C; *Legg.* X 904A), being clearly associated with αἰών, signifying an indefinitely long period (*cf.* detached note on Αἰών, p. 431); see esp.

Tim. 37, 38C. As used in later Greek and in particular in the Lxx, Apocr. Ps. Sol. N. T., and Patr. Ap., it retains this sense and association with αἰών in the sense just referred to. The supposition that it means "æonian," *i. e.*, "pertaining to the coming æon," is insufficiently supported by 1 Enoch 10¹⁰, and is definitely disproved by the evidence as a whole; as is also the suggestion of Brooke, *International Critical Commentary on 1 John* (1²) that it may be properly translated "spiritual."

9. τὸ δὲ καλὸν ποιοῦντες μὴ ἐνκακῶμεν, καιρῷ γὰρ ἰδίῳ θερίσομεν μὴ ἐκλυόμενοι. "And let us not be weary in doing that which is good; for in due season we shall reap, if we faint not." The thought of reaping, *i. e.*, of obtaining result from one's efforts, forms the link of connection between the preceding verses and this, in which, nevertheless, the apostle passes still further away from the thought that vv.⁷· ⁸ were introduced to enforce (viz., the support of teachers), to speak of persistence in well-doing in general and its reward. On τὸ καλόν as a general term for the morally good (it is scarcely used at all in N. T. in an æsthetic sense), see 1 Thes. 5²¹ Rom. 7¹⁸· ²¹, and *cf.* on ἐν πᾶσιν ἀγαθοῖς, v.⁶, and on τὸ ἀγαθόν, v.¹⁰.

As between the two readings ἐνκακῶμεν (or ἐγκακῶμεν) and ἐκκακῶμεν, the former is undoubtedly the original. B*D* read ἐνκ. אAB³ 31, 33, 326 ἐγκ. against CDᶜKLP al. pler. Clem. Chrys. Thdrt. which read ἐκκ. (FG ἐκκακήσωμεν). There is no sufficient evidence of the existence in N. T. times of the word ἐκκακέω, which apparently came into N. T. mss. from the usage of a later time.

Ἐνκακέω (from which ἐκκακέω apparently differs in form, but not in meaning; see Tdf. Ed. viii maj. 2 Cor. 4¹) appears first in Polybius and belongs, therefore, to the vocabulary of the post-classical literary language. See Nägeli, *Wortschatz des Ap. Paulus*, p. 32. It is not found in the Lxx or, so far as observed, in other Jewish writers before N. T. In N. T. it is found in Lk. 18¹ 2 Cor. 4¹· ¹⁶ Eph. 3¹³ 2 Thes. 3¹³ *et h.l.*; also in 2 Clem. 2²; Herm. *Mand.* 9⁸, and in Symm. (200 A. D.) in Gen. 27⁴⁶ Nu. 21⁵ Prov. 3¹¹ Isa. 7¹⁶. In Polyb. 4. 19¹⁰: ἐνεκάκησαν τὸ πέμπειν: "They neglected to send"; and in 2 Clem. 2²: τὰς προσευχὰς ἡμῶν ἁπλῶς ἀναφέρειν πρὸς τὸν θεὸν μὴ . . . ἐγκακῶμεν, it is in effect transitive, meaning "to neglect" and taking an object infinitive (or, if one prefers, is a verb of incomplete predication, requiring an infinitive or other equivalent form of expression to complete its meaning). In Philo, *Conf. ling* 51, (13), οὐκ ἐκκακούμενος (so mss.;

C. and W. read κακούμενος) ἐκνάμφθην, in 2 Thes. 3¹³, μὴ ἐνκακήσητε καλοποιοῦντες, and in the present passage the meaning of the verb is, apparently, "to grow weary." In these two N. T. passages the predication of the verb is completed by a participle in agreement with the subject. Cf. also Herm. Mand. 9⁸ᵗ: σὺ οὖν μὴ διαλίπῃς αἰτούμενος τὸ αἴτημα τῆς ψυχῆς σου, καὶ λήψῃ αὐτό· ἐὰν δὲ ἐκκακήσῃς καὶ διψυχήσῃς αἰτούμενος, σεαυτὸν αἰτιῶ καὶ μὴ τὸν διδόντα σοι. Cf. Mt. 11¹, and for the grammatical usage BMT 457, 459. In the remaining N. T. instances the verb may likewise be transitive, the subject being supplied from the context (so esp. Lk. 18¹ 2 Cor. 4¹) or intransitive "to be neglectful, slothful" (2 Cor. 4¹⁶ Eph. 3¹³).

Καιρῷ ἰδίῳ is paralleled, in N. T. at least, only in 1 Tim. 2⁶ 6¹⁵, and even then the plural is used. Yet the use of the separate words is not at all exceptional. On ἴδιος, meaning "appropriate, due," cf. 1 Cor. 3⁸ 15²³ Acts 1²⁵.

The participle ἐκλυόμενοι is conditional (BMT 436). ἐκλύω, used by classical writers from Homer down in a variety of meanings derived from the etymological sense "to loose," "set free," and in the Lxx and Apocr., occurs in N. T. in the passive only and with the meaning "to faint": (1) "to become exhausted physically" (Mt. 15³² Mk. 8³), (2) "to relax effort" (Heb. 12³, ⁵ et h.l.).

10. Ἄρα οὖν ὡς καιρὸν ἔχωμεν, ἐργαζώμεθα τὸ ἀγαθὸν πρὸς πάντας, μάλιστα δὲ πρὸς τοὺς οἰκείους τῆς πίστεως. "As therefore we have opportunity, let us do that which is good towards all, but especially towards those who are of the household of the faith." With this v. the exhortations of the paragraph reach the utmost point of generality. Because of the certainty of the result of their efforts (v.⁹ᵇ), therefore (ἄρα οὖν), the Galatians are exhorted, whenever they have opportunity, to do good to their fellow men in general, but with special care for the welfare of their fellow-Christians.

ℵB*31, 33, 102, al. read ἔχωμεν; AB³CDFGKLP al. pler. read ἔχομεν. The rarity of ὡς with the subjunctive without ἄν probably led to the change to the easier indicative. Transcriptional probability and the high authority of ℵB therefore both point to the subjunctive as the original.

Ἐργαζώμεθα is the reading of ℵBCDFG al.; AB³LP 31, 104, 234, 326, 1908, al. read —ομεθα. Intrinsic probability favours the subjunctive following the subjunctive in v.⁹. The weight of documentary authority is on the same side. Transcriptional probability, though on the side of the indicative, is not strong enough to outweigh the contrary evidence, especially in view of the frequency of itacistic changes. *Cf.* on θερίσομεν in v.⁹.

Ὡς ἔχωμεν is a conditional relative clause, ἄν being omitted as in a few other cases; *BMT* 307. On τὸ ἀγαθόν *cf.* on τοῖς ἀγαθοῖς v.⁶, but for τὸ ἀγαθόν, meaning "that which is advantageous," see Rom. 7¹⁸ 15². *Cf.* on ἀγαθωσύνη, 5²². The expression is not quite identical with τὸ καλόν, v.⁹, signifying, rather, what is beneficial to another than what is morally right. There is no decisive reason to limit the expression to either the spiritually or the materially beneficial; so far at least as concerns the principal statement ending with πάντας the language seems to be wholly general; on its use in relation to the phrase μάλιστα, etc., see below. πρὸς πάντας may be taken as limiting either ἀγαθόν, and meaning "in respect to" (*cf.* Eph. 4¹⁹) or the whole expression ἐργαζώμεθα τὸ ἀγαθόν and meaning "towards," as in 1 Thes. 5¹⁴ Eph. 6⁹ (Ell).

Though οἰκεῖοι (from Hesiod down; in N. T. in Eph. 2¹⁹ 1 Tim. 5⁸ *et h.l.*) was apparently used in later Greek without distinct suggestion of a household in the strict sense, yet in view of Paul's conception of the intimate unity of all believers (*cf.* 1 Cor. 3¹⁶, ¹⁷ 12¹²ff.) and the expression of this idea in terms borrowed from the idea of the house (1 Cor. 3⁹ *cf.* also Eph. 2¹⁹ 1 Tim. 3¹⁵) it is most probable that οἰκείους is here used with intention to characterise those to whom it refers as members of a household, though, of course, in a metaphorical sense. τῆς πίστεως denotes the (active) Christian faith, faith in Jesus Christ. *Cf.* on 1²² and detached note on Πίστις, Πιστεύω, p. 483. The genitive is a genitive of characteristic and the whole expression means "those who are members of that household, the distinguishing characteristic of which is the faith in Jesus Christ."

The qualification of the exhortation to do good to all men by μάλιστα . . . πίστεως, if intended as a general principle, represents a lapse from the universalistic principle of 5¹³, which really underlies the whole gospel of the apostle as against the particularism which the epistle opposes. To promote the spiritual welfare, *e. g.*, of those who have faith in preference to that of those who have not, is indefensible from the general point of view of the apostle. If, however, the apostle has specially in mind the physical needs of the Christian communities, such an exhortation might be judged to be consistent with or demanded by the general principle of love to one's neighbour. In time of famine or other general distress, the members of a Christian church composed of those who had recently come out of heathenism would, because of religious prejudice, be unlikely to receive any help at the hands of their non-Christian neighbours. Unless, therefore, their distress were relieved by their fellow-Christians, they would fare worse than the non-Christians. As the most needy, therefore, they would have a first claim. Moreover, the non-Christian members of the community would naturally expect the Christians most surely to manifest their love to one another. If, therefore, a Christian were left in distress this would be even more to the discredit of the new religion than if a non-Christian went hungry.

V. CONCLUSION OF THE LETTER (6[11-18]).

1. *Final warning against the judaisers* (6[11-16]).

In his own hand and in a larger character than the amanuensis has used, the apostle repeats briefly, but emphatically, his warning against the judaisers, and reaffirms his positive teaching that religion is wholly spiritual and in no way dependent on physical facts, such as Abrahamic descent and circumcision; he concludes with a benediction upon all who walk by this principle and a prayer for mercy upon the Israel of God.

[11]*See with how large letters I write to you with my own hand!* [12]*As many as wish to make a good showing in things pertaining to the flesh, these compel you to receive circumcision, only that they may not be persecuted because of the cross of the Christ.* [13]*For not even they that receive circumcision are themselves law-abiding, but they wish you to be circumcised that they may glory in your flesh.* [14]*But far be it from me to glory except in the cross of our Lord Jesus Christ, through whom a world hath been crucified to me and I to a world.* [15]*For neither is circumcision anything, nor uncircumcision, but a new act of creation.* [16]*And as many as shall walk by this rule, peace be upon them, and mercy upon the Israel of God.*

11. Ἴδετε πηλίκοις ὑμῖν γράμμασιν ἔγραψα τῇ ἐμῇ χειρί. "See with how large letters I write to you with my own hand!" At this point the apostle, who usually employed an amanuensis for the writing of his letters (*cf.* Rom. 16[22]), and doubtless had done so in the case of this letter also, took the pen in his own hand to write the concluding paragraph. *Cf.* similar instances in 2 Thes. 3[17] 1 Cor. 16[21] Col. 4[18]. His motives were probably two: first, the usual one of authenticating the letter; second, the special one of giving emphasis to certain of the main points of the letter; notice that vv.[11-16] are almost wholly devoted to the reiteration of ideas already expressed. This second motive led him also to write, somewhat humorously yet with serious purpose, in a larger character than his amanuensis had employed; the size of the letters would have somewhat the effect of bold-face type in a modern book, or double underlining in a manuscript, and since the apostle himself called attention to it, it would impress not only the one person who might be reading the letter to a congregation, but the listening congregation, also. Precisely how far Paul continued to write with his own hand, and how far he used the large characters, we have no certain means of knowing, but probably he did both through v.[16], at least. ἔγραψα is on this interpretation an epistolary aorist (B*MT* 44). For other examples of autographic portions of a dictated letter, see Cic. *ad Attic.* VIII 1[1]; XI 24; Aug. *Epist.* 146. *Cf.* Moff. *Introd.*, pp. 51, 88.

B* 33 read ἡλίκοις. Internal evidence is wholly indecisive, either form being good usage with no preponderance of temptation to change on either side. *Cf.* Bl.-D. 303; also Col. 2[1] Heb. 7[4]. This being the case, it is more probable that B* 33 have inadvertently modified the original than that all the rest of the authorities, including ℵACD al. have done so.

The interpretation of πηλίκοις γράμμασιν, as referring to the length of the letter (AV., "how large a letter"; so also Luth. Calv. Beng. Olsh., *et al.*) is here excluded by three considerations: (a) though γράμματα sometimes means "an epistle" (Acts 28[21]), Paul's invariable term for "epistle" is ἐπιστολή (so seventeen times); (b) such a meaning would have called for an accusative rather than a dative; and (c) this epistle is not notably long as compared with the apostle's other epistles. Zahn cites, as showing how the length of a letter would be spoken of, Heb. 13[22] 1 Pet. 5[12]; Ign. *Rom.* 8[2]; *Pol.* 7[3]. *Cf.* also Sief. *ad loc.* The use of ἔγραψα as an epistolary aorist is quite in accordance with Paul's habit. *Cf.* Phil. 2[28] Phm.[12, 19, 21] Col. 4[8]. ἔγραψα in 1 Cor. 5[9] is, of course, not epistolary but historical, having reference to an earlier letter, and most commentators take νῦν ἔγραψα in 5[11] in the same sense. It is much more probable, however, that the verb in the latter verse is epistolary as is suggested by νῦν, and that the apostle is contrasting what he is now writing unambiguously with what he previously wrote with the same intent, but so ambigu-

ously that the Corinthians misunderstood him. The reference of
ἔγραψα in the present passage to the whole letter or the previous portion, while still interpreting γράμμασιν of the characters in which the
letter is written (Ell. Alf. Wies. Zahn, *et al.*) is, therefore, not necessitated by ordinary late Greek or Pauline usage; while the improbability
that the apostle should have thought at the outset to use the pen
himself and to write in a noticeably large hand, and that he should
have kept up this strained and difficult method of emphasis through
all the pages of the letter, only now at the end calling attention to it,
is so great, especially in the case of a letter written to groups of people
and intended to be read aloud to them, as to amount to practical impossibility. The case of Cato, who, according to Plutarch, wrote his-
tories for his son, ἰδίᾳ χειρὶ καὶ μεγάλοις γράμμασιν (see Moff.
Introd. p. 88) is not at all a parallel one. That Paul wrote the letter
himself because unable to obtain a scribe, and in a large hand because
of some physical necessity, an accident to his hand or defect of his
eyesight, is in itself improbable in view of 1², and rendered more so
by the lack of any explanation to that effect in this sentence, in which
he evidently intends by his "large letters" to appeal to the feelings of
his readers. The objection that there were other parts of the letter
that equally with this called for emphasis, loses its force in view of
the fact that the following verses themselves repeat the chief things
that the apostle wishes to impress on the minds of the Galatians.

12. Ὅσοι θέλουσιν εὐπροσωπῆσαι ἐν σαρκί, οὗτοι ἀναγκάζουσιν ὑμᾶς περιτέμνεσθαι, μόνον ἵνα τῷ σταυρῷ τοῦ
χριστοῦ μὴ διώκωνται· "As many as wish to make a good
showing in things pertaining to the flesh, these compel you
to receive circumcision, only that they may not be persecuted
because of the cross of the Christ." Proceeding to the things
which he desires by large letters written with his own hand to
emphasise, the apostle alleges first the selfish motive of his
opponents. It is trouble for themselves that they wish to
avoid. Themselves members of the orthodox Jewish community, different from other Jews only in that they accepted
Jesus as the expected Messiah, they wish to remain in good
standing in the Jewish community, and to that end wish to be
able to point to converts from the Gentile world who have not
merely accepted Jesus as the Christ, but have also conformed
to those physical requirements of the Jewish law which from
the Jewish point of view were vital, but to Paul purely external

and physical. If they can do this they will escape that persecution which the apostle had himself suffered (5¹¹), and to which
they would be subject at the hands of their fellow-Jews as members of the Christian sect of the Jewish community, if they
favoured or did not successfully oppose its anti-legalistic tendency. τῷ σταυρῷ is a dative of cause. The word is, of course,
used by metonymy for the crucifixion of the Christ, or probably even more generally for the whole doctrine of salvation
through the crucified Jesus as against that of justification by
works of law. Cf. esp. 5¹¹, where Paul affirms that it is the
anti-legalism of the Christian position only that makes it offensive and an occasion of persecution. The use of the present
tense διώκωνται, denoting action in progress, suggests the possibility that they are already suffering persecution, in that case,
doubtless, not because of their own attitude but because of the
general tendency of the Christian movement.

’Ιησοῦ is added after Χριστοῦ by B 31 only. Eth. also has Jesu,
but follows its usual custom of placing it before Christi, also prefixing
domini to Jesu. There is a slight intrinsic probability in favour of
τοῦ Χριστοῦ only after σταυρός (see detached note on *Titles and Predicates of Jesus*, III, p. 398, and cf. 1 Cor. 1¹⁷ Phil. 3¹⁸). This fact,
together with the absence of any strong transcriptional probability on
either side favours the supposition that ’Ιησοῦ in B 31 is the product
of the scribal tendency to lengthen the titles of Jesus. Cf. on 2¹⁶.

Διώκωνται is the reading of אBD al. plu. Chr. Thdrt. Dam. Following ACFGKLP 31, 234, 429, 1908 al. plus.¹⁰ Euthal., Tdf. reads
-ονται. The indicative is probably the result of itacism. Cf. the
evidence on 6¹⁰ above and on 6⁹, ¹³ in Tdf. On the possibility of a
present indicative after ἵνα, see B*MT* 198; Bl.-D. 91, 369 and the
v. l. in Jn. 5²⁰ Tit. 2⁴.

Εὐπροσωπέω occurs here first in extant Greek literature, elsewhere
only in Chrys. and still later writers. Its meaning is clear, however,
from εὐπρόσωπος, "fair of face," "specious," in Aristoph. *Plut.* 976,
εὐπρόσωπον καὶ καλόν, in Luc. *Merced. Con.* 711: οὐχ ὁρῶ τὴν ἀπολογίαν
ἥτις εὐπρόσωπός σοι γένοιτο, and in Lxx, Gen. 12¹¹; from εὐπροσωπία,
"fair of appearance," Dion. Hal. etc.; from εὐπροσωπίζεσθαι, applied
to words, and meaning "to be fair" in Ps. 141⁶; and from σεμνοπροσωπέω,
"to assume a solemn face," Aristoph. *Nub.* 363. See further in Cremer
and Elsner. The term is evidently here used in a figurative sense.
ἐν σαρκί means "in the sphere of things that have their basis in the
body." σάρξ is here fundamentally physical in its meaning, but is

used by metonymy to include the whole sphere of life conditioned by the flesh; see detached note on Πνεῦμα and Σάρξ, II 5, and *cf.* 1 Cor. 1²⁶ 7²⁸; also Phil. 3¹ᶠᶠ·, though the meaning is not quite the same there. The whole expression describes those to whom it refers as desiring to stand well in matters whose real basis is physical rather than spiritual. Chrys., *ad loc.*, says that εὐπροσωπεῖν ἐν σαρκί is equivalent to εὐδοκιμεῖν παρ' ἀνθρώποις, "to be popular with men" —a paraphrastic interpretation. ἀναγκάζουσι is, of course, conative, as in 2¹⁴.

Of the present infinitive περιτέμνεσθαι two explanations suggest themselves: (1) As over against the aor., which would express the circumcision as a simple fact, and the perfect, which would express an existing state the result of a past fact, either of which would be suitable in speaking of those who without their own will were circumcised in infancy, Paul employs a present form (*cf.* 5². ³ 6¹¹) in speaking of the circumcision of Gentiles in mature life. As in verbs of effort progressiveness becomes conativeness (*cf.* B*MT* 11), so in this verb the present is the appropriate form to suggest voluntariness which necessarily accompanies circumcision under the circumstances here in mind. This idea is suggested by the English translation "receive circumcision." *Cf.* Moffatt's translation, "get circumcised." (2) There is some reason to believe that expressions of compulsion, consisting of a verb and dependent infinitive are thought of as constituting a unit, and as being as a whole either conative or resultative. It is true, at least, that the aorist of ἀναγκάζω is resultative and is in N. T. always followed by an aorist infinitive, and that the present and imperfect of ἀναγκάζω are conative and are followed by a present infinitive. Thus the present is found in Acts 26¹¹, Gal. 2¹⁴, and here; the aorist in Mt. 14²² Mk. 6⁴⁵ Lk. 14²³ Acts 29¹⁹ Gal. 2³.

WH. place a dash before μή, implying that the sentence is anacoluthic, Paul having intended when he wrote μόνον ἵνα to end the sentence with a positive expression. There is a certain basis for this punctuation in the fact that the apostle almost invariably places the μή of a negative ἵνα clause immediately after ἵνα, its absence from this position suggesting, therefore, that he intended to complete the clause with an unnegatived verb. Against this view, however, is the practical impossibility of supplying any such verb, of which τῷ σταυρῷ τοῦ Χριστοῦ could be the modifier. It is better, therefore, to suppose that Paul has in this case departed from his otherwise almost invariable custom and, as in 1 Cor. 2⁵ 2 Cor. 13¹⁰, interjected a phrase between ἵνα and μή.

13. οὐδὲ γὰρ οἱ περιτεμνόμενοι αὐτοὶ νόμον φυλάσσουσιν, ἀλλὰ θέλουσιν ὑμᾶς περιτέμνεσθαι ἵνα ἐν τῇ ὑμετέρᾳ σαρκὶ καυχήσωνται. "For not even they that receive circumcision

are themselves law-abiding, but they wish you to be circumcised that they may glory in your flesh." This sentence introduced by γάρ confirms that which is expressed by μόνον in
v.¹² (viz., that the only reason for their course was a desire to
escape persecution), by excluding the reason which the judaisers
probably themselves alleged as the motive of their conduct,
and which Paul assumes is the only alternative motive, namely,
a sincere zeal for the law. This zeal he disproves by the fact
that their converts, οἱ περιτεμνόμενοι, do not themselves
keep law, doubtless referring not to failure on the part of these
converts to attain to perfect conformity to the law, since such
failure would not disprove the zeal of the judaisers, but to the
fact that they do not undertake to keep it in full and are not
required by the judaisers to do so. See 5³ and notes there.
οἱ περιτεμνόμενοι, however, does not refer specifically to
those who among the Galatians had been circumcised, which
would have called for οἱ ἐν ὑμῖν περιτμηθέντες (or περιτετμημένοι). φυλάσσουσιν is a general present and the statement
refers in general to those who under the influence of the judaisers receive circumcision. νόμον has here the same sense as
in 5³, but is used qualitatively. "In your flesh" means "in the
fact that you have been circumcised," which would be the sign
of your conversion to legalistic Judaism.

The words θέλουσιν ὑμᾶς περιτέμνεσθαι repeat the thought of
ἀναγκάζ. ὑμ. περιτ., v.¹², and the clause ἵνα . . . καυχήσωνται expresses
in positive and emphatic form that of ἵνα μὴ διώκωνται. The phrase
ἐν τῇ ὑμετέρᾳ σαρκί, referring literally to the flesh in the material
sense as that in which circumcision takes place, is chosen in preference
to a pronominal phrase referring directly to the subject of περιτέμνεσθαι
the more distinctly to express the unworthy character of their boasting. On σαρκί here cf. the same word in 3². It is more literally employed than in v.¹² above. ἐν, literally denoting the sphere of the
boasting, suggests also ground, basis.

περιτεμνόμενοι is attested by ℵACDKP al. Mcion. f Vg. (qui cir-
cumciduntur) Syr. (psh. et harcl.) Sah. Arm.; Chr. Euthal. Thdrt. Dam.
περιτετμημένοι is the reading of BL al.⁵⁰ (F reads περιτέμνημι, G
περιτεμνηημένοι, both impossible readings, but probably attesting
the perfect, d g (qui circumcisi sunt) Goth. Boh. Eth. Victorin. Aug.
Hier. Ambrst. External evidence is not decisive. Transcriptional

probability favours -μνόμενοι, since the perfect would have been a wholly unobjectionable reading.

Against the common view held by Mey. (who reads περιτετμ.) Sief. Zahn, Ell. Ltft. Alf. that οἱ περιτ. designates the judaisers (Wies. and, according to Sief., Mathias hold the other view) the following reasons are decisive: (1) It is very doubtful whether Paul could have alleged in this unqualified way, and without explanation that the Jewish Christians did not keep the law. Rom. chap. 2, is scarcely a parallel case. (2) Had he wished to affirm it, the words οἱ περιτεμνόμενοι would have been superfluous, the subject of φυλάσσουσιν being the same as that of διώκωνται. This affirmation would have been most forcibly and clearly expressed by οὐδὲ γὰρ αὐτοὶ νόμ. φυλ. Had he wished to refer to the circumcision of the judaisers as emphasising their inconsistency in not keeping the law, he must have written not οἱ περιτ., but οὗτοι περιτ., "these, though circumcised." (3) The tense of the participle is in itself decisive. (a) Although a present participle may be used as a general present, designating all those who perform (or, in the passive, are subjected to) the action denoted by the verb, whether the mark of the class be the single or the habitual doing of it (BMT 123–126), yet it is not so employed, unless the mind is directed to the performance of the action, as distinguished from the resultant fact. There could have been no motive for such a distinction in this case if the apostle had intended to designate the judaisers (or the Jews). For this he must inevitably have written περιτετμημένοι.* (b) Throughout this epistle the present of περιτ. whether in participle, infinitive, or subjunctive, 5², ³ 6¹², ¹³ᵇ, means "to be circumcised" in the sense "to receive circumcision," "to get circumcised" (Moffatt), not in the sense "to be a circumcised person." (4) This conclusion is confirmed by 5³, which shows that the judaisers had not as yet endeavoured to bring the Galatians under obedience to the whole law. Against these reasons the absence of an expressed subject of θέλουσιν is of little weight. The statement concerning οἱ περιτεμ. reflecting, as it does, the attitude of the judaisers, the mind easily supplies as the subject of θέλουσιν after ἀλλὰ the judaisers who have been the principal subject of the discourse from the beginning of v.¹², and all possible ambiguity is excluded by the close

---

* Ellicott's assertion: "The use of the present may be fairly explained on the ground that St. Paul includes in the idea not merely their conformity to the rite (which strictly becomes a past act), but their endeavour thereby to draw others into the same state, which is a *present* and continuing act," ascribing to the present passive the ideas expressed by an aorist passive and a present active, is manifestly incorrect. In the passage cited by Ell. and at greater length by Ltft. *ad loc.*, from *Act. Petr. et Paul.*, § 63, the present περιτεμνόμενοι does seem to have something of the force of a perfect. But arguments drawn from the usage of this book, considerably later than Paul, are hardly strong enough to overthrow the clear evidence of Galatians itself. The οἱ ῥέοντες quoted by Ltft. from Plato, *Theæt.* 181A, is a nickname, which our participle quite certainly is not.

parallelism between θέλουσιν ὑμᾶς περιτέμνεσθαι, v.¹³ᵇ and ἀναγκάζουσιν ὑμᾶς περιτέμνεσθαι of v.¹².

14. ἐμοὶ δὲ μὴ γένοιτο καυχᾶσθαι εἰ μὴ ἐν τῷ σταυρῷ τοῦ κυρίου ἡμῶν Ἰησοῦ Χριστοῦ, δι' οὗ ἐμοὶ κόσμος ἐσταύρωται κἀγὼ κόσμῳ. "But far be it from me to glory except in the cross of our Lord Jesus Christ, through whom a world hath been crucified to me and I to a world." In striking contrast with the boasting of the judaisers, which has its sphere and basis in the mere material flesh of men, the apostle sets forth as *his* ground of boasting—note ἐμοί emphatic by position—the central fact of his gospel, the cross of Christ (*cf.* Rom. 1¹⁶ 1 Cor. 1²³ᶠ.) which has wrought a complete revolution in his own life. τῷ σταυρῷ undoubtedly has the same significance as in v.¹². See in v.¹⁵ the clear evidence that the doctrine of the cross is there also the antithesis to legalism. κόσμος is quite certainly employed here in the fifth of the meanings indicated in the note on Στοιχεῖα τοῦ κόσμου, p. 514, viz., "the mode of life characterised by earthly advantages." But the particular earthly advantages which the apostle has in mind are not, as in 1 Jn. 2¹⁵, etc., the sensual pleasures of riches and other like things, but, rather, those of which he speaks in Phil. 3³, ⁴. Paul's world, κόσμος, with which he severed his relation, when the cross of Christ acquired for him its new significance, was that of Israelitish descent, circumcision, the rank and dignity of a Pharisee, the righteousness that is in law, touching which he was blameless. To this world he became dead by the cross of Christ, because in Christ's death on the cross he saw a demonstration that God's way of accepting men was not on the basis of works of law, but on that of faith in Christ. *Cf.* 2¹⁹, ²⁰ 3¹³ 4⁴, ⁵ Rom. 3²¹ᶠᶠ. 4²⁵ 5¹⁸, ¹⁹. For evidence that the significance of the cross is in what it proves respecting God's real attitude towards men, see the extended discussion of 3¹³. The fulness of the expression τοῦ κυρίου ἡμῶν Ἰησοῦ Χριστοῦ adds weight to the utterance and reflects the emotion with which the statement is made; *cf.* detached note on the *Titles and Predicates of Jesus*, p. 393. As to what the apostle means by "boasting in the cross," see 1 Cor. 1¹⁸ᶠᶠ. Rom. 5², ³, ¹¹.

On μὴ γένοιτο, see on 2¹⁷. On the use of the dative with γένοιτο (here only in N. T. with μὴ γένοιτο), cf. Lk. 1³⁸; see also Mt. 8¹³ 9²⁹. The infinitive does not occur elsewhere in N. T. after μὴ γένοιτο, but is common in Lxx; cf. Gen. 44⁷· ¹⁷ Josh. 22²⁹ 24¹⁶ 1 Ki. 20 (21)³ 1 Mac. 9¹⁰ 13⁵ (cited by Ltft.); for the inf. after other forms of γίνομαι, cf. Acts 9³¹ Lk. 6¹² Mt. 18¹³. The use of κόσμος and κόσμῳ without the article gives to both words a qualitative emphasis; cf. Rom. 11¹⁵ 1 Cor. 3²² 2 Cor. 5¹⁹. ἐμοί and κόσμῳ are datives of relation; see on νόμῳ, 2¹⁹ and cf. Rom. 6²· ¹⁰· ¹¹ 7⁶. δι' οὗ, characterising the cross as that through the instrumentality of which he had wholly severed connection with his old world of Pharisaic dignity and legalism, leaves undescribed the process by which the cross achieved this result. For this unexpressed element of the apostle's thought, see on 2¹⁹· ²⁰, and especially on 3¹³· ¹⁴.

15. οὔτε γὰρ περιτομή τι ἔστιν οὔτε ἀκροβυστία, ἀλλὰ καινὴ κτίσις. "For neither is circumcision anything, nor uncircumcision, but a new act of creation." In these words the apostle gives a reason for glorying only in the cross of Christ (v.¹⁴ᵃ), especially as against those who glory in circumcision (v.¹³); yet not content to exclude circumcision only, he rejects every material ground of boasting, whether it be the circumcision of the Jew, or the uncircumcision of the Gentile. For doubtless the Gentile was just as proud of being uncircumcised as the Jew was of his circumcision. Cf. 5⁶, where to the περιτομή which is under discussion he adds, as here, οὔτε ἀκροβυστία. κτίσις is probably to be taken in its active sense, referring to the divine activity in the production of a new moral life (cf. Col. 3¹⁰), but the emphasis of the expression is not on this aspect of the matter but upon the radical transformation of character implied in the choice of such a word as κτίσις, "creation," and the addition of καινή, new. The fact referred to is that which is described in different terminology in 2¹⁹· ²⁰ Rom. 6⁴⁻⁶· ¹¹. What the apostle meant to affirm about καινὴ κτίσις he leaves to his readers to infer. The τι ἔστιν of the preceding clause suggests it, but, of course, conveys less than he meant; "is essential" is nearer his thought. Cf. 5⁶ 1 Cor. 7¹⁹.

οὔτε (some authorities οὐ) γάρ is attested by B 33, 1908 Syr. (psh. harcl. pal.) Sah.(?)Goth. Chr. Hier. Aug.; while ℵACDFGKLP al.

pler. d f g Vg. Boh. Sah.(?) Euthal. Thdrt. Dam. Victorin. Amb. Ambrst. read ἐν γὰρ Χριστῷ Ἰησοῦ οὔτε. Despite the weight of the group supporting the latter reading (*cf.* on 2¹³ 3²¹ 5²⁶ 6², ¹¹, ¹³) it is clearly a harmonistic corruption under the influence of 5⁶. As in 2¹⁶, the correct reading is preserved by B 33 al.

Κτίσις, in classical writers, from Pindar down, and not infrequent in Lxx and Apocr., is used in N. T. either (1) as a verbal noun, meaning "act of creation," Rom. 1²⁰, κτίσις κόσμου, or, (2) as a concrete noun equivalent to κτίσμα either (a) individually, "a created person or thing," Rom. 8³⁹ Heb. 4¹³, or (b) collectively, of the sum of created things, or the total of a particular class of created things: Rev. 3¹⁴ Rom. 8²² (Mk. 16¹⁵); the meaning in the difficult passage 1 Pet. 2¹³ need not be discussed here. The use of the same phrase, καινὴ κτίσις, in the concrete (passive) sense, 2 Cor. 5¹⁷, suggests the concrete meaning here, but the antithesis to περιτομή and ἀκροβυστία favours the verbal (actional) sense. The latter is also favoured by the parallel passages, 1 Cor. 7¹⁹: ἡ περιτομὴ οὐδέν ἐστιν, καὶ ἡ ἀκροβυστία οὐδέν ἐστιν, ἀλλὰ τήρησις ἐντολῶν θεοῦ, and Gal. 5⁶: οὔτε περιτομή τι ἰσχύει οὔτε ἀκροβυστία, ἀλλὰ πίστις δι' ἀγάπης ἐνεργουμένη, in both of which the second member of the antithesis is a term of action. In all three passages the term used is qualitative. A comparison of the second members in the three passages is instructive. In 5⁶ πίστις and ἀγάπη are purely ethical terms, descriptive of the fundamental moral attitude of the Christian. In 1 Cor. 7¹⁹ τήρησις ἐντολῶν is both a more external characterisation of the Christian life and more formal, in that no intimation is given of the content of the commandments. καινὴ κτίσις in the present passage is, on the one side, less definite as to the moral character of the new life than either of the other expressions, and, on the other hand, directs attention to the radical change involved rather than to the external expression or the moral quality of the life thus produced. Any close connection between this expression and the Hebrew בְּרִיָּה חֲדָשָׁה (a new creature), meaning "proselyte," is improbable.* To have used a phrase which would naturally be understood as meaning a proselyte would have been to render the sentence confused and self-contradictory. Had the expression been in current use with this meaning, Paul must at least have added ἐν Χριστῷ.

* Euthalius (Zacagnius, *Collect. Monum. Vet.* I 561; *Gallandi Bibl. Patr.* X 260) and after him Photius, *Amphiloch. Quest.* 183 (Migne 151), and a ms. of the eleventh century (Montfaucon, *Bibl. bibl.* I 195) express the opinion that the statement, 6¹⁸ οὔτε περιτομή τι ἐστιν οὔτε ἀκροβυστία ἀλλὰ καινὴ κτίσις, is a quotation from an apocryphal writing ascribed to Moses. Georgius Snycellus (*Chron.* Ed. Dind. I 48), whose statement, however, is probably based, like the others, upon that of Euthalius, specifies an apocalypse of Moses as the source of the quotation. The fact that the same epigrammatic saying recurs in very similar form (*cf.* above) in 5⁶ 1 Cor. 7¹⁹ is not unfavourable to the view that this is a quotation. But,

16. καὶ ὅσοι τῷ κανόνι τούτῳ στοιχήσουσιν, εἰρήνη ἐπ᾽ αὐτούς, καὶ ἔλεος καὶ ἐπι τὸν Ἰσραὴλ τοῦ θεοῦ. "And as many as shall walk by this rule, peace be upon them, and mercy upon the Israel of God." The apostle concludes this paragraph of brief reiterations of the chief ideas of the letter (*cf.* on v.[11]) with a benediction upon all whose life is conformed to the great principle for which he has been contending, viz., the essentially spiritual character of religion as against the ascription of fundamental religious value to any physical or material condition, however sanctioned. κανών, occurring in N. T. here and 2 Cor. 10[13-16] only, meaning properly "measuring rod" or "straight edge," is clearly shown by τούτῳ (referring to v.[15]) to have here its metaphorical sense of "principle." στοιχέω doubtless has here the same meaning as in 5[25] (*q. v.*), viz., "'o walk, to conduct oneself." While v.[15], to which τῷ κανόνι τούτῳ refers, is affirmative rather than imperative, yet the proposition which it affirms is of fundamental importance for the determination of conduct. He who recognises the value-lessness of such externals as circumcision and uncircumcision and the necessity of the new spiritual life will, on the one hand, be unmoved by the appeal of the judaisers to receive circumcision, and on the other seek, rather, to be led by, and to live by, the Spirit.

Καὶ ἔλεος is usually joined with εἰρήνη, as with it limiting ἐπ᾽ αὐτούς, the comma being placed after ἔλεος (so Tdf. WH. Ell. Ltft. Alf. Wies. Sief. Zahn). Against this interpretation, however, it is to be said: (a) The order εἰρήνη καὶ ἔλεος, if both words have reference to one class of persons, is illogical, placing effect first and cause afterwards. ἔλεος is joined with εἰρήνη elsewhere in benedictions in N. T. in 1 Tim. 1[2] 2 Tim. 1[2] 2 Jn. [3] Jude [2], always preceding εἰρήνη. Note, also, the often-repeated benediction, χάρις and εἰρήνη, in which χάρις, closely corresponding to ἔλεος in meaning, always precedes εἰρήνη. καὶ ἔλεος becomes, then, an afterthought, to which καὶ ἐπὶ τὸν

on the other hand, an apocryphon entitled "Apocalypse of Moses" is not otherwise known. The statement of the others (Euthalius, etc.) is general and vague. The extant so-called "Assumption of Moses" does not contain the sentence. But even though the passage should actually have been found in the text of some apocryphon of Moses as extant in Euthalius's day, that alone would by no means make clear what was the relation between this and the Pauline writing. Certainly the evidence as above displayed is not strong enough to prove that this is a quotation.

'Ισραὴλ τοῦ θεοῦ appends a second afterthought. (b) Though **Rom.**
9⁶ 1 Cor. 10¹⁸ show that Paul distinguished between Israel according
to the flesh and the Israel according to election or promise, and Rom.
2²⁹ Phil. 3³ suggest that he might use τὸν 'Ισραὴλ τοῦ θεοῦ of all believers in Christ, regardless of nationality, there is, in fact, no instance
of his using 'Ισραὴλ except of the Jewish nation or a part thereof.
These facts favour the interpretation of the expression as applying not
to the Christian community, but to Jews; yet, in view of τοῦ θεοῦ,
not to the whole Jewish nation, but to the pious Israel, the remnant
according to the election of grace (Rom. 11⁵), including even those who
had not seen the truth as Paul saw it, and so could not be included
in ὅσοι . . . στοιχ. In this case the benediction falls into two distinct parts. In the first the apostle invokes peace upon those who
recognise and act in accordance with the principle of v.¹⁵, and, in distinction from them, the mercy of God through which they may obtain
enlightenment and enter into peace, upon those within Israel who
even though as yet unenlightened are the true Israel of God. Against
the combined force of these two reasons the presence of καί after
ἔλεος is of little weight. It is quite explicable as slightly ascensive.
In view of the apostle's previous strong anti-judaistic expressions, he
feels impelled, by the insertion of καί, to emphasise this expression of
his true attitude towards his people. It can scarcely be translated
into English without overtranslating.

Κανών is believed to be ultimately of Semitic origin. *Cf.* Gregory,
Canon and Text, p. 15. It is found, however, in Greek from Homer
down in a great variety of usages at a greater or less remove from the
probable ground-meaning, "a tool or utensil made of reed or cane."
(1) Literally, of a large number of implements, most of which were
probably originally made of cane, the name being retained though
other material was later used in their construction: *e. g.,* the rods
across the hollow of the shield, through which the arm was passed:
Il. VIII 193; XIII 407; the shuttle or quill, by which the threads of the
woof were passed between those of the warp, *Il.* XXIII 761; in classical
times most frequently of the rule or straight edge used by masons and
carpenters: Soph. *Frag.* 421; Eur. *Troiad.* 6; Aristoph. *Av.* 999, 1002;
Plato, *Phil.* 56B; Æschin. 3²⁰⁰, etc. (in the same meaning, but metaphorically used: Aristoph. *Ran.* 799: Eur. *Supp.* 650); later of the
scribe's rule, Anth. Pal. 6⁶³; a curtain rod, Chares ap. Ath. 538D; the
keys or stops of a flute, Anth. Pal. 9. 365; the beam or tongue of a
balance, Anth. Pal. 11. 334. (2) Metaphorically. It is probably
upon the basis of the meaning most frequently found in classical times,
"a ruler or straight edge," that the word came to be used in a metaphorical sense, of anything regulative, determinative, a rule or stand·
ard. *Cf.* the similar transfer of meaning in our English word "rule."
It is so used of the written law conceived of as a whole, or a section

of it, Lycurg. 149. 4; of the good man, Arist. *Eth. N.* 3. 6 (1113 a³³);
of the Δορυφόρος of Polycleitus and the book explaining it: Pliny,
H. N. 34. 55; Galen, *Hippocr. et Plat.* V 3; of a general rule or
principle: *Anecdota Græca* (Bekker), 1180; Epict. *Diss.* I 28²⁸; Luc.
Halieus, 30; of a list of the chief epochs or eras, which served to determine intermediate dates, Plut. *Sol.* 27¹; and for other things of the
same general character.

In the Lxx the word is found but once, in the difficult passage,
Mic. 7⁴, where the translator either read a text differing from the
Massorah, or misunderstood the Hebrew The meaning is probably
"measuring rod" or "line." In the Apocr. it occurs only once,
Jdth. 13⁶ (⁸), for a rod used in the construction of a bed; in 4 Mac. 7²¹
it means "rule" or "standard."

In N. T., only Paul uses the word and that in but two passages:
2 Cor. 10¹³ ¹⁶, where the meaning probably is "measure" (others prefer
the meaning, "limit, boundary-line"), and in the present passage,
where it evidently refers to the preceding sentence, which it describes,
as a general rule or principle, serving as a standard. The use of κανών
to designate ecclesiastical statutes and ordinances, a fixed body of
Christian doctrines serving as a standard of correct teaching (sometimes conceived of as summed up in the pithy sentences of the Apostle's Creed), the clergy, the catalogue of martyrs or saints, or the collection of books accepted as authoritative for Christian doctrine and
practice, does not occur until later and belongs properly under a treatment of the ecclesiastical development of the word. In the last-
mentioned use it is (according to Zahn) not found until the middle
of the fourth century A. D., in Athanasius, *Decr. Syn. Nic.*; *cf.* also
Canon 59 of the Synod at Laodicea (Mansi II 574); Athanasius,
Festal Letter 39. For a fuller treatment of the word, see Zahn, *Grund-
riss der Gesch. des ntl. Kanons,*² pp. 1 *ff.*; *cf.* also Westcott, *The Canon
of the N. T.*⁵, App. A, pp. 504 *ff.*; Gregory, *Canon and Text*, pp. 15 *ff.*

Like πνεύματι in 5²⁵, τῷ κανόνι is a dative of means. On the use
of the future (στοιχήσουσιν) in a hypothetical clause see B*MT* 308.
Cf. Lk. 17³¹. On εἰρήνη, *cf.* on 1³. The verb to be supplied is an opta-
tive as in 1³ 6¹⁵, and frequently in similar connections.

2. *Appeal enforced by reference to his own sufferings* (6¹⁷).

17. Τοῦ λοιποῦ κόπους μοι μηδεὶς παρεχέτω, ἐγὼ γὰρ τὰ
στίγματα τοῦ Ἰησοῦ ἐν τῷ σώματί μου βαστάζω. "Henceforth let no man give me trouble; for I bear the marks of Jesus
in my body." This verse is best treated, as in WH., as a separate paragraph. V.¹⁸ is the benediction of the whole epistle,

hence not to be attached to v.¹⁷, and v.¹⁶ is the benediction concluding the paragraph begun at v.¹¹. With evidently deep feeling the apostle demands that henceforth he be spared the distress which his opponents have hitherto been inflicting upon him, and appeals to the scars which he has received in the service of Jesus, and which he in a figure describes as evidence that he belongs to Jesus.

Τοῦ λοιποῦ is doubtless here, as usually elsewhere, a genitive of time, meaning "henceforth." The interpretation of Zahn, which makes it equivalent to τῶν ἄλλων, a genitive of the whole limiting μηδείς and referring to the remainder of Israel, which is not τοῦ θεοῦ, is negatived by the fact that the familiar use of τοῦ λοιποῦ in the sense of "henceforth" would have made it necessary for Paul to employ τῶν ἄλλων to express the thought which this interpretation finds here. The interpretation of Wies. which takes τοῦ λοιποῦ in the sense "finally," equivalent to τὸ λοιπόν in Phil. 3¹ 4⁸, etc., is unsustained by any clear evidence of the use of the genitive τοῦ λοιποῦ in this sense. Eph. 6¹⁰ is the only example that is alleged for such usage, and neither text nor interpretation of this passage is quite certain.

Κόπος is frequent elsewhere in Paul in the sense of "labour, toil," 2 Cor. 6⁵ 1 Thes. 1³ 2⁹ 3⁵, etc. But the phrase κόπους παρέχειν clearly means, not "to impose toil," but "to give trouble"; cf. Sir. 29⁴ Mt. 26¹⁰ Mk. 14⁶ Lk. 11⁷ 18⁵. The use of the present imperative suggests an action already in progress. With μηδείς it means, "let no one continue to give, etc.," "let him cease giving"; cf. BMT 165.

By τὰ στίγματα Paul undoubtedly refers to the effects of his sufferings as an apostle (cf. 2 Cor. 6⁴⁻⁶ 11²³ff.), and as the ἐν τῷ σώματί μου shows, the physical effects, perhaps actual scars. The only doubt to which the phrase is subject concerns the value which he means to ascribe to these marks of his sufferings, or the figure of speech under which he means to present them. Elsner and Raphelius* find the explanation in a custom spoken of by Hdt. 2¹¹³, according to which a fugitive who took refuge in a temple and there received upon his body the marks of the god, could not thereafter be touched. Sief.

---

* Raphelius, *Annot. Philol. in N. T.*, II, p. 460 f., says: Videtur Paulus respicere ad morem illorum, qui, quod stigmata sacra gestarent, Deo sacri erant, quosque propterea nefas erat tangere, si modo ille mos Galatis notus fuit. Caussam certe hanc affert, cur nemo sibi molestias exhibere debeat, quod stigmata Domini Jesu portet. Mentionem hujus moris facit Herodotus (lib. 2. cap. 113). Erat in littore ad ostium Nili Herculis templum, quod nunc quoque est: ἐς τὸ ἢν καταφυγὼν οἰκέτης ὅτεῳ ἀνθρώπων ἐπιβάληται στίγματα ἱρά, ἑωυτὸν διδοὺς τῷ θεῷ, οὐκ ἔξεστι τούτου ἅψασθαι. ὁ νόμος οὗτος διατελέει ἐὼν ὅμοιος τὸ μέχρι ἐμοῦ ἀπ᾿ ἀρχῆς. τοῦ ὦν δὴ Ἀλεξάνδρου ἀπιστέαται θεράποντες πυθόμενοι τὸν περὶ τὸ ἱρὸν ἔχοντα νόμον, ἱκέται δὲ ἐζόμενοι τοῦ θεοῦ κατηγόρεον τοῦ Ἀλεξάνδρου, βουλόμενοι βλάπτειν αὐτὸν . . . Ceterum, quod Paulus dicit στίγματα βαστάζειν, Lucianus una voce

and Cremer, following many earlier interpreters, suppose the apostle
to be thinking of himself as the slave (or soldier) of Jesus, and of
the marks of his sufferings as comparable to the marks on the body
of a slave designating his ownership, or on that of a soldier, indicating the general under whom he serves; cf. Hdt. 7²³³; Diod. Sic. 34. 2¹;
Plut. *Nicias*, 29²; Deissmann, whom Zahn and M. and M. *Voc.* follow,
finds the suggestion of a charm, warding off attack, appealing especially to a papyrus of the third century A. D. (Papyrus J. 383 of the
Leyden Museum*), containing a spell, in which occur both the word
βαστάζω and the expression κόπους παρέχειν. The expression κόπους
παρεχέτω is favourable to the first or third of these views (note the
words οὐκ ἔξεστι τούτου ἄψασθαι in Hdt. 2¹¹³ and the precise phrase
κόπους παρέχειν in the papyrus). But it is doubtful whether the
usage described by Herodotus was prevalent in Paul's day and sur-
roundings, or at any rate familiar enough so that a bare allusion to it
would be intelligible. As concerns the third view, the appositeness
of the papyrus passage is greatly diminished by the fact that it makes
no reference to στίγματα; what the protected one bears being not
marks, but a miniature coffin of Osiris. On the other hand, the thought
of himself as a slave of Jesus is a favourite one with the apostle, and
the custom of branding or otherwise marking slaves was undoubtedly
familiar to the Galatians. These facts make it most probable that it
is the idea of himself as a slave of Jesus, marked as such by the scars
of his sufferings, that underlies the language of the apostle.

3. *Final benedictions* (6¹⁸).

18. Ἡ χάρις τοῦ κυρίου ἡμῶν Ἰησοῦ Χριστοῦ μετὰ τοῦ
πνεύματος ὑμῶν, ἀδελφοί· ἀμήν. "The grace of our Lord
Jesus Christ be with your spirit, brethren. Amen." The
concluding benedictions of all the letters ascribed to the apostle
Paul are alike in that they include the invocation of grace,
which, except in Colossians and the pastoral epistles, is specifi-

στιγματοφορεῖν effert, citatus in Lexico Graeco. Varius autem erat usus stigmatum. Nam
et servi in fronte iis notabantur, apud Romanos quidem fugitivi poenae causa, apud Thraces
vero, ut domini eorum noscerentur, et milites in manibus, cum militiae adscriberentur. . . .
Chrysostomus comparat cum vulneribus in bello acceptis. Sed ad scopum Pauli propius
accedere videtur, quod ex Herodoto citavimus. Vult enim ipse sacrosanctus et inviolabilis
haberi, propterea quod stigmata Domini Jesu in corpore suo gestet. Quanquam quocunque
Paulum respexisse dicas, certum tamen est, stigmatum nomine ipsum intelligere vibices ac
cicatrices ex plagis illis, lapidationibus et verberibus, quorum meminit 2 Cor. 11²³ *seqq.*
Quae signa erant manifesta, ipsum illorum similem non esse, qui circumcisionem urgebant,
ne ob crucem Christi persecutionem paterentur (v.¹²).

* Μή με δίωκε ὅδε· ανοχ παπιπετ[ον] μετουβανες· βαστάζω τὴν ταφὴν τοῦ Ὀσίρεως καὶ
ὑπάγω κατα[στ]ῆσαι αὐτὴν ε[ἰ]ς Ἀβιδος, καταστῆσαι εἰς ταστας καὶ καταθέσθαι εἰς [αλ]χας·
ἐάν μοι ὁ δεῖνα κόπους παράσχῃ, προσ (τ) ρέψω αυτὴν αὐτῷ. De.*BS.* p. 354.

cally called "the grace of the Lord Jesus Christ." Phil. 4²³ and Phm.²⁵ are like Galatians in using μετὰ τοῦ πνεύματος ὑμῶν instead of the usual μεθ' ὑμῶν. Ephesians only includes the invocation of peace, which is regularly found in the opening salutations of the apostle's letters. On the wholly exceptional form of 2 Cor., see p. 509. The expression "the grace of our Lord Jesus Christ" is to be taken at its full value; for, while the apostle closely associates the love of God manifest in Christ and the love of Christ (Rom. 8³⁵, ³⁹), he expressly ascribes to Christ in his earthly career a love for men and grace towards them (2²⁰ 2 Cor. 8⁹, etc.), and conceiving of Jesus as still living and in relation to men (1 Thes. 1¹⁰ Rom. 8³⁴, etc.) ascribes to him as thus living a gracious attitude towards men, manifest on the one hand in spiritual fellowship with them (2²⁰) and, on the other hand, in intercession for them (Rom. 8³⁴). The phrase μετὰ τοῦ πνεύματος ὑμῶν shows that it is the former that is here in mind. The sentence is, therefore, a prayer that the Galatians may have the indwelling gracious presence of the Lord Jesus Christ. By the addition of ἀδελφοί (cf. on 1¹¹) at the end of this letter, in which there is much of reproof and much strenuous exhortation, the apostle expresses his continued affection for the Galatians. Though the term itself is frequent in Paul's letters, in no other case does he add it to a concluding benediction. The addition of ἀμήν (cf. on 1⁵), appended to a doxology in 1⁵ Rom. 11³⁶ 16²⁷ Eph. 3²¹ Phil. 4²⁰, etc., and in Rom. 15³³ to a benediction (it is apparently a scribal addition in Rom. 16²⁴ 1 Cor. 16²⁴ 1 Thes. 3¹³ Phm. ²⁵), still further emphasises the strength and depth of the feeling with which the apostle brings to a close this remarkable letter. Though it was probably dictated rapidly, and was certainly composed under the stress of deep emotion, the six brief chapters of which it consists constitute one of the most important documents of early Christianity and one of the noblest pleas ever written for Christian liberty and spiritual religion.

APPENDIX.

DETACHED NOTES ON IMPORTANT TERMS OF PAUL'S VOCABULARY.

I. ΑΠΟΣΤΟΛΟΣ.*

I. CLASSICAL AND OTHER NON-CHRISTIAN USAGE.

The word ἀπόστολος is manifestly cognate with the verb ἀποστέλλω. In classical authors it is employed both as an adjective and as a noun. Joined with πλοῖος it was used much as our modern word "despatch" is, the phrase meaning "a despatch boat," i. e., a boat in commission. In Dem. 252[7], 262[15], etc., ἀποστόλος (paroxytone) alone signifies "a naval expedition." In Herodotus ἀπόστολος (proparoxytone) is used of a person, meaning an ambassador or delegate, a person commissioned by another to represent him. See 1[21]: ὁ μὲν δὴ ἀπόστολος ἐς τὴν Μίλητον ἦν. 5[38]: ἐς Λακεδαίμονα

---

* For other discussions of the subject see Lightfoot, *Commentary on Galatians*, pp. 92–101; Harnack, "Die Lehre der zwölf Apostel," in *Texte u. Untersuchungen*, II 93–118; Hincks, "Limits of the Apostolate," in *JBL*. 1895, pp. 37–47; Haupt, *Zum Verständnis des Apostolats*; Monnier, *La notion de l'apostolat*.

τριήρει ἀπόστολος ἐγίνετο.* In a similar but more general sense, it occurs in the Lxx (A) and Aq. in 1 Ki. 14⁶: ἐγώ εἰμι ἀπόστολος πρός σε σκληρός: "I am a hard messenger to thee," I bring thee heavy tidings. It is found also in Sym. at Isa. 18², but not elsewhere in the Greek O. T. In Jos. *Ant.* 17. 300 (11¹), ἀπόστολος apparently means "a despatching, a sending": ἀφίκετο εἰς τὴν Ῥώμην πρεσβεία Ἰουδαίων, Οὐάρου τὸν ἀπόστολον αὐτῶν τῷ ἔθνει ἐπικεχωρηκότος ὑπὲρ αἰτήσεως αὐτονομίας: "There came to Rome an embassy of Jews, Varus having granted the people the privilege of sending it for the purpose of asking for autonomy." The indirect evidence of Christian writers seems to show that in the post-Christian period the Jews used the term ἀπόστολος, or a Semitic term which was expressed in Greek by ἀπόστολος, (a) of persons despatched from Jerusalem to other cities, especially to gather the temple tribute; (b) of those who, after the destruction of Jerusalem, were associated with the patriarch in deliberations and in the carrying out of what was agreed upon. See the evidence in Ltft. pp. 93 *ff.*

II. NEW TESTAMENT USAGE IN GENERAL.

In the New Testament the term is used of persons only. Its general meaning, clearly seen in passages in which it is used in a non-technical sense, is "a delegate," "a representative," one commissioned by another to represent him in some way. Thus in 2 Cor. 8²³ and Phil. 2²⁵, it is used of persons delegated by a church to execute a commission.†

In Heb. 3¹ Jesus is spoken of as "the apostle and high priest (ἀπόστολος καὶ ἀρχιερεύς) of our confession" and is immediately afterwards characterised as faithful to him that appointed him.‡ In Jn. 13¹⁶ the word is used in such a way as almost to involve a definition of the word. "A servant is not greater than his master, nor a delegate (ἀπόστολος) greater than he that sent him."

III. THE APOSTLES OF CHRIST.

But in the majority of its occurrences in the New Testament the word is used of a class of persons in the Christian church, or among the followers of Jesus. The full expression was evidently ἀπόστολος Χριστοῦ, or ἀπόστολος Χριστοῦ Ἰησοῦ (2 Cor. 1¹ 11¹¹, etc.). But for this full expression ἀπόστολος alone is much more frequently used. It is found in nearly

* For exx. in inscriptions and papyri see Dittenberger, *Sylloge*, 153, and M. and M. *Voc. s. v.*; *cf.* also Nägeli, *Wortschatz des Apostels Paulus*, p. 23.

† In both cases a journey is involved, the matter to be attended to a financial one, and the person who makes the journey does not simply bear a message, but in a larger way represents the church. This may, indeed, be accidental coincidence, rather than decisive indication of the constant usage of the word. Yet compare the Jewish use of the term, as stated above.

‡ A similar idea of Christ is several times expressed in the Gospel of John, *e. g.*, Jn. 17³: "This is life eternal to know thee, the only true God, and Jesus Christ whom thou hast sent."

&ll the books of the New Testament, and was evidently in the apostolic age the common term for a well-known class in the church.

The earliest references to the apostles of Christ (reckoned by the date of the writing in which they occur) are found in the Pauline epistles, and bear witness not only to Paul's claim to be himself an apostle but to the existence of other members of the class, who were apostles before him (Gal. 1¹⁷). In the effort to trace the development of the apostolate it will be well therefore to begin by inquiring as to the identity of these apostles before Paul.

1. *The apostles before Paul.*—(a) The Twelve and their earliest designation. In the number of those who were apostles before him, Paul evidently includes Peter, and in all probability John (Gal. 1¹⁷⁻¹⁹ 2⁹). In the gospels there are frequent references to twelve disciples of Jesus, whom Mt. once calls the twelve apostles and Lk. refers to as the apostles, but who are most frequently spoken of simply as the Twelve. Of this company Peter and John were members. These facts do not warrant the assumption that the Twelve and the apostles are identical, especially in view of the apparent distinction between them in 1 Cor. 15⁵· ⁷; but they suggest the wisdom of beginning with an inquiry concerning the Twelve, while avoiding any presupposition as to their precise relation to the apostles.

The expression "the Twelve," οἱ δώδεκα, in 1 Cor. 15⁵, consisting simply of the numeral with prefixed article, taken in its context makes it evident that when the epistle was written this was a recognised title of a certain group who had been in his lifetime disciples of Jesus. This is made the more clear by the fact that, according at least to the third gospel and Acts, the company consisted at the time referred to, not of twelve, but of eleven persons. The existence of this company which Paul predicates for the time immediately after the resurrection, the gospels carry back into the lifetime of Jesus. All the four gospels frequently mention "the Twelve," οἱ δώδεκα, with evident reference to a company of Jesus' disciples (Mk. 4¹⁰ 6⁷ 9³⁵ 10³² 11¹¹ 14¹⁰, ¹⁷, ²⁰, ⁴³ Mt. 20¹⁷ [text uncertain] 26¹⁴, ⁴⁷ Lk. 8¹ 9¹,¹² 18³¹ 22³, ⁴⁷ Jn. 6⁶⁷, ⁷⁰, ⁷¹ 20²⁴).

It should be observed, however, that all the references in Mt. and all those in Lk., except 8¹ and 9¹², are parallel to passages in Mk. and probably derived from that source. Mk. (3¹⁴, ¹⁵), followed by the other synoptists, records the selection of these Twelve by Jesus, and Mt. and Mk. give the list of them by name (Mk. 3¹⁶⁻¹⁹ Mt. 10²⁻⁴; *cf.* also Acts 1¹³, ¹⁴). That such a company existed not only in Paul's day, when retrospectively at least it was referred to as the Twelve, but also in Jesus' own day—on this point there is no reason to question the testimony of the gospels.

It is not so clear by what name this company was known in the lifetime of Jesus. In Mk. 14²⁰ Jesus is said to have used the words, "one of the twelve," but this may mean only one of the twelve then at table with him. Jn. 6⁷⁰, "Have I not chosen you the twelve?" is also indecisive, especially

in view of the late date of the fourth gospel. Yet in view of the evidence
that this was a very early, probably the earliest now extant, name for the
inner circle of Jesus' disciples, and of the probability that even in Jesus'
ministry there was some common title for the company, it is not unlikely
that it was then known as "the Twelve." The persistence of the name,
even in the latest gospels, and its occurrence in Acts 6² show that it continued in use also to a late period in the apostolic age.

The phrase οἱ μαθηταί, frequent in all the gospels, probably often refers
to the Twelve, but is not in itself restricted to them. The expression οἱ
δώδεκα μαθηταί occurs in Mt. only (10¹ 11¹ 26²⁰), and is in all instances
clearly a secondary form of expression, due to the editor, not to his sources.

(b) The application of the term "apostles" to the Twelve. Reference
has been made above to the evidence that Peter and John, who were among
the Twelve, were also counted by Paul among those who were apostles
before him. Mt. 10² shows that when this passage of the first gospel took
its present form, all the Twelve were accounted apostles. Yet this designation of the Twelve as apostles is rather infrequent in the gospels. It occurs,
besides Mt. 10², in Mk. 3¹⁴ (on the text see below) 6³⁰ Lk. 6¹³ 9¹⁰ 17⁵ 22¹⁴ 24¹⁰
(perhaps also in Lk. 11⁴⁹). Of these passages Mt. 10² only uses the expression οἱ δώδεκα ἀπόστολοι, found elsewhere in N. T. in Rev. 21¹⁴, and in
early Christian literature in the title of the Διδαχή. In Mt. it is clearly
an editorial equivalent of οἱ δώδεκα μαθηταί in v.¹, which itself represents
the simple οἱ δώδεκα of Mk. 6⁷.

In Lk. 22¹⁴ οἱ ἀπόστολοι represents οἱ δώδεκα of Mk. 14¹⁷. In 17⁵ and
24¹⁰ we have no source with which to compare the Lukan form of the passages, but in view of 22¹⁴, the word ἀπόστολοι can not with confidence be
carried back to any older source than the editor of this gospel. In Lk. 9¹⁰,
however, the expression is taken over from Mk. 6³⁰, which therefore attests
the use of the term as a title of the Twelve as early as the date of the second
gospel, subject only to the possibility of an early and now unattested corruption of the text. Only Mk. 3¹⁴ and Lk. 6¹³ ascribe this usage to Jesus.*
The text of Mk. 3¹⁴ is open to some doubt. The words οὓς καὶ ἀποστόλους
ὠνόμασεν, though attested by אBCΔ al., and on this evidence included in
the text by WH. and set in the margin by RV., are rejected by Tdf. Tr.
Ws. Sd. The words are evidently in Mk. a scribal addition from Lk. 6¹³,
or in Lk. are taken over by the editor from Mk. In other words, we have
here a single witness, either the second evangelist or the third. Whatever
the date of this testimony it does not affirm that Jesus *at this time* gave to
the Twelve the name apostles, and does not necessarily mean that he at any
time conferred on them the *title* of apostles. If it is of late origin, it probably referred in the author's mind to the bestowal of a title, but if early

---

* The utterances of Lk. 11⁴⁹ and Jn. 13¹⁶ are ascribed to Jesus, and in both cases the term
ἀπόστολοι includes by implication his immediate followers, but it is not restricted to them
or employed as a title for them.

may have meant only that he was wont to speak of them as his messengers, using the term with descriptive rather than titular force.

According to Acts 1²¹⁻²⁶ there existed within the company of one hundred and twenty disciples of Jesus who gathered in Jerusalem after his death and resurrection, a smaller company having a distinct διαχονία. This smaller company constituted not an indefinite group, but an organic body of definite number and function. The context leaves no room for doubt that it is the Twelve that are here referred to. Note the list of the Twelve in v.¹³, the mention of Peter and Judas, vv.¹⁵, ¹⁶, and the implication of a definite number, within the company of the one hundred and twenty, which is to be kept complete. This passage purports to represent the ideas of the Twelve themselves very soon after the death and resurrection of Jesus. The Acts author by his use of the word "apostles" in vv.², ²⁶ attaches these ideas to the apostolate. The divergence between the conditions here implied as those of the apostolate and those which the rest of the book shows to have been regarded by the author himself as necessary, makes it improbable that the passage has been essentially modified from the source. For example, these conditions would have excluded Paul from the apostleship. Yet the general point of view of the Acts author forbids us to suppose either that he denied that Paul was an apostle, or that it was his intention to bring into prominence the conflict between the early Christian and the Pauline definition of apostleship. The reasonable explanation of the existence of this narrative is that the Acts author took it over substantially unchanged from some earlier source. As concerns the historicity of this source, it might conceivably have been an anti-Pauline source written with the purpose of excluding Paul from the apostolate. But two things are against this. First, Luke was evidently unaware of any such anti-Pauline bias in his source; and secondly, the word apostle does not occur in the body of the passage, as would almost certainly have been the case if it had been written to bear a part in the controversy over the apostolate. It seems probable, therefore, that this passage, which undoubtedly reflects the idea held at some period of the apostolic age as to the function and status of the Twelve at the beginning of that age, does in fact convey to us the thought of a very early period.

But a part of the same evidence which points to the early existence and recognition of the Twelve as a definite group with a distinct διαχονία indicates also that this group was not yet called the apostles. The Acts author, indeed, not only in this passage but throughout the first twelve chapters of Acts, assumes the identity of the Twelve and the apostles. But this identification belongs to the author, not to his sources. In the narrative of the selection of Matthias, the term apostle does not occur either in the speech of Peter or in the body of the narrative, but appears first in the statement of v.²⁶ that Matthias was numbered with the eleven apostles, thᵉ language of which is naturally referred to the Acts author rather than to an earlier source. While, therefore, the author of the source clearly conceived of "the Twelve" as constituting in this early period a definitely organised body, and the Acts author thought of them as the apostles, the evidence indicates that in the period of the events here recorded the Twelve were probably not as yet known as apostles.

In Gal. 1¹⁹ Paul applies the term "apostles" to a company some of whom at least were included in the Twelve. It is improbable that Paul would have used the term as he does in this passage unless those whom he there calls apostles were also so designated in their own circle. That he speaks of them as having been apostles before him implies that before he entered on his career as an apostle they were already exercising the function by virtue of which he now called them apostles, most naturally also that they bore the name before that time. Paul is thus in agreement with the Acts author in Acts 1²⁶, in that he carries the apostolic function at least back to a very early period in the history of the Christian community.

If now we compare this evidence with that of Lk.–Acts each will perhaps be found to throw light upon the other. It is clear, from evidence cited above, that when the gospel of Lk. was written, all the Twelve were counted as apostles, and that they were supposed to have constituted the original company of the apostles. To say "the apostles" when speaking of the life of Jesus was, therefore, equivalent to saying "the Twelve." From the usage of the third gospel that of the first twelve chapters of Acts differs only in that Matthias takes the place of Judas. With the latter portion of Acts, in which Paul and Barnabas also receive the title, we are not now concerned. What we have to note is that from the point of view of Lk.–Acts all the Twelve were apostles and had been such from the beginning. The apostle Paul also refers to certain of the Twelve as apostles, and though he does not definitely include *all* of them under the term, yet in the absence of any limitation of the title to a part of the Twelve, it is probable that he is in agreement with Luke on this point. The usage of Lk.–Acts in this respect would then be carried back to the date of Galatians at least, and by probable implication to a point a decade or two earlier, when Paul became an apostle. Further than this we can not go with confidence. It is not indeed impossible, in view of Mk. 3¹⁴ and the evidence of the early designation of the Twelve as apostles, that Jesus was wont to speak of the Twelve as his שְׁלִיחִים (messengers), or in Greek ἀπόστολοι. But in view of the fact that our earliest definite knowledge of its use with titular force comes from the sixth decade of the first century, and in view of the possibility that Mk. 3¹⁴ and Lk. 6¹³ may involve some antedating of the usage of a later period, we can not date the use of the term as a title applied pre-eminently or exclusively to the Twelve more definitely than between the middle of Jesus' ministry and the middle of the century, and can not say whether it was first used as a Hebrew or as a Greek term.

There are, indeed, four possibilities which with their subdivisions become seven. First, the term "apostle" may have been applied first of all to the Twelve (i) by Jesus in his lifetime, (ii) after the death of Jesus, and in either case have been gradually extended to include other men of like function in the church. Secondly, the term may have first been applied to a company that included both the Twelve and others (*e. g.*, the seventy) (i) in Jesus' lifetime, (ii) after his death, in either case subsequent additions being made to the company. Thirdly, the term may have been first applied to a company within the Twelve (i) in Jesus' lifetime, (ii) after his death, in either case the number being afterwards extended to include all the Twelve and some others also. Fourthly, the term may have been first applied after Jesus' death to a company of influential men, partly of the Twelve, partly not, *e. g.*, Peter, James, the Lord's brother, and John, and afterwards been extended as on the previous supposition. Bearing in mind these hypotheses we may pass to consider—

(c) The extent of the company of apostles before Paul. The evidence already cited tends to show that though Paul had personal relations with only a few of the Twelve, perhaps only with Peter and John, yet the expression "apostles before me" would on his lips have included, potentially, all the Twelve. It remains to inquire whether it would have included any others.

Reference has already been made to the fact that, according to Acts 1^{21-26}, within the larger company of Jesus' disciples, the Twelve constituted an organic body having a definite number and specific function. Eventual diminution of the number is potentially involved in the limitation (implied in the passage) of those from among whom vacancies may be filled; indeed this limitation implies the extinction of the body within a generation. But the passage makes no reference to such diminution, or to any possible increase of the number; it contemplates only the restoration and maintenance of the number which had been reduced by the treachery and death of Judas. That the Acts author by his v.^{26} associates these ideas with the apostles indicates that he supposed that in the early apostolic age there were twelve apostles, no more, no less. But the passage can not be cited as evidence that the early apostolic age itself held this opinion; for aside from the editorial setting in vv.$^{2, 26}$ it certifies only that in that period it was believed that the number of the Twelve was to be preserved intact for the time being, and presumably as long as there were among those who fulfilled the conditions here laid down competent persons to fill the vacancies as they occurred. Nothing is implied as to the opinion of the Acts author on the question how many apostles there might come to be.

Paul's inclusion of James among the apostles (Gal. 1^{19}) following closely upon the mention of those who were apostles before him (1^{17}) suggests, but does not necessarily imply, that James was an apostle before Paul was. It does, however, show that as early as when Paul wrote Galatians, probably at the time of the visit to Jerusalem to which he here refers, the apostolic body included others than the Twelve, *i. e.*, the original eleven and Matthias. But we do not know whether James was added to the Twelve, as Matthias was, by being elected to fill a vacancy, and acquired the title of apostle by virtue of his membership in the Twelve, or whether he became an apostle without being numbered with the Twelve. It is, however, distinctly improbable that the apostles and the Twelve were at the time when James became an apostle mutually exclusive bodies. This was clearly not the case when Paul wrote, nor when Acts was written. We have no evidence that it was the case when James became an apostle.

1 Cor. 9$^{3\text{ff.}}$ indicates clearly the existence of a class of apostles which included on the one side Paul and doubtless also Barnabas, and on the other, certain unnamed persons, whose standing as apostles was, however, quite assured and undisturbed. It may be safely assumed that "the rest of the apostles" here spoken of included those to whom in Gal. 1^{19} Paul refers as "those who were apostles before me." The mention of Cephas can not be understood as excluding him from the group of apostles, and since this is so, neither can it be assumed that the brethren of the Lord are so excluded. Yet the most probable explanation of the somewhat peculiar enumeration in v.^{5} is that the brethren of the Lord constituted as such a different group from the apostles (*i. e.*, that not all of the brethren of the Lord were apostles, as certainly not all of the apostles were brethren of the Lord), but that they occupied a position in the church, of dignity, influence, and privilege, similar to that enjoyed by the apostles. If we seek an explanation of this withholding of the name "apostle" from those to whom practically the same position was accorded, it seems to be suggested by v.^{1} compared with 15$^{5\text{-}7}$. V.^{1}, "Have I not seen Jesus our Lord?" suggests that to be a witness of the resurrection was now regarded as a condition of apostleship, as Acts 1^{22} shows that it was esteemed a condition of inclusion in the company of the Twelve, while 1 Cor. 15$^{5\text{-}7}$, mentioning specifically the epiphany to James, but none to his brothers, suggests that he alone of the brethren of Jesus enjoyed this privilege and distinction. If this is the correct explanation, the passage, though furnishing no specific names to add to the list of apostles before Paul, makes an important contribution to our knowledge of the limits of the apostolate on the non-Pauline side, suggesting that James was an apostle and his brethren not, though occupying a kindred position in the church, and that the reason for this discrimination was that he was a witness of the resurrection and they were not.

1 Cor. 15$^{3\text{-}8}$ manifestly requires careful consideration in connection with the question of the extent of the apostolate. It reads as follows:

For I delivered unto you first of all that which also I received: that he appeared to Cephas, then to the Twelve; then he appeared to above five hundred brethren at once, of whom the greater part remain until now, but some are fallen asleep; then he appeared to James; then to all the apostles. And last of all as to the child untimely born, he appeared to me also.

The phrase "all the apostles," used in a series such as that in which the phrase occurs here, might refer to a group entirely distinct from those previously mentioned, yet most naturally designates the whole of a group in distinction from a portion previously mentioned. Such portion may be found either in the Twelve (so, Chrysostom, who found in the phrase a reference to a band of apostles, including the seventy), or in James. The *prima facie* view of the language would also be that the phrase refers either to all who were apostles at the time of the event narrated or to all who were such at the time of writing. The latter hypothesis is, however, in this case improbable. For (i) the meaning "all who are now apostles" implies a detachment of the thought from the narrative that is improbable both in itself and because it would involve the mental addition to an original number of apostles of those who had subsequently acquired the title, and (ii) the phrase would strictly include Paul himself, whom, therefore, since he certainly was not present at the time referred to, he must have tacitly excepted. That he means "all the apostles" in distinction from the Twelve, with the implication that the latter constituted a part of the former, is also improbable in view of the remoteness of the mention of the Twelve and the intervention of the mention of the five hundred brethren and of James. The improbability of this view is further increased by the absence of any other evidence that there was at that time any such larger group. If, then, we set aside the hypothesis that the phrase means those who are now apostles, and the supposed reference to the Twelve, and if we assume precision of expression on Paul's part, we shall infer that he is speaking of a company which was composed of those who very soon after the death of Jesus were called apostles, and which included *all* such in contrast with James, who was only one of the company. In this case we shall conclude that James was at that time one of the apostles. But that Paul spoke with such precision of expression is, itself, by no means certain. Such a passage as 1 Cor. 9⁵, in which Paul speaks of "the rest of the apostles, and the brethren of the Lord, and Cephas," warns us against treating his enumerations as if they were drawn up by a statistician or a logician. If, as is probable, he means by James the same person to whom he refers in Gal. 1¹⁹ 2⁹, to affirm that at the time referred to he was not an apostle, would be indeed to beg the question at issue, but it is at least true that we have no evidence outside this passage that he was such, and that this passage is not decisive evidence on this point. It seems necessary, therefore, to reckon with certain other possibilities. Having in mind that James was not an apostle at the time referred to, or thinking of the five hundred as not being apostles, Paul may have used the expression "all the apostles" with the emphasis on "apostles" rather than on "all." Or, thinking of James as now an apostle, he may have been led half unconsciously to the use of a phrase including the word apostle to describe the next group, which, however, still meant all who were apostles at the time of the event referred to. Or without intention of comparison with any previously mentioned person or group, Paul, long accustomed to the term apostle, scarcely aware, indeed, of a time when the term was not in use, may have employed the expression "all the apostles" of all who were, at the time of the event referred to, members of the company which at the time of writing had long been known as the apostles. In itself the phrase would not tell us who these were. But in view of the other evidence we should naturally assume them to have been the Twelve, or rather, perhaps, the eleven. It may, indeed, be asked why, if the expression "all the apostles" is of identical content with "the Twelve," the apostle should have used the two instead of repeating the same phrase. A confident answer can not perhaps be given to this question, but instinctive desire for variety of expression combined with the intervention of the reference to the five hundred and to James may have been sufficient to lead him to say "to all the apostles," rather than "again to the Twelve." *

It seems impossible, therefore, to deduce from this passage any definite indication as to who constituted the apostles at the time of the epiphany which Paul here relates, or indeed that there was at that time any definite group of persons called apostles. Read in the light of the other evidence it distinctly implies the existence of a definite company of Jesus' disciples, known at the time of this epiphany or not much later as the Twelve, and a definite company then or afterwards known as the apostles. This passage itself does not define the extent to which these two companies were identical, but leaves unanswered the question whether they were mutually exclusive, partly identical or wholly so. The last view is, on the whole, more consistent with all the evidence.

The reference to "false apostles" mentioned in 2 Cor. will require consideration at a later point. It is sufficient at this point to note that Paul's attitude towards them renders it improbable that they were included in those whom he designates as having been apostles before him.

In Rom. 16⁷ mention is made of Adronicus and Junias as ἐπίσημοι ἐν τοῖς ἀποστόλοις. This is generally understood to mean that they were themselves of the number of the apostles and occupied a position of eminence among them. If this is correct, these men may well have been among those who were apostles before Paul, as he expressly says that they were Christians before he was. In that case, they were probably like the men referred to in 2 Cor. in that they constituted an early addition to the apostolic company and, like them, were apparently itinerant missionaries.

2. *The apostleship of Paul.*—With the conversion of Saul and his adoption for himself, or the ascription by others to him, of the title ἀπόστολος, that title enters upon a new stage of its history. It evidently passed from the Twelve, or the company of which they were a part, to him, not the reverse, but its application to him became the occasion of no little controversy.

* It is a tempting suggestion made by Valckenarius and cited by Heinrici in Mey. *Kom.* 8te Aufl., that for πᾶσιν we should read πάλιν; but in the absence of any external evidence the interpreter can scarcely avail himself of this way of escape.

Acts 13[1-3] relates that the company of prophets and teachers in the church at Antioch set apart two of their own number for a specific task, which though not sharply defined was apparently that of carrying the gospel into regions as yet unevangelised. There is a manifest parallel between this act and that of the one hundred and twenty in Jerusalem (Acts 1[15-26]), and it is not improbable that in this event we have an important step in the creation of an apostolate not authorised from Jerusalem or by the Twelve. But as in the case of Matthias, so in the case of Barnabas and Saul, there is no assertion that the term "apostle" was applied at the time of appointment, but only a subsequent reference to them as apostles by the Acts author, and no distinct evidence that those who took part in the Antioch incident looked upon it at the time as having any important bearing on the development of an office or the definition of a term.

For direct evidence as to the origin of Paul's assurance of his own apostleship and his conception of the functions of an apostle, we must depend upon his own letters. In 2 Cor. 8[23] and Phil. 2[25] he uses the term, with limitations, in the general sense of messenger or delegate. This evidence is valuable as showing what was for Paul the fundamental idea of the term, but it in no way obscures the fact that Paul applied the term to a certain limited number of persons, including himself and the Twelve, in a more specific sense. In the salutation of the Thessalonian letter (or letters if 2 Thes. be from Paul), he couples with his own name those of Silvanus and Timothy, and adds no title, but in 1 Thes. 2[6] he uses the term ἀπόστολος of himself, or of himself and one or more of his companions at Thessalonica, in such a way as to imply that to be an apostle of Christ carried with it either authority, or the right to be supported by his converts; it is impossible to say with certainty which is the implication of ἐν βάρει. In Gal. 1[1-2] he affirms his own apostleship with emphasis, and thereafter in the salutation of all the Pauline letters, except Phil. and Phm. the term ἀπόστολος is closely joined to the personal name Παῦλος. In all these cases the term is clearly restricted to Paul himself and is evidently of titular force. Gal. 1[1] and its context also make it clear that Paul's right to this title was disputed, and scarcely less so that the ground of objection was that the title and appointment had not been authorised in Jerusalem. To this his defence was not that he had been duly appointed, but that such appointment was unnecessary, and that he had never sought it, having received his apostleship by direct divine commission. In 1 Cor. 9[1] Paul couples the assertion of his apostleship with the affirmation that he had seen Jesus our Lord, evidently referring to the post-resurrection vision spoken of in 1 Cor. 15[8]. As therefore the Galatian passage suggests one element of the conditions of apostleship implied in Acts 1[21, 22], so the Corinthian passage suggests another. It is not, indeed, perfectly clear whether he conceded that such a vision of the risen Jesus was a necessary condition of apostleship or, only since he fulfilled it, preferred simply to affirm the fact and so avoid controversy on this point. On the one side, the general type of his thought, his emphasis on the purely spiritual as against the physical in religion, would favour the view that he did not attach vital importance to his having seen Jesus.* But, on the other hand, the great significance which he evidently attached to this particular experience, and his apparently careful avoidance of the ascription of apostleship to other missionaries of Christianity, such as Timothy, Titus, and Apollos, point to the conclusion that he included ability to bear personal testimony to the resurrection among the conditions of apostleship. We may concede that his view would have been more thoroughly self-consistent if he had attached no importance to this condition; but it seems on the whole probable, nevertheless, that he did include it in the necessary qualifications of an apostle.

If this is the case it was implied in the view both of Paul and his opponents that the apostleship could not last many years since the supply of those who fulfilled this condition would inevitably be exhausted within a generation. But it is probable that this consideration was deprived of any importance by their expectation of the consummation of the age by the coming of the Lord. *Cf.* Mt. 19²⁸.

3. *The false apostles.*—The mention by Paul of those whom he, in 2 Cor. 11¹³, characterises as "false apostles [ψευδαπόστολοι], deceitful workers, fashioning themselves into apostles of Christ," though adding, of course, none to the list of those whom he accounted apostles, throws considerable light on the whole problem of the conception of apostleship held in the apostolic age. The letter which has been preserved to us in part in chaps. 10–13 of what is commonly known as 2 Cor. shows clearly that there had been in Corinth certain persons who, claiming themselves to be apostles of Christ, denied Paul's right to that title. If 2 Cor. 3¹ (written a little later) refers, as it probably does, to the same persons, it suggests that these persons brought with them letters of commendation, and that not improbably their claim to the apostleship was supported by these letters. We have no means of knowing whether these men had been elected, as Matthias was, to fill a vacancy in the original Twelve, or were an addition to the Twelve. In any case, Paul's objection to their apostleship was not based on the method of their appointment, but on the spirit and purpose of the work they were doing. The expression "false apostles," however, confirms what the evidence previously examined implies, that to be an apostle was a definite fact. In other words, while neither Paul nor, so far as we know, the Jerusalem Christians were insisting on the maintenance of the number twelve, the term apostle still conveyed a definite meaning; it was not applied indiscriminately to any preacher or missionary of the Christian message.†

Cf. Hincks, "Limits of the Apostolate," in *JBL*. 1895, pp. 37–47.

† The assertion frequently made (see, *e. g.*, Robinson in *HDB*, art. "Apostle," and Robertson and Plummer on 1 Cor. 12²⁸) that the expression "false apostles" implies that the number of the apostles was indefinite is inaccurate and misleading. The expression

2 Cor. 10⁷ and 11²³ strongly suggest that among the qualifications which these persons affirmed that they possessed and Paul lacked was a certain relation to Christ. In all probability this was in part at least personal knowledge of him in his lifetime. This view is in some measure confirmed by 1 Cor. 1¹² (ἐγὼ δὲ Χριστοῦ) and 9¹, if, as is probable, the former passage refers to the same persons, or at least to the same movement, as 2 Cor. 10⁷ 11²³, and if 1 Cor. 9¹ conveys a veiled and passing allusion to that party, with which the apostle for some reason did not, in this letter, wish to deal openly.*   Cf. on the general situation Weizs. *Ap. Zeit.* p. 299, E. T. I 354, and Sanday in *Encyc. Bib.* I 905.

The time when these men set up their claim to be apostles is indicated only by the mention of them in the letter of Paul which is embedded in what is known as 2 Cor. This would point to a date in the early fifties as the time when they were in Corinth. How much sooner they claimed or were given the title of apostle we have no means of knowing. Whether elected to fill a vacancy in the number of the Twelve or added to that number, they may have been accounted apostles in Jerusalem even before Paul acquired the title. His subsequent denial of the title to them, when he discovered the spirit in which they were working, does not exclude the possibility of his having at first accounted them apostles. Such evidence as there is, however, would suggest that these were relatively late additions to the company of those who bore the title of apostles.

In Rev. 2² reference is also had to false apostles in the church at Ephesus, men who call themselves apostles and are not. Whatever the point of view of this portion of the Apocalypse, and whatever the test by which the Ephesians tried them and discovered that they were false, the passage testifies to the fact that to be an apostle was something definite and desirable.

4. *The usage of the latter part of Acts.*—Reference has already been made to the usage of the word "apostle" in the first twelve chapters of Acts. It remains only to observe that while in chap. 14 Paul and Barnabas are spoken of as apostles, the word occurs elsewhere only in chaps. 15 and 16, and always in the phrase οἱ ἀπόστολοι καὶ [οἱ] πρεσβύτεροι ἀδελφοί, designating the

shows only that there was difference of opinion as to who were apostles. It suggests no indefiniteness as to what it was to be an apostle, but quite the contrary, for had the term been of quite indefinite meaning (signifying, *e. g.*, only itinerant preacher), Paul would have had no motive to refuse it to the emissaries from Jerusalem, or, it may be added, to claim it for himself. Nor does the term of itself exclude definiteness of number; since an agreement, *e. g.*, that there could be but twelve apostles, would only have given acuteness to the question who were the genuine, who the spurious. *Cf.* the case of delegates to a political convention. Probably on neither side was the number definitely restricted, but the expression "false apostles" would not of itself prove this.

* It is not improbable that in 2 Cor. 5¹⁶ also there is an allusion to the same emphasis of Paul's opponents on personal knowledge of Jesus; in which case, however, the apostle's phrase ἐγνώκαμεν κατὰ σάρκα Χριστόν must be taken as a general expression inclusive of estimation of Christ on any basis of the physical and external, which estimation he now abjures, whatever may have been, in fact or according to the accusation of his opponents, the case in the past.

leading men of the church assembled in Jerusalem. While the epistles of Paul recognise the apostleship of James, and of Andronicus and Junias, and testify that others also claimed the title, which though denied by Paul was apparently conceded by others, the book of Acts makes no mention of any of these as apostles, but restricts the term to the Twelve with the addition of Paul and Barnabas.

5. *Summary of New Testament usage.*—These facts, respecting the usage of the word in the several N. T. books, suggest that the term was first used of a narrower circle, composed of the Twelve or including them and a limited number beside, then of a wider circle, and again in certain quarters of a narrower. They do not clearly indicate when the term was first applied to the Twelve except that it was at some time before the writing of Galatians. They do not show clearly whether the term was first applied to the Twelve only and afterwards to others, or whether it first arose as a title of a larger group including the Twelve. They suggest that while the Twelve were at first the eminent body among the followers of Jesus, and were known simply as the Twelve, the raising of James, and in a lesser measure of his brethren, to a place of influence in the Christian community only second, and in the case of James scarcely second, to that of the Twelve, gradually led to the partial displacement of the numerical term, the Twelve, by the more descriptive and honorific term "apostles." Not improbably from the beginning, this term included all the Twelve, but also James. Eventually all who like· these were regarded as founders of Christianity were called apostles. *Cf.* below on the function of the apostle. For this use of the term there was doubtless some preparation in earlier usage. This may have been furnished by the use of some such term as ἀπόστολοι or שׁליחים not as a title but as a term descriptive of the function of the Twelve. Subsequently, doctrinal differences led to the denial of the apostolic character of some of these later additions to the apostolic circle, each party denying the title to those whose views or character they disapproved, but none apparently questioning the apostolic title of the Twelve. The book of Acts represents a stage of the controversy and a circle of thought in which it was held that in the early days the Twelve were the only apostles and there was caution in recognising the legitimacy of any addition to that number except Paul and Barnabas. Of the persistence in other circles of another point of view, something will be said later in discussing the usage of the Διδαχή.

If this hypothesis be accepted as probable, we should reconstruct the history of the use of the term "apostle" in what we call the apostolic age somewhat as follows: In the midst of his ministry Jesus gathered about him a company of twelve disciples who companied with him, learning from him as pupils, and sharing in his work as his representatives. The earliest name that we can discover for this company was "the Twelve," a title which they not improbably bore even in Jesus' lifetime. Assured by their visions of him after his death that he still lived, they were impelled to continue their organisation such as it was, and to fill the vacancy caused by the treachery and death of Judas. They conceived it to be their function to testify to the resurrection of Jesus and in general to transmit the message of Jesus' life and teaching which they had received through their association with him. They were not ecclesiastical officers but bearers of a message. They continued for some time, precisely how long we can not tell, to be known as "the Twelve." With them were early associated the brothers of Jesus, of whom James was especially prominent, and these grew in influence. James being a witness of the resurrection and a man of weight and influence, assumed functions quite like those of the Twelve. This fact gradually led to the adoption of the term "apostles," which may or may not have already been applied to the Twelve, as the title of all who shared the functions of the Twelve.

Converted to an enthusiastic faith in Jesus by his Damascus vision, Paul felt himself called by God to become a preacher of the gospel message, as he conceived of it, to the Gentiles. This was for him a divine commission and he unhesitatingly appropriated to himself the title and function of an apostle of Christ, which he conceived himself to hold by direct divine authority, subject in no way to the control of those who were apostles before him.

When Paul had been at work for some years, there went out into the territory which he conceived to be his and into the churches which he had founded, certain men, perhaps by authorisation from Jerusalem, who denied Paul's apostleship, apparently either on the ground that he had not been a personal companion of Jesus, or had not been commissioned from Jerusalem, or both, and no doubt claimed for themselves what they denied to him. These men Paul in turn denounced as false apostles.

It is clear that there had grown up two contrasted views of the conditions of apostleship, having much in common but sharply differentiated on certain points. Both parties were agreed that to be an apostle was something very definite, and, as will appear later, were not widely divided as to what the function of an apostle was. Of the existence of a loose sense of the term as applied to apostles of Christ (2 Cor. 8[23] and Phil. 2[25] do not come into account here), either as the only meaning or parallel with a stricter sense, the books of N. T. give no evidence. The difference of opinion pertained chiefly to the conditions of apostleship. The party of Paul's opponents probably held respecting the apostolate substantially the position which Acts 1[21, 22] takes respecting the Twelve. An apostle must have known Jesus personally, must be able to bear witness to the resurrection, and must have been commissioned from Jerusalem. Paul denied the necessity of personal acquaintance with Jesus on earth, or of any commission whatever from men. On the basis of his Damascus vision he claimed to have seen Jesus and so to be a witness of the resurrection. Other condi-

378 GALATIANS

tions than this, he maintained, were purely spiritual, and apostleship came by unmediated divine commission.

How many of those who were eligible to apostleship under either of the two views eventually came to bear the name "apostle" it is impossible to state. We can definitely name only about twenty, but quite possibly it was given to all who having been sharers in the epiphanies of Jesus afterwards assumed positions of responsibility in the church, especially perhaps if they became itinerant preachers and founders of churches.

6. *The function of an apostle.*—For the interpretation of the epistles of Paul the question what he conceived to be the function of an apostle is of much more importance than the number of those to whom he conceived the title to be rightly applicable. Most of the evidence bearing on this point has been cited incidentally in the preceding sections, but may now be assembled and brought to bear on this phase of the subject.

In Mk. 3¹⁴, ¹⁵ we read: καὶ ἐποίησεν δώδεκα, οὓς καὶ ἀποστόλους ὠνόμασεν, ἵνα ὦσιν μετ' αὐτοῦ καὶ ἵνα ἀποστέλλη αὐτοὺς κηρύσσειν καὶ ἔχειν ἐξουσίαν ἐκβάλλειν τὰ δαιμόνια. This passage was evidently written or took its present shape when it was believed that Jesus himself created the apostolate and gave to its members the name apostles. It shows that at that time it was believed that the primary purpose for which Jesus chose the Twelve was that they should be his personal companions and helpers in his work. Learning from him by companionship with him, they were to share in his work by going out to announce his message and to do such things as he had himself been doing (*cf.* Mk. 9³⁸). Though this gospel was written long after the death of Jesus and when the Twelve had long been exercising a function largely created by conditions that arose after his death, and though the expression, "whom he also named apostles," probably shows the influence of later thought, yet with the exception of this phrase the horizon of the passage is wholly that of Jesus' lifetime, and there is in it no suggestion of any work to be done after Jesus' death.* This fact is strong evidence that the substance of the passage comes from a very early date, and embodies the recollection of the Twelve of their original conception of their primitive function.

But though this original appointment suggested no function extending beyond the period of the personal presence of Jesus, his death resulted not in the dissolution of the group but in the taking on of a new function. Those who had been his chosen companions in his lifetime became the witnesses of his resurrection. See above on Acts 1²¹⁻²⁶. The insistence upon personal companionship with Jesus, as a condition of membership in the body in the new period of its history, was doubtless in part because of

* This is the implication of the present tenses, ἀποστέλλη, κηρύσσειν, ἔχειν and ἐκβάλλειν, not, of course, in that they denote present time, but continued or repeated action, naturally, therefore, thought of as continuous with the time of ὦσιν μετ' αὐτοῦ. Had the thought been of a single subsequent sending out, following upon the period of the ὦσιν μετ' αὐτοῦ, the aorist ἀποστείλη must certainly have been used.

the relation between such companionship and ability to be a witness to the resurrection. But the inclusion of the phrase "from the baptism of John" indicates that the bearing of such testimony was not the full duty or the only function of the Twelve. They must also be able to testify to the deeds and words of Jesus before his death and even from the beginning of his public ministry, and carry forward his work as they only could do who knew him well. On the other hand witnessing to the resurrection was not an end in itself, but the means by which men were to be persuaded to accept him as Lord and Christ. The function of the apostle is therefore comprehensively the winning of men to faith in Jesus through the testimony to his resurrection, and building them up in such faith through the story of his life and teaching. There is thus a clear affinity between the thought of the two passages Mk. 3[14] and Acts 1[21-26]. The companionship with Jesus which in Mk. is a part of the purpose of the choice of the Twelve becomes in Acts a condition of membership in the body; and the function of the group, though new in that it includes and makes prominent the testimony to the resurrection, is in substance the same as that set forth in Mk. with only such modification as the death and subsequent epiphanies of Jesus, convincing them of his resurrection and messiahship, would naturally call for. Whether at the early period in which this conception of the function of the Twelve took shape they were already known as apostles, or, as suggested above, this name was only later applied to them, the passage in Acts shows that by the time of the writing of Acts the definition of function had become attached to the term "apostle," and there is no special reason to question that this took place in the process by which the term apostle was carried over to the Twelve or to that larger company of which they were the major part.

Paul's conception of the function of an apostle is conveyed by implication rather than by any express statement. The important passage 1 Cor. 12[28] indicates the place of high importance which he attached to it, and shows that he regarded apostleship rather as a commission conferred by divine endowment than an ecclesiastical office to which one was appointed or elected by men (see also Gal. 1[1]). That the function was local, τῇ ἐκκλησίᾳ referring to the church at Corinth, or generically to any local church, can not be assumed in view of Paul's use of ἐκκλησία in the larger sense in Gal. 1[13] 1 Cor. 15[9] Phil. 3[6] Col. 1[18, 24], and is against all other usage of the word ἀπόστολος. It is still more clear that in Eph. 4[11] the writer is thinking of the church at large. But neither of these passages gives a clear definition of the specific function of the apostle. The evidence that Paul regarded first-hand testimony to the resurrection as a part of the work of the apostle has already been discussed (cf. 2 above). That the preaching of the gospel was a part of it is clearly implied not only in such passages as Gal. 1[16] 1 Cor. 1[17] Rom. 1[1], but in practically all his references to his apostleship. But neither of apostleship in general nor of his own apostleship in particular would this have been an adequate definition. Not every preacher of the gospel was an apostle; nor was it given to Paul by virtue of his apostleship to preach the gospel without restriction. Limiting his own efforts to Gentile lands (Gal. 1^{16} $2^{8, 9}$) and within these lands to fields not already occupied by others, he disclaimed all intention of reproselytising to his own conception of Christianity converts already made by others (2 Cor. 10^{13} Rom. 15^{20}), and equally denied the right of others to attempt to win his converts to their views (Gal. $1^{8, 9}$ 5^{12}). We infer that according to Paul's conception the work of an apostle of Christ was that of planting Christianity. Endowed by the vision of the risen Christ with ability to testify to the resurrection, commissioned by God, and his commission attested by the signs of an apostle, viz., ability to work miracles and success in the work of the gospel (1 Cor. $9^{1, 2}$ 2 Cor. 12^{12}), possessed of a message for which no man was his authority (Gal. $1^{1, 11, 12}$), it belonged to the apostle not to follow in the footsteps of others, nor to build along the lines determined by other men's foundations, but himself to announce the gospel message, to found churches, and thus to fix the lines of the development of the new religion, or the new type of the Jewish religion. Disclaiming, indeed, lordship over the faith of his converts as against the working of the Spirit in their own hearts (2 Cor. 1^{24}), yet in the assured conviction of his own apostleship and his own possession of the Spirit (1 Cor. chap. 2), Paul did not hesitate on the one side to reprove, exhort, and even to command the churches which he had founded (1 Thes. 4^{2}; cf. 2 Thes. $3^{4, 6}$ 2 Cor. $13^{2, 10}$ et freq.), and, on the other, utterly to deny the right of others, whether true or false apostles, to assume such authority over these churches. To be an apostle of Christ was in Paul's thought to be divinely commissioned to found churches of Christ and, by virtue of such commission, to be independent of human authority.* It was such a commission and the right and duty to exercise it among the Gentiles, thus practically determining the character of Gentile Christianity as far as his work and influence extended, that Paul steadfastly claimed for himself.

Lacking any correspondingly definite expression of the conception of apostleship held by the other apostles, we can not say to what extent they would have agreed with Paul's definition of the function of an apostle. It is evident, however, that Paul's conception is closely akin to that which

* The work of the apostles as a whole might be defined (cf. Haupt, Zum Verständnis des Apostolats im N. T., p. 135) as the founding of the church. But since this is the work of no single man, one could not from Paul's point of view give this as the definition of the function of the apostle (sing.) without the addition of a limiting phrase defining the scope and territory within which the individual apostle was divinely commissioned to act. Yet neither, from Paul's point of view, was the founding of the church committed to any body of men to be achieved by them as a body. Whether it be due to the difference of judgment between himself and others whose apostleship he was nevertheless unwilling to deny, or to inherent individualism, the apostle held at any rate that to him was given his task and to the others theirs, which each was to accomplish, with recognition of the other's rights and duties, but not co-operatively as a duty laid on them all jointly.

underlies Acts 1²¹⁻²⁶, but that his is more sharply defined in respect to the independence of the apostle. It is evident, also, that precisely by reason of this peculiarity of Paul's view, it was well adapted to give rise to controversy. A conception of a college of apostles would have called for corporate action in the achievement of a common task. But Paul's individualism, his view that each apostle—he at least—had his own commission from God, and was responsible, therefore, to God and not to his fellow apostles, could scarcely fail to bring him into conflict with those who held the other conception. Paul's solution of the problem of conflicting claims that in fact arose was, as Gal. 2⁶⁻¹⁰ clearly shows, neither to deny the apostleship of the others and maintain his own only, nor to consent to submit mooted questions to a majority vote of a college of apostles, but to affirm the undiminished authority of each in his own field. The pillar apostles, on the other hand, without apparently denying his apostleship, did not at first recognise that it required them not to interfere with his work. Later, they conceded this in theory, but did not steadfastly conform to it in practice; while the more extreme members of the Jewish Christian party denied Paul's apostleship altogether.

Itinerancy was evidently an incidental rather than a cardinal feature of the apostle's work. The Twelve, according to Mk. 3¹⁴, were to go out from time to time. But Acts 1¹¹, ¹² makes no mention of itinerancy. The use of the phrase γυναῖκα περιάγειν in 1 Cor. 9⁵ suggests that the apostles generally and the brethren of the Lord were more or less itinerant, yet rather in the sense that they had frequent occasion to change their home than to be away from home. Paul, we know, was in "journeyings oft." Having no family he may perhaps be said to have had no home. Manifestly, also, the witness to the resurrection must go where they are to whom the testimony is to be borne, and the founder of churches can not remain seated in one place. Yet prolonged residence in a given place might be necessary to the accomplishment of a given apostle's task, and no definite limit could be set to the period of such residence. Like the modern missionary bishop, the apostle must be where his work called him, yet not necessarily always journeying. James the brother of our Lord was never, so far as our evidence shows, an itinerant preacher, nor does it seem probable that any one who, in the discharge of his function as a founder of Christianity, should find it expedient to take up permanent residence in a certain place, would on that account have been denied the title of apostle. Still less does the evidence of the N. T. permit us to suppose that itinerancy would of itself have entitled a preacher of the gospel to be called an apostle. Nor was the expression equivalent to "evangelist," or to the modern term, "missionary."

IV. CHRISTIAN USAGE IN THE SECOND CENTURY.

To the interpretation of the development of the apostolate and the usage of the word "apostle" hereinbefore set forth, the use of the word in the well-known passage in the Διδαχὴ τῶν δώδεκα Ἀποστόλων, chap. 11, seems at first sight to interpose an objection:

> But concerning the prophets and apostles, so do ye according to the ordinance of the gospel. Let every apostle, when he comes to you, be received as the Lord; but he shall not abide more than a single day, or if there be need, the second; and if he abide three days he is a false prophet. And when he departs let the apostle receive nothing save bread, until he find shelter. But if he ask for money he is a false prophet.

The first injunction manifestly has reference to Mt. 10⁴⁰: "He that receiveth you receiveth me, and he that receiveth me receiveth him that sent me." And this reference in turn associates the apostle here spoken of with the Twelve. Yet, on the other hand it is quite impossible to suppose that the following injunctions were intended to apply to the Twelve or arose in a time when they could have been so understood. For surely the Twelve never sank to so low a level in the esteem of the church that it was deemed necessary to prohibit their remaining more than two days at utmost in any one church, or receiving anything more than the food necessary to sustain them to their next stopping place. Apparently, therefore, the passage comes from a time when the apostles as a class were still so connected in thought with the Twelve that the sentence which the gospel applies to them could be applied to the then existing class of apostles, but when the still living members of the class had so far degenerated as to be regarded with suspicion and treated with extreme caution. Those to whom the term is here applied are itinerant prophets, living off the churches, but prohibited from receiving any money or subsisting upon any church for more than two days at a time. Violation of these rules proves them false prophets, but apparently does not deprive them of the title "apostles."

It should be borne in mind that this is the only extant passage in early Christian literature in which any such use of the term occurs. The term is found six times in Clem. Rom., once in so-called 2 Clement, 16 times in Ignatius, five times in the Epistle to Diognetus, five times in Hermas, and once in Barnabas (see Goodspeed, *Index Patristicus*). All of these instances are in line with the usage which from Acts we should infer prevailed in the latter portion of the apostolic age, most of them very clearly so. Clement of Rome, Barnabas, and Ignatius know of no apostles save the Twelve and Paul. In Clem. Rom. 47⁴ Apollos is expressly distinguished from the apostles: "For ye were partisans of apostles and of a man approved in their sight." Equally clear is the usage of 2 Clem. and Mart. Pol. The usage of Hermas is less clear and may perhaps be more nearly akin to that of the middle period of the apostolic age. He speaks once of forty apostles and teachers (Sim. 9. 15⁴) and twice of apostles and teachers, without mentioning their number (Sim. 9. 16⁵; 25²). These preached the gospel to the whole world and having fallen asleep preached also to those that had fallen asleep before them. The apostles preached to the twelve tribes (Sim. 9. 17¹), in which phrase there is, perhaps, a reminiscence of the twelve apostles. Of apostles still living Hermas makes no mention. From Ep. ad Diogn. 11¹: "Having become a disciple of apostles I came forward as a teacher of the gentiles," and the probability that this writing was produced not earlier than the third quarter of the second century, it might be inferred that the word is used of men of the second century. But the fact that, in the other instances in which it occurs in this fragment (11³, ⁶; 12⁵, ⁹), the word clearly has its usual reference to the great leaders of the church in the first century, makes it more likely that it has the same meaning here and that the writer intended to say that he accepted the teachings of the apostles, not that he knew them personally.

The usage of the Διδαχή remains therefore without parallel in the literature either of the first or of the second century. It is not, indeed, impossible that the persons here referred to were survivors of the company of five hundred witnesses of the resurrection whom Paul mentions in 1 Cor. 15⁶, but they had certainly ceased to exercise the functions which in an earlier period were the characteristic marks of an apostle, and which afterwards were regarded retrospectively as the signs of an apostle. In no strict sense can the use of the word in the Διδαχή be regarded as the survival of a primitive usage. Of the three ideas, preaching the gospel, founding the church, itinerancy, it was the first and second, not the first and third, which entered into the earliest use of the term as a designation of a class in the Christian community; and of these the second was what constituted the distinctive mark of an apostle; itinerancy was apparently neither a constant nor a necessary feature of apostleship.

A more probable explanation of the usage found in the Διδαχή is that it is an offshoot, probably local and rather temporary, from the general stream of usage in both first and second centuries arising out of the conditions of which we catch a glimpse in 2 Cor., a degenerate use of the term arising from the degeneracy of the class to whom it was applied. The conflict over the apostleship, reflected in the Galatian and Corinthian letters, led on the Jewish-Christian side, possibly on the Gentile-Christian also, to the designation and sending out of men as apostles, first, probably, of those only who had known Jesus in the flesh, but afterwards, perhaps, when no more such remained, of others. The name apostle thus became the designation of a class of itinerant Christian prophets which, for reasons no longer known, in time so degenerated that strenuous rules were laid down to prevent their unduly annoying the churches. But this was, after all, a relatively sporadic use of the term.* The main stream of usage in Christian circles remained the same. It was still commonly used of the founders

---

* *Cf.* the usage prevailing at about the same time in Jewish circles, mentioned under I above.

of the church, those men of the first generation, contemporaries of Jesus who put their stamp upon the new religious movement and had no successors.

II. ΠΑΤΗΡ AS APPLIED TO GOD.

The antecedents of the N. T. designation of God as Father are found, on the one side, in an ancient usage of the Greek world, and on the other in the religious thinking of the Hebrews.

I. CLASSICAL USAGE.

As early as Homer Zeus is designated as πατὴρ ἀνδρῶν τε θεῶν, and in later classical writers as πατήρ: Æsch. *Theb.* 512; Aristoph. *Achar.* 225; Pind. *Pyth.* 4[41]; Soph. *Trach.* 275: ὁ τῶν ἀπάντων Ζεὺς πατὴρ 'Ολύμπιος. On the question whether this title marked him as the progenitor of the race of gods and men, or emphasised his authority and watch-care over them, see Zinzow, "Ζεὺς πατήρ und θεός," in *ZkWkL.*, 1882, pp. 189 *f.* Diod. Sic. 5. 72[2] says of him, πατέρα διὰ τὴν φροντίδα καὶ τὴν εὔνοιαν τὴν εἰς ἅπαντας, ἔτι δὲ καὶ τὸ δοκεῖν ὥσπερ ἀρχηγὸν εἶναι τοῦ γένους τῶν ἀνθρώπων. *Cf.* also Plut. *Apoph. reg.* 15. Jos. *Ant.* 4. 262 (8[24]) speaks rather under the influence of his contact with the Greek world than of his Hebrew training when he calls God πατὴρ τοῦ παντός.

II. OLD TESTAMENT USAGE.

The O. T. writers speak of God as Father of men rather rarely, yet often enough to make it clear that they employed the term not in any literal or physical sense, or to designate a relation of God to all men, but to ascribe to him ethical relations to certain men or to a certain people analogous to those which a human father sustains to his sons. The relation which is in mind is sometimes authority, but especially love and watch-care. See Deut. 32[6] Isa. 63[16] Jer. 3[4, 19] 31[9] Mal. 1[6] 2 Sam. 7[14] 1 Chr. 17[13]; *cf.* Deut. 14[1] Hos. 11[1] Ps. 2[7]. The reference to creation in Mal. 2[10] is quite exceptional, but even here it is to be noticed that it is creation, not begetting or descent—hence, not fatherhood in a physical sense. In Ps. 2[7] the term "beget" is used, but it is evidently like the word "son" itself, employed in a purely figurative sense denoting an ethical or representative relationship. When God is said to be the Father of Israel, this affirmation is wholly religious, designating God's choice of the nation, and his love for it, and watch-care over it (Deut. 32[6-14]), and the designation of him as Father of the King of Israel or of the coming Messiah has the same significance. In the few instances in which it is used of individuals, Ps. 68[5] 103[13], it clearly refers to his compassionate love and care.

III. THE USAGE OF LATER JEWISH WRITERS.

In the later Jewish writers the term retains the same general significance in reference to the nation, present or future (Tob. 13[4] Wisd. 11[10] Jub. 1[24,]

**; *cf.* 2²⁰). Clear instances of the designation of God as Father of the Messiah do not seem to occur; for Test. XII Patr. Jud. 24² speaks of God not as Father of the Messiah, but as the Holy Father (see also Levi 18⁶), and Levi 17² employs the term only by way of comparison; the Ps. Sol. (17³⁸) designate the Lord as the King, not the Father of the Messiah. On the other hand, the designation of God as the Father of the pious individual or individuals appears more frequently than in the canonical writings. *Cf.* esp. Wisd. 2¹⁶⁻¹⁸: "He (the righteous) vaunteth that God is his father. Let us see if his word be true and let us try what shall befall him in the end of his life. For if the righteous man is God's son, he will uphold him, and he will deliver him out of the hands of his adversaries." See also Sir. 23¹˒⁴ Ps. Sol. 17²⁷, and Bous. *Rel. d. Jud.²*, pp. 432 *ff.*

IV. NEW TESTAMENT USAGE.

These facts make it evident that the N. T. teachers and writers found the term ready to their hands both in the thought and vocabulary of the Greek world and especially in their inheritance from their Hebrew ancestry; in the former as a designation of God's relationship to men in general and, in the latter, of his attitude towards those who were the especial objects of his love and approval. Its range of uses and the variety of the forms which the expression takes in N. T. is such as to make it necessary to give attention to these before considering the precise content of the term in the N. T. books.

A. THE FORMS OF EXPRESSION AND CONSTRUCTIONS OCCURRING IN N. T.

The term πατήρ is used in N. T. with reference to God:

1. Without the article and without other appellative so joined with it as to constitute with it a compound appellative.

(a) In the vocative (or nominative used as a vocative), alone: Lk. 11² 22⁴² 23⁴⁶ Jn. 11⁴¹ 12²⁷˒ ²⁸ 17¹˒ ⁵˒ ¹¹˒ ²¹˒ ²⁴˒ ²⁵; with other appellatives in apposition with it: Mt. 11²⁵ Lk. 10²¹ᵃ; with adjective or possessive limitations: Mt. 26³⁹˒ ⁴².

(b) In the predicate or in dependent construction with qualitative force: Jn. 1¹⁴ 5¹⁸ 8⁴¹ (with τὸν θεόν in apposition), ⁴² 2 Cor. 6¹⁸.

2. With the article, but without other appellative so joined with it as to constitute with it a compound appellative.

(a) Absolutely and without appositive: Mt. 11²⁶˒ ²⁷ 24³⁶ 28¹⁹ Mk. 13³² 14³⁶ Lk. 10²¹ᵇ˒ ²²ᵇ˒ ᶜ Jn. 1¹⁸ 3³⁵ 4²¹˒ ²³, and freq. in Jn. Acts 1⁴˒ ⁷ 2³³ Rom. 6⁴ 8¹⁵.

(b) Limited by a genitive referring to Jesus, as in the phrases, "my father," "his father," "thy father": Mt. 7²¹ 10³²˒ ³³ 11²⁷ 12⁵⁰ 20²³ 25³⁴ 26²⁹˒ ⁵³ Mk. 8³⁸ Lk. 2⁴⁹ 10²²ᵃ Jn. 5¹⁷ 8¹⁹ 10²⁵˒ ²⁹, and freq. in Mt. and Jn.

(c) Limited by a genitive referring to men: Mt. 6⁸˒ ¹⁵ 10²⁰˒ ²⁹ 13⁴³ Lk. 6³⁶ 12³⁰˒ ³²; no exx. in Jn.

(d) Limited by a participle or prepositional phrase: Lk. 11¹³ Jn. c⁴¹ 6⁴⁴, ⁵⁷ 8¹⁶, ¹⁸ 12⁴⁹.

(e) Limited by a genitive referring to Jesus, and an adjective, participle, or prepositional phrase: Mt. 7²¹ 10³², ³³ 12⁵⁰ 15¹³ 16¹⁷ 18¹⁰, ¹⁴, ¹⁹, ³⁵.

(f) Limited by a genitive referring to men, and an adjective, participle, or prepositional phrase: Mt. 5¹⁶, ⁴⁵, ⁴⁸ 6¹, ⁴, ⁶, ⁹, ¹⁴, ¹⁸, ²⁶, ³² 7¹¹ Mk. 11²⁵.

3. Joined with θεός to form a compound appellative.

(a) The two words standing without connective and neither word having the article: not found in the gospels or Acts; frequent in the Pauline epistles, and occasional in the general epistles: Rom. 1⁷, ἀπὸ θεοῦ πατρὸς ἡμῶν καὶ κυρίου Ἰησοῦ Χριστοῦ. 1 Cor. 1³ 2 Cor. 1² Gal. 1¹, ³ Eph. 1² 6²³ Phil. 1² 2¹¹ Col. 1² 1 Thes. 1¹ 2 Thes. 1¹, ² 1 Tim. 1² 2 Tim. 1² Tit. 1⁴ Phm. ³ 1 Pet. 1² 2 Pet. 1¹⁷ 2 Jn. ³ Jude ¹.

(b) The two words being joined by καί and the phrase preceded by the article, giving the expression ὁ θεὸς καὶ πατήρ; not found in the gospels or Acts; not infrequent in Paul: Rom. 15⁶, ἵνα . . . δοξάζητε τὸν θεὸν καὶ πατέρα τοῦ κυρίου ἡμῶν Ἰησοῦ Χριστοῦ. 1 Cor. 15²⁴ 2 Cor. 1³ 11³¹ Gal. 1⁴ Eph. 1³ 5²⁰ Phil. 4²⁰ 1 Thes. 1³ 3¹¹, ¹³ Jas. 1²⁷ 1 Pet. 1³ Rev. 1⁶.

4. In some eight or ten passages the words πατήρ and θεός are associated in other ways which are slight modifications of those already named. In five of them some uncertainty of text affects the question what form the original text contains. In Col. 1³ 3¹⁷, there occurs the phrase τῷ θεῷ πατρί. In Col. 1¹², ℵ31 read τῷ θεῷ πατρί, FG θεῷ τῷ πατρί, but the evidence is on the whole against the insertion of θεῷ. In Jn. 6²⁷ and Eph. 1¹⁷ ὁ θεός and ὁ πατήρ do not constitute a compound appellative, but stand in apposition, the relation being such as we commonly express in English by the word "namely." In Jn. 8⁴¹ ὁ θεός stands in similar relation with εἷς πατήρ, and in 1 Cor. 8⁶ ὁ πατήρ is in apposition with εἷς θεός. In Eph. 4⁶ we have εἷς θεὸς καὶ πατὴρ πάντων, which is simply the common form 3 b, with the numeral εἷς replacing the definite article. In Mt. 6⁸ ὁ θεὸς ὁ πατήρ is found in ℵ*B Sah., but most authorities omit ὁ θεός. It is bracketed by WH. Other editors do not admit it even to the margin. In 2 Thes. 2¹⁶ ὁ θεὸς ὁ πατήρ is read by most authorities. The ὁ before θεός is omitted by BD*K 33 and bracketed by WH. Before πατήρ it is doubtless genuine, though generally omitted by the Syrian authorities. Apparently we have here an expression unique in N. T.

Aside, therefore, from the four cases of distinctly detached apposition, the two cases of τῷ θεῷ πατρί (Col. 1³ 3¹⁷), the one case of [ὁ] θεὸς ὁ πατήρ (2 Thes. 2¹⁶), the one instance of εἷς θεὸς καὶ πατήρ (Eph. 4⁶), all the instances of θεός and πατήρ used together for which there is good textual evidence, have either the form θεὸς πατήρ (without article or connective) or ὁ θεὸς καὶ πατήρ (with both article and connective).

The first of these forms (see 3 a above) occurs in the genitive or dative only; in nineteen out of the twenty-one instances after a preposition, and ιιι the two remaining cases (Phil. 2¹¹ and 1 Pet. 1²) after a prepositional phrase. In nine of the twenty-one instances it is limited by ἡμῶν, the list of nine being almost identical with those which belong to the certainly genuine Pauline letters (1 Cor. 1³ 2 Cor. 1² Gal. 1³ Eph. 1² Phil. 1² Col. 1² Phm. ³ 2 Thes. 1¹, but cf. contra Gal. 1¹ 1 Thes. 1¹). In no instance in this group is the compound appellative followed by a genitive referring to Christ.

The second form (3 b above) is found in all cases except the vocative. In five of the fourteen it is followed by ἡμῶν; in six by a genitive referring to Jesus, in three there is no genitive limitation. In three instances it occurs after a preposition or prepositional adverb.

It thus appears that either form may be used in prepositional constructions, but that there is a decided preference for the shorter form after prepositions. Either form may be used in the genitive or dative, but only the longer form occurs in the nominative or accusative. Either form may be limited by ἡμῶν or be used without limitation, but only the longer form is limited by a genitive referring to Christ.

These facts show that the difference between the two expressions is one neither of meaning nor of definiteness, but only of the situations in which each is preferably used. In accounting for the omission of the article before θεοῦ πατρός it is to be borne in mind (1) that neither θεός nor πατήρ exhibit any special use of the article, the assertions commonly made to the contrary being without good basis, as is also the implication of Rob. p. 795, that θεός and ὁ θεός are used without distinction; the regular designation of God is ὁ θεός,* and the omission of the article indicates that the term is qualitative, or much more rarely indefinite, or comes under some other general rule for the use of nouns without the article; (2) that it is not due to the presence or absence of a limiting genitive; (3) that some compound names show a tendency to omit the article more freely than the single terms which compose the compound; this is true both of such names as Σίμων Πέτρος, composed of two proper names and of those like Ἰησοῦς Χριστός, which are in part appellative; it is apparently true of θεὸς πατήρ, since this expression is almost invariably anarthrous; (4) that prepositional phrases of a formulary or qualitative character tend to omit the article before the noun. This tendency is illustrated by ἐν κυρίῳ and ἐν Χριστῷ. It is apparently the combined influence of these two latter tendencies that gives rise to the expression ἀπὸ θεοῦ πατρός. The tendency to omit the article with compound names (in this case amounting to an almost invariable rule) excludes τοῦ θεοῦ πατρός; the preference for the non-articular form in prepositional phrases leads to the use of ἀπὸ θεοῦ πατρός rather than ἀπὸ τοῦ θεοῦ καὶ πατρός. Cf. 1 Thes. 1³ 3¹³ Jas. 1²⁷.

The fact of most importance for the interpreter is that the omission of

* The English use of "Lord" and "God" interestingly reverses the Greek use of κύριος and θεός in N. T. The Greek regularly says ὁ θεός, but in using κύριος of God usually employs it without the article. In English, on the other hand, we say "the Lord," but "God" (without the article). The usual Greek for "the Lord God" is κύριος ὁ θεός. Cf. Sl.Qn.

the article with the compound appellative does not affect the *meaning* of the expression.

In reference to the question whether πατρός in Gal. 1¹ and other passages in which no genitive is added designates God as Father of men or of Christ, it should be noticed: (i) The latter conception is several times unequivocally expressed in Paul (Rom. 15⁶ 2 Cor. 1³ 11³¹ Eph. 1³) and is, therefore, not intrinsically improbable here.   (ii) Yet in the Pauline epistles, when πατήρ, referring to God is joined by καί to a name of Christ, πατήρ prevailingly if not invariably designates God as Father of men.   In nine instances out of sixteen, viz., in Rom. 1⁷ 1 Cor. 1³ 2 Cor. 1² Gal. 1³ Eph. 1² Phil. 1² Phm. ³ 2 Thes. 1¹ 3¹¹ ἡμῶν is expressed; in three cases—1 Tim. 1² 2 Tim. 1² Tit. 1⁴— it is probably to be supplied in thought from the context; the probability is strong that in the remaining four cases—Gal. 1¹ Eph. 6²³ 1 Thes. 1¹ 2 Thes. 1², in which no genitive is expressed, that which is to be supplied in thought is ἡμῶν.   (iii) In the eight instances in the Pauline epistles in which πατήρ is used of God without genitive limitation and is not joined by καί to the name of Jesus (Rom. 8¹⁵ 1 Cor. 8⁶ 15²⁴ 2 Cor. 6¹⁸ Gal. 4⁶ Eph. 1¹⁷ Phil. 2¹¹ Col. 3¹⁷), there are several in which πατήρ unequivocally designates the relation of God to men; none in which it certainly designates God as Father of Christ, though several of them are usually so interpreted (esp. 1 Cor. 15²⁴ Phil. 2¹¹ Col. 3¹⁷).   These facts make it clear that πατήρ as a title of God is prevailingly used by Paul (it is otherwise in John) to designate the relation of God to men; and especially that when θεὸς πατήρ and κύριος Ἰησοῦς Χριστός are joined, the antithesis in thought is not that of the relation of Father and Son to one another, but of their respective relations to men. See Rom. 1⁷ 1 Cor. 1³ 2 Cor. 1², etc., esp. 1 Cor. 8⁶.   (iv) At the same time it must be remembered that in the two passages in which Paul specially discusses the relation of believers to God as sons of the Father he implies a causal relation between such sonship and the possession of the spirit of God's Son, Jesus Christ (Gal. 4⁴⁻⁷ Rom. 8¹⁵⁻¹⁷).   It is therefore contrary to the apostle's thought to draw a line of sharp distinction between the fatherhood of God to Christ and his fatherhood to men, and it may be that when πατήρ is used without genitive limitation, the emphasis is on God's fatherly attitude without specific reference to the persons to whom it is manifested.

When ἡμῶν, limiting πατρός after a preposition, is followed by καὶ κυρίου Ἰησοῦ Χριστοῦ, as in Gal. 1³, it is grammatically possible that κυρίου Ἰησοῦ Χριστοῦ should be joined by καί to ἡμῶν and along with it limit πατρός, rather than, like πατρός, be governed by the preposition.   That this is not in fact the case, but that καί joins κυρίου to θεοῦ πατρός and is with it governed by ἀπό is made clear by two facts: (i) This double conception, God as Father of us *and* of Jesus Christ, is nowhere unambiguously expressed in the Pauline letters; the second genitive καὶ κυρίου occurs only when θεο. πατρ. is itself in the genitive.   (ii) Though there is in the un-

doubtedly genuine letters of Paul no so perfectly clear example as that in
2 Thes. 1¹, ἐν θεῷ πατρὶ ἡμῶν καὶ κυρίῳ Ἰησοῦ Χριστῷ, where ἡμῶν limiting πατρί is followed not by κύρ. Ἰησ. Χρ. in the genitive but by a dative,
yet such other examples as Gal. 1¹ 1 Thes. 1¹ 3¹¹, where the structure of the
sentence removes all syntactical ambiguity, show that it was the apostle's
usual habit to associate the titles designating God and Christ together
after a preposition, not to join the latter with ἡμῶν, referring to men.

On the question whether when the form ὁ θεὸς καὶ πατήρ is followed
by ἡμῶν (Gal. 1⁴ Phil. 4²⁰ 1 Thes. 1² 3¹¹, ¹³) the genitive limits both θεός
and πατήρ or πατήρ only, translators and interpreters are divided. Vulg.
renders it uniformly by the ambiguous phrase "*deus et pater noster.*"
Weisz. usually reads, "*Gott unser Vater,*" entirely ignoring the καί (in
1 Thes. 1³, "*unser Gott und Vater*"). Sief. reads, "*Gott der auch unser
Vater ist,*" expressly rejecting the translation "*unser Gott und Vater.*"
Ell., followed by Alf., makes ἡμῶν limit πατήρ only, translating, "God and
our Father." Segond reads, "*notre Dieu et Père*"; RV. "our God and
Father." The last is undoubtedly correct; the arguments advanced for
restricting the limitation of ἡμῶν to πατήρ are quite inconclusive. The
statement of Alford (citing Ell., whom he misunderstands) that πατήρ is
regularly anarthrous is an error; πατήρ, whether referring to man or to
God, shows the regular use of the article; and the argument that ὁ θεός
is naturally used absolutely is of little weight in view of Paul's not infrequent use of ὁ θεὸς ἡμῶν (1 Cor. 6¹¹ 1 Thes. 2² 3⁹ 2 Thes. 1¹¹, ¹²), and ὁ θεός
μου (Rom. 1⁸ Phil. 1³ 4¹⁹). Nor is the appeal made by Sief. to the phrase
θεοῦ πατρὸς ἡμῶν (Rom. 1⁷ 1 Cor. 1³, etc.) of any weight, first because,
the phrase being different, it is by no means certain that the relation of
ἡμῶν is the same, and, second, because the probability is, as shown above,
that θεοῦ πατρός is itself a compound name, the whole of which, as a unity
including both elements, is limited in thought by ἡμῶν. Two nouns joined
by καί and having the article before the first only are always closely connected in thought, either as common predicates of one individual, or as
individuals constituting in some sense a unity. Even in the latter case,
when the objects are distinct, and only closely joined in thought, a genitive,
standing after either or before them both, commonly limits both. See
Lk. 14²¹ Phil. 1⁷, ²⁵ 2¹⁷ Eph. 3⁵ 1 Thes. 2¹² 3⁷ 2 Pet. 1¹⁰. Much more probably, therefore, would this be the case when the two nouns evidently designate the same person. The only fact that could suggest a restriction of
the relation of a genitive after two such nouns to the second would be its
manifest unsuitableness to limit the first.

Somewhat similar reasoning leads us to the conclusion that τοῦ κυρίου
ἡμῶν Ἰησοῦ Χριστοῦ when standing after ὁ θεὸς καὶ πατήρ (Rom. 15⁶
2 Cor. 1³ Eph. 1³ 1 Pet. 1³; *cf.* 2 Cor. 11³¹) is to be understood as limiting
both nouns. The expression "God of our Lord Jesus" does not, indeed,
occur in Paul (*cf.* Mk. 15³⁴ Mt. 27⁴⁶ Jn. 20¹⁷), but it can not be inferred from

this fact that Paul could not limit the compound appellative "God and Father" by a genitive referring to Jesus Christ, for neither does Paul use the phrase "Father of our Lord Jesus."

B. THE MEANING OF THE TERM, πατήρ, AS APPLIED TO GOD IN N. T.

1. Jas. 1^{17} stands quite alone in N. T. in its use of the term Father to designate God's relation to the heavenly bodies.

2. The conception that God is Father of all men is rarely expressed by N. T. writers. That he maintains to all men, and even to the lower animals, that attitude of love and watch-care which the term father expresses, is indeed explicitly affirmed. But even Mt. 5^{45} and Lk. $6^{35, 36}$ do not directly designate God as Father of all, but only of those who, as disciples of Jesus, are evidently looked upon as objects of divine approval. Nor is God called Father of all in Heb. 12^{7-9}, for the "we" of this passage apparently includes only Christians, or at most Jews and Christians. Only in Eph. 4^6, with which Eph. 3^{15} is seemingly in agreement in thought, does God seem definitely to be called Father of all, and even here it is not quite certain that "all" includes other than Christians. While, therefore, it may be properly said that the N. T. writers believe in the universal fatherliness of God, because they ascribe to him a relationship to all men which may naturally be included under that term, yet from the point of view of the N. T. *use of words*, the doctrine that God is the Father of all is definitely expressed, if at all, only in the Epistle to the Ephesians. Nor is this fact without significance; for it shows that the conception of God as Father so emphasised the ethical elements of fatherhood and in particular that of fellowship grounded in approval, that the N. T. writers were indisposed to use the term when the element of approval was not felt to be present.

3. The designation of God as Father of all who believe in Jesus is frequent in all parts of N. T. See examples under A. 2 c, f; 3 a, b above. While emphasising, especially when used in addressing God, the conception of his love and watch-care in which men may safely trust, yet by its all but universal restriction to use in relation to believers, and by the clear limitation of the correlative term "sons of God" to those who are like God (Mt. 5^{45}) or who are led by his Spirit (Rom. 8^{14-16}), it is evident that the term carries with it the idea not only of benevolent love such as God has for the world (Jn. 3^{16}) and as men are bidden to have for their enemies, but also such friendship and fellowship as is characteristic of the normal relation between a father and his children.

4. The designation of God as the Father of Jesus is, except in the fourth gospel, much less frequent in N. T. than the characterisation of him as Father of believers, yet it is found often enough to show that it is a familiar thought to the N. T. writers. It is found four times in the Pauline epistles (Rom. 15^6 2 Cor. 1^3 11^{31} Eph. 1^3), is ascribed by the synoptic gospels to

Jesus (see A. 2 b above), occurs very frequently in Jn., once in Heb. (1⁵, where it is expressly based upon the O. T. passage concerning the Son of David), in 1 Pet. 2 Jn. and Rev. In 1 Jn., as in the Gospel of John, ὁ πατήρ absolute frequently occurs in antithesis with ὁ υἱός, suggesting that the reference is to God as Father of Christ.

N. T. usage in general evidently has a twofold basis, on the one side in the conviction attested by the synoptic gospels that as Jesus could speak to other men of God as "your Father," so he could also think and speak of him as "my Father," and on the other, in that the ascription to him of messiahship carried with it the designation of God as his Father in the sense in which God was the Father of the Messiah (cf. esp. Heb. 1⁵). These two conceptions have, indeed, a common root in the conception of God's love and watch-care over those whom he approves, but the differentiation of the two ideas would probably be more present to early Christian thought than their common root. A comparison of the several books of N. T., with remembrance of the order of their development and of that of their sources, especially of the synoptists and the fourth gospel, indicates that the two conceptions developed in the order named, the conception of the fatherhood of God as pertaining to Jesus in a unique sense or degree gradually gaining ascendancy over the earlier idea that God is Father of all whom he approves, but even in its latest forms never wholly losing sight of the basal idea of fatherhood as consisting essentially in love. That "the Father loveth the Son and showeth him all things that he himself doeth," is still in the fourth gospel the fundamental element of fatherhood.

In respect to the thought of Paul in particular, it is to be noted (a) that he used the same form of expression in reference to Jesus as in respect to Christians, viz., "God and Father of us," "God and Father of our Lord Jesus Christ"; (b) that he expressly associated together the sonship of men by virtue of which they call God their Father and the sonship of Jesus, making the possession of the Spirit of the Son the ground or the consequence of the possession of the spirit of sonship (Rom. 8¹⁴⁻¹⁶ Gal. 4⁴⁻⁷); but (c) that he did not apparently join the two together in the expression, "the God and Father of us and of the Lord Jesus Christ"; (d) that though employing the expression "the God and Father of our Lord Jesus Christ," and once (2 Cor. 11³¹) "the God and Father of the Lord Jesus," he never used either "God of our Lord Jesus," or "Father of our Lord Jesus" alone; and (e) that he never enters into an exposition of the conception of the fatherhood of God in relation to Christ, and in particular never associates it with any statement respecting the origin of Jesus. From these facts it seems necessary to infer that, in common with the Jewish writers of the late pre-Christian period and with early Christian thought, Paul understood the divine fatherhood in a purely ethical sense, and associated it closely with the conception of the godhead (θειότης) itself, so that though one may say "our God," or "the Father," it is more congenial to say "our God and

Father." This conception of fatherhood holds in respect to God as the Father of Jesus also, and, indeed, especially in respect to him, God sustaining towards him in a pre-eminent degree those ethical relations which are expressed by the term Father, but having no relation to him as Father which can be thought of apart from the fact that he is God.

On the correlative idea of Jesus as "Son of God," see below on *The Titles and Predicates of Jesus*, V.

III. TITLES AND PREDICATES OF JESUS
Occurring in the Pauline Epistles.

I. THE TITLES ENUMERATED.

The following names and phrases are applied to Jesus in the Pauline epistles, as titles or predicates. For purposes of comparison instances occurring elsewhere in N. T. are indicated in the lists.*

1. Ἰησοῦς. (a) Without the article: Rom. 3²⁶ 10⁹ 1 Cor. 12³ 2 Cor. 4⁸ᵇ 11ᵃ⁺ 14ᵇ Phil. 2¹⁰ 1 Thes. 1¹⁰ 4¹⁴ᵃ (not elsewhere in Paul); Mt. 14¹ 20³⁰ 21¹⋅ ¹² 26⁵¹ Mk. 1⁹ Lk. 2⁵² 3²¹⋅ ²³ 4¹ Jn. 1⁴⁷⋅ ⁴⁸, etc. Acts 1¹⁶ 5³⁰, etc. Heb. 2⁹ 3¹ 6²⁰, etc.; 1 Jn. 2²² 5¹⋅ ⁵ Rev. 1⁹ 12¹⁷, etc.; not found in pastoral epistles, or 1 and 2 Pet. Jas. or Jude.

(b) With the article: Rom. 8¹¹ 2 Cor. 4¹⁰ᵃ⋅ ᵇ⋅ ¹¹ᵇ Gal. 6¹⁷ Eph. 4²¹ 1 Thes. 4¹⁴ᵇ (only instances in Paul); Mt. 2¹ Mk. 1¹⁴ Lk. 4⁸ Jn. 1³⁶, *et freq.*, in all the gospels; Acts 1¹¹⋅ ¹⁴, etc.; 1 Jn. 4³; not in pastoral epistles, Heb. 1 and 2 Pet. 2 and 3 Jn. Jude or Rev.

2. Χριστός. (a) Without the article: Rom. 5⁶⋅ ⁸ 6⁴⋅ ⁸ Gal. 1⁶⋅ ¹⁰, *et freq.*, in Paul, esp. in the phrase ἐν Χριστῷ, e. g.: Gal. 1²² 2¹⁷, etc.; rare in other parts of N. T., except 1 Pet. See Mt. 26⁶⁸ (voc.) Mk. 9⁴¹ Lk. 23² Jn. 1⁴¹ 9²² Acts 2³⁶ Heb. 3⁶ 9¹¹⋅ ²⁴ 1 Pet. 1¹¹ 2²¹ 3¹⁸ 4¹⋅ ¹⁴ 5¹⁰⋅ ¹⁴.

(b) With the article: Rom. 7⁴ 8³⁵ 9³⋅ ⁵ 14¹⁸ 15³⋅ ⁷⋅ ¹⁹ 16¹⁶ 1 Cor. 1⁶⋅ ¹²⋅ ¹⁷ 6¹⁵ᵇ 9¹² 10⁴⋅ ¹⁶ *bis* 11³ *bis* 12¹² 15¹⁵⋅ ²²⋅ ²³ᵇ 2 Cor. 1⁵ 2¹⁴ 3⁴ 4⁴ 5¹⁰⋅ ¹⁴ 9¹³ 10¹⋅ ⁵⋅ ¹⁴ 11²⋅ ³ (txt. unc.) 12⁹ Gal. 1⁷ 6² Eph. 1¹⁰⋅ ¹²⋅ ²⁰ 2⁵⋅ ¹³ᵇ 3⁴⋅ ⁸ 4¹²⋅ ¹³⋅ ²⁰ 5²⋅ ⁵⋅ ¹⁴⋅ ²³⋅ ²⁴⋅ ²⁵⋅ ²⁹ 6⁵ Phil. 1¹⁵⋅ ¹⁷ (txt. unc.) ²⁷ 3⁷⋅ ¹⁸ Col. 1⁷⋅ ²⁴ 2¹¹⋅ ¹⁷ 3¹⋅ ³⋅ ⁴⋅ ¹³ (txt. unc.) 1⁵⋅ ¹⁶ (txt. unc.) 4³ 1 Thes. 3² 2 Thes. 3⁵ (not elsewhere in Paul); less freq. in other parts of N. T. See Mt. 1¹⁷ 11² 16²⁰ 23¹⁰ Mk. 8²⁹ Lk. 4⁴¹ Jn. 7⁴¹ 11²⁷ 20³¹ Acts 2³¹ 8⁵ 9²² 17³ 18⁵⋅ ²⁸ 26⁶³ 1 Tim. 5¹¹ Heb. 3¹⁴ 5⁸ 6¹ 9¹⁴⋅ ²⁸ 11²⁶ 1 Pet. 4¹³ 5¹ 1 Jn. 2²² 5¹ 2 Jn. ⁹ Rev. 20⁶; after ἐν in 2 Cor. 2¹⁴ Eph. 1¹⁰⋅ ¹²⋅ ²⁰ only.

ὁ Χριστός, meaning "the Messiah," but not as a title or affirmed predicate of Jesus is found in Mt. 2⁴ 22⁴² 24⁵⋅ ²³ 26⁶³ Mk. 12³⁵ 13³¹ Lk. 3¹⁵ 20⁴¹ 22⁶⁷ 23³⁵⋅ ³⁹ 24²⁶⋅ ⁴⁶ Jn. 1²⁰⋅ ²⁵ 3²⁸ 4²⁹ 7²⁶⋅ ²⁷⋅ ³¹⋅ ⁴² 10²⁴ 12³⁴.

In a few passages ὁ χριστός is applied to Jesus, with the addition of unusual titles or limitations. Thus: ὁ χριστὸς ὁ βασιλεὺς Ἰσραήλ, Mk. 15³²; ὁ χριστὸς τοῦ θεοῦ, Lk. 9²⁰; ὁ χριστὸς αὐτοῦ, Acts 3¹⁸ 4²⁶ Rev. 11¹⁵.

* *Cf.* Middleton, *Use of the Article in Greek*, edited by H. G. Rose, Appendix II (by Rose), "A Table showing the various Appellations of our blessed Lord." etc.

3. Κύριος. (a) Without the article: Rom. 10⁹ 1 Cor. 7²²ᵇ, ²⁵ *bis* 10²¹ *bis*, etc. It is rather infrequent in Paul, except in the phrase ἐν κυρίῳ: Rom. 16⁸, ¹¹, ¹², ¹³, ²² 1 Cor. 7²²ᵃ, ³ᵇ 2 Cor. 2¹² Gal. 5¹⁰; a complete list is difficult to give because of the difficulty of deciding in all cases whether the reference is to God or Christ. It is rare in other parts of N. T. (Acts 2³⁶) except in the gospels as a title of respectful address (Mt. 8², ⁶, ⁸, etc.).

(b) With the article: 1 Cor. 4⁵ 6¹³, ¹⁴, ¹⁷ 7¹⁰, ¹² 9⁵ 11²⁶, ²⁷ Gal. 1¹⁹. Mk. 11³ and its repetition in Mt. 21³ are apparently the only cases in these gospels, but instances are much more frequent in Lk. Acts, and Jn.: Lk. 7¹³, ¹⁹ 10¹, ³⁹, ⁴¹ 11³⁹ 12⁴²ᵃ 13¹⁵ 17⁵, ⁶ 18⁶ 19⁸, ³¹, ³⁴ 22⁶¹ 24³⁴ Jn. 4¹ 6²³ 11² 20², ¹⁸, ²⁰, ²⁵ 21⁷, ¹² Acts 5¹⁴ 9¹, ¹⁰ᵃ, ¹¹, ¹⁵, ¹⁷, ²⁷, ²⁸, ³⁵, ⁴² 11¹⁶, ²¹ᵇ 13¹² 14²³ 22¹⁰ᵇ 26¹⁵ᵇ.

4. Ἰησοῦς Χριστός. (a) Without the article preceding: Rom. 1⁶, ⁸ 1 Cor. 3¹¹ Gal. 1¹, ¹² *et freq.* in Paul, Acts, the pastoral and general epistles; occurs also Heb. 10¹⁰ 13⁸, ²¹ Rev. 1¹, ², ⁵ Mt. 1¹ 16²¹ (txt. unc.) Mk. 1¹ Jn. 1¹⁷ 17³. In Mt. 1¹⁶ 27¹⁷, ²², occurs Ἰησοῦς ὁ λεγόμενος χριστός. In Acts 3⁶ 4¹⁰ we have Ἰησοῦς Χριστὸς ὁ Ναζωραῖος.

(b) With the article, in Mt. 1¹⁸ only. See 5 b below.

5. Χριστὸς Ἰησοῦς. (a) Without the article: Rom. 6³ 8¹¹ᵇ, ³⁴ 15¹⁶ 2 Cor. 1¹ (txt. unc.) Gal. 4¹⁴ Eph. 1¹ 2²⁰ Phil. 1¹, ⁸ Col. 1¹ 4¹², esp. freq. in the phrase ἐν Χριστῷ Ἰησοῦ; Rom. 3²⁴ 6¹¹ 8¹, ² 15¹⁷ 16³ 1 Cor. 1², ⁴, ³⁰ 4¹⁵, ¹⁷ 16²⁴ Gal. 2⁴ 3²⁶, ²⁸ 5⁶ Eph. 1¹ᵇ 2⁶, ⁷, ¹⁰, ¹³ 3⁶, ²¹ Phil. 1¹ᵇ, 2⁶ 2⁵ 3³, ¹⁴ 4⁷, ¹⁹, ²¹ Col. 1⁴ 1 Thes. 2¹⁴ 5¹⁸; found also in the pastoral epistles and Acts, but in no other books. In Rom. 1¹ 2¹⁶ 5¹⁷ 15⁵ 1 Cor. 1¹ 2 Cor. 4⁵ Gal. 2¹⁶ 3¹⁴ Phil. 1⁶ 2²¹ the mss. vary between Ἰησοῦ Χρ. and Χρ. Ἰησοῦ.

(b) With the article preceding: Gal. 5²⁴ (*cf. ad loc.*) Eph. 3¹ only. In Acts 5⁴² 18⁵, ²⁸ τὸν χριστόν is predicate; Mt. 1¹⁸ should probably read, τοῦ Ἰησοῦ Χριστοῦ.

6. Κύριος Ἰησοῦς. (a) Without the article: Rom. 14¹⁴ Phil. 2¹⁹ Col. 3¹⁷ 1 Thes. 4¹ Acts 7⁵⁹ Rev. 22²⁰ only. In Rom. 10⁹ and Phil. 2¹¹, probably also in 1 Cor. 12³ᵇ, κύριος is predicate.

(b) With the article preceding: 1 Cor. 5⁵ (txt. unc.) 11²³ 16²³ 2 Cor. 4¹⁴ᵃ 11³¹ Eph. 1¹⁵ 1 Thes. 2¹⁵ 4² 2 Thes. 1⁷ 2⁸ (txt. unc.); 2 Tim. 4²² (some texts); Phm.⁵; freq. also in Acts (8¹⁶ 11²⁰ 15¹¹ 16³¹ etc.) but not found in other books with conclusive ms. evidence.

7. Ἰησοῦς ὁ κύριος ἡμῶν: Rom. 4²⁴ 1 Cor. 9¹; or in transposed order: ὁ κύριος ἡμῶν Ἰησοῦς: 1 Cor. 5⁴ᵃ, ᵇ (txt. unc.) 2 Cor. 1¹⁴ 1 Thes. 2¹⁹ 3¹¹, ¹³ 2 Thes. 1¹²ᵃ; outside of Paul in 2 Pet. 1², Ἰησοῦς ὁ κύριος ἡμῶν, and Heb. 13²⁰, ὁ κύριος ἡμῶν Ἰησοῦς only.

8. κύριος Ἰησοῦς Χριστός and other phrases containing these three terms. (a) κύριος Ἰησοῦς Χριστός without the article: Rom. 1⁷ 1 Cor. 1³ 8⁶ 2 Cor. 1² Gal. 1³ Eph. 1² 6²³ Phil. 1² 3²⁰ 1 Thes. 1¹ 2 Thes. 1¹, ², ¹²ᵇ Phm. ³; outside the Pauline letters, in Jas. 1¹ only.

(b) With the article: Rom 13¹⁴ (txt. unc.) 1 Cor. 6¹¹ 2 Cor. 13³ Phil. 4²³ 2 Thes. 3⁶ Phm. ²⁵; outside of Paul in Acts 11¹⁷ 28³¹ Rev. 22²¹, with *vv. ll.* in the last case.

(c) In transposed order without the article: Χριστὸς Ἰησοῦς κύριος: 2 Cor. 4⁵.

(d) With the article repeated: ὁ χριστὸς Ἰησοῦς ὁ κύριος: Col. 2⁶.

(e) Ὁ κύριος ἡμῶν Ἰησοῦς Χριστός: Rom. 5¹, ¹¹ 15⁶, ³⁰ 1 Cor. 1², ⁷, ⁸, ¹⁰ 15⁵⁷ 2 Cor. 1³ 8⁹ Gal. 6¹⁴, ¹⁸ Eph. 1³, ¹⁷ 5²⁰ 6²⁴ Col. 1³ 1 Thes. 1³ 5⁹, ²³, ²⁸ 2 Thes. 2¹, ¹⁴, ¹⁶ 3¹⁸; also 1 Tim. 6³, ¹⁴ Acts 15²⁶ 20²¹ (txt. unc.) Jas. 2¹ 1 Pet. 1² 2 Pet. 1⁸, ¹⁴, ¹⁶ Jude 4, 17, 21.

(f) Ἰησοῦς Χριστὸς ὁ κύριος ἡμῶν: Rom. 1⁴ 5²¹ 7²⁵ 1 Cor. 1⁹, also Jude 25.

(g) Χριστὸς Ἰησοῦς ὁ κύριος ἡμῶν. (i) Without the article before Χριστὸς Ἰησοῦς: Rom. 6²³ 8³⁹ 1 Cor. 15³¹ 1 Tim. 1², ¹² 2 Tim. 1²; with μοῦ instead of ἡμῶν: Phil. 3⁸; (ii) With the article before Χριστὸς Ἰησοῦς: Eph. 3¹¹.

9. Υἱὸς θεοῦ, or υἱός with a pronoun referring to God: (a) Without the article with either word: Rom. 1⁴ (only instance in Paul); also in Mt. 14³³ 27⁴³, ⁵⁴ Mk. 1¹ (txt. unc.) 15³⁹ Lk. 1³⁵ Jn. 19⁷ Acts 13³³ Heb.1⁵ 5⁵.

(b) Υἱὸς τοῦ θεοῦ: Mt. 4³, ⁶ 8²⁹ (voc.) 27⁴⁰ Mk. 5⁷ (voc.) Lk. 4³, ⁹ 8²⁸ (voc.) Jn. 10³⁶ (txt. unc.); some of these are in conditional clauses.

(c) With the article before υἱός: ὁ υἱὸς τοῦ θεοῦ, or ὁ υἱὸς αὐτοῦ, ἑαυτοῦ, μοῦ, or ἴδιος, αὐτοῦ, etc., referring to God: Rom. 1³, ⁹ 5¹⁰ 8³, ²⁹, ³² Gal. 1¹⁶ 2²⁰ 4⁴, ⁶ Eph. 4¹³ 1 Thes. 1¹⁰ (no other examples in Paul); Mt. 2¹⁵ 3¹⁷ 17⁵ Mk. 1¹¹ 3¹¹ 9⁷ Lk. 3²² 4⁴¹ 9³⁵ Jn. 1³⁴, ⁴⁹ 3¹⁸ 5²⁵ 9³⁵ (txt. unc.) 11⁴ Acts 9²⁰ Heb. 6⁶ 7³ 10²⁹ 2 Pet. 1¹⁷ 1 Jn. 3⁸ 4¹⁰, ¹⁵ 5⁵, ⁹, ¹⁰ bis ¹¹ 12b, ¹³, ²⁰ª.

(d) With the article and other titles accompanying: ὁ υἱὸς αὐτοῦ Ἰησοῦς Χριστὸς ὁ κύριος ἡμῶν: 1 Cor. 1⁹; ὁ τοῦ θεοῦ υἱὸς Ἰησοῦς Χριστός: 2 Cor. 1¹⁹; ὁ υἱὸς αὐτοῦ Ἰησοῦς Χριστός: 1 Jn. 1³ 3²³ 5²⁰b; ὁ χριστὸς ὁ υἱὸς τοῦ ζῶντος θεοῦ: Mt. 16¹⁶ (cf. Mk. 14⁶¹ Mt. 26⁶³); ὁ χριστὸς ὁ υἱὸς τοῦ θεοῦ: Jn. 11²⁷ 20³¹; Ἰησοῦς ὁ υἱὸς τοῦ θεοῦ: Heb. 4¹⁴; Ἰησοῦς ὁ υἱὸς αὐτοῦ: 1 Jn. 1⁷; ὁ υἱὸς αὐτοῦ ὁ μονο- γενής: 1 Jn. 4⁹. Cf. 2 Jn. ³, Ἰησοῦς Χριστὸς ὁ υἱὸς τοῦ πατρός.

10. In the Pauline epistles σωτήρ is applied to Jesus in Phil. 3²⁰, yet here not precisely as a title. Cf. Lk. 2¹¹ Jn. 4⁴² Acts 5³¹ 13²³ 1 Jn. 4¹⁴. As a title of Jesus ὁ σωτὴρ ἡμῶν Χριστὸς Ἰησοῦς is found in 2 Tim. 1¹⁰; Χριστὸς Ἰησοῦς ὁ σωτὴρ ἡμῶν in Tit. 1⁴; Ἰησοῦς Χριστὸς ὁ σωτὴρ ἡμῶν in Tit. 3⁶; ὁ θεὸς καὶ σωτὴρ ἡμῶν Χριστὸς Ἰησοῦς in Tit. 2¹³; ὁ θεὸς ἡμῶν καὶ σωτὴρ Ἰησοῦς Χριστός in 2 Pet. 1¹; ὁ κύριος ἡμῶν καὶ σωτὴρ Ἰησοῦς Χριστός in 2 Pet. 1¹¹ 3¹⁸; without ἡμῶν in 2 Pet. 2²⁰.

11. θεός. The passages to be considered here are: Rom. 9⁵ Heb. 1⁸ Jn. 1¹, ¹⁸, 1 Jn. 5²⁰. Cf. also Phil. 2⁶.

II. ΊΗΣΟΥΣ.

Ἰησοῦς is a personal name, the Grecised form of the Hebrew name Joshua, יְהוֹשֻׁעַ, which etymologically means "saviour." To what extent this etymological sense of the word lingered in the use of the name itself in N. T. times, there is no definite indication. In Paul there is no trace of it, and elsewhere in N. T. in Mt. 1²¹ only. Probably it was usually as little in mind as is the meaning of the word Theodore at the present day.

III. ΧΡΙΣΤΟΣ.

A. JEWISH USAGE.

Χριστός is the Greek representative of the Hebrew מָשִׁיחַ, "anointed." The Hebrew word is applied in the literal sense to the high priest in Lev. 4³, ⁵, ¹⁶. As a substantive sometimes in the expression "the anointed of Yahweh," it is applied to the King of Israel: 1 Sam. 2¹⁰, ³⁵ 12³, ⁵ Ps. 18⁵¹ Lam. 4²⁰ Hab. 3¹³. It is used of Cyrus in Isa. 45¹. From its usage with reference to the King of Israel, perhaps under the influence of a messianic interpretation of Ps. 2², and Dan. 9²⁵ᶠ., it came to be employed as a title, eventually the most common and distinctive title, of the expected king and deliverer of Israel. But as the idea of a personal Messiah is not always associated with what may be broadly called the messianic hope (see Bous. *Rel. d. Jud.*², p. 255), so the term Χριστός is not always present when the expected deliverer is spoken of. See, *e. g.*, Test. XII Patr. Reub. 6⁷⁻¹²; Lev. 8¹⁴ 18¹ᶠᶠ. Jud. 24¹⁻³ Dan. 5¹⁰, ¹¹. Among the earliest instances of its use as a distinctive messianic title are 1 Enoch 48¹⁰ 52⁴. Charles, *Book of Enoch, ad loc.*, says these are the earliest cases. Nearly contemporaneous and more significant is Ps. Sol. 17³⁵ᵇ, ³⁶: "And a righteous king and taught of God is he that reigneth over them. And there shall be no iniquity in his days in their midst, for all shall be holy, and their King is Messiah, Lord (Χριστὸς κύριος)." The whole psalm is a most instructive reflection of the ideas of religion, and especially of the Messiah and the messianic deliverance which were held by the Pharisees in the last pre-Christian century. See also 18⁴, ⁸, and on the whole subject Schr., § 29; E. T. II, ii, pp. 129 *ff.*; Bous. *Rel. d. Jud.*², pp. 255 *ff.*

B. NEW TESTAMENT USAGE.

The evidence of N. T. leaves no room for doubt that the titular use of the term illustrated in Ps. Sol., in which it denotes an ideal expected character as distinguished from an identified historical person, had become common by the early part of the first Christian century, as it also shows even more clearly that early in the history of the Christian movement it was used as a descriptive title or personal name of Jesus.

As respects the degree of identification of the character designated by the term with the person Jesus, there are five uses of the term in N. T., in the first four of which it stands alone without other appellatives; in the fifth it is used with other titles of Jesus.

1. It designates "the Messiah" without identification of any person as such: Mt. 2⁴ 22⁴² Mk. 12³⁵ Lk. 2²⁶ 24²⁶ Jn. 7²⁶, ²⁷, ³¹, ⁴¹, ⁴² Acts 2³¹ 17³ᵃ.

2. It is used as the predicate of a proposition, the subject of which is affirmed to be the Messiah, the identification lying, however, not in the term but being effected by the proposition itself; or in a question, it is asked

whether one is to be identified with the Christ. Most frequently the sub-ject of the affirmation or question is Jesus (Mk. 8[29] 14[61] Mt. 16[16] 26[63] Lk. 9[20] 23[2] Jn. 7[41] 10[24] 11[27] 17[3b] Acts 17[3b] 18[5]), but occasionally others (Mt. 24[5, 23] Lk. 3[15]). For qualitative effect the article may be omitted: Acts 2[36].

3. It designates "the Messiah" as such, but with implied identification of the Messiah with Jesus; in other words, refers to Jesus, but to him specifically as the Christ: Mt. 1[17] 11[2] 23[10] Acts 8[5] Rom. 7[4] 9[3, 5] 14[18] 15[7, 19] 16[16] 1 Cor. 1[6, 13, 17] (txt. unc.) 9[12] 10[16] *bis* 12[12] 15[15] 2 Cor. 1[5] 2[12, 14] 3[4] 4[4] 5[10, 14] 9[13] 10[1, 5, 14] 11[2] 12[9] Gal. 1[7] 6[2] Eph. 1[10, 12, 20] 2[5, 13] 3[4, 8, 17] 4[12, 20] 5[2, 5, 14, 23, 24, 25, 29] Phil. 1[15, 27] 3[7, 18], etc.

4. It becomes a title or name of Jesus without discernible emphasis upon his messiahship, though this is perhaps usually in the background of the thought: Rom. 5[6, 8] 6[4, 8, 9] 8[9, 10, 17] 9[1] 10[4, 6, 7, 17] 15[8, 18, 20, 29] 16[5] 1 Cor. 1[12, 17] 2[16] 3[1, 23] 4[1, 10] *bis* 5[7] 6[15a] 7[22] 8[11, 12] 9[21] 11[1] 12[27] 15[3, 12, 13, 14, 16, 17, 18, 19, 20, 22, 23a] 2 Cor. 1[21] 2[10, 15, 17] 3[3, 14] 4[5] 5[17, 18, 19, 20] *bis* 6[15] 8[23] 10[7] *bis* 11[10, 13, 23] 12[2, 10, 19] 13[3] (?) Gal. 1[6, 10, 22] 2[4, 16, 17, 20, 21] 3[13, 16, 24, 27, 29] 4[19] 5[1, 2, 4] Heb. 3[6] 9[11, 24].

The line of distinction between the two classes of cases, 3 and 4, can not be clearly drawn. Broadly speaking, the instances in which the article is present in the Greek belong under 3, those in which it is absent under 4. But instances without the article may belong under 3, the article being omitted to give the word qualitative force. See, e. g., 1 Cor. 1[12] (cf. RV. margin); so, perhaps, 1 Cor. 2[16] and 2 Cor. 5[16], and probably Mk. 9[41]. It is possible also that in some cases the article is prefixed, as it is also to Ἰησοῦς or any proper name, without emphasising the titular significance. It is clear, however, that the word is often used purely as a proper name and that this fact is usually marked by the omission of the article. No examples of this usage of Χριστός alone, without the article (on Ἰησοῦς Χριστός, see below), occur in the gospels, except perhaps in Mk. 9[41]. Though the Pauline letters show clearly that it was current before the gospels were written, the gospel writers do not, with the one possible exception, impute it to the evangelic period or themselves employ it.

5. It occurs in combination with other titles of Jesus, forming with them compound appellatives. See I 4, 5, 8 above, and below.

In the epistles of Paul, which in time of writing precede all, or all but one, of the other N. T. books, we find the use of the term with reference to Jesus fully developed, and taken for granted. This is true even of the earliest letters. Paul's common titles for Jesus are "the Christ," "Christ," "the Lord Jesus Christ," and "our Lord Jesus Christ." Indeed, he finds no occasion to affirm that Jesus is the Christ, nor does he, outside of two or three passages of somewhat doubtful interpretation (see, e. g., 2 Cor. 10[14]; cf. Eph. 1[10, 12]), ever use the term in its primary sense of "the (unidentified) Christ." The major portion of the post-Pauline epistles exhibit substantially the same usage, but with a somewhat marked tendency to prefer the longer, compound titles. These facts show that comparatively early in the apostolic age the use of the term as a title or name of Jesus was already well established.

From the gospels and Acts we are able to see in part how this usage arose and was developed. Though undoubtedly written after the letters of Paul, and in many passages reflecting the usage of the period in which they arose (so, *e. g.*, clearly in Mt. 1¹ and Mk. 1¹; see also Mt. 11² 23¹⁰), they show clear traces of an earlier usage and thought. The gospel of Mk. represents Jesus as gathering his earliest disciples without asserting that he was the Christ or eliciting from them any acknowledgment of him as such. The first assertion of the messiahship was at Cæsarea Philippi, but the confession there made he charges them not to publish (8²⁹, ³⁰), and it is not again referred to except incidentally in conversation between Jesus and his disciples (9⁴¹), and by implication in the words of Bartimæus, till the trial of Jesus, when in response to the challenge of the high priest he openly declares that he is the Christ (Mk. 14⁶¹, ⁶²). The discussion of the lordship of the Messiah in 12³⁶ff. pertains to the Messiah as such, not to Jesus. This primitive tradition is somewhat modified in the other synoptic gospels, yet not so as materially to obscure it.

The fourth gospel represents the question whether Jesus was the Christ as playing a much larger and earlier part in the relation of Jesus to the Jewish people than the synoptic gospels imply. In this, as in other respects, the gospel has doubtless been affected by the distance between the events narrated and the writing of the book, and by the special purpose of the book as defined in 20³¹; but even in this gospel, there is an entire absence of the Pauline usages of Χριστός and ὁ χριστός, and Ἰησοῦς Χριστός occurs but once (17³) in narrative or discourse, the personal name Jesus being the one commonly used. Even in editorial passages Χριστός never occurs, ὁ χριστός but once (20³¹), and then not as a title but as a predicate, and Ἰησοῦς Χριστός but once (1¹⁷). The longer compound titles do not occur at all.

The book of Acts, on the other hand, furnishes examples of all the Pauline usages, the instances of the compound names being most frequent. The writer even represents Peter, at the beginning of the apostolic age, as commonly using the expression "Jesus Christ" and once "the Lord Jesus Christ." If this is historically correct, there must have been a very rapid development of usage immediately following the death and resurrection of Jesus. It is probable, however, that the author is here, to some extent, carrying back to the beginning of the apostolic age the usage of a later time. Acts 2³⁶ ascribes to Peter the view that by the resurrection and exaltation of Jesus God made him both Lord and Christ. If this means that the messiahship dates from the resurrection, this is a different conception from that which is implied in the third gospel, viz.: that it belonged to his public ministry (3¹⁵ff. 9²⁰), if not even dating from his birth (2¹¹, ²⁶). In the mind of the writer it may perhaps mean that what he was previously in purpose and by right he now became in fact and power (cf. Rom. 1⁴), or that he now became Lord as well as Christ.

The whole evidence points, therefore, to the conclusion that beginning with the use of "the Christ" as the name of the expected but as yet un-identified coming king (a usage in existence among the Jews before the appearance of Jesus) it was in his lifetime first questioned whether Jesus was the Christ, then affirmed by his disciples that he was; then with the birth of the conviction that Jesus was risen from the dead, reaffirmed with new confidence, and that out of this conviction, perhaps in part before Paul's day, but probably in larger part under his influence, there arose a variety of titles for Jesus, embodying this faith. These usages once devel-oped were carried back to a very limited extent into the gospel record and to a greater extent into the narrative of the early apostolic age, yet not so as wholly to obscure the underlying and more primitive usage.

But it still remains to inquire precisely what it meant in the first century to apply to Jesus or to any one else the term "Christ," not in its literal sense, "anointed," or as a mere proper name, but as a significant title. What did the early Christians mean when they affirmed that Jesus was the Christ? In particular how did this assertion differ from what they meant when they spoke of him as "Lord," or "Son of God"?

There is singularly little direct evidence to answer this question. The very familiarity of the term apparently made even indirect definition un-necessary. Yet such evidence as there is is sufficient to make it clear that as a descriptive title the word meant "deliverer," "saviour," with the added implication of divine appointment. Both elements of this meaning arise, of course, not from the etymology of the word, but from its employ-ment to designate the looked-for King of Israel, concerning whom men's chief thought was that he, sent by God, would deliver Israel. The element of divine appointment is specially suggested in Acts 2³⁶: "Him hath God made both Lord and Christ." But the word "Christ" complementary to the term "Lord" probably describes Jesus as Saviour. In the absence of any direct definition of the word in Paul's writings there is no more sig-nificant clue to the thought for which the term stands in his mind than the class of words with which he employs the expression ὁ χριστός, which, as pointed out above, is not a proper name but a significant title. It is important, therefore, to observe that he all but uniformly employs τοῦ χριστοῦ in preference to Χριστοῦ and even to other designations of Jesus after terms of soteriological significance. Thus he uses τὸ εὐαγγέλιον τοῦ χριστοῦ eight times (1 Thes. 3² Gal. 1⁷ 1 Cor. 9¹² 2 Cor. 2¹² 9¹³ 10¹⁴ Rom. 15¹⁹ Phil. 1²⁷) and only in 2 Thes. 1⁸ employs any other designation of Jesus after εὐαγγέλιον. After σταυρός he uses τοῦ χριστοῦ in 1 Cor. 1¹⁷ Gal. 6¹² (?) Phil. 3¹⁸, and only once any other name or title of Jesus (Gal 6¹⁴; but see also Col. 1²⁰). See also αἱ θλίψεις τοῦ χριστοῦ in Col. 1²⁴; and τὰ παθήματα τοῦ χριστοῦ in 2 Cor. 1⁵. After αἷμα or σῶμα, referring to his death τοῦ χριστοῦ is used in 1 Cor. 10¹⁶ *bis* Eph. 2¹³ Rom. 7⁴; but also τοῦ κυρίου in 1 Cor. 11²⁷. After ἀγάπη we find τοῦ χριστοῦ in Rom. 8³⁵ 2 Cor. 5¹⁴ Eph. 3¹⁹, and no instance of Χριστοῦ or other genitive referring to Jesus (yet *cf.* Gal. 2²⁰). Not all the instances of τοῦ χριστοῦ are clearly of this type; but the Pauline usage, as a whole, strongly suggests that by ὁ χριστός Paul meant "the Christ" in the sense of "the Deliverer," "the Saviour." Note, also, the rarity of σωτήρ as a title of Jesus in his vocabulary. Phil. 3²⁰ is the only instance in the certainly genuine letters, though it is frequent in the pastoral epistles.

From what the Christ was expected to deliver men—on this the thought of men undoubtedly varied greatly. When in Lk. 3¹⁵ it is said, "All men were in expectation and mused in their hearts whether John was the Christ," the meaning is doubtless that men were wondering whether John would be the national political deliverer for whom the nation was looking. In the trial scene in the synoptic gospels, the meaning of the term is probably similar.

Such passages as 1 Thes. 1¹⁰ Gal. 3¹³ Rom. 5⁹ show that in its negative aspect the salvation which the Christ brought to men was a deliverance from the condemnation of sin and the divine wrath against sinners. Yet it clearly had also its positive side, including both future glory (Rom. 5², ¹¹) and in the present life divine approval and the achievement of character. See, *e. g.*, Rom. 1¹⁶, ¹⁷ 3²¹⁻²⁴ 5¹⁻¹¹ chap. 8 Gal. 5¹⁹⁻²⁴ Phil. 3⁸⁻¹⁴.

It is the manifest intention of the fourth gospel to attach its doctrine of Jesus as the Christ to the Jewish idea of the Messiah (note its interpretation of the word "Christ" as the equivalent of the Hebrew "Messiah," 1⁴¹), and to claim for Jesus the fulfilment of that idea to the full. Yet it is scarcely less evident that the idea of the Christ which the fourth evangelist desired his readers to accept and hold had little in common with the Jewish idea of a political deliverer of the nation, except the bare idea of deliverance. See 20³¹, "that ye may believe that Jesus is the Christ, the Son of God; and that believing ye may have life in his name." See also 4⁴² where "the Saviour of the world" represents "the Christ" of v.²⁹. The author has attached his conception to its historical Jewish basis; he has retained the old term, but has so purged it of its political, and even of its apocalyptic, significance, and given it a purely religious meaning, that "the Christ" is in his thought chiefly a deliverer from death and from that which is the cause of death. "I am come that they may have life" represents the dominant point of view of the book, and "life" is a fundamentally ethical conception.

IV. ΚΥΡΙΟΣ.

A. CLASSICAL USAGE.

In classical Greek writers the substantive κύριος designates a person who has control over another person or thing, or persons or things, either by right of divinity, as in the case of the gods, or by right of ownership, as in the case of a master and his slave; or of position, as of a husband to his household, or of office, as in the case of a guardian or trustee.

In the Lxx this same word κύριος occurs hundreds of times, being employed as a translation of some twenty different Hebrew words and phrases. The two that are most important for our purpose are אָדוֹן, lord, and יהוה, Yahweh, the great majority of the occurrences of κύριος being translations of one or the other of these. אָדוֹן means "owner," "master," "lord," and is applied in various senses: to a man as the owner of property or as the master of a slave; to the husband as lord of the wife; to a prince as lord of the land; and even to God himself (Josh. 3¹¹). Applied to God, however, it usually takes the form אֲדֹנָי. The general tendency of the Lxx is to omit the article before κύριος when it translates יהוה.

In N. T. three elements enter into the meaning of the word: (i) ownership, (ii) right of service, (iii) right of obedience. Its correlative term is δοῦλος, "slave," or διάκονος, or οἰκέτης, "servant," most commonly the first. See Mt. 10²⁴, ²⁵ 18²⁷ 24⁴⁵⁻⁵⁰ 25¹⁹ Lk. 12⁴²⁻⁴⁷ 14²¹⁻²³ Jn. 13¹⁶ 15²⁰. The slave belongs to his master, owes him service and obedience. These three ideas are not, indeed, always equally prominent in the usage either of κύριος or δοῦλος, and in individual instances some one of them may altogether fall away. See, e. g., 2 Cor. 4⁵, where δοῦλος carries with it the idea of service only, being used by hyperbole for οἰκέτης or διάκονος. These conceptions are, however, the usual elements of the relation referred to by these words. κύριος then means:

1. The master of a slave in the ordinary human relation, or the owner of other property: Mt. 10²⁴, ²⁵ 15²⁷ 18²⁵, ²⁷, ³¹ 20⁸ 21⁴⁰ Mk. 13³⁵ Gal. 4¹ Eph. 6⁹.

In parables the meaning of the term is in itself the same as above; although the relation symbolised is, of course, one of an ethical and religious character: Mt. 24⁴², ⁴⁵, ⁴⁶, ⁴⁸, ⁵⁰ 25¹⁸, ¹⁹, ²⁰, ²¹, ²², ²³ bis ²⁴, ²⁶.

2. One who has rightful control of an institution, to whom it belongs, being, as it were, his property: Mt. 12⁸ Mk. 2²⁸, κύριος τοῦ σαββάτου.

3. Like the English "Mister" (Master) and the modern Greek κύριος, it is used as a term of polite address, expressing greater or less reverence, and implying greater or less authority according to circumstances; sometimes equivalent to "Rabbi" or "Master":

(a) addressed to a father by his son: Mt. 21²⁹.

(b) addressed to a Roman governor by his subjects: Mt. 27⁶³.

(c) addressed to Jesus by his disciples, and by the people: Mt. 17¹⁵ 18³¹ Mk. 7²⁸.

4. In the plural it is a generic term for deities, or for rulers, human and divine: Mt. 6²⁴ 1 Cor. 8⁵.

5. As a name for or title of God it represents the O. T. יהוה or אֲדֹנָי and varies in the precise thought which it conveys from a religious term distinctly expressive of the sovereignty of God to a proper name not sharply distinguished from the word θεός: Mt. 1²⁰, ²², ²⁴ 2¹³, ¹⁵, ¹⁹ 3³ 4⁷, ¹⁰ 5³³ 11²⁵ 21⁹, ⁴² 22³⁷, ⁴⁴ᵃ 23³⁹ 27¹⁰ 28² Mk. 1³ 5¹⁹ (?) 11⁹ 12¹¹, ²⁹, ³⁰, ³⁶ 13²⁰ Lk. 1⁶, ⁹, ¹¹, ¹⁵, ¹⁶, ¹⁷, ²⁵, ²⁸, ³⁸, ⁴⁵, ⁴⁶, ⁵⁸, ⁶⁶, ⁶⁸, ⁷⁶ 2⁹ᵃ, ᵇ, ¹⁵, ²², ²³ᵃ, ᵇ, ²⁴, ³⁹ 3⁴ 4⁸, ¹², ¹⁸, ¹⁹ 5¹⁷ 10²¹, ²⁷ 13³⁵ 19⁸ 20³⁷, ⁴² Jn. 1²³ 12¹³, ³⁸ᵃ, ᵇ Acts 1²⁴ 2²⁰, ²¹, ²⁵, ³⁴ᵃ, ³⁹ 3²² 4²⁶, ²⁹ 5⁹, ¹⁹ 7³¹, ³³, ⁴⁹ 8²⁶, ³⁹ 10³³ 11²¹ 12⁷, ¹¹, ¹⁷, ²³ 15¹⁷, ¹⁸ Rom. 4⁸, 9²⁸, ²⁹ 10¹³, ¹⁶ 11³, ³⁴ 12¹⁹ 14¹¹ 15¹¹ 1 Cor. 1³¹ (?) 2¹⁶ 3²⁰ 10⁹, ²² (?) ²⁶ 16¹⁰ (?) 2 Cor. 6¹⁷, ¹⁸ 8²¹ 10¹⁷ (?) 12¹ 1 Thes. 4⁶ 5² (?) 2 Tim. 2¹⁹ᵃ, ᵇ. Of these passages the following are most significant as indicating the meaning which the term bore in the N. T. period as applied to God: Mt. 4⁷, ¹⁰ 11²⁵ 22³⁷ Mk. 12²⁹, ³⁰ Lk. 10²¹, ²⁷. It is worthy of note that in the Pauline epistles the word is used of God chiefly in quotations from the O. T., the words θεός and πατήρ being the apostle's favourite titles for God, and κύριος being more commonly a title of Jesus. See especially 1 Cor. 8⁵, ⁶.

The N. T. follows the general usage of the Greek O. T. in that the word κύριος applied to God is usually without the article in Greek (as in English the word "God" is anarthrous). But both in the Greek O. T. and in N. T. the article is sometimes prefixed. So clearly in Gen. 12⁸ 18¹⁷ 39²³ Ex. 12⁴² 13¹² 14²⁵ 15¹ 16²³ 31¹⁵ Lev. 1² 2¹ 4³ 5¹⁵, etc. Mt. 5³³ Lk. 1⁶, ⁹, ²⁸ 2¹⁵, ²³ᵇ Acts 2²⁵ 4²⁶ 7³³ 15¹⁷ Rom. 15¹¹. In the letters of Paul there is a number of passages in which it is difficult to say whether the reference is to God or Christ.

6. As applied to Jesus (in addition to the instances falling under 3), it is sometimes used in a theocratic sense, ascribing to him supreme authority over men and the world of heavenly existences, subject only to that of God the Father: Rom. 10⁹ 1 Cor. 7²² 12³ Phil. 2¹¹, etc.

On the question what was the precise content of the term so used, and in particular whether it was identical in meaning with the term κύριος as applied to God the following facts have a bearing:

(a) יהוה, which, as stated above, is represented in the Lxx and in N. T. by κύριος, is never used with possessive suffixes. The expressions, "my Yahweh," "our Yahweh," never occur in O. T. But κύριος applied to Jesus is often accompanied by ἡμῶν. This suggests that κύριος as used of Jesus corresponds rather to אֲדֹנָי than to יהוה. See (c) below.

(b) The expression יהוה אֱלֹהִים is often applied in O. T. to God, as the Greek equivalent κύριος ὁ θεός is in the Lxx and N. T.; but the latter is never used of Jesus.

(c) In N. T. Ps. 110 is so quoted (Mt. 22⁴⁴ Mk. 12³⁶ Lk. 20⁴² Acts 2³⁴) as to apply the term יהוה to God, אֲדֹנָי to Jesus.

(d) In the Lxx יהוה is usually translated by κύριος without the article.

In N. T. this usage is generally followed, but, as indicated in 5 above, not invariably. For Jesus the regular term is ὁ κύριος, subject to the usual rules for the omission of the article.*

(e) The title κύριος was in the apostolic age beginning to be applied to the Roman emperors. In Acts 25²⁶ Festus speaks of Nero as ὁ κύριος. The term probably expressed supreme political authority. But, whatever its significance, it originated too late (Augustus and Tiberius refused it) to have marked influence on the early stages of the development of the term as a title of Jesus. See Dal. *WJ.* pp. 324 *ff.*

(f) The title κύριος as applied to Jesus, probably did not originate in Greek or in Hebrew. Even Paul took it over from the Aramaic, as appears in his use of the expression *Maran atha.* But *Mar* or *Maran* is a general term for lord, master, ruler; not a specifically religious term at all. See Case, "Κύριος as a Title for Christ," in *JBL.* 1907, pp. 151–161, especially p. 156. *Cf.* MacNeill, *The Christology of the Epistle to the Hebrews,* pp. 70 *ff.*

These facts indicate that κύριος, as applied to Jesus in N. T., is not, even in its highest sense, a term of nature or of identification with Yahweh, but of relationship (to men and the world).

What the precise relationship expressed by the term is, is indicated by the following facts:

(i) The distinctive Christian confession is that Jesus is κύριος: Rom. 10⁹ 1 Cor. 12³ Phil. 2¹¹; *cf.* 2 Cor. 4⁵.

(ii) κύριος and οἰκέτης or δοῦλος are used as correlative terms: 1 Cor. 7²¹⁻²⁴ 2 Cor. 4⁵ Rom. 14⁴; *cf.* Lk. 6⁴⁶ Col. 3²⁴. *Cf.* also the apostle's designation of himself as a slave of Christ: Rom. 1¹.

(iii) Despite the general practice stated in 5 and 6 (d) above, the lordship which is attributed to Christ, especially by Paul, is not sharply discriminated from that which is ascribed to God. The language which is used of God is to such an extent used also of Jesus that there are several passages in which it is impossible to determine with certainty whether the reference is to God or Jesus, and several in which the only choice is between assuming an application to God of the title usually employed of Jesus, or an ascription to Jesus of offices or titles generally ascribed to God. See, *e. g.,* Rom. 14⁶⁻⁹, where in v.⁶ the word κύριος is without the article, suggesting the reference to God, but in v.⁸ has the article, suggesting reference to Christ, which is confirmed by v.⁹; 2 Cor. 3¹⁶⁻¹⁸, where κύριος is without the article and refers to God in the O. T. quotation of v.¹⁶, in v.¹⁷ᵃ has the article, in

---

* As a title or name simply it has the article, as a rule. See, *e. g.,* Lk. 10¹ 17⁵· ⁶ Rom. 1⁴ 5¹· ¹¹ Gal. 1¹⁸ 6¹⁴. When the article is omitted the noun is (a) qualitative: Acts 2³⁶ Rom. 10⁹ 1 Cor. 7ⁿᵇ· ¹⁵ *bis* 10¹¹; (b) vocative: Acts 1⁶; (c) used in a fixed adverbial phrase, especially ἐν κυρίῳ: 1 Cor. 7²². ³⁹ 9¹· ² Gal. 5¹⁰, etc., though particularly in reference to this phrase is it difficult to determine with certainty whether the term refers to Christ or to God; or (d) joined by καί to a phrase, especially θεὸς πατήρ, which either itself has the article or is definite without it. See detached note on Πατήρ *as applied to God,* p. 386.

[17b, 18] is without it;* 2 Thes. 2[18], where κύριος is used with the article, and Phil. 4[9], where instead we have θεός; also 1 Cor. 10[15-22]. With Rom. 10[12-15] cf. 1 Cor. 1[2]; also with 1 Thes. 5[2] cf. 2 Thes. 2[2]; and with 1 Cor. 2[16] cf. Rom. 11[34].

(iv) The lordship which Jesus exercises since his resurrection is conceived of as delegated rather than original, having been bestowed by God after the death of Jesus on the cross. Yet on the other hand, Jesus possessed a lordship before the worlds were created, and was himself the agent of creation. The exaltation, therefore, to the present lordship is in part a restoration of a power temporarily laid aside. And while the present lordship is again, when it has accomplished its purpose, to give place to a supreme and unrivalled sovereignty of God the Father, yet during the period of its exercise, which is to extend beyond the coming of the Lord in the clouds, it is without limit in its authority over men, and extends even to "things in heaven" and "things under the earth." See 1 Cor. 8[5, 6] Phil. 2[9, 10] cf. 1 Cor. 15[24-28] Col. 1[15-18].

While, therefore, the sentence, "Jesus is Lord," which the apostle Paul several times quotes as the distinctively Christian confession (Rom. 10[9] 1 Cor. 12[3] Phil. 2[11]), was doubtless of variable content, according to the period in which it was used and the person uttering it, and while it does not in any case mean, "Jesus is God," being an assertion of function and authority rather than of nature, yet at its highest it ascribes to Jesus a lordship which is strictly theocratic in character. To accept him as Lord in this highest sense of the expression is to bow the will to him as God. This highest theocratic use of the term as applied to Jesus is most fully developed in the Pauline letters. The impression thus given that Christian thought is chiefly indebted to him for the development of the idea is confirmed by an examination of the gospels and Acts, the total evidence indicating that the term as applied to Jesus gradually acquired greater depth and significance, rising from a title of ordinary respect to a theocratic sense, but reaching the latter well within the lifetime of Paul.

In the gospel of Mk., the evangelist, though showing that he himself fully believed in the messianic or theocratic lordship of Jesus, and representing Jesus as having in somewhat veiled language claimed this for himself, yet does not represent Jesus' disciples as ever calling him Lord, or any of the people as doing so in any sense other than Sir or Master. The gospels of Mt. and Lk. modify this representation of the situation in Jesus' lifetime, yet on the whole in such a way as to make it clear that they are therein influenced chiefly by the usage of the later time in which they are writing. Particularly significant are the eschatological passages, Mt. 7[22]

* WH. suggest that κυρίου in v.[7] is a primitive error for κύριον, "dominant," a reading which would relieve the difficulty of interpretation and would obviously tempt to change to the more familiar κυρίου, but which one hesitates to adopt because of the rarity of the word κύριος as an adjective. it being found nowhere else in N. T.

and 25³⁷, ⁴⁴, in which Jesus, in his office of judge, at the last day, is addressed as Lord. In Acts the expression ὁ κύριος is frequently used in narrative passages as a name of Jesus, sometimes of the historic person, much more frequently of the risen and heavenly Jesus. Most significant is Acts 2³⁶, which ascribes to Peter at the beginning of the apostolic age the words, "Him hath God made both Lord and Christ," the implication being that this is achieved by his resurrection and exaltation. The association with the word "Christ" indicates that the word "Lord" is used in an exalted sense, probably exceeding the meaning of the word as addressed to Jesus in any passage in the third gospel. This, in a measure, confirms the evidence, derived from a comparison of the synoptic gospels, that the recognition of Jesus as Lord in the lofty sense of this passage arose first in the apostolic age and indicates that it was at first associated with him only as risen and exalted.

The usage of the fourth gospel is in essential features identical with that of Lk. and Acts, differing only in the greater frequency of the use of the word as a term of address to Jesus and in a clearer ascription of the term in a theocratic sense to the risen Jesus.

The total evidence tends, therefore, to indicate that the conception of Jesus as master or rabbi had its origin in Jesus' own lifetime and in his own teaching, but that the application of the term to Jesus in its higher senses is of later origin. The theocratic sense, so clearly and fully developed in Paul, is ascribed to the earlier apostolic age in Jn. 20²⁸ Acts 2³⁶, and to Jesus in Mt. 7²² 25³⁷, ⁴⁴. But the evidence as a whole points to the conclusion that (with the possible exception of Acts 2³⁶) all these passages, as well as Lk. 1⁴³ and 2¹¹, were modified by the usage of the Pauline period and that the higher, theocratic sense had its origin in the apostolic age, perhaps with Peter, more probably with Paul. *Cf.* Böhlig, "Zum Begriff Kyrios bei Paulus," in *ZntW*. 1913, pp. 23–37.

V. ΥΙΟΣ ΘΕΟΥ, ΥΙΟΣ ΤΟΥ ΘΕΟΥ.

A. CONCEPTION "SON OF GOD," IN THE OLD TESTAMENT.

In O. T. the term, "son of God," בֶּן אֱלֹהִים, with which may be included also the plural, "sons of God," בְּנֵי הָאֱלֹהִים, בְּנֵי אֱלֹהִים, and "my son," בְּנִי (when the possessive refers to God), is used in three different ways:

1. It is applied in the plural to angels, probably marking them as superhuman and like God in their mode of being: Job 1⁶: "Now there was a day when the sons of God came to present themselves before the Lord." See also Job 2¹ 38⁷ Ps. 89⁶ Gen. 6⁴. Of similar force is Dan. 3²⁵ (⁹²).

2. It is applied in the singular to the nation of Israel, marking it as chosen of God and brought into especially close relation with him, analogous to that of a son to his father: Ex. 4²², ²³: "Thou shalt say unto Pharaoh, Thus saith Yahweh, Israel is my son, my first-born, and I have said unto

thee, Let my son go." See also Deut. 14¹ 32⁶⋅ ¹⁸ Jer. 31⁹⋅ ¹⁹ (²⁰) Hos. 11¹:
"When Israel was a child, then I loved him, and called my son out of
Egypt." It is used also in the plural of the children of Israel: Hos. 1¹⁰:
"Where it was said unto them, Ye are not my people, it shall be said unto
them, Ye are the sons of the living God."

3. It is applied to the king of Israel, marking him as not only chosen of
God and brought into specially close relation to him, but also as exercising
authority as the representative of God: 2 Sam. 7¹⁴: "I will be his father,
and he shall be my son." See also Ps. 2⁷ 89²⁶⁻²⁷ 1 Chr. 17¹³⋅ ¹⁴ 22¹⁰.

The Hebrew phrase in all these latter cases is not definite or individualising, nor, on the other hand, indefinite, but qualitative.

B. USAGE IN JEWISH-GREEK.

The usage of υἱὸς θεοῦ in the Lxx corresponds substantially to that of
בְּנֵי אֱלֹהִים in the Heb. O. T. It is noticeable, however, that the singular
is never used with the article, but always as a qualitative expression without the article, and that the plural is definite only in Gen. 6⁴.

The term υἱὸς θεοῦ occurs not infrequently in the O. T. Apocrypha and
the Pseudepigrapha of the pre-Christian period, designating one who is
the object of divine love and care. It occurs most frequently in Wisd. Sol.
See 2¹⁸: "If the righteous man is God's son (υἱὸς θεοῦ) he will uphold him."
The plural is used in 5⁵: "How was he numbered ᴄmong sons of God, and
how is his lot among saints?" So also in 9⁷ 12¹⁹⋅ ²¹ 16¹⁰⋅ ²⁶ 18⁴. In 18¹³ the
singular is used, as in Hos. 11¹, of the people as a whole. The singular is
also found in Sir. 4¹⁰, but with special reference to an individual: "So shalt
thou be as a son of the Most High, and he shall love thee more than thy
mother doth." See also Jth. 9⁴⋅ ¹³ (plur.); 3 Mac. 6²⁸ (plur.); Ps. Sol. 17³⁰:
"For he shall know them that they are all sons of their God," υἱοὶ θεοῦ
εἰσιν αὐτῶν πάντες. Cf. detached note on Πατήρ as applied to God, p. 385.

The messianic use of the term in Jewish literature first appears in the
latter part of the first Christian century, in 4 Ezr.,* in 7²⁸⋅ ²⁹ (though the
phrase is of doubtful genuineness in 7²⁸, and Gunkel questions it in 29
also; cf. Gunkel in Ka.AP., and Bous. Rel. d. Jud.², p. 261 f.); 13³²⋅ ³⁷⋅ ⁵² 14⁹.
This book being definitely dated by internal evidence for the year 81 A. D.,
these passages are of capital importance. It is significant that (as Bousset
remarks) the Jewish passages in which the term "Son of God" is used of the
Messiah are those in which he is represented as in conflict with the people
and kings of the earth. This conception obviously suggests Ps. 2 as the
source of the idea, but as obviously suggests that there is little connection
between the Jewish and N. T. use of the term; since the latter has entirely
different associations and suggestions.

---

* The words "and my Son" in 1 Enoch 105² are in all probability an interpolation, if, indeed,
the whole passage is not. Cf. Charles, in Ch.AP. ad loc.; Dal.WJ. p. 269. Beer, in Ka.
AP., seems to accept the verse as genuine.

Apparently, therefore, we must seek not in Jewish but in Christian circles themselves the origin of the Christian usage of the title as applied to Jesus, or in so far as it has a basis in older usage must find this either (a) in the O. T. passages in which the king of Israel is called God's son, or (b) in those broader, more general, uses of the term in the O. T., which are themselves the basis of the application of the term to the king of Israel. It will appear from the examination of N. T. usage itself, on the one side, that these basal O. T. usages are familiar elements of Christian thought, and, on the other, that the application of the term to Christians in general is closely associated with its application in emphatic measure to Jesus.

One link of connection between Jewish and Christian usage must, however, be mentioned. The term "Christ" was in common use among the Jews as a title of the expected king and deliverer before the Christian era, and was early taken over by the Christians as a title of him whom they accounted to be this expected deliverer, viz., Jesus. Whether the usage was so associated with Ps. 2 that it involved a tacit reference to that psalm or not, it would certainly suggest it to many. And since in that psalm the one who is called the "Anointed" is also called "my son," that is, God's son, there was furnished in this way a possible basis for the application of the term "Son of God" to the Messiah by either Jews or Christians. It is doubtful, however, whether the Christian usage of the term was actually arrived at in this way. For, though the term "Son of God" was applied to the Messiah by Jews of the latter part of the first Christian century, there is no evidence that this usage was common either in the days of Jesus or in the lifetime of Paul that is sufficient to justify our assuming it as the basis for the interpretation of the Christian usage.*

C. USAGE OF THE NON-JEWISH WORLD.

The characterisation of a king as a son of God or of a particular god, was a wide-spread usage of the ancient world, but was not of uniform meaning. Dal.*WJ*. pp. 272 f., says: "When Asshurbanipal in his Annals . . . calls himself 'an offspring of Asshur and Bilit,' this means no more than a being destined from birth to the royal power. The kings of Egypt, on the contrary, were reckoned to be real 'descendants of the god Ra.' . . . The

---

* See Dal.*WJ*. pp. 268 ff.: "One may assume that as time passed the Christian exposition of Ps. 2 became a deterrent to its common use by the synagogue. But even for the earlier period it must be recognised as certain that Ps. 2 was not of decisive importance in the Jewish conception of the Messiah and that "Son of God" was not a common Messianic title. A hindrance to the use of בֶּן הָאֱלֹהִים or בַּר אֱלָהָא would have presented itself in the custom of not uttering the name of God; and this afterwards shows itself when Mark 14ᵘ gives the words of the Jewish high priest as ὁ υἱὸς τοῦ εὐλογητοῦ, a form ill adapted to become a current Messianic title. When God calls the Messiah his Son, this is merely meant as a sign of the exceptional love with which he above others is regarded," p. 272.

Cf. also Bous. *Rel. d. Jud.*², p. 262. "Dass der Titel 'Sohn' im Judentum an und für sich noch keinerlei metaphysische Bedeutung hat, bedarf keines weiteren Beweises."

Wendt, *Teaching of Jesus*, vol. II, p. 131, says that "this title was . . . neither a direct

royal style of old Egypt was continued by the Ptolemies. . . . Roman emperors also boasted frequently of divine progenitors. Sextus Pompeius called himself the son of Neptune; Domitian the son of Minerva; Caligula and Hadrian deemed themselves to be earthly manifestations of Zeus."

The Roman worship of rulers began with Julius Cæsar. Enthusiasm over his achievements led to the erection of statues which listed him among the deities. This was at first pure flattery taken seriously by no one. But with his assassination extravagant adulation crystallised into religious conviction. In the minds of the common people he became a god. In deference to this belief the senate conferred upon him the title *Divus* (deified) and ordered a temple erected for his worship. His successor, Augustus, disclaimed divine honours during his lifetime, but was deified immediately after his death. From that time on till the fall of the empire in the fifth century nearly every emperor was deified. Later, however, the honour lost much of its religious character and became largely a formality. Other members of the imperial family also were deified. The deification of a deceased emperor was accomplished by a formal vote of the senate, and was celebrated by appropriate ceremonies. See H. F. Burton, "The Worship of the Roman Emperors," in *Biblical World*, August, 1912, from which the above statements are condensed. *Cf.* also Case, *Evolution of Early Christianity*, chap. VII. The title "son of God," as applied to the Roman emperor of the first Christian century, was not, however, a characterisation of the emperor himself as divine, or of divine origin, but referred to the fact that his predecessor had been deified at death. See the inscription quoted by De.*BS*. p. 131, ὁ δᾶμος ὑπὲρ τᾶς αὐτοκράτορος Καίσαρος Θεοῦ υἱοῦ Σεβαστοῦ σωτηρίας Θεοῖς ἱλαστήριον, and that transcribed by Hogarth in *Journal of Hellenic Studies*, 1887, p. 358, in which the emperor apparently speaks of his imperial father as ὁ θεὸς πατήρ μου. *Cf.* also De.*BS*. pp. 166 *ff.* It is improbable, therefore, that this usage had any important influence on the Christian usage by which the term υἱὸς θεοῦ or ὁ υἱὸς τοῦ θεοῦ was applied to Jesus, still less, of course, on the use of the plural, υἱοὶ θεοῦ, as applied to believers in Christ. There is, indeed, a possible, not to say probable, parallelism in the apostle's mind between

designation of the Messianic dignity, nor did it bring into prominence that characteristic of the Messiah on which the Jews in the time of Jesus laid the chief stress. . . . In relation to this most essential characteristic of the Messiah [viz., that he was king of Israel] the traditional attribute, 'the Son of God,' denotes only an incidental notion of very indefinite content." Yet he holds that the term would be recognised as designating the Messiah. Thus, p. 130, "In the fact that the O. T. passages 2 Sam. 7[14] Ps. 2[7] 89[27f.], in which the theocratic king of Israel was designated the Son of God, were interpreted of the future Messianic king, lay the reason for this title of Son of God being considered as specially belonging to the Messiah." Even so much as this may be doubted. There is no clear evidence that a claim to be son of God would necessarily be understood as an affirmation of messiahship among the Jews of the first half of the first Christian century. One recognised as the Messiah would undoubtedly be conceived to be a son of God. But the converse would not follow.

the language in Rom. 1⁴, τοῦ ὁρισθέντος υἱοῦ θεοῦ . . . ἐξ ἀναστάσεως νεκρῶν, and an announcement such as might have been made in Rome that the emperor lately deceased had by decree of the senate been deified, raised to the rank of θεός. But the parallelism fails precisely in the fact that Paul uses υἱὸς θεοῦ instead of θεός: from which it must be inferred (since he can not possibly mean that by his resurrection from the dead his father has been made a god) that his term υἱὸς θεοῦ had its origin in and derived its meaning from a usage quite other than that of the application of this term to Augustus, or in similar sense to other emperors. *Cf.* H. F. Burton, *op. cit.*, p. 91.

D. NEW TESTAMENT USAGE.

1. *Pauline usage.*—Investigation of the use of the term by N. T. writers and teachers necessarily begins with that of Paul's epistles, since it is only in the light of their evidence that it is possible to judge how much of the usage of the gospels is of pre-Pauline origin. The clue to the meaning of the expression in Gal. 1¹⁶ is probably to be found in 2 Cor. 4⁴⁻⁶. Both passages seem to refer to the experience by which Paul abandoned Pharisaic Judaism to become a follower of Jesus the Christ; both refer to a process or act of divine revelation by which Paul gained a new conception of Jesus; it is reasonable, therefore, to take 2 Cor. 4⁴⁻⁶, in which Jesus is described as the image of God, and it is said that God shined in the apostle's heart to give the light of the glory of God in the face of Jesus Christ, as indicating the principal emphasis of the expression, "his Son," in Gal. 1¹⁶, and so to understand the term as referring especially to the resemblance of the Son to the Father.

In Rom. 8³ff. the post-resurrection Christ is identified with the Spirit of Christ and the Spirit of God, and in the same context is called God's own Son. It is hazardous to press the fact of this connection, both because there is a considerable interval between the two expressions, and because the expression "his own Son" is used in speaking of the sending of Christ into the world, while the other expressions are used of the post-incarnate Christ. It is probably safer, therefore, to interpret this passage by comparison with Rom. 8³², "He that spared not his own Son but delivered him up for us all," where the Son (incarnate) is evidently thought of as the special object of divine love, and with Rom. 5¹⁰, which, in the light of Rom. 5⁸, evidently emphasises the same aspect of the sonship.

In Gal. 4⁴ which apparently conceives of Christ as the Son of God before the incarnation, a different phase of sonship is made prominent. The purpose of his sending the Son is said to be that we might receive the spirit of adoption. And it is added that "because ye are sons, God sent forth the Spirit of his Son into our hearts, crying, Abba, Father." Two things are important here—first, that the apostle passes without jar from the idea of the pre-incarnate Son to that of the post-incarnate Son; and, second, that the aspect of the sonship which is emphasised is that of the filial spirit—the recognition of the divine fatherhood, in other words, intimacy of moral fellowship, which, belonging to Christ, becomes ours through the impartation of his Spirit to us. This connects the passage again with Rom. 8[9ff.], where the Spirit of Christ is identified with Christ and the Spirit of God. But it also recalls Rom. 8[14, 29], which make it clear that Paul used the term "son of God" to designate one who is in moral fellowship with God, governed by his Spirit, doing his will, like him in character, and that he applied the term in this sense both to Christ as *the* Son of God and to men as sons of God. These two uses, therefore, were related, but in two ways. In Gal. 4[4] God sends the Spirit of his Son into the hearts of men who are, and because they are, sons; in Rom. 8[14] it is implied that men become sons by the possession of the Spirit of God, which elsewhere Paul identifies with the Spirit of his Son. For the evidence that the expression, "born of a woman," in Gal. 4[4] can not be interpreted as referring to the virgin birth or as implying that, by virtue of divine procreation he is Son of God in a genealogical sense, see com. *ad loc.*

In 1 Cor. 15[28] it is noticeable that the expression "Son of God" is used of the post-incarnate Son, that it is made equivalent by the context to Christ (v.[23]), and that the whole context emphasises the idea of the exercise of power on behalf of God; yet it is, perhaps, also not without significance that it is only when he comes to speak of the surrender of power that the term "Son" is used. The term is therefore clearly employed in its theocratic sense—denoting one who, though subordinate to God, exercises for God power over all things.

In Col. 1[13-17], the expression "of his love" at once makes it clear that the expression is used in its affectional sense. With this, however, is closely associated in v.[15] the idea of moral likeness and in v.[17] that of vice-regal power. It is perhaps too much to say that the two latter ideas, as well as the first, are contained in the expression "his Son," but it is noteworthy that they follow in easy sequence upon it as if suggested by it.

Rom. 1[3-4] may be paraphrased as follows: " As a corporeally conditioned being, born Son of David (Messiah in the Jewish sense of the term or as predicted in the O. T.); as a holy and spiritually existent being, constituted Son of God with power (nearly equivalent to heavenly Messiah and Lord) by the resurrection from the dead." Thus the sonship with power, as contrasted with the sonship of his earthly life (*cf.* Phil. 2[7]), is based on moral likeness to God (note the word holiness) but consists essentially in the possession and exercise of theocratic power, that is, lordship over men and the world as God's representative. Note the immediately following words, "Jesus Christ our Lord," and *cf.* 1 Cor. 11[3] 12[12] Phil. 2[9-11]. Thus the two members of the parallelism express respectively the messiahship on its earthly and its heavenly side; in its pre-resurrection and its post-resurrection aspect.

We may then summarise the uses of the term by Paul as follows:

(a) The ethico-religious sense. In this sense Paul uses the term both of Christ and of men, though clearly assigning it to Jesus in unique measure, and in some cases basing the sonship of men on their possession of the Spirit of the Son.

(i) The affectional sense, denoting one who is the object of divine love: Gal. 3²⁶ 4⁴, ⁶, ⁷ Rom. 5¹⁰ 8³, ¹⁹ (*cf.* ²¹), ³² Col. 1¹³.

(ii) The moral sense, denoting one who is morally like God, being led by his Spirit, doing his will; as applied to Christ, consequently a revelation of God: Gal. 1¹⁶ 1 Cor. 1⁹ Rom. 8¹⁴ff., ²⁹.

(iii) With these two ideas Paul associates the idea of freedom, such as belongs to a son as distinguished from a slave: Gal. 4⁷ Rom. 8¹⁴⁻¹⁷.

(b) The official and theocratic sense, denoting one who exercises divine power for God; applied to Christ only: 1 Thes. 1¹⁰ 1 Cor. 15²⁸ 2 Cor. 1¹⁹ Rom. 1³, ⁴, ⁹.

Not all of these assignments are equally certain, and there is doubtless some blending of the different conceptions. But there are enough unambiguous cases under each head to justify the classification.

The official sense being applied to Christ only, it is natural that the two expressions "Christ" and "Son of God" approximate and to a certain extent blend in meaning. Through the union of the idea of the theocratic Son with that of the pre-existence of the Christ and with that of his resurrection and post-mundane power, there issues for Paul the thought of (i) the Son as the one Lord through whom the worlds came into being (1 Cor. 8⁶); (ii) the Son who, having laid aside his divine power on earth, lived under the law and died on the cross for men (Rom. 8³²); (iii) the Son, who, exalted to the right hand of God (Rom. 8³⁴; *cf.* Phil. 2¹¹) is again Lord of all till he surrender all things to the Father (1 Cor. 15²⁴⁻²⁸). Yet it is important to observe that, in Paul at least, each term retained its own fundamental meaning, Χριστός as an official term and the bearer of the inherited messianic idea as modified in Christian thought, υἱὸς [τοῦ] θεοῦ as a fundamentally ethical and religious term, connoting a certain moral and religious relation to God.

2. *Usage of the synoptic gospels and Acts.*—The instances of the term "son of God" that occur in the synoptic gospels and Acts may be best considered in the following groups:

(a) Those in which the expression "sons of God," υἱοὶ θεοῦ, designates those who are like God in moral character: Mt. 5⁹, ⁴⁵ Lk. 6³⁵; *cf.* Rom. 8¹⁴.

(b) One passage in which it designates those who are like God in that their mode of existence is supramundane: Lk. 20³⁶; *cf.* Job 1⁶.

(c) Those which record the personal religious experiences of Jesus, and use the term in the singular referring to him. Thus in the baptism, Mk. 1¹¹ Lk. 3²²: "Thou art my beloved Son" (ὁ υἱός μου ὁ ἀγαπητός), but in Mt. 3¹⁷: "This is my beloved Son"; in the transfiguration, Mk. 9⁷ Mt. 17⁵:

"This is my beloved Son" (ὁ υἱός μου ὁ ἀγαπητός), but in Lk. 9³⁵: "This is my son, the chosen" (ὁ υἱός μου ὁ ἐκλελεγμένος); in the temptation, Mt. 4³, ⁶ Lk. 4³, ⁹: "If thou art Son of God" (εἰ υἱὸς εἶ τοῦ θεοῦ). The context, esp. in the narrative of the baptism, but scarcely less clearly in the other accounts, emphasises the affectional sense of the term, the conception of the Son as object of the love and confidence of God. The use of the article, lacking in the narrative of the temptation, but present in all the other passages cited, designates Jesus as the one who was in an exceptional or unique degree the object of the divine approving love. This uniqueness doubtless suggests unique responsibility, and so conveys an intimation of the official or theocratic sense. But neither this fact nor the probability that in the apostolic age, when the theocratic sense was the common possession of Christian thought, it was understood chiefly in that sense, can conceal the fundamentally ethical sense of the term in these passages.

(d) The passages in which the demoniacs address Jesus as the Son of God, ὁ υἱὸς τοῦ θεοῦ, υἱὲ τοῦ θεοῦ, τοῦ Ὑψίστου: Mk. 3¹¹ Lk. 4⁴¹ Mt. 8²⁹ Mk. 5⁷ Lk. 8²⁸. There can be no doubt that in the passages as they stand, the expression is to be taken in a theocratic sense, probably nearly equivalent to "the Christ" in the Jewish sense. But several considerations combine to raise a doubt whether the original tradition which underlay the gospel record represented the demoniacs as calling Jesus the Son of God in this sense if, indeed, in any sense. Lexicographical evidence makes it doubtful, to say the least, whether "the Son of God" was in the life of Jesus in current use in an official sense. The gospel record makes it improbable that Jesus was in the beginning of his ministry recognised as the Christ; and the comparison of the statements of the several gospels shows such a tendency on the part of the evangelists to add such statements to the testimony of their sources as makes it probable that they are all, in fact, the product of the process of gospel-making. The cries of the demoniacs which tradition recorded, the evangelists, influenced by the thought of their own day, interpreted as affirmations of his divine sonship in a sense closely akin to messiahship.

(e) The records of the trial and crucifixion of Jesus. Here, also, the term which the evangelists report to have been used in the question of the high priest to Jesus (Mk. 14⁶¹ Mt. 26⁶³ Lk. 22⁶⁷, ⁷⁰) was doubtless understood by the gospel writers in a theocratic sense and nearly though not quite equivalent to "the Christ," which in Mt. and Mk. it follows immediately, and in Lk. in a separate question. But it is probable that, as in the preceding group and still more clearly in Mt. 16¹⁶ (see below), the words are an epexegetic addition of the evangelists. In Mt. 27⁴⁰, ⁴³ the term emphasises the ethical, affectional sense, yet is probably official also. It is, however, clearly an editorial expansion of the source. The words are not found in either Mk. or Lk., and though the parallelism of Mt. 27⁴⁰ with Lk. 23³⁵ suggests that Mk. originally had a similar expression, it does not imply that that expression contained the term "Son of God." The omission of the article before υἱός gives the phrase qualitative force. In Mk. 15³⁹ and the parallel Mt. 27⁵⁴, the expression, looked upon as an utterance of a Roman officer, would naturally be taken in its non-Jewish sense, "a son of a god," implying, perhaps, kingly authority, since such a title was usually employed of kings, but directly expressive of divine origin. In the thought of the evangelist it may have borne the ethical or the official meaning.

(f) In Mt. 16¹⁶, "the Son of the living God" (ὁ υἱὸς τοῦ θεοῦ τοῦ ζῶντος) is an unmistakable epexegetic addition to the Mk. source, which has only ὁ χριστός. The phrase is evidently theocratic. To Mt. 14³³ there is no parallel in either Mk. or Lk.: the verse is doubtless, like Mt. 27⁴⁰, ⁴³, an editorial addition. The article is lacking, the omission giving to the expression a qualitative force. There is nothing to indicate clearly whether it is ethical or official. In Mk. 1¹, υἱοῦ θεοῦ standing in the title of the gospel or of its opening section is manifestly editorial, whether proceeding from the original evangelist or an early scribe. In either case it is undoubtedly theocratic (cf. Rom. 1⁴ Jn. 20³¹). The absence of the article is due to the titular character of the whole expression, "The beginning of the gospel of Jesus Christ, Son of God."

(g) In Mk. 13³² and in its parallel in Mt. 24³⁶, and in Mt. 11²⁷ and its parallel Lk. 10²², Jesus uses the expression "the Son," ὁ υἱός, in antithesis to "the Father," ὁ πατήρ. The latter term clearly refers to God, and the former, without doubt, to Jesus himself. In itself the term bears its ethical sense, designating the one who is in closest fellowship and intimacy with God. Yet in Mt. 11²⁷, Lk. 10²² especially, the uniqueness of the sonship is so strongly emphasised as inevitably to suggest an official and theocratic sense, though clearly in the spiritual realm. The passage testifies to the early date at which this conception of Jesus' divine sonship was accepted by the church, but by its limitation of fellowship with God to those whom the Son admits to this privilege, in contradistinction to the synoptic teaching in Mk. 3³⁵ Mt. 5⁸, and, indeed, the immediate context, Mt. 11²⁵ Lk. 10²¹, it raises the question whether it is not the product of the same type of Christian thought of which the fourth gospel gives so abundant evidence, rather than a reflection of the earliest thought of the church or of Jesus' own thought.

(h) In the infancy narrative of Lk. the expression "Son of God," or its equivalent, occurs three times. The phrase in 1³² is υἱὸς Ὑψίστου, in 1³⁵ υἱὸς θεοῦ, and in 3³⁸ [υἱὸς] τοῦ θεοῦ. In the last-named passage the use and meaning of the term are quite exceptional. At the end of the genealogical line which traces the ancestry of Jesus backward, Seth is said to be son of Adam, and Adam son of God. The basis and content of the sonship is the fact that, as each preceding member of the line owed his existence to his immediate ancestor, so Adam owed his existence not to any man but directly to God.* It is improbable that the author meant to push the parallel so far as to ascribe to God a physical or biological paternity, such as that which Greek and Roman mythology sometimes ascribed to its gods, and quite certain that the term "son of God" as applied to Adam conveyed no implication respecting his nature. The first man is not other than man. In Lk. 1³² υἱὸς Ὑψίστου, used qualitatively, seems obviously to have the theocratic sense, but as the immediate context shows, with a distinctly Jewish colouring, akin to that which in Rom. 1³, ⁴ is expressed not by υἱὸς θεοῦ but by ἐκ σπέρματος Δαυείδ, and suggesting an influence of 2 Sam. 7¹⁴. The term is evidently nearly equal to Χριστός. Cf. Lk. 2¹¹, ²⁶. In 1³⁵ the meaning of the term is extremely difficult to determine with accuracy. Between the passage as it stands, including v.³⁴, and 3³⁸, there is a certain parallelism in that, as there Adam had no earthly father and owed his existence to the immediate activity of God, so here Jesus is represented as begotten without a human father and as owing his conception to the special exercise of divine power. But it can not perhaps be inferred that the content of the term is in both cases the same; it is possible that in 1³⁵ the writer thinks of this exceptional manner of Jesus' conception as differentiating him in nature from other men. If so, and if he thought that such differentiation of nature necessarily resulted from the exceptional relation of God to his conception, he has, of course, reasoned differently here from 3³⁸. If Adam, with no human parents, can be the product of divine creative power, yet as fully human as any other man, it can not be inferred as a matter of necessity that Jesus, with one human parent, becomes other or more than human, because the human paternity is replaced by divine creative power. Nor should it be overlooked that in no other passage of N. T. is divine sonship represented either as a biological fact or as physically conditioned. Of the impartation of the divine nature through a physical or biological process, or otherwise than in a purely spiritual and religious sense, or of its association with physical birth, there is no trace. From this point of view, therefore, the presumption is against the interpretation which would impute to the author the thought that by virtue of the exceptional condition of his conception Jesus was of divine or semi-divine nature.† Yet the context makes it improbable

* Cf. the statement of Philo, Opif. Mund. 140² (49): ἡ μὲν γὰρ ἡμετέρα γένεσις ἐξ ἀνθρώπων, τὸν (sc. Ἀδάμ) δὲ θεὸς ἐδημιούργησεν.

† This is the case, aside from any question as to the integrity or originality of the passage as it stands. But in fact, v.³⁴ is so out of harmony with the preceding context as to make it probable that it is an addition of a later hand than that of the author of the rest of the narrative. The preceding context, with its announcement to a maiden betrothed to a descendant of the house of David that she will bear a son who will be the promised Messiah, so obviously implies that this will take place in wedlock as to leave no ground or occasion for the question, "How shall this be, seeing I know not a man?" But with the omission of this verse, of the τῇ ἐμνηστευμένῃ αὐτῷ of 2⁵, and of the parenthetical ὡς ἐνομίζετο of 3²³, all of which are probably from the same hand, there disappears from the gospel all intimation of a conception without human paternity or of a divine sonship conditioned on or related to a

that the term here means no more than in 3³⁸, and the immediate association of the word ἅγιος, "holy," with the term υἱὸς θεοῦ, "son of God," and the parallel use of the expression πνεῦμα ἅγιον suggests that the term "Son of God" is here used in the ethical sense. Begotten of a mother overshadowed by the *Holy* Spirit, the child is *holy*: generated by the power of God the Highest, he is *son of God*. This is also favoured by the anarthrous use of almost all the terms in the sentence, suggesting a qualitative and ethical emphasis on them all. In that case, while the usage of the term is the familiar one which is found also in Mt. 5⁹, ⁴⁵, and in Rom. 8¹⁴, the passage is exceptional in that Jesus' divine sonship, ethically defined, is implied to result from, or to be associated causally with, the exceptional fact respecting his conception, viz., the replacement of human paternity by divine power. And if this be correct, then it appears that whereas the sonship with power is in Rom. 1⁴ carried back to the resurrection (its original possession, however, in 1 Cor. 8⁶ to the beginning of creation), and whereas in Mk. 1¹¹, the ethical sonship with theocratic implications is associated with the baptism of Jesus, the present passage associates its origin with the conception of Jesus in his mother's womb under the overshadowing of the Holy Spirit.

(i) In Acts the term occurs in 9²⁰ only. It is used here with reference to the exalted Jesus, doubtless in the theocratic sense.

3. *Usage of the Johannine writings.*—The term occurs more frequently in the fourth gospel than in the synoptic gospels, but the usage is less diverse. The title "the Son of God," as applied to Jesus, is, as in Paul and the synoptists, fundamentally ethical, marking him as in intimate fellowship with God, and the object of his love (1¹⁸ 5¹⁹, ²⁰). This is also the meaning of the term μονογενής, which refers not so much (if at all) to the generation of Jesus (*cf.* 1¹, ¹⁴) as to the uniqueness of his relation to God, describing him as possessing the love which a father has for his only son; *cf.* 3¹⁶, ¹⁸, and for the meaning of the term 1¹⁴, ¹⁸. But it should be observed that the expression μονογενὴς παρὰ πατρός in 1¹⁴ is not a predicate or title of Jesus, but a qualitative expression used by way of comparison, "glory as of an only begotten (son, sent forth) from a father (to represent him)"; and that in 1¹⁸ we should probably read μονογενὴς θεός, and interpret μονογενής as standing for μονογενὴς υἱός, with θεός in definitive apposition. But on the basis of its ethical sense the term is also theocratic, characterising Jesus as the representative and revelation of God (1¹⁴, ¹⁸ 3¹⁷, ³⁵ 5²², ²³, ²⁶ 10³⁶). In 1¹⁴ and in 1⁴⁹ there is probably an approximation to the idea of the Christ,

---

birth physically exceptional. The later writer, indeed, desiring, like his predecessor, to exalt Jesus, by the addition of v.³⁴ excluded human paternity and threw a different atmosphere around v.³⁵; but this does not destroy the original sense of the v., or even necessarily imply that the author of this v. gave to the divine sonship a physical or biological sense. His exclusion of human paternity does not necessarily carry with it the idea of a divine nature propagable by generation.

and that in the Jewish or early Christian sense, as in 11²⁷ and 20³¹ there is a manifest association, but not identification, of the term with the historically inherited idea of the Messiah. Here, as in Mt. 16¹⁶, the confession of Jesus as the Christ is naturally supplemented by the term "Son of God," not as a mere repetition, but as a term of additional and richer significance. In the gospel generally the term is thoroughly spiritualised, the Son being thought of as the revelation of the character and will of the Father (1¹⁸ 10³⁸, etc.), and the functions which are ascribed to him being in no way political or military (as they are in Ps. Sol. 17; cf. Acts 1⁶), but purely spiritual (3¹⁶, ³⁶ 6³⁹ 8³⁶). Even the judgment which is ascribed to the Son (5²²) is not primarily thought of as future or external, but as present and self-executing (3¹⁸); his great work is the impartation of eternal life as an immediate possession (3³⁶ 5²¹, ²⁴, ²⁵), and the conception of a future resurrection of righteous and wicked (5²⁸) is a secondary element unassimilated with the prevalent view of the book.

In the prologue the Christ, in his pre-existent state, is called the Word, ὁ λόγος. But in 1¹⁸ the Word is identified with the only begotten (Son) and 3¹⁷ 10³⁶ are most naturally interpreted as applying the term "Son" to him in his pre-existent state. There is at least no intimation that the Word becomes the Son by the incarnation. In 14¹³ and 20²¹, on the other hand, "the Son" is a title of the risen Christ. Most commonly, however, it refers to Jesus in his earthly life (1³⁴, ⁴⁹ 3³⁶ 5¹⁹⁻²⁶ 6³⁹ 8³⁶ 10³⁶ 11⁴, ²⁷ 17¹). In 19⁷ the Jews are said to have affirmed that he ought to die "because he made himself Son of God" (υἱὸς θεοῦ), the only instance of the qualitative use of the term in this gospel, as in 5¹⁸, they sought to kill him because he "called God his own Father, making himself equal with God." These passages probably imply that in the view of the writer the Jews understood the term as he himself did, and, on the other hand, that for him it expressed the possession on Jesus' part of full though delegated divine authority (1¹⁸ 5²²⁻²⁷ 10³⁰ 14⁹). This carries back into the earthly life of Jesus, and expresses more emphatically and explicitly what Paul affirmed of him as the risen and exalted Son.

In the fourth gospel the term "son of God" or "sons of God," υἱὸς θεοῦ or υἱοὶ θεοῦ, as a title of believers, is displaced (1¹² 11⁵²) by τέκνα θεοῦ, which Paul also uses as a synonym of υἱοὶ θεοῦ (Rom. 8¹⁴, ¹⁶, ¹⁷). The exclusion of υἱοὶ θεοῦ from Jn. is generally, and probably correctly, ascribed to the writer's desire to distinguish more sharply between Jesus and his followers than would seem to be done by using υἱοὶ θεοῦ of them.

In no book of N. T. does the term "Son of God" occur as frequently in proportion to its length as in 1 Jn. In 3⁸ 5⁵, ¹⁰ᵃ, ¹², ¹³, ²⁰ᵃ we have ὁ υἱὸς τοῦ θεοῦ; in 4¹⁰ 5⁹, ¹⁰ᵇ, ¹¹ ὁ υἱὸς αὐτοῦ; in 1³ 3²³ 5²⁰ᵇ ὁ υἱὸς αὐτοῦ Ἰησοῦς Χριστός; in 1⁷ Ἰησοῦς ὁ υἱὸς αὐτοῦ; in 4⁹ ὁ υἱὸς αὐτοῦ ὁ μονογενής; in 2²², ²³ bis ²⁴ 4¹⁴ 5¹² bis ὁ υἱὸς, in every case except those in 5¹² in antithesis with ὁ πατήρ. In 2 Jn. ³ occurs the expression Ἰησοῦς Χριστὸς ὁ υἱὸς τοῦ πατρός, and in v.⁹ ὁ υἱός in antithesis with ὁ πατήρ. The term is never anarthrous in either epistle. It is clear from the use of the term in its various forms that there are those who deny that Jesus is the Son of God, and the term is, perhaps in part by reason of the controversy over it, thoroughly familiar and needs no definition. In themselves, these letters do not clearly indicate precisely what phase of its meaning is chiefly in mind, but read in the light of the clearer passages of the fourth gospel, they leave no doubt that it bears here the same general meaning as there, and that by the title, "the Son of God," Jesus is described as being the unique revelation and representative of God. The constant designation of God as the Father, alongside of the term " Son " applied to Jesus, emphasises the intimacy of relation between them and the representative character of the Son. A comparison of 1 Jn. 2²² 4¹⁵ with 5¹ illustrates the familiar approximation of the term to "the Christ," but even the latter term has evidently largely left behind its Jewish messianic associations, and the functions of the Son of God are spiritual and universal. See 1³, ⁷ 3⁸ 4¹⁰ (cf. 2²) ¹⁴.

As in the fourth gospel, the children of God are called in the epistle τέκνα θεοῦ, not υἱοὶ θεοῦ (1 Jn. 3¹, ², ¹⁰ 5²).

In Rev. the " Son of God," ὁ υἱὸς τοῦ θεοῦ, is found in 2¹⁸ only. It manifestly refers to the exalted Jesus, but what phase of its meaning is emphasised, the context does not show. In 21⁷ it is said of him that overcometh that he shall be to God a son, υἱός, the expression clearly designating the victor as the object of God's approving love.

4. *Usage of the other N. T. books.*—The phrase "Son of God" does not occur in the pastoral epistles, nor in any of the general epistles except 1 and 2 Jn.

In the Epistle to the Hebrews great emphasis is laid upon the pre-existence of Jesus, and upon his post-resurrection exaltation and authority. In the former period powers above those of the angels are ascribed to him, even the word God, θεός, being used of him. In the latter all things are put in subjection to him. In both these periods he is spoken of as Son of God, and this term is, moreover, expressive of his exaltation. Yet in the period of his sufferings, also, he was Son. In all the instances in which the term is used of Jesus, it is apparently to be taken in an official or theocratic sense and for the writer evidently far surpasses in content the term "Christ." What is conveyed respecting nature is by implication of the context only. See 1², ⁵, ⁸ 3⁶ 4¹⁴ 5⁵, ⁸ 6⁶ 7¹ 10²⁹. But the term is also used of believers (12⁵⁻⁸), with emphasis upon the fact that as a father God chastens those whom he receives as sons.

5. *Summary.*—From the whole history of the usage of the term in N. T., it appears that the basis of that usage is in the use of the term in a purely ethical and religious sense, in which it is applied in O. T. to the nation of Israel and in Wisd. Sol. and Ps. Sol. to the pious individual, designating him as the object of divine love and approval.

In their portrayal of Jesus' religious experiences the oldest evangelic sources use the term with the article, marking its application to him in unique degree to express his consciousness of exceptionally intimate fellowship with God and divine approval, with probable suggestion of the consequent duty and responsibility resting upon him. These documents furnish the best basis we possess for determining Jesus' own use of the term and conception of himself which he expressed by it. It is impossible to trace with accuracy and certainty the connection between the representation of Jesus' consciousness which underlies the usage of the synoptic gospels and the Pauline usage. But it is clear that the latter also, whether under the influence of the type of Christian thought that is reflected in the synoptists or independently, like the synoptists, takes its starting-point from the general religious use of the term and, alongside of the use of the term in the plural to designate pious men, applies it in a unique degree, and with consequent heightening but without essential change of meaning, to Jesus. On the other hand, through association of the term with "the Christ" and with the doctrine of the pre-existence of Jesus as the Word of God and the Lord, through whom God exercised creative power, it came to be in the Pauline letters the bearer of the most exalted conception of Jesus held by the early church, surpassed only in that respect by the term θεός itself. Yet it is to be observed that in no passage of N. T. does it take on a clearly physical or biological sense, implying that Jesus was, by reason of exceptional facts respecting his paternity, of divine nature; nor is it, apart from any such facts, ever in the strict sense a term of nature. True to this extent to its O. T. ancestry, it is always a term descriptive of the religious and ethical relationship between God and Christ, and of the function of Jesus in the field of relationship between God and man.

Into the difficult question in how many of the passages named above in I 11 (p. 394) θεός is used of Jesus and what sense the term bears when applied to him or to the λόγος, who became flesh (Jn. 1¹, ¹⁴), it is not necessary to enter here, since the word is not so used in Galatians. On the question whether Paul so uses the term, the reader should consult S. and H. on Rom. 9⁵ and the literature there referred to. On the other passages see esp. Westcott on Heb. 1⁸ and 1 Jn. 5²⁰.

The discussion of σωτήρ also lies outside the scope of this work, since it is not found in Galatians.

IV. 'ΕΚΚΛΗΣΙΑ.

A cursory examination of the N. T. instances of the words ἐκκλησία and συναγωγή is sufficient to show (i) that συναγωγή is commonly used of the Jewish place of worship, or of the congregation meeting there, and ἐκκλησία, on the other hand, all but invariably of the Christian assembly or community, and (ii) that ἐκκλησία most commonly designates a local assembly of Christians, less frequently the whole body of Christians in the world. The reason for the distinction between the two terms, and the order of development of the two usages of ἐκκλησία are more difficult to ascertain.

I. Ἐκκλησία denotes in classical Greek, according to its etymology, "a summoned assembly," and by usage "an assembly of citizens summoned for legislative business." At Athens the term was applied to the assembly of all citizens, as distinguished from the local assemblies which were called κύριαι; see L. and S. *s. v.*

II. In O. T. the assembly of Israel is sometimes called עֵדָה, sometimes קָהָל. The latter corresponds approximately in etymological meaning and usage to the Greek ἐκκλησία; the former, cognate with the verb יָעַד, "to appoint," signifies primarily an assembly met by appointment. In usage the two words are nearly synonymous, as an examination of the respective articles in BDB. will show. Both have their most frequent use in reference to the people of Israel, either as gathered in assembly, or as constituting a community. But while the company of the Israel of the Exodus is usually called עֵדָה (Nu. 27¹⁷ 31¹⁶ Josh. 22¹⁶, ¹⁷; BDB. speak of it as a *term. tech.* in this sense in P), sometimes also קָהָל (Exod. 16³ Lev. 4²¹ 16³³ Nu. 16³, etc.), עֵדָה practically disappears from Chr. Ezr. and Neh. (occurring but once, 2 Chr. 5⁶), and the community of Israel is called קָהָל (2 Chr. 31¹⁸ Ezr. 2⁶⁴ Neh. 7⁶⁶, etc.).

III. In the Pentateuch, where both words occur frequently, the Lxx translate both by συναγωγή down to and including Deut. 5²². From this point on, with few exceptions, ἐκκλησία regularly stands for קָהָל, συναγωγή for עֵדָה. This holds also of 2 Chr. 5⁶, where the עֵדָה יִשְׂרָאֵל, but represented as assembled together, is translated συναγωγὴ Ἰσραήλ.

IV. In the Apocrypha both words occur in both senses, but while ἐκκλησία is used only of Israel and more frequently than συναγωγή of the community as such, συναγωγή is used also of other companies, even of "sinners," and occurs also in the sense of a collection of material things, as of money, or of water. ἐκκλησία never occurs in the plural. συναγωγαί (plur.) occurs once, Sir. 24²³, but the Syriac, which has the sing., indicates that the Hebrew read קָהָל, having reference to the Jewish community, the house of Jacob, and that the Lxx have substituted for this idea that of the "synagogues" of the dispersion. In Ps. Sol. neither word occurs of the Jewish community as a whole. συναγωγή occurs three times (10⁸ 17¹⁸, ⁴⁸), in the plural of the congregations (or synagogues) of Israel; in the one instance of the singular (17⁵⁰) it also refers to Israel, but is probably used in a literal sense, "a gathering together." The one instance of ἐκκλησία (10⁷) stands in parallelism with συναγωγαί and apparently expresses qualitatively what the other term expresses concretely.

V. These examples, though few in number, indicate what N. T. itself makes far more clear, that by the end of the pre-Christian period the local

Jewish congregations—"synagogues," by this time widely developed both in the dispersion and in Palestine (see Bous. *Rel. d. Jud.*[2], pp. 197 *f.*)— were universally known as συναγωγαί and the term ἐκκλησία, formerly used by preference for the Jewish assembly or community, had fallen into disuse. There is perhaps no more probable explanation of this shift of usage than that the common use of ἐκκλησία in the Greek-speaking world to designate a civil assembly (*cf.* Acts 19[39]) led the Jews as they spread through that world and established their local congregations to prefer what had previously been the less used term, συναγωγή.

On the other hand, when, in the same regions in which these Jewish συναγωγαί existed, the Christians established their own assemblies they, finding it more necessary to distinguish these from the Jewish congregations than from the civil assemblies, with which they were much less likely to be confused, chose the term ἐκκλησία, which the Jews had discarded.

If this be the correct explanation of the distinction between συναγωγή and ἐκκλησία in N. T., it suggests, also, that the use of the term in reference to the Christian church arose first on Gentile soil, and with reference to the local congregations, but that the development of the ecumenical meaning was the easier because of the usage of קָהָל with reference to Israel as the covenant people of God, and the representation of this term in the Lxx by ἐκκλησία. This is in a measure confirmed by the use of the term in Paul's letters. In all those that precede Col. it is used in a large preponderance of instances in the local sense (1 Thes. 1[1] 2[14] 2 Thes. 1[1, 4] Gal. 1[1, 22] 1 Cor. 1[2] 4[17] 6[4] 7[17] 11[16] 14[33, 34] 16[1, 19] 2 Cor. 1[1] 8[1, 18, 19, 23, 24] 11[8, 28] 12[13] Rom. 16[1, 4, 5, 16, 23] Phil. 4[15] Phm. [2]). In 1 Cor. 11[18] 14[19, 28, 35] ἐν ἐκκλησίᾳ is a qualitative phrase meaning "in assembly," "publicly." For another instance of qualitative usage see 1 Cor. 14[4]. In 1 Cor. 14[5, 12, 23] it is local but perhaps used generically. The latter is probably the case in 12[28]. In Gal. 1[13] 1 Cor. 10[32] 15[9] Phil. 3[6], however, we find ἡ ἐκκλησία used not of a local church but of the whole body of Christians. In Gal. 1[13] 1 Cor. 10[32] 15[9] there are added the words τοῦ θεοῦ, and in Gal. 1[13] 1 Cor. 15[9] Phil. 3[6] the reference is to the Christian community which Paul persecuted before his conversion. That he does not mean the local church in Jerusalem, but the body of Christian believers as such, is indicated by the fact that the persecution extended beyond Jerusalem, by the addition of τοῦ θεοῦ, by the absence of any local designation (*cf.* 1 Cor. 1[2] 11[16] 2 Cor. 1[2] 1 Thes. 2[14]) and especially by the use of precisely the same phrase ἡ ἐκκλησία τοῦ θεοῦ in 1 Cor. 10[32], where a reference to the church at Jerusalem is impossible, and to any local church improbable. The facts as a whole show that when he wrote Gal. and 1 Cor., Paul had not only learned to think of each local Christian body as ἡ ἐκκλησία τοῦ θεοῦ in that particular place, but had also already formed the notion of the entire body of believers in Christ as constituting the קָהָל of God, ἡ ἐκκλησία τοῦ θεοῦ, and that though he used the expression but rarely, it was that which came most naturally to his lips when he was speaking of his persecution of the Christians. In Phm. ᵉ ἐκκλησία is used in the local sense. In Col. there are two instances of the local sense (4¹⁵, ¹⁶), but also two perfectly clear instances of the œcumenical sense (1¹⁸, ²⁴). In Eph. the œcumenical sense only is found (1²² 3¹⁰, ²¹ 5²³, ²⁴, ²⁵, ²⁷, ²⁹, ³²). In Tit. (3⁵, ¹⁵ 5¹⁶) it is apparently used in the local sense, but in 3¹⁵ qualitatively and in 5¹⁶ generically taken. In Acts it is prevailingly local (5¹¹ 8¹, ³ 11²², ²⁶ 12¹, ⁵ 13¹ 14²³, ²⁷ 15³, ⁴, ²², ⁴¹ 16⁵ 18²² 20¹⁷), but there is a trace of the larger sense in 9³¹, and perhaps in 20²⁸. In 19³², ⁴¹ it is used in the Greek sense of an assembly, a company of people, and in 19³⁹ of a civil assembly in particular. In 7³⁸, like עֵדָה, but also occasionally קָהָל, in the Pentateuch, it is used of the congregation of Israel in the wilderness. Heb. 2¹² is a quotation from the Lxx of Ps. 22²² (²³), and the term is apparently qualitative. In 12²³, though translated by EV. "the . . . church," it signifies simply "an assembly." In Jas. 3 Jn. and Rev. it is used in the local sense exclusively. In Mt. 16¹⁸ it is used in the œcumenical sense, in 18¹⁷ in the local sense, generically taken.

Both uses of ἐκκλησία are thus in evidence from an early period, but the local sense, for which there was a basis in the Jewish use of this term in translation of קָהָל, and especially in the current Greek usage, is undoubtedly primary. On the other hand, the fact that Paul's earlier letters preceding Rom. are all addressed to a church or group of churches, while from Rom. on the word ἐκκλησία does not appear in the salutation, does not warrant the inference that in framing the idea of the œcumenical he had abandoned that of the local church, for though the Christian community in Rome is nowhere in the epistle spoken of as constituting a church, this may very well be due to the fact that it was not organised as a single community, and in Phil. Phm. and Col. the apostle still uses ἐκκλησία of the local body.

Nor can there be imported into the word, on the basis of its etymology, the thought that the church is "called out" from the world and separated from it. For however congenial to N. T. thought it is to think of the church in this way (2 Cor. 6¹⁴⁻¹⁸), the substitution of an etymological sense for that of current usage is foreign to Paul's habit of mind.

V. ῞ΕΤΕΡΟΣ AND ῎ΑΛΛΟΣ.

In his *Historical Commentary on St. Paul's Epistle to the Galatians*, p. 262, Ramsay maintains that "when the two words are pointedly contrasted with one another, ἕτερος means 'a second,' 'another of the same kind' . . . while ἄλλος implies difference of kind." In defence of this doctrine Ram. cites Hom. *Il.* XIII 64; XXI 22; Thuc. 2. 40²ᶠ·; Plato, *Protag.* 329D–330D, and Aristot. *Polit.* 2. 5² (1263 a⁹). The Homeric passages are indecisive, Ram. really begging the question when he assumes that because ὄρνεον ἄλλο probably refers to a bird of a different species, and ἰχθυες ἄλλοι to fishes of a different species, it is this difference of species rather than individual non-identity within the class of birds and fishes that is indicated by the word ἄλλος. Similarly indecisive are the passages from Thucydides and Aristotle. The passages from Plato illustrate the otherwise well-known fact that ἄλλος may be used to express not simply non-identity but qualitative difference; but also prove that ἕτερος and ἄλλος standing in close connection may be synonymous. See also Eur. *Or.* 345 *ff.*: τίνα γὰρ ἔτι πάρος οἶκον ἄλλον ἕτερον | ἢ τὸν ἀπὸ Θεογόνων γάμων, | τὸν ἀπὸ Ταντάλου, σέβασθαί με χρή; "For what other house, other than that which sprang from divine nuptials, the house that descended from Tantalus, ought I more to reverence?" *Cf.* also Aristot. *Metaph.* 4. 3¹ (1014 a²⁹ᶠ·): μηκέτ' εἰς ἄλλας φωνὰς ἑτέρας τῷ εἴδει αὐτῶν, "no longer (divisible) into other vocables of a different kind (*lit.* different in their kind)." *Cf.* l. 33, where the same idea is expressed by μηκέτι εἰς ἄλλα εἴδει διαφέροντα.

Of the important evidence of the Lxx and N. T. Ram. takes no account. The former (including that of both canonical and apocryphal books) shows that broadly speaking the two words are synonymous. Both words are used much more frequently in the enumerative sense, meaning "an additional one," than in the differentiative sense, meaning "(another) of a different kind." But both are used in both senses, and in six instances of pairs of passages, otherwise practically identical, ἕτερος is used in one member of the pair, and ἄλλος in its parallel. *Cf.* Gen. 8¹⁰ and 41³; Exod. 8¹⁰ and 20³; I Sam. 10⁹ and Ezek. 11¹⁹; Deut. 24² and I Sam. 10⁶; Lev. 6¹¹ and I Sam. 28⁸, Gen. 19¹² and Judg. 11³⁴. On the other hand, in so far as there is a distinction between the two words ἄλλος is enumerative and ἕτερος differentiative. It is of little significance that the preponderance of enumerative over differentiative cases is slightly greater in the case of ἄλλος (9 to 1) than in that of ἕτερος (8 to 1). More decisive is the use of ἄλλος in Job 37²² and Dan. 4⁷ [¹⁰], and the regular employment of θεοὶ ἕτεροι for "strange gods," whose worship is forbidden. The very prohibition or reprobation of such worship excludes the thought that they were conceived of as other gods of the same class as Yahweh, and marks them as foreign, different. See Deut. 5⁷ 6¹⁴ 8¹⁹ 11¹⁶, ²⁸ Josh. 23¹⁶ 24² Judg. 2¹², etc.

The situation in N. T. is much the same. The near approach of the words to identity of meaning is illustrated in Mt. 16¹⁴ I Cor. 12¹⁰ and in Mk. 4⁵⁻⁹ Mt. 13⁵⁻⁸, compared with Lk. 8⁶⁻⁸. Gal. 1¹⁹ shows the use of ἕτερος in the additional or enumerative sense. But its characteristic meaning appears in Mt. 6²⁴ Lk. 14³¹ (*cf.* Jn. 14¹⁶) 23⁴⁰ Acts 23⁶ Heb. 7¹¹, ¹³, and esp. in Mk. 16¹² Lk. 9²⁹ 2 Cor. 11⁴. In some of these passages ἄλλος might perhaps have been used, but no such instances actually occur in N. T. Most instructive is I Cor. 15³⁹⁻⁴¹, in which both words occur in apparently similar senses. Yet this also illustrates the real difference between the two words. ἄλλος is used in the subject when simply enumerating the various

kinds of flesh; ἕτερος in predicate to affirm that they are different.   This
passage is specially significant for our present purpose, because it shows how
Paul distinguished the terms.   Taken with the other evidence, it leaves no
room for doubt that for Paul ἕτερος suggested difference of kind more
distinctly than did ἄλλος and that the latter, in contrast with ἕτερος, signified simply numerical non-identity.   *Cf.* Rob. pp. 747 *ff.*

VI. ΕΥΑΓΓΕΛΙΟΝ.

The word εὐαγγέλιον is found in Greek writers from Homer down, bearing in extant exx. from the classical period the sense "reward for good
news."   In the Lxx it is used in the plural in this sense (2 Sam. 4¹⁰ 18²²),
once at least (in the Swete text) in the sense "good news" (2 Sam. 18²⁵),
in which sense it appears also in later Greek writers.   *Cf.* Frame on 1 Thes. 1⁵
and reff. given there.   In N. T. it is used only in the singular, only in the
sense "good news," and only with reference to the good news of salvation
as announced by Jesus, or (and especially) as achieved through him.   Its
usage is so preponderatingly Pauline (in the Pauline letters sixty times, of
which ten instances are in Eph. 2 Thes. and the pastorals; in 1 Pet. and
Rev. each once; in Mk. seven times; in Mt. four, in Acts two, in Lk. not at
all) as to suggest that the Christian use of the term probably originated
with Paul.

I.   It is most frequently used in a doctrinal sense, signifying the great
body of teaching concerning salvation which constituted the apostle's
message (Rom. 1¹⁶) and which because it came to him from God by revelation of Jesus Christ to him (1 Thes. 2⁴ Gal. 1¹¹, ¹²) he called "the gospel of
God" (1 Thes. 2², ⁸, ⁹ 2 Cor. 11⁷ Rom. 15¹⁶), or "the gospel of the Christ"
(Gal. 1⁷ 2 Cor. 9¹³ Phil. 1²⁷), sometimes also "my (or our) gospel" (1 Thes. 1⁵
2 Cor. 4³ Rom. 2¹⁶ [16²⁵]; *cf.* Gal. 1¹¹ 2²), but most frequently simply "the
gospel" (Gal. 2⁵, ¹⁴ Rom. 1¹⁶ 10¹⁶, etc.).   It has a similar doctrinal sense in
Eph. 1¹³ 3⁶ 6¹⁵ Acts 15⁷ 20²⁴ 1 Pet. 4¹⁷ Rev. 14⁶.   So also, but with special
reference to the message of the kingdom as announced by Jesus, in Mk.
1¹⁴, ¹⁵ Mt. 4²³ 9³⁵; perhaps also Mk. 13¹⁰ Mt. 24¹⁴.

II.   In a few instances the term is used with special reference to certain
historic events which, having soteriological significance, are themselves a
part of the good news.   So in 1 Cor. 15¹.   This is more clearly the sense
in 2 Tim. 2⁸, and is perhaps the meaning in Mk. 14⁹.   The clearest instance
is in Mk. 1¹.   But even here (unless the verse is a title added by a later
hand; see Menzies, *The Earliest Gospel, ad loc.;* Swete, *ad loc.*) it does not
denote the book, but the series of events and teachings that from the
point of view of the writer constitute the good news.

III.   The term is also employed by metonymy in a practical sense.
The message requires to be proclaimed and is accordingly not infrequently
conceived of objectively as a thing requiring service, so that the word
denotes the gospel-work, the whole task of making the message known and

securing its acceptance. In this sense Paul calls it "a gospel of God" (Rom. 1¹), or "the gospel of his Son," or "of the Christ" (1 Thes. 3² Rom. 1⁹ 15¹⁹ 1 Cor. 2¹² 9¹² 2 Cor. 10¹⁴), or "the gospel" (1 Cor. 9¹⁴ᵇ˙ ²³ 2 Cor. 8¹⁸ Phil. 2²² 4³ Phm. ¹³). It is in this sense probably that the word is used in Mk. 8³⁵ 10²⁹; cf. 1 Cor. 9²³.

It should be observed, however, that these three uses can not be sharply distinguished. They differ only in the emphasis that is laid on different aspects of one conception rather than by sharp discrimination of meaning.

VII. ΧΑΡΙΣ.

I. Χάρις, a word of the same root as χαίρω and χαρά, is used in Greek writers from Homer down to the present day. It is very frequent in classical authors and has a wide range of usage, including "gracefulness," "attractiveness," the quality of giving pleasure (so in Homer, Hesiod, Thucydides, et al.), "graciousness," "kindness," "good-will towards another" (so in Hesiod, Thucydides, Æschylus, Sophocles), or "an act of kindness" (so from Homer down); and the effect of kindness, viz., "thanks" (so, very often, from Homer down), or of grace, viz., "pleasure," "gratification" (Pindar, Euripides, et al.). From this last-named usage there arose, also, the use of χάριν with the force of a preposition, meaning "for the sake of," "because of."

II. In the Lxx χάρις is the usual translation of חֵן (as ἔλεος is of חֶ֫סֶד). Like the Greek term in its classical usage, חֵן signifies "gracefulness," "elegance" (Prov. 22¹¹ 31³⁰), but much more frequently "favour," "approval," and, usually in the phrases which have no exact parallel in the classical usage of χάρις, מָצָא חֵן, "to find favour," and נָתַן חֵן "to cause to obtain favour." In itself the term has no religious significance, being used of the obtaining of the approval both of men (Gen. 30²⁷ 39²¹) and of God (Ex. 33¹²ᶠ˙ 2 Sam. 15²⁵). The meanings of χάρις not expressed by the Hebrew חֵן are rather rare in the Lxx and other Jewish-Greek writers.

III. In N. T., while retaining nearly all the classical usages, it takes on, under the influence of Christian thought, and especially in Paul, certain distinctly new shades of meaning. Its uses are:

1. As in classical Greek and the Lxx: gracefulness, attractiveness: Lk. 4²², τοῖς λόγοις τῆς χάριτος.

2. As in classical Greek and the Lxx: kindly disposition, favourable attitude towards another, approval: Lk. 2⁵²: προέκοπτεν . . . χάριτι παρὰ θεῷ καὶ ἀνθρώποις. In this sense the word occurs in phrases derived from the Hebrew through the Lxx: εὑρεῖν χάριν, "to find favour," both in relation to the favour of God towards men and of men towards one another (Lk. 1³⁰ Acts 7⁴⁶): δοῦναι χάριν, "to cause to obtain favour" (Acts 7¹⁰; though in Jas. 4⁶, apparently under the influence of Christian thought, a different interpretation is put upon the same phrase as quoted from Prov. 3³⁴); and ἔχειν χάριν (Acts 2⁴⁷), not in the sense which this phrase

usually has in classic writers, "to have gratitude," but as the equivalent of the Heb. חֵן נָשָׂא, a meaning found, however, in Plut. *Dem.* 7⁷. Favour or kindness of a given type may be individualised, giving rise to the expression, ἡ χάρις αὕτη (2 Cor. 8⁶), meaning "this sort of kindness" (to your fellow-Christians), and πᾶσα χάρις (2 Cor. 9⁸), meaning "every form of (divine) favour."

3. As in classical Greek and Apocr. but not in the Lxx, and rare in N. T.: kindly feeling because of benefit received, thanks: Lk. 6³², ³³, ³⁴ 1 Tim. 1¹².

4. As in classical Greek and Apocr. but not often in the Lxx: an expression of kindness, a benefit: 2 Cor. 1¹⁵; or bounty: 1 Cor. 16³.

5. In a sense found neither in classical Greek nor in the Lxx, but apparently first occurring in N. T.* and especially frequent in Paul: "favour towards men contrary to their desert." This usage is illustrated in the employment of κατὰ χάριν and κατὰ ὀφείλημα to express directly antithetical conceptions (see Rom. 4⁴, ¹⁶); in accordance with it also ἔργα νόμου (on man's part) and χάρις (on God's part) are mutually exclusive as possible grounds of acceptance with God (Rom. 3²¹⁻²⁴ 6¹⁴, ¹⁵ 11⁵, ⁶ Gal. 5⁴). Grace in this sense is attributed only (a) to God in his relations to sinful men (Rom. 3²¹⁻²⁴ 5¹⁵ 1 Cor. 15¹⁰ Eph. 1⁶, ⁷), and (b) to Christ (Acts 15¹¹ Rom. 5¹⁵ 1 Cor. 16²³ and frequently in benedictions), inasmuch as the gracious attitude of God towards men is also that of Christ (2 Cor. 8⁹ *cf.* Rom. 5⁸ with Gal. 2²⁰), and it is in the work, especially the death, of Jesus that the divine grace is manifested (Rom. 3²⁴ 5² Eph. 1⁶, ⁷). It is the basis of the whole work of salvation, characterising and underlying God's action in the gift of Christ for men (Rom. 5⁶; *cf.* 2), in the justification of believers (Rom. 3²⁴), in the blessings bestowed on believers (1 Cor. 1⁴ Phil. 1⁷), and consummating the whole work (Rom. 5², ¹⁰). It is not possible to determine in every case in which the grace of God or of Christ is spoken of whether this special aspect of it as manifested to the sinful and undeserving is distinctly present to the mind or not. But the prominence of this thought in the thinking of the apostle Paul makes it almost certain that in his benedictions he thinks of grace as specifically divine favour to the sinner, manifested in Christ.

VIII. ΕΙΡΗΝΗ.

Εἰρήνη is one of those N. T. words which show clearly the influence both of the classical sense of the term and of the Hebrew word of which it became the recognised representative.

---

* In I Enoch (Giz.) 5⁷ (⁸) the word is used apparently as a synonym of ἔλεος (*cf.* 5⁶), and with reference to those who have been sinful. But it is not clear that the fact of their sin and non-desert is in mind in the use of the word, and in any case, since the *Greek* is, according to Charles, not earlier than the eighth century, the passage throws no light on the pre-Christian or early Christian use of the Greek word.

I. In classical writers εἰρήνη means "a state of harmony," "freedom from, or cessation of, war or strife": Hom. *Il.* II 797: αἰεί τοι μύθοι φίλοι ἄκριτοί εἰσιν, ὡς ποτ' ἐπ' εἰρήνης· πόλεμος δ' ἀλίαστος ὄρωρεν: "Words without limit are always dear to thee, as in days of peace; but war without respite is upon us." Xen. *Cyr.* 3. 2¹², ἀλλ' εἰρήνην βουλόμενος ποιῆσαι Ἀρμενίοις καὶ Χαλδαίοις. Cf. *Hell.* 7. 1²⁷; Plato, *Rep.* 465B: εἰρήνην πρὸς ἀλλήλους οἱ ἄνδρες ἄξουσι: "Men will maintain peace with one another."

II. The Hebrew שׁלוֹם, on the other hand, has as its fundamental idea "soundness," "prosperity," "well-being," and acquires the sense of harmony between persons or nations, freedom from strife and war, only as a secondary meaning, and apparently because such freedom from strife is conceived of as a necessary condition of well-being. Its range of meaning in O. T. is as follows:

1. Well-being, welfare, prosperity.

(a) In general, well-being, welfare: 1 Sam. 25⁶: "Peace be both unto thee, and peace be to thy house, and peace be unto all that thou hast." See also 1 Sam. 17¹⁸, ²² Ps. 29¹¹ 122⁶, ⁷; so the Aramaic שׁלם in the salutation of a letter: Ezr. 4¹⁷ 5⁷ Dan. 3³¹ (4¹) 6²⁵ (²⁶), and in the modern Hebrew salutation, *shalom elekem,* "Good morning."

(b) Specifically, safety: 2 Sam. 3²¹, ²³ Isa. 38¹⁷.

(c) Specifically, prosperity, success: 2 Sam. 11⁷ Ps. 73³·.

2. Harmony, freedom from or cessation of war or strife: Josh. 9¹⁵: "And Joshua made peace with them, and made a covenant with them, to let them live." See also Lev. 26⁶ Deut. 20¹⁰, ¹¹ Judg. 4¹⁷·. In the positive sense of friendship: Ps. 41¹⁰·. Of reconciliation between God and man in the turning away of the divine anger: Ps. 85⁸ Isa. 53⁵ 57¹⁹·. The subjective sense of "tranquillity," "quietness of mind," is perhaps less certainly vouched for, but is probably found in such passages as Gen. 15¹⁵ Ex. 18²³ Ps. 4⁹ 37³⁷ Isa. 32¹⁷ Jer. 30⁵·.

III. The N. T. usage of εἰρήνη follows that of the O. T. שׁלוֹם more closely than that of the classical εἰρήνη; it distinctly includes the meaning, "tranquillity of mind." Its range of meaning and use is as follows:

1. Harmony, absence of strife.

(a) Between nations or between man and man: Mt. 10³⁴: μὴ νομίσητε ὅτι ἦλθον βαλεῖν εἰρήνην ἐπὶ τὴν γῆν· οὐκ ἦλθον βαλεῖν εἰρήνην ἀλλὰ μάχαιραν. See also Lk. 14³² Acts 7²⁶ Heb. 12¹⁴, etc.

(b) Reconciliation between God and man: Eph. 2¹⁷·.

2. Prosperity, well-being, safety.

(a) In general, with reference to external conditions or without exclusive reference to spiritual conditions, especially in salutations: 1 Cor. 16¹¹: προπέμψατε δὲ αὐτὸν ἐν εἰρήνῃ. See also Mt. 10¹³ Lk. 11²¹ Acts 16³⁶ Jas. 2¹⁶·.

(b) Specifically, spiritual well-being, that state into which men are brought by the grace and mercy of God in delivering them from the evil of sin, nearly equivalent to salvation in the broad sense: Rom. 8⁶: τὸ δὲ φρόνημα τοῦ πνεύματος ζωὴ καὶ εἰρήνη. See also Rom. 16²⁰ Eph. 6¹⁵·.

3. Tranquillity of mind, which comes from the assurance of being reconciled with God and under his loving care: Jn. 14²⁷: εἰρήνην ἀφίημι ὑμῖν, εἰρήνην τὴν ἐμὴν δίδωμι ὑμῖν. See also Jn. 16³³ Rom. 5¹ 15³³ Phil. 4⁷ Col. 3¹⁵·.

The occurrences of the word in the apostolic salutations fall almost of necessity, by the fact that they are in salutations, under the second general sense, and by the association with the term "grace," as well as the evidently religious character of the whole course of thought, under the second subdivision.

IX. ΑΙΩΝ AND ΑΙΩΝΙΟΣ.

In discussing the New Testament usage of the word αἰών it is necessary to distinguish among the influences affecting it (a) classical usage of αἰών, (b) O. T. usage of עוֹלָם, with the union of these two in the Lxx and the Jewish-Greek writers, and (c) the idea of the two ages; this was of relatively late origin, but whether it was born on Greek or Semitic soil is not wholly clear.

I. CLASSICAL USAGE OF ΑΙΩΝ.

The Greek αἰών is connected by etymologists with αἰεί, ἀεί, Skr. *âyu*, Lat. *ævum*, Germ. *ewig*, Eng. *aye*. It occurs in three senses:

1. Lifetime, life. So in Homer, Pindar, Herodotus, the tragedians, Plato, Xenophon, and Aristotle. See Æsch. *Eumen.* 315, ἀσινὴς δ' αἰῶνα διοιχνεῖν, "to go through life unharmed." By metonymy it denotes "one's lot in life," Eur. *Andr.* 1215, or "a generation," Æsch. *Theb.* 744; in Dem. 295² ὁ μέλλων αἰών apparently means "posterity," though possibly it falls under the next meaning. In an inscription of 37 A. D. (Dittenberger, *Sylloge²*, 364⁹) it means "age" (of human history).

2. An indefinitely long time; sometimes with an adjective, μακρός, ἄπαυστος. See Æsch. *Supp.* 574, 582; *Ag.* 554; Aristot. *Mund.* 5 (397 a³¹).

3. In philosophic language, "time without limit," "eternity"; so notably in Plato, *Tim.* 37C–38, τὸν αἰῶνα, "forever"; and Aristot. *Cael.* 1. 9¹⁵ (279 a²³ff.), where αἰών, meaning lifetime of a man, and αἰών, denoting the period of existence of the universe, are associated.

II. THE HEBREW עוֹלָם.

The etymology of this term affords no safe guidance in determining the meaning. In usage it signifies "a period of indefinite duration, time without limits, except such as are set by the context or the nature of the thing spoken of." Cremer, accepting its relation etymologically to עלם, "to hide," defines it as "a time whose end or beginning escapes perception." It is used with reference to:

1. Past time stretching indefinitely backward, as in Gen. 6⁴, "the mighty men of old": Josh. 24² Ps. 93² Prov. 8²³, etc.

2. Much more frequently, time stretching indefinitely forward, with no limit except that which is set by the author's thought of the nature of the thing of which he is speaking: Deut. 15[17]: "He shall be thy servant for ever"; 2 Sam. 12[10]: "The sword shall not depart from thy house for ever"; Ps. 29[10]: "The Lord sitteth as king for ever." It is probably not correct to say that in such passages as Deut. 15[17] and 1 Sam. 1[22] the word denotes a lifetime, or that in Ps. 29[10] it signifies eternity. The extent of the forward look depends upon the author's thought about the nature of the thing spoken of, but the meaning of the word remains the same, "time bounded by no known or discernible limit."

To emphasise the idea of the length of the time the plural is sometimes used: 1 Ki. 8[13]: "I have surely built thee a house of habitation, a place for thee to dwell in for ever" (עוֹלָמִים); Ps. 61[5] 145[13] Isa. 26[4].

III. THE USAGE OF ΑΙΩΝ IN THE LXX.

In the Lxx αἰών, though occasionally used to translate עַד and other words of nearly the same significance as עוֹלָם, is in so large a proportion of its occurrences the translation of the latter that its usage is practically identical with that of this word.

1. It occurs in prepositional phrases meaning "from of old," such as ἀπ' αἰῶνος (Ps. 118 [119][52] Jer. 2[20]), ἀπὸ τοῦ αἰῶνος (1 Chr. 16[36]), ἐξ αἰῶνος (Prov. 8[21]), πρὸ αἰῶνος (Ps. 73 [74][12]), πρὸ τῶν αἰώνων (Ps. 54 [55][20]).

2. It stands in prepositional phrases, meaning "for ever," i. e., for the indefinite future, such as εἰς αἰῶνα (1 Chr. 16[15]); εἰς αἰῶνα αἰῶνος (Ps. 18 [19][10]); εἰς τὸν αἰῶνα (Deut. 15[17] et freq.); εἰς τὸν αἰῶνα τοῦ αἰῶνος (Ps. 144 [145][1]); εἰς τοὺς αἰῶνας τῶν αἰώνων (Ps. 83 [84][5]); ἕως αἰῶνος (1 Sam. 1[22]); ἕως τοῦ αἰῶνος (Josh. 4[7]); ἕως τοῦ αἰῶνος τῶν αἰώνων (Lxx Dan. 7[18]); δι' αἰῶνος (Deut. 5[29] Isa. 60[21]).

3. It is used without prepositions, meaning "an indefinitely long time," either (a) in the past, ἡμέρας αἰῶνος (Deut. 32[7]); νεκροὺς αἰῶνος (Ps. 142 [143][3]); γενεὰ αἰῶνος (Isa. 51[9]); λαὸς αἰῶνος (Ezek. 26[20]); or (b) in the future, βασιλεύων τὸν αἰῶνα (Ex. 15[18]); see also Isa. 25[2] Ps. 65 [66][7] 144 [145][13]; Lxx Dan. 5[4], though in the last-named example τοῦ αἰῶνος may mean "of the world." In Eccl. 3[11], τὸν αἰῶνα ἔδωκεν ἐν καρδίᾳ αὐτῶν, it seems to stand by metonymy for "the conception of eternity," or "the ability to conceive of eternity."

4. Quite exceptional is Ps. 89 [90][8], in which αἰών has its classical meaning, "lifetime"; cf. v.[9].

IV. THE IDEA OF THE TWO AGES.

Speculation as to the future history of the world and the beginnings of the idea that world-history can be divided into periods of fixed length appear as early as the book of Daniel, and in Ethiopic Enoch (Bous. Rel. d. Jud.[2], pp. 278 ff.), but the clear evidence of a definitely framed doctrine of

the two ages, עוֹלָמִים, this age and the age to come, does not appear among
Jewish writers before the last pre-Christian century. In the Greek fragments of the Ethiopic Enoch there are several phrases (some of them new)
illustrating the familiar meanings of αἰών, "a long, undefined period" (9⁴ 10³· ⁵
14⁵ 21¹⁰ 22¹¹ 27³). But in 16¹, ὁ αἰὼν ὁ μέγας τελεσθήσεται, a passage assigned
by Charles to the second century B. C. and dated about 170, there appears the
thought of an age of limited extent, which is further defined as lasting ten
thousand years. Cf. 18¹⁶ 21⁶·. The phraseology reminds one of the Stoic notion of the great conflagration, itself related to Platonic influence. Cf. Bous.,
op. cit., p. 568. If the translation correctly represents the Hebrew original, we
may perhaps discover in this passage both the first occurrence of the idea
in Semitic literature and the clue to its appearance in Hebrew thought. If,
further, αἰών here stands for עוֹלָם, we have the earliest traceable instance of this word in this sense. In the Slavonic Enoch, said by
Charles to have been written 1–50 A. D., occur the expressions, "the great
æon," "the endless æon," over against which is set the present æon of
woes (61² 65⁷· ⁸ 66⁶, cited by Bous., op. cit., p. 280). To the famous teacher
Hillel, a contemporary of Herod the Great, are ascribed the words: "He
who acquires for himself the words of the law acquires for himself the life
of the age to come" (Pirke Aboth ii. 7, cited by Dal.WJ., p. 150). But
the authenticity of the ascription is doubted by some. The earliest rabbinic witness to the use of the two phrases "this age" and "the age to
come" is Yokhanan ben Zakkai, who flourished about 80 A. D. (Dal.WJ.,
loc. cit.). These passages give no indication of the boundary-line between
the two ages. The age to come would seem to be the life after death.
Similar ideas appear also in 4 Esd. (81 A. D.). In this latter book "this
age" and "the coming, endless age" are clearly distinguished. See 4²· ²⁷
6⁹ 7¹², ²⁹⁻³¹, ⁴⁷, ¹¹²f. 8¹f., ⁵². In 7¹¹³ the day of judgment is said to be the
boundary-line between the two ages. In 6⁷⁻¹⁰ it seems to be implied that
the new age begins with and includes the period of Israel's dominion, or the
messianic times. But in 7²⁹ the new age begins after the days of the Messiah. This seems to indicate that the variation of view on this point
found in later Jewish writings antedated 4 Esd., and this, in turn, suggests that the idea of the two ages had been for some time prevalent in
Jewish thought.

On the other hand, there is reason to doubt whether this conception was
wide-spread before the Christian era or early in the Christian period. Ps.
Sol. (ca. 60 B. C.) use αἰών frequently in the familiar sense of the Lxx (see
2³⁸, ⁴¹ 3¹³, ¹⁵ 8⁷, ³¹ 9²⁰ 11⁸, ⁹ 15¹⁵), adding the expression εἰς αἰῶνας (8³¹)
and showing a special fondness for the phrase εἰς τὸν αἰῶνα καὶ ἔτι, but
never use the word in reference to the two ages. Philo uses αἰών not infrequently for the period of a man's life. See Ebriet. 195 (47); Sobr. 24 (5);
Abr. 271 (46). He employs it in the usual sense of an indefinitely long
time, in the phrase not elsewhere observed, μέχρι τοῦ παντὸς αἰῶνος.

See *Cher.* 2 (1); *Quod deus sit* 2 (1). In *Mut. nom.* 12 (2) ἐν τῷ καθ' ἡμᾶς αἰῶνι means "in the present age," the present period of the world's existence, in contrast with the eternity before the world came into being, which is described as πρὸ αἰῶνος. In *Præm. et pæn.* 37 (6) occurs the expression τὸν ἔμπροσθεν αἰῶνα, meaning the earlier part of a man's life, the part preceding the experience under consideration. *Cf.* also *Sacr. Caini et Abel* 76 (21). But there is apparently no trace of the antithesis between this age and the coming age. Concerning the various forms which the doctrine took and the different definitions of what belonged to each age, see Dal. *WJ.* pp. 147 *ff.*; Schr. pp. 544 *ff.*, E. T., ii 177–79; Charles, art. "Eschatology of the Apocryphal and Apocalyptic Literature" in H*DB.* I 741 *ff.*, and *Hebrew, Jewish, and Christian Eschatology,*[2] chaps. V–VIII.

V. NEW TESTAMENT USAGE OF ΑΙΩΝ.

The result of these different usages appears in the New Testament in the existence of three senses of the term, for the most part clearly distinguishable from one another.

1. An indefinitely long period, a period without assignable limits. This sense is found, as in the Lxx, chiefly in prepositional phrases, which, expressing with varying emphasis the idea of indefinite or unending continuance, are translated by the word "forever," or with a negative "never." The simplest and most frequent of these expressions is εἰς τὸν αἰῶνα, which occurs in N. T. 27 times: Mt. 21[19] Mk. 3[29] 11[14], etc.. There are but two instances in Paul: 1 Cor. 8[13] 2 Cor. 9[9]. For contemporary exx. of this phrase and of εἰς αἰῶνα, see M. and M., *Voc. s. v.* The intensive εἰς τοὺς αἰῶνας occurs six or eight times: Lk. 1[33] Rom. 1[25] 9[5] 11[36] 2 Cor. 11[31] Heb. 13[8]. The still stronger form, εἰς τοὺς αἰῶνας τῶν αἰώνων, found but once in the Lxx, is a well-established idiom in N. T., occurring two or three times in the Pauline epistles: Rom. 16[27] (?) Gal. 1[5] Phil. 4[20], twice in the pastorals 1 Tim. 1[17] 2 Tim. 4[18], and 11 times in Rev. Other slightly variant forms also occur in single instances. The expressions referring to past time are less frequent, but by no means lacking: Acts 3[21] 15[18] 1 Cor. 2[7] Eph. 3[9, 11] Col. 1[26] Jude [25]. The great variety of prepositional phrases employing this word in the Lxx, Apoc., and N. T. is extraordinary.

2. One of the two great periods of the world's history, distinguished as ὁ αἰὼν οὗτος and ὁ αἰὼν ὁ μέλλων or ὁ ἐρχόμενος: Mt. 12[32] Mk. 10[30] Lk. 16[8] 18[30]. The boundary-line between the two ages is doubtless for N. T. writers generally the future coming of Christ. Mt. specifically indicates that ἡ συντέλεια τοῦ αἰῶνος, the consummation of the age, doubtless of the then present age, is at the coming of Christ for judgment, Mt. 13[39, 40, 49] 24[3] 28[20].

3. In the plural, world, universe. This meaning is, perhaps, not established beyond all doubt, but it seems nearly certain that it must be assumed for Heb. 1[2] and 11[3]; *cf.* Wisd. 13[9] 14[6] 18[4] and Jos. *Ant.* 1[272] (18[6]).

From the point of view of the date of the literature, the Pauline epistles furnish the first evidence for the acceptance by Christians of the idea of the two ages. The expression "this age," ὁ αἰὼν οὗτος, occurs seven times in the unquestionably genuine epistles: Rom. 12² 1 Cor. 1²⁰ 2⁶ (bis) ⁸ 3¹⁸ 2 Cor. 4⁴. In Gal. 1⁴ there occurs also the expression "the present evil age," ὁ αἰὼν ὁ ἐνεστὼς πονηρός. Only in Ephesians, among the epistles ascribed to Paul, do the two expressions, "this age," "the coming age," occur together (1²¹). In 2⁷ we have "the coming ages." In the pastoral epistles, 1 Tim. 6¹⁷ 2 Tm. 4¹⁰ Tit. 2¹², we find the expression "the present age," ὁ νῦν αἰών.

In the eight passages first named the emphasis of the apostle's thought is upon the ethical characteristics of the present age. Note esp. 1 Cor. 1²⁰ (where he uses "world," κόσμος, as a synonym for "this age"); Rom. 12² Gal. 1⁴. The distinctly apocalyptic passages, however, 1 Thes. 4¹³⁻¹⁸ 5²² 1 Cor. 15²² (cf. Phil. 1⁶), leave no doubt that Paul held the doctrine of Eph. 1²¹ respecting the two ages, and that 2 Thes. 2¹⁻¹², whether from his pen or not, is substantially in accordance with his thinking. His thought about the character of the age to come, and the extent to which the apocalyptic ideas associated with it pervaded Paul's thinking, may be gathered from such passages as 1 Thes. 2¹⁹ 3¹³ chaps. 4, 5, 1 Cor. 15²³⁻²⁸ 2 Cor. 5¹⁻¹⁰ Phil. 1⁶, ¹⁰ 2¹⁶.

1 Thes. 4¹⁵ shows that the apostle believed himself to have the authority of Jesus for his expectation of the apocalyptic coming of the Lord. But it does not follow from this, nor is it probable, that Paul was the first in the Christian church to hold this view, and that it passed from him to the Jewish Christian body. The absence of any indication of any controversy over the matter, such as arose over other points on which he held views different from those of his predecessors in the Christian community, and the evidence of the early chapters of Acts that the primitive church already accepted the doctrine, make it much more probable that the apostle found the doctrine already in the church, and that if ἐν λόγῳ κυρίου refers, as many interpreters, ancient and modern (cf. Frame ad loc.), hold, to a revelation-experience of the apostle, this experience confirmed or amplified a view already held. If, as is more probable, it is, with Frame et al., to be understood as referring to an uttered word of Jesus, it shows, indeed, that the apostle himself supposed his inheritance of thought on this point to have had its ultimate origin in the teaching of Jesus himself. The latter view is, as is well known, confirmed by the testimony of the gospels as they stand, but not so certainly by their older sources. The latter leave it at least doubtful whether Jesus accepted the two-age eschatology or used its phraseology. The expression, "the consummation of the age," which Mt. 13³⁹, ⁴⁰, ⁴⁹ 24³ and 28²⁰ ascribe to Jesus, is found in this gospel only. In 24³ it is manifestly an editorial addition to the source (Mk. and Lk. agree in reporting the question in a simpler form without this phrase), and this fact, together with its occurrence nowhere else in the N. T. (cf., however,

Heb. 9²⁶) makes it probable that in the other passages also it is an interpretative gloss of the editor, reflecting the thought of his time as to what
Jesus held, but not traceable to any early source. The situation is similar
in respect to all the passages in which Jesus is represented as speaking of
the coming age in contrast to the present age (Mt. 12³² Mk. 10³⁰ Lk. 18³⁰
20³⁴ᵇ, cf. Lk. 16⁸). Only in Mk. 10³⁰ does the oldest source attest this
expression as coming from Jesus, and here the absence of this phraseology
from Mt. (19²⁹), whose predilection for the idea of the two ages would
have tended to prevent his omitting it while taking over the rest of the
passage, makes it highly probable that it was lacking in the original form
of Mk., and that it owes its presence in Lk. (18³⁰) to the same impulse or
influence that accounts for it in Lk. 20³⁴ᶠ· In that case its presence in
Mk. is due to the influence of the other gospels upon the original Mk.,
of which there is considerable evidence. Cf. Burton, Some Principles of
Literary Criticism, p. 25; Sharman, The Teaching of Jesus about the Future,
pp. 57, 93, 95, 256.

In Mk. 4¹⁹ the absence of the word "this" makes it improbable that there
was here, at least in the original form of the expression, any reference to
the two ages. Cf. Lk. 8¹⁴.

The phrases "this age" and "the coming age" do not occur in Acts, nor
are they found in the fourth gospel. Both these books bear evidence in
other ways of being influenced by eschatological ideas similar to those of
Paul, and implicitly, too, by the conception of the two ages, but it is not
probable that here, any more than in the synoptic gospels, these conceptions are traceable to Jesus.

It is in any case, however, clear that the two-age eschatology was for
Paul not a product of his own thinking, but an inheritance accepted on
what he believed to be the authority of Jesus. That it was shared by
practically all N. T. writers, even by the author of the fourth gospel to
a certain extent, appears from the passages quoted above from the synoptists, and from such passages as Jn. 6³⁹, ⁴⁰ Jas. 5⁷, ⁸ 1 Pet. 1⁵ 2 Pet. 3⁴ 1 Jn. 2¹⁸
Jude ¹⁸ Rev. 1³.

VI. ΑΙΩΝΙΟΣ.

The adjective αἰώνιος is found first in Plato. From Plato down to N. T.
times it is used, with no apparent change in meaning, in the sense, "enduring for an indefinitely long time," "perpetual," "eternal," referring both
to the past and (perhaps throughout its history, certainly in N. T., rather
more frequently) to the future. For classical usage see Plato, Rep. 363D;
Legg. X 904A; post-classical, e. g., Diod. Sic. 1. 1⁵. Cf. the statement of
M. and M. Voc.: "In general the word depicts that of which the horizon is
not in view, whether the horizon be at an infinite distance . . . or whether
it lies no farther than the span of a Cæsar's life."

The Lxx translates by means of it only עוֹלָם and cognates, modifying διαθήκη (Gen. 17⁷ 1 Chr. 16¹⁷), νόμιμος (Ex. 27²¹ Nu. 10⁸), etc. The phrase ζωὴ αἰώνιος, so frequent in N. T., occurs first in Dan. 12². The Apocrypha show no noteworthy deviation from previous usage. ζωὴ αἰώνιος occurs in 4 Mac. 15² Ps. Sol. 3¹⁶ (¹²). A similar phrase, αἰώνιος ἀναβίωσις ζωῆς, occurs in 2 Mac. 7⁹. In I Enoch 15⁴· ⁶ we find the phrase πνεύματα ζῶντα αἰώνια.

In N. T. the phrase ζωὴ αἰώνιος occurs 43 times. In Jn. and 1 Jn., in Acts, and in Gal. (6⁸) the adjective is used in this phrase exclusively. The feminine αἰωνία is found 2 Thes. 2¹⁶ Heb. 9¹². Its force is, as everywhere else in ancient Greek, purely temporal and quantitative. Cf. M. and M. *Voc. s.v.* The qualitative conception sometimes ascribed to it lies wholly in the noun ζωή, with which it is joined. It has no association with ὁ αἰὼν οὗτος or ὁ μέλλων αἰών. It came into existence before these terms were in use, and its kinship of meaning is not with them, but with the αἰών of Plato, meaning "for ever." See also in N. T., Mk. 3²⁹.*

X. ᾿ΕΝΕΣΤΩΣ.

᾿Ενεστώς is the perf. part. of ἐνίστημι, which in the pres. mid. means "to impend," "to threaten," "to begin," in the aor. act. "impended," "threatened," "begun," but in the perf. with the proper force of a perfect of existing state (*BMT.* 75, 154), "to have begun," "to be present." Examples of this use of the perf. appear especially in the participles ἐνεστώς and ἐνεστηκώς.

Thus, in classical writers: Æschin. 2⁵⁸, ἔτι τοῦ πολεμοῦ τοῦ πρὸς Φίλιππον ὑμῖν ἐνεστηκότος. Aristot. *Rhet.* 1. 9¹⁴ (1366 b²¹), κατὰ τὸν ἐνεστῶτα καιρόν. In the grammarians, ὁ ἐνεστὼς χρόνος signifies "the present tense." See also Xen. *Hell.* 2. 1⁶, τῶν ἐνεστηκότων πραγμάτων. Polyb. 1. 18³⁸ 1. 60⁷⁵ 2. 26². The usage of the Jewish Greek writers is the same. See 1 Esdr. 9⁶ 1 Mac. 12⁴⁴ 2 Mac. 3¹⁷ 6⁹ 12³. The participle is used in this sense only in O. T. Apocr. It does not occur in the Lxx (can. bks.).

In N. T. the participle has but one meaning, "present." See Rom. 8³⁸ 1 Cor. 3²², in both of which it stands in antithesis with μέλλοντα; 1 Cor. 7²⁶ 2 Thes. 2² Heb. 9⁹. The translation of RV. in 1 Cor. 7²⁶, "that is upon us," and 2 Thes. 2², "is just at hand," is in both cases evasive of the real meaning, as is the comment of Robertson and Plummer on 1 Cor. *ad loc.* See Frame on Thes. *ad loc.* See also Ep. Barn. 1⁷: τὰ παρεληλυθότα, καὶ τὰ ἐνεστῶτα, καὶ τῶν μελλόντων δοὺς ἀπαρχὰς ἡμῖν γεύσεως, and 5³: ὅτι καὶ τὰ παρεληλυθότα ἡμῖν ἐγνώρισεν, καὶ ἐν τοῖς ἐνεστῶσιν ἡμᾶς ἐσόφισεν, καὶ εἰς τὰ μέλλοντα οὐκ ἐσμὲν ἀσύνετοι.

In Gal. 1⁵ τοῦ αἰῶνος τοῦ ἐνεστῶτος undoubtedly refers to what is

---

* The first, and apparently the only occurrence of αἰώνιος in a meaning other than that given, which is known to present-day lexicographers, is in Herodian (238 A.D.) 3. 8¹², where he refers to the *ludi sæculares* given by Severus in the words: αἰωνίους δε αὐτὰς ἐκάλουν οἱ τότε, ἀκούοντες τριῶν γενεῶν διαδραμουσῶν ἐπιτελεῖσθαι.

more commonly called ὁ αἰὼν οὗτος; for "present" is the only clearly
established sense of the word ἐνεστώς, and the apostle's twice-repeated
antithesis between ἐνεστῶτα and μέλλοντα (Rom. 8³⁸ 1 Cor. 3²²), together
with the use of the word μέλλων in connection with αἰών to designate the
future age, apparently a recognised and current usage (Mt. 12³² Eph. 1²¹
Heb. 6⁵), makes it especially difficult to give to ἐνεστώς in connection with
αἰών any other sense than its usual one, "present."

XI. 'ΑΠΟΚΑΛΥΠΤΩ AND 'ΑΠΟΚΑΛΥΨΙΣ.

A comparison of the N. T. instances of the words ἀποκαλύπτω and
φανερόω shows that the two terms have a certain area of usage in common,
so that in certain connections either might be used and the difference of meaning be but slight. Thus both are used in general expressions about manifesting or revealing that which is hidden: Mt. 10²⁶ Mk. 4²². Both are used of
the revelation of divine righteousness in the gospel: Rom. 1¹⁷ 3²¹. Both
are used of the manifesting of Christ at his second coming, yet neither
frequently: Lk. 17³⁰ (only instance of ἀποκαλύπτω) Col. 3⁴ 1 Pet. 5⁴ 1 Jn.
2²⁸ 3². Both are used of the revelation of the mystery of Christ: Eph. 3⁵
Rom. 16²⁶. In general, however, the distinction between the two words is
maintained.

Φανερόω throws emphasis on the fact that that which is manifested is objectively clear, open to perception. It is thus suitably used of an open and
public announcement, disclosure, or exhibition: 1 Cor. 4⁵ 2 Cor. 2¹⁴ 4¹⁰, ¹¹
Eph. 5¹³.

'Αποκαλύπτω, on the other hand, refers primarily to the removal of what
conceals, an uncovering, and in some cases the choice of the word seems to
be due to the thought of a previous concealment. But for some reason
ἀποκαλύπτω has evidently come to be used especially of a subjective revelation, which either takes place wholly within the mind of the individual
receiving it, or is subjective in the sense that it is accompanied by actual
perception, and results in knowledge on his part: Rom. 8¹⁸ 1 Cor. 2¹⁰ 14³⁰
Eph. 3⁵.

This distinction is illustrated even in some passages in which the words
seem at first sight to be used interchangeably. Thus in Rom. 1¹⁷ Paul,
using a present tense and by this fact and the context indicating that he
is speaking of what is constantly taking place as the result of the preaching of the gospel, writes δικαιοσύνη γὰρ ἐν αὐτῷ ἀποκαλύπτεται, i. e., men
are coming to perceive the divine way of righteousness. But in 3²¹, speaking, as the use of the perfect tense and the context show, of a fact once
for all made clear, he writes νυνὶ δὲ χωρὶς νόμου δικαιοσύνη θεοῦ πεφανέρωται.
The distinction between ἀποκαλύπτεται in 1¹⁸ and ἐφανέρωσεν in 1¹⁹ is less
obvious and perhaps less real. The former verb is probably chosen in part
because of the ἀποκαλύπτεται in v.¹⁷, the apostle having in mind that, parallel to the revelation of the righteousness of God, there is also in progress

a revelation of divine wrath, the revelation in both cases taking place in experience. The tense of ἐφανέρωσεν, on the other hand, indicates that he is summing up all God's past disclosure of himself as a single fact and the use of the subject, ὁ θεός, shows that he has specially in mind the divine activity.

Especially significant in its bearing on the interpretation of Gal. 1¹⁶ is the comparison of 1 Cor. 2¹⁰ (see also Eph. 3⁴, ⁵), in which ἀποκαλύπτω is used, with 2 Cor. 4¹⁰, ¹¹, in which φανερόω is employed. In 1 Cor. 2¹⁰ a revelation through the Spirit is spoken of, and in Eph. 3⁵ in the spirit: the latter phrase probably means in the realm of spirit, i. e., of the mind of the prophet, thus emphasising the subjective character of the revelation. In 2 Cor. 4¹⁰, ¹¹, on the other hand, the reference is evidently not to the perception in the minds of those to whom the disclosure was made, but to the disclosure itself. In harmony with this distinction between the two words is the fact that φανερόω is several times used in speaking of the appearance of Christ in the flesh (Jn. 2¹¹ 1 Tim. 3¹⁶ Heb. 9²⁶ 1 Pet. 1² (bis) 3⁵, ⁸ 1 Pet. 1²⁰); three times of his appearance after the resurrection (Jn. 21¹ [bis] ¹⁴, and four times of his future coming (Col. 3⁴ 1 Pet. 5⁴ 1 Jn. 2²⁸ 3²), while ἀποκαλύπτω is never used of the first or second of these events and but once (Lk. 17³⁰; cf. 2 Thes. 1⁷) of the third. ἀποκαλύπτω is indeed used, also, in 2 Thes. 2³, ⁶, ⁸ of the appearance of the man of sin, but probably here with reference to the disclosure and perception of his true character. The total evidence leaves no room for doubt that the presumption is strongly in favour of the view that ἀποκαλύπτω has reference to a disclosure to the human mind involving also perception and understanding by the mind.

᾿Αποκάλυψις occurs first, so far as observed, in the Lxx: 1 Sam. 20³⁰ (the only instance in can. bks.); see also Sir. 11²⁷ 22²² 42¹. In general it corresponds in meaning to ἀποκαλύπτω, signifying properly " an uncovering, disclosing, laying bare." It acquired by association the idea of a corresponding perception (possible or actual) of that which was disclosed, but does not so preponderatingly as ἀποκαλύπτω suggest the idea of actual perception.

N. T. usage of ἀποκάλυψις is as follows:

1. An appearance or manifestation of a person, a coming, or coming to view; used of the coming of Christ, nearly equivalent to ἐπιφάνεια: 1 Cor. 1⁷ 2 Thes. 1⁷ 1 Pet. 1⁷, ¹³ 4¹³.

2. A disclosure of a person or thing such that its true character can be perceived: Lk. 2³² Rom. 2⁵ 8¹⁹ 16²⁵.

3. A divine revelation or disclosure of a person in his true character, of truth, or of the divine will, made to a particular individual, and as such necessarily involving the perception of that which is revealed; by metonymy, that which is revealed: 1 Cor. 14⁶, ²⁶ 2 Cor. 12¹, ⁷ Gal. 1¹² 2² Eph. 1¹⁷ 3³ Rev. 1¹. In the first group the emphasis is upon the objective appearance of the person; in the second on the disclosure of a person or truth, the revela-

tion of him or it in its true character; in the third on the divine source of the revelation and its perception by the individual to whom it was made. *Cf.* Milligan, *Com. on Thes.* pp. 149 *f.*

XII. 'IOΥΔΑΙΑ.

The precise extent of the territory covered by the word Judæa is difficult to determine. 'Ιουδαία is the feminine form of the adjective 'Ιουδαῖος (derived from Hebrew יְהוּדָה). Like other similar adjectives, Γαλιλαία, Συρία, etc., it designates a country, χώρα (see Mk. 1⁵; Jos. *Ant.* 11⁴ [1²]) being omitted. The country designated by it was of variable extent. In the Lxx, as the translation of יְהוּדָה used in a territorial sense (1 Sam. 23³), it denotes the territory ruled by David or that of the southern kingdom (2 Chr. 11⁵). In 1 and 2 Mac. it designates substantially the same territory, as inhabited by the Jews of the Maccabæan period (1 Mac. 3³⁴ 5¹⁸ 9⁵⁰ 10³⁸; *cf.* v.³⁰; 11²⁰, ³⁴ 2 Mac. 1¹¹ 11⁵). The military successes of the Maccabees extended the territory under their dominion, probably in part at least, with a corresponding extension of the term Judæa. Herod the Great ruled over all the territory on both sides of the Jordan from the desert to the Mediterranean, to Phœnicia and Syria on the north, and to Idumæa (inclusive) on the south. His title was king of Judæa. But whether the whole of the territory ruled by him was included under the term Judæa is not wholly clear. On Herod's death Augustus, substantially confirming Herod's will except as to the title given Archelaus, assigned to him Idumæa, Judæa, and Samaria, with the title of Ethnarch (Jos. *Bell.* 2. 93 *f.* [6³]). When, ten years later, Archelaus was removed, his territory was made a Roman province and placed under a procurator (Jos. *Bell.* 2. 117 [8¹]), who apparently bore the title, "Procurator of Judæa" (Lk. 3¹; *cf.* Jos. *Bell.* 2. 169 [9²]). From 41 to 44 A. D. Herod Agrippa I again ruled, with the title of king, over all the territory which had previously belonged to his grandfather, Herod the Great (Jos. *Bell.* 2. 215 [11⁶]; *Ant.* 18. 252 [7²] 19. 274 [5¹]). On the death of Herod Agrippa I his kingdom again came under Roman procurators with the title "Procurator of Judæa" (*Ant.* 19. 363 [9²]), and this condition of affairs continued until 53 A. D., when Ituræa, Trachonitis, etc., subsequently increased also by a portion of the former tetrarchy of Herod Antipas, was given to Herod Agrippa II (Jos. *Ant.* 20. 158 *f.* [8⁴]). Josephus speaks of Cuspius Fadus as procurator (ἔπαρχος) of Judæa "and of the entire kingdom" (*Ant.* 19. 363 [9²]), rather suggesting that Judæa was not the name of the whole territory. But *cf.* *Ant.* 20. 97 (5¹). Also in speaking of the addition to the kingdom of Agrippa I he speaks of the country of his grandfather Herod as Judæa and Samaria (*Ant.* 19. 274 [5¹]). And in *Bell.* 3. 35–58 (3¹⁻⁵), speaking of the period just preceding the Roman War, he divides the whole country of the Jews into Galilee, Peræa, Samaria, and Judæa. Yet, having in *Bell.* 2. 247 *f.* (12⁸) stated that Felix had been made procurator of Samaria, Galilee, and

Peræa, and in 2. 252 f. (13²) that certain toparchies in the vicinity of the
Sea of Galilee were given to Agrippa, he adds that over the *rest* of Judæa
he made Felix procurator. *Cf.* also Jos. *Bell.* 2. 265 (13⁶). Similarly in
Acts Luke seems commonly to use Judæa in the narrower sense (Acts. 1⁸
8¹ 9³¹ 11¹), in 12¹⁹ and 21¹⁰ even excluding by implication Cæsarea, which
was the residence of the procurator of Judæa. Only in 2⁹ 10³⁷ 26²⁰ 28²¹
is a larger sense, inclusive of Samaria and Galilee, probable. Mt. 19¹
on the other hand (*cf. contra* Mk. 10¹) bears witness to the inclusion of Peræa
under the term Judæa. While, therefore, under the influence of the numerous political changes which Palestine underwent in the last century B. C.
and the first century A. D., the term Judæa was probably used in at least
three different senses: (a) the territory south of Samaria and west of the
Jordan, (b) the Roman province, which, as in the days of Pilate, *e. g.*, included Samaria and Idumæa, (c) the kingdom of Herod the Great, and after
him of Agrippa I, yet alike in the O. T., Apocr., N. T., and Josephus,
the first, with some vagueness as to exact extent, remains the prevalent
usage. Whether Paul, under the influence of his predilection for the
Roman usage of geographical terms, employed it in 1 Thes. 2¹⁴ Gal. 1²²
2 Cor. 1¹⁶ Rom. 15³¹ in its Roman sense, or as Josephus usually does, in
its narrowest sense, must for lack of decisive evidence remain uncertain.
It is worthy of note, however, that all these letters were written in the
period of the procuratorships that followed the death of Herod Agrippa I,
and all the passages are explicable as referring to the Roman province of
Judæa.

XIII. 'AMAPTIA AND 'AMAPTANΩ.

I. CLASSICAL USAGE.

'Αμαρτία and ἁμαρτάνω are derived etymologically from α and μέρος, the
primary significance of the verb being therefore "to have no part in," but
more commonly in usage, "to miss the mark," "to fail to attain." In a
physical sense it is used in Hom. *Il.* V 287, of a spear missing the mark, and
in other similar applications in Æschylus, Sophocles, and Antipho. So also
from Homer down in such derived senses as "to fail of one's purpose," "to
lose," "to neglect." But it had also acquired as early as Homer and retained throughout the classical period a distinctly ethical sense, "to do
wrong, to err, to sin." See numerous exx. in L. & S.

The noun ἁμαρτία first appears in Æschylus and ἁμάρτημα in his contemporary Sophocles. Neither word seems to have been employed in a
physical sense, but both are used of non-moral defects and of sin in
the strictly ethical sense. By its termination ἁμαρτία would naturally
mean the quality of an act or person, "defectiveness," "sinfulness." In
the former of these senses it is found in Plato, *Legg.* I 627D, ἕνεκα . . .
ὀρθότητός τε καὶ ἁμαρτίας νόμων ἥτις ἐστι φύσει, "in the interest of the
right and wrong of law, whatever it is by nature." *Legg.* II 668C: σχολῇ

τήν γε ὀρθότητα τῆς βουλήσεως ἢ καὶ ἁμαρτίαν αὐτοῦ διαγνώσεται: "He will scarcely be able to discern the rightness or wrongness of its intention" (sc. of a musical or poetic composition). For the latter, more ethical sense, see Plato, Legg. II 660C: λοιδορεῖν γὰρ πράγματα ἀνίατα καὶ πόρρω προβεβηκότα ἁμαρτίας οὐδαμῶς ἡδύ: "For it is not at all pleasant to censure things that are incurable and far advanced in evil." But it is also found in the more concrete sense of a "fault," an "error," either non-ethically of an error of judgment, or ethically of a wrong deed; in the former sense in Thuc. i. 32⁵, δόξης δὲ μᾶλλον ἁμαρτία. In the latter sense it occurs in Æschyl. Ag. 1198, παλαιὰς τῶνδε ἁμαρτίας δόμων, "ancient crimes of this house." Antipho 127³⁵: οὐ τῇ ἑαυτοῦ ἁμαρτίᾳ . . . ἀπέθανεν. Cf. Dem. 248²⁵: ἔστω δ' ἀδικήματα πάνθ' ἃ πέπρακται καὶ ἁμαρτήματ' ἐμά. For discussion of classical usage, see Butcher, *Aristotle's Theory of Poetry and Fine Art*², pp. 311 ff.; Kendall in *Classical Review*, XXV, 195-7. For interesting exx. from the papyri, see M. and M. *Voc. sub* ἁμαρτάνω.

II. HEBREW USAGE OF חָטָא, חַטָּאָה AND חַטָּאת.

These Hebrew words, the common originals of ἁμαρτάνω and ἁμαρτία in the Lxx, have etymologically the same meaning as the Greek terms, viz., "to miss (the mark)," "a missing (of the mark)." The verb is occasionally used (in Kal and Hiph.) in this original sense: Job 5²⁴ Prov. 19²; but far more frequently in an ethical sense, "to sin"; occasionally against man: Gen. 42²² 1 Sam. 19⁴, ⁵, but in the great majority of cases, expressly or by implication, against God: Gen. 20⁶ Ex. 32³³ Eccl. 7²⁰ *et freq.* Of the modified senses of the various conjugations it is unnecessary to speak. The nouns are always used in an ethical sense, signifying:

1. An act of sin: (a) *proprie:* Deut. 21²² Ps. 51⁹ Mic. 6⁷ Hos. 4⁸ *et freq.*; possibly in 1 Ki. 8³⁵ 2 Chr. 6²⁶ Ezek. 18²⁴ Ps. 51⁵ in the sense of "the committing of sin"; but *cf.* Ezek. 18²¹, ²⁸, which seem to show that even repentance was thought of as the turning from deeds committed or which might be committed rather than expressly as the abandonment of a course of action in progress. (b) With special reference to responsibility and consequent guilt: Deut. 15⁹ 24¹⁵, ¹⁶ Gen. 18²⁰ Nu. 16²⁶; (c) With special reference to the penalty or consequence of sin: Lev. 20²⁰ 24¹⁵ Isa. 53¹² Zech. 14¹⁹.

2. (חָטָא not so used.) A sin offering: Lev. 7³⁷ 2 Chr. 29²¹, ²³, ²⁴.

III. USAGE OF THE SEPTUAGINT.

In the Lxx (can. bks.) ἁμαρτάνω is found about 170 times, being in all but 21 of these a translation of חָטָה in one or another of its conjugations. Its meaning is practically identical with the usual ethical sense of the Hebrew original; that the latter is often translated also by ἀδικεῖν only emphasises the fact of the ethical character of the word in the minds of the Lxx.

Of the nearly 500 instances of ἁμαρτία in the Lxx about four-fifths **are**
translations of חטא or חטאת, and the word has the same variety of meaning as the Hebrew terms, except that a sin offering is expressed by
περὶ ἁμαρτίας or τὸ περὶ ἁμαρτίας, the word ἁμαρτία therefore retaining
its usual meaning, "sin." See Lev. 9[2, 3, 7, 10, 15, 22], etc.

IV. USAGE OF THE APOCRYPHA AND PSEUDEPIGRAPHA.

The usage of the Apocr. is in general similar to that of the Lxx (can.
bks.). The words are always ethical. ἁμαρτάνω is frequently used in
speaking of sin against God (1 Esd. 1[24] 6[15] Jdth. 5[20] 2 Mac. 7[18]), or in
his sight (Susan. 23), sometimes against men (Sir. 7[7] Ep. Jer. 14), and
occasionally against one's own soul (Sir. 19[4], cf. Tob. 12[10]); yet it is doubtless thought of as related to God as the supreme power whose authority it
contravenes and who will punish it.

'Αμαρτία is used most frequently of deeds of sin, commonly in the plural
(Tob. 3[3, 5] Sir. 2[11], etc.), sometimes in the singular in the same sense (Tob.
3[14] 4[21]) or qualitatively (Sir. 10[13] 19[8]), occasionally collectively (Tob. 12[9]
1 Esd. 7[8]). In a few passages it means "the doing of sin," rather than
the deed, Sir. 8[5] 21[2], but esp. 25[24] 46[7]. It apparently does not occur in
the sense of "sinfulness."

Under the influence of the developing legalism of this period the conception of sin among the Palestinians in general tended to become legalistic,
and sin to be regarded as the violation of commandments (Tob. 3[1-5] 4[5]
Jub. 15[34] 21[4-22], chap. 50; Toy, *Judaism and Christianity*, pp. 205 *ff.*; Bous.
Rel. d. Jud.[2], pp. 145 *ff.*, Ch.*AP.*, II 9).

Atonement for sins is thought of as achieved by sacrifice (Jub. 6[2] 34[18]),
or by compensatory, meritorious deeds, especially almsgiving (Tob. 4[9-11]
12[8, 9]). Of attempt to define in more explicit ethical terms what it is that
makes sin sinful there is little trace.

On the other hand, there appears in this period an effort, of which there
is little trace in O. T., to discover the origin of sin. Among the Palestinians
there arises the doctrine of the evil impulse. According to Ryssel, quoted
in Bous. *Rel. d. Jud.*[2], pp. 462 *f.*, it is to be found as early as Sir. (21[11 a]);
clearly in 4 Esd. (3[20ff.] 4[30] 7[48, 92] 8[53] 14[34]), the Pirke Aboth (IV 1) and
then frequently in the rabbinic literature. As interpreted, no doubt correctly, by Porter ("The Yeçer Hara" in *Biblical and Semitic Studies by
Members of the Faculty of Yale University*, pp. 93–111) and Bous. (*op. cit.*,
p. 465) this impulse has its seat in the soul, not in the body of men. The
Palestinians never found the seat of moral evil in matter. Philo, affected
by Greek thought, especially by Plato, wavers in his opinion, sometimes
seeming to find the cause of sin in the materiality of the body, sometimes
tracing it to the work of demons in the creation of man, sometimes to man's
free choice of pleasure. Adam and Eve were originally morally indifferent,
as is every infant of their posterity, but made choice of evil. The indi-

ΑΜΑΡΤΙΑ 439

vidual man is a free moral agent, tempted to sin by his body but able to
choose the life of the spirit. See Siegfried, *Philo von Alexandria*, pp. 242 *ff.*
A noteworthy element of Philo's doctrine is that intention is of equal importance with fulfilment, yet does not become guilty until it is fulfilled
(*Quod. det. pot.* 96–99 [26]). See B*SSF.* p. 163. Sir. once traces the
sin of the race to Eve (25²⁴), and 2 Bar. once intimates the same (47⁴²),
but the common doctrine of 2 Bar. (17² 54¹⁵, etc.) and of 4 Esd.
(3²¹ 4³⁰ 7¹¹⁶ff.) is that the sin of men began with Adam, and that death is
its consequence, yet this is not conceived of as excluding the moral responsibility of the individual (2 Bar. 54¹⁵, ¹⁹). The connection which the Ethiopic Enoch finds between the sin of men and that of the fallen angels is an
exceptional view. The transmutation of the serpent of Gen., chap. 3,
into Satan and the tracing of the beginnings of human sin to the devil
begin as early as the first half of the first century B. C. (Wisd. Sol. 2²⁴).
On the whole subject see the full and informing discussion in Bous., *op. cit.*,
pp. 459–70.

V. NEW TESTAMENT USAGE.

In N. T. both verb and noun are used in the ethical sense only. The
influence of the etymology of the word is to be seen in the fact that there
is still in some cases clearly, probably always in fact, in the background of
the conception the idea of a standard to which action ought to but does not
conform. The standard is usually conceived of as set by God (Rom. 3²³;
cf. 1²³⁻³², esp. ³²), rarely by the civil power (Acts 25⁸).

The nouns ἁμαρτία and ἁμάρτημα are also always ethical. ἁμάρτημα,
which occurs only in Mk. 3²⁸, ²⁹ Rom. 3²⁵ 1 Cor. 6¹⁸ [2 Pet. 1⁹], is always,
in accordance with its termination, an act of sin. ἁμαρτία, which occurs
much more frequently, is never used in its strictly abstract sense, "sinfulness," but, formally defined, has two usages:

1. The committing of sin, the doing of that which is not in accordance
with the will of God, equivalent to τὸ ἁμαρτάνειν, *peccatio*, as distinguished
from *peccatum*: Rom. 6¹: ἐπιμένωμεν τῇ ἁμαρτίᾳ; see also Rom. 5¹², ¹³, ²⁰, ²¹
6², ⁶ᵇ, ¹³, ¹⁴, ¹⁶, ¹⁷, ¹⁸, ²⁰, ²², ²³ (?); most of the instances in chap. 7; 8², ³ᵃ, ᵒ
1 Cor. 15⁵⁶ 2 Cor. 5²¹ᵃ Gal. 2¹⁷ Jn. 8⁴⁶ 16⁹ Heb. 4¹⁵. The word is never
used in this sense in the synoptic gospels, or Acts, and is mainly confined
to Paul and John. In this sense it is frequently personified, or semi-
personified, being spoken of as one would speak of a person—a demon or
Satan (see, *e. g.*, Rom. 6¹²: μὴ οὖν βασιλευέτω ἡ ἁμαρτία ἐν τῷ θνητῷ ὑμῶν
σώματι . . . μηδὲ παριστάνετε τὰ μέλη ὑμῶν . . . τῇ ἁμαρτίᾳ), or as a force
having existence independent of the sinner;* see esp. Rom. 5¹², ¹³ 7⁵, ²⁰.

* The opinion of Dib.*Gwt.* pp. 114–124, that Paul sometimes not simply rhetorically
personifies but actually personalises sin, thinking of it as a demon, is scarcely justified by
the evidence. Dib. himself holds that he more frequently uses the word in a non-personalised
sense, and that it is not possible always to draw with certainty the line between image and
actuality.

Rom. 5¹²⁻²¹ shows that Paul applied the term both to the violation of known law (cf. Rom. 1¹⁸ff·) and to conduct of the same character produced, where there was no law, under the impelling influence of the hereditary tendency derived from Adam. To the former only Paul apparently applies such terms as παράπτωμα and παράβασις (see Rom. 5¹⁴ff· Gal. 3¹⁹); cf. the discriminating discussion by E. P. Gould, "Paul's Doctrine of Sin," in *Baptist Review*, 1880, pp. 216–235.

2. Sin committed, the deed as distinguished from the doing of it—*peccatum*.

(a) Generically, when no reference is had to specific forms of sin: Mt. 1²¹: σώσει τὸν λαὸν αὐτοῦ ἀπὸ τῶν ἁμαρτιῶν αὐτῶν. Mk. 2⁵: ἀφίενταί σου αἱ ἁμαρτίαι. This is the use in all the instances in the synoptic gospels except Mt. 12³¹. So also in Jn. 8³⁴ᵃ (b ?), ⁴⁶ 15²², ²⁴ 19¹¹ 20²³ Acts 2³⁸ (and always in Acts except 7⁶⁰) Rom. 4⁷, ⁸ 8³ᵇ, ¹⁰ 11²⁷ 1 Cor. 15³, ¹⁷ 2 Cor. 11⁷ Heb. 1³, and generally in this epistle; 1 Jn. 1⁹, and generally in this epistle. It is used in this sense, in the singular and without the article, qualitatively (meaning, however, not sinfulness, but having the quality of sin) in Rom. 14²³ 1 Jn. 5¹⁷ Jas. 4¹⁷.

(b) Specifically, when reference is had to a particular deed or a particular kind of sinful deed: Mt. 12³¹: πᾶσα ἁμαρτία καὶ βλασφημία ἀφεθήσεται τοῖς ἀνθρώποις, ἡ δὲ τοῦ πνεύματος βλασφημία οὐκ ἀφεθήσεται. See also Acts 7⁶⁰.

(c) Collectively, the singular for the plural: Jn. 1²⁹: Ἴδε ὁ ἀμνὸς τοῦ θεοῦ ὁ αἴρων τὴν ἁμαρτίαν τοῦ κόσμου. See also Rom. 3⁹, ²⁰.

(d) By metonymy, for a sin-bearer: 2 Cor. 5²¹: τὸν μὴ γνόντα ἁμαρτίαν ὑπὲρ ἡμῶν ἁμαρτίαν ἐποίησεν.

It is obvious that the distinction between 1 and 2, having reference to a difference not in content but only in point of view, may easily reach a vanishing point. Thus the context of 1 Jn. 3⁵ shows that "to take away sins" means to cause them to cease to be done; in other words, it is the doing of sin that is to cease, but the writer has in thought objectified the deeds and spoken of them as things to be removed. So also in Jn. 8²⁴, to "die in your sins," is probably synonymous with to "die in your sin," in 8²¹, the meaning in both cases being to die while still sinning; though it is possible that the plural phrase means to "die in the condemnation caused by your sins." *Cf.* also Rom. 6¹⁰ 7⁵, and the exx. cited under חטא, 1 (a).

As concerns the material content of ἁμαρτία, there was evidently room for wide difference of opinion among those who used the term. Unlike such words as πορνεία, κλοπή, and φόνος, which in themselves describe the external character of the deeds to which they refer, and φθόνος and ὀργή, which describe an inward disposition, ἁμαρτία by etymology and usage describes the acts denoted simply as failing to conform to a standard (implied to be right), and among Jews and Christians conceived to be set by God. One's conception of the standard set by God would therefore determine to what things the term ἁμαρτία would be applied.

In the type of Pharisaism which finds expression in Jub., and which is reflected in the gospels and in the controversial letters of Paul, we find a distinctly legalistic conception of sin. Basing the teaching on law and making much of its specific and especially its more external commands, literally interpreted, it tended to emphasise the external. This tendency Jesus opposed (see esp. Mt., chaps. 5, 6), yet not to the extent of making righteousness and sin matters wholly of disposition or intention (*cf.* above on Philo). He included both external and internal acts under the category of sins (see esp. Mk. 7²¹), and demanded deeds as well as disposition (Mt. 7²⁴⁻²⁷). He did not find his standard of what was right and wrong in the statutes of the law, but in some more ultimate criterion. Yet he does not expressly state any single principle of sin to which all sins may be reduced. We may roughly classify the acts and dispositions which he reproved and evidently included under the term sin as (a) sins of the flesh and the sensual mind: fornication, adultery, encouragement of sensual thought. (b) Sins of conduct or attitude towards other men: theft, covetousness, hatred, lack of compassion, unwillingness to forgive. (c) Attitude towards truth: refusal to accept truth when it is presented, captious demand for evidence, hypocrisy, and profession without deeds. (d) Attitude towards God: ingratitude, unwillingness to trust him.

Remembering that Jesus summed up all righteous action under the single term "love," and observing that in all the things which he calls sin there is an element of selfishness, in the sense of grasping things for one's self regardless of the welfare of others, or excessive self-assertion, this may be understood to be the characteristic quality of sin, viz., isolation of one's self from the world in which one lives, refusal to live in reciprocally beneficial relations to the community of which one is an integral part. But Jesus does not himself explicitly state the matter thus. So far as the gospels report, he seems rather immediately to have recognised certain acts as sin and to have assumed that his hearers' consciences would give concurrent judgment.

In his writings the apostle Paul emphasised the internal, yet not to the exclusion of the external. Under the conception of sin he included outward acts and inward thoughts and feelings: on the one side murder, fornication, drunkenness, and on the other envy, malice, jealousies, wraths, etc.

In Rom., chap. 7, he seems to indicate that while he was yet a Pharisee there was the beginning of the perception that the law extended its dominion to the feelings as well as to outward deeds, and that wrong feelings as well as wrong outward acts were sin. The commandment "Thou shalt not covet," which in his Pharisaic days brought dormant sin to life was a prohibition not of action but of desire. Yet the clear perception of the spiritual character of the law and the transfer of emphasis in the conception both of righteousness and sin from the external deeds to the internal attitudes of heart and the principle of love apparently came only with his conversion.

Yet he nowhere clearly indicates that even after his conversion he worked out for the generic idea of sin a definition corresponding to that which he found for righteousness in the idea of love.   For while in Rom. $1^{18\text{ff.}}$ he finds the ground of divine condemnation of sin in the suppression of truth possessed, yet this is probably not to be taken as a definition of sin, but as the basis of guilt.   Jas. 4^{17} similarly makes conduct not in accordance with one's knowledge of good to be sin, but does not affirm the converse, and hence does not thereby define sin.

The gospel of John takes fundamentally the same position as the synoptists and Paul.   Instead of defining sin, it assumes that its character is known, and puts especial emphasis on rejection of the light, especially as manifested in failure to believe in Jesus, and finds in such rejection the ground of the divine judgment (3^{19} 9^{41} 15^{22} 16^9).

The statement of 1 Jn. 3^4 must be understood in view of the fact that it is part of the author's polemic against the Antinomians, who justified their unrighteousness on the ground that they were not under law; yet, in view of the whole character of the letter, the law here referred to must be understood, not in the legalistic sense of the term, but as denoting the divine will in general.

Of the origin of sin and the relation of its origin to personal responsibility, there is no direct discussion in the synoptic gospels, but there are one or two passages which have an important bearing on Jesus' thought on the subject.   These gospels record him as speaking of Satan or the devil as tempting men to sin (Mk. 1^{13} Mt. $13^{19,\ 38}$) and of men as exerting a like influence on one another (Mk. 8^{33}).   He speaks of physical conditions also as being the occasion of sin.   But he never ascribes to any of these influences compelling power.   Indeed, in Mk. $7^{14\text{-}23}$, discussing the question of what defiles a man morally, he expressly finds the cause of sin, both internal and external in the man himself, the heart.   It is of special importance to note that he does not say either that outward acts *prove* the heart (that is, as the context shows, the inner self, which is the source of action) to be sinful, as if its character were already fixed (*e. g.*, by heredity) and could only *manifest* itself, or that inward conditions *determine* the outward, but that from the heart proceed evil thoughts, and that these *defile* the man.   He thus makes the man the generator of his own character and deeds.   Whatever he may have thought of heredity or of physical forces as related to sin, they were not, according to this passage, the causes of it.

Paul, agreeing in large measure with 4 Esd. and 2 Bar., makes sin a racial matter, beginning with Adam, and passing down to his descendants, both before and after the coming of law, not being imputed, however, where there is no law (Rom. $5^{12\text{ff.}}$).   In the individual, also, sin has its two stages corresponding to the two stages of the experience of the race (after Adam).   It is first a dormant force (presumably hereditary and from Adam), then on the coming of the commandment becomes an active

force and an actual practice (Rom. 7⁸⁻¹³), as in the race it issued in transgression (Gal. 3¹⁹). In his representation of responsibility for sin the
apostle is apparently not quite uniform. Consistent in his view that
there is guilt only where law is, he seems in Rom. 5¹³, ¹⁴ to imply that it
exists only where there is explicit published law, but in 1¹⁸⁻²¹⁶ clearly holds
that suppression of truth, violation of law, however revealed, involves
guilt. So, also, death is in Rom. 5¹³, ¹⁴ traced, not to the sin which being
against law is imputed, but to the primal sin of Adam, shared by his descendants, but not imputed to the individual descendant who was not
under law. On the other hand, in Rom. 7⁸⁻¹³, its cause is found in the conscious disobedience of known commandments. Personal responsibility is
even more explicitly set forth without reference to heredity in 1¹⁸ 2⁶, the
basis of condemnation being, as pointed out above, in the suppression of
truth and action contrary to it.

In this conception of sin as a force dormant in the individual until the
coming of the commandment (Rom. 7⁸⁻¹³), the thought of the apostle approximates the rabbinic idea of the evil impulse (yeçer hara). Yet the
Pauline ἁμαρτία differs from the yeçer hara in that the latter designates
not the doing of sin, but a force operative in the conscious life and impelling
one to evil conduct, while with Paul ἁμαρτία is primarily the doing of sin,
and when used by metonymy denotes the impulse, tendency, or habit which
is dormant till roused to life by the commandment. Nor is sin identified
with the yeçer hara in Jas. 1¹⁵, where if ἐπιθυμία denotes the evil impulse it
is expressly distinguished from sin, being made the cause of it.

The fourth gospel, like the synoptists, connects sin with the devil; but
as clearly insists upon personal responsibility, and finds the ground of condemnation, which is death, in resistance to light possessed. See above,
p. 442.

Similar is the doctrine of James except that the evil impulse, ἐπιθυμία,
furnishes the force that tends to sin. But the fatalistic view is expressly
rejected, personal responsibility affirmed and grounded in the possession
of knowledge of the good. As in other N. T. writers death is the penalty
of sin. See Jas. 1¹²⁻¹⁵ 4¹⁷.

In all these writers, therefore, sin is non-conformity to the divine standard of character and conduct, and, whatever the influence contributing to
it, involves individual guilt, whenever its non-conformity to the standard
of right is perceived by the wrong-doer.

XIV. ΝΟΜΟΣ.

I. CLASSICAL USAGE.

Νόμος (from νέμω) means properly "that which is distributed, appor-
tioned, appointed." From this primary meaning to the meaning which
it came later to have, "law" very much in the present, technical sense of

the English word, "statute," "ordinance," or "a body or code of statutes," the development of νόμος has not as yet been traced with sufficient fulness and exactness to make assured statements possible. The lexicons are all deficient at this point. The following outline, however, is believed to give an approximately correct representation of classical usage. The word first appears in Greek literature in Hesiod. From Hesiod down to N. T. times at least, the general idea underlying all its uses in extant non-biblical literature seems to be that of the expression of the thought or will of one mind or group of minds intended or tending to control the thought or action of others. Where it first appears in Hesiod, it may perhaps best be defined as an established way of doing things which seems imposed upon men or animals by some necessity outside of themselves, this necessity being in most, if not in all cases, referred to the will of the gods (Hes. *Theog.* 66, 417; *Op.* 276, 388). It is distinguished from δίκη, on the one hand, in that it is not necessarily moral—in fact, νόμος may be quite opposed to δίκη, Hes. *Op.* 276—and, on the other, from ἦθος, probably by the greater fixity and necessity attaching to it. In later authors two distinguishable senses appear. On the one hand, there is found a laxer usage, sometimes closely approaching, though probably never quite arriving at, the meaning "custom, convention." See Pind. *Isth.* 2. 55; Pind. ap. Hdt. 3³⁸; Hdt. 4³⁹; Aristot. *Eth. Nic.* I 3² (1094 b¹⁶). On the other hand, it means what we most commonly mean by "law," *i. e.*, a rule of action prescribed by authority. In this general sense:

1. It may refer to a single rule, the authority issuing it and enforcing it (a) being conceived of as divine (*cf.* Æsch. *Eum.* 448; Soph. *Trach.* 1177; in the plur. Soph. *Ant.* 453); or (b) conceived to be of human origin (Pind. *Nem.* 10⁵¹). In the plural the word is used of a collection or code of laws, obtaining in a state (Aristot. *Rhet.* 2²³ [1398 b⁸ff.]); so especially of Solon's laws at Athens; Draco's laws were called by the older name, θέμιστες.

2. In the singular collectively, it may denote a written civil code, νόμος ἴδιος, or a body of unwritten principles, νόμος κοινός, equivalent to δίκαιον, the principles being chiefly ethical and common to all men: Aristot. *Rhet.* I 10³ (1368 b⁷ff.) *Rhet. ad Alex.* 1 (2) (1421 b,³⁵ff.). According to L. V. Schmidt, *Die Ethik der alten Griechen*, p. 202, the sharp distinction of ἔθη "customs," from νόμος "law," does not appear until post-classical times, *e. g.*, Polyb. 6. 47¹. φύσις is at times distinguished from νόμος (Plato, *Prot.* 337D: "For by nature like is akin to like, whereas law is the tyrant of mankind, and often compels us to do many things that are against nature"; Aristot. *Eth. Nic.* I 3² [1094 b¹⁶]); at other times it is made the basis of νόμος, *e. g.*, by the Stoics. But the term νόμος φύσεως did not, either in the Stoics' usage (*cf.* F. C. French, *The Concept of Law in Ethics*, chap. I, § 4, pp. 6 *ff.*) or in that of other writers (*e. g.*, Plato, *Tim.* 83E, where it probably means simply "demands of nature") mean to the ancient mind what "law of nature" means in modern scientific terminology, a

formula expressing the observed regular recurrence of an event or a sequence of events in nature. The meaning, "musical mode or strain," "a kind of ode," in which νόμος is also found, is easily derivable from the etymological ground meaning of the word. It is, in fact, merely an application of this meaning to music. It seems never to have had any appreciable influence upon νόμος meaning "law."

II. HEBREW USAGE OF תּוֹרָה.

תּוֹרָה (cf. הוֹרָה, "to point out the way") means primarily "direction" given to another. It is of frequent occurrence in O. T., signifying:

1. Direction, instruction concerning a specific matter, such as offerings, etc., (a) an oral direction or decision, as of priest or judge: Deut. 17[11] Jer. 18[18] (cf. Mic. 3[11], and Driver, *Joel and Amos*, p. 230, in *Cambridge Bible for Schools*). (b) A formulated rule or statute, concerning a specific matter: Lev. 6[9]: "This is the law of the burnt offering." See also Ex. 12[49] Lev. 14[7] Nu. 5[29], *et freq.* in Lev. and Nu. In 2 Ki. 17[9], quite exceptionally in the sense "custom," "manner."

2. Ethical and religious instruction: (a) In general, the instruction or advice of parent, prophet, or sage: Prov. 6[20]: "My son, keep the commandment of thy father, and forsake not the law of thy mother." See also Ps. 78[1] Prov. 4[2] 13[14]. (b) Specifically the will of God announced by a prophet; reference being had not to a code or definitely formulated body of statutes, but to the will of God in general, as defined by the context. Hence, the revealed will of God: Mic. 4[2]: "For out of Zion shall go forth the law, and the word of Yahweh from Jerusalem." See also Ex. 13[9] 16[4, 28] Ps. 40[8] (9) Zech. 7[12] Isa. 1[10] 2[3] 5[24] 42[24], etc. Jer. 6[19] Lam. 2[9].

3. A definitely formulated body of statutes, or ordinances, whether ethical, religious, or civil, but in general in accordance with the Hebrew conception of the origin of the law, conceived of as divinely authorised: (a) The substance and content of such law; used especially of the law of Moses in whole or in part: Deut. 1[5] (and elsewhere in Deut.), of the body of ethical and religious instructions, contained in that book; Ex. 24[12], the law written on tables of stone; Josh. 8[31] 2 Ki. 14[6] 23[25], the law of Moses; 1 Chr. 22[12] Ps. 78[5, 10] Dan. 9[10], *et freq.* (b) The book containing the law: Neh. 8[2, 8]. In 1 Ki. 2[3] 2 Chr. 23[18], also, the reference is in a sense to the book, but still to its content, its requirements, not to the material book—and these passages therefore belong under (a) rather than here.

III. USAGE OF THE SEPTUAGINT.

Νόμος, used by the Lxx by far most frequently for תּוֹרָה, but also occasionally for חֻקָּה, הֹק, דָּת, etc., differs very slightly in force and usage from תּוֹרָה, chiefly in that it is employed somewhat more frequently of a specific statute, and occasionally as the translation of דָּת for the civil law of a heathen nation or the royal decree of a heathen king: Ezr. 7²⁶: νόμον τοῦ θεοῦ καὶ νόμον τοῦ βασιλέως. Esth. 1¹⁹, κατὰ τοὺς νόμους Μήδων καὶ Περσῶν. Esth. 1²⁰, ὁ νόμος ὁ ὑπὸ τοῦ βασιλέως.

IV. USAGE OF THE APOCRYPHA AND PSEUDEPIGRAPHA.

Νόμος in the Apocr. and Pseudepig. differs from הּיָרָה in the Hebrew, and νόμος in the Lxx, chiefly in that on the one side the meaning "direction," "instruction," is disappearing, the word tending to denote more constantly a definitely formulated statute or code, and on the other in that this latter conception is in the process of being generalised into that of law in the abstract, *i. e.*, apart from the question of the particular form of its expression. Usage may be formulated as follows:

1. A formulated statute or decree, whether ethical, religious, or civil. 1 Mac. 2²², τὸν νόμον τοῦ βασιλέως. 10³⁷: πορευέσθωσαν τοῖς νόμοις αὐτῶν. 13³ Wisd. 9⁵: ἐν συνέσει κρίσεως καὶ νόμου. 2 Mac. 2²² 3¹, etc. It is a peculiarity of the style of 2 Mac. that it commonly uses the term νόμοι (pl.) to denote that body of statutes and instruction which elsewhere in O. T. and N. T. is usually called הּיָרָה, νόμος (sing.).

2. Ethical and religious instruction. This sense, so frequently expressed by הּיָרָה, is rarely expressed by νόμος in the Apocr. In Sir. 44¹⁹: "Abraham kept the law of the Most High," "law" means in general "will," unless the passage involves an anachronism or the conception (found in the later Jewish writings) of the law as antedating Moses. In Wisd. 6¹⁸ νόμοι apparently means "precepts" or "instructions" of Wisdom. But it is evident that in this period νόμος is surrendering the general meaning "instruction" and coming to denote something more formal and fixed.

3. A formulated body of statutes, ordinances, or instructions. Used with reference to: (a) The law of Israel, usually spoken of as "the law of Moses," the "law of the Most High," or, simply, "the law." (i) The content of the law, usually its rules and precepts: 1 Esd. 1³³, ἐν τῷ νόμῳ κυρίου. 5⁵¹, ὡς ἐπιτέτακται ἐν τῷ νόμῳ. 8³ Tob. 1⁸ (א) Wisd. 16⁶ Sir. prol. (*bis*) 2¹⁶ 9¹⁵ 1 Mac. 1⁴⁹, ⁵², ⁵⁶, ⁵⁷ 2 Mac. 1⁴ 2², ³ Ps. Sol. 14¹ *et freq.* In Sir. it is sometimes used with special reference to the ethical contents of the law in distinction from its ceremonial prescriptions: Sir. 35¹: ὁ συντηρῶν νόμον πλεονάζει. 32¹⁵: ὁ ζητῶν νόμον ἐμπλησθήσεται αὐτοῦ. See also 32²⁴. In 2 Mac. 2¹⁸ 10²⁶, it refers especially to the promises of the law. (ii) The book containing the law: 1 Esd. 9³⁹, ⁴⁰ᵃ, ⁴⁶; Sir. prol. *ter.* (b) With primary reference still to the divine law given to Israel, νόμος is used with emphasis upon its authoritative character as law, rather than on the form of its embodiment in the law of Moses, and thus approximates the conception of (divine) law as such, without reference to the specific form in which it has been expressed. It is difficult or impossible, especially by reason of the laxity in the use of the article in the Apocrypha, to draw a sharp line of distinction between the instances that belong here and those

which fall under 3 a (i). But there can be no doubt that some of the instances in Wisd. and Sir. of νόμος without the article, belong here. Wisd. 2¹² 6⁴ Sir. 19²⁰: ἐν πάσῃ σοφίᾳ ποίησις νόμου, see also v.²⁴. This general sense of the term is especially clear when with descriptive epithets added it is used qualitatively; thus in Sir. 45⁵, νόμος ζωῆς καὶ ἐπιστήμης, "a law of life and knowledge."

4. By metonymy νόμος denotes a force or custom which, being put forth as a guide of action, has the effect of law: Wisd. 2¹¹; cf. 14¹⁶.

It is especially important to observe that הוֹרָה in Heb. and νόμος in the Lxx and Apocr. denote law in the imperative sense; it is the address of one will to another demanding obedience. It is not a mere statement of usage or custom. It is not the formula in accordance with which certain things customarily or invariably happen. It is a command, instruction, a body of teaching or demands to which obedience is required. Cf. Classical Usage, p. 444, fin.

V. NEW TESTAMENT USAGE.

In N. T., as in classical writers, O. T., and Apocr., νόμος is employed in the imperative, not in the declarative sense. It is not the formula expressing a general fact, but a principle, or statute, or body of instruction, which calls for obedience. Any exceptions to this statement are due simply to a lax use of the word as the equivalent of γραφή or to conscious metonymy. The conception that law proceeds from God so pervades N. T. that the word νόμος itself conveys the thought of divine law unless the context gives it a more general reference. Especially by reason of the extensive and varied use of the term by the apostle Paul in his controversial writings, its usage is much more complex than in the O. T. books.

To understand its development it is necessary to have in mind the points at issue in the controversy in which Jesus and, even more explicitly, Paul, were involved through their opposition to Pharisaic ideas of righteousness and law.

The common reference of the term among the Jews was, of course, to the legislative system ascribed to Moses. This was par eminence ὁ νόμος. On the basis of this system Pharisaism had erected what at least tended to become a rigid external legalism, according to which God demanded obedience to statutes, and approved or disapproved men according as they rendered or failed to render such obedience.* Ethical principles and motives were in large measure lost sight of, not character, but deeds of obedience to statutes, counted as assets in the counting-room of the Great Accountant.

* It must, of course, be recognised that different views prevailed among Jewish, and even among Pharisaic thinkers, as is illustrated, e. g., in the more strenuous legalism of the book of Jubilees, and the more liberal views of the almost precisely contemporary Testament of the Twelve Patriarchs. See Ch.AP. II 294. Besides that extreme type of legalism which Paul opposed, other views were held then and later, some of them closely approximating certain aspects of Paul's own thought. But the evidence seems to indicate that the view against

The Gentile did not obey, he did not even know, the statutes of the law; he had therefore no standing before God; the publican did not conform to the statutes as Pharisaism interpreted them; therefore he was accursed. This rigid legalism was indeed tempered in one respect, viz., by the ascription to God of favouritism towards the Jew as the son of Abraham, whose covenant relation to God was sealed by the rite of circumcision,* a qualification however, which served only more completely to de-ethicalise the law. Over against this legalism reached by an exclusive emphasis on statutes, both Jesus and Paul discover in the law certain fundamental ethical principles, and declare that in them the law consists, and that by the subjection of the life to them men become the objects of divine approval (Mt. 7¹² 22⁴⁰ Gal. 5¹⁴: ὁ γὰρ πᾶς νόμος ἐν ἑνὶ λόγῳ. Rom. 13⁸: ὁ γὰρ ἀγαπῶν τὸν ἕτερον νόμον πεπλήρωκεν. There thus arises a purely ethical sense of the word, representing a conception of law at the opposite extreme from that held by the Pharisees.

But the controversies of Paul also forced him to meet his opponents more nearly on their own ground and to employ the word "law" with yet other shades of discrimination of meaning. The Pharisaic doctrine of God's partiality for the Jew rested upon an interpretation of the covenant with Abraham according to which God had made certain promises to the seed of Abraham. Instead of directly controverting the Pharisaic definition, which the legalistic language of O. T. rendered somewhat difficult, Paul at times, and to a certain extent, takes the Pharisaic opponent on his own ground and attacks his conception of law through an attack upon his notion of the covenant. Respecting this he maintains first that it was not legalistic, but ethical, essentially a covenant not of circumcision and with the circumcised seed of Abraham, but of faith and with those that entered into relation with God through faith. This is the substance of his contention in Gal. 3⁶⁻⁹, where the expression "sons of Abraham" is practically equivalent to participators in the Abrahamic covenant. Again he contends that this covenant of faith was not set aside by the law that came in through Moses, but that it remained in force through the whole period of the law, conditioning the law, so that, whatever function the law had, man's relation to God was never determined by law alone viewed as the expression of a legalistic system. This is his contention in Gal. 3¹⁷. In this argument

which Paul contended was very influential in his day, and it is in any case that with which in our effort to understand N. T. usage we are chiefly concerned. *Cf.* Bous. *Rel. d. Jud.*², pp. 136–150, esp. p. 145: "Was wir von Hillel und Schammai und ihren beiderseitigen Schulen wissen, das stimmt ganz zu dem Bilde das wir von den Schriftgelehrten und Pharisäern zu machen gewohnt sind."

* The nature of the position which Paul was combating appears in the fact that the stress of his argument in Rom., chap. 2 (esp. vv.¹⁷⁻²⁹), is against the thought that the Jew, just because he is a Jew, possessed of the law and circumcised, is secure of God's favour. Only as an appendix does he in 3⁹⁻²⁰, in answer to the contention of him who might set up the claim of sinlessness, declare that there is in fact no one who can successfully make such a claim.

Paul does not deny but rather admits that the law, *if viewed by itself* and in detachment from the ethicalism of the covenant that preceded it and properly conditioned it, and from the ethicalism that underlay its very statutes themselves, was legalistic, a body of statutes demanding obedience and denouncing penalties on all who failed fully to obey them; he could himself speak of the law in this sense (Gal. 3[10, 11]).   What he denied was that the law so understood was ever intended to constitute the whole and sole basis on which man stood before God and was judged by him.   But it will be evident that while Paul's essential view remains unchanged, the precise meaning of the term as used by him varies not only according as he is viewing the law as the embodiment of ethical principles or as a code of statutes, but also according as, while bearing in mind its character as a code of statutes, he thinks of it in distinction from or as combined with and conditioned by the ethicalism of the covenant.

If now it be borne in mind that Paul also maintained that the law as a system of statutes ceased to be in force when Christ came, we may perhaps aid ourselves to grasp the apostle's thought by the following diagram:

Let *abcd* represent the covenant with Abraham, never abrogated, interpreted by Paul as essentially ethical in character and permanent.   Let *klmn* represent the same covenant as the Pharisee interpreted it, making it the basis of a permanent favouritism of God towards Israel.   Let *ef* and *gh* together represent the law that came in through Moses; *ef* its statutes, *gh* its underlying ethical principles.   The statutes according to Paul are in force from Moses to Christ; the ethical principles are of permanent validity.   *Cf.* also Mt. 5[18].   But it is not always pertinent to make these distinctions.

If, then, Paul is speaking in simple, historical fashion without reference to the controversies that had gathered around the term "law" and compelled discrimination between its different phases and aspects, or if in the midst of such controversy he desires to speak of that objective thing which both he and his opponents had in mind, however much they differed in their interpretation of its significance, then he ignores all the distinctions indicated by *ef* and *gh* or the relation of these to *bc* or *lm*, and means by the law simply the system that came in through Moses. This is clearly the case in Rom. 2¹⁸, κατηχούμενος ἐκ τοῦ νόμου. So also in Rom. 2¹², ὅσοι ἐν νόμῳ ἥμαρτον, except that he is here speaking qualitatively of *such* a system as that of Moses, a concrete objection expressive of the will of God as such.

But Rom. 2¹²⁻¹⁶ shows clearly that alongside of this conception of law Paul held also another which differed from this precisely in that it lacked the idea of expression in a concrete objective system. The teaching of this passage is of prime importance for the understanding of Paul's conception of law and his use of the term. In v.¹² Paul classifies sinful men (those previously described in v.⁸ as οἱ ἐξ ἐριθίας καὶ ἀπειθοῦντες τῇ ἀληθείᾳ πειθόμενοι δὲ τῇ ἀδικίᾳ and in v.⁹ as οἱ κατεργαζόμενοι τὸ κακόν), into two classes, ὅσοι ἀνόμως ἥμαρτον and ὅσοι ἐν νόμῳ ἥμαρτον. It is evident therefore that there is a sense of the word "law" which represents something that not all men possess, and the context makes it clear that this is law such as the Jew possessed, law definitely promulgated in concrete objective form. But v.¹⁴ affirms that all in fact possess law, that those who are without law, νόμον μὴ ἔχοντες, are in truth a law to themselves; *i. e.*, possess a knowledge of God's will, though not in concrete objective form as the Jews have it. It does not indeed follow that the term νόμος as used in the expression ἑαυτοῖς εἰσὶν νόμος signifies specifically a law not in objective form. Indeed it is more probable that the word νόμος in this phrase is broad enough to cover any revelation of God's will, whether definitely promulgated or not. For in the connection of v.¹³, οὐ γὰρ οἱ ἀκροαταὶ νόμου δίκαιοι παρὰ τῷ θεῷ, ἀλλ' οἱ ποιηταὶ νόμου δικαιωθήσονται, with v.¹²ᵇ it is involved that νόμου in v.¹³ covers such a law as is referred to in v.¹², the law the possession of which is the distinguishing mark of the Jew; and in the relation of v.¹⁴ to v.¹³ it is equally involved that νόμου of v.¹³ covers the law which is possessed by those who have no such objective law. For the purpose of v.¹³ is to prove that the Gentiles τὰ μὴ ἔχοντα νόμον are also ἀκροαταὶ νόμου in that ἑαυτοῖς εἰσὶν νόμος. But if νόμος in v.¹³ has this inclusive sense, signifying revelation of God's will without reference to the form of revelation, then it is superfluous to give to νόμος in ἑαυτοῖς εἰσὶν νόμος a more specific sense. For though it is clear from the rest of the verse that the law referred to was in fact not in concrete objective form, the aim of the apostle is plainly not by the term νόμος to affirm this specific quality but rather to affirm that which it has in common with νόμος previously spoken of. This passage therefore furnishes clear evidence that Paul employed νόμος of divine law both in a more and in a less specific sense, using it either to denote an objective revelation of God's will such as is found in O. T. (with the article that revelation itself) or for revelation of God's will as such without reference to the form of its expression; in the latter case, therefore, with a meaning broad enough to include both such a law as that of O. T. and the law which the Gentile possessed in himself. This use of the term, therefore, not only ignores the distinction between *ef* and *gh*, but also eliminates from the meaning of the term all thought of the form in which the will of God is made known to men.

But it is of capital importance to observe that when Paul is thus speaking of divine law in the most general sense, he affirms that the doers of law are justified before God, Rom. 2¹³. Nor can it be affirmed that this is a purely theoretical statement of which there are and can be no examples. For not only is there no hint of hypothetical character in the categorical statement of the verse, but the impossibility of joining v.¹⁶, ἐν ᾗ ἡμέρᾳ κρίνει ὁ θεός, etc., with v.¹⁵ compels the recognition of vv.¹⁴, ¹⁵ as a parenthesis and the connection of v.¹⁶ with v.¹³, whereby the definitely objective and unhypothetical character of the assertion is clearly established. This view of the passage is moreover confirmed by the self-consistency which the argument thus acquires, and by the perfectly objective character of the statement to the same effect in vv.⁶⁻¹¹, in which the apostle clearly affirms that God will judge men according to the motive and conduct of their lives, and to those who by patient continuance in good work seek for glory and honour and incorruption, will render eternal life, and to every one that doeth good, glory and honour and peace. This is substantially the doctrine of the prophets, that God approves and saves those who work righteousness, whose purpose it is to do God's will. (*Cf.* detached note on Δίκαιος, etc., II A. 4, p. 462.)

But the apostle does not always speak thus inclusively of both elements of the law, or so ignore the distinction between them. Indeed oftener than otherwise he seems to have clearly before him the distinction between the specific statutory requirements of the law and its ethical principles; yet he can apply the term νόμος to either the one or the other. Thus if he is speaking, as the exigencies of controversy often compelled him to speak, of the law as a body of statutes, distinct alike from the covenant, *abc*, which preceded them and ran parallel to them, and from the element of ethical principle, *gh*, which underlay and ran through them, a legalistic system which constituted not the whole of that régime under which by divine appointment the Jew lived from Moses to Christ, but an element of it, then he calls this, *ef*, the law, and means by νόμος a purely legalistic system. This is most clearly the case in such passages as Gal. 3¹⁰, ¹¹: ὅσοι γὰρ ἐξ ἔργων νόμου εἰσὶν ὑπὸ κατάραν εἰσίν· γέγραπται γὰρ ὅτι ἐπικατάρατος πᾶς ὃς οὐκ ἐμμένει πᾶσιν τοῖς γεγραμμένοις ἐν τῷ βιβλίῳ τοῦ νόμου τοῦ ποιῆσαι αὐτά. ὅτι δὲ ἐν νόμῳ οὐδεὶς δικαιοῦται παρὰ τῷ θεῷ δῆλον, etc. That in this and other like passages Paul is not using νόμος in the same sense as in Rom. 2¹²⁻¹⁶ is evident because in the one he expressly affirms that no one is justified by works of law and as clearly implies that the reason is that law demands an absolutely complete and full obedience to its demands, such as no man in fact renders, while the other implies that they and they only are accepted of God who are doers of law, thereby distinctly implying that in the actual judgment of God men are approved for doing the things that are required by the law. The explanation of the difference lies in a difference in the meanings of the term "law," of which the passages themselves furnish the evidence. In the passage in Gal. Paul is speaking not of law in its totality and actuality as the revealed will of God, as is seen in that he sets the law in antithesis to other declarations of scripture which he evidently accepts as expressing the will of God (3¹²), but of the legalistic element in O. T., isolated and set off by itself, that element which if it were expressive of the whole will of God would be simply a sentence of universal condemnation. In the other passage, on the contrary, he is speaking of the revealed will of God as a whole, whether expressed in O. T. as a whole or revealed in the conscience of the Gentile, but in which in either case God is disclosed not as judging without mercy, condemning every one in whom is found any shortcoming or transgression, but as approving him who does good, who with patient continuance in well-doing seeks for glory and honour and incorruption, and condemning those who work that which is evil, who disobey the truth and obey iniquity (Rom. 2⁶⁻¹¹). Of law in the sense which is gained by isolating the purely legalistic element of O. T. and speaking of it by itself, Paul can say very different things from that which he says of the law as the will of God broadly and justly understood.

It is of great importance for the understanding of Paul to recognise that law in the legalistic sense was an actual, not a merely hypothetical existence, yet that it was never alone and by itself the basis of God's action towards men. There never was a period of pure legalism except in the erroneous thoughts of men. Might not one argue in somewhat the same way about the law of war? Had he maintained that this legalistic element thus isolated in fact before the coming of Christ held full sway in God's government of the world, unqualified by covenant or ethical principle, he would have predicated for this period an absolute legalism, which would have pronounced sentence of condemnation on every man who in any respect failed to fulfil all the commands of the law. It might even seem that he does this in Gal. 3¹⁰⁻¹². But against this are the reasons already urged: first, that in this very passage he cites O. T. as teaching the precise contrary of this legalism, making faith the basis of acceptance with God (Gal. 3¹¹); and second, that in Rom. 2⁶⁻¹⁶, he likewise clearly makes the basis of divine acceptance, not legalistic—a perfect conformity to all the things written in the book of the law—but ethical, character as shown in purpose and conduct. And when we examine his language in the passage in Gal., we find that he does not say that God deals with men on the basis of such legalism, or that law so understood actually held unqualified sway, but only that law in that sense in which it can be set over against the other teaching of scripture, pronounces such sentence. It is necessary, therefore, to understand him as here isolating law in thought and affirming of it that which is true of it as a legal system pure and simple, but not affirming that it constituted the total basis of God's relation to men.

Had Paul qualified this absolute legalism by the Pharisaic notion of God's covenant (that is, if separating *ef* both from *bc* and from *gh*, he had combined it with *lm* and called this the law), he would have used the term practically as the Pharisee used it, and if he had believed this to represent God's actual attitude to men, he would have held the Pharisaic doctrine. He does indeed show that he is familiar with this notion of law, and in speaking of the Jewish position, notably in Rom. 2[17], he comes so near to using the term in this sense that we should not seriously misrepresent his thought if we should take the term as representing this Pharisaic thought. Yet even here it is perhaps best to suppose that Paul was using the term in a sense which represented for him a reality, viz., as referring to the law as an actual historic régime. *Cf.* 2 (a), p. 455.

But Paul did not always emphasise the purely legalistic element when he resolved law into its elements. In truth, it was rather the element of ethical principle than that of formulated statute, *gh* rather than *ef*, that represented for Paul the true will of God, the real νόμος. And when he was free from the stress of controversy which compelled him to shape his use of terms in large part by that of his opponents, he could use the word with exclusive emphasis upon the ethical principles of the law. This he clearly does in Gal. 5[14]: ὁ γὰρ πᾶς νόμος ἐν ἑνὶ λόγῳ πεπλήρωται, ἐν τῷ ἀγαπήσεις τὸν πλησίον σου ὡς σεαυτόν. This he does also in Rom. 13[8]: ὁ γὰρ ἀγαπῶν τὸν ἕτερον νόμον πεπλήρωκεν. See also v.[10]. That the term νόμος is used in the former passage in a sense which not simply emphasises the ethical principle which is at the heart of the law, but does so to the exclusion of the statutory requirements of the law, is clear from the fact that, while the apostle fervently exhorts the Galatians not to yield obedience to the command to be circumcised, he clearly implies that the law as he is here speaking of it, is to be fulfilled by them. In this passage, therefore, the element of ethical principle, *gh* in the diagram, is isolated and treated as constituting the law. And this meaning once clearly established by such passages as those cited is then seen to satisfy best the requirements of the context of not a few other passages.* See 2 (d), p. 458.

* That the line of discrimination between law to be fulfilled and law not to be obeyed is between the ethical principle and the statutes as such, not between ethical and ceremonial statutes, is shown by Paul's bold application of his principle in 1 Cor. 6[12] (*cf.* also 10[23]), where he refuses to condemn even unchastity on the ground that it is unlawful, but strenuously condemns it because it destroys one's fellowship with Christ.

It might seem that this meaning of the word is identical with that assigned above to Rom. 2¹⁴, ἐαυτοῖς εἰσὶν νόμος. Nor is it needful to suppose that the law as spoken of in the two classes of passages is of different content. The elements of the concept are, however, different in the two cases. The distinction which Rom. 2¹⁴ makes is (a) that between law objectively promulgated, and law, whether objectively promulgated or not, νόμος in τὰ μὴ νόμον ἔχοντα signifying a law thus objectively promulgated and νόμος in ἐαυτοῖς εἰσὶν νόμος, denoting a disclosure of the divine will without reference to whether it is so promulgated or not. In Gal. 5¹⁴ the distinction that is in mind is (b) that between statutes and ethical principles, and ὁ νόμος means the law inclusive of ethical principles, and exclusive of statutes (save as these are involved in the principles). These two distinctions are by no means equivalent; for, while a law not definitely promulgated can not easily be thought of as consisting in statutes, yet it is not impossible that the law which men create for themselves or which their conduct reflects should take the form of rules rather than principles, and it is by no means impossible that a law definitely and formally promulgated should be expressed in principles, or reduced to a single principle, rather than in a multiplicity of specific statutes. Indeed it is of a law definitely promulgated that Paul seems to be speaking in Gal. 5¹⁴ and 6². Moreover, the two passages differ in this, that, while in Rom. 2¹⁴ distinction (b) is not at all present to the mind, and distinction (a) furnishes the solution of the paradox of the sentence, in Gal. 5¹⁴ on the other hand, distinction (a) is alien to the thought of the passage (though it is in fact a definitely promulgated law of which the apostle is speaking), and distinction (b) is distinctly present, and ὁ . . . νόμος denotes law as consisting of ethical principles, not law as consisting of statutory rules.

For the formulation of a complete exhibit of N. T. usage account must also be taken of the fact that most, if not all, of these various senses of the word may be used either specifically with reference to the law in question, this definiteness of reference being usually indicated by the article, or without the article, qualitatively, the thing referred to being often the same historic fact that would be denoted by ὁ νόμος, but the word describing it not as *the* law, but as *a* law or as law, having the qualities for which the term stands.* Such an exhibit must also include certain less frequent senses of the word not specifically mentioned above.

The arrangement of meanings in the following tabulation† is in the main that which is suggested by genetic relations. The first meaning, though of comparatively infrequent occurrence in N. T., is probably closer to the original sense, both of the Greek νόμος and of the Hebrew הוֹרָה, than

---

* See Slaten, "The Qualitative Use of Νόμος in the Pauline Epistles" in *AJT.* 1919, pp. 213–217, and Sl*QN*. pp. 35–40.

† If any reader approaches such a tabulation of usage with a presumption in favour of finding, in Paul at least, but one meaning of the word, rather than a variety of meanings, such presumption ought to be overthrown by an examination of the passages already discussed. See, *e. g.*, Rom. 3³¹ 7²³ 8²· ³· ⁴, in each of which Paul clearly sets law over against law. Or compare Rom. 2¹³ with Rom. 3²⁰ and Gal. 2¹⁶, in which formally contradictory

those which follow. But it is the second meaning that is the real starting-point of N. T., and especially of Pauline, usage. To Paul ὁ νόμος was, save in exceptional cases, the revealed will of God, and the primary reference of the term was to the revelation of that will in O. T.

1. A single statute or principle, ethical, religious, or civil (cf. Pind. Nem. 10. 51; Ex. 12⁴⁹ Lev. 6⁹, etc.): Rom. 7²ᵇ, ἀπο τοῦ νόμου τοῦ ἀνδρός, "from the statute concerning marriage"; Rom. 7³ Heb. 8¹⁰ 10¹⁶.

2. Divine law, the revealed will of God in general, or a body of statutes, ordinances, or instructions expressing that will. Under this head fall the great majority of all the N. T. instances of the word. But for the purposes of the interpreter, and for reasons indicated above, it is necessary to recognise four specific modifications of the general sense above stated.

(a) Divine law, expression of the divine will, viewed as a concrete fact, or as a historic régime of which such expression is the characteristic feature. The expression may be mandatory, or condemnatory, or approbatory, since will may be expressed in any of these ways. In this use the term is colourless as concerns the distinction between general principles and specific statutes, and as respects the qualification of the statutory system by any other elements of divine revelation; it refers simply to divine revelation as a concrete, historic fact without further definition of it.

Most frequently it is the law of O. T., or more specifically, the Mosaic code that is referred to, and this reference is indicated by the prefixing of the article designating the well-known or previously mentioned law. So in Mt. 11¹³: πάντες οἱ προφῆται καὶ ὁ νόμος ἕως Ἰωάννου ἐπροφήτευσαν. 12⁵ 22³⁶ 23²³ Lk. 2²², ²⁴, ²⁷, ³⁹ 10²⁶ 16¹⁶ Jn. 1¹⁷: ὁ νόμος διὰ Μωυσέως ἐδόθη. 7¹⁹ᵃ, ᵇ, ²³, ⁴⁹ 8 [⁵]. ¹⁷ Acts 6¹³ 7⁵³ 15⁵ 18¹³ 21²⁰, ²⁴, ²⁸ 22³, ¹² 23³ Rom. 2¹⁸, ²⁰, ²³ᵇ 3¹⁹ᵃ, ᵇ 4¹⁶ 1 Cor. 9⁸, ⁹ 14³⁴ Heb. 7⁵, ¹⁹, ²⁸ᵃ, ᵇ 9¹⁹, ²² 10¹. When the reference to the O. T. law is indicated by the addition of Μωυσέως or Κυρίου the article is sometimes omitted. See Lk. 2²³ (cf. Acts 13⁴⁹, which, however, probably falls under (c); Heb. 10²⁸).

When the law viewed simply as a concrete fact or historic régime is spoken of qualitatively so that while the thing chiefly or even exclusively in mind is the O. T. law, yet it is thought of not specifically as the O. T. system but simply in its character as law (historically or concretely viewed), the article is regularly omitted: Heb. 7¹², ¹⁶ 8⁴ 10⁸.* Naturally examples of this usage

---

assertions are made about law. Or, again, compare Rom. 6¹⁴, 7⁴ and Gal. 2¹⁹ 5¹ with Rom. 8⁴ and Gal. 5¹³, ¹⁴, which disclose a similar antithesis of statement concerning law, which can be resolved only by recognising that Paul uses the term νόμος in different, if not even antithetical, senses.

* It might seem as if these and the previously cited examples from Heb. properly belong under (c), "law viewed as a purely legalistic system," since the author evidently has specially in mind the sacrificial and ritual elements of the law, and in 7¹⁶ characterises it as a law of carnal commandment. But since there is in this epistle no antithesis between different conceptions of law, such as is so clearly marked in Paul, it is gratuitous to assign to the author of Heb. those specialised meanings which are demanded in the case of Paul; it is truer to the point of view of the author of the Epistle to the Hebrews to assign all these instances to the category of law viewed simply as a concrete historic régime.

occur in close connection with instances with the article.   It is this sense of νόμος, concrete, objective expression of the will of God, qualitatively thought of, that underlies both clauses of Rom. 2¹²: ὅσοι γὰρ ἀνόμως ἥμαρτον, ἀνόμως καὶ ἀπολοῦνται, καὶ ὅσοι ἐν νόμῳ ἥμαρτον, διὰ νόμου κριθήσονται.   It is law in this sense that the Gentiles lack and the Jews possess.   It is in the same sense of νόμος that the Gentiles are described in v.¹⁴ as τὰ μὴ νόμον ἔχοντα and νόμον μὴ ἔχοντες. This is also the most probable sense in 2¹⁷, ²³, and in 3³¹ᵃ, ᵇ.*

But the context of 2¹², ¹⁴ in which of those who are described as νόμον μὴ ἔχοντες it is immediately affirmed, ἐαυτοῖς εἰσὶν νόμος, shows clearly that Paul could also use the term νόμος without including the idea of concrete, objective expression, as in a code.   Hence we recognise a second specific sense of νόμος denoting divine law:

(b) Divine law in general, the will of God made known to men, but without reference to the manner of its expression, inclusive therefore of law as a historic régime, and of any other less objective forms of expression of the divine will.†

As in the preceding usage, so here also the term may be used with the

---

* It would be easy to judge that Rom. 5¹³: ἄχρι νόμου, 5²⁰: νόμος παρεισῆλθεν, should be classed here on the ground that these passages clearly refer to the law as a concrete historic fact.   That they do refer to the concrete historic fact is undoubtedly true, but not to it *simply* as such.   A careful study of the context makes it clear that the apostle is thinking not of the whole institution of law, inclusive of all the elements of the system, and of this whole simply as a historical fact, but only of the legalistic element and aspect of the system, of law isolated from all other elements of divine revelation and set over against these other elements.   These instances, therefore, belong not here but under (c).

Similarly Gal. 3¹⁷ might seem to demand classification under the historic sense.   For while it is evident that in Gal., chap. 3, generally, it is the law legalistically interpreted that Paul is contending against, yet in 3¹⁷ the expression "which came four hundred and thirty years afterwards" seems to give to the word "law" to which it is attached an unequivocally historical sense.   Yet it is also to be recognised that in his assertion that the law does not annul the covenant it is the displacing of the covenant by the principle of legalism that he is contending against.   So that while it may be said that what he affirms both in the participial phrase and in the negative predicate οὐκ ἀκυροῖ obviously applies to the law historically understood, yet it is his thought of the legalistic element or interpretation of the law which leads Paul to make the statement.   Thus his full thought would probably be expressed in some such fashion as this.   "The law which came four hundred and thirty years afterwards, which you affirm established the principle of justification by law, and in which I do not deny such a principle may be found, does not annul the promise."   It seems necessary, therefore, to assign all the instances in this chapter to this head.

It is noticeable that the use of νόμος in the concrete historic sense, frequent in other parts of the N. T. is infrequent in Paul.   It was a natural result of the controversies in which Paul was engaged and in connection with which he had chief occasion to use the term that when he spoke of the law or of law it was with some special aspect of the law in mind —either that which his own thought emphasised or that which his opponents made prominent.

† It is important to observe that this use of the term does not designate law without concrete historic expression, as the law of conscience or of the mind; concrete historic expression is not denied of the thing referred to, but is eliminated from the definition.   The relation of (a) and (b) is illustrated, not by the categories, "black horse" and "not-black horse," but by "black horse" and "horse."

article and be definite, or without the article, and in that case be qualitative or indefinite: Rom. 2¹³: οὐ γὰρ οἱ ἀκροαταὶ νόμου δίκαιοι παρὰ [τῷ] θεῷ, ἀλλ' οἱ ποιηταὶ νόμου δικαιωθήσονται. *Cf.* p. 451. The qualitative force of the term without the article can be expressed in English by translating: "For not the law-hearers . . . . but the law-doers, etc." Here belongs also, as indicated above, Rom. 2¹⁴ᵈ: ἑαυτοῖς ἐισὶν νόμος. In 2¹⁴ᵇ: τὰ τοῦ νόμου ποιοῦσιν, it is impossible to tell with certainty whether τοῦ νόμου means the concrete historic law (of the Jew), the requirements of which the Gentile meets, though ignorant of the fact that they are so required, or more generally the law of God, without reference to the form of its presentation. In τὸ ἔργον τοῦ νόμου, v.¹⁵, the latter is quite clearly the meaning, and from this it may perhaps be inferred that the meaning is the same in v.¹⁴ᵇ.

Since meaning (b) is simply (a) with the elimination of the idea of concrete, objective promulgation, it is easy to pass from the one sense to the other, and sometimes difficult to decide in which sense the term is employed. This is the case in Rom. 2²⁵ᵃ, ᵇ, ²⁶, ²⁷ᵃ, ᵇ. Yet it is probable that in all these cases the term represented in the apostle's mind the more generalised conception, and so that these instances fall under (b).

The extreme of generalisation of the conception of the law of God is represented in Rom. 3²⁷, διὰ ποίου νόμου, and though in the answer to this question, ἀλλὰ διὰ νόμου πίστεως, the content of the law is indicated by the word πίστεως, in both question and answer νόμου itself is wholly colourless as respects mode of expression. Similar to this latter case is Rom. 9³¹, where νόμον δικαιοσύνης signifies a law through which righteousness could be achieved, but the word conveys no intimation *pro* or *con* respecting definite promulgation of such a law in a concrete system.

The two preceding usages, differing by the inclusion or exclusion in the concept of the idea of concrete, historic expression, are alike in that both ignore the distinction between general ethical principle and specific statutes. From these we pass then to the two uses to which this latter idea is of fundamental importance, and which are distinguished from one another precisely in that one emphasises statutes and the other principle. The first of these reflects most strongly the influence of Pharisaic thought, of which Paul's defence of his own conception compelled him to take account.

(c) Divine law viewed as a purely legalistic system made up of statutes on the basis of obedience or disobedience to which it justifies or condemns men as matter of debt without grace; the law detached in thought and distinguished from all other elements or aspects of divine revelation, whether it be the ethical principle that underlay it, or the covenant that preceded it and qualified it, or the ethicalism that is demanded by the facts concerning the law written in the heart of the Gentile. All the instances of the word in this sense occur in the Pauline epistles. The occasion for such a use of the word by Paul was, as pointed out above, in the controversies in which he was engaged. The possibility of its occurrence, as representing a reality and not merely an idea, lies in the fact that there are in the O. T. certain passages which taken by themselves and strictly interpreted are expressive of pure legalism. The apostle might perhaps have challenged the strictly legalistic interpretation of such passages as Deut. 27²⁶, which he quotes in Gal. 3¹⁰: "Cursed is everyone who continueth not in all the things that are written in the book of the law to do them." He chose rather, admitting and even insisting upon the strictly legalistic meaning of these passages, to take, in effect, the position that such legalism was but one element of the revelation of the divine will, citing against it the Abrahamic covenant (Gal. 3¹⁵ff·) and the utterance of prophecy (Gal. 3¹²) and the psalmist (Rom. 4⁶ff·).

Used with the article (occasionally with other defining qualifications), the word in this sense refers to the legalistic element in the O. T., or to the O. T. or any part of it, looked at as Paul's opponents looked at it, as through and through legalistic. Without the article it is qualitative, designating law as such legalistically understood, usually no doubt with special thought of the legalism of the O. T. or of later Judaism, yet without strict or exclusive reference to these.

That instances of the word in this legalistic sense should occur in close connection with other usages, and that it is sometimes difficult to determine with certainty the meaning in adjacent instances, is not strange, since the entity referred to is in any case in part or in whole the same, and many assertions could be made of law in more than one sense of the word. Espe-cially is it the case that the definite and the qualitative uses occur in close connection. The following list avoids a confusing minuteness of classifica-tion by citing all the examples of the legalistic sense without further sub-division: Acts 13³⁹ Rom. 3²⁰ᵃ, ᵇ 3²¹ᵃ, ²⁸ 4¹³, ¹⁴, ¹⁵ᵃ, ᵇ 5¹³ᵃ, ᵇ, ²⁰ 6¹⁴, ¹⁵ 7⁴, ⁵, ⁶, ⁷ᵃ, ᵇ, ᶜ, ⁸, ⁹, ¹², ¹⁴, ¹⁶ 8²ᵇ, ³ 10⁴, ⁵ 1 Cor. 9²⁰ᵃ, ᵇ, ᶜ, ᵈ (cf. also ἄνομος in v.²¹) 15⁵⁶ Gal. 2¹⁶ᵃ, ᵇ, ᶜ, ¹⁹ᵃ, ᵇ, ²¹ 3², ⁵, ¹⁰ᵃ, ᵇ, ¹¹, ¹², ¹³, ¹⁷, ¹⁸, ¹⁹, ²¹ᵃ, ᵇ, ᶜ, ²³, ²⁴ 4⁴, ⁵, ²¹ᵃ, ᵇ 5², ⁴, ¹⁸ Eph. 2¹⁵ Phil. 3⁵, ⁶, ⁹ 1 Tim. 1⁸, ⁹. Of this list a few examples will suf-fice to illustrate the usage: Gal. 3¹⁰: ὅσοι γὰρ ἐξ ἔργων νόμου εἰσὶν ὑπὸ κατάραν εἰσίν. 3¹¹: ὅτι ἐν νόμῳ οὐδεὶς δικαιοῦται παρὰ τῷ θεῷ δῆλον. Rom. 3²¹: νυνὶ δὲ χωρὶς νόμου δικαιοσύνη θεοῦ πεφανέρωται. 10⁴: τέλος γὰρ νόμου Χριστὸς εἰς δικαιοσύνην παντὶ τῷ πιστεύοντι.

But as pointed out above, p. 448, the legalistic use of νόμος is for the apostle Paul a case of adaptation, and the meaning which is congenial to his own thought is almost the exact opposite viz.:

(d) Divine law conceived of as reduced to the ethical principle which constitutes its permanent element and essential demand, the perception of which deprives the statutes as such of authority—law as centralised and summed up in love.*

---

* Conformity to this principle fulfils law, but even this is, in Paul's view, the result not of obedience to it in a strict and legal sense of the word "obedience," but of an impulse and

This use of the word is by no means exclusively Pauline. It is found also in the gospels and in Jas. When the reference is to the O. T. law looked at as embodying the great ethical principle, to which it is indeed reducible, or to the law of God inclusively viewed, without reference to the mode of its expression, the word is used with the article. When the law is qualitatively viewed, the word is without the article.

This is clearly the sense of ὁ νόμος in Mt. 7¹²: οὗτος γάρ ἐστιν ὁ νόμος καὶ οἱ προφῆται. The addition of the words καὶ οἱ προφῆται makes it evident that it is the law of God as expressed in O. T. that is specially in mind. See also Mt. 22⁴⁰. Not less certainly is this the meaning in Mt. 5¹⁷, ¹⁸ Lk. 16¹⁷, if these words come from Jesus, since it is beyond question clear that Jesus regarded many statutes of the law as invalid or no longer valid, and only the central ethical principle of the law as of perpetual force. Gal. 5¹⁴, ὁ γὰρ πᾶς νόμος ἐν ἑνὶ λόγῳ πεπλήρωται, ἐν τῷ Ἀγαπήσεις τὸν πλησίον σου ὡς σεαυτόν, and Rom. 13⁸, ¹⁰ are clear vouchers for this usage in Paul, and clear expressions of his view of the fundamental meaning of the law. In both cases it is the law of God with special reference to its expression in O. T. that is in mind. It is difficult to say with certainty whether Rom. 7²², ²³ᵇ, ²⁵ᵃ Gal. 5²³ 6² should be classed here or regarded as examples of the more general sense indicated under (b). Here also belong probably all of the instances in Jas.: 1²⁵ 2⁸, ⁹, ¹⁰, ¹¹, ¹² 4¹¹.*

3. By a metonymy due to the prominence given by the Jews to the law of O. T. ὁ νόμος designates the books that contain the law even when they are thought of without special reference to the law which they contain, but simply as scripture. Hence ὁ νόμος [καὶ οἱ προφῆται] becomes a name either for the books of Moses or for the scriptures in general without restriction either to the books of Moses or to the mandatory portions of other books: Lk. 24⁴⁴ Jn. 1⁴⁵ 10³⁴ 12³⁴ 15²⁵ Acts 13¹⁵ 24¹⁴ 28²³ Rom. 3²¹ᵇ.

4. By elimination of the idea of the divine authority of law, which indeed is not intrinsic in the word, but an acquired element of its meaning as usually employed in both O. T. and N. T., νόμος comes to mean law as such without reference to its source or authority. The thing actually spoken of may be Jewish or Roman law, or law without discrimination, but in any case without thought of its character as divine or human. It may be spoken of generically or definitely with the article, or qualitatively or

---

power from within, begotten and maintained by the Spirit, by the indwelling Christ. But this element of the apostle's thought does not strictly belong to his idea of law. Strictly defined, law as here conceived is the will of God comprehended in a single principle. That the principle is love, and that fulfilment of it is achieved by the indwelling Spirit rather than by "obedience" are both synthetic, not analytic judgments.

* In Jas. 2¹⁰, ¹¹, while mentioning specific commands, the author as clearly affirms the unity of the whole law and in v.⁸ finds this unity in the principle of love. By his characterisation of the law in 1²⁵ 2¹² as a law of liberty he emphasises the principle that the law is not only centralised in one principle but even so must address itself not to the man from without but be operative from within, being written on the heart.

indefinitely without it: Jn. 7⁵¹ 8¹⁷ 18³¹ 19⁷ᵃ, ᵇ Acts 18¹⁵ 23²⁹ 25⁸ Rom. 7¹ᵃ, ᵇ 7²ᵃ
1 Tim. 1⁹.

5. By metonymy, a force or tendency which, tending to produce action of a certain kind, has the effect of law, may itself be called νόμος: Rom. 7²¹, ²³ᵃ, ᶜ, ²⁵ᵇ 8²ᵃ.*

XV. ΔΙΚΑΙΟΣ, ΔΙΚΑΙΟΣΥΝΗ, AND ΔΙΚΑΙΟΩ.

Few words of the N. T. vocabulary have been more frequently or more thoroughly discussed than those of this group. There remains little ground for dispute concerning their fundamental meaning. Yet on some points of great importance for the understanding of this epistle and the Pauline thought in general interpreters are not wholly agreed. It seems necessary, therefore, to undertake a fresh investigation of the whole subject.†

I. CLASSICAL USAGE.

A. Δίκαιος is fundamentally a forensic or court term in the sense that it denotes conformity to a standard or norm (δίκη) not conceived of as defined in the word itself. It differs thus from ἀγαθός and καλός, which, so to speak, contain within themselves their own norm. δίκη being primarily established custom, conceived of as the norm for human conduct (chiefly for the conduct of men towards one another), is nevertheless a norm to which men are bound to conform. δίκαιος is accordingly as applied to men and their actions a moral term, and means, "conforming to that which is required, to what is right in relation to others." ὁ δίκαιος is the man whose action is according to δίκη; he does what is right; he renders to

---

* It might seem that τοῦ νόμου τῆς ἁμαρτίας καὶ τοῦ θανάτου of Rom. 8²ᵇ must by the connection and the similarity of phraseology refer back to νόμῳ ἁμαρτίας in Rom. 7²⁵, and so be assigned here instead of to 2 (c); or else 7²⁵ and with it 7²¹, ²³ᵃ, ᶜ, be assigned to 2 (c). It is undoubtedly true that the fuller phrase in 8²ᵇ does refer to the shorter one in 7²⁵; but a careful study of the passage will lead to the conclusion that this reference does not involve identification of the things referred to. Speaking in 7²¹, ²³, ²⁵ of that force for evil which in v.¹⁷ and ²⁰ he calls ἁμαρτία, and designating it as a νόμος because it stands opposed to the νόμος τοῦ θεοῦ (vv.²¹, ²²), with such a turn of words as the apostle delights in he substitutes for it in 8²ᵇ its companion in bringing failure and defeat, the law in its legalistic sense. If, as is possible, we take τοῦ νόμου τῆς ἁμαρτίας καὶ τοῦ θανάτου as designating the same thing spoken of in 7²ᵇ, then the change in the reference of νόμος will come in between vv.¹ and ²; for τοῦ νομου in v.² must evidently mean the law in the proper sense of the term, that which is spoken of in the first part of chap. 7.

† Of the abundant literature the following monographs and articles may be cited: Kautzsch, *Die Derivate des Stammes* צדק *im alttest. Sprachgebrauch.* Tübingen, 1881; Cremer, *Biblisch-theologisches Wörterbuch der neutest. Gräcität*¹⁰, pp. 296–330; Morison, *Critical Exposition of the Third Chapter of . . . Romans*, pp. 163–207; Stevens, Wm. A., "On the Forensic Meaning of Δικαιοσύνη," in *AJT*. 1897, pp. 443–450; Davies, "The Righteousness of God in St. Paul," in *JThSt.* II 198–206; Drummond, Jas., "On the Meaning of 'Righteousness of God' in the Theology of St. Paul," in *Hibbert Journal*, 1902–3, pp. 83–95; Ropes, "Righteousness and 'the Righteousness of God' in the O. T. and in St. Paul," in *JBL.* 1903, Pt. II, pp. 211–227; Skinner, art. "Righteousness" (O. T.) in *HDB.*; Stevens, Geo. B. art. "Righteousness" (N. T.) in *HDB.*; Addis, art. "Righteousness" in *Encyc. Bib.*; Sanday and Headlam, *The Epistle to the Romans*, pp. 24–39.

others their rights; he exacts also his own. The word is thus employed either in the broad sense, "right" (Hom. *Od.* XVIII 413; Bacchyl. 10 [11], 123; Thuc. 3. 40³; Plato, *Gorg.* 507B; Aristot. *Eth. Nic.* 5. 1¹ᶠ· [1129 a³· ⁷]), or in the more specific sense, " just " (Hes. *Op.* 270 *ff.*; Hero(n)das 2⁸⁶: γνώμη δικαίᾳ κρίσιν διαιτᾶτε. Dem. 12¹), rendering to each what he has the right to claim. τὸ δίκαιον signifies, " that which is right (in general) " (Hdt. 1³⁹ 7¹³⁷; Æsch. *Prom.* 187; Aristot. *Eth. Nic.* 5. 1¹[1129 a⁵]) or " that which is due from one man to another " (Thuc. 3.54¹; Dem. 572¹⁴), and this either as one's duty, one's rights, or one's (penal) deserts. Though in the older Greek literature (Hom. *Od.* VI 120) to be δίκαιος included also the discharge of obligations to the gods and τὸ δίκαιον was conceived of as having the sanction of divine authority, yet especially in the later classical writers its predominant reference is to the mutual relations of men, and the conception of divine sanction is by no means constantly present. Least of all are the gods themselves spoken of as δίκαιοι or their conduct and character conceived of as the standard of human conduct. Though δίκαιος is frequently used in a non-moral sense even here there is usually a reference to a standard outside the thing itself, or a demand requiring to be satisfied, as when the word means, " exact " (applied to numbers), fitting, suitable, genuine (Hdt. 2¹⁴⁹; Xen. *Mem.* 4. 4⁵; Æsch. *Ag.* 1604; Luc. *Hist. conscr.* 39).

B. Δικαιοσύνη is: 1. The character of the δίκαιος, and that usually in the narrower sense of justice: Hdt. 1⁹⁶ 7⁵²; Aristot. *Rhet.* 1. 9⁷ (1366 b⁹): ἔστι δὲ δικαιοσύνη μὲν ἀρετὴ δι' ἣν τὰ αὑτῶν ἕκαστοι ἔχουσι, καὶ ὡς ὁ νόμος, ἀδικία δὲ δι' ἣν τὰ ἀλλότρια, οὐχ ὡς ὁ νόμος. But *cf. Eth. N.* 5. 1¹⁴ (1129 b²⁵ᶠᶠ·). 2. The business of a judge: Plato, *Gorg.* 464B, C.

C. Δικαιόω is used in two chief senses: 1. To deem right, to think fit, etc.: Hdt. 1⁸⁹; Thuc. 1. 140¹; Soph. *Ph.* 781. 2. To do one justice, and chiefly *in malam partem*, to condemn, to punish: Thuc. 3. 40⁴; Plut. *Cat. Maj.* 21⁴; Dion. Cass. 48. 46⁴; Polyb. 3. 31⁹. Cremer (p. 319) in an approximately exhaustive examination of the usage of the word in classical and other non-biblical Greek writers found no instance of the use of the term with a personal object in the sense "to make righteous."

II. HEBREW USAGE OF צֶדֶק AND ITS COGNATES.

Like the Greek δίκαιος the Hebrew words from the root צדק are (so far as the evidence enables us to judge) fundamentally forensic in sense, expressing agreement with a standard or norm, not conceived of as defined in the word itself. Whether when the term first passed from the presumably original physical sense (of which, however, there is no clear trace in extant Hebrew usage), the norm was conceived to be furnished by the objective standard of the object itself, or by the idea of God or of man (Kautzsch), or as seems more probable by the demand of the circumstances of a given case (Cremer) does not materially affect the meaning of the word as used in O. T. Actual extant usage may be classified as follows:

A. צֶדֶק signifies:

1. Conformity to an existing standard, which though conventionally established creates an obligation to conform to it: Lev. 19³⁶; Deut. 25¹⁵, etc.

2. Righteousness, action which is what it ought to be, and this in any degree, whether conceived of as absolutely such as it ought to be, or approximately so, or spoken of qualitatively without reference to the degree of conformity: Ps. 18²⁴ 45⁷ Eccl. 3¹⁶ 7¹⁵ Isa. 1²¹ 32¹ 59⁴, etc.

3. Righteousness in relation to others, justice, the rendering to each of that which is due, either that which he has the right to claim, or that which he deserves; esp. justice in judging: Lev. 19¹⁵ Deut. 1¹⁶ Job 31⁶ Eccl. 5⁷ Isa. 11⁴ Jer. 11²⁰.

4. Specifically of God's righteousness in distinguishing between the righteous and the wicked, rendering punishment to the latter and giving deliverance to the former. The conception underlying this use of the term is that a righteous God must distinguish in his dealings between the wicked man, who neither fears God nor deals justly with men, and the righteous man, who though he be not perfect but is indeed often confessedly a sinner, yet relatively speaking lives uprightly and trusts in God. The righteousness of God in this aspect of it involving the deliverance of the upright is often spoken of in parallelism with salvation, but without losing sight of the basis of such salvation in the discriminating righteousness of God: Ps. 7¹⁷ 35²⁴⁻²⁸ Isa. 41¹⁰ 42⁶ 45⁸ᵃ, ¹³ 51⁵. With the same underlying conception the righteousness of the ones that are saved is spoken of: Isa. 62¹, ²; yet here, also, without converting צֶדֶק into a mere synonym for salvation. The uprightness of the people, their loyalty to God is still expressed in the term.*

B. צְדָקָה is used with substantially the same range of meaning as צֶדֶק, only lacking instances of the first sense. The second usage, 2, is llustrated in Deut. 6²⁵ 9⁴ 2 Sam. 22²¹, etc. In Gen. 15⁶ there is obvious reference to the requirement of God, and צ signifies that conduct or attitude of mind which God desires, and which renders man acceptable to him. The forensic sense of the term is, therefore, especially clear here, throwing into the background the usual moral content of the term. Usage 3 is illustrated in Jer. 22³ Ezek. 45⁹; usage 4 in Ps. 36⁷ (⁶), ¹¹ (¹⁰) 51¹⁶ (¹⁴) Isa. 45⁸ᵇ 51⁶, ⁸ 56¹ Mic. 7⁹. For its application to the saved see Isa. 48¹⁸ 54¹⁷. In one passage only is the term used, with an apparent forgetfulness of the

* Ropes, *JBL.* 1903, Pt. II, p. 219, holds that in Second Isaiah the ground of the vindication of Israel, by virtue of which the righteousness of God is salvation, is not in Israel's character or suffering, but lies rather in Jahweh himself, who for his own name has redeemed his servant whom he knew, chose, and loved." Ropes calls this a profounder view than that of the psalmists, which finds the basis in the moral excellence and conscious piety of the worshipper. This is partly true respecting Isa., but only partly, and it is not the view which controls Paul, as Rom., chaps. 1, 2, show; Rom. 8³⁰ is apparently the nearest approximation to an expression of it.

conception of discriminating righteousness, to denote acceptance by God and consequent deliverance (Ps. 69²⁷). There are also a few passages in which it is apparently used of a just cause, a being in the right in a given case. *Cf* 1. under צָדִיק and see 1 Ki. 8³² 2 Chr. 6²³.

C. צָדִיק (applied to persons only, except in Deut. 4⁸) signifies:

1. With a formal and purely forensic rather than moral sense, in the right in a particular case or in an assertion: Ex. 23⁸ Prov. 18¹⁷ Isa. 41²⁶. Yet this sense can not always be sharply distinguished from 3 below. See Deut. 25¹ Prov. 17¹⁵, ²⁶ 18⁵.

2. Innocent, free from guilt in a particular matter: Gen. 20⁴.

3. Righteous, in moral conduct and character, what one ought to be, whether absolutely and perfectly so: Ps. 145¹⁷ Eccl. 7²⁰; or in a more general sense of those who are upright in purpose and life: Gen. 6⁹ Ps. 1⁵ 14⁵ 64¹⁰ Prov. 21²⁶. In Deut. 4⁸ it is applied to the law as inculcating righteousness.

4. Just, rendering to one what is due, especially in punishing the wicked: Ps. 7⁸, ¹⁰ (⁹, ¹¹) Jer. 12¹ Lam. 1¹⁸.

These terms are, therefore, much more distinctly than the corresponding Greek terms, δίκαιος and δικαιοσύνη, religious terms. They are applied to God himself, and though this use is probably not the earliest, it has certainly profoundly affected the terms as applied to men. See Ps. 7⁸, ¹⁰ (⁹, ¹¹) 89¹⁴ 96¹³ 97², ⁶ Jer. 11²⁰ Ezr. 9¹⁵ Hos. 14⁹ Zeph. 3⁵. The righteous man owes duties to God as well as to his fellow men: Ps. 18²⁰⁻²⁴ Isa. 51¹, ⁷; and the obligations of righteousness are imposed by divine authority: Gen. 18¹⁹ Deut. 16¹⁸⁻²⁰ Isa. 5¹⁶ Ps. 119⁷, ⁷⁵, etc. It is a natural result of this difference that the conception of justice, that which one owes to another and which that other can claim, as compared with righteousness, that which is required by morality or divine authority, is much less prominent than in the Greek use of δίκαιος and its cognates. Indeed it is not entirely clear that to the Hebrews the distinction existed at all. Justice is to them perhaps simply righteousness as manifested in particular relations, especially in judging.

D. In צֶדֶק the legal and formal sense which appears in צָדִיק predominates, though not, it would seem, to the entire exclusion of a moral-forensic sense. *Cf.* Kautzsch, *op. cit.* pp. 15–17.

In the Kal conj. it means:

1. To be in the right in a given case or in one's assertion: Gen. 38²⁶ Job 9¹⁵ 33¹².

2. To carry one's case, to prevail: Job 9² 11² 25⁴ 40⁸ Ps. 143² Isa. 43⁹, ²⁶.

3. To be righteous, צָדִיק in the moral sense (this use Cremer denies): Job 35⁷ Ps. 19¹⁰ (⁹).

The Niphal occurs in Dan. 8¹⁴ only, where it means, to be put to rights, to be made such as it should be.

The Piel means, to declare or show one in the right (Job 32² 33³²), to show one, or cause one to appear, righteous, but relatively, not absolutely: Jer. 3¹¹ Ezek. 16⁵¹, ⁵².

In the Hiphil the meanings are:

1. To do one justice: 2 Sam. 15⁴ Ps. 82³.

2. To declare one to be in the right, to cause one to carry one's case, to give judgment for one; when used of one accused, it means to acquit: Ex. 23⁷ Deut. 25¹ 1 Ki. 8³² 2 Chr. 6²³ Job. 27⁵ Prov. 17¹⁵ Isa. 5²³ 50⁸.

3. To give one standing, to cause one to be accepted: Isa. 53¹¹ Dan. 12³. While it can not perhaps be categorically denied that in these two passages the Hiphil is a moral-causative term, meaning "to make righteous" (the Lxx read ἀπὸ τῶν δικαίων τῶν πολλῶν, which suggests a different Heb. txt.), yet in view of the prevailingly forensic sense of the term and the fact that it is at least possibly applicable to these passages, there seems no sufficient ground for taking it here in a purely causative sense.

In the Hithpael the meaning is, to clear one's self, to cause one's self to appear in the right: Gen. 44¹⁶.

III.   USAGE OF THE SEPTUAGINT.

In the Lxx the terms δίκαιος, δικαιοσύνη, and δικαιόω stand as the regular representatives of צַדִּיק, צֶ֫דֶק. צְדָקָה, and צָדַק, and though other Hebrew words are occasionally rendered by δίκαιος, etc., and words of the צדק group are sometimes rendered by other Greek words than δίκαιος, etc., the correspondence is nevertheless very close.*

A. Δίκαιος. The analysis given above for צַדִּיק may stand for δίκαιος save that there must be added as a meaning applied to things (weights and measures), conforming to the accepted standard (cf. צֶ֫דֶק, 1), and as a meaning of the neuter, generally used substantively (representing צֶ֫דֶק. מִשְׁפָּט, etc.) right, just, that which is one's due, justice: Deut. 16²⁰ Prov. 18⁵ 29²⁶.

B. Δικαιοσύνη. The analysis of צְדָקָה may stand for δικαιοσύνη, the usage 1 under צֶ֫דֶק disappearing through the use of δίκαιος to represent it in the passages which belong there.

C. Δικαιόω is used to render צָדַק, the Piel and Hiphil of the latter corresponding to the active of the former, and the Kal to the passive (or to δίκαιός εἰμι, or δίκαιος φαίνομαι). In all the examples cited under II D above, except Dan. 8¹⁴, the Hebrew word is represented in the Lxx by some word of the δίκαιος group.

IV.   USAGE OF THE APOCRYPHA AND PSEUDEPIGRAPHA.

A. Δίκαιος. In the Apocryphal books δίκαιος is used as in the Lxx except that there are apparently no examples of the meanings, "in the right" (unless in Susan. 53), "innocent." The meaning, "righteous," applied both to persons, God and men, and to actions, occurs in Tob. 3² 14⁹

---

* On the noteworthy exceptions, cf. Ryle and James, *The Psalms of Solomon*, note on 16¹⁵; Hatch, *Essays in Biblical Greek*, pp. 49 f.

Wisd. 2¹⁰ 3¹ Sir. 10²⁸ 2 Mac. 9¹²; the meaning "just," applied to God in Wisd. 12¹⁵, to men in Tob. 14⁹ (?); to judgment in 2 Mac. 9¹⁸. The use of the neuter in the sense "just," that which is right, one's rights, or one's (penal) deserts is specially frequent; 1 Mac. 7¹² 11³³ 2 Mac. 11¹⁴ 13²² Wisd. 14³⁰.

In Ps. Sol. δίκαιος applied to men designates the upright who in general are on God's side, and who are approved of God; they are not the sinless, but like the צַדִּיקִים of the prophets those who observe the law of God, and trust in him as distinguished from the sinner: 2³⁸ 3⁴⁻⁸ 9⁴ 15⁸, etc. This is its use, also, in the Ethiopic Enoch so far as the Greek text is extant: 1¹, ², ⁸ 10¹⁷ 22⁹ 25⁴ 27³ (Giz) 10³ (Syn). The word is not used of God in Enoch; in Ps. Sol. it is applied to God and his judgments to designate him as righteously discriminating between the righteous and the sinner (2¹², ¹⁹, ³⁶; cf. v.³⁸; 5¹ 8⁸ 9⁴ 10⁶), and to the Messiah in a similar sense (17³⁵).

B. Δικαιοσύνη in the Apocryphal books has all the usages of the same word in the Lxx, except that there are no perfectly clear instances of the meaning, "justice." Possible instances are 1 Mac. 2²⁹ Wisd. 9³ Sir. 45²⁶. When used in the sense of (human) "right conduct" it is with an even clearer implication than is common in the canonical books that it is righteousness which makes men acceptable to God, and this righteousness is conceived of in a more external, legalistic way than in the prophets: Tob. 12⁹ 14¹¹ Wisd. 1¹⁵. There are clear instances of the term applied to God to denote his righteousness in discriminating between the righteous and the wicked among men, whether in punishing the wicked or in saving the righteous: Wisd. 5¹⁸ 12¹⁶ Sir. 16²² Bar. 1¹⁵ 2⁶, ¹⁸.* It is worthy of notice that in the book of Wisdom, also, and in 1 Mac. the term is used with such special emphasis upon the conception that righteousness (i. e. of men) is the basis of acceptance with God and consequent salvation as to be almost the equivalent of "acceptance with God," "condition of salvation": Wisd. 14⁷ 15² 1 Mac. 2⁵². Specially significant is Wisd. 15²: τὸ γὰρ ἐπίστασθαί σε ὁλόκληρος δικαιοσύνη, καὶ εἰδέναι σου τὸ κράτος ῥίζα ἀθανασίας, in which the author endeavours to sum up in one act or moral attitude the content of righteousness, that which makes one acceptable to God and secures immortality. He differs from Tob. and from Gen. 15⁶ in his conception of what constitutes righteousness, but not in his definition of the concept itself. To the prophets generally, it is right living towards God and men that makes men acceptable to God; to Tob. right living, especially almsgiving; to the writer of Gen. 15⁶ it is faith; to the author of Wisd. 15² knowledge of God. But to all of them that which makes men acceptable to God is by virtue of that fact righteousness, δικαιοσύνη. In Ps. Sol. δικαιοσύνη is used in two senses corresponding to those of δίκαιος. The

---

* In chaps. 4, 5 of Bar. a "righteousness which comes from God" is spoken of, reminding one of Isa. 54¹⁷ Rom. 3²¹ and esp. Phil. 3⁹. But the post-Christian date of these portions of Bar. must be borne in mind.

righteousness of men is their good conduct which makes them acceptable to God and the objects of his salvation: 1² 5²⁰ 9⁹ 14¹. The righteousness of God is manifest in his discrimination between the righteous and the wicked, not indeed in punishing without mercy all wrong-doing, but in saving the saints, the δίκαιοι, and in punishing the sinner: 2¹⁶, Ps. 8 and 9. Of the same nature is the righteousness of the Messiah, 17²⁸, ³¹, ⁴², ⁴⁵, though including, also, personal freedom from sin: 17⁴¹. The usage of Enoch corresponds to the first of the two senses just named: 10¹⁶, ¹⁸ 12⁴ 13¹⁰ 14¹ 32³.

C. Δικαιόω is used in Tob. in the passive with the sense, " to be rightly assigned, to belong." In Sir. it means: (1) " to do justice to," and this with reference to the sinner in the sense, " to punish": Sir. 42²; (2) " to recognise or declare to be right or righteous," δίκαιος; Sir. 7⁵ 10²⁹ 13²². It occurs most frequently in the passive: Sir. 18²; and of sinners, in the sense, " to be acquitted, to be declared innocent": Sir. 9¹² 23¹¹ 26²⁹ 34 (31)⁵; once in the sense " to be accepted " (of God), apparently with the idea of forgiveness rather than acquittal, yet not with exclusive reference to the negative side. δίκαιόω does not appear in the book of Enoch. In Ps. Sol. it is used exclusively in the sense, " to recognise as just or righteous," and with reference to men's recognition of the righteousness of God and his judgments: 2¹⁶ 3³, ⁵ 4⁹ 8⁷, ²⁷, ³¹ 9³. It occurs twice in Test. XII Patr.: in Sim. 6¹ in the sense, " to acquit "; in Dan. 3³, meaning, " to justify, to deem right."

V. SUMMARY OF PRE-CHRISTIAN USAGE.

From this general survey of Greek and Hebrew usage certain facts appear which may properly be summarised before taking up N. T. usage.

1. Both the Greek and Hebrew words, and all the terms of each group are in general, and in Jewish usage with increasing clearness, forensic terms, in the sense that they imply a comparison with some standard; the verb in particular in a large proportion of cases expressing a judgment concerning such conformity, not signifying the bringing of a person or thing into it.

2. In Hebrew usage and the Greek usage of Semitic writers the terms are prevailingly moral as well as forensic; i. e., the standard is ethical, not merely conventional or legal. The acts by virtue of which a man is esteemed righteous are acts which are conceived of as having moral character. The terms are therefore prevailingly moral-forensic. Formally defined, righteousness is that which conforms to the true or recognised standard of conduct or meets the divine demand. Materially defined, it consists in certain acts or in a certain moral state believed to be good.

3. Alike in respect to its formal definition and in respect to the material content of the conception there is a variation in different periods and among various writers. (a) There is great difference in the clearness with which the standard is conceived of as being set by God, or divinely sanctioned. Among the Greeks this sense of divine requirement was in general feeble.

In O. T. צֶדֶק sometimes denotes conformity to a standard primarily conventional, and only secondarily fixed by divine authority. In many other cases the conception of a divine sanction, though probably not wholly absent, is thrown into the shade by emphasis upon the material content of righteousness. In other cases, however, in O. T. and later Jewish writings, notably such as Gen. 15⁶ Job 9² Deut. 6²⁵ 24¹³ Ps. 71² Wisd. 15³ Tob. 13⁶ Ps. Sol. 1², the conception of righteousness as required by God and as constituting the ground of acceptance with him is clearly present, so that the term approaches the formal sense, "acceptance with God." In general, it is clear that in the latter part of the pre-Christian period, at least, the conception of divine requirement is always included in that of righteousness, and δικαιοσύνη used in reference to men signifies either that conduct and character which satisfy God's requirement and make one acceptable to him, or more abstractly, acceptance with him. (b) In respect, also, to the material content of righteousness conceptions vary. The Greek definition of the content of δικαιοσύνη would differ greatly from the Hebrew, the former, e. g., emphasising justice more than the latter. Among the Hebrews, also, there is no little variation; sometimes the emphasis is laid on right, equitable conduct towards men, sometimes on mercy and almsgiving, sometimes on the strict observance of rites and ceremonies, sometimes on a trustful, reverential attitude towards God. This variation simply reflects the difference in the conceptions of what was required by God and acceptable to him, as held in different ages and by different men.

4. The Jews (it was otherwise with the Greeks) prevailingly ascribed righteousness to God, both in the general sense that he did what was right, and specifically in the sense that he discriminated, in his attitude towards men and in his dealing with them, between the righteous and the wicked. Moreover, while freely recognising the sinfulness of "the righteous," they did, in fact—this is specially true of the writers of Isa. 40–66, many of the canonical Psalms, such as Ps. 65, 71, 85, and 143, and of Ps. Sol.— rely not alone on the mercy of God for salvation, but on his righteousness. So far is this appeal to God's righteousness carried that in numerous passages in Isa. 40–66 and the Psalms, God's righteousness, sometimes even the righteousness of the saints, is equivalent in the content of the thing referred to (not in the definition of the conception itself) to salvation. In Ps. 71² "thy righteousness" apparently signifies, "acceptance with thee and consequent salvation by thee." This usage of the *word* does not appear in the latest pre-Christian books; but the conception of divine and human righteousness which underlies it is unmistakably present and strongly predominant.

5. With rare and doubtful exceptions the verbs δικαιόω and צָדַק are not moral-causative but judicial and forensic in force. It is especially clear that in Jewish-Greek usage δικαιόω is purely, or all but purely, a moral-forensic term (note the usage of the Apocr. and of Ps. Sol.), being

used prevailingly in the sense "to recognise or declare as δίκαιος" either positively, "to recognise as righteous" (Sir. 18², Ps. Sol. *u. s.* IV C), or in the negative and restricted sense, "to acquit" (Sir. 23¹⁴ 26²⁹), or in a more general sense, "to accept," with the implication of forgiveness (Sir. 18²²).

VI. NEW TESTAMENT USAGE.

A. Δίκαιος in N. T. is clearly a moral-forensic term, meaning, in general, conforming to the true standard, meeting the ethical requirements under which one is placed. In the main it follows closely the usage of the Lxx and later Jewish writings, but as applied to men emphasises even more than O. T. the conception of divine requirement, fulfilment of which renders one acceptable to God, and as applied to God has even more exclusive reference to the righteousness of his dealings with men. *Cf.* the usage of Ps. Sol. Its uses may be classified as follows:

1. (a) Of persons: Upright, righteous in conduct or purpose, satisfying the ethical requirements of God and so acceptable to him. Usually employed qualitatively without reference to the degree of conformity to the standard, or denoting approximate conformity: Mt. 5⁴⁵ 10⁴¹ 13¹⁷, ⁴³, ⁴⁹ 23²⁸, ²⁹ 25³⁷, ⁴⁶ Lk. 1⁶, ¹⁷ 2²⁵ 14¹⁴ 15⁷ 18⁹ 20²⁰ 23⁵⁰ Acts 10²² 24¹⁵ Rom. 5⁷ 1 Tim. 1⁹ Heb. 10³⁸ 12²³ Jas. 5¹⁶ 1 Pet. 3¹² 4¹⁸ 2 Pet. 2⁷, ⁸ Rev. 22¹¹. In Mt. 9¹³ Mk. 2¹⁷ Lk. 5³² Acts 3¹⁴ 7⁵² 22¹⁴ Rom. 3¹⁰ Jas. 5⁶ 1 Pet 3¹⁸ 1 Jn. 2¹ 3⁷ᵇ the righteousness referred to is evidently conceived of as perfect, fully satisfying the divine requirement. In Mt. 23³⁵ 27¹⁹ Lk. 23⁴⁷, the negative element, innocence, is emphasised.

(b) Of action: Right, such as it ought to be, conforming to the moral requirement of God: Lk. 12⁵⁷ Acts 4¹⁹ Eph. 6¹ Phil. 1⁷ 2 Pet. 1¹³. In Rom. 7¹² the commandment of God is spoken of as δίκαιος, *i. e.*, requiring what is right. In 1 Jn. 3¹² the works of Abel are said to be righteous, apparently emphasising their acceptableness to God.

2. In the cases named above there is a varying emphasis upon the forensic element, acceptable to God, neither the moral nor the forensic element being wholly absent, but the former predominating. In certain other passages the forensic element so clearly predominates that the term approximates or even reaches the sense, acceptable to God, yet always with the implication that such acceptance rests upon some fact of moral significance. Rom. 1¹⁷ 2¹³ 5¹⁹ Gal. 3¹¹ Heb. 11⁴ 1 Jn. 3⁷ᵃ.

3. Righteous, satisfying the requirements of a true ethical standard in dealing with others. Used in this sense especially of God, not, however, as rendering to each his deserts without mercy,* but as discriminating between righteous and wicked, and treating each in accordance with his character: Jn. 17²⁵ Rom. 3²⁶ 2 Tim. 4⁸ 1 Jn. 1⁹ Rev. 16⁵; with a like meaning used of God's judgments: 2 Thes. 1⁵, ⁶ Rev. 15³ 16⁷ 19²; of the judgment of

---

* It is worthy of notice that neither in O. T. nor in N. T. is righteousness conceived of as excluding mercy; it forbids treating a man worse than he deserves but not better.

Christ: Jn. 5³⁰; and of men, in the sense, right in discriminating according to the facts: Jn. 7²⁴; of the action of men affecting others, it means, right, that which one ought to do in relation to others: Mt. 20⁴ Phil. 4⁸ Col. 4¹. In these three passages it is possible that δίκαιος means, just, i. e., what others have a right to claim. But there is no clear evidence that δίκαιος ever has this sense in biblical Greek. The meaning as given above is therefore more probable.

B. The usage of δικαιοσύνη corresponds quite closely to that of δίκαιος, the word denoting, in general, the character or position of one who is δίκαιος. Neither the moral nor the forensic element can be lost sight of.

1. Conduct and character which satisfy the ethical requirements of God, and so render one acceptable to him. As in the case of δίκαιος, so the noun also may be used simply qualitatively, or with reference to an approximate conformity, or of an ideal, perfect fulfilment of divine requirements: Mt. 3¹⁵ 5⁶, ¹⁰, ²⁰ 6¹, ³³ (?) 21³² Lk. 1⁷⁵ Jn. 16⁸, ¹⁰ Acts 10³⁵ 13¹⁰ 24²⁵ Rom. 6¹³, ¹⁶, ¹⁸, ¹⁹, ²⁰ 8¹⁰ 10⁵ 14¹⁷ 2 Cor. 6⁷, ¹⁴ 9⁹, ¹⁰ 11¹⁵ Eph. 4²⁴ 5⁹ 6¹⁴ Phil. 1¹¹ 1 Tim. 6¹¹ 2 Tim. 3¹⁶ Tit. 3⁵ Heb. 1⁹ 5¹³ 7² 11³³ 12¹¹ Jas. 1²⁰ 3¹⁸ 1 Pet. 2²⁴ 3¹⁴ 2 Pet. 2⁵, ²¹ 3¹³ 1 Jn. 2²⁹ 3⁷, ¹⁰ Rev. 22¹¹.

2. Acceptance with God. With a stronger emphasis upon the forensic element, δικαιοσύνη sometimes approaches or even reaches the sense, acceptance with God, or ground of acceptance with God. The question at issue between Paul and his opponents was in what way or on what ground men became acceptable to God, he maintaining that it was faith that rendered men acceptable to God, they that it was certain inheritances and deeds comprehended under the term, " works of law," or "law." This discussion gave rise to such terms as "righteousness by faith," and "righteousness by law," in which just by reason of the fact that the question at issue was what made men acceptable to God, the term "righteousness" was necessarily without emphasis on this or that condition of acceptance. In another direction, also, the emphasis on the forensic element modified in some cases the meaning of the term. In Jewish thought acceptance with God involved for one who has sinned provision respecting the sins of the past. And since, according to Paul, "all have sinned and are destitute of the divine approval," forgiveness is included in righteousness, either distinctly and explicitly, or by implication. Thus the present sense differs from the preceding in two respects, viz., in that the term itself lays less emphasis on the conduct and character which form the basis of acceptance with God, and that it more distinctly includes forgiveness. Rom. 4³, ⁵, ⁶, ⁹, ¹¹, ¹³, ²² 5¹⁷, ²¹ 9³⁰, ³¹ 10⁴, ⁶, ¹⁰ 1 Cor. 1³⁰ Gal. 2²¹ 3⁶, ²¹ 2 Tim. 4⁸ Jas. 2²³ Heb. 11⁷. On Gal. 5⁵ and Phil. 3⁹, which may with almost equal propriety be assigned to this or to the preceding class, see below, p. 471.

These passages differ somewhat among themselves in the degree of the emphasis upon the forensic element and of the consequent subordination of the moral element, so much so, indeed, that they might even seem to fall into two distinct classes. Thus, in Rom. 4¹¹, in σφραγίδα τῆς δικαιοσύνης τῆς πίστεως, a seal attesting the fact of acceptance with God through faith, and still more in 5¹⁷, in the expression οἱ τὴν περισσείαν τῆς χάριτος καὶ [τῆς δωρεᾶς] τῆς δικαιοσύνης λαμβάνοντες, it seems clear that the noun is purely forensic, expressing in itself simply the fact of acceptance, πίστεως indicating the ground of acceptance. On the other hand, in Rom. 4⁵: λογίζεται ἡ πίστις αὐτοῦ εἰς δικαιοσύνην (cf. 4³), faith being spoken of as reckoned for, as the equivalent of, righteousness, the latter might be thought to include the conception of right conduct which makes one acceptable to God, not in the sense that πίστις itself constituted such conduct, but in the sense that it was accounted equivalent to such conduct, acceptable in lieu of it, the very point of the expression lying in the fact that faith was accounted equivalent to something that could not be directly predicated of it. On the other hand, it may be maintained that in Rom. 4¹³: οὐ γὰρ διὰ νόμου ἡ ἐπαγγελία . . . ἀλλὰ διὰ δικαιοσύνης πίστεως, πίστεως is most naturally taken as a genitive of description (appositional), and that δικαιοσύνη πίστεως means righteousness which consists in faith; and it may be further contended that this is also the meaning of δικαιοσύνη in vv.³, ⁵, ⁶, ¹², these passages referring not to a crediting of faith as something different from what it really is but a recognition of it as being, in fact, of the quality of righteousness, the moral attitude towards God which God desires and which therefore renders men acceptable to God. In this case, also, we should have a sense of the word δικαιοσύνη in which the moral element would be distinctly present, but the relation between faith and righteousness would be not that of an equivalence for purposes of justification, created by divine fiat, but (qualitative) moral identity. But it is probable that both these views over-emphasise the distinction of meaning among the passages cited above. The conception of value imputed contrary to fact is not involved in the phrases λογισθῆναι εἰς or λογισθῆναί τινι, which simply express the idea that a certain thing is valued at a certain value, or credited to a person, without implication that such valuation or crediting is otherwise than according to the facts. See note on chap. 3⁶. Nor is the notion of value attributed contrary to fact involved in the teaching of Rom. 4¹⁻⁶. For while this passage expressly affirms that God's acceptance of Abraham was not on grounds of merit, ὀφείλημα, that is, not on a commercial, bookkeeping basis, by which God demanded and Abraham rendered a quantitatively complete satisfaction of the divine claims, yet it by no means follows that in evaluating Abraham's faith at righteousness, God reckoned it as something else than it was. It meets the requirements of the passage and it better accords with the apostle's strenuous insistence upon the conformity of God's judgments with reality (Rom. 2¹⁻¹⁶, esp. vv.², ⁶) to suppose that the thought which underlies his language here is that faith is really acceptable to God, qualitatively a satisfaction of his requirements, the attitude towards God which he desires men to sustain.

Yet it does not follow, nor is it on the whole probable, that in these verses Paul means by the *word* δικαιοσύνη right conduct, with the emphasis on the moral element. The atmosphere of the whole passage is so distinctly forensic that it is better to suppose that the word δικαιοσύνη itself is employed in a predominantly forensic sense, meaning, " basis of acceptance with God," and that while there is no implication that the accounting of faith as righteousness involved an element of fiction, yet neither is there any direct reference to the moral quality of faith.* It is the value which God gave to Abraham's faith of which the apostle is speaking; what it was in that faith that warranted such a valuation is not here the prominent thought.

In Phil. 3⁶, ⁹ δικαιοσύνη ἡ ἐν νόμῳ, ἐκ νόμου is such righteousness as is attainable in the sphere of law, and from (obedience to) law. It is, in fact, as the context implies, so insufficient as to be worthless, no true righteousness at all. The moral and forensic elements are so conjoined in this passage that it is difficult to assign the instances decisively to this head or the preceding. The moral—or at least the active—element seems to predominate in v.⁶, the forensic (but without exclusion of the moral) in v.⁹.

In Gal. 5⁵ the use of the words ἐλπίδα and ἀπεκδεχόμεθα show that δικαιοσύνης does not refer to that divine acceptance of the believer of which Paul usually speaks in using the verb δικαιόω, but to something still to be obtained. On the other hand, the use of δικαιοῦσθε in v.⁴ indicates that the term is not employed with an exclusively ethical emphasis, but that, on the contrary, the forensic element is distinctly present. These facts require us to take the term as having reference to that future justification of which Paul speaks in Rom. 2¹³, ¹⁶. Yet inasmuch as such future justification is itself based not on faith, even conceived of as qualitatively righteous, but on the achieved character of the justified person, exclusive emphasis on the forensic element is improbable. The righteousness which is hoped for is ethical-forensic, with the forensic element distinctly but not exclusively in mind, and, by the very fact that it is hoped for, still in the future.

Probably altogether similar is the meaning of τὴν [δικαιοσύνην] διὰ πίστεως Χριστοῦ and τὴν ἐκ θεοῦ δικαιοσύνην ἐπὶ τῇ πίστει of Phil. 3⁹, ¹⁰. These phrases also refer to the future and the context emphasises both ethical and forensic elements in such way as to make it impossible to exclude either from these phrases or to determine with certainty on which the emphasis lies. Concerning Rom. 1¹⁷ 3²¹, ²² 10³, which are closely related to the passages already considered, but yet constitute a group by themselves, see 4 below.

3. Out of the fundamental meaning of the term (1, above) there arises

---

* V.⁷ indicates that in such acceptance of him who believes there is involved forgiveness of past sins. But this, though it confirms the judgment that the apostle's thought is moving on the forensic plane, is, as compared with the idea of positive acceptance, only incidental, not the key to the central point of view of the passage.

through its use in reference to relations to others, the more specific sense: righteousness in dealing with others in accordance with their conduct and character. The term is used in this sense exclusively of God (and Christ). In Acts 7³¹ Rev. 19¹¹, the discrimination between the righteous and the wicked, issuing in the punishment of the latter and the salvation of the former is in mind (cf. also Rom. 2⁵, δικαιοκρισία, and 2 Thes. 1⁵, ⁶). In Rom. 3⁵, ²⁵, ²⁶ the necessity that the righteous God shall manifest his disapproval of sin is emphasised. In 2 Pet. 1¹ δικαιοσύνη τοῦ θεοῦ denot⁻⁻ the impartial righteousness of God manifested in the salvation of Gentiles as well as of Jews.

4. Inasmuch as the way of acceptance with God is prescribed and provided by God (being bestowed not on grounds of merit but on condition of faith), such acceptance with him may be called God's righteousness, δικαιοσύνη θεοῦ, the genitive denoting source: Rom. 1¹⁷ 3²¹, ²² 10³. This usage is most closely related to the O. T. usage in Isa. and Ps. (see exx. under II A 4, also under IV, B). But the thought of Paul, so far as expressed, differs in two respects from that of his predecessors, the prophets and psalmists. (a) While the prophet finds in the righteousness of God, which discriminates between the righteous and the wicked, the basis of salvation for the righteous, and so associates the two that the same term seems at times to express both, or at least to express one with a distinct implication of its basis in the other, Paul rarely so conjoins the divine discriminating righteousness with human salvation. This conception (expressed in N. T. in 1 Jn. 1⁹; cf. 2 Thes. 1⁵, ⁶ Rom. 2⁵) the apostle leaves behind not by denying but simply by ignoring it; to him the divine righteousness is brought under suspicion not so much by failure to save as by a neglect to punish sin (see Rom. 3²⁵, ²⁶ and 3 above). (b) The salvation of men is with Paul grounded in the grace of God. Though affirming that the final judgment of God will be on the basis of conduct and character (Rom. 2¹³⁻¹⁶; cf. Gal. 5⁵ and discussion of it above), and regarding faith as itself satisfying God's fundamental requirement (see B. 2 above, p. 469), he yet clearly maintains that justification is the gracious acceptance of sinners on the ground of faith. These two peculiarities of the Pauline thought, which are evidently but the opposite sides of one fact, find their occasion, or the occasion of their expression, in two related facts: (1) He was opposing the Pharisaic legalism which, being a distortion and corruption of the prophetic doctrine that the righteous God accepts and approves righteous men, could only be met by an emphasis upon the divine grace in salvation which threw quite into the background the conception of the divine righteousness as the basis of salvation. Even when the apostle adopts for a moment the prophetic point of view, emphasising the discriminating righteousness of God (Rom., chap. 2) it is for the sake of insisting that this righteousness will bring about the punishment of impenitent Israel. (2) Closely connected with this is the fact that the apostle held a stricter and

more consistent, though less legalistic, view of sin than did those Pharisees and Pharisaic Christians whose views he was opposing. While recognising with the prophets the discrimination of men into two classes, the righteous and the wicked, and maintaining that God approves and accepts the former, he yet maintained, also, that there were none who, being perfectly righteous, could be accepted on grounds of personal merit. The righteousness of God, therefore, in its purely forensic aspect and apart from grace, could not of itself bring salvation to any. While, therefore, it is a tempting position to take, that δικαιοσύνη θεοῦ in Rom. 1¹⁷, etc., is the personal righteousness of God conceived of as the basis of salvation, as in Isa. 56¹, etc., yet this position is not sustained either by the context of the passages in question or by the general position of Paul concerning the relation of divine righteousness and human salvation, or by the history of the usage of the word in the period between Isaiah and Paul.

C. Δικαιόω in N. T. signifies, to recognise, declare, accept as δίκαιος. It is a moral-forensic term, and this not only in that this is the force of δίκαιος as taken up into the verb, but, also, in that the verb itself (like ἀξιόω and ὁσιόω), is declarative rather than strictly causative. Its various senses are as follows:

1. To recognise or declare one to be (in the proper ethical sense) δίκαιος. (a) Negatively: to declare or to show to be innocent: Lk. 10²⁹ 1 Cor. 4⁴. (b) Positively: to recognise or declare to be right or righteous, such declaration or acceptance involving no element of grace or pardon: Mt. 11¹⁹ Lk. 7²⁹, ³⁵ 16¹⁵ Rom. 3⁴ 1 Tim. 3¹⁶.

2. With a greater emphasis upon the forensic element in the meaning of δίκαιος (acceptable to God), the verb means, to recognise as acceptable (to God), to accept; in the passive, to be accepted (by God). As in the instances of the corresponding sense of δικαιοσύνη, the ground of acceptance is not implied in the word itself and in many passages is the very point under discussion. It is, however, always evident that the term refers to a judgment broadly and fundamentally moral; the underlying sense of δίκαιος is still moral-forensic, not simply legal-forensic save in Rom. 6⁷, where Paul draws an illustration from the purely legal realm. We may recognise six sub-classes of passages in which the word occurs with the sense above indicated: (a) Those in which a positive ground of acceptance is spoken of and this ground is certain deeds or conduct, there being no implication that the justification spoken of involves pardon for sin or grace: Mt. 12³⁷ Rom. 2¹³ Jas. 2²¹, ²⁴, ²⁵. (b) Those in which a positive ground is spoken of, but this ground is either faith or works of law, the latter being declared to be inadequate. In these passages there is no reference to pardon as an element of justification, and the justification is indicated to be an act of grace only by the implication conveyed in ἐκ πίστεως, οὐκ ἐξ ἔργων νόμου, etc. The explicit mention of positive ground of justification in the passages which deny the possibility of justification on the grounds

named, ἔργα νόμου, shows that the term is not merely negative, meaning simply, to pardon: Rom. 3²⁰, ²⁸, ³⁰ 4² 5¹ Gal. 2¹⁶, ¹⁷ 3⁸, ¹¹, ²⁴ 5⁴. (c) Those in which the word is used with no limitation save that of a direct object; the force of the word is apparently the same as in the passages under (b): Rom. 3²⁶ 8³⁰, ³³. (d) In Rom. 3²⁴ 4⁵ 5⁹ 1 Cor. 6¹¹ Tit. 3⁷ there is a distinct recognition that the acceptance referred to involves an element of pardon and grace; those who are accepted not being in personal character δίκαιος, but ἄδικος and ὑπόδικος. It should be observed, however, that in some of the passages under (b) this is only a little more remotely implied, that no sharp line of discrimination can be drawn between the two classes, and that the verb itself retains in both cases the same meaning. (e) In Rom. 6⁷ the context demands the meaning, to declare free or set free, the penalty having been suffered. In this case the unrighteousness of the person is presumed, but there is no element of grace or pardon, the release being based on the suffering of the penalty. Though this instance is quite exceptional, it serves to show how broad is the meaning of the word. In itself it contains no assertion concerning the character of the person, and no implication of pardon. These are conveyed, when conveyed at all, by the context. (f) In two passages, Lk. 18¹⁴ Acts 13³⁹, the emphasis upon the negative element of pardon is so strong as almost to give to the word the meaning, to pardon.* These are instances of a semi-metonymy, by which the term which denotes the whole of the act is used with chief or exclusive reference to a part of it which is involved in every ordinary case of the whole as applied to wrong-doers. The reduction of Paul's term, δικαιόω, to a purely negative sense, "to pardon," is definitely excluded by the evidence. Over against these two passages, neither of them in Paul's epistles, and neither of them quite certainly referring exclusively to pardon, there is the decisive evidence of the passages in which a positive ground of justification, ἔργα νόμου, is mentioned and its adequacy denied. See under (a) above. For the context makes it clear that works of law are thought of as inadequate not to secure the forgiveness of admitted sinners, but to win approval on ground of merit, which would leave no occasion for forgiveness. The argument of Rom. 1¹⁸–3²⁰, as of Gal. 3¹⁰ff. is to the effect, not that men who seek justification on a legalistic basis fail of forgiveness for their sins, but that failing to meet God's requirements, and being held responsible for that failure, they are in need of forgiveness, and must be accepted, if at all, on grounds of grace. Forgiveness is an element of the justification which men obtain through faith, by grace; but is not included in the justification which they (vainly) seek by works of law. It can not therefore exhaust the meaning of the term.

* To these might perhaps be added Rom. 4⁵: τὸν δικαιοῦντα τὸν ἀσεβῆ, were it not for the next clause, λογίζεται ἡ πίστις αὐτοῦ εἰς δικαιοσύνην, which evidently involves a positive element.

XVI. ΠΙΣΤΙΣ AND ΠΙΣΤΕΥΩ.

I. CLASSICAL USAGE.*

A. Πίστις, used in Greek writers from Hesiod down, is employed in two distinct senses, the active and the passive, the latter the more frequent.

1. The active sense: faith, confidence, trust.

(a) As exercised towards another: Soph. *O. C.* 950; Plato, *Phaed.* 275A.

(b) As enjoyed by one, exercised towards him by others; hence credit, trust in the commercial or legal sense: Dem. 962⁵; Polyb. 8. 21³; Plut. *Cic.* 41³: καὶ τὴν οὐσίαν αὐτῆς ὁ Κικέρων ἐν πίστει κληρονόμος ἀπολειφθεὶς διεφύλαττεν.

(c) In an intellectual sense with reference to a proposition: conviction, confident belief; in Plato it is distinguished from ἐπιστήμη, knowledge, in that the latter implies the actuality of the thing believed, while πίστις affirms only subjective certainty (Plato, *Rep.* 601E); in Aristotle from δόξα, opinion (*Anim.* 3. 3⁸ [428 a²⁰], which, however, it is said to follow; for though δόξα may be true or false, it is impossible not to believe those things which one thinks). In the religious realm, πίστις denotes general belief in the existence and power of the gods, not personal faith and confidence in them: Plato, *Legg.* XII 966D.

(d) By metonymy, probably connected with (b): that with which one is entrusted, an office, as the expression or result of the confidence reposed in one: Polyb. 5. 41².

2. The passive sense: trustworthiness, faithfulness, or the pledge or assurance of it.

(a) Personal fidelity, faithfulness: Hdt. 8¹⁰⁵; Xen. *An.* 1. 6³; Aristot. *Mor. Magn.* II 11⁵ (1208 b²⁴); Polyb. 1. 43³.

(b) Pledge or promise of good faith, assurance of fidelity: Hdt. 3⁷⁴ Thuc. 5. 30³; Xen. *Cyr.* 7. 1⁴⁴.

(c) Token of a compact, guarantee: Soph. *O. C.* 1632; Æsch. *Fr.* 394 (290).

(d) Evidence, proof, as presented in court: Polyb. 3. 100³; or in argument: Aristot. *Rhet.* 3. 13² (1414 a³⁵).

B. Πιστεύω, found in Greek writers from Æschylus down, is used in a sense corresponding to the active sense of πίστις:

1. To believe, to trust.

(a) To trust, to put confidence in, to rely upon, whether of persons or things; the object is in the dat.: Eur. *Or.* 1103: Xen. *An.* 3. 1²⁹ 5. 2⁹; Thuc. 5. 112².

(b) In an intellectual sense, to believe a person, or his word or statement. The name of the person, or the noun denoting his word, is in the dat., the word expressing the content of his statement in the acc.: Soph. *El.* 886;

---

* This treatment of classical usage is mainly based on Cremer.

Plato, *Phaed.* 88C; Æsch. *Pers.* 800; Eur. *Hel.* 710. Followed also by an inf. with subj. acc.: Plato, *Gorg.* 524A. Since believing one's word and putting confidence in one are in experience closely related, a sharp discrimination can not always be made between (a) and (b).

2. To entrust, to commit, with the acc. of the thing committed and dat. of the person to whom it is entrusted: Xen. *Mem.* 4. 4¹⁷.

II. HEBREW USAGE OF אֵמוּן ,אֱמוּנָה ,הֶאֱמִין, AND אֱמֶת

A. אֱמוּנָה in O. T. The primary sense of the root אמן is, apparently, to be firm, lasting, enduring. This sense appears in a few uses of the noun.

1. Steadiness, stability.

(a) Of physical things, steadiness, firmness: Ex. 17¹⁵.

(b) Of institutions, stability: Isa. 33⁶: "And there shall be stability in thy times."

2. In a moral sense, steadfastness, faithfulness.

(a) In judgment or statement, fidelity to the facts, or in conduct, to one's statements, especially to one's promises; faithfulness, honesty in judgment: Ps. 33⁴: "For the word of the Lord is right, and all his work is done in faithfulness"; Prov. 12²²: "Lying lips are an abomination to the Lord, but they that deal truly (with faithfulness) are his delight"; Hos. 2²²: "I will even betroth thee unto me in faithfulness"; Isa. 11⁵: "And righteousness shall be the girdle of his loins and faithfulness the girdle of his reins." See also Ps. 36⁶ 40¹¹ (¹⁰) 88¹² (¹¹) 89 2 (¹), ³ (²), ⁶ (⁵), ⁹ (⁸), ²⁵ (²⁴), ³⁴ (³³), ⁵⁰ (⁴⁹) 92³ (²) 96¹³ 98³ 100⁵ 119³⁰, ⁷⁵, ⁸⁶, ⁹⁰, ¹³⁸ 143¹ Prov. 12¹⁷ Jer. 5¹, ³ 7²⁸ 9² Lam. 3²³.

(b) Fidelity to one's obligations or official duties; conscientiousness, honesty in dealing: 2 Ki. 12¹⁵: "Moreover they reckoned not with the men into whose hands they delivered the money to give to them that did the work; for they dealt faithfully." See also 1 Sam. 26²³ 2 Chr. 19⁹ 31¹² 34¹².

(c) In a more strictly religious sense, steadfast adherence to God: Hab. 2⁴: "But the righteous shall live by his faithfulness."

3. A trust, an office: 1 Chr. 9²², ²⁶, ³¹ 2 Chr. 31¹⁵, ¹⁸.

B. אֵמוּן and אֱמֶת (the latter much more frequent in O. T. than the former) have substantially the same range of meanings as אֱמוּנָה, except that neither of them seems to have been used in a physical sense. אֵמוּן (Deut. 32²⁰ Isa. 26² Prov. 13¹⁷, etc.) is rendered by πίστις in the Lxx in Deut. 32²⁰ only. אֱמֶת is translated by πίστις in Prov. 3³ 14²² 15²⁷ (16⁶) Jer. 35 (28)⁹ 39 (32)⁴¹ 40 (33)⁶. In nearly ninety instances it is rendered by ἀλήθεια, which is also frequently used in translating אֱמוּנָה.

C. הֶאֱמִין in O. T. means:

1. To stand still, to be steady: Job 39²⁴, of a horse.

2. To believe a statement, or a person making a statement.

(a) *Proprie*, without clear implication of anything else than this: 1 Ki.

10⁷: "I believed not the words, until I came, and mine eyes had seen it." See also Gen. 45²⁶ 2 Chr. 9⁶ Prov. 14¹⁵ Job 9¹⁶ 15²² 29²⁴ Jer. 12⁶ 40¹⁴ Lam. 4¹².

(b) To believe a statement, or a person making a statement, or, with reference to a fact, to accept its evidence, with an implication of conduct corresponding thereto, especially a corresponding trust in the person who speaks or to whom the fact or statement pertains; usually with ל, but occasionally with ב: Gen. 15⁶: "And he believed (in?) Yahweh, and he counted it to him for righteousness." See also Ex. 4¹, ⁵, ⁸, ⁹ 1 Sam. 27¹² 2 Chr. 32¹⁵ Ps. 78³² 106¹², ²⁴ Hab. 1⁵ Isa. 7⁹ 53¹ Jer. 12⁶.

3. With a personal object, or an object treated as personal, when there is no specific reference to a statement made, to trust, to put confidence in; usually with ב.

(a) *Proprie:* Deut. 1³²: "In this thing ye did not believe (in?) Yahweh your God." See also Job 4¹⁸ 15¹⁵, ³¹ 39¹² Mic. 7⁵ Judg. 11²⁰.

(b) With the idea of trust there is sometimes associated that of recognition of one's character or standing; used with reference to Yahweh, his prophets and his commandments: Ex. 14³¹: "And the people feared Yahweh and they believed in Yahweh, and in his servant Moses." See also Ex. 19⁹ Ps. 119⁶⁶ 2 Chr. 20²⁰. Used with reference to God the emphasis is sometimes clearly upon the element of trust, confidence, reliance: Nu. 14¹¹ Ps. 27¹³ 78²² 116¹⁰ Isa. 28¹⁶ Dan. 6²⁴. Some of these, perhaps, belong under (a). In other cases the emphasis is almost as clearly on the recognition of authority and character, which calls for obedience: Nu. 20¹² Deut. 9²³ 2 Ki. 17¹⁴ Jn. 3⁵ Isa. 43¹⁰.

4. To have assurance of: Deut. 28⁶⁶ Job 24²².

III. USAGE OF THE SEPTUAGINT.

A. Πίστις represents אֱמוּנָה in all the phases of its meaning except the first, "steadiness," "stability." Though occasionally used to translate other words, *e. g.*, אֱמֻן, the meanings of which are closely similar to those of אֱמוּנָה, the analysis of the meanings of the latter word may, with the omission of 1, stand also for πίστις.

B. Πιστεύω is the regular representative in the Lxx of הֶאֱמִין in the Hebrew, though the latter is rendered by ἐμπιστεύω in Deut. 1³² Judg. 11²⁰ 2 Chr. 20²⁰; by καταπιστεύω in Mic. 7⁵, and by the passive of πείθω in Prov. 26²⁵. The meanings of πιστεύω are the same as those of the Hebrew verb, with the probable exception of the physical sense, to stand still. For though the Lxx have πιστεύω, in Job 39²⁴ it is not clear what sense they intended to give the words, and the passage is not sufficient evidence that the Greek word had the physical sense. The usual construction with πιστεύω in the Lxx is a dat. of the person or thing believed or trusted (representing both ל and ב after the Hebrew verb). See Gen. 15⁶ 45²⁶ Ex. 4¹ Jn. 3⁵, etc. Other constructions, such as ἐν with the dat. (Ps. 77

(78)[22] Jer. 12⁶ Dan. 6²⁸), ὅτι with a clause (Job 9¹⁶ 15³¹), and the infinitive (Job 15²² Ps. 26 (27)¹²) are rare.

IV. USAGE OF THE APOCRYPHA AND PSEUDEPIGRAPHA.

A. Πίστις. The usage of the noun in these books shows clearly the influence of the Greek usage as distinguished from the Hebrew. It means:

1. In the passive sense: faithfulness, truthfulness, sincerity: Wisd. 3¹⁴ Sir. 15¹⁵ 40¹² 41¹⁶ 46¹⁵ 1 Mac. 10²⁷, ³⁷ 14³⁵ 3 Mac. 3³. In 4 Mac. 15²⁴ 16²² 17² the passive meaning seems more probable, though the active sense is in all cases possible.

2. In the active sense: faith, confidence.

(a) Towards God: Sir. 1²⁶ (²⁷) 49¹⁰, though in both these cases the passive meaning is possible.

(b) Between men, credit: Sir. 22²³ 27¹⁶ 37²⁶.

3. A pledge of faith or friendship: 3 Mac. 3¹⁰; cf. Jos. Ant. 20. 62 (3²).

B. Πιστεύω means:

1. To believe a statement, or a person making a statement.

(a) Proprie, without clear implication that anything else is involved: 1 Esd. 4²⁸ Tob. 2¹⁴ 5² (⁵) 10⁸ (⁵) 14⁴ (⁵) bis Sir. 19¹⁵ Dan. Susan. 41 1 Mac. 10⁴⁶.

(b) To believe, with implication of the assumption of the corresponding attitude of trust or adherence; the following are possible instances: Sir. 13¹¹ 1 Mac. 1³⁰ (A).

2. To trust, to put confidence in.

(a) Proprie: Wisd. 16²⁶ (dat.) 18⁶ Sir. 2⁶, ⁸, ¹⁰, ¹³ 11²¹ 12¹⁰ 35 (32) ²³ 36³¹ (²⁸) Dan. Susan. 53 Lxx (pass.) 1 Mac. 7⁷ 2 Mac. 3¹².

(b) To put confidence in and to accept, yielding allegiance to: Jdth. 14¹⁰ (dat.) Wisd. 12² (ἐπί with acc.).

3. Absolutely: to be confident, to be at ease: Sir. 35 (32)²¹.

4. To entrust (dat. and acc.): Wisd. 14⁵ 1 Mac. 8¹⁶ 2 Mac. 3²².

V. NEW TESTAMENT USAGE.

Πίστις and πιστεύω, as used in N. T., clearly show the influence alike of the Greek usage of the words and of the Hebrew thought of which they became the vehicle. The words are Greek, the roots of the thought are mainly in the experience and writings of the Hebrew prophets and psalmists. Yet in important respects the usage of the N. T. has moved away from that of both lines of its ancestry.

Thus while πίστις in the Lxx and Apocr. is almost exclusively passive in sense, and in classical writers apparently about as often passive as active, in N. T. it is in a large proportion of cases active, signifying not "faithfulness," but "faith."

Again, while in the Greek writers the terms are prevailingly intellectual or ethical, i. e., are used of an intellectual or moral attitude, in either case in a sphere other than that of religion, and in Jewish-Greek (following in this the Hebrew) prevailingly ethical, in N. T. πίστις is employed almost exclusively in the religious realm, and πιστεύω prevailingly so. Πιστεύω is indeed used of an acceptance of a proposition of religious signifi- cance without any corresponding moral act or attitude (see 1, (b), under πιστεύω), but such a use of πίστις is very rare. See below, πίστις, II 1. While always including or involving acceptance of truth, that which is called πίστις in N. T. carries with it also the volitional action which such acceptance calls for. See Mt. 9²⁸, ²⁹ Mk. 11²²⁻²⁴ Rom. 10⁹ff. 2 Thes. 2¹³ Heb. 11⁶ Jn. 20³¹. It is true that in certain instances such as Heb. 11¹, ³ the emphasis is so laid upon the apprehension and acceptance of truth rather than upon the corresponding volitional action, as to seem to imply that volitional action (except as involved in the will to believe) is not strictly speaking included in faith. But it is clear from the remainder of the chapter that the writer intends to apply the term πίστις only to a belief which exerts a determinative influence on conduct. If, therefore, volitional action is not strictly included in the term πίστις it is involved in the act itself. In Jas. 2¹⁴⁻²², it is true also that πίστις is used of a purely intellectual holding of a religious proposition. But this usage is quite exceptional in N. T., and, moreover, the whole argument of this passage is aimed at showing that such faith is futile, and the usage of the rest of the letter indicates that in this passage the writer is merely adopting the verbal usage of another whose views he does not hold, and whose usage of words is different from his own usual employment of them.

Once again, while in the Lxx (representing הֶאֱמִין) and Apocr., πιστεύω, followed by words referring to God or persons or things represent- ing God, is often used to express the attitude of the religious man, and while this use of the word furnishes the principal basis or point of attach- ment for the development of N. T. usage, it becomes much more frequent and important in N. T. than in O. T. In short, both πίστις and πιστεύω are in N. T. prevailingly religious rather than intellectual or ethical terms, πίστις is active rather than passive, and both are employed with much greater frequency than in preceding literature, either Greek or Hebrew.

These facts are to such an extent characteristic of N. T. as a whole that while its several portions exhibit considerable difference in their emphasis upon the different elements or aspects of faith, yet these differences do not necessitate a separate lexicographical treatment for the different writers.

The prominence of the verb and the fact that πίστις is active, so that the idea expressed by it is more definitely expressed by the verb with its various limitations, make it expedient that the verb should precede the noun.

A. Πιστεύω has the following meanings:

1. To accept as true, to believe a proposition, or a person making a state- ment. The thing believed is expressed by an accusative, or by a clause

introduced by ὅτι; once by an infinitive with subject accusative (Acts 15¹¹); once by a dative (Acts 24¹⁴); once by εἰς with the accusative (1 Jn. 5¹⁰ᶜ); the name of the person making the statement, or the impersonal thing which is thought of as bearing testimony, is in the dative (Mt. 21²⁵, ³² Jn. 5⁴⁶, etc.), very rarely with a preposition (Mk. 1¹⁵ Lk. 24²⁵); the verb is sometimes used absolutely when the context indicates what limitation is intended.

(a) The thing believed may be any fact of every-day life: Jn. 9¹⁸ 1 Cor. 11¹⁸; even a thing wholly false: 2 Thes. 2¹¹: εἰς τὸ πιστεῦσαι αὐτοὺς τῷ ψεύδει.

(b) It may be a proposition of religious significance, the verb designating a merely intellectual assent to it, without implying (the context may even exclude) any corresponding moral attitude. This is most clearly so in Jas. 2¹⁹: καὶ τὰ δαιμόνια πιστεύουσιν καὶ φρίσσουσιν. Other probable examples are: Mt. 24²³, ²⁶ Mk. 13²¹ (16¹³, ¹⁴) Jn. 2²² 3¹² 4²¹ 8⁴⁵, ⁴⁶ Acts 8¹³ 15¹¹ 26²⁷ Rom. 6⁸ 13⁷ 1 Thes. 4¹⁴ 1 Jn. 4¹.

(c) But in the great majority of cases the thing believed is a proposition pertaining to God or Christ, the person believed is God or Christ, or some one bringing the divine message; and it is more or less clearly implied that the belief itself is accompanied by the conduct corresponding thereto, especially by a corresponding trust in the person who is believed, or to whom the statement pertains: Jn. 5²⁴: ὁ τὸν λόγον μου ἀκούων καὶ πιστεύων τῷ πέμψαντί με ἔχει ζωὴν αἰώνιον. See also Mt. 8¹³ 9²⁸ 21²², ²⁵, ³² Mk. 1¹⁵ (ἐν) 5³⁶ 9²³, ²⁴ 11²³, ²⁴ 15³² Lk. 1⁴⁵ 8¹², ¹³, ⁵⁰ 20⁵ 22⁶⁷ 24²⁵ Jn. 1⁵⁰ (⁵¹) 4⁴⁸, ⁵⁰ 5²⁴, ³⁸, ⁴⁴, ⁴⁶, ⁴⁷ 6³⁰, ⁶⁹ 8²⁴ 10²⁵, ²⁶, ³⁷, ³⁸ 11¹⁵, ²⁶ᵇ, ²⁷, ⁴⁰, ⁴² 12³⁸, ³⁹ 13¹⁹ 14¹⁰, ¹¹, ²⁹ 16²⁷, ³⁰, ³¹ 17⁸, ²¹ 19³⁵ 20⁸, ²⁵, ²⁹, ³¹ Acts 4⁴ 8¹² 13⁴¹ 24¹⁴ 27²⁵ Rom. 4⁵, ¹⁷, ¹⁸ 10⁹, ¹⁶ 2 Cor. 4¹³ Gal. 3⁶ 2 Thes. 1¹⁰ Jas. 2²³ Heb. 11⁶ 1 Jn. 3²³ 5¹, ⁵, ¹⁰ᵇ, ᶜ.

2. To trust, to put confidence in, to commit one's self to; usually with the added idea of recognition of the character or standing of the one trusted and allegiance to him. The object, which is always a word referring to Christ (except in Jn. 12⁴⁴ᶜ—even here implied, not expressed—14¹ Acts 16³⁴ Rom. 4²⁴ 9³³) is most commonly introduced by the preposition εἰς, but sometimes by ἐπί with dat. or acc., and is in a few cases expressed by a simple dative. The verb in this sense is not infrequently used absolutely, the context supplying the object and construction. In Jn. 14¹ Rom. 9³³ 10¹¹ 1 Pet. 2⁶ 2 Tim. 1¹² Tit. 3⁸ Heb. 4³, the idea of trust is probably prominent, perhaps to the exclusion of any other. Usually that of acceptance and adherence is in the foreground: Gal. 2¹⁶: καὶ ἡμεῖς εἰς Χριστὸν Ἰησοῦν ἐπιστεύσαμεν. Mt. 18⁶ 27⁴² Mk. 9⁴² Jn. 1¹² 2¹¹, ²³ 3¹⁶, ¹⁸ (bis) ³⁶ 4³⁹ 6²⁹, ³⁰, ³⁵, ³⁶, ⁴⁰ 7⁵, ³¹, ³⁸, ³⁹, ⁴⁸ 8²⁴, ³⁰, ³¹ 9³⁵, ³⁶, ³⁸ 10⁴² 11²⁵, ²⁶ᵃ, ⁴⁵, ⁴⁸ 12¹¹, ³⁶, ³⁷, ⁴², ⁴⁴, ⁴⁶ 14¹² 16⁹ 17²⁰ Acts 9⁴² 10⁴³ 11¹⁷ 14²³ 16¹¹, ³⁴ 18⁸ 19⁴ 22¹⁹ Rom. 10¹⁴ Phil. 1²⁹ 1 Tim. 1¹⁶ 3¹⁶ 1 Pet. 1⁸ 1 Jn. 5¹⁰ᵃ, ¹³.

The construction πιστεύω εἰς, which is found in all the passages cited under 2, except Mt. 27⁴² Acts 9⁴² 11¹⁷ 16³¹ 22¹⁹ Rom. 4²⁴ 9³³ 10¹¹ 1 Pet. 2⁶ 1 Tim. 1¹⁶ (ἐπί) Jn. 6³⁰ 8³¹ Acts 16³⁴ 18⁸ᵃ (dat.) Jn. 6⁸⁴ 9³⁸ 1 Tim. 3¹⁶ (absolutely), appears for the first time in N. T. The rarity of the construction in the synoptic gospels and Acts (Mt. 18⁶ Mk. 9⁴² Acts 10⁴³ 14²³ 19⁴), its appearance in Paul and Acts alongside of the Lxx construction πιστεύω ἐπί with approximately equal frequency, and its entire displacement of the latter usage in the Johannine writings, suggest the probability that it first came into literary use in the Christian (perhaps Pauline) circles of the apostolic age, as being more exactly expressive of the Christian feeling respecting the relation of the believer to Christ, especially in its aspect of acceptance and adherence, than any previously current phraseology. It may have been previously used colloquially, or have been coined colloquially in Christian circles. It is used with an impersonal object in 1 Jn. 5¹⁰ᶜ only.

3. To have faith, referring to Christian faith as such without emphasis upon any special aspect of it: Rom. 1¹⁶: δύναμις γὰρ θεοῦ ἐστὶν εἰς σωτηρίαν παντὶ τῷ πιστεύοντι. See also Mk. 9⁴² Acts 2⁴⁴ 4³² 5¹⁴ (?) 11²¹ 13¹², ³⁹, ⁴⁸ 14¹ 15⁵, ⁷ 17¹², ³⁴ 18⁸ᵇ, ²⁷ 19², ¹⁸ 21²⁰, ²⁵ Rom. 3²² 4¹¹ 10⁴, ¹⁰ 13¹¹ 15¹³ 1 Cor. 1²¹ 3⁵ 14²² 15², ¹¹ Gal. 3²² Eph. 1¹³, ¹⁹ 1 Thes. 1⁷ 2¹⁰, ¹³ 1 Pet. 2⁷ Jude ⁵.

4. To have confidence, to be bold: Rom. 14²: ὃς μὲν πιστεύει φαγεῖν πάντα. The basis of this confidence is indicated by v.¹ to be Christian faith; yet the verb here apparently means simply, to have confidence, the allusion to πίστις in the Christian sense lying not in the verb, but in its power to recall the πίστις of v.¹.

5. To entrust (followed by acc. and dat., or in the passive by acc.): Jn. 2²⁴: αὐτὸς δὲ Ἰησοῦς οὐκ ἐπίστευεν αὐτὸν αὐτοῖς. See also Lk. 16¹¹ Rom. 3² 1 Cor. 9¹⁷ Gal. 2⁷ 1 Thes. 2⁴ 1 Tim. 1¹¹ Tit. 1³.

B. Πίστις has the following senses:
I. The passive sense: faithfulness, fidelity to one's promises or obligations.

1. *Proprie*, of the fidelity of God to his promises, or of the faithfulness of men to one another: Mt. 23²³ Rom. 3³ Gal. 5²² Tit. 2¹⁰.

2. Evidence, assurance: Acts 17³¹.

II. The active sense: faith, belief, trust.

1. Belief of a proposition, or of a person, intellectual assent simply as such: Jas. 2¹⁴⁻²⁶.

2. Belief of the truth concerning, and corresponding trust in, a person including or involving the attitude of will and conduct which such belief calls for, especially the committal of one's self to him to whom the truth pertains. The object of faith in this sense is in N. T. almost always explicitly or by implication God or Christ; rarely the truth or a truth.

(a) Apprehension and acceptance of the truth concerning God or Christ with the emphasis on this intellectual element: Heb. 11³: πίστει νοοῦμεν κατηρτίσθαι τοὺς αἰῶνας ῥήματι θεοῦ. *Cf.* v.¹.

(b) Belief in the power and willingness of God, as revealed in the pre-Christian period, to bless, help, and save, and a corresponding trust and obedience; used of the faith of Abraham: Rom. 4⁹, ¹¹, ¹², ¹³, ¹⁹, ²⁰ Heb. 11⁸, ⁹, ¹⁷; of that of other O. T. characters: Heb. 4² 11⁴, ⁵, ⁷ (*bis*) ¹¹, ¹³, ²⁰⁻³⁹.

(c) Of essentially the same type is the faith in God which Jesus, in the synoptic gospels, enjoins his disciples to exercise: Mk. 11²²: ἔχετε πίστιν θεοῦ. See also Mt. 17²⁰ 21²¹ Lk. 17⁵, ⁶ 18⁸; and that which is spoken of in Jas. 1³, ⁶.

(d) Belief in the power and willingness of Jesus to do a certain thing, heal the sick, deliver from peril, forgive sins, accompanied by a committal of one's self to him in reference to the matter in question: Mt. 9²⁹: κατὰ τὴν πίστιν ὑμῶν γενηθήτω ὑμῖν. *Cf.* v.²⁸: πιστεύετε ὅτι δύναμαι τοῦτο ποιῆσαι; see also Mt. 8¹⁰ 9², ²² 15²⁸ Mk. 2⁵ 4⁴⁰ 5³⁴ 10⁵² Lk. 5²⁰ 7⁹, ⁵⁰ 8²⁵, ⁴⁸ 17¹⁹ 18⁴². Closely akin to this is the faith in the name of the risen Jesus, which secured the healing of the sick, Acts 3¹⁶ 14⁹. In Jas. 5¹⁵ it is not clear whether the faith referred to is thought of as faith in God or in Christ.

(e) The acceptance of the gospel message concerning Jesus Christ, and the committal of one's self for salvation to him or to God as revealed in him. Such faith is often spoken of specifically as faith in Jesus Christ, less often as faith in or towards God, very frequently simply as faith, or the faith, its specifically Christian character as based upon the Christian revelation and involving acceptance of the gospel message being implied in the context.

The large number of cases which fall under this head divide themselves into several classes, differing, however, only in the greater or less clearness with which the nature and object of the faith is expressed, or in the emphasis upon one or another phase of it.

(i) Those in which the object of the faith is distinctly expressed by an objective genitive or prepositional phrase. The article is sometimes prefixed and the faith is definitely identified as the faith in Christ Jesus or towards God: Acts 20²¹: τὴν εἰς θεὸν μετάνοιαν καὶ πίστιν εἰς τὸν κύριον ἡμῶν Ἰησοῦν. See also Acts 24²⁴ Eph. 1¹⁵ 3¹² Col. 1⁴ 2⁵, ¹² 1 Thes. 1⁸ Jas. 2¹ Rev. 2¹³ 14¹². Sometimes it is omitted, giving the phrase a qualitative force: Rom. 3²², ²⁶ Gal. 2¹⁶ (*bis*) 3²² Phil. 3⁹ᵃ Heb. 6¹ (πίστεως ἐπὶ θεόν). Occasionally the noun is without the article, but the qualifying phrase is preceded by an article agreeing with πίστις, giving the sense, "faith," or "a faith which is," etc. So in Gal. 2²⁰ Acts 26¹⁸ 1 Tim. 3¹³ 2 Tim. 1¹³ 3¹⁵.

(ii) Those in which πίστις is accompanied by a subjective genitive or equivalent phrase indicating by whom the faith is exercised. The article is in this case almost invariably present. The object of the faith is usually indicated, more or less definitely, by the context, but occasionally directly expressed, such cases falling at the same time under the preceding head: Lk. 22³² Rom. 1⁸, ¹² 1 Cor. 2⁵ 15¹⁴, ¹⁷ 2 Cor. 1²⁴ᵃ 10¹⁵ Phil. 2¹⁷ Col. 1⁴ 2⁵ 1 Thes. 1⁸ 3², ⁵, ⁶, ⁷, ¹⁰ 2 Thes. 1⁴ 2 Tim. 2¹⁸ Phm. ⁵, ⁶ Heb. 13⁷ Jas. 1⁸ 1 Pet. 1⁷, ²¹ 2 Pet. 1⁵ 1 Jn. 5⁴ Jude ²⁰ Rev. 2¹⁹ 13¹⁰. Without the article: Tit. 1¹.

(iii) Those in which, though there is neither objective nor subjective limitation, the distinctly Christian character of the faith is clearly implied in the context. The article sometimes occurs marking the faith either as that just previously spoken of, as in Rom. 3[30b] 2 Cor. 1[24b] Phil. 3[9b], or as that referred to in the accompanying phrase, as in Gal. 1[23], or, most frequently, as the well-known (Christian) faith, as in Gal. 6[10]. For other examples with the article, see Acts 6[7] (πολύς τε ὄχλος τῶν ἱερέων ὑπήκουον τῇ πίστει) Acts 13[8] 14[22] 15[9] 16[5] Rom. 3[31] 10[8, 17] (the article is possibly generic in this case) 11[20] 1 Cor. 16[13] 2 Cor. 4[13] 13[5] Gal. 1[23] 3[14, 23, 25] Eph. 3[17] 4[13] 6[16] Phil. 1[25, 27] Col. 1[23] 2[7] 1 Thes. 1[3] 2 Thes. 3[2] 1 Tim. 1[19b] 3[9] 4[1, 6] 5[8, 12] 6[10, 12, 21] 2 Tim. 1[5] 2[18] 3[8, 10] 4[7] Tit. 1[13] 2[2] Heb. 12[2] 1 Pet. 1[9] 5[9] Jude 3. *Cf.* also Eph. 4[5].* When the article is omitted the noun has a qualitative force, as in Acts 11[24] 14[27] Rom. 1[5, 17] (*ter*) 5[1] 9[30, 32] 10[6] 16[26] 2 Cor. 8[7] Gal. 3[2, 5, 8, 9, 24] 5[5, 6] Eph. 2[8] 6[23] 1 Thes. 5[8] 2 Thes. 1[11] 1 Tim. 1[2, 4, 5, 14, 19a] 2[7, 15] 4[12] 6[11] 2 Tim. 2[22] Tit. 1[4] 2[10] 3[15] Heb. 10[22] 1 Pet. 1[5] 2 Pet. 1[1].†

(iv) Those which refer to Christian faith as a belief in the power and willingness of God to work through men in the gifts of the Spirit; used both definitely and qualitatively: Rom. 12[3, 6] 1 Cor. 12[9] 13[2, 13].

(v) Those which speak of Christian faith with special reference to the element of reliance upon God for acceptance with him apart from works of law and merit, and its consequent power to free one from the scruples of legalism or asceticism; used both definitely and qualitatively: Rom. 14[1, 22, 23] (*bis*) 1 Tim. 4[6] (?).

(f) Faith without reference to the distinction between faith in God as revealed in the O. T. period and faith as the acceptance of the gospel message; the term thus signifies faith as the attitude towards God of the man who accepts and believes whatever accredits itself to him as from God, and commits himself in trustfulness and obedience to God, whether towards God as known in the O. T. period or as revealed in Christ. In the nature

* In certain of these cases by a semi-metonymy, faith, as the central principle of Christianity and the determinative factor of the Christian life, stands almost for Christianity itself, without, however, wholly losing its own proper meaning of (active) faith. See 1 Tim. 1[19b] 3[9] 4[1] 5[8] 6[10, 21] 2 Tim. 3[8] Tit. 1[13] 2[2] Jude 3. Out of this usage there undoubtedly grew in time the use of πίστις to denote Christianity and in particular the beliefs of Christianity. But it is doubtful whether this stage of development is reached in N. T. Gal. 1[23] 2 Tim. 4[7], sometimes regarded as examples of this usage, are certainly not such, and are not even to be classed with those cited above. πίστις in these two passages has its proper and usual N. T. sense of (active) faith in Christ.

† These anarthrous cases form a transition from those in which the reference is distinctly to the belief of the gospel and faith in Christ, or in God as revealed in Christ, to those in which (see f. below) faith is spoken of without reference to the extent of the revelation and without distinction between its O. T. type and its N. T. form. Respecting some of the passages cited above, e. g., Gal. 3[7, 8, 9], it may fairly be questioned on which side of the line they belong. That the line of distinction can not be sharply drawn and that N. T. writers easily pass from one conception to the other is a result and evidence of the fact that faith, whether directed towards the God revealed in O. T. or towards Christ or God as revealed in the gospel, is conceived of as always essentially the same in character.

of the case the word in these instances is qualitative and hence without the article or accompanied by the generic article. See Rom. 3[27, 28, 30] 4[14, 16a] 9[30, 32] 2 Cor. 5[7] Gal. 3[7, 12] Heb. 6[12] 10[38, 39] 11[6] Jas. 2[5]. In Rom. 1[17c] Gal. 3[11], though the quotation is from O. T. and אֱמוּנָה of the original meant "faithfulness," Paul evidently takes πίστις in the active sense—an interpretation which is not wholly without basis in the O. T. passage, since אֱמוּנָה there denotes a steadfast adherence to God which implies faith in the active sense as an essential element of the experience. In Rom. 4[16b] ἐκ πίστεως 'Αβραάμ means "of an Abrahamic faith," i. e., possessing a faith which like that of Abraham was exercised outside of the régime of law.

Two elements of the apostle Paul's conception of faith are worthy of special attention. On the one hand, he conceived of faith in Christ as issuing in a vital fellowship of the believer with Christ, by which Christ becomes the compelling and controlling force in the believer's moral life (Gal. 2[20] 5[6]). On the other hand, he laid great stress upon the essential identity of such faith in God as existed in the O. T. period and the Christian type of faith. The doctrine of faith in Christ is defended by an appeal to the faith of Abraham, and the permanence and continuity of the principle of faith as the determinative element of God's demand upon men urgently maintained. The union of these two elements in his idea of Christian faith, viz., its higher possibilities and normal destiny, and its essential identity with the more primitive faith of an older period is an important fact for the understanding of his thought.

Neither idea, however, is peculiar to Paul. The former permeates the fourth gospel, though usually expressed in terminology other than that of Paul. The latter appears in almost all parts of N. T. According to the synoptic gospels Jesus teaches men to believe in God and invites them to have faith in him, apparently assuming that the production of the one faith will generate the other, and, indeed, expressly affirming that he that receives him receives him that sent him (Mk. 9[37]). The fourth gospel expresses the same thought more explicitly in terms of faith (12[44]) and reiterates it in other forms. In the Epistle to the Hebrews Christians are exhorted to maintain their faith in Christ by O. T. examples of faith in God.

It is involved, implicitly if not explicitly, in this recognition of the essential identity of pre-Christian and Christian faith that while all faith has of necessity an intellectual element, the intellectual content of faith is not a fixed quantity. Faith may differ in different persons and in the same person at different times. It is capable of development and of waning, and this both in respect to the content of the truth apprehended and in respect to the intensity or firmness with which it is exercised. See Mt. 15[28] Lk. 7[9] 17[5, 6] 22[32] Acts 6[5] 14[22] 16[5] Rom. 1[17] 4[19, 20] 12[6] 1 Cor. 13[2] 2 Cor. 8[7] 10[15] Phil. 1[25] Col. 1[23] 2[5] 1 Thes. 3[10] 2 Thes. 1[3] 1 Tim. 4[1] 5[12] 6[10] Jas. 2[5, 22].

To what extent Paul influenced early Christian usage of the words πιστεύω and πίστις and the idea of faith associated with them; to what extent he was himself influenced by earlier Christian thought, is not easy to determine with accuracy. In the synoptic gospels, aside from a single instance which by its exceptional use of Pauline phraseology (Mt. 18⁶; the phrase πιστεύω εἰς in Mk. 9⁴² is in all probability not original, but a harmonistic addition from Mt. 18⁶, and in the latter an editorial modification of the source), betrays an influence of the Pauline usage, the conception of faith is simple and relatively elementary. On the one hand, it includes the idea of trust in God frequently expressed in O. T. by נבטה and in the Lxx by πέποιθα and ἐλπίζω, and, on the other hand, that of confidence in the willingness and ability of Jesus to do certain things, usually to heal sickness or rescue from danger, rarely to forgive sins. It is never so used as to imply that faith in Jesus necessarily involved any formal definition of his person or mission; it is not, for example, employed in relation to Peter's confession of the messiahship of Jesus (Mk. 8²⁹ and parallels).

When the early church accepted Jesus as the Messiah, and confession that he was Lord and Christ became the keynote of the new religious movement that attached itself to his name, both the volitional and the doctrinal element of faith (cf. under πιστεύω, 1 (c) and 2) became more definite and more prominent. Yet the simple use of the word "faith" continued (Acts 3¹⁶), and it is not possible to determine from the early chapters of Acts precisely to what extent confession of Jesus in explicit doctrinal terms became associated with the word πίστις. The noun is infrequent, and the verb occurs almost wholly in narrative passages, which doubtless reflect the usage of the period when Acts was written rather than of that of the events.

There can be little doubt that it was largely to Paul that the Christian movement owed that strong emphasis on faith, and the prominence of the word in the Christian vocabulary which is reflected in N. T. as a whole. Clearly the emphasis on "faith" and "works of law" as antithetical conceptions is mainly due to him. That Jesus was, like Paul after him, a non-legalist, the evidence seems clearly to prove. But there is no reason to think that he developed a sharp antithesis between law and faith. The early church believed in Jesus as the Christ, but it was not, for the most part at least, consciously anti-legalistic, and it apparently did not occur to the early apostles to set faith and works or faith and law in antithesis to one another. To Paul, also, we doubtless owe the conception of faith as creating a mystical union with Christ, which appears in his letters, and of the influence of which the post-Pauline literature gives evidence. In this case as in so many others, Paul was a most important factor in the creation of the Christian vocabulary, not by inventing words, but by making them the bearers of his new thought or emphasis.

See the excellent discussion in W. H. P. Hatch, " The Pauline Idea of Faith," in *Harvard Theological Studies*, II, Cambridge, 1917.

XVII. ΠΝΕΥΜΑ AND ΣΑΡΞ.*

I. ΠΝΕΥΜΑ.

A. Πνεῦμα appears first among Greek writers in Æschylus. Its meanings in writers down to and including Aristotle are "wind," "air," "breath," "life." The meaning "spirit" does not appear. Xenophanes is said by Diogenes Laertius, IX 2. 3 (19), to have been the first to say that the soul, ψυχή, is πνεῦμα, but the context shows that by this statement Xenophanes did not mean that the soul is (immaterial) spirit, but rather, as against the views of his predecessors that the soul lives after death as a shade, he affirms that everything that comes into being is also subject to extinction, and that the soul is but breath or air. To Anaximenes, a contemporary of Xenophanes, Plutarch, *Plac. phil.* 1³, ascribes the words: οἷον ἡ ψυχή, φησιν, ἡ ἡμετέρα ἀὴρ οὖσα συγκρατεῖ ἡμᾶς καὶ ὅλον τὸν κόσμον πνεῦμα καὶ ἀὴρ περιέχει. The passage shows that in Xenophanes' day it was held that the soul was air; it suggests that ἀήρ and πνεῦμα are nearly synonymous terms, and that both are used of a substance supposed to control the world, and hence in some sense of cosmic significance. Cicero says that Anaximenes made air God, but he did not, so far as we know, say either that πνεῦμα was God or that God was πνεῦμα, nor do we know of any other pre-Aristotelian writer who did so. Of Heraclitus, who found the origin of all things in fire, yet also, according to Aristotle, said that the origin of all things was soul, ψυχή, Siebeck, *op. cit.*, says that he thinks of πνεῦμα as that which connects the soul with the surrounding air, which is itself thought of as more or less soul or spirit. Epicharmus speaks of earth (*i. e.*, the body) as going to earth in death, and of πνεῦμα as going above. Yet no pre-Aristotelian writer apparently uses πνεῦμα as an individualising term or as the equivalent of soul. From Xenophanes down to N. T. times ψυχή, soul, is an individual and functional term whose definition was not in that of which it was composed but in its functions; it is the seat of life, feeling, thought. πνεῦμα, on the other hand, is a term of substance, defined not by its functions, which are very variable, but by its qualities. *Cf.* the terms "knife" and "steel," "sword" and "bronze." Aristotle distinguishes between in-

---

* For fuller discussion see Holsten, *Zum. Evangelium des Paulus u. Petrus*, pp. 365 *ff.*, Rostock, 1868; Wendt, *Die Begriffe Fleisch und Geist*, Gotha, 1878; Dickson, *St. Paul's Use of the Terms Flesh and Spirit*, Glasgow, 1883; Gunkel, *Die Wirkungen des heiligen Geistes*, Göttingen, 1888; Schoemaker, "The Use of רוח in the O. T. and of πνεῦμα in the N. T.," in *Journal of Biblical Literature*, 1904, pp. 13–67; Wood. *The Spirit of God in Biblical Literature*, N. Y. 1904; Siebeck, "Neue Beiträge zur Entwickelungsgeschichte des Geist-Begriffs," in *Archiv für Geschichte der Philosophie*, Bd. XXVII, 1914, pp. 1–16; Burton, *Spirit, Soul, and Flesh: The Usage of Πνεῦμα, Ψυχή and Σάρξ in Greek Writings, and Translated Works from the Earliest Period to* 180 A. D. *and of their Equivalents . . . . in the . . . . Old Testament*, Chicago, 1918; also articles of which the above-mentioned monograph is an expansion and revision, published under the same title in *AJT.* Oct., 1913; Jan., 1914; July, 1914; Oct., 1914; July, 1915; Oct., 1915. The following discussion is in part a reproduction and in part a condensation of this book and these articles.

born air, σύμφυτον πνεῦμα, and air which is inhaled from without. But he also speaks of πνεῦμα in a sense which he expressly distinguishes from πνεῦμα meaning the air of which wind is composed, and apparently, also, from the σύμφυτον πνεῦμα, describing it as the substance which is in both plants and animals, and permeates all, διὰ παντὸς διήκει, and is both living and generative, *Mund.* 4 (394 b. [10f.]). Thus in ancient writers πνεῦμα is neither the soul nor God, but a substance identical with or akin to air, but possessing, according to some writers, intelligence, according to others being the substance of which the soul is composed, and to others a sort of soul-stuff or world-stuff, the basis of all life, if not of all existence.

In post-classical Greek writers, the principal meanings of πνεῦμα, in order of frequency, are "wind," "life," "air." The meaning "breath" drops out, or is absorbed in the meaning "life." In one passage in Dionysius Halicarnassensis (*Antiq.* i[31]) the word is used of a demon, perhaps under Hebrew influence. The Stoics made much use of the term πνεῦμα. Chrysippus affirmed that the ultimate reality was πνεῦμα moving itself (Stob. *Ecl.* i. 17[4]) and the Stoics generally held this monistic view. Their πνεῦμα has both material and "spiritual" qualities. Affirming that the soul is σῶμα, by which the Stoics meant not only that it was real but that it possessed physical qualities, and, on the other hand, that it is πνεῦμα (Zeno calls it πνεῦμα ἔνθερμον; and Chrysippus, according to Galen, σύμφυτον ἡμῖν συνεχὲς παντὶ τῷ σώματι διῆκον), they indicate both that the πνεῦμα has intellectual qualities and that the soul itself has physical qualities. The πνεῦμα, of which the soul is composed, is σῶμα, but is permeated with λόγος, and the organs of sense-perception are called πνεύματα νοερά, the πνεῦμα extending from the governing part of the soul to the organs of sense-perception. Posidonius was, so far as we know, first among the Greeks to say that God was πνεῦμα, to which he added νοερὸν καὶ πυρῶδες. Two hundred years before Posidonius, Menander used the phrase πνεῦμα θεῖον in a way to show that some of his contemporaries ascribed to it the control of human affairs, but how far it was individualised and personalised does not appear, and it remains that with rare if any exception, πνεῦμα is to the end of the first Christian century still a term of substance, not of functions, and a name not of God or the human soul, but of the substance of which both are composed, a refined and ethereal substance, yet still a substance and not yet thought of as immaterial. Akin to this, but probably to be distinguished from it, is πνεῦμα as a permeating principle or force. Aristotle's language leaves it uncertain whether in his day it was thought of as extending to all existence or to animate things only. Plutarch discusses the distinction between the souls of men and irrational animals, the principle of growth in plants, and the force of cohesion in stones, but does not call either of the latter πνεῦμα. Galen, in the second century, calls the power of cohesion ἑκτικον πνεῦμα, and finally Sextus Empiricus, in the third century, groups all these things together under the common term πνεῦμα.

The use of similar language in Philo shows that this terminology was already in use in the first century. In this century, in which the N. T. arose and, as will presently appear, πνεῦμα was in very common use among Christians, it occurs rather rarely in extant Greek literature, but is found in Plutarch, Cornutus, Epictetus, and Dio Chrysostom. It has the following four senses: "wind," "air," "breath," "the medium or bearer of psychic energy" (nervous fluid). The most notable fact here is the almost total absence of the meaning "spirit."

B. The term in Hebrew which corresponds most nearly to πνεῦμα in Greek is רוּחַ. It bears three meanings, which, in order of frequency, are: "spirit," "wind," "breath." The genetic order is probably "wind," "spirit," "breath." As spirit it denotes the Spirit of God, the spirit of man, and an evil spirit or demon. רוּחַ is also probably originally a term of substance, and retained throughout the O. T. period a trace of this meaning in the clinging to it of a quantitative sense, as is illustrated in Elisha's request for a double portion of Elijah's spirit (2 Ki. 2⁹). But by an early development of meaning רוּחַ came to be used of the Spirit of God, as that through which the power of God was manifested (Gen. 1²), and in the later period as the power of God operative in the ethical and religious life of the people (Isa. 61¹ Ps. 51¹³ [¹¹]). In O. T. it was also used of the spirit of man, first probably meaning "strength," "courage," "anger," etc. (Judg. 8³ Prov. 18¹⁴), then the seat of these and other qualities, and finally the seat of mentality, though this last usage is late and rare (Job 20²). Alike, therefore, in the starting point and in the general range of usage there is a large measure of parallelism between the Hebrew רוּחַ and the Greek πνεῦμα, which made it inevitable that the latter should become the translation and recognised representative of the former. But there is also a marked difference between the usage of the two words, especially in the fact that the Hebrews so much earlier associated the term with God, making it, however, not a predicate of God (the O. T. never says God is רוּחַ), but an individualising name for an expression or manifestation of God.

C. In Jewish-Greek literature, including Greek works by Jewish authors, down to 100 A. D., whether translations of Semitic originals or originally composed in Greek, πνεῦμα bears three meanings, in order of frequency, as follows: "spirit," "wind," "breath." As "spirit" the term denotes the Spirit of God, the spirit of man, and superhuman beings both good and evil. Genetic relations can scarcely be spoken of, usages being inherited rather than developed. In the Lxx we find for the first time the expression πνεῦμα θεοῦ (Gen. 1² 41³⁸) and πνεῦμα ἅγιον (Ps. 50 [51]¹¹), the latter a translation of the Hebrew רוּחַ קֹדֶשׁ, probably modelled on the πνεῦμα θεῖον which Menander's usage proves to have existed among the Greeks and which itself occurs occasionally in the Lxx (Job 27³ 33⁴). The entire usage in Jewish-Greek shows far more influence of the Hebrew view than of Greek thought.

D. N. T. usage of πνεῦμα, like that of other Jewish-Greek literature, is strongly influenced by the ideas which come from O. T., which it follows much more closely than it does that of Greek writers in general. Yet it also shows, especially in Paul, peculiarities of its own, which were probably in the main not derived from outside but developed within the circle of Christian thought. Of the characteristics of N. T. usage which differentiate it from non-Jewish-Greek, and to a certain extent from all previous usage, the following are the most important: (a) πνεῦμα is no longer prevailingly a substantial term, as in Greek writers, but, with few exceptions, individualising as in Jewish-Greek, following the Hebrew. (b) Its most frequent use is with reference to the Spirit of God. For this there is only the slightest precedent in the non-Jewish Greek writers. N. T., especially Pauline, usage shows a marked advance even on Jewish-Greek. (c) The relation of πνεῦμα to ψυχή is almost wholly new, having only partial precedent in Philo. Whereas in Greek writers generally ψυχή is the term which definitely conveyed the idea of life and mentality, and πνεῦμα is a term of substance, in itself conveying no idea of mentality, and ranging all the way from "wind" or "air" to an extremely refined substance of which God and the soul are composed, and while in the nearly contemporaneous Hermetic literature πνεῦμα is definitely graded below ψυχή in the scale of being, πνεῦμα in N. T. assumes a position of definite superiority to the ψυχή. This is due not to the degradation of ψυχή, but to the elevation of πνεῦμα. The former is still, as in the Greek usage generally, the general term for the seat of life, feeling, thought, and will. But πνεῦμα, having now become an individualised term and as such a name both for the soul of man and the Spirit of God, is used as the seat of the moral and religious life of man. (d) πνεῦμα is now used as a generic term for incorporeal beings, including in Paul those who have heavenly bodies. For this usage there is no exact previous parallel, though it has its basis in the application of the term πνεῦμα to God and to the demons. A product of this usage and the preceding, or at least related to them, is the antithesis here formed for the first time between ψυχικός and πνευματικός, which in Paul is applied to bodies, designating them as suitable, on the one hand, to a ψυχή, a soul in an ordinary material body, and on the other to a πνεῦμα, i. e., a soul no longer embodied in the ordinary sense (1 Cor. 15[44f.]); but also to men in a religious sense, distinguishing one who has not and one who has the Spirit of God (1 Cor. 2[14f.]). The latter usage appears also in Jude, v.[19]. (f) There is a clear distinction between the work of the Spirit of God in producing the so-called χαρίσματα, such as tongues, prophecy, etc., and the operation of the same spirit in producing ethical results, and a depreciation of the former as compared with the latter. This appears first in Paul, and is perhaps original with him. See Gunkel, *Die Wirkungen des heiligen Geistes*, pp. 62–97, esp. 77 *ff.*

The meanings of πνεῦμα in N. T. arranged in the order of their probable genetic relationships are as follows:

I.   Wind: Jn. 3⁸ᵃ: τὸ πνεῦμα ὅπου θέλει πνεῖ καὶ τὴν φωνὴν αὐτοῦ ἀκούεις, ἀλλ' οὐκ οἶδας πόθεν ἔρχεται, καὶ ποῦ ὑπάγει.   See also Heb. 1⁷.

II.   Breath, breath of life: 2 Thes. 2⁸: καὶ τότε ἀποκαλυφθήσεται ὁ ἄνομος ὃν ὁ κύριος ['Ιησοῦς] ἀνελεῖ τῷ πνεύματι τοῦ στόματος αὐτοῦ.   See also Rev. 11¹¹ 13¹⁵.

III.   Spirit: an incorporeal, sentient, intelligent, willing being, or the element by virtue of which a being is sentient, intelligent, etc.

A.   Embodied, viz., human spirit, that element of a living man by virtue of which he lives, feels, perceives, and wills; variously viewed:

1. As the seat of life, or that in man which constitutes him a living being. Lk. 8⁵⁵: καὶ ἐπέστρεψεν τὸ πνεῦμα αὐτῆς, καὶ ἀνέστη παραχρῆμα.   See also Mt. 27⁵⁰ Lk. 23⁴⁶ Jn. 19³⁰ Acts 7⁵⁹ Jas. 2²⁶.

2. As the seat of emotion and will, especially of the moral and religious life, including thought as concerned with religion: Mk. 14³⁸: γρηγορεῖτε καὶ προσεύχεσθε, ἵνα μὴ ἔλθητε εἰς πειρασμόν· τὸ μὲν πνεῦμα πρόθυμον ἡ δὲ σὰρξ ἀσθενής.   See also Mt. 26⁴¹ Mk. 8¹² Lk. 1⁴⁷ Jn. 4²³, ²⁴ᵇ 11³³ 13²¹ Acts 17¹⁶ 18²⁵ 19²¹ 20²² Rom. 1⁹ 2²⁹ 7⁶ 8¹⁶ 12¹¹ 1 Cor. 4²¹ 7³⁴ 16¹⁸ 2 Cor. 2¹³ 7¹, ¹³ Gal. 6¹, ⁸, ¹⁸ Eph. 4²³ Phil. 4²³ 2 Tim. 4²² Phm. ²⁵ Jas. 4⁵ 2 Pet. 3⁴. It sometimes seems to denote the human spirit as permeated with or dominated by the divine Spirit, either ethically (Jn. 3⁶ᵇ), or ecstatically (1 Cor. 14¹⁴, ¹⁵, ¹⁶).

3. As the seat of consciousness and intelligence: 1 Cor. 2¹¹: τίς γὰρ οἶδεν ἀνθρώπων τὰ τοῦ ἀνθρώπου εἰ μὴ τὸ πνεῦμα τοῦ ἀνθρώπου τὸ ἐν αὐτῷ; see also Mt. 5³ Mk. 2⁸ Lk. 1⁸⁰.

4. Generically, without reference to these distinctions: Rom. 8¹⁰: εἰ δὲ Χριστὸς ἐν ὑμῖν, τὸ μὲν σῶμα νεκρὸν διὰ ἁμαρτίαν, τὸ δὲ πνεῦμα ζωὴ διὰ δικαιοσύνην.   See also 1 Cor. 5³, ⁴ Phil. 1²⁷ Col. 2⁵ 1 Thes. 5²³ Heb. 4¹² 12⁹ (?) Rev. 22⁶.

B.   Unembodied or disembodied spirit: more exactly, a sentient, intelligent, volitional being whose mode of life is not conditioned by a body in the ordinary sense of the term; used of various beings so conceived, the specific reference being indicated by limitations of the word or by the context; thus of:

1. The Spirit of God, viewed as:

(a) The cause of extraordinary phenomena in human experience, such as prophecy, tongues, healings, etc.: 1 Cor. 12⁴: διαιρέσεις δὲ χαρισμάτων εἰσίν, τὸ δὲ αὐτὸ πνεῦμα.   See also Mt. 10²⁰ 12¹⁸, ²⁸, ³¹, ³² 22⁴³ Mk. 3²⁹ 12³⁶ 13¹¹ Lk. 1¹⁵, ¹⁷, ⁴¹, ⁶⁷ 2²⁵, ²⁶, ²⁷ 4¹⁸ 10²¹ 12¹⁰, ¹² Jn. 7³⁹ (bis) 20²² Acts 1⁵, ⁸, ¹⁶ 2⁴, ¹⁷, ¹⁸, ³³, ³⁸ 4⁸, ²⁵, ³¹ 5³, ⁹, ³² 7⁵¹, ⁵⁵ 8¹⁵, ¹⁷, ¹⁸, ¹⁹, ²⁹ 9¹⁷ 10¹⁹, ⁴⁴, ⁴⁵, ⁴⁷ 11¹², ¹⁵, ¹⁶, ²⁸ 13², ⁴, ⁹, ⁵² 15⁸, ²⁸ 16⁶ 19², ⁶ 20²³, ²⁸ 21⁴, ¹¹ 28²⁵ Rom. 15¹⁹ 1 Cor. 2¹⁰, ¹²ᵇ, ¹³, ¹⁴ 7⁴⁰ 12³, ⁷, ⁸, ⁹, ¹¹, ¹³ 14² Gal. 3², ³, ⁵ Eph. 3⁵ 1 Thes. 5¹⁹ 1 Tim. 4¹ Heb. 2⁴ 3⁷ 9⁸ 10¹⁵ 2 Pet. 1²¹ 1 Jn. 4²ᵃ, ⁶ᵃ Rev. 1¹⁰ 2⁷, ¹¹, ¹⁷, ²⁹ 3⁶, ¹³, ²² 4² 14¹³ 17³ 21¹⁰.   In Acts 16⁷ 1 Pet. 1¹¹ Rev. 19¹⁰ (?), the Spirit in this sense is identified with that of the risen Jesus.

(b) Active in an extraordinary way in the conception of a child: Mt. 1[18]: εὑρέθη ἐν γαστρὶ ἔχουσα ἐκ πνεύματος ἁγίου. See also Mt. 1[20] Lk. 1[35].

(c) Operative in the human spirit for the production of ethical results: Rom. 8[4]: ἵνα τὸ δικαίωμα τοῦ νόμου πληρωθῇ ἐν ἡμῖν τοῖς μὴ κατὰ σάρκα περιπατοῦσιν ἀλλὰ κατὰ πνεῦμα. See also Mt. 3[11] Mk. 1[8] Lk. 3[16] Jn. 3[5, 6a, 8b] 14[17, 26] 15[26] 16[13] Acts 9[31] Rom. 5[5] 8[2, 5, 6, 9, 13, 14, 15b, 16a, 23, 26, 27] 9[1] 14[17] 15[13, 16, 30] 1 Cor. 2[4] 3[16] 6[11, 19] 2 Cor. 1[22] 3[3, 6, 8, 17, 18] 4[13] 5[5] 6[6] 13[13] Gal. 4[6] 5[5, 16, 17, 18, 22, 25] Eph. 1[13, 17] 2[18, 22] 3[16] 4[3, 30] 6[17, 18] Phil. 2[1] 3[3] Col. 1[8] 1 Thes. 1[5, 6] 4[8] 2 Thes. 2[13] 2 Tim. 1[14] Tit. 3[5] Heb. 10[29] 1 Pet. 1[2] 4[14] Jude vv. 19, 20. In Rom. 8[9c] Phil. 1[19] Heb. 9[14], the Spirit in this sense is identified with that of the risen Jesus.

(d) The mind of God: 1 Cor. 2[11]: οὕτως καὶ τὰ τοῦ θεοῦ οὐδεὶς ἔγνωκεν εἰ μὴ τὸ πνεῦμα τοῦ θεοῦ.

(e) Operative in the external world: Acts 8[39]: ὅτε δὲ ἀνέβησαν ἐκ τοῦ ὕδατος, πνεῦμα κυρίου ἥρπασεν τὸν Φίλιππον. Cf. I above.

(f) Generically, without specific reference to the form of activity: Lk. 4[14]: καὶ ὑπέστρεψεν ὁ Ἰησοῦς ἐν τῇ δυνάμει τοῦ πνεύματος εἰς τὴν Γαλιλαίαν. See also Mt. 3[16] 4[1] 28[19] Mk. 1[10, 12] Lk. 3[22] 4[1] (bis) 11[13] Jn. 1[32, 33] (bis) 3[34] Acts 1[2] 6[3, 5, 10] 10[38] 11[24] Rom. 8[11] (bis) Gal. 3[14] 4[29] Eph. 4[4] 5[18] Heb. 6[4] 1 Pet. 1[12] 1 Jn. 3[24] 4[13] 5[6, 8] Rev. 22[17].

2. The spirit of man separated from the body after death:

(a) In a heavenly mode of existence: Acts 23[9]: οὐδὲν κακὸν εὑρίσκομεν ἐν τῷ ἀνθρώπῳ τούτῳ. εἰ δὲ πνεῦμα ἐλάλησεν αὐτῷ ἢ ἄγγελος—. See also 1 Cor. 5[5] Heb. 12[23].

(b) A ghost, spectre, shade, visible on earth: Lk. 24[37]: πτοηθέντες δὲ καὶ ἔμφοβοι γενόμενοι ἐδόκουν πνεῦμα θεωρεῖν. See also Lk. 24[39].

(c) In Sheol: 1 Pet. 3[19]: ἐν ᾧ καὶ τοῖς ἐν φυλακῇ πνεύμασιν πορευθεὶς ἐκήρυξεν.

3. An angel: Heb. 1[14]: οὐχὶ πάντες εἰσὶν λειτουργικὰ πνεύματα εἰς διακονίαν ἀποστελλόμενα διὰ τοὺς μέλλοντας κληρονομεῖν σωτηρίαν;

4. A demon: Acts 8[7]: πολλοὶ γὰρ τῶν ἐχόντων πνεύματα ἀκάθαρτα βοῶντα φωνῇ μεγάλῃ ἐξήρχοντο. See also Mt. 8[16] 10[5] 12[43, 45] Mk. 1[23, 26, 27] 3[11, 30] 5[2, 8, 13] 6[7] 7[25] 9[17, 20, 25] (bis) Lk. 4[33, 36] 6[18] 7[21] 8[2, 29] 9[39, 42] 10[20] 11[24, 26] 13[11] Acts 5[16] 16[16, 18] 19[12, 13, 15, 16] 1 Tim. 4[1] Rev. 16[13, 14] 18[2].

5. Without reference to these distinctions, referring qualitatively to any being not corporeally conditioned, or to all such, or to a group (other than any of the above), defined by the context; used both of beings conceived of as actually existing, and, especially as a descriptive term in negative expressions, of beings presented merely as objects of thought: Jn. 4[24a]: πνεῦμα ὁ θεός, καὶ τοὺς προσκυνοῦντας αὐτὸν ἐν πνεύματι καὶ ἀληθείᾳ δεῖ προσκυνεῖν. (The first instance only falls under this head.) Rom. 8[15]: οὐ γὰρ ἐλάβετε πνεῦμα δουλείας πάλιν εἰς φόβον, ἀλλὰ ἐλάβετε πνεῦμα υἱοθεσίας. See also Lk. 9[55] Acts 23[8] Rom. 1[4] 11[8] 1 Cor. 2[12a] 12[10] 14[12, 32] 15[45] 2 Cor. 11[4] 12[18] Eph. 2[2] 2 Thes. 2[2] 1 Tim. 3[16]* 2 Tim. 1[7] 1 Pet. 3[18] 4[6] 1 Jn. 4[1] (bis) 2b, 3, 6b Rev. 1[4] 3[1] 4[5] 5[6].

*Cf. 1 Enoch 20[6], ἐπὶ τῷ πνεύματι.

C. Generically, without reference to the distinction between embodied and unembodied spirit: Jn. 6⁶³ (bis) 1 Cor. 6¹⁷ Heb. 12⁹ (?).

II. ΣΑΡΞ.

Σάρξ bears throughout Greek literature the meaning "flesh," but is sometimes used by metonymy for the whole body. In the Lxx it translates בָּשָׂר, and takes over from the Hebrew certain other derived meanings, e. g., "kindred," and "a corporeal living creature." In N. T. certain further developments of meaning appear, and the word becomes one of the most important for the purposes of interpretation, especially of the Pauline epistles. Its meanings are as follows:

1. Flesh: the soft, muscular parts of an animal body, living or once living: Lk. 24³⁹: ψηλαφήσατέ με καὶ ἴδετε, ὅτι πνεῦμα σάρκα καὶ ὀστέα οὐκ ἔχει καθὼς ἐμὲ θεωρεῖτε ἔχοντα. See also Jn. 6⁵¹ (bis) ⁵², ⁵³, ⁵⁴, ⁵⁵, ⁵⁶, ⁶³ 1 Cor. 15³⁹ (quater) ⁵⁰ Jas. 5³ Rev. 17¹⁶ 19¹⁸ (quinquies) ²¹.

2. Body: the whole material part of a living being: 2 Cor. 12⁷: διὸ ἵνα μὴ ὑπεραίρωμαι, ἐδόθη μοι σκόλοψ τῇ σαρκί. See also Mt. 26⁴¹ Mk. 14³⁸ Jn. 1¹³ (?) Acts 2²⁶, ³¹ Rom. 2²⁸ 1 Cor. 5⁵ 2 Cor. 4¹¹ 7¹ 10³ᵃ Gal. 2²⁰ 3³ 4¹³, ¹⁴ 6⁸ (bis) ¹³ Eph. 2¹¹ᵇ, ¹⁵ 5²⁹ Phil. 1²², ²⁴ Col. 1²², ²⁴ 2¹, ⁵, ¹³ 1 Tim. 3¹⁶ Heb. 9¹⁰, ¹³ 10²⁰ 12⁹ 1 Pet. 3¹⁸, ²¹ 4¹ (bis) ², ⁶ 1 Jn. 2¹⁶ 4² 2 Jn. ⁷ Jude ⁷, ⁸, ²³. By metonymy, for embodiment, incarnation: Heb. 5⁷. With αἷμα, the whole phrase signifying, the body: Heb. 2¹⁴.

3. By metonymy: the basis or result of natural generation.

(a) The basis of natural generation and of kinship (the body, or the body plus whatever is concerned with generation and kinship): Jn. 3⁶ᵃ: τὸ γεγεννημένον ἐκ τῆς σαρκὸς σάρξ ἐστιν. (Only the first instance falls under this head. Cf. 6 below.) See also Rom. 4¹ 9³, ⁵, ⁸ 1 Cor. 10¹⁸ Gal. 4²³, ²⁹ Eph. 2¹¹ᵃ.

(b) As a collective term, equivalent to "kindred": Rom. 11¹⁴: εἴ πως παραζηλώσω μου τὴν σάρκα καὶ σώσω τινὰς ἐξ αὐτῶν. In this use the term passes beyond the limits of the physical and comes to include all the elements of a human being.

4. A corporeally conditioned living being: usually referring exclusively to man, yet sometimes including all corporeal living beings, and in any case designating the beings referred to not as human but as corporeal: Mt. 16¹⁷: μακάριος εἶ, Σίμων Βαριωνᾶ, ὅτι σὰρξ καὶ αἷμα οὐκ ἀπεκάλυψέν σοι ἀλλ' ὁ πατήρ μου ὁ ἐν [τοῖς] οὐρανοῖς. See also Mt. 19⁵, ⁶ 24²² Mk. 10⁸ 13²⁰ Lk. 3⁶ Jn. 1¹⁴ 17² Acts 2¹⁷ Rom. 1³ 3²⁰ 8³ᵇ, ᶜ (?) 1 Cor. 1²⁹ 6¹⁶ Gal. 1¹⁶ 2¹⁶ Eph. 5³¹ 6¹² 1 Pet. 1²⁴.

5. By metonymy: the creature side, the corporeally conditioned aspect of life, the external as distinguished from the internal and real, or the secular as distinguished from the strictly religious: Jn. 8¹⁵: ὑμεῖς κατὰ τὴν σάρκα κρίνετε, ἐγὼ οὐ κρίνω οὐδένα (cf. 7²⁴). See also 1 Cor. 1²⁶ 7²⁸ 2 Cor. 5¹⁶ (bis) 7⁵ 10² 11¹⁸ Gal. 6¹² Eph. 6⁵ Col. 3²² Phm. ¹⁶.

6. The product of natural generation apart from the morally transforming power of the Spirit of God; all that comes to a man by inheritance rather than from the operation of the divine Spirit. The term as thus used does not exclude, may even specifically include, whatever excellent powers, privileges, etc., come by heredity, but whatever is thus derived is regarded as inadequate to enable man to achieve the highest good: Phil. 3⁴: εἴ τις δοκεῖ ἄλλος πεποιθέναι ἐν σαρκί, ἐγὼ μᾶλλον. Note the context. See also Jn. 3⁶ᵇ Rom. 6¹⁹ 7⁵, ¹⁸, ²⁵ 8³ᵃ 2 Cor. 1¹⁷ Phil. 3³.

7. That element in man's nature which is opposed to goodness, that in him which makes for evil; sometimes thought of as an element of himself, sometimes objectified as a force distinct from him, this latter usage being, however, rather rhetorical: Rom. 8⁶: τὸ γὰρ φρόνημα τῆς σαρκὸς θάνατος. See also Rom. 8⁴, ⁵, ⁷, ⁸, ⁹, ¹² (bis) ¹³ 13¹⁴ Gal. 5¹³, ¹⁶, ¹⁷, ¹⁹, ²⁴; perhaps Eph. 2³ (bis) Col. 2¹¹, ¹⁸, ²³ 2 Pet. 2¹⁰, ¹⁸, though in all these latter cases σάρξ may itself mean simply body, and the implication of evil lie in other members of the sentence.

In 6 all the good that comes to man by nature is credited to the σάρξ, the evil of it is its moral inadequacy; in 7 the right impulses are credited to the νοῦς or the ἔσω ἄνθρωπος, and the σάρξ becomes a force positively and aggressively evil.

It has often been contended (see Schweitzer, Paul and His Interpreters, p. 86) that the σάρξ, which, according to Paul, is a force that makes for evil (6 above), is at the same time the body (2 above), and that it is to the compelling force of the body as such that, in his view, sin is due. If this is the case he must logically, at least, hold that the touch of the flesh is essentially polluting, and that there can be no salvation except through the release of the soul from the body. That Paul associated the tendency to sin with the body is undoubtedly true (1 Cor. 9²⁷) and is evidenced by the very fact of his using σάρξ for the power that makes for evil. But that he identified σάρξ as meaning body and σάρξ as meaning the force that makes for moral evil, that he ascribed either to the flesh as physical or to the evil impulse which he called σάρξ, compelling force, seems thoroughly disproved by the evidence. It is often assumed that this view was the current conception in Paul's day. It is true that from before the time of Plato there is manifest a tendency to regard the body as by virtue of its materiality injurious to the intellectual or moral interests of man. Apparently, also, comparatively early in the Christian period the Gnostics had developed the view which Paul is alleged to have held, viz., that "flesh" and "spirit" represent an antithesis which is at the same time substantial and ethical, that sin in the universe is a necessary consequence of the matter in it, and that it must be where matter is. But the evidence does not seem to warrant the conclusion that this development had already taken place in the N. T. period. Weber, in his Theologie des Talmud, maintained that rabbinism found the seat of the evil impulse, yeçer hara, in the flesh. But

Porter* has shown the incorrectness of that view, and Bous. affirms that Palestinian Judaism did not find the cause of sin in matter (*Rel. d. Jud.*², pp. 459 *ff.*).　While, therefore, it is evident that there was in Paul's intellectual world a soil out of which he might have developed such an idea, it is his own letters that must show whether he did or not, and they, in fact, show that he did not.　The conspectus of usages given above shows that the term was no longer the simple one that it was in classical Greek.　It had taken on new meanings from the Hebrew בָּשָׂר, and developed still others not found in the Hebrew word.　In this process of development, the steps of which it is fairly easy to trace, the distinctly physical sense is left behind.　Even in 3 b, as also clearly in 4 and 5, the term is no longer purely material.　Nor is it so in 6.　Under the term as so used (see Phil. 3³ᶠ·) the apostle includes all that comes as the sequel of natural generation, both physical and immaterial, both good and evil, but especially the good. When he finally passed by another metonymy to isolate under this same term "flesh" the evil element of heredity it is very improbable that he at the same time added the idea of the exclusively physical, which had already been dropped at a much earlier point.　And this conclusion is confirmed by the fact that we find usage 6 in a later letter than that in which 7 appears, which indicates that in the development of meaning 7 the apostle has not left 6 behind.　To these considerations it is to be added that Paul nowhere ascribes compelling power to the σάρξ in either sense of the word.　The life in the flesh may be a life of faith and of victory over evil (Gal. 2²⁰), and in faith there is a force to overcome the flesh in its worst sense (Rom. 6¹, ² Gal. 5¹⁶, ²², ²³).　Finally it must be said that so far from sharing the feeling that is expressed by Plato, Seneca, and Plutarch, that true blessedness is achieved only by getting rid of the body, Paul retained the feeling, derived from his Hebrew ancestry, that the soul could not be wholly happy without a body.　*Cf.* 1 Cor., chap. 15; 2 Cor., chap. 5; 1 Thes. 5²³; Rom. 8¹¹. We conclude, therefore, that while to Paul the body is inferior to the soul and needs to be kept in subjection, and while there is a force in man that makes for evil, which he calls σάρξ, yet this force is not the body, and neither it nor the body exercises a compelling influence for evil upon the soul of man.

It might perhaps have been expected that inasmuch as Paul frequently uses πνεῦμα and σάρξ in antithesis it would always be the same meanings that would be contrasted.　Such, however, proves not to be the case.　On the contrary, the numerous meanings of the two terms give rise to a number of antitheses between them.　In Gal. 6⁸ 1 Cor. 5⁵ 2 Cor. 4¹¹ Rom. 2²⁸, ²⁹ Col. 2⁵, the contrast is between the flesh, or the body, and the spirit of man, an antithesis that in most Greek writers would have been expressed by σῶμα and ψυχή; but in most of the passages cited there is an emphasis on the religious capacity of the πνεῦμα that would not have been conveyed

---

* "The Yeçer Hara: A Study in the Jewish Doctrine of Sin," in *Biblical and Semitic Studies, by Members of the Faculty of Yale University,* New York and London, 1901.

by ψυχή. In Gal. 6⁸ the sowing to the flesh is the devotion of one's goods (see v.⁶) and energies to the satisfaction of the demands of the body; sowing to the spirit is devoting these things to the development of the spirit-life, which is both intellectual and religious. In Gal. 3² the flesh is, as in the preceding cases (see esp. Rom. 2²⁸, ²⁹), the physical flesh, that in which the cricumcision which they were urged to accept took place; but the spirit is the Spirit of God, which they received (v.²) when they accepted the gospel, and by which miracles were wrought among them (v.⁵). In Gal. 4²³ σάρξ, as in Rom. 9³, ⁵, ⁸, is clearly the basis of natural generation, the contrast being with the promise in fulfilment of which Isaac was born extraordinarily; in the application of the allegory ὁ γεννηθεὶς κατὰ σάρκα (v.²⁹) refers to the Jew who depends upon his heredity for salvation (the word thus verging towards meaning 6) in contrast with one whose life is according to the Spirit of God, or possibly with one who has been born according to the Spirit, an idea suggested in Rom. 6⁴ and further developed in Jn. 3⁶. In Rom. 1³, despite the similarity of the phrases to those in Gal. 4²³, ²⁹, σάρξ is probably to be taken as denoting a corporeally conditioned being, and πνεῦμα as a generic term for an unembodied being (III B 5), κατά meaning "viewed as" and the whole passage indicating the high rank of Jesus, first, among earthly (corporeally conditioned) beings, and, secondly, among holy heavenly (not corporeally conditioned) beings. Somewhat similar is the contrast in 1 Tim. 3¹⁶, but σάρξ probably denotes the body or the corporeally conditioned mode of life, and πνεύματι, by a further metonymy suggested by the desire to parallel ἐν σαρκί, denotes an incorporeal mode of being rather than an incorporeal being. In Phil. 3³ πνεῦμα manifestly denotes the Spirit of God, and σάρξ, as already pointed out, all that man obtains by heredity. In Rom. 7⁵ σάρξ probably means the totality of the life apart from the Spirit (as in Phil. 3³), while πνεῦμα in 7⁶ stands for the human spirit as the seat of religious life. In Rom. 8⁴⁻¹¹ there is, as indicated above, a gradual transition from this meaning of σάρξ to the more positively ethical sense, while in vv.¹², ¹³ there is probably a return to the earlier meaning. Throughout these verses πνεῦμα denotes the Spirit of God, and sometimes the Spirit of Christ identified with the Spirit of God. The absence of the article gives the phrases in which it is lacking a qualitative force, by which it approximates to the generic sense, as inclusive of the divine and human spirit, but the term probably always retains in the apostle's mind a reference to the divine Spirit. In Gal. 5¹⁷⁻²⁵ the flesh is the force that makes for sin, and πνεῦμα is the divine Spirit, the omission of the article having the same effect as in Rom., chap. 8.

XVIII. ΔΙΑΘΗΚΗ.*

I. CLASSICAL USAGE.

Of the usage of Greek writers to and including Aristotle, an extended examination has been made by Dr. F. O. Norton.† Of two hundred and twelve writers whose extant remains were examined the word was found in only nine, viz., Aristophanes, Lysias, Isocrates, Isæus, Plato, Demosthenes, Aristotle, Dinarchus, and Hyperides. Among these writers Isæus is the most important. The following is substantially Norton's tabulation of uses, slightly changed as to form:

1. Arrangement, disposition, testamentary in character.

(a) In the plural, of the single provisions of a will, but not designating the will as a whole: Isæ. 1²⁴, εἰ γὰρ δή, ὦ ἄνδρες, ὡς οὗτοί φασιν, ἐν ταῖς νῦν γεγραμμέναις διαθήκαις ἔδωκεν αὐτοῖς τὴν οὐσίαν: "For if now, O men, as these men say, in the present written provisions he gave you the property. . . ."

(b) In the plural, of the sum total of the provisions of the will, so that the plural is equivalent to "will" and can be so translated: Lys. 19³⁹: ὁ γὰρ Κόνωνος θάνατος καὶ αἱ διαθῆκαι, ἃς διέθετο ἐν Κύπρῳ, σαφῶς ἐδήλωσαν ὅτι πόλλοστον μέρος ἦν τὰ χρήματα ὧν ὑμεῖς προσεδοκᾶτε: "For the death of Conon and the will which he made in Cyprus plainly showed that the money was a very small part of what you expected." See also Isæ. 2¹⁴; Dem. 27¹³.

(c) In the singular, of a will or testament as a whole: Plato Legg. XI 923C, ὃς ἂν διαθήκην γράφῃ τὰ αὐτοῦ διατιθέμενος: "whoever writes a will disposing of his possessions." See also Aristoph. Vesp. 584, 589; Dem. 46²⁵.

2. An arrangement or agreement between two parties in which one accepts what the other proposes or stipulates; somewhat more one-sided than a συνθήκη. It may include provisions to be fulfilled after the death of the party making the stipulations, but is not strictly testamentary in character. Isæ. 6²⁷: καὶ γράψας διαθήκην, ἐφ' οἷς εἰσήγαγε τὸν παῖδα, κατατίθεται μετὰ τούτων Πυθοδώρῳ: "And having written out an agreement, by which he introduced the boy (into his φρατρία), he deposited it, with their con-

---

* For other literature, see Westcott, *The Epistle to the Hebrews*, pp. 298-302; Fricke, *Das Exegetische Problem Gal.* 3²⁰, pp. 16-18, Leipzig, 1879; Schmiedel, art. "Galatians" in *Encyc. Bib.* II 1609; Conrat, "Das Erbrecht in Gal. 3¹⁵⁻⁴¹" in *ZntW.* vol. V. pp. 204 ff.; Riggenbach, "Der Begriff der Διαθήκη in Hebräerbrief," in *Theologische Studien Theodor Zahn . . . dargebracht*, Leipzig, 1908; Norton, *A Lexicographical and Historical Study of Διαθήκη, from the Earliest Times to the End of the Classical Period*, Chicago, 1908; Ferguson, *The Legal Terms Common to the Macedonian Inscriptions and the New Testament*, pp. 42-46, Chicago, 1913. Behm, *Der Begriff Διαθήκη im Neuen Testament*, Naumburg, 1912; Lohmeyer, Διαθήκη: *Ein Beitrag zur Erklärung des neutestamentlichen Begriffs*, Leipzig, 1913; reviewed by Moffatt, in *Review of Theol. and Phil.* 1913, p. 338; Moulton and Milligan, *Vocabulary of the Greek Testament*, p. 148; Vos, "Hebrews, the Epistle of the Diatheke," in *Princeton Theological Review*, 1915, pp. 587-632; 1916, pp. 1-61.

† *Op. cit. supra.*

currence, with Pythodorus." The close relation between the two general meanings of the word are illustrated in Isæ. 4¹², in which διαθήκη, meaning a will, is classed among συμβόλαια, agreements or contracts: περὶ μὲν γὰρ τῶν ἄλλων συμβολαίων οὐ πάνυ χαλεπὸν τοὺς τὰ ψευδῆ μαρτυροῦντας ἐλέγχειν· ζῶντος γὰρ καὶ παρόντος τοῦ πράξοντος, καταμαρτυροῦσι· περὶ δὲ τῶν διαθηκῶν πῶς ἄν τις γνοίη τοὺς μὴ τἀληθῆ λέγοντας, κτλ. See also Isæ. 10¹⁰ Plato, Legg. XI 922 A–C. In Aristoph. Av. 435-461, διαθήκη denotes a compact: μὰ τὸν 'Απόλλω 'γὼ μὲν οὔ, ἢν μὴ διάθωνται γ' οἵδε διαθήκην ἐμοὶ ἥνπερ ὁ πίθηκος τῇ γυναικὶ διέθετο ὁ μαχαιροποίος, μήτε δάκνειν τούτους ἐμέ.

Among Norton's further conclusions from his investigation are the following: (a) The custom of will-making among the Greeks arose from the adoption of an heir. (b) Adoption *inter vivos* was irrevocable except by mutual agreement; but adoption by will became operative at death, and such adoption and the will might be revoked at the discretion of the testator. (c) A διαθήκη in the sense of a covenant was revocable only by mutual consent.

II. USAGE OF THE HEBREW בְּרִית.

In the Lxx διαθήκη occurs over three hundred times, in a very large majority of cases as the translation of בְּרִית. This Hebrew word uniformly signifies "covenant," "compact." It is often used of a mutual agreement between men, most commonly between kings or peoples: Gen. 14¹³ 21²⁷, ³² Ex. 23³² Deut. 7² Josh. 9⁶, ⁷, ¹¹, ¹⁵, ¹⁶ 1 Sam. 11¹ 2 Sam. 3¹², ¹³, ²¹ 5³ 1 Ki. 5¹² 20³⁴ 2 Chr. 23¹ [Lxx otherwise] ³ Isa. 33⁸ Ezr. 16²¹, etc. It is still more commonly employed of a covenant between God and men, in which case the initiative being thought of as wholly with God, the compact assumes in general the form of a gracious promise on God's part to do certain things, accompanied by the imposition of certain conditions and obligations upon men. The word in its various instances emphasises, now the mutuality of the relation (Gen. 17²⁻¹⁴; *cf.* Lev. 26⁹, ¹⁵ and context); now the promises of God (Gen. 9⁹, ¹¹ 15¹⁸ Lev. 26⁴⁵ Ps. 89³ᶠ·, ³⁴); and now the obligations laid upon the people and assumed by them (Ex. 19⁵ 24⁷, ⁸; *cf.* Gen. 17¹⁴); but in general carried the suggestion both of divine initiative and of mutuality. Only rarely are men said to make a covenant with God (2 Ki. 11¹⁷ 23³ 2 Chr. 34³¹), and even in these passages the act is perhaps thought as an acknowledgment of the obligation imposed by God.

The word is of frequent occurrence in the Zadokite Fragment, the product of a sect of Jews who withdrew to Damascus, where they established "the New Covenant," "the Covenant of Repentance." This work is assigned by Charles to a period between 18 B. C. and 70 A. D. See Schechter, *Fragments of a Zadokite Work*, Cambridge, 1910; Ch.*AP.* II, pp. 785-834. The בְּרִית here spoken of is always a covenant with God, or established by God. Thus 6⁴: "In accordance with the covenant which God established with Israel." In 4². ³ it is conceived of as existing from the time of Abraham. The "New Covenant entered into in the land of Damascus" (9²⁸) is apparently a covenant to return to the law of Moses (19¹⁻¹⁴). See also 1⁴. ¹². ¹⁵ 2¹ 4⁹ 5¹ 7¹² 8³. ¹¹. ¹⁵. ²¹ 9¹¹. ¹². ¹⁵. ²⁵. ³⁷. ⁴¹. ⁴⁹. ⁵¹ 10² 11² 16⁷. ¹² 20⁸ (Charles' notation).

III. USAGE IN JEWISH–GREEK.

The Lxx use διαθήκη in the sense of the Hebrew בְּרִית. The basis of this usage is on the one side in the use of the term διαθήκη by classical writers to denote a compact not testamentary in character, as in the examples cited under 2 above (esp. Aristoph. *Av.* 435–61), and, on the other, in the fact that the ordinary Greek word for "compact," συνθήκη, was probably felt to be inappropriate to express the thought of the Hebrew בְּרִית, the latter being commonly used not for a compact between two parties of substantially the same rank, but for a relationship between God and man graciously created by God, and only accepted by man.

Of special significance as showing that the employment of the word in this sense was not a mere translator's expedient, but that it reflected a real usage of the language is the fact that the O. T. Apocrypha, both Alexandrian and Palestinian, use διαθήκη uniformly in the sense of "covenant," with the possible exception of a few instances in which by metonymy it means "a decree," "ordinance" (Sir. 14¹². ¹⁷ 16²² 45¹⁷), and that both of the covenant of God with men, usually with Israel (2 Esd. 10³ Wisd. 18²² Jdth. 9¹³ Sir. 11²⁰ 17¹² 24²³ 28⁷ 39⁸ 42² 44¹¹. ¹⁸. ²⁰. ²² 45⁵. ⁷. ¹⁵. ²⁴. ²⁵ 47¹¹ Bar. 2³⁵ 1 Mac. 1¹⁵. ⁵⁷. ⁶³ 2²⁰. ²⁷. ⁵⁰. ⁵⁴ 4¹⁰ 2 Mac. 1² 7³⁶ 8¹⁵), and of a compact between men (Sir. 38³³ 41¹⁹ 1 Mac. 1¹¹ 11⁹). In the latter sense συνθήκη is also used, and in 2 Mac. it is uniformly the case that διαθήκη is used of God's covenant with Israel, and συνθήκη of covenants between men. Only once in the Apocrypha is συνθήκη used of a covenant of God with men (Wisd. 12²¹).

In the sense of "covenant" it occurs also in Ps. Sol. 9¹⁹ 10⁵ 17¹⁷; Test. XII Pat. Benj. 3⁸ (perhaps a Christian interpolation).*

In the sense of "testament," meaning not an instrument conveying property, but the message which one about to die leaves to his posterity, it is found in Test. XII Pat. Reub. 1¹; Naph. 1¹; Gad. 1¹; Ash. 1¹; Jos. 1¹, and in the title of the work and of each of the twelve parts of it.

Not possessing the two treatises on διαθῆκαι which in *Mut. nom.* 52 (6) Philo says he had written, we are dependent on the exegesis of a few passages for our knowledge of his usage. The word occurs in *Leg. alleg.* III 85 (28); *Sac. Ab.* 57 (14); *Quod det. pot.* 67 (19); *Quis rer. div.* 313 (62); *Mut.*

* The same idea is expressed in Jub. 1⁵. ¹⁰ 6⁴. ¹⁰. ¹¹. ¹⁶. ¹⁷. ³⁵ 14 ¹⁸. ²⁰ 15⁴. ⁹. ¹¹. ¹³. ¹⁴. ¹⁹. ²¹. ²⁶. ²⁸. ²⁹. ³⁴ 16¹⁴ 20³ 21⁴. ¹¹ 22¹⁵. ³⁰ 23¹⁶. ¹⁹ 24¹¹ 30²¹ 33⁹ 48⁸; but as the Greek of none of these passages is extant, they can be cited only as evidence of the currency of the idea in Jewish circles in the second century B. C., not directly of the usage of διαθήκη. The covenants here spoken of are the covenant with Noah (6⁴ᶠᶠ·), with Abraham (14¹⁸. ²⁰ 15⁴. ⁹. ¹¹) with Moses on Mt. Sinai (1⁵), etc. The covenant with Abraham is interpreted with special reference to circumcision.

nom. 51, 52 (6); 57, 58 (8); 263 (45); *Som.* II 223, 224 (33); *Spec. leg.* II
(Third, Fourth, and Fifth Com.) 16⁴. These passages, of which the most
significant are those from *Mut. nom.*, do not seem to sustain the verdict of
Cremer, p. 1008, and of Riggenbach (*op. cit.* p. 313) that Philo uniformly
uses the word in the sense "testament." Only in *Spec. leg.* II 16⁴ is this
clearly its meaning. Elsewhere "covenant" is the more probable meaning.
Both in the quotations from the Lxx and also in his own language he uses
phrases that imply mutuality. See *Mut. nom.* 52, 58. Note also that
in 58 he says that there are many kinds of διαθῆκαι, and in *Som.* II that
the διαθήκη is established as on the foundation of the soul of the righteous
man; neither of which things could appropriately be said of wills. It is
true that Philo repeatedly emphasises the element of grace which the
διαθήκη involves; but this fully comports with the fact that διαθήκη is in
his thought and usage not a contract in general (for this he uses συνθήκη in
Leg. ad Cai. 37 [6] but a covenant between God and man, and that he is
fully in agreement with the O. T. conception of the nature of that covenant.
There is, moreover, an entire absence in the passages of any of those things
which are characteristic of a will as distinguished from a covenant, as, *e. g.*,
its becoming effective after the death of the testator; an idea which is,
indeed, excluded by the fact that God is the maker of the διαθήκη. Even
if (as is probably not the case) Philo's usage is based on the idea of a testament, it has so departed from its starting point as to constitute practically
a new sense of the word.

In Josephus διαθήκη uniformly means "a will," "testament," or "testamentary provision," the plural being most frequent, meaning a "will."
In *Ant.* 13. 349 (13¹) it refers to the will of Cleopatra; in *Ant.* 18. 156 (6³)
to that of Bernice; always elsewhere apparently to the will of Herod the
Great. See *Ant.* 17. 53 (3²), 78 (4²), 146 (6¹), 188 (8¹), 195 (8²), 224–249
(9⁴⁻⁷) *passim*, 332 (11⁵); *Bell.* 1. 451 (23²), 573 (29²), 588 (30²), 600 (30⁷), 625
(32²), 645 (32⁷), 664 (33⁷), 669 (33⁸); 2. 2 (1¹), 20–38 (2³⁻⁷) *passim*, 99 (6³).
For a treaty between nations, or agreements between men, Josephus uses
συνθήκη (συνθῆκαι) *Ant.* 5. 55 (1¹⁶), 6. 230 (11⁸); *Bell.* 1. 586 (30³), 7. 221
(7¹) *et freq.*; and for the making of an agreement συντίθεσθαι, *Ant.* 1. 212
(12¹), 300 (19⁶), 339 (21¹) *et freq.* The absence of διαθήκη in the sense of
"covenant" is apparently to be explained by his failure ever to speak of the
covenant of God with his people, though it is also significant of his feeling
that διαθήκη was not the suitable word in his day and circle of thought for
an agreement between equals that in referring to agreements of this character which in the Lxx are called διαθῆκαι he uniformly employs some
other form of expression. See Riggenbach (*loc. cit. sup.*).

IV. USAGE IN LATER NON-JEWISH GREEK.

In the Greek papyri edited by Petrie, Mahaffy, Grenfell and Hunt,
Hogarth, Goodspeed, *et al.*, διαθήκη occurs frequently, always in the sense

of "testament," "will." Many of these are dated in the first and second centuries, a few as early as the reign of Augustus. See, *e. g.*, *BGU*. I 19. ii. 5; 75. ii. 8; 187[5]; 326. i. 1, 3; 327[2]; 340[10]; 361. ii. 19; II 388. iii. 5; 448[13]; 464[7]; 592. i. 6, 10; ii. 7; 613[30]; III 786. ii. 3; 896[8]; IV 1037[36]; 1113[5]; 1149[25]; 5151[7, 22]; *Pap.* Gd. *Cairo*, 29. iii. 3; *Pap. Lond.* I 77[47], etc.; II 127[6, 19]; 261[14]; P. Oxyr. I 75[12, 31]; 105[3] *et freq.*; 106[13, 21]; 107[7]; II 249[24]; III 482[34]; 489 *et freq.* *Cf.* M. and M. *Voc.* p. 148.

The following passage from Arius Didymus of the first century A. D. (quoted by Mullach, *Frag. Phil. Gr.* II, p. 87[4ff.] is significant. οὐδένα γοῦν οὕτως ὠμὸν εἶναι καὶ θηριώδη τὴν φύσιν, ὅς οὐκ ἄν σπουδάζοι μετὰ τὴν ἑαυτοῦ τελευτὴν εὐδαιμονεῖν τὰ τέκνα, καὶ καλῶς ἐπανάγειν μᾶλλον ἢ τοὐναντίον. Ἀπὸ ταύτης γοῦν τῆς φιλοστοργίας καὶ διαθήκας τελευτᾶν μέλλοντας διατίθεσθαι, καὶ τῶν ἔτι κυοφορουμένων φροντίζειν, ἐπιτρόπους ἀπολιπόντας καὶ κηδεμόνας, καὶ τοῖς φιλτάτοις παρατιθεμένους καὶ παρακαλοῦντας ἐπικουρεῖν αὐτοῖς: "No one certainly is so cruel and brutal in his nature that he would not be concerned that his children should after his death be prosperous and get on well rather than the contrary. It is this parental affection, indeed, that leads those about to die to make a will and to provide for those who are still unborn, leaving them stewards and guardians, and committing them to their best beloved and exhorting them to care for them."

From the usage, therefore, of writers before N. T. or approximately contemporaneous with it there emerge two distinct meanings of the word. "Testament" or "testamentary provision" is the most frequent use in classical writers, and is the invariable sense in Josephus and the papyri. The meaning "covenant" is very infrequent in classical writers, but is the almost invariable meaning in the Lxx, in the O. T. Apocr., both translated and original, both Alexandrian and Palestinian, and in the Pseudepigr. and Philo. The essential distinction between the two meanings is that in a testament the testator expresses his will as to what shall be done after his death, esp. in respect to his property; the covenant is an agreement between living persons as to what shall be done by them while living. This distinction requires qualification only by the fact that in rare cases, as is illustrated by the exx. from Isæus, a διαθήκη may be both contractual and testamentary in character. It is of prime importance to observe that in the διαθήκη (ברית) between God and men, so often spoken of in O. T., the initiative is with God, and the element of promise or command is prominent; but that it still remains essentially a covenant, not a testament. In their emphasis on the former fact some modern writers seem to lose sight of the latter.

V. NEW TESTAMENT USAGE.

If with the facts above established in mind, the N. T. examples are examined, it becomes evident that in the great majority of these "covenant"

in the O. T. sense of בְּרִית and as just defined is the more appropriate meaning. See, *e. g.*, Mt. 26²⁸ Mk. 14²⁴ (with their allusion to Ex. 24⁸) Lk. 1⁷²
(with its clear reference to the covenant of God with Israel; *cf.* also 1 Mac.
1¹⁵, ⁶³) Lk. 22²⁰ (with allusion to Jer. 31³¹) Acts 3²⁵ and 7⁸ (with their explicit
reference to Gen. 12³ and 17¹⁰). In the passages in Hebrews, 7²² 8⁶, ⁸⁻¹⁰,
etc., despite the contrary arguments of Cremer, Riggenbach, *et al.*, the most
probable meaning of the word, except in 9¹⁶, ¹⁷, is "covenant," the meaning which it clearly has in the passages quoted from the Lxx. It is noteworthy that the argument continues after these verses on the same lines as
before them and unaffected by them. They are most probably a parenthetical attempt of the author to enforce his position by appeal to the facts
concerning διαθήκη in a different sense (as a modern preacher discussing
law in the imperative, moral, sense will parenthetically confirm his argument by appeal to the characteristics of law in the wholly different sense
in which it is used in modern science), or possibly even a gloss of an early
scribe. *Cf.* M. and M. *Voc. s. v.* The identification of the old covenant
with the law is paralleled in Sir. 24²³ Ps. Sol. 10⁵; 2 Cor. 3⁶, ¹⁴, etc.

This is also the usage, prevailingly at least, of Paul. Rom. 9⁴, with its
reference to the privileges of Israel; Rom. 11²⁷, with its quotation of Isa. 59²¹;
1 Cor. 11²⁵, which, whether it be interpreted in the light of Mk. 14²⁴ (written
later than Paul, but doubtless reflecting a tradition antedating his writing),
or of Jer. 31³¹, yields the same meaning; 2 Cor. 3⁶, ¹⁴, with their contrast
between the new covenant and the old, the latter clearly referring to the
O. T. law; Gal. 4²⁴ and Eph. 2¹², are all most naturally interpreted as speaking of a "covenant" in the O. T. sense; none of them (except Heb. 9¹⁶ff·)
sustains the meaning "testament."

So far from its being self-evident (as Cremer affirms) that the word means
"testament" in Gal. 3¹⁵, ¹⁷ the evidence of such meaning must be found
in the passage itself, without presumption in its favour. That evidence is
apparently conflicting. Certain elements of the context are consistent
with the meaning "testament," and apparently in its favour. Thus v.¹⁸
speaks of that which is to be obtained through the διαθήκη as κληρονομία,
a word commonly translated "inheritance." Again, in v.²⁹, with evident
reversion to the thought of the κληρονομία, the phrase κατ' ἐπαγγελίαν
κληρονόμοι, "heirs according to promise," occurs. The word κληρονόμοι
in turn becomes the occasion of the analogical argument of 4¹⁻⁵, in which
κληρονόμος clearly means "heir," not, indeed, one who has received his
inheritance, nor necessarily one who is to receive it after the death of his
father, but one who is to enter into a possession not yet his. On the other
hand, the διαθήκη of which 3¹⁷ speaks is, in the O. T. passage there referred
to, clearly a covenant. Either, therefore, the apostle, availing himself of
the ambiguity of the Greek word, speaks of that as a testament which in
the passage to which he is referring was conceived of as a covenant, or beginning with the idea of the covenant he has at some point between 3¹⁷ and 4¹

introduced the idea, if not of the testament, at least the related notion of
an heir. As bearing on the decision between these alternatives the following facts must be considered: (a) It is against the theory that διαθήκη in
3¹⁷ is a will that it is expressly said to have been made by God. For a will
becomes effective only on the death of the maker of it. The case of a
father making a will and his son receiving an inheritance on the death of
the father may be used to illustrate by analogy the relation of God and the
believer, as is perhaps the case in 4¹ff.; but it is more difficult to suppose
that the incongruous element of the death of God should either be involved
in the argument of vv.¹⁵⁻¹⁷ or, though implied in the language, be ignored in
silence when the will is directly called God's. (b) The διαθήκη of v.¹⁵
must be a covenant, not a will, for of the διαθήκη here spoken of it is said
οὐδεὶς ἀθετεῖ ἢ ἐπιδιατάσσεται, and this is true of an agreement, which
once made can not be modified (except, of course, by mutual agreement of
the parties to it, an exception too obvious to receive mention), but is not
true of a will. Ramsay's argument (Com. pp. 349–370) that because Paul
speaks of the διαθήκη as irrevocable he must have had in mind a will, and
specifically a Greek will by which a son was adopted into a family and made
an heir, fails of convincingness, and his conclusions have been disproved
by Norton at several points. (i) His contention that a Greek will of this
period ipso facto involved the adoption of a son, so that one accustomed to
Greek usage would at once understand by διαθήκη a will adopting a son,
is not borne out by the evidence (Norton, op. cit. pp. 39–55. Cf. also the
passage quoted above from Ar. Did., from which it appears that at the date
of that passage a will was thought of primarily as a provision for the children of one's body). (ii) The evidence does not show that a Greek will,
whether involving adoption or not, was irrevocable (Norton, pp. 63–68).
That adoption within the lifetime of the father was irrevocable after it had
gone into effect does not carry with it the irrevocability of a will adopting
a son at death, still less the irrevocability of wills in general. Nor can the
mention of adoption in 4⁵ be accepted as evidence that Paul here has in
mind an adoptive will; so essential an element of his argument must have
been stated here, not remotely suggested many lines later. The evidence
of the papyri and of Josephus can not be cited for the custom in respect to
Greek wills, but as showing what ideas Paul would associate with the word
διαθήκη, meaning "a will," it is not without significance that both the
papyri and Josephus show clearly that the wills of which they speak are
revocable. In respect to Josephus, see Bell. i. 664 (33⁷), 668 f. (33⁸);
Ant. 17. 78 (4²). (iii) Ramsay overlooks the fact that if v.¹⁶ be from
Paul he here makes Christ the son and heir, and that it is foreign to Paul's
thought in this epistle to think of Christ as son and heir by adoption. Cf.
Schm., art. "Galatia," in Encyc. Bib. II 1609.

To suppose that v.¹⁵ ignores the maker of the will, affirming in effect that
no one but the maker of the will can modify it, is to reduce it to absurdity,

since the precise purpose of the argument is to show that God, the maker of the διαθήκη, could not by the law that came in later nullify the former. Nor can the force of this fact be evaded by appealing* to v.¹⁹ as evidence that Paul thought of the law as given by angels, hence not from God; for δι᾽ ἀγγέλων does not describe the law as proceeding from the angels, but only as being given by their instrumentality, and the whole argument of vv.¹⁹⁻²² implies that the law proceeded from God. Only then, in case the apostle's argument in vv.¹⁵⁻¹⁷ involves the application to the διαθήκη . . . . θεοῦ of statements true of a διαθήκη ἀνθρώπου only after the death of the testator, which would deprive the argument not only of convincingness but even of speciousness, can the διαθήκη be a will.

If with this evidence against the meaning "testament," we reconsider the evidence of κληρονομία and κληρονόμος, we do not find that this furnishes any substantial evidence in favour of it. For κληρονομία does not at all uniformly mean "inheritance" in the strict sense of the word, but often "possession," occurring as the translation of מֹרָשָׁה and in reference to the possession which is promised to the seed of Abraham in the covenant. See note on κληρονομία, chap. 3¹⁸. κληρονομίαν, in 3¹⁸, therefore, constitutes no argument for taking διαθήκη in 3¹⁷ in the sense of "will." On the contrary, by association it rather suggests the covenant. κληρονόμος, in 3²⁹, undoubtedly reverts to the κληρονομία of 3¹⁸. In the Lxx, where this word occurs infrequently, it always means "an heir," and this is also its meaning even in the passages cited by L. & S. for the meaning "possessor" (Isoc. 109 e; Dem. 603 fin.). See also Plut. Cic. 41³. Yet in these latter passages the word is used tropically, and though in Rom. 8¹⁷ it means "heir," it can not be taken in the strict sense of that word. So here, also, as the reference to κληρονομίαν implies, it probably means, not "one inheriting under a will," but "destined recipient of the promised possession." The use of κληρονόμοι at this point doubtless leads to its employment in the illustration in 4¹ff. probably with a closer approximation to the usual sense of the term, though even here there is no reference to a will or the death of the father, and the term quite possibly means "one who is to come into possession of property at a later time." But whatever the exact sense of κληρονόμος here, it is more reasonable to recognise a shift of meaning at this point, or a gradual shift from 3¹⁵ to this point, than from this point to carry back into διαθήκη in vv.¹⁵, ¹⁷, the meaning "testament," which is at variance with the evidence of that passage itself.

If appeal be made from the evidence of the passage to the usage of the readers, and it be said that to them διαθήκη could mean only "testament," it must be answered (a) it is not certain that the meaning "covenant" was wholly unknown to them. See the evidence respecting classical usage above. (b) The assumption (of Ram., e. g.) that the Galatians, being Gentiles, must have understood διαθήκη in the common Greek sense, ignores

* Schmiedel, art. "Galatians," in Encyc. Bib. II 1611.

the fact, of capital importance for the interpretation of Gal. 3^{15ff.}, that throughout chaps. 3 and 4 Paul is replying to the arguments of his judaising opponents, and is in large part using their terms in the sense which their use of them had made familiar to the Galatians. See detached note on *Sons of Abraham*, p. 156. Nor is the general assumption that Paul's usage is governed by that of his Greek readers sustained, but rather discredited, by a study of Paul's vocabulary in general, which clearly shows that he is strongly influenced by the usage of the corresponding Hebrew terms. *Cf.*, *e. g.*, πνεῦμα and σάρξ, νόμος, δικαιοσύνη and ἁμαρτία. Whether Paul, like many modern preachers, used his own vocabulary in his own sense and left to his readers to gather that sense from his way of using it, or whether the meanings which Greek words had acquired among the Greek-speaking Jews were more familiar to the common people among the Greeks, or among Christians in particular, than the remains of the literary Greek of that period would lead us to suppose—whatever the reason, a study of the apostle's use of words shows clearly that he was not at all limited in his use of them to meanings that can be proved to exist by the evidence of contemporary Greek writings. His own writings must furnish the decisive evidence as to the meaning which he attached to them.

To take κατὰ ἄνθρωπον as meaning "I am using terms in a Greek, not a Hebrew sense," as Ramsay in effect does, is quite unjustified by the usage of that expression. If, indeed, it could be shown that according to the usage familiar in Galatia a testament, διαθήκη, was irrevocable, then it would be evident that Paul's argument would on that account have appealed more effectively to the Galatians, since the most discriminating readers would observe the double sense of the word. But even in that case it would remain probable that by διαθήκη Paul meant simply a covenant.

The contention of Halmel, *Über römisches Recht im Galaterbrief*, that διαθήκη refers to a Roman will, is refuted by the fact that the Roman will was revocable by the maker of it.

In favour of the view advocated by Hauck in *Th.St.u.Kr.* 1862, pp. 517 *f.*, and adopted also by Bous. (*SNT. ad loc.*), that διαθήκη signifies a stipulation (legal instrument), in a sense broad enough to cover both "will" and "covenant," there can be cited some classical examples of διαθήκη referring to an agreement that included stipulations of a testamentary character (*cf.* Norton, pp. 30–38), but against it is the fact that it brings the statement οὐ ἀθετεῖ, etc., into conflict with the facts, since it is now well established that both Greek and Roman wills were revocable by the maker. For that reason the διαθήκη here must not be broad enough to include a will.

It remains, therefore, that while it is by no means impossible that Paul should, availing himself of the more common usage of διαθήκη in the Greek-speaking world at large, have converted the "covenant" with Abraham into a "will," and based an argument concerning it on the usage of the Greek world in respect to wills, yet the evidence of usage and the passage tends strongly to the conclusion that this is not what he did, but that, though in 4¹ he arrived by successive shadings of thought at the idea of an heir, by διαθήκη 3¹⁵, ¹⁷ he meant not "will," but "covenant," in the sense of the O. T. בְּרִית. This conclusion is in harmony with the usage of N. T. generally (except Heb. 9¹⁶ff.) and with the whole context in Galatians. A covenant or compact duly executed is irrevocable; not to fulfil it is a breach of faith. "It is evident, first, that the essential thing in the covenant, distinguishing it from ordinary contracts or agreements, was the oath under the solemn and terrible rites in use—a covenant is an intensified oath, and in later times the term 'oath' is usual as a synonym of covenant. And, secondly, as the consequence of these solemnities, that the covenant was an inviolable and immutable deed. Hence a frequent epithet applied to covenants is 'eternal' (2 Sam. 23⁵, Lk. 24⁸). The penalty of breaking the covenant was death through the curse taking effect" (Davidson, in HDB. I 510; see more fully there, and cf. Gen. 15¹³⁻¹⁸ 26²⁸ 31⁴⁴ff.). The O. T. covenant involved promises (see ἐπαγγελίαι, v.¹⁶), and might be spoken of with practically exclusive reference to the element of promise or with special reference to the possession (κληρονομία) which they receive to whom the covenant pertains.

To the conclusion that it is in this sense that Paul uses the word, it should be added that for the determination of his argument in its essential and important features it is, after all, a matter of little consequence whether διαθήκη meant, for him, a covenant or a testament. The proposition for which he is contending is clear, namely, that the principle of faith which he conceives to have been revealed to Abraham in the promises to him is not displaced, as the basis of God's relationship to men, by the legalism which he discovers in the law. Whether he conceived of the revelation to Abraham as a divinely initiated, yet in a sense mutual, covenant, or, tropically speaking, a will, and whether in his effort to present his thought to the Galatians he availed himself of the characteristics of covenants between men, or of the usage in respect to wills is a matter of the surface of his thought rather than the substance.

XIX. ΣΠΕΡΜΑΤΙ AND ΣΠΕΡΜΑΣΙΝ.

For the interpretation of the argument which is made to turn on the distinction between σπέρματι and σπέρμασιν the following data must be considered:

1. The word זֶרַע, rendered by σπέρμα in the Lxx, is used sometimes of the seed of plants (Gen. 1¹¹, ¹², ²⁹, etc.) sometimes of the *semen virile* (Lev. 15¹⁶, ¹⁷, ¹⁸), but is most commonly a collective noun meaning "posterity." In a few cases it is used of a single person (Gen. 4²⁵ 21¹³ 1 Sam. 1¹¹ 2 Sam. 7¹² 1 Chr. 17¹¹), but in most if not all of these instances designates such person not as an individual but as constituting, or (qualitatively)

as belonging to, the posterity of the parent spoken of. The plural, זַרְעֵיכֶם, occurs in 1 Sam. 8¹⁵, meaning "seeds of grain," "grain." In post-biblical language a plural זַרְעָתָא and זַרְעִיּוֹת is found, meaning "races" or "families," in the former case races existing side by side. See Levy, *Neu-hebräisches u. Chaldäisches Wörterbuch*, Leipzig, 1876–1889.

2. In Greek writers σπέρμα has nearly the same usage as the Hebrew זֶרַע, but occurs much more frequently in the plural. (a) For the seed of plants, it occurs in the singular or plural, and from Hesiod down. See Hes. *Op.* 446, 471; Xen. *Oec.* 17⁸, ¹⁰; Epict. *Diss.* 4. 8³⁶. In the papyri the plural is the common term for grain. See *Pap. Amh.* II 61³ (B. C. 163); *Pap. BM.* II 97, 98, 201; III 122, etc. (all from the first century A. D.); *BGU.* I 20³, ¹⁰, 31¹ (second century A. D.) *et freq. Pap. Kar.* contains 91 examples in as many grain receipts, many of them dating from A. D. 158–9; (b) the meaning *semen virile* is illustrated in Pind. *Pyth.* 3²⁷, etc., Eurip., and in Epict. *Diss.* 1. 9⁴; 1. 13²; (c) as a singular collective for offspring, posterity, it is among the Greeks a poetic term (Æsch. *Fr.* 295, *Cho.* 503); (d) the use of the word for an individual is also chiefly poetic in Greek writers; thus in the singular in Pind. *Ol.* 9⁹¹; Æsch. *Prom.* 705; *Cho.* 234; Soph. *Ph.* 364, etc. The use of the plural σπέρματα for descendants is rare in classic writers (Æsch. *Eum.* 909, Soph. *O. C.* 600; once even in Plato, *Legg.* IX 853C).

3. In Jewish-Greek σπέρμα is used (a) of the seeds of plants: in the singular in Gen. 1¹¹, ¹², ²⁹ Deut. 28³⁸ 1 Ki. 18³², etc.; in the plural in 1 Sam. 8¹⁵ Ps. 126⁶ Isa. 61¹¹ Dan. (Th.) 1¹², ¹⁶; 1 Enoch 28² (for the seeds of trees); (b) of the *semen virile*, Lev. 15¹⁶, ¹⁷, ¹⁸; (c) in the singular as a collective term for posterity: Gen. 9⁹; 15³, ⁵, and very frequently in Lxx. So also in Ps. Sol. 9¹⁷ 17⁵ 18⁴, of the seed of Abraham and David. In 1 Enoch 22⁷ it is used of the posterity of Cain, and in the phrase σπέρμα ἀνθρώπων, meaning "men." In a few passages it is apparently used of a race, nation, or group of people without distinct reference to their descent from a common ances-tor: Prov. 11¹⁸: σπέρμα δικαίων; Isa. 57⁴ 65²⁵; so also in Ps. Sol. 17⁸, ¹¹; (d) in the singular for a single person, in Gen. 4²⁵ 21¹³ 1 Sam. 1¹¹ 2 Sam. 7¹² 1 Chr. 17¹¹; (for זֶרַע) Deut. 25⁵; (for בֵּן) Susan. 56; but in all these instances the term itself is probably not individualising, but is to be under-stood as the Hebrew term is explained above; (e) in the plural for descend-ants: Dan. (Th.) 11³¹; 4 Mac. 18¹; Jos. *Ant.* 8. 200 (7⁶). Of σπέρματα used in the sense of זַרְעִיּוֹת of late Hebrew, meaning "lines of descent," there are apparently no examples in either Jewish or non-Jewish Greek.

4. In N. T. σπέρμα is used: (a) for vegetable seed, both in the singular as a collective term (Mt. 13²⁴ *et freq.*) and in the plural (Mt. 13³² 1 Cor. 15³⁸); in Rom. 9²⁹ figuratively for the remnant of a nation from which it may spring anew; (b) for *semen virile*: Heb. 11¹¹; (c) in the sense, "race," "pos-terity": Mk. 12²⁰, ²¹, ²² Jn. 7⁴² 8³³ Rom. 1³ 4¹³, etc. An instance of the noun used by implication of a single person, qualitatively, as in the Lxx, occurs in 2 Cor. 11²².

5. The retention of the καί in the phrase καὶ τῷ σπέρματι in Gal. 3¹⁶ indicates that the apostle has in mind a passage in which not simply τῷ σπέρματι, but καὶ τῷ σπέρματι occurs; hence, Gen. 13¹⁵, or 17⁸, in both of which the promise pertains to the possession of the promised land, or 17⁷, in which the promise of God is that he will be the God of the seed of Abraham. Both these promises would doubtless be interpreted by Paul as involving the promise of divine favour, the promise that they to whom it pertained should be the people of God.

6. In the O. T. passages to which Paul must be supposed to refer in Gal. 3¹⁶ it is beyond all question clear that זֶרַע in Hebrew and σπέρμα in the Lxx are used collectively, signifying "posterity." See esp. Gen. 13¹⁶ 15⁵ 17⁷⁻⁹. Yet it must also be noticed that the promise that the land should be given to the seed of Abraham does not necessarily involve the participation of all the seed in that possession (the assertion that a man left his property to his family does not necessarily mean that all the members of the family share in it); and, moreover, that even in Gen. (see 21¹², quoted by Paul in Rom. 9⁷), there is a clear intimation of a division among the descendants of Abraham and the promise to Abraham's seed is restricted to the descendants of Isaac. This does not modify the meaning of the terms זֶרַע and σπέρμα, but by suggesting a distinction among the seed of Abraham, perhaps prepares the way for the thought that there is a seed which is the heir of the promises, and a seed which is such only in that it is descended from Abraham.

7. Of the suggestion thus afforded by Gen. 21¹² Paul, in fact, avails himself in Rom. 9⁶ᶠᶠ·, using the word σπέρμα in v.⁷, qualitatively, of Abraham's descendants without distinction, but in v.⁸ to designate those who are heirs of the promise. In the following verses of this passage, also, he argues that the separation between the seed of Isaac and Ishmael was followed by other like divisions, culminating in the creation of a new people—those that are called, not from the Jews only but also from the Gentiles (v.²⁴).

8. In Rom. 4¹¹⁻¹⁸ Paul interprets the seed of Abraham, to whom the promises were to be fulfilled in the collective sense and as including all that believe, both Jews and Gentiles. This is also the view distinctly expressed in the immediate context of the present passage (v.²⁹).

9. In this same passage, vv.²⁸, ²⁹, the apostle has also expressed the thought that believers, the seed of Abraham, are all one person (εἷς) in Christ Jesus. The sentence is ambiguous, but its thought may be kindred with that expressed in 1 Cor. 12¹², that believers constitute one body, and that body Christ, or akin to the identification of a race or family with its ancestor; cf. Rom. 9⁶, ⁷, ¹³, ³¹. Thus for the interpretation of Χριστός in the present verse as referring to all believers as a single body or race designated by its head, there are if not exact parallels, yet close analogies, and these in the immediate context.

These considerations suggest three possible interpretations of Gal. 3¹⁶:

(a) That σπέρμα is to be taken as meaning an individual descendant (*cf.* 1 and 3 above), and ἑνός as one person, σπέρματα as meaning descendants, and πολλῶν many persons, and Χριστός is to be understood of Jesus personally. The thought then is, "He says not to the seeds, meaning many persons, but to his seed, meaning one person, viz., Christ."

(b) That σπέρμα means a single line of descent, ἑνός one such line, σπέρματα lines of descent, πολλῶν many such lines, and Χριστός is to be understood of the one line of spiritual descendants, that spiritual race of which Christ is the head; so Dalmer and Zahn. *Cf.* also Bacon, *JBL.* 1917, pp. 139 *ff.*, who makes the plurality which Paul denies, that of Jew and Gentile (see Rom. 4¹⁶), bond and slave, etc., and the unity the one undivided body of Christ.

(c) That σπέρμα and σπέρματα are to be understood as designating respectively one and many individuals (as in 1), and Χριστός as a personal name, yet as standing not for Jesus alone and strictly as an individual, but for him as the head of a race or community; *cf.* 9 above.

Could it be shown that σπέρματα was in Paul's day current in the sense which is expressed by זַרְעֻיִּות in late Hebrew, the second of these interpretations would probably have the strongest claim to acceptance as being most consistent with the attested usage of words and the apostle's usual interpretation of Abraham's seed, though it would involve a use of Χριστός not precisely paralleled elsewhere in Paul. Nor is it impossible that Paul, assuming it to be self-evident that σπέρμα in this connection could mean nothing else than posterity, has invented for it so used a plural; as in English one might say, "He speaks not of posterities, but of posterity" (*cf.* Ltft. *ad loc.*, who in defence of a different interpretation makes a similar suggestion). If the absence of evidence of such a use of σπέρματα, and especially the fact that Paul must, it would seem, have expressed this idea more clearly than by the bare words ὅς ἐστιν Χριστός without intimation of their mystical or corporate meaning (*cf.* 1 Cor. 12¹² and Sief. *ad loc.*) deter us from adopting this view, it will be necessary to choose between (a) and (c). Of these the first is open to no serious objection on purely lexical grounds. For while the use of the singular σπέρμα is not precisely identical with that found in the passages cited in 3 (d) above, it is approximately so (see esp. Gen. 4²⁵), and the classical examples, 2 (d), clearly show that such a meaning is not foreign to Greek usage; the sense ascribed to the plural is verified both by classical and late Greek usage. But its interpretation of Χριστός in a strictly individual sense implies a conception of the seed of Abraham as a single person which is in conflict with the apostle's everywhere else expressed notion of the seed of Abraham and even with the immediate context (v.²⁹). The third view is open to the objection, obviated by the second, that it takes the *word* σπέρμα (in the singular) in a sense different from that which it has elsewhere in Paul. But since it takes the word in a sense vouched for by examples from Greek writers, and retains the apostle's usual conception of the thing referred to, it must probably be preferred to either of the other possible views. The argument thus interpreted may be paraphrased as follows: And when God said "and to thy seed" he spoke not of many persons, the descendants of Abraham in general, but of one person, and that one Christ, who is the head of that people to which belong all that are joined to him by faith.

But it is difficult to accept even the most probable of these interpretations as an expression of the apostle's thought, not because he is incapable of adopting a rabbinic method of interpretation, but because of the inharmoniousness of such an interpretation with his other references to the passage, and because the sentence contributes little to the force of his argument at this point. It is, moreover, not in harmony with the thought of vv.²⁸, ²⁹, where the word "seed" is used collectively and predicated not of Christ but of those who are Christ's. These considerations raise the question whether the whole sentence from οὐ λέγει to Χριστός is not a primitive corruption, and due to an early editor rather than to Paul. There is significant evidence to which due attention has not usually been given (yet *cf.* Lake, *The Earlier Epistles of St. Paul*, pp. 366 *f.*) that at so early a period that the evidence of it is now chiefly, though not wholly, internal and not documentary, the epistles of Paul were collected and edited. To this process we may assign the bringing together into one epistle of the parts of three or more letters that are now to be found in so-called 2 Cor.; the similar gathering into one of all the extant fragments of Paul's letters to the Philippians; the addition of 16¹⁻²³ to the Epistle to the Romans; the appending of the doxology of Rom. 16²⁵⁻²⁷, if not also the benediction of 2 Cor. 13¹³, both of these latter quite unlike the conclusion of Paul's other letters; and doubtless certain other editorial changes in the original text. That these processes were not accomplished solely by paste and scissors, but involved some addition of at least short phrases or sentences is evident. It is not, therefore, improbable that in connection with this process occasional comments on the text were added either directly to the text or to the margin, but in either case so early as to have become incorporated into the parent of all extant manuscripts. As respects the present sentence it is evident that the omission of it leaves a consistent connection, τοῦτο δὲ λέγω taking up the thought appropriately after καὶ τῷ σπέρματι αὐτοῦ and that the interjected sentence is complete in itself, and such a comment as an early editor might make. The objection to the first of the above-named interpretations that it conflicts with the apostle's conception of Christ as elsewhere expressed would, of course, not apply if it is an editorial remark, and on this hypothesis this interpretation is probably to be preferred to either of the others.

Ltft.'s view that σπέρματα is, so to speak, a coined plural, "a forced and exceptional usage," and that the apostle "is not laying stress on the particular word used, but on the fact that a singular noun of some kind, a collective term is employed, where τὰ τέκνα or οἱ ἀπόγονοι, for instance, might have been substituted, encounters the difficulty that, making the contrast between seeds and seed, between many and one, a contrast not between many persons and one person, but between many persons and one body of persons, it is unsupported by intimation of the passage that such is the nature of the intended contrast; rather does the clause ὅς ἐστιν Χριστός seem directly to exclude it. To have expressed this thought would have required a collective term—σώματος, e. g., after ἑνός or at least ὅς ἐστιν τὸ σῶμα Χριστοῦ in place of ὅς ἐστιν Χριστός. Ell. apparently wavers between understanding σπέρμα and Χριστός of Christ personally and taking them inclusively as denoting "not merely the spiritual posterity of Abraham but him in whom that posterity is all organically united."

XX. TA ΣΤΟΙΧΕΙΑ ΤΟΥ ΚΟΣΜΟΥ.*

The meaning of τὰ στοιχεῖα τοῦ κόσμου has been discussed from the early Christian centuries, and is still in dispute. στοιχεῖον is found in Greek writers from Plato on; in later Greek writers it is of very frequent occurrence. It is related to στοῖχος, "a line," "a row," "a rank," and its fundamental meaning is apparently "standing in a row," hence "an element of a series."

Grouping in one conspectus usage from Plato to Plutarch, with occasional use of later passages, yields the following table of meanings:

1. An element of speech, a letter of the alphabet, or, more exactly, the elementary sound for which it stands: Plato, *Crat.* 422A: (ὀνόματα) ἃ ὡσπερεὶ στοιχεῖα τῶν ἄλλων ἐστὶ καὶ λόγων καὶ ὀνομάτων, "(names) which are, as it were, elements of all other words and names." See also Plato, *Polit.* 277E, *et freq.*; Plut. *Quest conv.* IX, Prob. 3¹; Philo, *Opif. mund.* 127 (42). It is expressly distinguished from the syllable, because the latter can be broken up into diverse elements, in Aristot. *Metaph.* 6. 17¹² (1041 b³¹); *Poet.* 20. 1 *ff.* (1456 b²⁰ff.); *Categ.* 9(12). 3 (14 a³⁹ff.).

Κατὰ στοιχεῖον means "alphabetically," or by metonymy, "in order," Plut. *Defect. orac.* 23.

By metonymy, the elements or ultimate parts of anything are called

* Of the abundant literature upon the subject the following works are of special note: Neander, *Planting and Training of the Christian Church*, Bk. III, chap. 9; Bk. VI, chap 1; Schneckenburger, "Was sind die στοιχεῖα τοῦ κόσμου?" in *Theol. Jahrbuch*, 1848, pp. 444-453; Hilgenfeld, *Der Galaterbrief*, pp. 66 *ff.*; Hincks, "The Meaning of the Phrase τὰ στοιχεῖα τοῦ κόσμου in Gal. 4¹ and Col. 2⁸," in *JBL*. 1896, Pt. I, pp. 183 *ff.*; Spitta, *Der zweite Brief Petrus u. d. Br. d. Judas*, pp. 263 *ff.*; Everling, *Die paulinische Angelologie u. Dämonologie*, pp. 65 *ff.*; Diels, *Elementum;* Deissmann, art. "Elements" in *Encyc. Bibl.*; Pfister, "Die στοιχεια τοῦ κόσμου in den Briefen des Apostels Paulus," in *Philologus*, LXIX. 1910, pp. 410 *ff.*; Kennedy, *St. Paul and the Mystery Religions*, pp. 24 *ff.*, 61 *ff.*; Clemen, *Primitive Christianity*, pp. 106 *ff.*, 109 *f.*; Reitzenstein, *Poimandres*, pp. 71, 74, 80.; Sieffert, *Der Brief an die Galater* (in Meyer series, 9th ed.), pp. 235 *ff.*; Dibelius, *Die Geisterwelt im Glauben des Paulus*, pp. 78-85, 227-230.

στοιχεῖα: as of things in general: Xen. *Mem.* 2. 1¹, Plato, *Polit.* 278C; of a state: Aristot. *Pol.* 5. 9⁵ (1309 b¹⁶); *cf.* Isoc. 18 a (2¹⁶); of a discourse: Aristot. *Rhet.* 1. 6¹ (1362 a²¹); 2. 22¹³ (1396 b²¹, ²²); Dion. Hal. *Comp. verb.* 2.

2. One of the component parts of physical bodies. According to Diogenes Laertius first used by Plato in this sense. Empedocles employed the term ῥιζώματα and Anaxagoras σπέρματα, though Aristot. *Metaph.* 1. 4⁶ (985 a³²); 2. 3² (998 a²⁸), ascribes the use of στοιχεῖον to Empedocles, and Diogenes Laertius (II 1¹; IX 3²) employs it in speaking of the views of other pre-Socratic philosophers. Sometimes identified with ἀρχή, sometimes distinguished from it: Plato, *Tim.* 48B: λέγομεν ἀρχὰς αὐτὰ τιθέμενοι στοιχεῖα τοῦ παντός: "We call them (fire, water, air, earth) principles, regarding them as elements of the totality." See also Plato, *Theæt.* 201E; 202B, etc.; Aristot. *Meteor.* 1. 1¹ (338 a²²), etc.

By metonymy, anything that is small, simple and indivisible is called στοιχεῖον. Aristot. *Metaph.* 4. 3⁴ (1014 b³). Likewise, by metonymy, the term στοιχεῖον is applied to a genus, because it has one definition: Aristot. *Metaph.* 4. 3⁵ (1014 b⁹).

Among the Stoics, as testified by Diogenes Laertius and other witnesses, the term was in common use for the four elements, earth, water, air, fire, which were distinguished from the two ἀρχαί, θεός (λόγος) and ὕλη (οὐσία). See, *e. g.*, Diog. Laert. VII 1⁶⁸ᶠ· (134 *f.*); III 1¹⁹ (24); V 1¹³ (32); VIII 2¹² (76); IX 3² (21). Similarly in other writers influenced by Stoicism: Wisd. 7¹⁷ 19¹⁸; Philo, *Quis rer. div.* 197 (41), etc.; 4 Mac. 12¹³; Epict. *Diss.* 3¹³, ¹⁴; Plut. *Aristid.* 6⁴; Herm. *Vis.* 3. 13³; Just. Mart. *Dial.* 62²; Athenag. 22¹, ⁸.

By Philo and Plutarch the term was applied also to the sea, as one of the parts of the earth: Plut. *Quest. conv.* VIII, Prob. 8²; *Aq. an Ign.* 8ᵇ; Philo, *Opif. mund.* (131) 45.

In Orac. Sib. 2²⁰⁶ it is said: τότε χηρεύσει στοιχεῖα πρόπαντα τὰ κόσμου, and the στ. τ. κ. are defined as ἀήρ, γαῖα, θάλασσα, φάος, πόλος, ἤματα, νύκτες; in 8³³⁷ as ἀήρ, γαῖα, θάλασσα, φάος πυρὸς αἰθομένοιο, καὶ πόλος οὐράνιος, καὶ νύξ, καὶ ἤματα πάντα. In 3⁸⁰, where the language is otherwise very similar to 2²⁰⁶, τά is omitted and κόσμου apparently limits the verb in the sense of "order." As χηρεύσει naturally requires a genitive to complete its meaning and the τά after its noun is in any case awkward. it is a question whether it should not be omitted in 2²⁰⁶ and 8³⁷. In any case, we have here an exceptional conception of the στοιχεῖα, including two of the Stoic four elements, the sea, which Philo and Plutarch also call στοιχεῖον, and four others which may be called semi-astronomical.

By metonymy, στοιχεῖον denotes that in which qualities inhere: Plut. *Defect. orac.* 10.

3. A premise or fundamental proposition of a demonstration: Aristot. *Metaph.* 2. 3²ᶠᶠ· (998 a²⁶): καὶ τῶν διαγραμμάτων ταῦτα στοιχεῖα λέγομεν ὧν αἱ ἀποδείξεις ἐνυπάρχουσιν. See also Plut. *Marcell.* 17⁵, and *cf.* Aristot. *Metaph.* 4. 3² (1014 a³⁶ᶠᶠ·) cited under 4 below. Apparently it is

in this sense that the word was applied by later writers to Euclid's work on mathematics, and that of Archimedes. Aristot., *Metaph.* 4. 3⁴ (1014 b³ᶠᶠ·), apparently using στοιχεῖον and ἀρχή as synonyms, calls the unit and the point ἀρχαί, but only by implication στοιχεῖον. In *Topica* 8. 3⁶ (158 b³⁵), 8. 14 (12)⁸ (163 b²⁴); *Cat.* 9 (12)⁴ (14 a³⁹) στοιχεῖον is applied to a line or circle. It is in a kindred sense, also, that Aristot. uses στοιχεῖον of the even and the odd, the limited and the unlimited, as the fundamental elements of things, *Metaph.* 1. 5² (986 a¹).

Aristoph. *Eccl.* 652, in which τὸ στοιχεῖον means the shadow on a sundial, seems to imply the meaning "a line." See also Plut. *Soll. anim.* 29.

4. With a force closely akin to the preceding, sometimes scarcely distinguishable from it: a simple or elementary principle of knowledge or instruction. Isoc. 18 a (2¹⁶): ταῦτα γὰρ στοιχεῖα πρῶτα καὶ μέγιστα χρηστῆς πολιτείας ἐστιν. Nicolaus Com. 1. 30 (Meineke *Com. Frag.* IV 579): στοιχεῖα μὲν ταῦτ' ἐστι τῆς ὅλης τέχνης. See also Plato, *Legg.* VII 790C; Aristot. *Metaph.* 4. 3² (1014 a³⁵); Plut. *Lib. ed.* 16; Cornut. 14; Heb. 5¹²; and *cf.* Xen. *Mem* 2. 1¹, cited under 1.

5. Aristotle, having in mind the previous senses of the word, employs it as an inclusive term to cover two or more of them, defining it as "that from which as a constituent first principle, indivisible into other kinds of things, things of another kind are produced": *Metaph.* 4. 3² (1014 a²⁶⁻³¹): στοιχεῖον λέγεται ἐξ οὗ σύγκειται πρώτου ἐνυπάρχοντος ἀδιαιρέτου τῷ εἴδει εἰς ἕτερον εἶδος. *Cf. Metaph.* 2. 3²ᶠᶠ· (998 a²³ᶠᶠ·); 6. 17¹² (1014 b³¹); 12. 10 (1086 b); *Categ.* 9 (12)⁴ (14 a³⁹ᶠᶠ·). Plutarch in *Com. not.* 48, 49 says: οὐ γὰρ στοιχεῖον οὐδ' ἀρχὴ τὸ μεμιγμένον, ἀλλ' ἐξ ὧν μέμικται, and a little later refers to the four πρῶτα στοιχεῖα. *Cf.* also *Prim. frig.* 7. But in *Plac. phil.* 1¹⁻³ he distinguishes στοιχεῖον from ἀρχή, expressly defining στοιχεῖα as σύνθετα, composite, as distinguished from ἀρχή, which is not dependent upon anything that existed before.

6. A heavenly body, star, sun, constellation, etc.

(a) A constellation: Diog. Laert. VI 9² (102): οὗτος (*sc.* Μενέδημος), καθά φησιν Ἱππόβοτος,* εἰς τοσοῦτον τερατείας ἤλασεν, ὥστε Ἐρινύος ἀναλαβὼν σχῆμα περιήει . . . ἦν δὲ αὐτῷ ἡ ἐσθὴς αὕτη . . . πῖλος Ἀρκαδικὸς ἐπὶ τῆς κεφαλῆς, ἔχων ἐνυφασμένα τὰ δώδεκα στοιχεῖα. So also in "A Syriac Life of Clement of Rome," in *Bulletin of John Rylands Library*, Vol. IV, No. 1, p. 88.

---

* Diels, *Elementum*, p. 45, places Hippobotos at latest in the first Christian century; but von Christ, *Gesch. d. gr. Lit.* II 1⁴, p. 68, declines to fix his date except as after Sotion, who belongs in the second century B. C., and before Diogenes Laertius (*ca.* 200 A. D.). It must also be remembered that the employment of στοιχεῖα by Diogenes Laertius in reciting the statement of Hippobotos is not conclusive evidence that Hippobotos used the word, for Diogenes, though stating in III 1¹⁹ (24) that Plato was the first to employ it in philosophy, elsewhere uses it in quoting the opinions of pre-Socratic philosophers. See II 1¹; IX 3¹ (21). Our first decisive evidence of the use of στοιχεῖον in an astronomical sense is, therefore, that of the Christian writers of the middle of the second century.

(b) In the general sense of a heavenly body, a star or planet: Just. Mart. *Trypho*, 23²: ὁρᾶτε ὅτι τὰ στοιχεῖα οὐκ ἀργεῖ οὐδὲ σαββατίζει. Just. Mart. *Apol.* II 5²: ὁ θεὸς τὸν πάντα κόσμον ποιήσας καὶ τὰ ἐπίγεια ἀνθρώποις ὑποτάξας καὶ τὰ οὐράνια στοιχεῖα εἰς αὔξησιν καρπῶν καὶ ὡρῶν μεταβολὰς κοσμήσας. Ep. *ad Diogn.* 7²: οὗ (*sc.* τοῦ θεοῦ) τὰ μυστήρια πιστῶς πάντα φυλάσσει τὰ στοιχεῖα. See also Theoph. *ad Autol.* 1⁴, and Theod. *Comm.* on Gal. and Col. *Cf.* Aristides, *Apol.*, chaps. III, IV, V. But the usage seems to show that the term here, while including the heavenly bodies, includes also fire and earth—hence that the word means not the stars or sun, but the physical elements of which these are composed. *Cf.* exx. from Orac. Sib. under 2.

By metonymy a great man, a light, a star: Eus. *Hist. Eccl.* III 31; V 24, in both cases quoting from Polycrates.

7. A spirit or demon. This meaning might possibly be ascribed to the word in Manetho 4⁶²⁴ (*ca.* 300 B. C.): ταῦτα τοι οὐρανίων ἄστρων στοιχεῖα τέτυκται. But the context does not require anything other than the familiar classical usage of the word (physical) elements, and in view of the date of the passage any other meaning is improbable. Everling, *Die paulinische Angelologie und Dämonologie*, cites as an example of this usage Test. Sal. § 34.* On the basis of mss. HLPVW, C. C. McCown in his (unpublished) work, *Testamentum Salamonis*, reads as follows (§ VIII): καὶ ἦλθον πνεύματα ἑπτὰ συνδεδεμένα καὶ συμπεπλεγμένα εὔμορφα τῷ εἴδει καὶ εὔσχημα. ἐγὼ δὲ Σολομῶν ἰδὼν ταῦτα ἐθαύμασα καὶ ἐπηρώτησα αὐτά· ὑμεῖς τίνες ἐστέ; οἱ δὲ εἶπον· ἡμεῖς ἐσμὲν † στοιχεῖα τοῦ κοσμοκράτορος τοῦ σκότους. καί φησιν ὁ πρῶτος· ἐγὼ εἰμι ἡ Ἀπάτη, etc. Deissmann (*Encyc. Bib.* art. "Elements") cites the Orphic Hymns 65⁴, in which Hephæstus is called στοιχεῖον ἀμεμφές, and the Hermes Trismegistus, in which the gods come as στοιχεῖα before the supreme God. This evidence, confirmed also by modern Greek usage, leaves no doubt that στοιχεῖον did eventually come to mean an "angel," "spirit," or "god." What is not clear is that this usage belongs to the first century A. D. That the Jewish writers ascribed a spirit or angel to various physical objects is clearly shown from 1 Enoch 60¹¹⁻²¹; Jub. 2²ff. cited by Bous. (*Rel. d. Jud.*², p. 372), but not that they were called στοιχεῖα. Bous. cites 2 Enoch 16⁷ as evidence of this. But aside from the fact that we have not the Greek text of this book and hence can not say for certain that στοιχεῖα occurred in this passage, the occurrence of the word "elements," between the words "spirits" and "angels" scarcely proves that this word itself means "angels." Chaps. 12¹ and 15¹ identify the elements of the sun with the Phœnixes and Chalkydri, which are flying creatures, with feet and tails in the form of a lion,

---

* This is the notation of Conybeare in his translation, published in *Jewish Quarterly Review*, IX 1-45.

† For στοιχεῖα, etc., VWGl. read τὰ λεγόμενα στοιχεῖα οἱ κοσμοκράτορες τοῦ σκότους τούτου. P: ἐκ τῶν τριάκοντα τριῶν στοιχείων τοῦ κόσμου τοῦ σκότους. HI: στοιχεῖα τοῦ κοσμοκράτορος, omitting καί φησιν ὁ πρῶτος, etc., and adding τὸ ὄργανον τοῦ θ[εοῦ].

a crocodile's head, and twelve wings like those of angels, but do not make them angels or spirits. Tatian, *Oratio ad Græcos*, chap. 12, says that there is a spirit (πνεῦμα) in the stars, the angels, the plants, the water, in men, in animals. This is the same inclusive use of πνεῦμα which appears in Sextus Empiricus (B *SSF*. pp. 139 f.), but involves no use of στοιχεῖον in this sense. In chap. 21 Tatian says he can not be persuaded to worship τῶν στοιχείων τὴν ὑπόστασιν. But the στοιχεῖα are apparently the material elements of the world into which by allegorical interpretation the Greeks resolve their deities (see context), not the deities themselves.

Apparently, therefore, there is no definite evidence that στοιχεῖον meant "spirit," "angel," or "demon" earlier than Test. Sal., which in its present form is post-Christian, and may not be earlier than the third or fourth century, to which McCown assigns it. See Deissmann, *op. cit.* col. 1260; *cf.* Harnack, *Altchristliche Litteratur*, I 858.

Of the various meanings of κόσμος (in Greek literature from Homer down) the following only need to be taken into account:

1. The world in the physical sense, with greater or less inclusiveness, but not with exclusive reference to the earth: Wisd. 11¹⁷: οὐ γὰρ ἠπόρει ἡ παντοδύναμός σου χεὶρ καὶ κτίσασα τὸν κόσμον [ἐξ] ἀμόρφου ὕλης. Jn. 17⁵: πρὸ τοῦ τὸν κόσμον εἶναι. Acts 17²⁴: ὁ θεὸς ὁ ποιήσας τὸν κόσμον καὶ πάντα τὰ ἐν αὐτῷ. See also Plat. *Tim.* 27A; Aristot. *Cæl.* 1¹⁰ *fin.* (280 a²¹).

2. The firmament, the universe exclusive of the earth: Isoc. 78 c: τῆς γὰρ γῆς ἀπάσης τῆς ὑπὸ τῷ κόσμῳ κειμένης δίχα τετμημένης, καὶ τῆς μὲν 'Ασίας, τῆς δὲ Εὐρώπης καλουμένης. . . . Deut. 4¹⁹: καὶ μὴ ἀναβλέψας εἰς τὸν οὐρανὸν καὶ ἰδὼν τὸν ἥλιον καὶ τὴν σελήνην καὶ τοὺς ἀστέρας καὶ πάντα τὸν κόσμον τοῦ οὐρανοῦ πλανηθεὶς προσκυνήσῃς αὐτοῖς καὶ λατρεύσῃς αὐτοῖς, ἃ ἀπένειμεν Κύριος ὁ θεός σου αὐτὰ πᾶσιν τοῖς ἔθνεσιν τοῖς ὑποκάτω τοῦ οὐρανοῦ. *Cf.* also Philo, *Vita Mosis*, III 133 (14).

3. The world of humanity: Wisd. 2²⁴: φθόνῳ δὲ διαβόλου θάνατος εἰσῆλθεν εἰς τὸν κόσμον. Rom. 3⁶: ἐπεὶ πῶς κρινεῖ ὁ θεὸς τὸν κόσμον. See also Jn. 3¹⁶, ¹⁷, ¹⁹ Rom. 5¹² 11¹².

4. The sinful world, humanity as alienated from God: 2 Cor. 7¹⁰: ἡ δὲ τοῦ κόσμου λύπη θάνατον κατεργάζεται. See also 1 Jn. 3¹, ¹³ 15¹⁸.

5. The mode of life which is characterised by earthly advantages, viewed as obstacles to righteousness: Gal. 6¹⁴: δι' οὗ ἐμοὶ κόσμος ἐσταύρωται κἀγὼ κόσμῳ. See also Mt. 16²⁶ 1 Jn. 2¹⁵ Jas. 1²⁷ 4⁴.

The phrase τὰ στοιχεῖα τοῦ κόσμου occurs in N. T. three times, Gal. 4³ and Col. 2⁸, ²⁰. Instances of its earlier occurrences have not been pointed out, the nearest approximation being perhaps in Wisd. 7¹⁷, εἰδέναι σύστασιν κόσμου καὶ ἐνέργειαν στοιχείων, where κόσμος is used in the first sense named above and στοιχείων apparently in the second of its meanings. Orac. Sib. 2²⁰⁶; 8³³⁷ contain the phrase στοιχεῖα τὰ κόσμου, but, as pointed out above, the text is open to suspicion. Of the various meanings that have been proposed for the phrase the following are most worthy of consideration:

1. The meaning suggested by Wisd. 7¹⁷, viz., the physical elements of the universe. This interpretation is adopted by Beng. and Zahn, who find in it a reference to the fact that the Mosaic law not only fixes its sacred days and periods by the movements of the heavenly bodies, but contains many commands pertaining to physical matters; in a similar sense by Holsten; by Neander (*Planting and Training*, Bk. III, chap. 9; Bk. VI, chap. 1) with reference to material elements in both Judaism and heathenism (he makes no mention of the heavenly bodies), and by various others with varying specific application.

2. The meaning attested for στοιχεῖα by Justin Martyr, *et al.*, and expressly advocated as that of τὰ στ. τ. κόσμ. in Gal. and Col. by Theodoret in his commentaries on those epistles, viz. the heavenly bodies, which the Galatians worshipped before their conversion and to which they would be doing reverence again if they should adopt the Jewish observance of days and weeks and months. "For before, he says, ye were deemed worthy of the calling, ye served those that are not by nature gods, deifying the elements; but now the Master, Christ, has freed you from this error; and I do not know how you are going back into the same error. For when ye keep Sabbaths and new moons and the other days, and fear the transgression of these ye are like those who deify the elements." Theodoret on Gal. 4. This interpretation generally adopted by the fathers has also found wide acceptance in more recent times. Hilg. (*Galaterbrief*, pp. 66 *ff.*) holds to this interpretation, but with the added suggestion that the apostle is thinking of the heavenly bodies as living beings, gods of the Gentiles and in his own view lower gods (*cf.* Deut. 4¹⁹), which have an influence on the lives and destinies of men, and which as heavenly bodies control the cycle of Jewish feasts. So similarly Diels, *Elementum*, pp. 50 *f.*; Bous. S*NT.* *ad loc.*; Clemen, *Primitive Christianity*, p. 106 *ff.*; *contra*, Kennedy, *St. Paul and the Mystery Religions*, pp. 24, 25, 60 *f.*

3. The spirits that are associated with the στοιχεῖα in the physical sense, whether stars or other existences, and so angels and spirits in general. So Ritschl, *Rechtfertigung u. Versöhnung*, Vol. II, pp. 252 *f.* (who finds in the passage a reference to the angels through whom the law was given, but who are also associated with the phenomena of nature [Ps. 104⁴], the thunderings of Mt. Sinai being the evidence of their presence at the giving of the law); Spitta, *Zw. Br. Petrus u. Judas*, pp. 263 *ff.*; Everling, *Die paulinische Angelologie und Dämonologie*, pp. 65 *ff.*, with inclusion of the angelic powers to which the Jews were subjected and the deities of the Gentiles. Similarly, Dib. *Gwt.* pp. 78 *ff.*, but with characterisation of the difference between this and the preceding view as unimportant.

4. The elements of religious knowledge, possessed by men: a description applicable both to the Gentile religion of the Galatians and to Judaism before Christ. Under this term are included ritual observances, but the reference is not to them exclusively nor to them as ritual, but as elemen-

tary, adapted to children. So substantially Tert. (*Adv. Marc.* V 4) Hier. Erasm. Calv. Wies. (but with reference to O. T. only) Mey. Ell. Ltft. Sief. *et al.* with reference to Jews and Gentiles.

The ancient world undoubtedly believed in numerous supernatural beings, intermediary between God and men. No doubt, also, Paul shared this belief to a large extent. He believed in Satan and angels, and apparently in numerous "principalities and powers." He seems to have attributed real existence to the heathen gods, though denying their deity; quite probably he identified them with the "principalities and powers." Thus they played for him an important part in the religion of the Gentiles. In Judaism, also, the angels had a place in that the law was given through them; and though they are not represented as hostile to God or Christ, they might be thought of as such in the sense that they, or the law which came through them, were in rivalry with Christ. It is also true that στοιχεῖα was very widely used of the elements of the physical world, and that there was a tendency to extend this use from the four ultimate elements to the parts of the world in a looser sense, including the sea and the sky, day and night. In Christian writers later than the N. T., possibly, also, in other writers who antedated Paul, the heavenly bodies are called στοιχεῖα. Before deciding, however, that it was to any of these things, either the elements of the physical world, or the heavenly bodies, or to any spirits which inhabited them, that Paul referred, the following facts must be considered:

1. Precisely the phrase τὰ στοιχεῖα τοῦ κόσμου has not been observed elsewhere than in the two passages in the Pauline epistles. Neither Sap. 7⁷ nor Orac. Sib. 2²⁰⁶; 8³³⁷, nor Manetho 4⁶²⁴ have just this phrase, nor furnish more than a suggestion as to the meaning of the Pauline expression. Nor can it be assumed to be identical with the τὰ στοιχεῖα of the philosophers or the τὰ οὐράνια στοιχεῖα of Justin Martyr. The decisive word as to the meaning of Paul's phrase must be found, if at all, in Paul himself.

2. There is no clear evidence that τὰ στοιχεῖα had in Paul's day come to be used of deities or other like beings; for even if the evidence of Diogenes Laertius be supposed to prove the use of στοιχεῖον in an astronomical sense in the first century, the fact that a star might be called στοιχεῖον and that a star might be worshipped does not give to στοιχεῖον the meaning "deity"; as the fact that a cow is an animal and is worshipped does not make "animal" mean "god." While, therefore, τὰ στοιχεῖα τοῦ κόσμου might mean the stars or planets, the view that it means the spirits that dwelt in or controlled the heavenly bodies has but indirect and slender support.

3. The use of τὰ στοιχεῖα in v.⁹ as synonymous with τα. στ. τ. κοσμ. of v.³ suggests that probably the emphatic element of the phrase is conveyed by στοιχεῖα. This is confirmed by the addition of the adjectives ἀσθενῆ καὶ πτωχά. *Cf.* also Heb. 5¹² in which the στοιχεῖα are depreciated because of their elementary character.

4. The context of the phrase in v.³ and of the synonymous expression in

v.⁹, esp. the reference to the possible acceptance of the Jewish law by the Gentile Galatians as a re-enslavement to the elements, shows that whatever the precise meaning of the words στοιχεῖα and κόσμου, the whole expression ὑπὸ . . . δεδουλωμένοι (v.³) and the similar language of v ⁹ refers inclusively to the condition, both of the Jews as men under law, and of idol-worshippers. See in com. *ad loc.* on the reference of ἡμεῖς.

5. The tacit assumption that τὰ στοιχεῖα τοῦ κόσμου, to which the Galatians were formerly in bondage, were precisely the same as those to which they were on the point of returning, is unwarranted. It is, indeed, to be assumed that the phrase has the same meaning in both cases, but it is entirely possible that it is descriptive rather than directly identifying, and denotes a category inclusive of those things to which the Galatians were enslaved and those to which they are now in danger of returning.

6. The contention of Everling, Bousset, and Dibelius that because v.⁸ affirms that the Galatians were in bondage to gods that by nature are not such, therefore the στοιχεῖα to which v.³ speaks of them (and the Jews) as being in bondage must be personal beings, gods, is without good foundation. The same fact may be, and often is expressed both in personal and impersonal terms. Does it follow from Rom. 6¹⁷ and ²² that ὁ τύπος διδαχῆς is God? Especially is it the case that personal terms may be used by way of illustration to describe an impersonal fact. It no more follows that the στοιχεῖα are personal because of the previous ἐπιτρόπους καὶ οἰκονόμους than that ὁ νόμος is personal because personified as παιδαγωγός. With the recognition of this fact and of the absence of any reference to spirits in this connection the chief support of Everling's view falls to the ground.

7. On the other hand, the close connection of ὅτε ἦμεν νήπιοι in v.³ with ὑπὸ τὰ στοιχεῖα obviously suggests the meaning "elementary teachings." Not only so, but the whole passage from 3²³ to 4⁷, if not also to 4⁹, is permeated with the thought that the Jewish system which the Galatians are being urged to take up is imperfect, adapted to childhood, and the whole purpose of the argument is to dissuade the Galatians from accepting this system on the ground that it is childish, fitted, like their old idol-worship, for the infancy of the race. Like other passages of the epistle, it appeals not only to their reason, but to their emotions.

8. The adjectives ἀσθενῆ and πτωχά have no appropriateness as applied to the heavenly bodies, and but little with reference to the physical elements of the material universe, but appropriately describe the elements of an imperfect religious system as compared with the full truth of the revelation in Christ.

9. The mention of days, months, and years in v.¹⁰ suggests the possibility of a reference to the heavenly bodies by whose movements the recurrence of these periods is fixed. The mention of meat and drink in the context of Col. 2⁸,²⁰ (see v.¹⁶) suggests a possible reference of στοιχεῖα to the material elements of the earth. But this latter explanation will with difficulty

apply to Gal. 4³·⁹, as the planetary explanation will not apply to Col. 2⁸·²⁰. The element that is common to both, and is emphasised in Col., is that the στοιχεῖα represent an imperfect type of teaching; in Gal. described as temporary and ended by the coming of Christ, in Col. as proceeding from men (v.⁸), and also as temporary and abolished in Christ (¹⁴·¹⁷). While, therefore, it is possible that in Gal. Paul has reference to the heavenly bodies as, on the one side, formerly objects of worship by the Gentiles, and, on the other, as governing the cycle of Jewish observances, and in Col. to the physical elements of the universe, it is more probable that the phrase means the same in both cases, and in both cases has reference to the elementary and imperfect teachings of religion.

10. Aside from the debatable question of the meaning of τὰ στ. τ. κόσμ. it is entirely clear that the things which Paul was dissuading the Galatians from accepting were, in fact, requirements of the law; as those from which he dissuaded the Colossians were dogmas of religion urged in the name of Judaism or some system of kindred spirit. To find the ground of the description of obedience to them as a bondage to τὰ στοιχεῖα τοῦ κόσμου in a remote and unsuggested connection between them and the heavenly bodies, or the physical elements of the universe, or the spirits of these elements, when the phrase is directly applicable to them in a sense appropriate to and suggested by the context and sustained by contemporary usage, is to substitute a long and circuitous course of thought for a short, direct, and obvious one.

While, therefore, the discovery of convincing evidence that στοιχεῖα was in current use as a designation of the heavenly bodies conceived of as living beings, or of spirits that inhabit all existences, might make it possible that it was to these that Paul referred, this would become probable only on the basis of new evidence, and even then the contextual evidence is against it. The evidence as it stands favours the simple view proposed by Tert. and advocated by Erasm. Th. Crem. Ltft. Sief. *et al.* The words τοῦ κόσμου are most naturally understood as referring to the world of humanity (*cf.* Col. 2⁸, παράδοσιν ἀνθρώπων, and 2²², ἐντάλματα καὶ διδασ-καλίας τῶν ἀνθρώπων), yet, in view of the inclusion of the law in the content of the phrase, not as a genitive of source, but of possession, the whole expression meaning "the rudimentary religious teachings possessed by the race."*

* If the fact that στοιχεῖα is rather infrequently used in the sense of elementary teachings, while the physical sense is very common, seems to necessitate understanding τὰ στ. τ.κ. as in some sense physical or related to the physical sense, the interpretation most consonant with the evidence would be to understand στ. in that loose and inclusive sense in which it is employed in Orac. Sib. as including both the physical constituents of the world, and the sky and stars. To the στοιχεῖα in this sense, the Jews might be said to be enslaved in the ordinances pertaining to physical matters, such as food and circumcision, and also as the context suggests in the observance of days fixed by the motions of the heavenly bodies, while the bondage of the Gentiles to them would be in their worship of material images and heavenly bodies.

XXI. 'ΑΓΑΠΑΩ AND 'ΑΓΑΠΗ.

I.   The verb ἀγαπάω is used in classical writers from Homer down, signifying with reference to persons, "to be fond of," "to love," "to desire"; with
reference to things, "to be contented with," "to take pleasure in."   If we
seek a more definite statement of the content of the term, it appears that
there are three elements which with more or less constancy and in varying
degrees of emphasis enter into the thought expressed by the word: (a) "to
admire," "to approve," "to recognise the worth of," "to take pleasure in,"
(b) "to desire to possess" (c) "to be well-disposed towards," "to wish to
benefit."   The first of these elements appears distinctly in Plato, *Rep.*
330B, C, yet blended with or shading into the second: τούτου ἕνεκα ἠρόμην,
ἦν δ' ἐγώ, ὅτι μοι ἔδοξας οὐ σφόδρα ἀγαπᾶν τὰ χρήματα, τοῦτο δὲ ποιοῦσιν ὡς
τὸ πολὺ οἳ ἂν μὴ αὐτοὶ κτήσωνται· οἱ δὲ κτησάμενοι διπλῇ ἢ οἱ ἄλλοι ἀσπάζον-
ται αὐτά.   ὥσπερ γὰρ οἱ ποιηταὶ τὰ αὐτῶν ποιήματα καὶ οἱ πατέρες τοὺς παῖδας
ἀγαπῶσι ταύτῃ τε δὴ καὶ οἱ χρηματισάμενοι, περὶ τὰ χρήματα σπουδάζουσιν
ὡς ἔργον ἑαυτῶν, καὶ κατὰ τὴν χρείαν ᾗπερ οἱ ἄλλοι.   The third element is
present, if at all in this example, only by suggestion in the words καὶ οἱ
πατέρες τοὺς παῖδας ἀγαπῶσι.   There is, indeed, but slight trace of this
element of meaning in the word as used by non-biblical writers of the pre-
Christian period.

II.   In the Lxx ἀγαπάω translates several Hebrew words, but in the great
majority of cases (about 130 out of 160) the Kal of אָהֵב, which is also
rendered in a few cases (10) by φιλέω.   אָהֵב is used with much the same
range of meaning as our English word love.   Thus, *e. g.*, it is used of the
love of a parent for a child, Gen. 25²⁸; of a husband for a wife, Gen. 29¹⁸, ³²;
of sexual love in which the element of passion and desire of possession is
prominent, 2 Sam. 13¹, ⁴; of the love of friend for friend and of a people for
a leader, 1 Sam. 18¹, ³, ¹⁶; of God's love for Israel, Deut. 4³⁷ Hos. 11¹; of the
love of men for God, Ex. 20⁶ Deut. 6⁵ 11¹; of the love of men for material
things, Hos. 9¹; and much more frequently for the love of immaterial things,
good or evil, such as righteousness or peace, and their opposites, Ps. 4³ (²)
11⁷ (⁶) 33⁵ Prov. 12¹.   It is evident that into the thought of the Hebrew
word enter all three of the elements named above, the emphasis upon
the several elements varying in the various instances very greatly, even
in some cases to the exclusion of one element or another.   The element of
admiration, approval, recognition of worth, is doubtless always present,
whether one speak of the love of men for women, of men for men, of men
for God, of men for righteousness, or even of God for men.   In the case
of the love of men for God it becomes worship, adoration, or at least
approaches this; in the case of friends, it involves mutual admiration;
when it is goodness that is loved, it is the object of approval and delight.
The desire to possess is likewise usually present; in a gross form in such a
case as 2 Sam. 13¹⁻⁴ Hos. 9¹; of an elevated type in the love of men for

righteousness. The desire to benefit can not, of course, be included when the object is impersonal; it may be said to be driven out by desire to possess in such a case as 2 Sam. 13¹⁻⁴; in the case of men's love for God it becomes desire to serve the person loved (Deut. 11¹, ¹³); in the case of God's love for men and in such injunctions as Lev. 19¹⁸, ³⁴ Deut. 10¹⁹ the desire to benefit is the prominent element.

III. In the N. T. usage of ἀγαπάω the same elements appear, the word being used of personal friendship where the element of admiration, usually accompanied with desire to benefit, is prominent (Mk. 10²¹ Lk. 7⁵ Jn. 11⁵ 13²²); of God's attitude towards Jesus, where approval is evidently the chief element of the thought and the word approximates the meaning of ἐκλέγω, "to choose" (Jn. 3³⁵ Eph. 1⁶); of the love of God for men of good character, where the meaning is much the same save in degree of emphasis (2 Cor. 9⁷); of the love of God and of Christ for even sinful men (Jn. 3¹⁶ Gal. 2²⁰ Heb. 12⁶ 1 Jn. 4¹⁹ᵇ), where benevolence, desire to benefit, is the chief element; of the love which men are bidden to have for God and for Christ, and of Christ's love for God, in which admiration is raised to adoration, and includes readiness to serve (Mt. 22³⁷ Jn. 14¹⁵, ²¹, ³¹ Rom. 8²⁸ 1 Cor. 8³ 1 Jn. 4²⁰ᵃ); of the love which men are bidden to have for one another, even their enemies, in which the willingness and desire to benefit is prominent, and in the case of enemies admiration or approval falls into the background (Mt. 22⁴⁹ Jn. 13³⁴ᶜ Rom. 13⁸, ⁹ Eph. 5²⁵, ²⁸ 1 Jn. 2¹⁰); and finally of the love of things, when admiration and desire to possess are prominent, to the entire exclusion of desire to benefit (Lk. 11⁴³ Jn. 12⁴³ 1 Jn. 2¹⁵).

As concerns ἀγαπάω and φιλέω, it is to be observed that while in the biblical writers, at least, the two terms have a certain common area of usage in which they may be used almost interchangeably, yet in general φιλέω emphasises the natural spontaneous affection of one person for another, while ἀγαπάω refers rather to love into which there enters an element of choice, and hence of moral character. It is consistent with this distinction that ἀγαπάω is never used with the meaning "to kiss" (which φιλέω sometimes has) and is rarely used of sexual love (but see 2 Sam. 13¹, ⁴ Cant. 1³, ⁴, ⁷ 3¹⁻⁴, as against the too strong statements of Grimm and Cremer, s. v. φιλεῖν; and cf. also exx. in Th.); that φιλεῖν is never used in the command to men to love God or men, and very rarely of God's love to men (but see Jn. 16²⁷); but that either term may be used of honourable love between man and man, into which there enters more or less of the element of choice and decision. Cf. Jn. 11³, ³⁶ (φιλέω) with 11⁵ (ἀγαπάω) and Jn. 20² with 21⁷.

IV. Ἀγάπη, unlike the verb, and certain others of its cognates which occur from Homer down, appears first in the Lxx, and thereafter is almost wholly limited to biblical and Christian writers. Cf. M. and M. Voc. s. v. In the Lxx (can. bks.) it is used chiefly of love between the sexes (see 2 Sam. 13¹⁵ and the eleven instances in Cant.; but are these latter possibly due to an allegorical interpretation of the book?). But in Wisd. and in Philo it is employed in a nobler sense; in Wisd. 3⁹ and Philo, *Quod deus immut.* 69 (14) of the love of God, and in Wisd. 6¹⁸ of the love of wisdom. *Cf.* M. and M. *Voc. s. v.* This sense becomes the prevailing one in N. T., wholly displacing the use with reference to love between the sexes. Nor are there any clear instances of ἀγάπη in reference to ordinary human friendship, personal affection. The desire to possess is also rarely present as a prominent element; 2 Thes. 2¹⁰ is apparently the only N. T. instance, and here appreciation is perhaps equally prominent. On the other hand, ἀγάπη is used freely of God's approving attitude towards Jesus (Jn. 15¹⁰ 17²⁶); of the love of God and of Christ towards men, even sinful men (Rom. 5⁵, ⁸ 8³⁵, ³⁹ 1 Jn. 3¹, ¹⁶ 4⁹, ¹⁰, ¹⁶); of the love which men are bidden to have for God (Lk. 11⁴² Jn. 5⁴² 1 Jn. 2⁵, ¹⁵ 4¹⁸ 5³; the only clear example in the Pauline epistles is 2 Thes. 3⁵); and with especial frequency in Paul of the love which men have or are enjoined to have towards one another (Jn. 15¹³ Rom. 12⁹ 13¹⁰ 14¹⁵ 1 Cor. 13¹, ², ³, ⁴, ⁸, ¹³ 14¹). It must again be emphasised that these several elements are not mutually exclusive, only one being present in a given instance of the word; the distinction is one of emphasis and prominence, not of exclusive expression.

The use of ἀγαπήσεις in Gal. 5¹⁴, quoted from Lev. 19¹⁸, follows the Lxx, and is in accordance with the uniform habit of the biblical writers to use ἀγαπάω rather than φιλέω of the love which men are bidden to exercise towards their fellow men. The verb in this passage and the noun in all the instances occurring in this epistle (5⁶, ¹³, ²²) while including the element of appreciation, recognition of worth, which is fundamental to all the meanings of both verb and noun, evidently lay chief stress upon the desire and will to benefit, which issues in efforts for the well-being of another. The verb in Gal. 2²⁰ has essentially the same meaning and emphasis, but being used by Paul of the love of Christ for himself, a confessedly sinful man, still further emphasises the element of benevolence.

It is love of this type, of which recognition of worth is the foundation, and desire to benefit the leading element, that Paul exalts in his remarkable panegyric in 1 Cor. chap. 13, and of which he says in Rom. 13¹⁰ that love is the fulfilment of law, and in Gal. 5⁶:

"In Christ Jesus neither circumcision availeth anything nor uncircumcision, but faith, working through love."

INDEXES.

I. ENGLISH WORDS, SUBJECTS, AND AUTHORS.

Authors, ancient and modern, are cited in this list only when they are specially important or their opinions are quoted and discussed. Their names are printed in small capitals. Words in italic type are those which occur in the translation of the letter. A number in bold-face type indicates a page on which the word is discussed. Words in ordinary Roman type denote subjects referred to in the Epistle or in the Commentary, including the Introduction and the Appendix. Grammatical forms and syntactical usages are referred to only when they are regarded as for some reason specially important.

which Paul received his gospel, 41–43, 50, 51; sent forth from God, 216, to deliver them that are under law, 219, that they might receive the adoption, 220; the sons of God receive his Spirit, 221; he is the basis and cause of Christian liberty, 83, 270; object of faith, 120 f., 123, 138 f., 196 f.; cf. 202; basis of justification, 124; his crucifixion participated in by Paul, 135; he lives in the believer, 136 f.; cf. 248; not distinguishable in experience from the Spirit, 137; manifested his love in his gift of himself for men, 139 (cf. 11); his death evidence that righteousness is not through law, 140; set forth to the Galatians, crucified, 143; delivered men from the curse of the law, 168–171; became a curse for us, 171 ff., in order that we might receive the blessing of the Spirit, 176; the law a means of bringing men to him, 200; by baptism into him they acquire his standing, 203; in him all distinctions are abolished, 206 ff.; those who are his are heirs of the promise to Abraham, 208; they who have the Spirit of the Son recognise God as Father, 223; relation of Gentile believers to Christ destroyed by receiving circumcision, seeking to be justified in law, 272, 275; in him neither circumcision nor uncircumcision avails anything, but faith working through love, 279 f.; they who are his have crucified the flesh, 319; the Galatians exhorted to fulfil the law of the

Christ, 329; his cross an occasion of persecution, 349, and the ground of glorying, 354; the apostle received as Jesus Christ by the Galatians, 242; bears in his body the marks of Jesus, 359 f.

Jew, Jews, 108, 111, 119, 206.
Jewish Christians, 108 f.; eating with Gentiles, lix f., 116.
Jews: religion of, 46; attitude towards Gentiles, lix, 104.
John, 94.
JOSEPHUS: use of geographical terms, xxxiii; use of διαθήκη, 499.
Joy, 312, 314.
Jubilees, doctrines of the book of, 158.
Judaisers, see "Opponents of Paul."
Judea, 62 f., 435 f.; churches of, 62 f.
Justify, 119, 123 f., 159, 165, 201, 275, 460 ff.

Kindness, 312, **315**.
Kingdom of God, 310 ff.

LAKE, K., l, 509.
Law, 119 f., 123 f., 132 f., 140, 147, 151, 163 ff. (esp. 170), 182, 184, 187, 192 ff., 198, 200, 216, 218, 219, 252, 274, 275 f., 293 f., 302, 318, 329, 351 f., **443** ff.
Law: curse of, 163 ff., 168–172; freedom of Gentile Christians from, 82, 270, 291 f.; of Jewish Christians, 112 ff.; to be fulfilled by Christians, 293 f.; the law of the Christ, 329; see also **443** ff.
Leaven, 283.
Legalists in the early church, see "Opponents of Paul."

II. GREEK WORDS AND PHRASES.

This index includes all the words in the Epistle, and a few important words discussed in the Introduction or Appendix. The lists of occurrences in the Epistle are complete, except when otherwise indicated. When examples of special usages are given, the completeness of the lists of these is not guaranteed. A number in bold-face type indicates a page on which the word is discussed.

ἀββά, 223 f.

'Αβραάμ, 153, 155, 159, 162, 175, 180, 186, 208, 252.

ἀγαθός, 335, **338**, 345.

ἀγαθωσύνη, 312, 316.

ἀγαπάω, 139, 293, **296**, **519** f.

ἀγάπη, 279 f., 293, 312, **314**, **520** f.

Ἀγαρ, 258 (bis).

ἄγγελος, 25, 189, 242.

ἀγνοέω, 62.

ἄγω, 302.

ἀδελφοί, 8, 35, **36**, 177, 236, 264, 267, 286, 291, 325, 362.

ἀδελφὸς τοῦ κυρίου, 60 f.

ἀδικέω, 237.

ἀθετέω, 140, 178, 180.

αἷμα, 53.

αἵρεσις, 304, **309**.

αἰών, 13, 16, **426** ff.

αἰώνιος, 339, **343**, **431** f.

ἀκαθαρσία, 304, **305**.

ἀκοή, 147, 151.

ἀκούω, 43, 64, 252.

ἀκροβυστία, 91, **92** f., 279, 355.

ἀκυρόω, 182, **184**.

ἀλήθεια, 85, 109, 281; ἡ ἀλήθεια τοῦ εὐαγγελίου, 85, 109.

ἀληθεύω, 244.

ἀλλά, 5, 75, 91, 195, et freq.

ἀλλάσσω, 250.

ἀλληγορέω, 253, **254** ff.

ἀλλήλων, 293, 297, 300, 323, 329.

ἄλλος, 22 ff., 283, **420** f.

ἁμαρτία, 11, 125 f., 195, **436** ff.

ἁμαρτωλός, 119, 125, **127** ff.

ἀμήν, 16, 361 f.

ἄν, with ind., 32, 193; with subj., 189.

ἀναβαίνω, 67, 69.

ἀναγκάζω, 75 f., 111, 115, 349; always of the attempt to subject Gentile Christians to the law.

ἀνάθεμα and ἀνάθημα, 25, **28**, 30.

ἀναλίσκω, 297.

ἀναπληρόω, 329, **330**.

ἀναστατόω, 288, **289**.

ἀναστροφή, 43, **44**.

ἀνατίθημι, 70, **71**.

ἀνέρχομαι, 54, 58.

ἀνήρ, 264.

ἀνθίστημι, 102.

ἄνθρωπος, 3, 4 f., 30, 32 (bis), 37, 38, 40, 88, 119, **120**, 177, 178, 274, 325, 339; κατὰ ἄνθρωπον, 37, **38**, 177.

ἀνόητος, 143, 148.

ἀντίκειμαι, 300.

'Αντιόχεια, 102.

ἀπεκδέχομαι, 277, **278**.

ἀπέρχομαι, 55.

ἀπό, 3, 4, 11, 18, 86, 103, 147, 257, 275.

III. BIBLICAL PASSAGES, NOT IN GALATIANS, DISCUSSED IN THIS COMMENTARY.

Gen., chap. 12: 157.
Gen. 12³, 160 f.
Gen. 13¹⁵, 181 f., 507.
Gen., chap. 17 (esp. vv. ⁷, ⁸): 157; cf. 181 f., 507.
Gen. 21¹⁰, 267.

Lev. 18⁵, 167.
Lev. 19¹⁸, 296.

Deut. 27²⁶, 164.
Deut. 32⁶⁻¹⁴, 384.

Ps. 2⁷, 384.

Isa. 54¹, 264.

Hab. 2⁴, 166 f.

Mt. 4³, ⁶, 411.
Mt. 5⁴⁵, 390.
Mt. 11²⁷, 412.
Mt. 16¹⁶, 412.
Mt. 27⁴⁰, ⁴³, 411.

Mk. 1¹, 412.
Mk. 1¹¹, 410 f.
Mk. 3¹¹, 411.
Mk. 3¹⁴, 366, 378 f.
Mk. 3¹⁵, 378.
Mk. 9⁷, 410 f.
Mk. 13³², 412.
Mk. 14⁶¹, 411.

Lk. 1³², 412 f.
Lk. 1³⁴, ³⁵, 413.

Lk. 3³⁸, 412.
Lk. 4³, ⁹, 411.
Lk. 6¹³, 366.
Lk. 6³⁵, ³⁶, 390.
Lk. 10²², 412.

Jn. 1¹⁴, 414.

Acts 1²¹⁻²⁶, 367, 370, 379.
Acts, chaps. 10, 11, 15: 115.
Acts 13¹⁻³, 373.
Acts 16⁶, xxxi ff.
Acts 18²³, xxxviii ff.

Rom. 1¹⁷, 433, 472 f.
Rom. 1³, ⁴, 409.
Rom. 2¹², 456.
Rom. 2¹²⁻¹⁶, 450 f., 452.
Rom. 2¹³, 457.
Rom. 2¹⁴, 454.
Rom. 3²¹, ²², 472.
Rom. 3²⁷, 457.
Rom. 4¹⁻⁶, ¹¹⁻¹³, 470 f.
Rom. 4¹¹⁻¹⁸, 507.
Rom. 5¹³, 456.
Rom., chap. 7: 441.
Rom. 8³ᶠᶠ·, 408.
Rom. 10⁹, 403.
Rom. 16⁷, 372.

1 Cor. 9¹, 370, 373.
1 Cor. 9³ᶠᶠ·, 370.
1 Cor. 12³, 403.
1 Cor. 12²⁸, 379.
1 Cor. 15³⁻⁸, 370 ff.; cf. 373.
1 Cor. 15²⁸, 409.